# ZAGATSURVEY®

# 2006

# MOVIE GUIDE

**Editor: Curt Gathje**

**Coordinator: Larry Cohn**

Published and distributed by
ZAGAT SURVEY, LLC
4 Columbus Circle
New York, New York 10019
Tel: 212 977 6000
E-mail: movies@zagat.com
Web site: www.zagat.com

# Acknowledgments

We appreciate the help of the DC Independent Film Festival, as well as the Arizona Film Society, MSC Film Society, Olympia Film Society, Peachtree Film Society, University Film Society and Yale Film Society.

Thanks also to the following who worked on this guide: our associate editor, Griff Foxley, and our editorial assistant, Jason Briker, as well as Carol Bialkowski, Kimberly Butler, Ed Dwyer, Gwen Hyman, Marilyn Laurie, David Margolick, Joshua Mooney, Pia Nordlinger, Maura O'Connell, Bernard Onken, Jane Rosenthal, Arthur Schlesinger Jr. and Bill Wolf. In addition, this guide would not have been possible without the hard work of our staff, especially Augustine Chan, Reni Chin, Liz Daleske, Schuyler Frazier, Jeff Freier, Shelley Gallagher, Natalie Lebert, Mike Liao, Dave Makulec, Emily Parsons, Troy Segal, Robert Seixas, Daniel Simmons, Sharon Yates and Kyle Zolner.

# Contents

# About This Survey

Over the past 26 years, Zagat Survey has become the leading publisher of consumer-based leisure guides. In the last few years, we've expanded our scope beyond restaurants and hotels to cover entertaining, golf, music, movies, nightlife, shopping and tourist attractions. Now we are proud to bring you this fourth edition of the ultimate moviegoers' guide, a compilation of 1,355 great films, as rated by our surveyors.

With over 12,000 participants in this *Survey*, seeing an average of 2.2 movies per week (or 1.4 million films annually), and with each surveyor separately rating the films they've seen for Overall Quality, Acting, Story and Production Values, we hope to have achieved a uniquely reliable guide.

Of our surveyors, 54% are women, 46% men; the breakdown by age is 17% in their 20s; 33%, 30s; 20%, 40s; 18%, 50s; and 12%, 60s or above. Though living in all parts of the country and coming from highly diverse backgrounds, these people share one common trait – they are all movie lovers. In producing the reviews contained in this guide, our editors have done their best to synopsize these surveyors' opinions, with exact comments shown in quotation marks. We thank each of these participants. Being based entirely on their ratings and comments, this guide is really "theirs."

To help you find the best movie for any occasion, we have prepared a number of Top Ratings lists (pages 8–32), as well as 65 handy indexes. Though the vast majority of the films in this book are currently available on DVD, we have flagged those that are not yet available with the following icon – ∅.

**To vote in any of our upcoming *Surveys*, just register at zagat.com.** Each voter will receive a free copy of the resulting guide (or a comparable reward). Subscribers to zagat.com have access to restaurant and hotel ratings and reviews for 70 cities worldwide and receive ZagatWire, our monthly e-mail newsletter, as well as getting up to 25% off on your purchases at our online Shop.

Since there is always room for improvement, we invite your comments, suggestions and even criticisms of this guide so that we can revise future editions. Please contact us at movies@zagat.com or by mail at Zagat Movies, 4 Columbus Circle, New York, NY 10019. We look forward to hearing from you.

New York, NY
September 12, 2005

*Nina and Tim*

Nina and Tim Zagat

# What's New

For this fourth edition of our *Movie Guide,* we've surveyed the new releases of the last 12 months and included the 40 highest rated herein (see page 8). An analysis of these winners says something about the national moviegoing mood.

Predictably, **franchise sequels** were big, with *Harry Potter and the Prisoner of Azkaban, Spider-Man 2* and *Star Wars Episode III* doing boffo biz, though **independent films** were well represented by such offbeat entries as *Before Sunset, Crash, Garden State, Sideways* and *The Woodsman.* **Biopics** gave the big-screen treatment to a millionaire (*The Aviator*), a sexologist (*Kinsey*) and a singer (*Ray*). **Animation** continued to up the technological ante with productions like *The Incredibles, Madagascar, Polar Express* and *Robots.* This year's **sports**-themed flicks – *Coach Carter, Friday Night Lights* and *Million Dollar Baby* – all featured a charismatic coach as the central character, while **martial arts** provided some kicks with *Hero, House of Flying Daggers* and *Kung Fu Hustle.* **Foreign language** standouts included *Bad Education, Hero, House of Flying Daggers* and *Maria Full of Grace.*

As for the year's hottest players, six top-billed actors garnered double berths in the Top 40: **Joan Allen** (*The Bourne Supremacy, The Upside of Anger*), **Don Cheadle** (*Crash, Hotel Rwanda*), **Gael García Bernal** (*Bad Education, The Motorcycle Diaries*), **Natalie Portman** (*Garden State, Star Wars Episode III*), **Jamie Foxx** (*Collateral, Ray*) and **Zhang Ziyi** (*Hero, House of Flying Daggers*). In the director's chair, **Zhang Yimou** scored twice for his chopsocky duo *Hero* and *House of Flying Daggers.*

**New to This Edition:** In addition to the Top 40, we've also added 60 additional reviews, for a grand total of 100 more titles than our last edition. To further guide you to the right movie for any occasion, we have split our 'best of' lists in the front of this guide into two categories: classic films (those made before 1960) and modern ones (made 1960 to date).

**DVD Candidates:** We again asked voters to name their favorite films not available on DVD that should be. This year's mentions included *The African Queen, Becket, The Conformist, El Cid, Enchanted April, The Heiress, High Anxiety, Isadora, Julia, King Kong, Kiss of the Spider Woman, Lady Sings the Blues, The Magnificent Ambersons, Morocco, 1900, O Lucky Man!, Performance, Reds, Repulsion, Sergeant York, An Unmarried Woman, Valley of the Dolls, Yentl* – and anything with "Mae West." Hollywood, are you listening?

New York, NY
September 12, 2005

Curt Gathje

# Ratings & Symbols

**Film Name, U.S. Release Date, Director & Cast,**
**Running Time, MPAA Rating**

Zagat Ratings

See symbols below

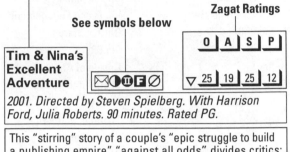

Tim & Nina's Excellent Adventure

2001. Directed by Steven Spielberg. With Harrison Ford, Julia Roberts. 90 minutes. Rated PG.

This "stirring" story of a couple's "epic struggle to build a publishing empire" "against all odds" divides critics: "inspiring" ("outdoes *Citizen Kane*") vs. "strictly snoozeville" ("Bill and Ted's adventure was much better"); while most applaud Harrison Ford's "sensitive" portrayal of Tim ("amazing makeup job"), some feel Julia Roberts' take on Nina is just a "reprise of her role in *Pretty Woman*"; P.S. the black-and-white 3-D shots can be "nauseating", especially the dinner scenes in bed.

**Review, with surveyors' comments in quotes**

Movies with highest overall ratings and greatest popularity are listed in BLOCK CAPITAL LETTERS.

⌧   Oscar winner for Picture, Acting, Direction, Screenplay
◑   Filmed in Black & White
Ⅱ   Inspired a Sequel
🄵   Foreign Language film
∅   Not yet on DVD

**Ratings** are on a scale of **0** to **30**:

| 0 | Overall | A | Acting | S | Story | P | Production Values |
|---|---|---|---|---|---|---|---|
| 25 | | 19 | | 25 | | 12 | |

| | | |
|---|---|---|
| **0–9** poor to fair | **20–25** very good to excellent | |
| **10–15** fair to good | **26–30** extraordinary to perfection | |
| **16–19** good to very good | ▽ low response/less reliable | |

# Top Ratings*

Excludes films with low voting, unless indicated by a ▽.

## New Releases

*28* Hotel Rwanda
*27* Million Dollar Baby
*26* Incredibles, The
    Crash
    Ray
*25* Finding Neverland
    Maria Full of Grace
    Hero
    Enron: Smartest Guys
*24* Vera Drake
    House of Flying Daggers
    Harry Potter/Prisoner
*23* Star Wars III/Revenge of Sith
    Motorcycle Diaries
    Kung Fu Hustle
    Bad Education
    Aviator, The
    Sideways
    Notebook, The
    Being Julia

*22* Spider-Man 2
    Very Long Engagement
    Garden State
    Sin City
    Upside of Anger
    Shaun of the Dead
    Kinsey
*21* Phantom of the Opera
    Before Sunset
    Woodsman, The
    Polar Express
    Fahrenheit 9/11
    Collateral
    Bourne Supremacy
    Madagascar
    Friday Night Lights
    Hitch
    Coach Carter
*20* Robots
    Interpreter, The

---

* Indicates a tie with film above

# Favorite Films of All Time

Each surveyor has named his or her five favorite films. The most frequently named movies are:

1. Godfather, The
2. Casablanca
3. Star Wars
4. Gone with the Wind
5. Shawshank Redemption
6. Braveheart
7. Lord of Rings/Fellowship
8. Citizen Kane
9. Godfather Part II
10. Raiders of the Lost Ark
11. American Beauty
12. When Harry Met Sally
13. Beautiful Mind
14. It's a Wonderful Life
15. African Queen
16. Schindler's List
17. Matrix, The
18. Princess Bride
19. Wizard of Oz
20. Annie Hall
21. Usual Suspects*
22. Pretty Woman
23. Sound of Music
24. Moulin Rouge! (2001)
25. Pulp Fiction
26. 2001: A Space Odyssey
27. Gladiator
28. Affair to Remember
29. Breakfast at Tiffany's
30. Goodfellas*
31. Almost Famous
32. Saving Private Ryan
33. Singin' in the Rain*
34. Apocalypse Now
35. Lawrence of Arabia
36. Bridget Jones's Diary
37. Star Wars V/Empire*
38. Shrek
39. Silence of the Lambs*
40. Animal House
41. Forrest Gump
42. All About Eve
43. Top Gun
44. Blade Runner
45. Memento*
46. E.T.
47. Chocolat
48. Graduate, The
49. Dr. Strangelove
50. To Kill a Mockingbird*
51. Dirty Dancing
52. Airplane!
53. Blazing Saddles*
54. Shakespeare in Love*
55. Die Hard
56. Doctor Zhivago*
57. Harry Potter/Sorcerer's Stone
58. American Pie
59. American President
60. Willy Wonka
61. 12 Angry Men
62. As Good As It Gets
63. English Patient*
64. Ferris Bueller's Day Off
65. Rear Window
66. Amadeus
67. Caddyshack
68. Chinatown*
69. Fargo
70. Good Will Hunting*
71. Maltese Falcon
72. Sixth Sense
73. Dead Poets Society
74. Grease*
75. Great Escape
76. Producers, The
77. Roman Holiday
78. Bridge on the River Kwai
79. L.A. Confidential
80. Moonstruck*
81. My Fair Lady*
82. Fight Club
83. Fugitive, The
84. Hunt for Red October*
85. One Flew Over Cuckoo's ...*
86. Being John Malkovich
87. Out of Africa*
88. Birdcage, The
89. Cast Away*
90. Sleepless in Seattle*
91. Some Like It Hot*
92. Titanic*
93. Young Frankenstein
94. Gosford Park
95. West Side Story
96. Billy Elliot
97. Clockwork Orange
98. Thelma & Louise*
99. Breakfast Club
100. North by Northwest

# Overall Quality

(See page 32 for Top Foreign Language Films.)

## Classic (Pre-1960)

| | |
|---|---|
| **29** Casablanca | **27** Sweet Smell of Success |
| **28** Wizard of Oz | Snow White |
| Lady Eve | Philadelphia Story |
| Singin' in the Rain | Woman of the Year |
| Rear Window | Treasure of Sierra Madre |
| It Happened One Night | Notorious |
| Citizen Kane | Searchers, The* |
| All About Eve | Brief Encounter |
| African Queen | Duck Soup |
| Third Man | It's a Wonderful Life |
| Best Years of Our Lives | Christmas Carol |
| Grapes of Wrath | Witness for the Prosecution |
| On the Waterfront | Big Sleep |
| Paths of Glory | Night of the Hunter |
| Fantasia | Streetcar Named Desire |
| Bridge on the River Kwai | Stalag 17 |
| Some Like It Hot | Quiet Man |
| Sunset Boulevard | Top Hat |
| All Quiet/Western Front | Vertigo |
| Gone with the Wind | Rebecca |
| North by Northwest | Roman Holiday |
| High Noon | Place in the Sun |
| 12 Angry Men | Wuthering Heights* |
| Double Indemnity | Now, Voyager |
| Maltese Falcon | 39 Steps |

## Modern (1960 to Date)

| | |
|---|---|
| **29** Godfather | Chinatown |
| Godfather Part II | Apocalypse Now |
| Schindler's List | Lord of Rings/Fellowship |
| Lawrence of Arabia | Patton |
| To Kill a Mockingbird | Annie Hall |
| **28** Star Wars | Sting, The |
| Shawshank Redemption | Chicago |
| Pianist, The | Lord of Rings/Two Towers |
| Finding Nemo | Gandhi |
| Dr. Strangelove | Great Escape |
| Lord of Rings/Return | Million Dollar Baby |
| Man for All Seasons | Wild Bunch |
| Lion in Winter | Princess Bride |
| Hotel Rwanda | Graduate, The |
| Sound of Music | Goodfellas |
| Psycho | Toy Story |
| Raiders of the Lost Ark | Days of Wine and Roses |
| **27** One Flew Over Cuckoo's ... | Doctor Zhivago |
| My Fair Lady | Breaker Morant |
| Usual Suspects | Mary Poppins |
| West Side Story | **26** E.T. |
| Taxi Driver | Shrek |
| Young Frankenstein | MASH |
| Silence of the Lambs | Saving Private Ryan |
| Manchurian Candidate | Fiddler on the Roof |

# By Genre

## Action/Adventure

**Classic**
- **27** Treasure of Sierra Madre
- **25** Adventures of Robin Hood
  - Mutiny on the Bounty
  - King Kong
  - Captains Courageous
- **23** Captain Blood
  - War of the Worlds
  - Mark of Zorro
- **22** Around the World in 80 Days
- **21** Tarzan the Ape Man

**Modern**
- **29** Lawrence of Arabia
- **28** Star Wars
  - Lord of Rings/Return
  - Raiders of the Lost Ark
- **27** Lord of Rings/Fellowship
  - Lord of Rings/Two Towers
  - Great Escape
- **26** Star Wars V/Empire
  - Magnificent Seven
  - Spartacus

## Americana

**Classic**
- **28** Best Years of Our Lives
  - Grapes of Wrath
- **27** It's a Wonderful Life
- **26** Meet Me in St. Louis
  - Mr. Smith Goes to Washington
- **25** Yankee Doodle Dandy
  - All the King's Men
- **24** Oklahoma!
  - East of Eden
  - Giant

**Modern**
- **29** To Kill a Mockingbird
- **26** Christmas Story
- **25** Music Man
  - Badlands
  - Seabiscuit
- **24** Stand by Me
  - American Graffiti
  - Far From Heaven
  - Forrest Gump
  - Straight Story

## Animated

**Classic**
- **28** Fantasia
- **27** Snow White
- **26** Pinocchio
  - Cinderella
  - Bambi
  - Lady and the Tramp
- **25** Peter Pan
  - Sleeping Beauty
- **24** Dumbo
  - Alice in Wonderland

**Modern**
- **28** Finding Nemo
- **27** Toy Story
- **26** Shrek
  - Beauty and the Beast
  - Shrek 2
  - Incredibles, The
  - Monsters, Inc.
- **25** Lion King
- **24** Iron Giant
  - Little Mermaid

## Biography

**Classic**
- **29** Napoléon∇
- **25** Yankee Doodle Dandy
- **24** Sergeant York∇
- **23** Diary of Anne Frank
  - Anastasia
- **22** Pride of the Yankees

**Modern**
- **29** Lawrence of Arabia
- **28** Man for All Seasons
- **27** Patton
  - Gandhi
- **26** Raging Bull
  - Amadeus
  - Becket
  - Ray
  - Last Emperor
  - Funny Girl

# Top Overall

## Children/Family

**Classic**
- 28 Wizard of Oz
- 27 It's a Wonderful Life
  Christmas Carol
  David Copperfield▽
- 24 Jungle Book▽
  National Velvet
  Old Yeller
- 23 Lili▽
  Father of the Bride
- 22 20,000 Leagues Under Sea

**Modern**
- 28 Sound of Music
- 27 Princess Bride
  Mary Poppins
- 26 E.T.
  Christmas Story
  Willy Wonka
- 25 Whale Rider
- 24 Oliver!
  Black Stallion
  Harry Potter/Prisoner

## Comedy

**Classic**
- 28 Some Like It Hot
- 27 Woman of the Year
  Mister Roberts
- 26 Adam's Rib
  Great Dictator
  Harvey
- 25 Auntie Mame
  Lavender Hill Mob
- 24 Bishop's Wife
- 23 Mr. Blandings

**Modern**
- 27 Young Frankenstein
  Annie Hall
  Graduate, The
- 26 This Is Spinal Tap
  When Harry Met Sally
  Manhattan
  Local Hero
- 25 Waiting for Guffman
  Blazing Saddles
  Tootsie

## Crime

**Classic**
- 28 Rear Window
  On the Waterfront
- 26 Arsenic and Old Lace
  Anatomy of a Murder
- 25 Lavender Hill Mob
  Dial M for Murder
  To Catch a Thief
  Public Enemy▽
- 24 Angels with Dirty Faces
- 23 High Sierra▽

**Modern**
- 29 Godfather, The
  Godfather Part II
- 27 Usual Suspects
  Sting, The
  Chicago
  Goodfellas
- 26 Pulp Fiction
  Mystic River
- 25 Fargo
  In Cold Blood

## Cult

**Classic**
- 29 Casablanca
- 28 Wizard of Oz
  All About Eve
  Fantasia
- 27 It's a Wonderful Life
- 26 Red Shoes
- 25 Forbidden Planet
- 21 5,000 Fingers of Dr. T.▽
- 20 7th Voyage of Sinbad

**Modern**
- 28 Star Wars
  Shawshank Redemption
  Dr. Strangelove
  Sound of Music
- 27 Manchurian Candidate
  Princess Bride
- 26 Monty Python/Holy Grail
  Blade Runner
  Willy Wonka
- 25 Harold and Maude

## Drama

**Classic**
- **28** Citizen Kane
  - Best Years of Our Lives
  - Grapes of Wrath
  - On the Waterfront
  - Paths of Glory
  - High Noon
  - 12 Angry Men
- **27** Witness for the Prosecution
  - Streetcar Named Desire
  - Quiet Man

**Modern**
- **29** Godfather, The
  - Godfather Part II
  - Schindler's List
  - To Kill a Mockingbird
- **28** Shawshank Redemption
  - Pianist, The
  - Lion in Winter
  - Hotel Rwanda
- **27** Taxi Driver
  - Million Dollar Baby

## Dramedy

**Classic**
- **28** All About Eve
  - African Queen
- **27** Dinner at Eight▽
  - It's a Wonderful Life
  - Stalag 17
  - Sullivan's Travels▽
  - Women, The*▽
- **26** Mr. Smith Goes to Washington
- **25** Sabrina
  - Ninotchka▽

**Modern**
- **27** One Flew Over Cuckoo's . . .
  - Sting, The
- **26** Breakfast at Tiffany's
  - Crimes and Misdemeanors
  - Sense and Sensibility
  - Charade
  - Bend It Like Beckham
  - Cool Hand Luke
- **25** Apartment, The
  - Fargo

## Epic

**Classic**
- **28** Bridge on the River Kwai
  - Gone with the Wind
- **26** Ben-Hur
- **25** Mutiny on the Bounty
  - Gunga Din
- **24** Ten Commandments
  - Giant
- **22** Around the World in 80 Days
- **20** King Solomon's Mines
- **19** Robe, The▽

**Modern**
- **29** Lawrence of Arabia
- **27** Gandhi
  - Doctor Zhivago
- **26** Last Emperor
  - Braveheart
  - Spartacus
- **25** Empire of the Sun
- **24** Longest Day
  - Zulu
  - Once Upon a Time . . .

## Fantasy

**Classic**
- **28** Wizard of Oz
- **27** Christmas Carol
- **26** Harvey
- **25** Miracle on 34th Street
  - King Kong
  - Lost Horizon
- **24** Ghost and Mrs. Muir
- **21** 5,000 Fingers of Dr. T.▽
- **20** Topper
  - 7th Voyage of Sinbad

**Modern**
- **28** Lord of Rings/Return
  - Raiders of the Lost Ark
- **27** Lord of Rings/Fellowship
  - Lord of Rings/Two Towers
  - Princess Bride
  - Mary Poppins
- **26** Willy Wonka
- **24** Indiana Jones/Last Crusade
  - Pirates of the Caribbean
  - Brazil

# Top Overall

## Film Noir

**Classic**
- 28 Third Man
  - Sunset Boulevard
  - Double Indemnity
  - Maltese Flacon
- 27 Sweet Smell of Success
  - Big Sleep
  - Night of the Hunter
  - Laura
- 26 Touch of Evil
  - Strangers on a Train

**Modern**
- 27 Chinatown
- 26 Blade Runner
  - L.A. Confidential
  - Memento
- 25 Cape Fear
- 24 Body Heat
  - Blood Simple
- 23 Seven
- 22 Last Seduction
  - Dead Again

## Horror

**Classic**
- 25 Frankenstein
  - Bride of Frankenstein
- 24 Dracula
  - Invasion of Body Snatchers
- 23 Thing, The
- 22 Invisible Man
- 21 House of Wax
- 20 Wolf Man
  - Fly, The
- 16 Godzilla

**Modern**
- 25 Exorcist, The
  - Shining, The
- 24 Rosemary's Baby
- 23 Thing, The
- 22 Poltergeist
  - Halloween
  - Carrie
  - Evil Dead
  - Night of the Living Dead
- 21 Omen, The

## Musical

**Classic**
- 28 Wizard of Oz
  - Singin' in the Rain
- 27 Top Hat
  - King and I
- 26 American in Paris
  - Band Wagon
  - Meet Me in St. Louis
- 25 Yankee Doodle Dandy
  - White Christmas
- 24 Gigi

**Modern**
- 28 Sound of Music
- 27 My Fair Lady
  - West Side Story
  - Chicago
  - Mary Poppins
- 26 Fiddler on the Roof
  - Cabaret
  - Funny Girl
- 25 Music Man
  - That's Entertainment!

## Romance

**Classic**
- 29 Casablanca
- 28 Lady Eve
  - It Happened One Night
  - African Queen
  - Gone with the Wind
- 27 Philadelphia Story
  - Notorious
  - Brief Encounter
  - Quiet Man
  - Top Hat

**Modern**
- 27 Annie Hall
  - Graduate, The
  - Doctor Zhivago
- 26 Room with a View
  - Charade
  - Manhattan
  - Romeo and Juliet
- 25 Harold and Maude
  - Apartment, The
  - Tootsie

## Sci-Fi

**Classic**
- 25 Forbidden Planet
- Day the Earth Stood Still
- 24 Invasion of Body Snatchers
- 23 War of the Worlds
- Thing, The
- 22 20,000 Leagues Under Sea
- 20 Fly, The
- 19 Journey to Center of the Earth
- 16 Godzilla

**Modern**
- 28 Star Wars
- 26 E.T.
- Stars Wars V/Empire
- Blade Runner
- 2001
- 25 Matrix, The
- Alien
- 24 Star Wars VI/Return of Jedi
- Close Encounters
- Terminator, The

## Thriller

**Classic**
- 28 Rear Window
- Third Man
- North by Northwest
- 27 Notorious
- Night of the Hunter
- Vertigo
- 39 Steps
- 26 Gaslight
- Strangers on a Train
- 25 Lifeboat

**Modern**
- 28 Psycho
- 27 Taxi Driver
- Silence of the Lambs
- Manchurian Candidate
- 26 Jaws
- Pulp Fiction
- Memento
- Seven Days in May
- Sixth Sense
- 25 Wait Until Dark

## War

**Classic**
- 29 Casablanca
- 28 Paths of Glory
- Bridge on River Kwai
- All Quiet on Western Front
- 27 Stalag 17
- Caine Mutiny
- Mister Roberts
- 26 Twelve O'Clock High
- 25 Gunga Din
- For Whom the Bell Tolls

**Modern**
- 29 Schindler's List
- 28 Pianist, The
- Hotel Rwanda
- 27 Apocalypse Now
- Patton
- Great Escape
- 26 MASH
- Saving Private Ryan
- Henry V
- Deer Hunter

## Western

**Classic**
- 28 High Noon
- 27 Searchers, The
- Ox-Bow Incident▽
- Stagecoach
- 26 Red River
- Shane
- 24 Oklahoma!
- She Wore a Yellow Ribbon
- 23 Fort Apache
- Rio Bravo▽

**Modern**
- 27 Wild Bunch
- 26 Butch Cassidy
- Unforgiven
- Magnificent Seven
- 25 Outlaw Josey Wales
- Man Who Shot Liberty Valance
- 24 Good, the Bad and the Ugly
- Little Big Man
- Silverado
- 23 McCabe & Mrs. Miller

# Top Overall

## By Decade

### 1910s/1920s
29 Napoléon▽
28 Greed▽
   General, The
   Gold Rush▽
27 Intolerance▽
   Potemkin
   Metropolis
26 Cabinet of Dr. Caligari
25 Birth of a Nation
24 Cocoanuts, The

### 1930s
28 Wizard of Oz
   It Happened One Night
   All Quiet/Western Front
   Modern Times
   Gone with the Wind
27 Snow White
   Duck Soup
   Top Hat
   Wuthering Heights
   39 Steps

### 1940s
29 Casablanca
28 Lady Eve
   Citizen Kane
   Third Man
   Best Years of Our Lives
   Grapes of Wrath
   Fantasia
   Double Indemnity
   Maltese Falcon
27 Philadelphia Story

### 1950s
28 Singin' in the Rain
   Rear Window
   All About Eve
   African Queen
   On the Waterfront
   Paths of Glory
   Bridge on the River Kwai
   Some Like It Hot
   Sunset Boulevard
   North by Northwest

### 1960s
29 Lawrence of Arabia
   To Kill a Mockingbird
28 Dr. Strangelove
   Man for All Seasons
   Lion in Winter
   Sound of Music
   Psycho
27 My Fair Lady
   West Side Story
   Manchurian Candidate

### 1970s
29 Godfather, The
   Godfather Part II
28 Star Wars
27 One Flew Over Cuckoo's ...
   Taxi Driver
   Young Frankenstein
   Chinatown
   Apocalypse Now
   Patton
   Annie Hall

### 1980s
28 Raiders of the Lost Ark
27 Gandhi
   Princess Bride
   Breaker Morant
26 E.T.
   Raging Bull
   Amadeus
   Star Wars V/Empire
   Right Stuff
   Henry V

### 1990s
29 Schindler's List
28 Shawshank Redemption
27 Usual Suspects
   Silence of the Lambs
   Goodfellas
   Toy Story
26 Saving Private Ryan
   Beauty and the Beast
   Pulp Fiction
   L.A. Confidential

### 2000s
28 Pianist, The
   Finding Nemo
   Lord of Rings/Return
   Hotel Rwanda
27 Lord of Rings/Fellowship
   Chicago
   Lord of Rings/Two Towers
   Million Dollar Baby
   Spirited Away
26 Shrek
   Shrek 2
   Beautiful Mind
   Incredibles, The
   Crash
   Ray
   Rabbit-Proof Fence
   Fog of War
   In America
   Monsters, Inc.
   Memento
   Bend It Like Beckham

# By Director

**Robert Aldrich**
25 Flight of the Phoenix
22 Whatever Happened to ...
21 Dirty Dozen

**Woody Allen**
27 Annie Hall
26 Crimes and Misdemeanors
Manhattan

**Pedro Almodóvar**
26 Talk to Her
25 All About My Mother
24 Women on the Verge ...

**Robert Altman**
26 MASH
23 McCabe & Mrs. Miller
Player, The

**Hal Ashby**
26 Being There
25 Harold and Maude
23 Coming Home

**Bruce Beresford**
27 Breaker Morant
24 Driving Miss Daisy
16 Double Jeopardy

**Ingmar Bergman**
27 Seventh Seal
26 Wild Strawberries
Fanny and Alexander

**Bernardo Bertolucci**
26 Conformist, The
Last Emperor
17 Last Tango in Paris

**Peter Bogdanovich**
23 Last Picture Show
22 Paper Moon
21 What's Up, Doc?

**Kenneth Branagh**
26 Henry V
24 Hamlet
22 Dead Again

**James L. Brooks**
25 Terms of Endearment
23 Broadcast News
22 As Good As It Gets

**Mel Brooks**
27 Young Frankenstein
26 Producers, The
25 Blazing Saddles

**Richard Brooks**
25 Elmer Gantry
In Cold Blood
Cat on a Hot Tin Roof

**Tim Burton**
22 Big Fish
21 Edward Scissorhands
20 Batman

**James Cameron**
24 Terminator, The
23 Aliens
20 Abyss, The

**Frank Capra**
28 It Happened One Night
27 It's a Wonderful Life
26 Arsenic and Old Lace

**Charlie Chaplin**
28 City Lights
Modern Times
26 Great Dictator

**Joel Coen**
25 Fargo
24 Blood Simple
23 Raising Arizona

**Chris Columbus**
24 Harry Potter/Sorcerer's
Harry Potter/Chamber
20 Mrs. Doubtfire

**Francis Ford Coppola**
29 Godfather, The
Godfather Part II
27 Apocalypse Now

**George Cukor**
27 My Fair Lady
Philadelphia Story
26 Adam's Rib

**Michael Curtiz**
29 Casablanca
26 Mildred Pierce
25 Yankee Doodle Dandy

**Jonathan Demme**
27 Silence of the Lambs
25 Stop Making Sense
24 Philadelphia

**Stanley Donen**
28 Singin' in the Rain
26 Charade
24 Funny Face

**Clint Eastwood**
27 Million Dollar Baby
26 Unforgiven
Mystic River

**Blake Edwards**
27 Days of Wine and Roses
26 Breakfast at Tiffany's
24 Pink Panther

# Top Overall

**Federico Fellini**
27 La Strada
Nights of Cabiria
26 8½

**Victor Fleming**
28 Wizard of Oz
Gone with the Wind
25 Captains Courageous

**John Ford**
28 Grapes of Wrath
27 Searchers, The
Quiet Man

**Milos Forman**
27 One Flew Over Cuckoo's ...
26 Amadeus
20 Hair

**Bob Fosse**
26 Cabaret
24 All That Jazz
20 Sweet Charity

**John Frankenheimer**
27 Manchurian Candidate
26 Seven Days in May
22 Birdman of Alcatraz

**Stephen Frears**
24 Dangerous Liaisons
23 Dirty Pretty Things
22 Grifters, The

**Terry Gilliam**
26 Monty Python/Holy Grail
24 Brazil
22 Twelve Monkeys

**Christopher Guest**
25 Waiting for Guffman
24 Best in Show
23 Mighty Wind

**Lasse Hallström**
25 My Life As a Dog
22 Chocolat
What's Eating Gilbert Grape

**Curtis Hanson**
26 L.A. Confidential
21 Wonder Boys
16 Hand That Rocks the Cradle

**Howard Hawks**
27 Big Sleep
Bringing Up Baby
26 Red River

**George Roy Hill**
27 Sting, The
26 Butch Cassidy
22 Slap Shot

**Alfred Hitchcock**
28 Rear Window
North by Northwest
Psycho

**Ron Howard**
26 Beautiful Mind
24 Apollo 13
22 Parenthood

**John Hughes**
23 Ferris Bueller's Day Off
22 Breakfast Club
Sixteen Candles

**John Huston**
28 African Queen
Maltese Falcon
27 Treasure of Sierra Madre

**James Ivory**
26 Room with a View
24 Remains of the Day
22 Howards End

**Peter Jackson**
28 Lord of Rings/Return
27 Lord of Rings/Fellowship
Lord of Rings/Two Towers

**Lawrence Kasdan**
24 Body Heat
Silverado
23 Big Chill

**Philip Kaufman**
26 Right Stuff
21 Unbearable Lightness of Being
19 Invasion of Body Snatchers

**Elia Kazan**
28 On the Waterfront
27 Streetcar Named Desire
25 Splendor in the Grass

**Stanley Kramer**
26 Inherit the Wind
Judgment at Nuremberg
25 Guess Who's Coming to Dinner

**Stanley Kubrick**
28 Dr. Strangelove
Paths of Glory
26 2001: A Space Odyssey

**Akira Kurosawa**
29 Seven Samurai
Rashomon
27 Ran

**David Lean**
29 Lawrence of Arabia
28 Bridge on the River Kwai
27 Brief Encounter

**Ang Lee**
26 Sense and Sensibility
25 Eat Drink Man Woman
24 Crouching Tiger

**Spike Lee**
23 Malcolm X
   Do the Right Thing
21 25th Hour

**Mike Leigh**
24 Vera Drake
   Secrets & Lies
23 Topsy-Turvy

**Sergio Leone**
24 Good, the Bad and the Ugly
   Once Upon a Time in America
19 Fistful of Dollars

**Richard Lester**
24 Hard Day's Night
22 Three Musketeers
   Funny Thing Happened . . .

**Barry Levinson**
25 Rain Man
   Diner
23 Natural, The

**Joshua Logan**
24 South Pacific
   Picnic
21 Camelot

**George Lucas**
28 Star Wars
24 American Graffiti
23 Star Wars III/Revenge of Sith

**Baz Luhrmann**
23 Moulin Rouge!
   Strictly Ballroom
19 Romeo + Juliet

**Sidney Lumet**
28 12 Angry Men
26 Pawnbroker, The
24 Fail-Safe

**David Lynch**
24 Elephant Man
   Straight Story
22 Blue Velvet

**Terrence Malick**
25 Badlands
23 Days of Heaven
19 Thin Red Line

**Louis Malle**
27 Au Revoir Les Enfants
24 Atlantic City
21 My Dinner with Andre

**Joseph L. Mankiewicz**
28 All About Eve
25 Sleuth
24 Ghost and Mrs. Muir

**Michael Mann**
25 Insider, The
22 Last of the Mohicans
   Heat

**Penny Marshall**
23 Big
22 Awakenings
20 League of their Own

**Anthony Minghella**
22 Cold Mountain
   English Patient
18 Talented Mr. Ripley

**Vincente Minnelli**
26 American in Paris
   Band Wagon
   Meet Me in St. Louis

**Michael Moore**
24 Roger & Me
22 Bowling for Columbine
21 Fahrenheit 9/11

**Mike Newell**
24 Enchanted April
21 Four Weddings and a Funeral
20 Donnie Brasco

**Mike Nichols**
27 Graduate, The
25 Who's Afraid of V. Woolf?
22 Silkwood

**Alan J. Pakula**
26 Sophie's Choice
25 All the President's Men
20 Klute

**Alan Parker**
24 Midnight Express
23 Mississippi Burning
21 Life of David Gale

**Alexander Payne**
23 Sideways
22 Election
21 About Schmidt

**Arthur Penn**
25 Miracle Worker
   Bonnie and Clyde
24 Little Big Man

**Wolfgang Petersen**
28 Das Boot
20 In the Line of Fire
18 Air Force One

# Top Overall

**Roman Polanski**
*28* Pianist, The
*27* Chinatown
*24* Rosemary's Baby

**Sydney Pollack**
*25* Tootsie
Out of Africa
*24* Way We Were

**Otto Preminger**
*27* Laura
*26* Anatomy of a Murder
*23* Exodus

**Robert Redford**
*25* Ordinary People
*22* River Runs Through It
*21* Quiz Show

**Rob Reiner**
*27* Princess Bride
*26* This Is Spinal Tap
When Harry Met Sally

**Franklin J. Schaffner**
*27* Patton
*26* Papillon
*23* Planet of the Apes

**Martin Scorsese**
*27* Taxi Driver
Goodfellas
*26* Raging Bull

**Ridley Scott**
*26* Blade Runner
*25* Alien
*23* Gladiator

**Bryan Singer**
*27* Usual Suspects
*24* X2
*19* X-Men

**Steven Soderbergh**
*23* Traffic
*21* Out of Sight
Erin Brockovich

**Steven Spielberg**
*29* Schindler's List
*28* Raiders of the Lost Ark
*26* E.T.

**George Stevens**
*27* Woman of the Year
Place in the Sun
*26* Shane

**Oliver Stone**
*25* Platoon
*22* Wall Street
*20* Born on the Fourth of July

**John Sturges**
*27* Great Escape
*26* Magnificent Seven
*24* Bad Day at Black Rock

**Quentin Tarantino**
*26* Pulp Fiction
*25* Kill Bill Vol. 2
*24* Reservoir Dogs

**François Truffaut**
*27* 400 Blows
Day for Night
*24* Jules and Jim

**Gus Van Sant**
*24* Good Will Hunting
*19* My Own Private Idaho
Drugstore Cowboy

**Peter Weir**
*25* Gallipoli
*24* Year of Living Dangerously
Dead Poets Society

**Orson Welles**
*28* Citizen Kane
*26* Touch of Evil
*25* Lady from Shanghai

**James Whale**
*25* Frankenstein
Bride of Frankenstein
*22* Invisible Man

**Billy Wilder**
*28* Some Like It Hot
Sunset Boulevard
Double Indemnity

**Robert Wise**
*28* Sound of Music
*27* West Side Story
*25* Day the Earth Stood Still

**William Wyler**
*28* Best Years of Our Lives
*27* Roman Holiday
Wuthering Heights

**Terence Young**
*25* Wait Until Dark
*23* From Russia with Love
Dr. No

**Robert Zemeckis**
*24* Forrest Gump
Who Framed Roger Rabbit
*23* Back to the Future

**Fred Zinnemann**
*28* Man for All Seasons
High Noon
*26* From Here to Eternity

**subscribe to zagat.com**

# Acting

| | |
|---|---|
| *29* Godfather Part II | Raging Bull |
| Godfather, The | Adam's Rib |
| All About Eve | Philadelphia Story |
| One Flew Over Cuckoo's . . . | Sweet Smell of Success |
| Monster | Inherit the Wind |
| Ray | White Heat |
| Lion in Winter | Mystic River |
| Taxi Driver | Cries and Whispers |
| On the Waterfront | Sophie's Choice |
| Becket | My Left Foot |
| To Kill a Mockingbird | Night of the Hunter |
| Schindler's List | Midnight Cowboy |
| Pianist, The | Born Yesterday |
| Brief Encounter | Kind Hearts and Coronets |
| African Queen | Grapes of Wrath |
| *28* Hotel Rwanda | Chinatown |
| Casablanca | Vera Drake |
| Beautiful Mind | Woman of the Year |
| Million Dollar Baby | Apartment, The |
| Streetcar Named Desire | Caine Mutiny |
| Silence of the Lambs | Sunset Boulevard |
| Days of Wine and Roses | Sleuth |
| 12 Angry Men | Witness/Prosecution |
| Gandhi | Bridge on the River Kwai |
| Man for All Seasons | American History X |
| Lady Eve | It Happened One Night |
| Patton | Hours, The |
| Shawshank Redemption | Third Man |
| Lawrence of Arabia | Dr. Strangelove |
| Now, Voyager | Mrs. Brown |

# By Lead Actor

**Woody Allen**
*26* Annie Hall
 Crimes and Misdemeanors
*24* Manhattan

**Julie Andrews**
*25* Sound of Music
*24* Mary Poppins
 Victor/Victoria

**Ann-Margret**
*26* Carnal Knowledge
*24* Grumpy Old Men
*18* Bye Bye Birdie

**Fred Astaire**
*24* Funny Face
*23* Top Hat
*21* Band Wagon

**Lauren Bacall**
*27* To Have and Have Not
 Big Sleep
*26* Key Largo

**Alec Baldwin**
*27* Glengarry Glen Ross
 Cooler, The
*24* Hunt for Red October

**Anne Bancroft**
*28* Miracle Worker
*27* Graduate, The
*25* Agnes of God

**Antonio Banderas**
*24* Women on the Verge
*21* Tie Me Up! Tie Me Down!
*19* Interview with the Vampire

**Alan Bates**
*27* Zorba the Greek
*25* Unmarried Woman
*23* Rose, The

**Kathy Bates**
*26* About Schmidt
*25* Fried Green Tomatoes
*24* Misery

# Top Acting

**Warren Beatty**
25 Bonnie and Clyde
   Splendor in the Grass
23 McCabe and Mrs. Miller

**Annette Bening**
27 Being Julia
   American Beauty
26 Grifters, The

**Ingrid Bergman**
28 Casablanca
27 Notorious
   Gaslight

**Gael García Bernal**
26 Bad Education
25 Motorcycle Diaries
24 Y Tu Mamá También

**Juliette Binoche**
24 English Patient
   Unbearable Lightness of Being
   Chocolat

**Humphrey Bogart**
29 African Queen
28 Casablanca
   Caine Mutiny

**Helena Bonham Carter**
26 Howards End
   Room with a View
25 Fight Club

**Kenneth Branagh**
28 Henry V
26 Hamlet
25 Rabbit-Proof Fence

**Marlon Brando**
29 Godfather, The
   On the Waterfront
28 Streetcar Named Desire

**Jeff Bridges**
25 Seabiscuit
24 Fisher King
23 Last Picture Show

**Matthew Broderick**
26 Glory
24 Election
22 Ferris Bueller's Day Off

**Yul Brynner**
27 Anastasia
26 King and I
21 Ten Commandments

**Ellen Burstyn**
27 Requiem for a Dream
26 Alice Doesn't Live Here
24 Exorcist, The

**Richard Burton**
29 Becket
27 Who's Afraid of V. Woolf?
18 Cleopatra

**Nicolas Cage**
26 Adaptation
25 Moonstruck
24 Leaving Las Vegas

**James Cagney**
28 White Heat
27 Mister Roberts
25 Yankee Doodle Dandy

**Michael Caine**
28 Sleuth
26 Man Who Would Be King
   Quiet American

**Leslie Caron**
23 Gigi
   Lili
   American in Paris

**Jim Carrey**
24 Eternal Sunshine
22 Truman Show
   Man on the Moon

**Charlie Chaplin**
28 City Lights
27 Great Dictator
26 Modern Times

**Don Cheadle**
28 Hotel Rwanda
27 Crash
17 Family Man

**Cher**
26 Silkwood
25 Moonstruck
24 Mask

**Julie Christie**
26 Doctor Zhivago
23 McCabe and Mrs. Miller
19 Fahrenheit 451

**Montgomery Clift**
27 From Here to Eternity
   Place in the Sun
25 Red River

**George Clooney**
23 O Brother, Where Art Thou?
21 Out of Sight
   Thin Red Line

**Glenn Close**
26 Dangerous Liaisons
24 Big Chill
23 Fatal Attraction

**Jennifer Connelly**
28 Beautiful Mind
27 House of Sand & Fog
Requiem for a Dream

**Sean Connery**
26 Man Who Would Be King
25 Wind and the Lion
24 Hunt for Red October

**Chris Cooper**
27 American Beauty
26 Adaptation
25 Lone Star

**Gary Cooper**
26 High Noon
For Whom the Bell Tolls
23 Beau Geste

**Kevin Costner**
26 Upside of Anger
24 Silverado
22 Bull Durham

**Joseph Cotten**
28 Third Man
27 Gaslight
23 Magnificent Ambersons

**Joan Crawford**
26 Women, The▽
25 Grand Hotel▽
Mildred Pierce

**Russell Crowe**
28 Beautiful Mind
Insider, The
27 L.A. Confidential

**Tom Cruise**
27 Rain Man
26 Few Good Men
24 Collateral

**Billy Crystal**
25 When Harry Met Sally
21 Analyze This
20 City Slickers

**Tony Curtis**
28 Sweet Smell of Success
27 Some Like It Hot
19 Operation Petticoat

**John Cusack**
26 Grifters, The
24 Being John Malkovich
23 Bullets Over Broadway

**Willem Dafoe**
25 Platoon
Shadow of the Vampire
24 Mississippi Burning

**Matt Damon**
26 Saving Private Ryan
25 Good Will Hunting
21 Talented Mr. Ripley

**Bette Davis**
29 All About Eve
28 Now, Voyager
27 Dark Victory

**Geena Davis**
25 Thelma & Louise
24 Accidental Tourist
20 League of Their Own

**Daniel Day-Lewis**
28 My Left Foot
25 In the Name of the Father
24 Age of Innocence

**James Dean**
27 East of Eden
24 Rebel Without a Cause
23 Giant

**Benicio Del Toro**
28 Usual Suspects
27 21 Grams
24 Traffic

**Judi Dench**
28 Mrs. Brown
27 Iris
25 Shakespeare In Love

**Catherine Deneuve**
25 Belle de Jour
Indochine
23 Dancer in the Dark

**Robert De Niro**
29 Taxi Driver
28 Raging Bull
Deer Hunter

**Johnny Depp**
27 Finding Neverland
25 Pirates of the Caribbean
What's Eating Gilbert Grape

**Cameron Diaz**
24 Being John Malkovich
19 There's Something About Mary
18 Mask, The

**Leonardo DiCaprio**
25 What's Eating Gilbert Grape
Aviator, The
24 Catch Me If You Can

**Kirk Douglas**
27 Paths of Glory
24 Seven Days in May
Spartacus

# Top Acting

**Michael Douglas**
25 China Syndrome
24 Traffic
   Wonder Boys

**Richard Dreyfuss**
24 Apprenticeship of D. Kravitz
23 Goodbye Girl
   American Graffiti

**Faye Dunaway**
28 Chinatown
25 Network
   Bonnie and Clyde

**Clint Eastwood**
28 Million Dollar Baby
26 Unforgiven
23 Outlaw Josey Wales

**Mia Farrow**
26 Crimes and Misdemeanors
25 Hannah and Her Sisters
   Rosemary's Baby

**Sally Field**
27 Norma Rae
25 Steel Magnolias
   Absence of Malice

**Ralph Fiennes**
29 Schindler's List
24 End of the Affair
   English Patient

**Albert Finney**
27 Two for the Road
24 Tom Jones
22 Big Fish

**Laurence Fishburne**
26 What's Love Got to Do with It
22 Boyz N the Hood
19 Matrix, The

**Henry Fonda**
28 12 Angry Men
   Lady Eve
   Grapes of Wrath

**Jane Fonda**
27 On Golden Pond
26 Coming Home
25 China Syndrome

**Harrison Ford**
24 Fugitive, The
   Raiders of the Lost Ark
   Witness

**Jodie Foster**
28 Silence of the Lambs
   Accused, The
26 Alice Doesn't Live Here

**Brendan Fraser**
27 Gods & Monsters
26 Quiet American
16 Mummy, The

**Morgan Freeman**
28 Million Dollar Baby
   Shawshank Redemption
27 Driving Miss Daisy

**Clark Gable**
28 It Happened One Night
27 Gone with the Wind
25 Mutiny on Bounty (1935)

**Judy Garland**
26 Wizard of Oz
   Star is Born
24 Meet Me in St. Louis

**Richard Gere**
26 Chicago
25 Primal Fear
24 Unfaithful

**Mel Gibson**
25 Year of Living Dangerously
   Gallipoli
24 Braveheart

**Whoopi Goldberg**
27 Color Purple
21 Ghost
18 Sister Act

**Cuba Gooding Jr.**
25 Radio
22 Boyz N the Hood
   Jerry Maguire

**Cary Grant**
28 Philadelphia Story
   His Girl Friday
27 Bringing Up Baby

**Hugh Grant**
23 Bridget Jones's Diary
   Love Actually
   About a Boy

**Alec Guinness**
28 Kind Hearts and Coronets
   Bridge on the River Kwai
26 Lavender Hill Mob

**Gene Hackman**
26 Conversation, The
   Unforgiven
   French Connection

**Tom Hanks**
27 Philadelphia
26 Road to Perdition
   Forrest Gump

**Ed Harris**
*28* Beautiful Mind
*27* Glengarry Glen Ross
*26* Pollock

**Rex Harrison**
*27* My Fair Lady
*25* Ghost and Mrs. Muir
*18* Cleopatra

**Ethan Hawke**
*27* Training Day
*25* Dead Poets Society
*23* Before Sunset

**Audrey Hepburn**
*27* My Fair Lady
   Two for the Road
*26* Roman Holiday

**Katharine Hepburn**
*29* Lion in Winter
   African Queen
*28* Adam's Rib

**Charlton Heston**
*24* Touch of Evil
*23* Ben-Hur
*21* Ten Commandments

**Dustin Hoffman**
*28* Midnight Cowboy
*27* Graduate, The
   Rain Man

**Philip Seymour Hoffman**
*25* Happiness
   25th Hour
*23* Magnolia

**William Holden**
*28* Born Yesterday
   Sunset Boulevard
   Bridge on the River Kwai

**Judy Holliday**
*28* Adam's Rib
   Born Yesterday
*24* Bells Are Ringing

**Anthony Hopkins**
*28* Silence of the Lambs
*27* Elephant Man
   Remains of the Day

**Dennis Hopper**
*23* Easy Rider
   Blue Velvet
*22* Hoosiers

**Holly Hunter**
*26* Thirteen
*25* Broadcast News
*24* Piano, The

**William Hurt**
*25* Children of a Lesser God
   Body Heat
   Kiss of the Spider Woman

**Angelica Huston**
*26* Crimes and Misdemeanors
   Grifters, The
*24* Prizzi's Honor

**Jeremy Irons**
*27* Being Julia
*25* French Lieutenant's Woman
*24* Mission, The

**Scarlett Johansson**
*26* Ghost World
*24* Lost in Translation
*23* Girl with a Pearl Earring

**Shirley Jones**
*27* Elmer Gantry
*24* Music Man
*22* Oklahoma!

**Tommy Lee Jones**
*27* Coal Miner's Daughter
*24* Fugitive, The
*20* Men in Black

**Diane Keaton**
*26* Annie Hall
   Something's Gotta Give
*24* Manhattan

**Gene Kelly**
*28* Inherit the Wind
*26* Singin' in the Rain
*23* American in Paris

**Grace Kelly**
*27* Rear Window
*26* High Noon
*25* To Catch a Thief

**Deborah Kerr**
*27* From Here to Eternity
*26* King and I
*25* Affair to Remember

**Nicole Kidman**
*28* Hours, The
*25* Others, The
*24* Cold Mountain

**Ben Kingsley**
*29* Schindler's List
*28* Gandhi
*27* House of Sand & Fog

**Kevin Kline**
*28* Sophie's Choice
*24* Fish Called Wanda
   Big Chill

## Top Acting

**Burt Lancaster**
*28* Sweet Smell of Success
*27* Elmer Gantry
Atlantic City

**Jessica Lange**
*28* Frances
*27* Tootsie
*24* Cape Fear

**Jude Law**
*26* Road to Perdition
*24* Cold Mountain
*21* Talented Mr. Ripley

**Janet Leigh**
*26* Psycho
*24* Touch of Evil
*18* Bye Bye Birdie

**Jack Lemmon**
*28* Days of Wine and Roses
Apartment, The
*27* Odd Couple

**Laura Linney**
*26* You Can Count on Me
Kinsey
*25* Primal Fear

**Myrna Loy**
*27* Best Years of Our Lives
*25* Thin Man
*24* Mr. Blandings . . .

**Shirley MacLaine**
*28* Apartment, The
*27* Being There
*26* Terms of Endearment

**Fred MacMurray**
*28* Apartment, The
*27* Double Indemnity
*17* Absent-Minded Professor

**Tobey Maguire**
*25* Seabiscuit
*24* Wonder Boys
Cider House Rules

**John Malkovich**
*26* Dangerous Liaisons
Killing Fields
*25* Shadow of the Vampire

**Fredric March**
*28* Inherit the Wind
*27* Best Years of Our Lives
*24* Seven Days in May

**Marx Brothers**
*25* Duck Soup
Night at the Opera
*24* Animal Crackers

**James Mason**
*26* North by Northwest
Star Is Born
*24* Lolita

**Matthew McConaughey**
*25* Lonestar
*24* Amistad
*21* Contact

**Frances McDormand**
*27* Fargo
*25* Man Who Wasn't There
Blood Simple

**Kelly McGillis**
*28* Accused, The
*24* Witness
*18* Top Gun

**Ewan McGregor**
*24* Big Fish
*23* Moulin Rouge!
*22* Trainspotting

**Ian McKellen**
*27* Gods & Monsters
*26* Lord of Rings/Return
*25* Lord of Rings/Fellowship

**Steve McQueen**
*27* Papillon
*26* Sand Pebbles
Great Escape

**Ray Milland**
*25* Lost Weekend
*24* Dial M for Murder
*23* Beau Geste

**Liza Minnelli**
*25* Cabaret
*21* Arthur
*19* New York, New York▽

**Marilyn Monroe**
*27* Some Like It Hot
*23* Seven Year Itch
*21* Gentlemen Prefer Blondes

**Yves Montand**
*27* Jean de Florette
*26* Wages of Fear
*25* Z

**Julianne Moore**
*28* Hours, The
*27* Far From Heaven
*24* End of the Affair

**Viggo Mortensen**
*26* Lord of Rings/Return
*25* Lord of Rings/Fellowship
Lord of Rings/Two Towers

**Bill Murray**
25 Rushmore
24 Lost in Translation
   Royal Tenenbaums

**Liam Neeson**
29 Schindler's List
26 Kinsey
24 Mission, The

**Paul Newman**
27 Cat on a Hot Tin Roof
   Cool Hand Luke
26 Sting, The

**Jack Nicholson**
29 One Flew Over Cuckoo's . . .
28 Chinatown
27 Five Easy Pieces

**Nick Nolte**
25 Affliction
24 Cape Fear
21 Prince of Tides

**Edward Norton**
28 American History X
25 Fight Club
   Primal Fear

**Kim Novak**
26 Vertigo
24 Picnic
22 Bell, Book and Candle

**Laurence Olivier**
28 Sleuth
27 Wuthering Heights
   Rebecca

**Ryan O'Neal**
23 Paper Moon
20 What's Up, Doc?
18 Barry Lyndon

**Haley Joel Osment**
25 Sixth Sense
   Secondhand Lions
20 A.I.: Artificial Intelligence

**Peter O'Toole**
29 Lion in Winter
   Becket
28 Lawrence of Arabia

**Al Pacino**
29 Godfather Part II
   Godfather, The
28 Insider, The

**Gwyneth Paltrow**
25 Shakespeare In Love
24 Royal Tenenbaums
23 Emma

**Guy Pearce**
27 L.A. Confidential
25 Memento
24 Adventures of Priscilla . . .

**Gregory Peck**
29 To Kill a Mockingbird
26 Cape Fear (1962)
   Roman Holiday

**Sean Penn**
28 Mystic River
27 21 Grams
26 Dead Man Walking

**Joe Pesci**
28 Raging Bull
27 Goodfellas
24 Casino

**Michelle Pfeiffer**
26 Dangerous Liaisons
25 I Am Sam
24 Age of Innocence

**Brad Pitt**
25 Fight Club
23 Seven
   Twelve Monkeys

**Christopher Plummer**
28 Insider, The
26 Man Who Would Be King
25 Sound of Music

**Sidney Poitier**
27 In the Heat of the Night
   Guess Who's Coming to Dinner
26 Lilies of the Field

**William Powell**
27 Mister Roberts
25 Thin Man
   My Man Godfrey

**Dennis Quaid**
27 Far From Heaven
23 Postcards from the Edge
22 Rookie, The

**Claude Rains**
28 Casablanca
   Now, Voyager
27 Notorious

**Robert Redford**
26 Sting, The
   Butch Cassidy
   All the President's Men

**Vanessa Redgrave**
26 Julia
23 Blowup
21 Camelot

## Top Acting

**Lee Remick**
28 Days of Wine and Roses
27 Anatomy of a Murder
21 Omen, The

**Burt Reynolds**
26 Deliverance
21 Boogie Nights
15 Longest Yard

**Tim Robbins**
28 Shawshank Redemption
   Mystic River
23 Player, The

**Julia Roberts**
23 Erin Brockovich
22 Pretty Woman
19 My Best Friend's Wedding

**Edward G. Robinson**
27 Double Indemnity
26 Key Largo
21 Ten Commandments

**Geoffrey Rush**
27 Elizabeth
25 Pirates of the Caribbean
   Shine

**Kurt Russell**
26 Silkwood
23 Miracle
22 Tombstone

**Rosalind Russell**
28 His Girl Friday
25 Auntie Mame
24 Picnic

**Meg Ryan**
25 When Harry Met Sally
22 Sleepless in Seattle
20 You've Got Mail

**Eva Marie Saint**
29 On the Waterfront
26 North by Northwest
23 Exodus

**Susan Sarandon**
27 Atlantic City
26 Dead Man Walking
25 Thelma & Louise

**Peter Sellers**
28 Dr. Strangelove
27 Being There
24 Lolita

**Omar Sharif**
28 Lawrence of Arabia
26 Doctor Zhivago
25 Funny Girl

**Martin Sheen**
27 Apocalypse Now
   Badlands
23 Wall Street

**Jean Simmons**
27 Elmer Gantry
24 Spartacus
21 Guys and Dolls

**Frank Sinatra**
27 From Here to Eternity
26 Manchurian Candidate
23 On the Town

**Will Smith**
24 Six Degrees of Separation
21 Hitch
20 Men In Black

**Sissy Spacek**
27 Badlands
   Coal Miner's Daughter
26 In the Bedroom

**Kevin Spacey**
28 Usual Suspects
27 L.A. Confidential
   American Beauty

**James Spader**
24 Secretary
20 Sex, Lies & Videotape
17 Stargate

**Rod Steiger**
29 On the Waterfront
28 Pawnbroker, The
27 In the Heat of the Night

**James Stewart**
28 Philadelphia Story
27 Rear Window
   Anatomy of a Murder

**Ben Stiller**
24 Royal Tenenbaums
21 Meet the Parents
19 There's Something About Mary

**Meryl Streep**
28 Sophie's Choice
   Hours, The
26 Adaptation

**Barbra Streisand**
25 Funny Girl
   Way We Were
21 Prince of Tides

**Donald Sutherland**
27 Ordinary People
25 MASH
24 Six Degrees of Separation

**Elizabeth Taylor**
27 Who's Afraid of V. Woolf?
Cat on a Hot Tin Roof
Place in the Sun

**Charlize Theron**
29 Monster
24 Cider House Rules
19 Italian Job

**Emma Thompson**
27 Sense and Sensibility
Remains of the Day
26 Howards End

**Billy Bob Thornton**
27 Sling Blade
26 Monster's Ball
25 Man Who Wasn't There

**Uma Thurman**
26 Pulp Fiction
24 Kill Bill Vol. 2
22 Kill Bill Vol. 1

**Spencer Tracy**
28 Adam's Rib
Inherit the Wind
Woman of the Year

**John Travolta**
26 Pulp Fiction
19 Saturday Night Fever
Face/Off

**Jean-Louis Trintignant**
26 Conformist, The
25 Z
24 Man and a Woman

**Kathleen Turner**
25 Body Heat
24 Prizzi's Honor
Accidental Tourist

**John Turturro**
24 Barton Fink
23 Quiz Show
O Brother, Where Art Thou?

**Jon Voight**
28 Midnight Cowboy
26 Coming Home
Deliverance

**Max Von Sydow**
27 Seventh Seal
24 Exorcist, The
20 Minority Report

**Christopher Walken**
28 Deer Hunter
25 Man on Fire
24 Catch Me If You Can

**Denzel Washington**
27 Philadelphia
Training Day
26 Hurricane

**John Wayne**
25 Red River
Searchers, The
Quiet Man

**Sigourney Weaver**
25 Year of Living Dangerously
23 Holes
22 Alien

**Orson Welles**
28 Third Man
27 Citizen Kane
Jane Eyre

**Gene Wilder**
26 Producers, The
Young Frankenstein
22 Blazing Saddles

**Tom Wilkinson**
26 In the Bedroom
24 Eternal Sunshine
23 Girl with a Pearl Earring

**Robin Williams**
26 Awakenings
25 Dead Poets Society
Good Will Hunting

**Bruce Willis**
26 Pulp Fiction
25 Sixth Sense
23 Twelve Monkeys

**Kate Winslet**
27 Finding Neverland
Sense and Sensibility
25 Heavenly Creatures

**Reese Witherspoon**
24 Election
23 Importance of Being Earnest
21 Pleasantville

**Natalie Wood**
25 Splendor in the Grass
24 West Side Story
Rebel Without a Cause

**Renée Zellweger**
26 Chicago
24 Cold Mountain
23 Bridget Jones's Diary

**Catherine Zeta-Jones**
26 Chicago
25 Traffic
17 Mask of Zorro

# Top Story

## Classic (Pre-1960)

29 Casablanca
28 All Quiet on Western Front
   Paths of Glory
   Witness for the Prosecution
   Grapes of Wrath
   Wizard of Oz
   Best Years of Our Lives
   Double Indemnity
   Rear Window
   Christmas Carol
27 All About Eve
   Wuthering Heights
   Citizen Kane
   Wages of Fear
   12 Angry Men
   Bridge on the River Kwai
   39 Steps
   Place in the Sun
   Strangers on a Train
   Dial M for Murder
   Gone with the Wind
   It's a Wonderful life
   Rebecca
   Searchers, The
   Sunset Boulevard

   Third Man
   Brief Encounter
   Maltese Falcon
   Anatomy of a Murder
   North by Northwest
   Stalag 17
   Laura
   Lady Eve
   Vertigo
26 Sweet Smell of Success
   Some Like It Hot
   Diary of Anne Frank
   Twelve O'Clock High
   Gaslight
   D.O.A.
   Notorious
   High Noon
   Pinocchio
   Woman of the Year
   Caine Mutiny
   Jane Eyre
   It Happened One Night
   Miracle on 34th Street
   Snow White
   African Queen

## Modern (1960 to Date)

29 Godfather
   To Kill a Mockingbird
   Schindler's List
28 Godfather Part II
   Shawshank Redemption
   Usual Suspects
   Star Wars
   Manchurian Candidate
   Hotel Rwanda
   Seven Days in May
27 Man for All Seasons
   Henry V
   Great Escape
   Dr. Strangelove
   Raiders of the Lost Ark
   Breaker Morant
   Romeo and Juliet
   Lord of Rings/Return
   Psycho
   Christmas Story
   Pianist, The
   House of Games
   Sting, The
   One Flew Over Cuckoo's . . .
   Killing Fields

   Lord of Rings/Fellowship
   Princess Bride
   Lawrence of Arabia
   Inherit the Wind
   Sixth Sense
   Lion in Winter
   West Side Story *
   Gandhi
   My Fair Lady
   Memento
   Sound of Music
   Wait Until Dark
   Fiddler on the Roof
   Silence of the Lambs
26 Doctor Zhivago
   Lord of Rings/Two Towers
   Chinatown
   All the President's Men
   Producers, The
   Sleuth
   Star Wars V/Empire
   E.T.
   Willy Wonka
   Goodfellas
   Magdalene Sisters

# Top Production Values
## Classic (Pre-1960)

29 Fantasia
   Wizard of Oz
   Gone with the Wind
28 Singin' in the Rain
   Citizen Kane
   Ben-Hur
   Bridge on the River Kwai
   Third Man
27 North by Northwest
   Searchers, The
   King and I
   American in Paris
   Casablanca
   Quiet Man
   Sunset Boulevard
   Snow White
   Red River
   Ten Commandments
   Rear Window
26 Band Wagon
   Paths of Glory
   Top Hat
   Some Like It Hot
   Notorious
   Lady from Shanghai

   Vertigo
   African Queen
   Bambi
   Night of the Hunter
   Touch of Evil
   Sweet Smell of Success
   Gigi
   All About Eve
   Moulin Rouge
   Red Shoes
   Cinderella
   Star Is Born
   Woman of the Year
   Pinocchio
   42nd Street
   Laura
   Meet Me in St. Louis
   On the Waterfront
   Lady Eve
   Song of the South
25 Double Indemnity
   Lady and the Tramp
   Around the World in 80 Days
   Best Years of Our Lives
   Stagecoach

## Modern (1960 to Date)

29 Lord of Rings/Return
   Finding Nemo
   Lord of Rings/Two Towers
   Lawrence of Arabia
   Lord of Rings/Fellowship
   Godfather
   Star Wars
   Chicago
   Godfather Part II
   Schindler's List
28 Star Wars V/Empire
   Matrix, The
   Last Emperor
   Saving Private Ryan
   Toy Story
   Raiders of the Lost Ark
   Pianist, The
   Shrek 2
   Doctor Zhivago
   Sound of Music
   Shrek
   Monsters, Inc.
   Incredibles, The
   Apocalypse Now
   Star Wars VI/Return of Jedi

   Star Wars III/Revenge of Sith
   Nightmare Before Christmas
27 2001
   Beauty and the Beast
   West Side Story
   Jurassic Park
   My Fair Lady
   Patton
   Braveheart
   Brazil
   Gandhi
   Last Samurai
   Blade Runner
   Harry Potter/Sorcerer's
   Wild Bunch
   E.T.
   Who Framed Roger Rabbit
   Fantasia 2000
   Psycho
   Lion King
   Frida
   Harry Potter/Prisoner
   Barry Lyndon
   Master and Commander
   Moulin Rouge!

# Top Foreign Language Films

| | | | |
|---|---|---|---|
| 29 | Seven Samurai | | Wild Strawberries |
| | Rashomon | | Amarcord |
| 28 | Shoah | | Black Orpheus |
| | Children of Paradise | | Fanny and Alexander* |
| | Beauty and Beast (1947) | | Z |
| | Grand Illusion | | Cries and Whispers |
| | Das Boot | | Talk to Her |
| 27 | Ran | | Alexander Nevsky |
| | Bicycle Thief | | Amélie |
| | Seventh Seal | | M |
| | Life Is Beautiful | | Diabolique |
| | La Strada | 25 | Blue Angel |
| | Au Revoir Les Enfants | | Antonia's Line |
| | Jean de Florette | | Garden of Finzi-Continis |
| | Nights of Cabiria | | Maria Full of Grace |
| | Triumph of the Will* | | Farewell My Concubine |
| | 400 Blows | | La Dolce Vita |
| | Wages of Fear | | All About My Mother |
| | Spirited Away | | Hero |
| | Day for Night | | My Life As a Dog |
| 26 | Cinema Paradiso | | Like Water for Chocolate |
| | Conformist, The | | Breathless |
| | City of God | | Eat Drink Man Woman |
| | Babette's Feast | 24 | Jules and Jim |
| | 8½ | | Crouching Tiger |

## By Country

**France**

- **28** Children of Paradise
  - Beauty and Beast (1947)
  - Grand Illusion
- **27** Au Revoir Les Enfants
  - Jean de Florette
  - 400 Blows
  - Wages of Fear
  - Day for Night
- **26** Black Orpheus
  - Z
  - Amélie
  - Diabolique
- **25** Breathless
- **24** Jules et Jim
  - La Cage Aux Folles
  - Triplets of Belleville

**Germany**

- **28** Das Boot
- **26** M
- **25** Blue Angel
- **24** Wings of Desire
- **23** Run Lola Run
  - Tin Drum∇

**Italy**

- **27** Bicycle Thief
  - Life Is Beautiful
  - La Strada
  - Nights of Cabiria
- **26** Cinema Paradiso
  - Conformist, The
  - 8½
  - Amarcord
  - Garden of Finzi-Continis
- **25** La Dolce Vita

**Japan**

- **29** Seven Samurai
  - Rashomon
- **27** Ran
  - Spirited Away
- **23** Akira

**Sweden**

- **27** Seventh Seal
- **26** Wild Strawberries
  - Fanny and Alexander
  - Cries and Whispers
- **25** My Life As a Dog
- **20** Elvira Madigan

# Movie Directory

### About a Boy
**21 | 23 | 22 | 21**
*2002. Directed by Chris Weitz, Paul Weitz. With Hugh Grant, Toni Collette, Nicholas Hoult, Rachel Weisz. 101 minutes. Rated PG-13.*
This "wonderfully funny romantic comedy" features Grant's "best work" as a "rich, self-absorbed" "skirt-chaser pretending to be a single dad" who strikes up a "sweet friendship" with a "lonely young boy" and "redeems himself in the end"; those who "expect the usual superficial" "chick-flick fluff" are "pleasantly surprised" by this "clever" adaptation of the Nick Hornby novel.

### About Schmidt
**21 | 26 | 20 | 21**
*2002. Directed by Alexander Payne. With Jack Nicholson, Kathy Bates, Hope Davis, Dermot Mulroney. 125 minutes. Rated R.*
It's a "change of pace for Nicholson" ("no eyebrow raising"), who plays a "lethargic" "Middle America everyman" trying "to give his life purpose before it's too late" in this "heartbreaking" yet "hilarious" dramedy "guaranteed to scare anyone approaching retirement"; though it "drags at times", the "brilliant acting overcomes any plot shortcomings" – and the "Kathy Bates hot-tub scene" "will leave your head spinning."

### Absence of Malice
**21 | 25 | 21 | 20**
*1981. Directed by Sydney Pollack. With Paul Newman, Sally Field, Bob Balaban. 116 minutes. Rated PG.*
"Newman and Field ignite the screen" in this "textured" "hard-hitting" courtroom drama demonstrating how "guilt by association" causes a "newspaper to ruin a man's career"; most say that the "irresponsible press" is a topic made for the movies, but some feel this "slight" effort "should have been better" – starting with the "not-believable ending."

### Absent-Minded Professor, The ❶⓫
**19 | 17 | 19 | 17**
*1961. Directed by Robert Stevenson. With Fred MacMurray, Nancy Olson, Keenan Wynn. 97 minutes. Rated PG.*
Despite its "charming", "classic Disney" formula, this "bouncy tale" involving an invention dubbed "flubber" divides voters: flubbergasted fans claim it "stands up well over time", but deflators find it "kinda corny", adding it "may not appeal" to small fry, since its black-and-white cinematography "looks old"; although popular enough to inspire a couple of remakes, the "original is the best."

### Abyss, The
**20 | 19 | 19 | 25**
*1989. Directed by James Cameron. With Ed Harris, Mary Elizabeth Mastrantonio. 146 minutes. Rated PG-13.*
"Eye-popping" special effects – notably the "breakout use of morphing" – are the raison d'être of this "underwater opus", a "fun" cocktail comprised of a "little sci-fi, a little action and a little romance"; it's also a little "long" and "sputters" at the finale, so diehards recommend the (even longer) "director's cut", which "fleshes out the far-too-abrupt ending in the original version."

### Accidental Tourist, The
**20 | 24 | 21 | 19**
*1988. Directed by Lawrence Kasdan. With William Hurt, Kathleen Turner, Geena Davis. 121 minutes. Rated PG.*
This "zany" romantic drama about love, loss and "alphabetizing the groceries in your cupboard" is "as good as" Anne Tyler's best-seller and might "break and mend your heart in one sitting"; its "perfect cast" includes a "terrific" Hurt and an "offbeat", "pitch-

perfect" Davis (who "copped an Oscar"), though some argue the picture is "too quirky" and "inert" for mainstream audiences.

### Accused, The ✉    23 | 28 | 23 | 21

*1988. Directed by Jonathan Kaplan. With Kelly McGillis, Jodie Foster, Bernie Coulson. 108 minutes. Rated R.*

Not for the "faint of heart", this "white-knuckle" thriller about a gang rape and its courtroom consequences is "based on true events" and dominated by a "phenomenal" Foster, who won a "thoroughly deserved" Oscar for her "captivating performance"; the "excruciating", "very graphic" reenactment of the crime is "definitely for mature audiences" – but far from gratuitous given the picture's "socially responsible" message.

### Ace Ventura: Pet Detective ⓤ    15 | 16 | 12 | 14

*1994. Directed by Tom Shadyac. With Jim Carrey, Courteney Cox, Sean Young. 86 minutes. Rated PG-13.*

The "vulgar", "puerile humor" of this "silly, turn-your-brain-off" comedy about a pet detective tracking down a kidnapped dolphin was "Carrey's breakthrough", though some would "rather eat dirt" than sit through it; still, the "rubber-faced" star is so "over the top" that few notice this venture is "inanely short on plot."

### Adam's Rib ◑    26 | 28 | 25 | 23

*1949. Directed by George Cukor. With Spencer Tracy, Katharine Hepburn, Judy Holliday. 101 minutes. Not Rated.*

"Chemistry abounds" in this "sparkling" matchup of Tracy and Hepburn, "probably the best pairing" of these "two pros", who are so "delightful" that many "wish they'd made even more movies together"; plotwise, this "battle-of-the-sexes" comedy concerns "married attorneys on opposing sides of a case", but fans say it's worth watching for the "effortless comedic timing" alone.

### Adaptation    22 | 26 | 21 | 22

*2002. Directed by Spike Jonze. With Nicolas Cage, Meryl Streep, Chris Cooper. 114 minutes. Rated R.*

"You'll either love or hate" this "story within a story within a story", a "dark", "twisted" "head trip" about a screenwriter trying to adapt an unadaptable book; some find it "confusing", and even fans feel the "ending seemed to belong to a different film" ("perhaps that's the point"), but still "it's one of the most original movies ever made", bolstered by "superb acting."

### Addams Family, The ⓤ    17 | 19 | 16 | 20

*1991. Directed by Barry Sonnenfeld. With Anjelica Huston, Raul Julia, Christopher Lloyd. 102 minutes. Rated PG-13.*

That "creepy, kooky" family spawned from the "*New Yorker*" cartoons and popularized by the '60s TV series makes its "ookie" screen debut with all its "madcap", ghoulish antics intact; "like MTV's *The Osbournes*", the story revolves around "misunderstood but lovable" types doing "quirky, offbeat" things.

### Adventures of Priscilla, Queen of the Desert, The    23 | 24 | 22 | 22

*1994. Directed by Stephan Elliott. With Terence Stamp, Guy Pearce, Hugo Weaving. 104 minutes. Rated R.*

"Outlandish drag queens" and the "Australian outback" collide in this "razor-sharp" road comedy, a "flaming romp" about "boas, false eyelashes" and a bus "ride through the desert"; highlights include Stamp's "campy" performance as a "post-op transsexual looking for love" and a "fabulous" soundtrack that will thrill "ABBA fans"; P.S. yup, "that's really Guy Pearce!"

### Adventures of Robin Hood, The    25 | 22 | 24 | 24

*1938. Directed by Michael Curtiz, William Keighley. With Errol Flynn, Olivia de Havilland. 102 minutes. Not Rated.*
This "swashbuckliest swashbuckler of them all" is the "definitive telling" of the tale, filmed in "gorgeous Technicolor" and "acted with verve" by a "charismatic" Flynn and a "perfect" de Havilland; ok, it might be "a bit dated", but its "lightning-quick dialogue", "exciting" swordplay and those famous "green tights" are "still engaging" enough to inspire a "whole genre of films" – plus a "whole lot of parodies."

### AFFAIR TO REMEMBER, AN    26 | 25 | 25 | 23

*1957. Directed by Leo McCarey. With Cary Grant, Deborah Kerr, Richard Denning. 119 minutes. Not Rated.*
The "ultimate chick flick", this "three-hankie tearjerker" begins with a "glamorous" "shipboard romance" that turns "tragic" after an "unexpected twist" at the "Empire State Building"; though the "inspiration for many other weepies" (notably *Sleepless in Seattle*), this one's the "standard", thanks to the "captivating banter", ultra-"suave Grant" and some "classic NY" scenery; just don't bother to see it with your boyfriend – men "don't get it."

### Affliction    20 | 25 | 19 | 19

*1998. Directed by Paul Schrader. With Nick Nolte, Sissy Spacek, James Coburn. 113 minutes. Rated R.*
Granted, it's "grim, grim, grim", but this "disquieting" adaptation of Russell Banks' novel of "family dysfunction" in New Hampshire is still "eminently watchable" due to its "strong performances": Nolte's "wrenching" work and Coburn's "scary", Oscar-winning turn in particular; though admittedly a "great exposé on abuse", some of the afflicted find it so "mind-numbingly downbeat" that they want to "slash their wrists" afterward.

### AFRICAN QUEEN, THE ⊠∅    28 | 29 | 26 | 26

*1951. Directed by John Huston. With Humphrey Bogart, Katharine Hepburn, Robert Morley. 105 minutes. Not Rated.*
"Curmudgeonly riverboat captain" Bogie and "feisty missionary" Hepburn "sizzle" as they take a "trip up a hellish river" and "discover love, courage" and the "best use of leeches since the Middle Ages" in this "beautifully crafted" drama; its "legendary reputation" owes a lot to Huston's "no-nonsense direction", James Agee's "witty" screenplay, the fine "location shots" of "deepest Africa" and, of course, that "undeniable chemistry" between the two shining stars; in sum, "they don't make 'em like this anymore."

### After Hours    21 | 20 | 22 | 19

*1985. Directed by Martin Scorsese. With Griffin Dunne, Rosanna Arquette, Teri Garr. 96 minutes. Rated R.*
From the ever-"creative" Scorsese comes this "offbeat" cult curio, a "pitch-black comedy" set in '80s SoHo recounting the after-hours adventures of a "straight-laced guy" out on the town and out of cash in a "pre-ATM" world; the "numerous subplots" (involving an "ice cream truck", a "headbanger nightclub" and a potty-mouthed sculptress) strike the straightlaced as "confusing"

verging on "weird", but most tout its "razor-sharp performances" and "deft" wit.

### Age of Innocence, The
22 | 24 | 22 | 26

*1993. Directed by Martin Scorsese. With Daniel Day-Lewis, Michelle Pfeiffer, Winona Ryder. 139 minutes. Rated PG.*
"Scorsese does Edith Wharton justice" in this "exquisite period drama" concerning "forbidden love" among "upper-class NYers" in the "opulent" "Gilded Age"; Day-Lewis gives a "subtle, understated" performance as the "tortured" lover, while the "gorgeous production" supplies a "sumptuous feast for the eyes" that "captures the smallest details in a languorous way" – maybe that's why the pace is a little on the "slow" side.

### Agnes of God
21 | 25 | 22 | 19

*1985. Directed by Norman Jewison. With Jane Fonda, Anne Bancroft, Meg Tilly. 98 minutes. Rated PG-13.*
Make sure to "be in a serious mood" for this "disturbing" yet "powerful" drama about a "hysterical nun who may or may not be pregnant"; while there's some mighty "serious acting by some great women", voters split on the story ("compelling" vs. "convoluted") and the overall quality ("thought-provoking" vs. "underbaked"); either way, it's "worth sitting through just for the ending."

### A.I.: Artificial Intelligence
16 | 20 | 15 | 23

*2001. Directed by Steven Spielberg. With Haley Joel Osment, Jude Law, Frances O'Connor. 146 minutes. Rated PG-13.*
"*Pinocchio*" meets "*Blade Runner*" in this "mesmerizing" tale of a "robot boy who wants to be loved" in a devastated, tech-sprawled future; while the "brilliant" Osment brings real life to this artificial world, the scenario is a "strange mélange", one part Stanley Kubrick's "brooding" vision (he first optioned the story), one part Spielberg's "sugar"-coated "sentimentalism"; biggest "downer": that "Amazingly Inept ending."

### Air Force One
18 | 19 | 18 | 21

*1997. Directed by Wolfgang Petersen. With Harrison Ford, Gary Oldman, Glenn Close. 124 minutes. Rated R.*
The "furrowed-browed" Ford plays a "butt-kicking" American president whose plane is hijacked by a "Russian madman" in this "escapist" thriller, a gripping mix of "edge-of-your-recliner suspense" and multi-"million-dollar stunts"; granted, cynics nix its "far-fetched", "action-by-the-numbers" plot but admit that this piece of "harmless, jingoistic fun" "works best with a big bowl of popcorn" nearby.

### Airplane! ①
24 | 19 | 20 | 19

*1980. Directed by Jim Abrahams, David Zucker, Jerry Zucker. With Robert Hays, Julie Hagerty, Lloyd Bridges, Leslie Nielsen, Peter Graves, Robert Stack. 88 minutes. Rated PG.*
"Funny as heck", this "laugh-a-second spoof" mocks "'70s-era disaster films" with a "scatter-gag" barrage of "relentless slapstick", "constant plays on words" and the "best appearance by Ethel Merman in decades"; granted, it's "infantile" and some of the humor might be perceived as "politically incorrect" today, but there are so many "one-liners you'll remember years later" – 'don't call me Shirley!' – that it's no surprise this flick "launched a thousand imitators."

### Airport ⑪
17 | 15 | 18 | 18

*1970. Directed by George Seaton. With Burt Lancaster, Helen Hayes, Dean Martin, George Kennedy. 137 minutes. Rated G.*
The "first" and arguably the "best" of the "disaster flick" genre, this "gripping", "old-fashioned" drama unfolds on one particular night when nothing's going right at a major airport; given the "big, lumbering production" with a bevy of nearly "out-of-work actors" spouting "soap opera–city" dialogue, it's become a "guilty pleasure", though in its heyday it inspired "myriad sequels and spoofs."

### Akira ⬛
23 | – | 21 | 26

*1988. Directed by Katsuhiro Otomo. Animated. 124 minutes. Rated R.*
"Defining the anime genre", this "groundbreaking" "classic" "based on the Japanese comic book" is "blazingly kinetic", though "more violent than it needs to be" and thus "not for younger viewers"; the "confusing" sci-fi plot (something to do with "how power corrupts") might "make you wonder if something was lost in translation", but it's so "visually stunning" you won't care.

### Aladdin
24 | – | 22 | 25

*1992. Directed by Ron Clements, John Musker. Animated. 90 minutes. Rated G.*
Disney's "fast-moving" animated version of the Aladdin story is "stolen" by Robin Williams' "infectiously manic", "whirlwind" vocal performance as a "genius" genie; overall, its "likable characters" and "humorous storyline" appeal to both "adults and kids alike", while the "enchanting" Oscar-winning soundtrack will leave you "singing for days."

### Alamo, The
18 | 18 | 20 | 21

*1960. Directed by John Wayne. With John Wayne, Richard Widmark, Laurence Harvey. 167 minutes. Not Rated.*
A "big-as-Texas" slice of "Americana", this "entertaining" rendition of the Battle of the Alamo still "appeals as a period film", although it strikes some as "overblown", "hokum history" with a "surprisingly boring" Wayne as Davy Crockett; even so, that "slam-bang, operatic finale" "mostly justifies" the "dreary opening hour."

### Alexander Nevsky ⊙⬛
26 | 22 | 25 | 26

*1938. Directed by Sergei Eisenstein. With Nikolai Cherkassov. 107 minutes. Not Rated.*
"Propaganda" was never better than this "exceptional" war epic, made to rally Soviet support for Stalin; shot in "haunting" black-and-white and set to a "superb Prokofiev score", it recounts the trials and tribulations of a 13th-century Russian prince, and even if the "clanky" script "ultimately collapses under the weight of all the ideological baggage", it's still a "triumph of expressionism" from "genius" director Eisenstein.

### Alfie ⑪
22 | 26 | 22 | 20

*1966. Directed by Lewis Gilbert. With Michael Caine, Shelley Winters, Vivien Merchant. 114 minutes. Not Rated.*
This "little charmer" of a drama stars the "phenomenal" Caine in the career-making role of a "philandering playboy who gets his comeuppance" after dalliances with a flock of '60s birds; although it seems "a bit dated" and might be "politically incorrect" today,

its "brutally honest" script still "asks the important questions" –
and there's an "excellent" Sonny Rollins score as a bonus.

### Alice Doesn't Live Here Anymore ✉    24 | 26 | 23 | 21
*1974. Directed by Martin Scorsese. With Ellen Burstyn, Kris
Kristofferson, Jodie Foster. 112 minutes. Rated PG.*
In this "early Scorsese" drama, Burstyn won an Oscar for her role
as a "blue-collar" gal "trying to find herself" after a marriage
breakup, and the "poignant", very "real" outcome marked a
"watershed" for "feminists" in a "time when men and women were
changing their roles."

### Alice in Wonderland    24 | – | 25 | 25
*1951. Directed by Clyde Geronimi, Wilfred Jackson, Hamilton
Luske. Animated. 75 minutes. Rated G.*
Disney's wonderfully "wacky" animation transforms Lewis Carroll's
children's book into an "intelligent cartoon" rife with "hidden
messages" and a slightly "schizophrenic" edge to boot; indeed,
"family entertainment" mavens say this "imaginative" production
is such a "terrific adaptation" that it "almost makes you forget the
classic Tenniel illustrations."

### Alien ⑪    25 | 22 | 25 | 26
*1979. Directed by Ridley Scott. With Sigourney Weaver, Tom
Skerritt, Veronica Cartwright. 117 minutes. Rated R.*
"Often imitated but never equaled", this "fierce" sci-fi "horror
classic" could pass as a "Hitchcock-in-space" thriller thanks to
its "jaw-dropping visuals" and "heart-pounding" plot about an
outer space "survey team" that inadvertently brings a "new guest"
home to dinner; "Weaver rocks" in "macho-man" mode and is
only upstaged by the "slimy", "really gross" title character, the
"best movie monster this side of Frankenstein."

### Aliens ⑪    23 | 21 | 22 | 26
*1986. Directed by James Cameron. With Sigourney Weaver,
Michael Biehn, Bill Paxton. 137 minutes. Rated R.*
This "second installment" in the Alien franchise is just as
"scream-out-loud scary" as its predecessor, with a "*Rambo*-
esque" emphasis; expect the "same high-quality production
values" and "edge-of-your-seat tension", and if there's debate as
to whether it "trumps" or "just lives up to" the original, one thing's
certain: Weaver is still one "bad-ass" chick.

### ALL ABOUT EVE ✉◑    28 | 29 | 27 | 26
*1950. Directed by Joseph L. Mankiewicz. With Bette Davis, Anne
Baxter, Gary Merrill. 138 minutes. Not Rated.*
"Fasten your seatbelts" – the "ladies lunch on each other" in
this "scalding", "wickedly funny" look at the "vicious world of
showbiz"; a "boffo" Davis is "electrifying" as the "fading star"
(opposite a "strong" Baxter as the rising one), but both are
indebted to Mankiewicz's "perfect script", a "catty" catalog of
"sharp-tongued dialogue" that "puts today's scenarios to shame";
in sum, this is one of the "best backstage bitchfests of all time."

### All About My Mother ✉🄵    25 | 26 | 25 | 23
*1999. Directed by Pedro Almodóvar. With Cecilia Roth, Penélope
Cruz, Marisa Paredes. 101 minutes. Rated R.*
Though "all the major characters are women", this "captivating
story" via Spanish director Almodóvar is definitely "not a chick

flick": rather, this "unusual", Oscar-winning drama about a mother searching for her dead son's transsexual dad provides a very "modern definition of what makes a family"; fans single out Roth's "stunning" work and Cruz's "breakout performance" – that is, when they're not "crying their hearts out" or "laughing their heads off."

### All Dogs Go to Heaven ⓤ        17 | – | 17 | 18

*1989. Directed by Don Bluth, Gary Goldman, Dan Kuenster. Animated. 89 minutes. Rated G.*
"Great for toddlers and young children", this "cute" animated flick about a "ghostly canine" sent from heaven to do good on earth might be a "non-Disney film" but still boasts "Disney quality"; surveyors split on the end result: a "listless, uninspired cartoon" vs. a "wonderfully sweet tearjerker."

### ALL QUIET ON THE                28 | 26 | 28 | 25
### WESTERN FRONT ⊠◑

*1930. Directed by Lewis Milestone. With Lew Ayres, Louis Wolheim, Raymond Griffith. 131 minutes. Not Rated.*
"One of the first anti-war films" (and the "last word" on the subject for many), this "devastating" WWI saga is a "harrowing" glimpse at the "unglorious nature" of battle; over 75 years later, it "still packs a wallop", and though a bit "slow" by modern standards, this "faithful adaptation of the novel" will "stay with you."

### All That Jazz        24 | 23 | 22 | 26

*1979. Directed by Bob Fosse. With Roy Scheider, Jessica Lange, Ann Reinking, John Lithgow. 123 minutes. Rated R.*
A "brilliantly original" "autobiopic" from Bob Fosse about Bob Fosse, this "prescient" drama might be "self-indulgent" and plainly "inspired by 8½", but it's also a "warts-and-all" "character sketch" with, no surprise, "imaginative choreography"; look for a "great star turn" by Scheider and lots of "sardonic" dialogue.

### All the King's Men ⊠◑        25 | 26 | 25 | 22

*1949. Directed by Robert Rossen. With Broderick Crawford, John Ireland, Mercedes McCambridge. 109 minutes. Not Rated.*
The "American dream goes sour" in this "classic political drama" adapted from the Pulitzer Prize–winning novel about the rise and fall of a Huey Long–esque politician "corrupted by power"; this Best Picture winner is memorable for its "strong story" – and "even stronger acting by Crawford" (who also won a statuette).

### All the President's Men        25 | 26 | 26 | 23

*1976. Directed by Alan J. Pakula. With Robert Redford, Dustin Hoffman, Jason Robards. 138 minutes. Rated PG.*
"History comes alive" in this "truth-is-stranger-than-fiction" account of the "Watergate" scandal, a "riveting", torn-"from-the-headlines thriller" that "captures you every time" "even though you know the outcome"; as reporters Woodward and Bernstein, Redford and Hoffman are truly "memorable" (ditto those "ties and sideburns"), and in the end this "gripping" effort brings "clarity to the events of that confusing time."

### ALMOST FAMOUS ⊠        23 | 24 | 24 | 22

*2000. Directed by Cameron Crowe. With Billy Crudup, Frances McDormand, Kate Hudson. 122 minutes. Rated R.*
"Almost perfect" filmmaking, director Crowe's "feel-good" "semi-autobiographical story" about his work as a "teenage *Rolling*

*Stone* reporter" "on the road with a rock band" is half "coming-of-age" romance, half unadulterated "love song" to the '70s; while Crudup's "underrated" portrayal of a rocker and McDormand's "outstanding" mom earn kudos, "Hudson steals the show" as the "vulnerable groupie."

### Along Came a Spider
16 | 20 | 18 | 18 |
*2001. Directed by Lee Tamahori. With Morgan Freeman, Monica Potter, Michael Wincott. 104 minutes. Rated R.*
Playing a forensic psychologist trying to rescue a senator's daughter from a psychopathic kidnapper, "Freeman carries" this "better-than-average" thriller adapted from the James Patterson book; but even though this "prequel of sorts to *Kiss the Girls*" is "competent" enough, foes fret it's "pretty predictable" and "close to thrill-free", except for that "nice twist at the end."

### Altered States
19 | 20 | 20 | 20 |
*1980. Directed by Ken Russell. With William Hurt, Blair Brown, Bob Balaban. 102 minutes. Rated R.*
"Sometimes you don't know which end is up" in this "mind-bending" sci-fi "journey" starring Hurt as a scientist experimenting with sensory deprivation via an isolation chamber and select hallucinogens; although the "trippy" visuals and "convoluted" plot were considered "shocking" at the time, it may now look "like a relic from another era."

### Amadeus ✉
26 | 27 | 25 | 27 |
*1984. Directed by Milos Forman. With F. Murray Abraham, Tom Hulce, Elizabeth Berridge. 158 minutes. Rated PG.*
"Genius thwarted by mediocrity" is the theme of this "lively" Mozart biopic that's admittedly "not historically accurate", given its depiction of the "tortured" composer as something of a cross between a "twerp" and a "rock god"; awash in "lush period details", "timeless music" and "surprisingly nuanced performances" by Abraham and Hulce, it even manages to "make classical music seem racy" – and was quite the Oscar magnet, taking home eight of them.

### Amarcord ✉🅵
26 | 25 | 25 | 26 |
*1975. Directed by Federico Fellini. With Magali Noël, Bruno Zanin, Pupella Maggio. 127 minutes. Rated R.*
"Fellini's warmhearted look back to his childhood", this Foreign Language Oscar winner is a "wonderful depiction" of "small-town life" in 1930s "fascist Italy", an "evocative" film that's simultaneously "lyric, tragic, vulgar and comic"; fans say this "beautiful reminiscence" reveals the famed director "at his most accessible" – and most "surreal."

### Amélie 🅵
26 | 26 | 24 | 25 |
*2001. Directed by Jean-Pierre Jeunet. With Audrey Tautou, Mathieu Kassovitz. 122 minutes. Rated R.*
"Sweet as *sucre*", this "candy-coated" "picture postcard" of a romance concerns a "modern-day Pollyanna from Montmartre" "who wants to fix everyone's life" to make up for "what's missing in hers"; in the title role, a "new star has arrived" in "gamine" Tautou, a "21st-century Audrey Hepburn" whose "doe-eyed", "cute-as-a-button" looks alone will "put a huge grin on your face"; indeed, this "brimming-with-goodwill" picture is so "magical", you'll "hardly notice the subtitles."

## AMERICAN BEAUTY ✉    24 | 27 | 23 | 24
*1999. Directed by Sam Mendes. With Kevin Spacey, Annette Bening, Wes Bentley, Thora Birch. 121 minutes. Rated R.*
The "desperation of modern suburban life" is the theme of this "engrossing" Best Picture winner that polarizes viewers: fans hail this tale of a man's "midlife awakening" and "resurrection" as a "truthful commentary on American society", but thornier types fuss it's a "pretentious", "angry" tract "disguised as existentialist philosophy"; nonetheless, there are plenty of bouquets for Spacey's "dead-on" performance and Alan Ball's "seriously meaty", "rapierlike screenplay."

## American Graffiti ⓤ    24 | 23 | 23 | 23
*1973. Directed by George Lucas. With Richard Dreyfuss, Ron Howard, Cindy Williams. 110 minutes. Rated PG.*
"Spot future stars" (including an early Harrison Ford) in this "end-of-an-era" dramedy that "launched a dozen careers" and proves that "Lucas once directed actors, not just pixels"; "covering one night" in 1962 – "but what a night" – it "captures a time and place" in teenage, West Coast America by mixing "cool cars", "period jukebox hits" and "Wolfman Jack" into a "classic growing-up story" that really "makes nostalgia compelling."

## American History X    25 | 28 | 24 | 23
*1998. Directed by Tony Kaye. With Edward Norton, Edward Furlong, Beverly D'Angelo. 119 minutes. Rated R.*
"Neo-Nazi violence" and "racism" lie at the heart of this "scalding" drama about "white supremacists" that's "like a punch in the gut" thanks to the "gifted" Norton's "all-too-convincing" portrait of a "scary" "skinhead"; though surely "horrifying", this "powerful" film will also "make you think."

## American in Paris, An ✉    26 | 23 | 22 | 27
*1951. Directed by Vincente Minnelli. With Gene Kelly, Leslie Caron, Oscar Levant. 113 minutes. Not Rated.*
A "debonair" Kelly and "beautiful Caron" "dance up a storm" in this "unforgettable" Gershwin musical that might tempt you to "visit Paris"; sure, the "silly story" is a bit "hackneyed", but "who cares?" when the production's so "visually compelling" (especially that climactic ballet "integrating Impressionist art" in its settings); no surprise, it took home six Oscars, including Best Picture.

## American Pie ⓤ    19 | 16 | 18 | 18
*1999. Directed by Paul Weitz. With Jason Biggs, Shannon Elizabeth, Tara Reid. 95 minutes. Rated R.*
"You'll never look at an apple pie the same way" after a gander at this "drop-dead funny" slice of "raunch" about some teenage dudes, "hormones a-raging", who "vow to lose their virginity on prom night"; while bluenoses berate its "toilet humor" as "moronic", "baked-goods" buyers say its "laugh-a-minute" plot is an "intelligent gross-out", the "Gen-X" version of "*Porky's.*"

## American President, The    21 | 22 | 21 | 21
*1995. Directed by Rob Reiner. With Michael Douglas, Annette Bening, Martin Sheen. 114 minutes. Rated PG-13.*
"Only in Hollywood" could the "President openly date a lobbyist", but no one "believes it for a second – or cares" – since this "feel-good" romance is so darned "entertaining"; voters like Douglas'

"humanized" Chief Exec and Bening's "luminous" gal pal but reject the "rose-colored" script and its "telegraphed happy ending", sighing "pass the popcorn."

### American Splendor
`23 | 25 | 22 | 22`

*2003. Directed by Shari Springer Berman, Robert Pulcini. With Paul Giamatti, Hope Davis, Harvey Pekar. 101 minutes. Rated R.*
An "average slob" gets the big-screen treatment in this "subversive" biopic of underground comics scribe Harvey Pekar, a "schlubby" "anti-hero" complete with a "file-clerk" day job; deftly employing "three parallel realities" – "actors, cartoons" and Harvey himself – to tell its story, this "offbeat" picture is nothing if not "original", though some feel it "falls short of its potential" and wonder "what does it amount to in the end?"

### American Tail, An ⑪
`21 | – | 21 | 22`

*1986. Directed by Don Bluth. Animated. 77 minutes. Rated G.*
"One of the first good non-Disney" pieces of animation, this "wonderful" "story of the immigrant experience" follows the adventures of a Russian mouse separated from his kin after arriving in America; a "real family favorite", its "clever" concept with a "touch of pathos" makes many "hearts melt."

### American Werewolf in London, An ⑪
`20 | 17 | 21 | 21`

*1981. Directed by John Landis. With David Naughton, Jenny Agutter, Griffin Dunne. 97 minutes. Rated R.*
"Filmed with style and wit", this "tragicomic gorefest" "shows some bite" as it follows the misadventures of two American "zombies" abroad; best remembered for its "transformation scene" combining "superior makeup" and "amazing special effects" – and second-best known for Agutter's "hot shower scene" – this one's so "suspenseful and creepy" that it "helped revitalize the horror genre" in the early '80s.

### Amistad
`21 | 24 | 22 | 24`

*1997. Directed by Steven Spielberg. With Morgan Freeman, Djimon Hounsou, Matthew McConaughey. 152 minutes. Rated R.*
Examining the "dark underside of American history", this "little-known" true story of 19th-century "Africans forced into slavery" "starts on a slave ship and culminates in court"; while some say this "gripping", "difficult" story is an "underappreciated" Spielberg opus, others find it so "heavy-handed" and "manipulative" that they're left "out to sea."

### Analyze This ⑪
`18 | 21 | 18 | 18`

*1999. Directed by Harold Ramis. With Robert De Niro, Billy Crystal, Lisa Kudrow. 103 minutes. Rated R.*
"*Sopranos*" nuts see some familiar plot threads in this "funny Mafia movie" featuring the "hilarious pairing" of "De Niro as a mobster with anxiety attacks" and Crystal as his reluctant shrink; though some analysts shrug it off as a "flat" "trifle", supporters call it an "amusing send-up" that may be "ridiculous, but it works."

### Anastasia ✉
`23 | 27 | 24 | 23`

*1956. Directed by Anatole Litvak. With Ingrid Bergman, Yul Brynner, Helen Hayes. 105 minutes. Not Rated.*
The Oscar-winning, ever "appealing" Bergman and a "great" Brynner make quite a "combo" in this dramatic biography of Anastasia, the legendary daughter of the last Russian czar and

pretender to the throne – or is she?; told with "sympathy and empathy", it's a "cuddle-up-with-your-honey" picture with acting "so good you find yourself rooting for those inept royals"; "is it true?" – c'mon, "does it matter?"

### Anastasia
20 | – | 19 | 22

*1997. Directed by Don Bluth, Gary Goldman. Animated. 94 minutes. Rated G.*
"Disney isn't the only one" making "amazing animation" these days: this cartoon version of a lost (and found) Russian princess is an "astonishingly good feature", although it "doesn't seem to be kid material"; still, it's a "visually appealing" extravaganza oozing "style", even if the "bat steals the show."

### Anatomy of a Murder ◗
26 | 27 | 27 | 24

*1959. Directed by Otto Preminger. With James Stewart, Lee Remick, Ben Gazzara. 160 minutes. Not Rated.*
Stewart "pulls out all the stops" as a "down-to-earth" lawyer in this courtroom drama that's a "spellbinding" look at a "sensational" "backwoods" revenge killing; "considered risqué" in the '50s given Remick's "sultry" turn and its use of the then-verboten word "'panties'", it remains as "riveting" as ever; P.S. "Duke Ellington and his band" lay down the cool progressive jazz soundtrack.

### Andromeda Strain, The
20 | 18 | 25 | 20

*1971. Directed by Robert Wise. With Arthur Hill, David Wayne, James Olson, Kate Reid. 131 minutes. Rated G.*
"Science provides the thrills" in this piece of "thinking man's sci-fi" based on the early "Michael Crichton thriller" concerning a "dangerous" virus from outer space; though it may be "low-tech" (with "out-of-date special effects" and "sprayed-on perspiration"), it supplies enough "palpable tension" to keep things "interesting."

### Angels with Dirty Faces ◗
24 | 24 | 22 | 20

*1938. Directed by Michael Curtiz. With James Cagney, Pat O'Brien, Humphrey Bogart. 97 minutes. Not Rated.*
Two toughs from the slums take different career paths – one becoming a "lowlife", the other a priest – in this "cautionary melodrama" from the days when "good was good and bad was bad"; "cliché-ridden" though it may be, it was designed to "scare the bejesus out of would-be delinquents" – or at least have them "doing Cagney impersonations for weeks" afterward.

### Animal Crackers ◗
26 | 24 | 18 | 20

*1930. Directed by Victor Heerman. With the Marx Brothers, Lillian Roth, Margaret Dumont. 97 minutes. Rated G.*
"Hooray for Captain Spaulding!"; this "timeless" Marx Brothers "romp" is best remembered for Groucho's "priceless entrance" and "fabulously stupid" quips ("I shot an elephant in my pajamas, but how he got in my pajamas, I'll never know"); needless to say, the "storyline isn't the point" here, but the "zany" pace doesn't leave time for logic anyway.

### ANIMAL HOUSE
24 | 20 | 21 | 20

*1978. Directed by John Landis. With John Belushi, Tim Matheson, Tom Hulce, John Vernon. 109 minutes. Rated R.*
"Raunchy and vulgar", this much-admired "granddaddy of the frat boy gross-out comedies" features the much-"missed" Belushi "at his side-splitting best" as Bluto Blutarsky, a "seven-year college"

vet; "no, it ain't Shakespeare", but rather a "textbook" study of "toga parties", "road trips", "food fights" and "anarchic libidos on parade" that's so much of a "guy's movie" that some fellas say they "thought it was a documentary."

### Anna and the King
19 | 21 | 21 | 24

*1999. Directed by Andy Tennant. With Jodie Foster, Chow Yun-Fat, Tom Felton. 148 minutes. Rated PG-13.*
Take a "trip to Thailand" via this "touching" romance that's a "nonmusical rendition" of *The King and I*, based on the true story of Brit school teacher Anna Leonowens; though "slow" pacing and the "absence of chemistry" between Foster and Yun-Fat leave things "rather flat", at least this "lush" production ("magnificent scenery", "elaborate costumes") is "gorgeous to look at."

### Annie
19 | 19 | 20 | 20

*1982. Directed by John Huston. With Albert Finney, Carol Burnett, Aileen Quinn, Tim Curry. 126 minutes. Rated PG.*
Little Orphan Annie's "rags-to-riches" saga morphs into a "colorful" "children's musical" with a "splendid cast" in this "stylized" "adaptation of the comic strip" that first bowed on Broadway; parents say it's "perfect for kids", and even those who find it "bloated" and "boring" find themselves leaving the theater humming 'Tomorrow.'

### ANNIE HALL ✉
27 | 26 | 25 | 24

*1977. Directed by Woody Allen. With Woody Allen, Diane Keaton, Tony Roberts. 93 minutes. Rated PG.*
"Every neurotic's favorite comedy", this Oscar-winning Allen film about an "insecure" "Jewish nebbish" smitten with a nutty, "la-di-da"–spouting "shiksa" is "among his deftest creations"; its "pitch-perfect NY" setting, "pure-genius script" and "very funny" set pieces (the "lobster-cooking episode", the "split-screen family dinner scene") make for "essential Woody."

### Antonia's Line ✉ 🅵
25 | 26 | 25 | 24

*1995. Directed by Marleen Gorris. With Willeke van Ammelrooy, Els Dottermans. 102 minutes. Rated R.*
"About women and for women", this "liberating" drama recounts 50 years in one lady's life, told in "flashback" from her "death bed"; "shockingly feminist" to chauvinists, its "charming performances" and "empowering message" are so "unforgettable" that it more than "deserves the Best Foreign Film Oscar" it received.

### Antwone Fisher
23 | 26 | 24 | 22

*2002. Directed by Denzel Washington. With Derek Luke, Denzel Washington, Joy Bryant. 120 minutes. Rated PG-13.*
"Buy a box of tissues before you rent" this "inspiring true-life story about a boy from the 'hood who makes something of himself despite many obstacles"; this "emotional roller coaster" is "wonderfully acted" and represents a "terrific directorial debut by Denzel", who "manages to bring realism to what could have been a manipulative storyline."

### Antz
20 | – | 19 | 23

*1998. Directed by Eric Darnell, Tim Johnson. Animated. 87 minutes. Rated PG.*
Opinion splitz on this fully computer-animated feature about an insect's "rebellion" against conformity; fans buzz that this "highly

creative" film "for all ages" tells a "well-executed" story, yet drones swat it for "ugly animation" and a "subversive socialist subtext" that's "not recommended" for "younger children"; P.S. Woody Allen's voice-over as a "neurotic ant is a must-hear."

### Apartment, The ✉️◑          25 | 28 | 25 | 23
*1960. Directed by Billy Wilder. With Jack Lemmon, Shirley MacLaine, Fred MacMurray. 125 minutes. Not Rated.*
"Sex in the big, bad city" has never been as "realistic" or "touching" as in this "sad-edged romance", recounting the exploits of a "hapless" "junior exec in love with his boss' mistress"; it pits a "baby-faced" Lemmon opposite a "tender" MacLaine and "understated" MacMurray, and besides being "very amusing", it's also a "powerful social comment masquerading as comedy."

### APOCALYPSE NOW          27 | 27 | 25 | 28
*1979. Directed by Francis Ford Coppola. With Martin Sheen, Marlon Brando, Robert Duvall. 153 minutes. Rated R.*
The "Vietnam nightmare" meets Joseph "Conrad's *Heart of Darkness*" in this "landmark" Coppola opus that's one part "gut churner", one part "acid trip" as it examines the "insanity of war"; true, it's "long", the "last half hour is disappointing" and many wonder "what the heck Brando's saying", but ultimately this "sprawling" "meditation on the human mind" just plain "grabs you"; P.S. the expanded version (*Apocalypse Now Redux*) divides voters.

### Apollo 13          24 | 24 | 25 | 26
*1995. Directed by Ron Howard. With Tom Hanks, Bill Paxton, Kevin Bacon, Gary Sinise. 140 minutes. Rated PG.*
"Even though you [presumably] know the outcome", this "space race" drama based on the "remarkable true story" of the "perilous voyage of Apollo 13" stays "suspenseful"; with a roster of "big-name actors" exuding the "right stuff", it delivers "get-up-and-cheer escapism" that might be "a tad corny" but will "make you proud to be an American" – "isn't history wonderful?"

### Apprenticeship of Duddy Kravitz, The ∅          22 | 24 | 24 | 20
*1974. Directed by Ted Kotcheff. With Richard Dreyfuss, Micheline Lanctôt, Jack Warden. 120 minutes. Rated PG.*
A "nice Jewish boy in Montreal comes of age" and tries to ascend the "slippery slope of success" in this "little-known comic gem" "tinged with sadness"; a "moving" adaptation of Mordecai Richler's novel, it's a "genius" "showcase for Dreyfuss" as the titular "hustling" "mensch."

### Armageddon          15 | 14 | 14 | 21
*1998. Directed by Michael Bay. With Bruce Willis, Billy Bob Thornton, Ben Affleck, Liv Tyler. 144 minutes. Rated PG-13.*
An "asteroid hurtles toward the earth" in this "high testosterone" "explosionfest" with a "far-fetched" "patriotic story" involving a "*Dirty Dozen*–style space mission" and "tongue-in-cheek heroics"; foes say this "blockbuster" is "all budget and no brain" with "state-of-the-art special effects as the real star of the film."

### Around the World in 80 Days ✉️          22 | 20 | 22 | 25
*1956. Directed by Michael Anderson. With David Niven, Cantinflas, Shirley MacLaine. 175 minutes. Rated G.*
"It's the scenery, stupid" that makes this globe-trotting "epic" "travelogue" based on "Jules Verne's classic book" "worth

watching", though lots of "stars popping up in cameo roles" add to the "visual cornucopia"; however, some find it a "boring", "three-hour ride" and "can't believe" it snagged a Best Picture Oscar.

### Arsenic and Old Lace ◑     26 | 26 | 25 | 22 |
*1944. Directed by Frank Capra. With Cary Grant, Priscilla Lane, Raymond Massey. 118 minutes. Not Rated.*
"Elderberry wine" makes for "murderous fun" in this "macabre" black comedy about two "vengeful old ladies" killing off bachelors while "chewing the scenery"; as their nephew, a "frantic" Grant "hams it up unashamedly" and delivers the "world's best double takes" in this "funny" adaptation of the Broadway hit.

### Arthur ⑪     20 | 21 | 19 | 19 |
*1981. Directed by Steve Gordon. With Dudley Moore, Liza Minnelli, John Gielgud. 117 minutes. Rated PG.*
There's "not a dull moment" in this "silly" yet "tender" romantic comedy about a "falling-down-drunk" millionaire looking for love; although top billing goes to "sexy short guy" Dudley Moore opposite "Liza Minnelli as Liza Minnelli", this "priceless" picture arguably belongs to Gielgud, who delivers its most "classic line" – "I'll alert the media" – "as if he were playing Hamlet."

### As Good As It Gets ✉     22 | 25 | 21 | 21 |
*1997. Directed by James L. Brooks. With Jack Nicholson, Helen Hunt, Greg Kinnear. 139 minutes. Rated PG-13.*
Fans feel the "title says it all": this "smart comedy" about the "unlikely pairing" of a "cantankerous" "obsessive-compulsive jerk" and a "kooky" "single-mom waitress" crackles with "sharp", "NY neurotic" dialogue; but even though both Hunt and Nicholson grabbed Oscars for their "tour-de-force" turns, some shrug they "play themselves" in this "overhyped" and "overrated" flick.

### Asphalt Jungle, The ◑     24 | 24 | 24 | 23 |
*1950. Directed by John Huston. With Sterling Hayden, Louis Calhern, Sam Jaffe. 112 minutes. Not Rated.*
Sure, this "prime example of juicy film noir" is one of the "original caper" pictures, about a "carefully planned" "jewel heist gone terribly wrong", but it's also appealing for an "early" turn by Marilyn Monroe in a "blow-you-away" bit part; otherwise, this "dark tale" of "greed" and "emotion" supplies enough "twists and compelling characters" to make it "one of Huston's most underrated films."

### Atlantic City     24 | 27 | 22 | 22 |
*1980. Directed by Louis Malle. With Burt Lancaster, Susan Sarandon, Kate Reid. 104 minutes. Rated R.*
This "valentine to a lost city" pairs a "stunning" Lancaster and Sarandon as unlikely lovers "trying to redeem their lives" in the "bleak atmosphere" of a "dying" town; "sad, bittersweet" and "overlooked", it boasts a "superb" John Guare script full of "characters worth caring about" but is most remembered for the scene of "our heroine bathing herself with sliced lemons."

### Atlantis: The Lost Empire     16 | – | 14 | 21 |
*2001. Directed by Gary Trousdale, Kirk Wise. Animated. 95 minutes. Rated PG.*
Centering on the search for the "legendary" sunken civilization, this "sophisticated action" flick is a Disney production featuring

elements of "Jules Verne" and "Japanese anime" but no "song-and-dance numbers" or cute talking animals; though its blend of traditional and CGI animation is "visually stunning", some say the story's "subpar" and a bit "too violent for minors."

## Auntie Mame                    25 | 25 | 24 | 25 |
*1958. Directed by Morton DaCosta. With Rosalind Russell, Forrest Tucker, Coral Browne. 143 minutes. Not Rated.*
"Defining diva-dom for generations", this "stylish" comedy about a wide-eyed kid's "wacky rich" auntie stars a "larger-than-life Russell" as a "great old broad"–cum–"force of nature"; it might be "overlong and underplotted", but "great one-liners" barbed with "sharp wit" ("life is a banquet and most poor suckers are starving to death") assure its rep as the "campiest of camp classics."

## AU REVOIR LES ENFANTS ⊟∅      27 | 26 | 27 | 24 |
*1987. Directed by Louis Malle. With Gaspard Manesse, Francine Racette. 104 minutes. Rated PG.*
"Powerful and haunting", this "must-see" drama explores "anti-Semitism" in WWII "occupied France" via its depiction of a "Jewish boy hidden" in a French school; though there's certainly "no happy ending" here, it "brings the events of the Holocaust to a personal level" so devastatingly that you'll "never forget" it.

## Austin Powers:                 19 | 18 | 17 | 19 |
## International Man of Mystery ⓤ
*1997. Directed by Jay Roach. With Mike Myers, Elizabeth Hurley, Michael York. 90 minutes. Rated PG-13.*
"No-brainer" alert: this "shagadelic" "spoof of James Bond movies" delivers "tons of laughs" with "dumb" jokes and overall "retro '60s silliness" – "oh, behave!" – courtesy of "comic genius" Myers in a dual role as a spy with "mossy teeth" and a villain with a pet pussycat; there's debate over its "crude" "toilet humor" but wide agreement that you needn't "bother with the sequel."

## Aviator, The                   23 | 25 | 22 | 27 |
*2004. Directed by Martin Scorsese. With Leonardo DiCaprio, Cate Blanchett, Kate Beckinsale, John C. Reilly, Alec Baldwin, Alan Alda. 170 minutes. Rated PG-13.*
Martin Scorsese takes off with a "bottomless budget" in this "sweeping" biopic of "eccentric" gazillionaire Howard Hughes, where the lift-off is supplied by "sumptuous" production design (including one of the "most realistic plane crashes" ever filmed) and Cate Blanchett's "dead-on", Oscar-grabbing take on Kate Hepburn; more debatable is Leo's title turn ("formidable" or "hollow"), though most agree on the "too-long" running time and "soulless", "conventional" windup.

## Awakenings                     22 | 26 | 23 | 20 |
*1990. Directed by Penny Marshall. With Robert De Niro, Robin Williams, John Heard. 121 minutes. Rated PG-13.*
A true story about the search for a "cure for comatose patients" gets "thought-provoking" treatment in this "touching" drama, featuring Williams "playing it straight" for a change opposite a "memorable" De Niro; while some berate its "sentimental", "hanky-wringing" edge, most find it both "amusing and moving", despite the "potentially mawkish" subject matter.

### Awful Truth, The ✉◗
▽ 25 | 25 | 24 | 22

*1937. Directed by Leo McCarey. With Irene Dunne, Cary Grant, Ralph Bellamy, Alexander D'Arcy. 91 minutes. Not Rated.*
"Two spoiled rich people" on the verge of divorce try to "win each other back" in this "laugh-out-loud" romantic comedy top-billing the "classic combo" of Grant and Dunne; it's "one of the better screwball" pictures "from the golden age of Hollywood" with enough "crackling dialogue" and sheer "fun" to leave nostalgics sighing "they don't make 'em like this anymore."

### Babe ⓘ
25 | 22 | 25 | 26

*1995. Directed by Chris Noonan. With James Cromwell, Magda Szubanski, Danny Mann. 89 minutes. Rated G.*
"Believe the hype": fans are in "hog heaven" over this "porcine" comedy about a "talking pig" who "wants to be a sheepherder so he won't get eaten"; "cute without being cutesy", it features Oscar-winning "computer effects" that allow "animals to interact" with humans so realistically that it may "turn you into a vegetarian."

### Babette's Feast ✉🅵
26 | 26 | 26 | 25

*1987. Directed by Gabriel Axel. With Stéphane Audran, Bibi Andersson, Jarl Kulle. 102 minutes. Rated G.*
"Sumptuous enough to make vegetarians drool" (though "slow as molasses"), this "classic foodie" dramedy is an "unusual" tale based on the Isak Dinesen story about the "power of redemption" cooked up in one "magnificent meal"; "still mouthwatering after all these years", this "intriguing" Danish treat is so "delectable" and "savory" that it could be the "Zagat signature movie."

### Baby Boom
19 | 20 | 20 | 18

*1987. Directed by Charles Shyer. With Diane Keaton, Sam Shepard, Harold Ramis. 103 minutes. Rated PG.*
"Career vs. home and family" is the theme of this "very '80s" "light comedy" starring a "sharp, understated" Keaton as a "woman who wants it all" – and gets it when she inherits a baby and hooks up with Shepard; though tough guys dismiss it as a "feel-good chick flick", "warm-and-fuzzy" folk find it a "likable" tale of "triumphant romance."

### Backdraft
18 | 18 | 18 | 23

*1991. Directed by Ron Howard. With Kurt Russell, William Baldwin, Scott Glenn, Robert De Niro. 132 minutes. Rated R.*
"Big fires and cute firemen" sum up the appeal of this disaster thriller aflame with a "stellar cast" and some mighty "eye-opening", "amazingly realistic" special effects; ok, the "melodramatic storyline's a bit soft" and the actors struggle with the "moronic dialogue", but the action sequences will "keep you hanging on until the end."

### Back to the Future ⓘ
23 | 20 | 25 | 24

*1985. Directed by Robert Zemeckis. With Michael J. Fox, Christopher Lloyd, Lea Thompson. 111 minutes. Rated PG.*
A "time-traveling DeLorean" propels the "delectably dimpled Fox" into a "fun ride to the past" (and an opportunity to observe his parents as "goofy teenagers") in this "perfect blend of sci-fi, fantasy and pop culture"; "irrepressibly entertaining" and very popular, it spawned an "incredible ride" at the Universal theme park as well as two "terrible sequels."

### Bad Day at Black Rock
24 | 28 | 24 | 22

*1955. Directed by John Sturges. With Spencer Tracy, Robert Ryan, Anne Francis. 81 minutes. Not Rated.*

This "taut little thriller" is "mean, lean" moviemaking about "bigotry and intolerance" in a "small town with a secret", starring an "excellent" Tracy in "one of his more unusual roles"; although somewhat "forgotten" today, it's "just as relevant as it was in the post-McCarthy '50s", "giving you plenty to think about" as it "profiles American prejudices."

### Bad Education 🄵
23 | 26 | 23 | 24

*2004. Directed by Pedro Almodóvar. With Gael García Bernal, Fele Martínez, Daniel Giménez Cacho. 106 minutes. Rated R.*

"Bad boy" director Almodóvar proves he's at the "head of the class" with this "visually hypnotic", "gender-bending" mystery that pays homage to both "film noir" and "Hitchcock"; boasting a "bravura" performance by rising star Bernal (who's just as "sexy in drag"), this "out-there" flick is rife with "racy", "taboo"-smashing material (e.g. "drugs", "transvestites", "priest abuse") and "not for the easily offended."

### Badlands
25 | 27 | 24 | 24

*1973. Directed by Terrence Malick. With Martin Sheen, Sissy Spacek, Warren Oates. 95 minutes. Rated PG.*

The "banality of evil" is dissected in this "dark, disturbing" depiction of a true-life teen crime spree; playing "shallow", "disaffected" lovers on the run, a "very young" Spacek and Sheen are "first rate", while Malick's "trademark sweeping cinematography" acts as "visually stunning" counterpoint to the "bitingly tragic" story; in short, it's "gutsy", "twisted" and "not nearly as well known as it should be."

### Bad News Bears, The 🅤
18 | 16 | 19 | 15

*1976. Directed by Michael Ritchie. With Walter Matthau, Tatum O'Neal, Vic Morrow. 102 minutes. Rated PG.*

A "must-see for any Little Leaguer", this "cute" sports comedy pitches a story about a curmudgeonly drunk roped into coaching a "truly awful" kids' baseball team; though perhaps "better then than now" (with "foul but funny language" that might raise parental eyebrows), its sequels are definitely "bad news for moviegoers."

### Bad Santa
18 | 20 | 17 | 17

*2003. Directed by Terry Zwigoff. With Billy Bob Thornton, Tony Cox, John Ritter, Bernie Mac. 91 minutes. Rated R.*

"Rude, crude and awfully funny", this "fearless" black comedy toplines Thornton as a "burnt-out", "mean-spirited" Santa who robs department stores with his partner, a "potty-mouthed" elf; no question, it's "sick, sick, sick" and "definitely not for kids" ("it ain't rated R for nothing"), but "twisted" types label it the "perfect antidote to phony Christmas cheer."

### Bad Seed, The 🄾
22 | 23 | 25 | 20

*1956. Directed by Mervyn LeRoy. With Nancy Kelly, Patty McCormack, Eileen Heckart. 129 minutes. Not Rated.*

"Not for the faint of heart", this "very creepy" thriller is the story of a "perky little deranged girl" who's the "world's most evil child" (think "Ted Bundy in a pinafore"); "unsettling and unforgettable" in its time, it's still "way, way over the top", and even if the

Broadway play "had a better ending", this one will positively "send chills down your spine."

### Bambi
26 | – | 25 | 26

*1942. Directed by David Hand. Animated. 70 minutes. Rated G.*
"Don't forget those tissues" before settling into this dear coming-of-age story that's best remembered for the "absolutely heart-wrenching" "death of Bambi's mother", a "cruel lesson in life" that will "make you think twice about showing it" to young children; otherwise, it's arguably the "most beautiful" example of vintage Disney animation, "warm and fuzzy" but "not mawkish."

### Bananas
23 | 20 | 22 | 19

*1971. Directed by Woody Allen. With Woody Allen, Louise Lasser, Carlos Montalban. 82 minutes. Rated PG-13.*
"For Allen purists mostly", this "early" comic romance "relies heavily on sight gags and slapstick humor" in its "anarchic" story of a nebbish turned "Latin American dictator" that's a "zany" satire to some, but "intermittently funny shtick" to others; P.S. hang on for a "young" Sylvester Stallone's cameo as a "thug on the subway."

### Band Wagon, The
26 | 21 | 20 | 26

*1953. Directed by Vincente Minnelli. With Fred Astaire, Cyd Charisse, Nanette Fabray. 111 minutes. Not Rated.*
A "worthy companion to *Singin' in the Rain*", this "solid musical" comedy boasts the "most romantic moment in movie history" – the "hauntingly lovely 'Dancing in the Dark' number in Central Park" – performed by Astaire and Charisse in "top form"; thanks to its "fantastic music" and "delightful cast", nostalgists sigh "they don't make 'em like this anymore."

### Bang the Drum Slowly
23 | 25 | 24 | 18

*1973. Directed by John Hancock. With Michael Moriarty, Robert De Niro, Vincent Gardenia. 96 minutes. Rated PG.*
Moriarty and De Niro deliver "two moving performances" in this memorably "sad" drama about a hayseed baseball catcher with a terminal illness and the star pitcher who befriends him; both a "real tearjerker" and a "powerful story of friendship", it's a "well done", "humbling" experience that still has "staying power."

### Barfly
18 | 21 | 17 | 16

*1987. Directed by Barbet Schroeder. With Mickey Rourke, Faye Dunaway, Frank Stallone. 100 minutes. Rated R.*
"Down and out" in LA the Charles Bukowski way, this "painful look" at "burnt-out alcoholics" stars Rourke and Dunaway as "rummies on the skids" uttering "heavy dialogue" over "tacky/cool" background music; some swat it for being "relentlessly depressing", but for most it's a "gritty, poignant look at the fringes of society" with some mighty "great acting" as a bonus.

### Barry Lyndon
20 | 18 | 21 | 27

*1975. Directed by Stanley Kubrick. With Ryan O'Neal, Marisa Berenson, Leon Vitali. 184 minutes. Rated PG.*
"Kubrick's classic adaptation" of the Thackeray novel depicts the "rise and fall of an Irish lad whose luck finally runs dry" with "amazing period detail" and "gorgeous photography"; but although this "thing of beauty" is a "feast for the eyes", the "acting's from hunger" and the "dull, plodding" pace leaves some sighing "what you see isn't what you get."

### Barton Fink
20 | 24 | 19 | 22

*1991. Directed by Joel Coen. With John Turturro, John Goodman, Judy Davis, Michael Lerner. 116 minutes. Rated R.*
"Delightfully weird", this Coen brothers drama about a gone-Hollywood playwright with a colossal case of writer's block "alternates between fascinating and frustrating" given a "surreal", "terribly odd" storyline that's "brain candy" for intellectuals; despite "fantastic acting" from an "exceptional" Turturro and "absolutely sinister" Goodman, this "out-there" picture is "not for everyone."

### Basic Instinct
19 | 19 | 20 | 19

*1992. Directed by Paul Verhoeven. With Michael Douglas, Sharon Stone, Jeanne Tripplehorn. 123 minutes. Rated R.*
Aside from Stone's notorious "uncrossed legs" "money shot", this "leering erotic thriller" offers enough "noir-esque dialogue" and "gratuitous sex" to make for one "highly provocative" "hormone movie"; though detractors deem it "unintentionally funny trash", "mired in leftover '80s hedonism", fans find it "surprisingly entertaining" – just "don't make the mistake of watching it with your parents."

### Basquiat
17 | 20 | 19 | 17

*1996. Directed by Julian Schnabel. With Jeffrey Wright, Benicio Del Toro, David Bowie. 108 minutes. Rated R.*
It "feels as though you've lived, not just watched" this "insightful biopic" about the rise and fall of a "promising prodigy imploding" in the NY art scene; directed by fellow artist Schnabel, "excellently scored" by ex–Velvet Undergrounder John Cale and featuring a "beautifully cast" Bowie as pop conduit Andy Warhol, it's a "dark", tragic ride that "ends abruptly – like Basquiat's life did."

### Batman ⑪
20 | 19 | 19 | 24

*1989. Directed by Tim Burton. With Michael Keaton, Jack Nicholson, Kim Basinger. 126 minutes. Rated PG-13.*
The "first and best of the bat franchise", this "brilliantly shot" fantasy-adventure flick reflects the "dark side of the comic book" thanks to the "dynamic duo" of "visionary" director Burton and "top-notch" "caped crusader" Keaton; Nicholson's an "awesome" Joker and the *"Blade Runner"*–esque Gotham City is "realized to stunning effect", so even if the "sequels stink", this one "rocks."

### Batman Returns ⑪
16 | 17 | 15 | 21

*1992. Directed by Tim Burton. With Michael Keaton, Danny DeVito, Michelle Pfeiffer. 126 minutes. Rated PG-13.*
The "last of the dark deco Batman" pictures, this "freak show of a sequel" is "another atmospheric Burton production" that keeps Keaton as the caped crusader and is "spiced up" by a "sizzling" Pfeiffer playing an "S&M version of Catwoman"; spoilsports say "they should've stopped" after the original, bemoaning what happens when "marketing takes over a movie."

### Battle of Algiers, The ❶🄵
▽ 28 | 23 | 27 | 27

*1967. Directed by Gillo Pontecorvo. With Jean Martin, Yacef Saadi. 117 minutes. Not Rated.*
"Terrorism and military response" are the up-to-the-minute subjects of this "decades-ahead-of-its-time" feature delineating the Algerian struggle for independence from French rule; the

"riveting" footage is "so lifelike" that it "looks like a documentary", but even as a "docudrama" it remains "timely, essential" viewing.

### Beau Geste ◑
25 | 23 | 25 | 22

*1939. Directed by William A. Wellman. With Gary Cooper, Ray Milland, Robert Preston. 120 minutes. Not Rated.*
"Heroic heroes and villainous villains" populate this "ultimate" war picture about "friendship and honor" that's "perhaps the best Foreign Legion movie" ever made; ok, there are "no special effects" and it might seem "corny" today, but it still supplies plenty of "first-class adventure" right up to that "majestic ending."

### BEAUTIFUL MIND, A ✉
26 | 28 | 25 | 25

*2001. Directed by Ron Howard. With Russell Crowe, Ed Harris, Jennifer Connelly. 134 minutes. Rated PG-13.*
"What *Rain Man* did for autism", this "absorbing" Oscar winner about a "brilliant mathematician's" battle with mental illness "does for schizophrenia", revealing the "thin line between genius and insanity"; "phenomenally acted" by Crowe and Connelly, it "celebrates the triumph of the human spirit" – though foes say its "Hollywoodized" script "strays too far from historical accuracy."

### BEAUTY AND THE BEAST ◑🄵
28 | 25 | 27 | 28

*1947. Directed by Jean Cocteau. With Jean Marais, Josette Day, Marcel André. 93 minutes. Not Rated.*
Enter a "highly stylized universe" in this "hallucinatory" take on the classic "fairy tale" that's both "dreamlike" and "complex" owing to "Cocteau's wit and imagination"; "still unsurpassed by more lavish productions", this "amazing visual feast" demonstrates the artistry possible with "ancient technology" – and enough "sexuality beneath the surface" to keep things throbbing.

### Beauty and the Beast
26 | – | 25 | 27

*1991. Directed by Gary Trousdale, Kirk Wise. Animated. 84 minutes. Rated G.*
A "sensational score" complements the cast of "lovable characters" in this "magical milepost" that "set the bar for a new wave of animated classics"; told with a "fresh approach", it has an "intelligent" "heroine with chutzpah" trilling "catchy", "singable songs" that will "keep tots of all ages entranced"; in short, this "modern masterpiece" – the first animated film ever nominated for Best Picture – is nothing less than "Disney at its high-flying best."

### Becket ✉∅
26 | 29 | 26 | 26

*1964. Directed by Peter Glenville. With Richard Burton, Peter O'Toole, John Gielgud. 148 minutes. Not Rated.*
"Big drama writ large", this biopic about England's King Henry II and his "deep bond with Thomas Becket" features the "brilliant teaming" of "two high-powered actors" – the "winning" O'Toole and "wonderful" Burton – in "histrionic, bellowing performances"; sure, it's "a bit talky", but otherwise this "beautifully filmed period piece" is living proof of the way "history should be experienced."

### Bedazzled ∅
20 | 19 | 21 | 16

*1967. Directed by Stanley Donen. With Dudley Moore, Peter Cook, Raquel Welch. 104 minutes. Not Rated.*
This "immensely clever" "takeoff on the Faust legend" relocated to "swinging '60s London" is a "wickedly funny" comedy full of

"vintage Brit humor" and "witty" "double entendres" in its story of "poor dweeb Moore selling his soul" to the devil in exchange for "true love"; ok, it may be "slow in spots", but it's still "far superior to the 2000 remake."

### Beethoven ❶ 16 | 14 | 16 | 16

*1992. Directed by Brian Levant. With Charles Grodin, Dean Jones, Bonnie Hunt, Stanley Tucci. 87 minutes. Rated PG.*

"Dog lovers" dig this "cute" exercise in "good, clean family fun" about a "slobbery", "scene-stealing" St. Bernard who wreaks havoc in the house while deftly avoiding the clutches of an evil vet; though grumps growl about the "average acting", "predictable storyline" and "laboratory villains", "kids love it" – enough said.

### Beetlejuice 20 | 19 | 21 | 22

*1988. Directed by Tim Burton. With Michael Keaton, Geena Davis, Alec Baldwin, Winona Ryder. 92 minutes. Rated PG.*

"Netherworld antics" animate this "demented haunted-house comedy", a "bizarre" yet "enchanting" flick from "twisted" director Burton that's "endlessly inventive and endearingly funny"; built around a "genius" performance by Keaton as the "wonderfully disgusting" title character, it's also notable for a "macabre" turn from Ryder as a very "unusual teenager."

### Before Night Falls 22 | 26 | 22 | 20

*2000. Directed by Julian Schnabel. With Javier Bardem, Johnny Depp, Olivier Martinez. 133 minutes. Rated R.*

Based on the true life story of "gay Cuban poet" Reinaldo Arenas, this "historically significant" biodrama is a "serious" reminder not to "take freedom for granted" as it details the hero's struggles against an "oppressive regime" bent on "silencing" him; look for an "excellent" Bardem in a "beautiful", "fully realized" performance.

### Before Sunset 21 | 23 | 20 | 21

*2004. Directed by Richard Linklater. With Ethan Hawke, Julie Delpy. 80 minutes. Rated R.*

After their "magical" one-night "chance encounter" in *Before Sunrise*, Hawke and Delpy – now "older and somewhat wiser" – meet again in "atmospheric" Paris for a one-day "second chance" in this "intelligent romance"; while their "nonstop", "meandering" conversation seems to "drag" for some, it's like a "fairy tale" for those mesmerized by the stars' "amazing chemistry."

### Being John Malkovich 22 | 24 | 24 | 22

*1999. Directed by Spike Jonze. With John Cusack, Cameron Diaz, John Malkovich, Catherine Keener. 112 minutes. Rated R.*

"'Original' does not even begin to describe" this "surreal romp" that mixes "dark fantasy" with "smart comedy" in its "off-the-wall" story of a regular guy who finds a portal that takes him "inside the head" of actor John Malkovich; though it "rewards rather than insults the audience's intelligence", it's definitely "not for everybody", being either "engrossing", "audacious fun" or "confusing as hell."

### Being Julia 23 | 27 | 21 | 24

*2004. Directed by István Szabó. With Annette Bening, Jeremy Irons. 104 minutes. Rated R.*

Bening "steals the show" with her "luminous" portrayal of a "fading English actress undertaking one last fling" with a young Yank in this "enjoyable" Brit "comedy of manners" based on the Somerset Maugham novella; overall, it's a "fluffy period piece" perhaps best suited for devotees of the "theatuh", but it's still "worth watching" all the way through for that "deliciously wicked climax."

### Being There
26 | 27 | 25 | 23

*1979. Directed by Hal Ashby. With Peter Sellers, Shirley MacLaine, Melvyn Douglas. 130 minutes. Rated PG.*
"Politics and hypocrisy" get a skewering in this "classic allegory" about a "slow-thinking" gardener who proves that "80 percent of life is just showing up"; "Sellers glows" in this "faithful" adaptation of Jerzy Kosinski's story, which "requires patience with its slow pace" but does "allow you to form your own conclusions."

### Bell, Book and Candle
22 | 22 | 22 | 21

*1958. Directed by Richard Quine. With Kim Novak, James Stewart, Jack Lemmon. 106 minutes. Not Rated.*
Stewart and Novak "have fun with witchcraft" in this romantic comedy based on the Broadway hit about a "man falling for a woman who's a witch"; fans claim that this "old chestnut" was responsible for many cats being "named Pyewacket" and note that the "enchanting" title refers to the Roman Catholic rite of exorcism.

### Belle de Jour
24 | 25 | 23 | 23

*1968. Directed by Luis Buñuel. With Catherine Deneuve, Jean Sorel. 101 minutes. Rated R.*
Deneuve was "never sexier" than in this "marvelously perverse" French drama, a peek at the "dark side" of a "chichi housewife" pent up in "bourgeois" wedlock whose "S&M fantasies" compel her to take a "side job" at the local bordello; more "Dali painting" than *Playboy* centerfold, it's a "stylish", "complex" window into director Buñuel's "surreal world", and the leading lady's "intense", "alluring" performance spices up the "slow" spots.

### Bells Are Ringing
24 | 24 | 22 | 22

*1960. Directed by Vincente Minnelli. With Judy Holliday, Dean Martin, Fred Clark. 127 minutes. Not Rated.*
A "funny" Broadway musical becomes a "fine vehicle" for the "wonderful" Holliday in this story of a singing switchboard girl hung up on a playwright (the slightly "out-of-his-league" Martin); yet despite a "classic" score and a "famous song" ('The Party's Over'), some say this "stage-bound" production's "outdated."

### BEND IT LIKE BECKHAM
26 | 24 | 25 | 23

*2003. Directed by Gurinder Chadha. With Parminder K. Nagra, Keira Knightley, Jonathan Rhys-Meyers. 112 minutes. Rated PG-13.*
"Bend it like anything you want" – this "thoroughly entertaining", "cross-cultural feel-good movie" about an "Indian girl in England who wants to play soccer" scores with its "empowering" storyline and "fantastic ensemble acting"; a "true delight" "for young and old alike", it's the "best ethnic-themed movie since *My Big Fat Greek Wedding*" – "but no TV series, please."

### Ben-Hur ✉
26 | 23 | 25 | 28

*1959. Directed by William Wyler. With Charlton Heston, Jack Hawkins, Stephen Boyd. 212 minutes. Rated G.*
Unleashed four decades "before Gladiator", this "bigger than big" sword-and-sandals "masterpiece" features Heston exuding "hammy", bare-chested "bravura" as a Judean prince betrayed

into Roman slavery only to seek payback via "breathtaking" bouts of action (including that "stunner" of a "chariot race"); a colossal hit and major Oscar magnet, it epitomizes the "grand Hollywood historical epic", built on "biblical" bedrock.

### Benji ⏱ | 19 | 16 | 18 | 17 |
*1974. Directed by Joe Camp. With Patsy Garrett, Peter Breck. 86 minutes. Rated G.*
The "must-see" flick for the "mid-'70s" single-digit demo, this fetching "doggy adventure" features a star turn from a "cute", shaggy-browed mutt who trots to the rescue after his young owners are kidnapped; nostalgists recall a "sappy" but "wonderful" "childhood favorite", albeit with "low-rent" production values.

### Best in Show | 24 | 25 | 23 | 22 |
*2000. Directed by Christopher Guest. With Christopher Guest, Eugene Levy, Catherine O'Hara. 90 minutes. Rated PG-13.*
"Three woofs" and "four paws up" for this "quirky riot" of a mockumentary about a "gaggle of fanatical dog show participants" and their "pedigreed pooches"; the wacky repartee makes for a "beautifully inappropriate", "laugh-a-minute satire" that "can be viewed 100 times without becoming dog-eared."

### BEST YEARS OF OUR LIVES, THE ✉◑ | 28 | 27 | 28 | 25 |
*1946. Directed by William Wyler. With Myrna Loy, Fredric March, Dana Andrews, Teresa Wright. 172 minutes. Not Rated.*
"Have the Kleenex handy" – there's no denying the "pure heart" of this "compelling" drama exploring the "uneasy readjustment" of WWII "vets coming home" to Main Street USA; its all-around "riveting" acting and "no-miss script" perfectly capture the "next-door" post-war mood, taking Best Picture (plus six more Oscars) and resonating as a "quintessentially American period piece."

### Beverly Hills Cop ⏱ | 20 | 19 | 19 | 19 |
*1984. Directed by Martin Brest. With Eddie Murphy, Judge Reinhold, John Ashton. 105 minutes. Rated R.*
This action/comedy "breakthrough" is a "star vehicle" for Murphy, cast as an "inner-city" flatfoot with a "trademark laugh" who upstages his "goofy" El Lay counterparts in pursuit of a friend's killer; though the typically "'80s" foolery and "cheesy storyline" have cooled over time, this "hoot" still works as "feel-good" fare to fill a "Saturday afternoon."

### BICYCLE THIEF, THE ✉◑🅕 | 27 | 26 | 27 | 24 |
*1948. Directed by Vittorio De Sica. With Lamberto Maggiorani, Enzo Staiola. 93 minutes. Not Rated.*
"Poetry put on film", this early slice of "Italian neorealism" is "so sad" but so "beautifully executed" that it's ultimately "not a downer"; using "nonprofessional actors" in a drama of a father and son searching impoverished post-war Rome for the stolen bike that's key to their livelihood, De Sica tugs hearts with a "timeless pathos" that's most "affecting" for its "charm and simplicity."

### Big | 23 | 24 | 24 | 22 |
*1988. Directed by Penny Marshall. With Tom Hanks, Elizabeth Perkins, Robert Loggia. 104 minutes. Rated PG.*
Getting literal with its "inner child", this "cute" "kid-in-a-man's-body" comedy stars a "winning", "never-so-lovable" Hanks, who "makes the movie" (and moves into the big time) as a 13-year-old

who "becomes an adult overnight" and gains entrée to NYC's corporate playground; though some of the "fantasy" is "on the sappy side", a large contingent calls it "most rewatchable."

### Big Chill, The                23 | 24 | 22 | 21
*1983. Directed by Lawrence Kasdan. With Glenn Close, William Hurt, Kevin Kline, Jeff Goldblum, Mary Kay Place, JoBeth Williams, Tom Berenger. 105 minutes. Rated R.*
Trace the tracks of their tears as this '60s-era "nostalgia" trip tries to "define a generation" via a "superb ensemble", an "iconic soundtrack" and the "soul-searching" premise of "boomers regathering" at a friend's funeral (fun fact: Kevin Costner "plays the stiff"); anyone bummed by the "contrived" setup and "smug" "yuppie angst" can still groove to the "perfect" tune selection.

### Big Fish                22 | 24 | 23 | 25
*2003. Directed by Tim Burton. With Ewan McGregor, Albert Finney, Billy Crudup, Jessica Lange. 125 minutes. Rated PG-13.*
The "guy equivalent of a chick flick", this "bittersweet" story of a "complicated father-and-son relationship" reels in sentimentalists with equal parts of "whimsy and schmaltz"; "less twisted" than director Burton's usual fare, it still has its "oddball" moments via a "patchwork", *"Forrest Gump"*–like script, and if cynics yawn it's "sappy" and "slow", many more laud its "vivid imagery and good message" – plus, it's a relief to "see McGregor without a light saber" for a change.

### Big Heat, The ◑                ▽ 24 | 23 | 25 | 23
*1953. Directed by Fritz Lang. With Glenn Ford, Gloria Grahame, Lee Marvin, Carolyn Jones. 90 minutes. Not Rated.*
"Considered daring in its time", this "ultimate noir picture" features a rogues' gallery of hard-boiled "tough guys" and gals in a story about an honest cop "obsessed with getting revenge" following his wife's murder; though tepid types say the heat's "cooled off over the years", there's "one horrifying scene" involving a pot of "scalding hot coffee" that's still quite a "shocker."

### Big Lebowski, The                20 | 22 | 19 | 20
*1998. Directed by Joel Coen. With Jeff Bridges, John Goodman, Julianne Moore, Steve Buscemi. 117 minutes. Rated R.*
The brothers Coen "strike again" with this "shaggy-dog" comedy, an "homage to slobs" that gets rolling when Bridges' "aging" "slacker/stoner character" and his "bizarre bowling buddies" become embroiled in a surreal kidnapping; though an "acquired taste" and certainly "strange for its own sake" ("dude, where's my plot?"), it has "cult" followers citing "quotable" lines and swearing "you'll laugh."

### Big Night                24 | 26 | 23 | 23
*1996. Directed by Campbell Scott, Stanley Tucci. With Stanley Tucci, Tony Shalhoub, Minnie Driver. 107 minutes. Rated R.*
"Yum": this "quirky", "thoroughly enjoyable" dramatic "feast" tracks two "Italian immigrant brothers" in their "endearing" effort to keep their restaurant and culinary "vision" alive on the '50s-era Jersey coast; hailed as an "overlooked gem", its slow-simmering pace allows admirers to "savor" "brilliant performances" that are rivaled only by "stunning food shots" – "don't catch it on an empty stomach."

## BIG SLEEP, THE ◑     27 | 27 | 24 | 24
*1946. Directed by Howard Hawks. With Humphrey Bogart, Lauren Bacall, Martha Vickers. 114 minutes. Not Rated.*
"Whodunit? who cares?" as long as the legendary Bogie and Bacall keep up the "snappy" patter and "heavy-lidded" "chemistry" in this "dizzying" film noir "classic" featuring Bogart as "fast-talking" gumshoe Philip Marlowe prowling Raymond Chandler territory (1940s Los Angeles at its most "atmospheric"); if the notoriously "incomprehensible plot" is seriously in need of a clue, at least the "crackling" pace and "salty" repartee always "entertain and enthrall."

## Bill & Ted's Excellent Adventure ⓤ     15 | 10 | 15 | 13
*1989. Directed by Stephen Herek. With Keanu Reeves, Alex Winter, George Carlin. 90 minutes. Rated PG.*
"Two goof-offs" about to flunk out of high school time-travel to the past in a desperate attempt to graduate in this "totally tubular" slacker comedy, a budding "cult classic" that just may be "better than you remember it"; sure, this "sophomoric", "truly mindless" flick could have "typecast Keanu" forever, and even if it's "not very good, it's still lots of fun, dude."

## Billy Elliot     25 | 26 | 25 | 23
*2000. Directed by Stephen Daldry. With Julie Walters, Jamie Bell. 110 minutes. Rated PG-13.*
It takes *Swan Lake* to break the "working-class shackles" of a Northern England mining town in this "coming-of-age" drama about a "boy who loves ballet" and his hardscrabble dad; behind the "thick British accents", fans discover a "captivating" if "unlikely tale" propelled by "talent, desire" and lots of "fancy footwork", with an "uplifting" finale that's apt to inspire "a good cry."

## Birdcage, The     22 | 25 | 22 | 22
*1996. Directed by Mike Nichols. With Robin Williams, Nathan Lane, Gene Hackman, Dianne Wiest. 117 minutes. Rated R.*
Reset in South Beach, director Nichols' "slick" take on the "classic" French farce *La Cage aux Folles* soars "over the top" on the wings of the "perfect comedic combination" of Williams and Lane, cast as a pair of "flamboyant" gay cabaret owners obliged to "play it straight" for their son's "uptight" in-laws-to-be; busy with burlesque and "insight", it's widely welcomed as a "laugh-out-loud" "blast", though holdouts chirp "stick with the original."

## Birdman of Alcatraz ◑     22 | 25 | 22 | 20
*1962. Directed by John Frankenheimer. With Burt Lancaster, Karl Malden, Thelma Ritter. 147 minutes. Not Rated.*
Lancaster is "at the top of his game" in this saga of "a man, a prison and some birds", the "fascinating" bio of Rock lifer Robert Stroud, who struggles under the screws' authority but "finds love and friendship" when he becomes a famed ornithologist; it's generally judged a "keeper" as a "gritty" but "entertaining" penal drama that's also a "touching" "examination of survival."

## Birds, The     24 | 20 | 24 | 25
*1963. Directed by Alfred Hitchcock. With Tippi Hedren, Rod Taylor, Jessica Tandy. 119 minutes. Rated PG-13.*
"Nature strikes back, Hitchcock style", in this "improbably terrifying" "nail-biter" about "birds gone mad" that "still packs

enough of a punch" to leave the timid "traumatized"; though critics aren't chirping about the "hokey", "no-rhyme-or-reason" plot that takes "too long to get going", ultimately you'll "never think of pigeons in the same way" after a gander at this one.

### Birth of a Nation, The ◑    25 | 20 | 19 | 27
*1915. Directed by D.W. Griffith. With Lillian Gish, Mae Marsh, Henry B. Walthall. 190 minutes. Not Rated.*
A "masterful" technical feat that could be the "most influential movie ever made", Griffith's "landmark" silent epic "wrote the book" on "camera movement" and "cinema as storytelling" while offering a "morally irresponsible" version of Reconstruction replete with "blatantly racist" "stereotyping" and the "Ku Klux Klan presented as heroes"; so even though this work marks the "birth of the feature" film, be prepared for a storyline that's a "mess" – "even by 1915" standards.

### Bishop's Wife, The ◑    24 | 24 | 24 | 23
*1947. Directed by Henry Koster. With Cary Grant, Loretta Young, David Niven. 105 minutes. Not Rated.*
Although "less well known" than some of its "holiday movie" peers, this "Christmasy" romance stars Grant as a "guardian angel" blessed with "elegance and style" ("duh!") who's sent to "restore faith" to a clergyman and his spouse but "falls in love" along the way; overall, it's an "amusing, touching" display of "old-fashioned" "star power" that sentimental souls will "never forget."

### Blackboard Jungle ◑    23 | 24 | 22 | 19
*1955. Directed by Richard Brooks. With Glenn Ford, Anne Francis, Vic Morrow, Sidney Poitier. 101 minutes. Not Rated.*
See "the '50s in a new way" via this "gritty" drama, a standout of the "juvenile delinquent genre" set in an "inner-city school" where "danger is only a heartbeat away" as idealistic teacher Ford is forced to "tame" a horde of punks; notable for Hollywood's "first use of a rock 'n' roll" soundtrack, it may "feel a bit dated", though cynics shrug "schools haven't changed" that much.

### Black Hawk Down    23 | 21 | 23 | 26
*2001. Directed by Ridley Scott. With Josh Hartnett, Ewan McGregor, Tom Sizemore. 144 minutes. Rated R.*
It's "hard to watch, but it's even harder to turn away" from this "astoundingly gripping" (and "surprisingly accurate") account of a 1993 Mogadishu "military misadventure", which pitted a handful of U.S. Army Rangers against a huge enemy force; "Scott puts you on the ground with the soldiers", "brilliantly showing the total chaos of the Somalian battle" in all its "gory", "graphic" and "grueling" detail; indeed, even peaceniks agree this "salute to our servicemen" "doesn't simplify or sensationalize" combat.

### Black Orpheus ✉ 🄵    26 | 23 | 25 | 25
*1959. Directed by Marcel Camus. With Marpessa Dawn, Breno Mello. 100 minutes. Rated PG.*
"Brazilian backdrops" and "bossa nova" rhythms cast their "spell" over Greek legend in this "enchanting", "lyrical" foreign flick, an "exotic retelling" of the Orpheus and Eurydice myth transposed to "modern-day Rio" during Carnival; "sexy", "lush" and full of "beautiful shots" of "cinema verité" revelry, it takes its Dionysian devotees to Hades and back in "unmatched" style – and oh, that "moving-in-your-seat" soundtrack!

### Black Stallion, The ❶    24 | 20 | 23 | 25
*1979. Directed by Carroll Ballard. With Mickey Rooney, Kelly Reno, Teri Garr. 118 minutes. Rated G.*
Equestrians of "all ages" ponder the "bond between boy and horse" in this "captivating" family film about an Arabian steed who's shipwrecked with a youngster on a desert island only to be entered in a turf race after they're rescued and resettled to a Western ranch; though saddled with a "somber" side, it "wins the roses" with a "skillful blend" of "breathtaking" scenery and "luminous cinematography."

### BLADE RUNNER    26 | 22 | 25 | 27
*1982. Directed by Ridley Scott. With Harrison Ford, Rutger Hauer, Sean Young, Daryl Hannah. 117 minutes. Rated R.*
This "awesome" "blueprint" for "modern sci-fi" is a "visually stunning" picture best watched with "your brain switched on"; an ultra-"stylish" "noir take" on LA as a 21st-century "dystopia" where "commercialism and biotech run amok", it's also a "hard-boiled" "morality play" with one of "Ford's best acting jobs" as a PI "hunting cyborg replicants while falling in love with one"; connoisseurs run right for the "superior director's cut."

### Blazing Saddles    25 | 22 | 23 | 23
*1974. Directed by Mel Brooks. With Cleavon Little, Gene Wilder, Harvey Korman, Madeline Kahn. 93 minutes. Rated R.*
"You'll never look at a horse the same way" after a peek at this "hilarious", "decidedly un-PC" comedy via Mel Brooks, an "off-the-wall" Wild West "spoof" that "insults everyone" with a mix of "slapstick", "eminently quotable one-liners" and infamously "tasteless" routines (like the sound effects–ridden "campfire scene"); most call it "enjoyable" if "overdone."

### Blood Simple    24 | 25 | 25 | 22
*1984. Directed by Joel Coen. With Frances McDormand, John Getz, Dan Hedaya. 97 minutes. Rated R.*
"Complex" is more like it as the Coen brothers' first feature "pumps new blood" into the "low-budget crime thriller" in this "brilliant" "film noir homage" filled with "wicked" "thrills delivered with a drawl"; it's a "twisty", "nerve-jangling" tale of betrayal and revenge in a dusty Texas town, told with a "quirky" slant that "foreshadows" the filmmakers' "masterpiece, *Fargo*."

### Blowup    26 | 23 | 25 | 25
*1966. Directed by Michelangelo Antonioni. With David Hemmings, Vanessa Redgrave, Sarah Miles. 111 minutes. Not Rated.*
"Forget *Austin Powers*", baby, "this is the *real* Swinging London": a "riveting existential thriller" that tracks a happening fashion photographer obsessed by both Redgrave and a "mysterious death in a park"; hipsters hail it as an "enigmatic" (or "infuriating") milestone of the "alienation genre" possessed by the "spirit of the '60s" – and that tasty "period flavor" is still "too cool for words."

### Blue Angel, The ❶❺    25 | 27 | 24 | 22
*1931. Directed by Josef von Sternberg. With Marlene Dietrich, Emil Jannings. 99 minutes. Not Rated.*
Behold the "magnificent Dietrich" "at her best" in this "Weimar-era" German drama, the story of "naughty Lola", a garter-flashing chanteuse who "seduces an old fool" of a schoolmaster and

expedites his "descent into the gutter"; though it's a "dated" dose of "ennui and moral rot" in a "world now lost", fräulein Marlene's "tour-de-force", career-launching turn is "music to the eyes."

### Blues Brothers, The 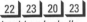 22 | 19 | 19 | 21
*1980. Directed by John Landis. With John Belushi, Dan Aykroyd, John Candy. 133 minutes. Rated R.*
"Ignore the plot" and "get out the popcorn" for this "good-time" comedy, powered by Belushi and Aykroyd on a "full tank of gas" as sibs Jake and Elwood, who accept a "mission from God" to provoke "hilarity" and find out "how many cars they can wreck"; if it's (ahem) "not a critics' choice", those with a hankering for "hot" "soul 'n' blues" numbers liberally chased with "dumb fun" insist "you gotta love it."

### Blue Velvet 22 | 23 | 20 | 23
*1986. Directed by David Lynch. With Kyle MacLachlan, Isabella Rossellini, Dennis Hopper. 120 minutes. Rated R.*
"One sick puppy of a movie", this pretty "kinky" yet totally "enthralling" look at the "seedy underbelly" "beneath the surface of suburbia" is "love-it-or-hate-it" filmmaking from the "warped" mind of "surrealist auteur Lynch"; despite applause for Hopper's "creepy" portrayal of the "gas-inhaling pervert" ("worth seeing for the Pabst Blue Ribbon scene alone"), sensitive souls find the flick "ugly, pointless" and "not as good as its reputation."

### Bob and Carol and Ted and Alice 17 | 19 | 17 | 17
*1969. Directed by Paul Mazursky. With Natalie Wood, Robert Culp, Elliott Gould, Dyan Cannon. 104 minutes. Rated R.*
"Remember the '60s?" – this "social satire" of wannabe swingers experimenting with free love "captures the era to a T", though what was once "hip 'n' happening" seems more "quaint" today; still, many find themselves "laughing at the outfits, the decor", the "dated" dialogue and that "priceless" ending.

### Body Heat 24 | 25 | 25 | 23
*1981. Directed by Lawrence Kasdan. With William Hurt, Kathleen Turner, Richard Crenna, Mickey Rourke. 113 minutes. Rated R.*
"Whew!" this "palpably steamy" "noir thriller" stars "what-a-babe" Turner as a trophy wife who "burns up the screen" as she seduces "small-town lawyer" Hurt into a "spiraling" web of "deceit" that "keeps you guessing" to the last frame; in short, it's a sexed-up "version of the old help-me-kill-my-husband story", a kind of "*Double Indemnity* for a new generation."

### Bonnie and Clyde 25 | 25 | 24 | 25
*1967. Directed by Arthur Penn. With Warren Beatty, Faye Dunaway, Gene Hackman, Estelle Parsons. 111 minutes. Not Rated.*
More a piece of "film history than real history", this "stunning" 1930s "crime-spree" biopic "broke a lot of old rules" in its "revisionist" take on the title characters, real-life "losers" reconceived by Beatty and Dunaway as the "screen's best-ever antiheroes"; the "letter-perfect" cast, "impeccable" direction and "gorgeously gory" photography all add up to way-"ahead-of-its-time" moviemaking, even if the "indelible images" of the "bloody ballet at the end" unsettle the squeamish.

**Boogie Nights**                    19 | 21 | 19 | 19
*1997. Directed by Paul Thomas Anderson. With Mark Wahlberg, Burt Reynolds, Julianne Moore. 152 minutes. Rated R.*
Set in the '70s "disco era", this "dead-on look" at the "ins and outs (so to speak) of the porn industry" features "inspired performances" – "Burt returns!", "Marky Mark grows up!" – even if the "XXX film stars" portrayed "don't have much going on upstairs"; though the "sex-drugs-and-roller-skates" plot is "shamelessly entertaining" for the "first 2/3" of the picture, the "violent", "depressing" final act can be "emotionally draining."

**Born Free** Ⓤ                    24 | 19 | 24 | 23
*1966. Directed by James Hill. With Virginia McKenna, Bill Travers, Geoffrey Keen. 95 minutes. Rated PG.*
The "theme song alone" is enough to set off "shameless weeping" as this "well-told" family flick unfolds, focusing on a husband and wife in "wild Africa" and their effort to "protect the lioness Elsa"; a "major tearjerker" in its day, it remains "vivid" for boomers who tell of "loving it as a child" even though it's "so sad."

**Born on the Fourth of July** ✉            20 | 21 | 20 | 20
*1989. Directed by Oliver Stone. With Tom Cruise, Kyra Sedgwick, Willem Dafoe. 145 minutes. Rated R.*
"Cruise excels" in one of Stone's "most accomplished works", a "potent", "well-done" bio of Vietnam vet Ron Kovic that's an "intense", "heart-wrenching" study of "flag-waving patriotism"; though it draws fire for being "contrived" and "overwrought", it does offer convincing "proof that Tom can act."

**Born Yesterday** ✉◑                26 | 28 | 25 | 23
*1950. Directed by George Cukor. With Judy Holliday, Broderick Crawford, William Holden. 103 minutes. Not Rated.*
"Still magical today", this "zany" screwball comedy has to do with a "not-so-dumb blonde" who undergoes a *My Fair Lady*–like transformation and "breaks out of her bimbo chains"; thanks to a unique voice and "great timing", the "perfectly cast" Holliday took home an Oscar for her "pure gold" performance, a "pièce de résistance" that the 1993 remake "can't match."

**Bourne Identity, The** Ⓤ            20 | 19 | 20 | 21
*2002. Directed by Doug Liman. With Matt Damon, Franka Potente, Chris Cooper. 119 minutes. Rated PG-13.*
An "amnesiac" CIA assassin struggles to recover his identity in this "adrenaline-rush" thriller based on the Robert Ludlum best-seller that features "riveting action" scenes (including "one of the better car chases in recent memory"), but only "decent chemistry" between the leads; though Matt's performance provokes debate – "cool and capable" versus "lightweight" – in the end the scenic European "locations redeem the picture."

**Bourne Supremacy, The**            21 | 21 | 21 | 23
*2004. Directed by Paul Greengrass. With Matt Damon, Joan Allen, Julia Stiles. 108 minutes. Rated PG-13.*
Damon is "re-Bourne" as a "secret agent turned wanted man" out for "payback" in this "sharp-shooting sequel", a "spy caper with a brain" that's "as good as the original", packing fresh "cat-and-mouse action", "high-tech twists" and "gorgeous" Euro backdrops; its "herky-jerky" camera coverage can be "dizzying",

though, so "take Dramamine" during those "fantastic" car chases that are one "wicked ride."

### Bowling for Columbine
**22 | – | 21 | 19**

*2002. Directed by Michael Moore. Documentary. 120 minutes. Rated R.*

Moore's "provocative" yet "surprisingly funny" docudrama is a "punch in the jaw to anyone who is completely pro-gun"; "even if the events were staged, the message massaged and the view decidedly one-sided", it's still an "important movie" that "everyone should see", so "watch it before passing judgment" – "you'll have something to talk about for hours."

### Boys Don't Cry ✉
**23 | 27 | 23 | 21**

*1999. Directed by Kimberly Peirce. With Hilary Swank, Chloë Sevigny, Peter Sarsgaard. 118 minutes. Rated R.*

Turning a "dark situation" into a "tough" study of "intolerance", this "disturbing" drama is a "faithful telling of the story of Teena Brandon", a small-town girl who "dresses and acts the part" of a boy, leading to "powerful" complications; though the Oscar-winning Swank is "beyond convincing", the "brutal" ending is "not easy to watch", but "will stay with you" – "unfortunately, it's true."

### Boys on the Side
**15 | 18 | 15 | 16**

*1995. Directed by Herbert Ross. With Whoopi Goldberg, Mary-Louise Parker, Drew Barrymore. 117 minutes. Rated R.*

"Girl power" is alive and well in this "epitome of a chick flick" charting the offbeat adventures of three gals headed cross country; the "touching" story, one part road movie and one part feminist tract, proves that "friendship is a great thing", while also demonstrating that "Drew can act if she picks the right material."

### Boyz N the Hood
**23 | 22 | 24 | 21**

*1991. Directed by John Singleton. With Ice Cube, Cuba Gooding Jr., Laurence Fishburne. 107 minutes. Rated R.*

The "gangsta flick" that "sets the bar" for the competition "keeps it real" as it takes a "hard-core" look at ghetto "gang wars in South Central" LA; an "important" breakthrough with some "surprising acting turns", it's a "fantastic first film" from Singleton, whose later work doesn't "get anywhere near this one."

### BRAVEHEART ✉
**26 | 24 | 25 | 27**

*1995. Directed by Mel Gibson. With Mel Gibson, Sophie Marceau, Catherine McCormack. 177 minutes. Rated R.*

"It's got everything" say fans of this "awe-inspiring" medieval "history lesson" about an "underdog" Scottish hero ("Mel in a kilt" and "war paint") "knocking heads" in an anti-Brit "rebellion"; the "gory", "hackin'-and-hewin'" battles, "heartfelt" acting and "huge scope" help justify Gibson's Best Director win, even if some warn of three "long", "melodramatic" hours.

### Brazil
**24 | 23 | 23 | 27**

*1985. Directed by Terry Gilliam. With Jonathan Pryce, Robert De Niro, Bob Hoskins. 131 minutes. Rated R.*

Even as "fantasy", Monty Python alum Gilliam's "twisted", "utterly original" vision of a "part-Orwell, part-Python" future is "a little out there"; it demands "perseverance" – what with its "baffling" "whirlwind" of "bizarre" effects and chin-scratching "black comedy" plot about one man's struggle with a "Kafka-esque" "bureaucracy" – but rewards those who hang in there with a "totally crazy ride."

**Breaker Morant**                     27 | 27 | 27 | 24

*1980. Directed by Bruce Beresford. With Jack Thompson, Edward Woodward, Bryan Brown. 107 minutes. Rated PG.*

"Guy's-flick" fans salute this "solid Aussie" drama of "kangaroo" justice, a "small masterpiece" in its "gripping" depiction of "betrayal" at a military trial during the Boer War; told with "moving realism", it tackles the "question of morals in warfare" using a "top-notch" cast to "demonstrate bravery" and "bravura", turning the fate of "appointed scapegoats" into an "inspiration."

**BREAKFAST AT TIFFANY'S**            26 | 26 | 24 | 24

*1961. Directed by Blake Edwards. With Audrey Hepburn, George Peppard, Patricia Neal. 115 minutes. Rated PG.*

In the "role she was born to play", a "mesmerizing" Hepburn brings Truman Capote's "messed-up" "free spirit" Holly Golightly to life in "peerless style"; fans find everything about it "irresistible" – "Henry Mancini's divine score", Audrey's "timeless clothes", the "love-letter-to-NY" cinematography – and call this "dream-making, heartbreaking" tribute to the "power of romance" their "all-time favorite."

**Breakfast Club, The**               22 | 21 | 22 | 19

*1985. Directed by John Hughes. With Emilio Estevez, Anthony Michael Hall, Judd Nelson, Molly Ringwald. 92 minutes. Rated R.*

Any card-carrying "child of the '80s" is apt to "know all the lines" of this "engaging" high school yukfest, a "Gen-X" "time capsule" about a group of "Brat Pack all-stars" "stuck in detention" and left to compare and contrast "confused personalities"; a "hoot" with a "sensitive" side, it's rerun "ad infinitum", since it "speaks to teenagers in a way that *American Pie* will never be able to."

**Breaking Away** ✉                   24 | 21 | 24 | 20

*1979. Directed by Peter Yates. With Dennis Christopher, Dennis Quaid, Daniel Stern. 100 minutes. Rated PG.*

A "rousing ride", this "*Rocky*-esque" "Hoosier tale" is a "coming-of-age" drama on two wheels, with Christopher leading a cast of "cutie-pie" "underdogs" as a cyclist who pedals straight into a "town-and-gown" "class conflict"; it's cheered on as a "big-hearted" "buddy film" that delivers a "socko" bike race finale.

**Breaking the Waves**                23 | 27 | 20 | 20

*1996. Directed by Lars von Trier. With Emily Watson, Stellan Skarsgård. 153 minutes. Rated R.*

"Be prepared" for "emotionally devastating" doings in this "raw" drama of "delusion" and "doomed romance" about a "dimwitted girl" who "sacrifices everything for her paralyzed husband"; most pronounce it "strange" yet "so well done it's painful" (the "musical interludes give one time to weep"), though foes call it a "silly" parable that's a most "depressing" picture of "female martyrdom."

**Breathless** ◑🅕                    25 | 24 | 21 | 23

*1961. Directed by Jean-Luc Godard. With Jean-Paul Belmondo, Jean Seberg. 87 minutes. Not Rated.*

"So hip" and as "refreshing" now as at its debut, this French "New Wave masterpiece" breathes "pure pleasure" into a "silly gangster story" with "luscious" leads Belmondo and Seberg as lovers on the lam (even the late-'50s Paris setting is a "terrific character"); while scholars speak of genre-"defining" technical feats – the "jump cut is born!" – most simply find it "charming" and way "ahead of its time."

### Bride of Frankenstein, The ◑    | 25 | 21 | 23 | 23 |
*1935. Directed by James Whale. With Boris Karloff, Colin Clive, Elsa Lanchester. 75 minutes. Not Rated.*
Bolt-necked Frankie gets "his one shot at love" in this "excellent sequel" to the hoary "'30s horror classic", wherein Karloff reprises his signature role with "panache" and Lanchester's shocked fiancée simply has "great hair"; fright fiends cherish the "creepy" results as "campy", "funny" and not a little "whacked."

### BRIDGE ON THE RIVER KWAI, THE ✉ | 28 | 28 | 27 | 28 |
*1957. Directed by David Lean. With William Holden, Alec Guinness, Jack Hawkins. 161 minutes. Rated PG.*
Those "stiff upper lips" do some "memorable" whistling in director Lean's "grand", "engrossing" Japanese POW camp epic, an "old-fashioned" yarn about the "timeless themes" of "honor", "conviction" and the "madness" of war; a lock for the top Oscars of 1957, it "succeeds" mightily with "great performances" – led "heart and soul" by a "hubris"-afflicted Guinness – enhanced by "splashy" scenery and an "explosive ending."

### Bridges of Madison County, The | 19 | 23 | 20 | 20 |
*1995. Directed by Clint Eastwood. With Clint Eastwood, Meryl Streep, Annie Corley. 135 minutes. Rated PG-13.*
Director/leading man Eastwood unveils his "gentle side" in this "bittersweet" romance recounting the "middle-aged" passion between a "roving" photographer and a "lonely housewife"; some cite the "banal", "snail's-pace" plot as a big "yawn", but to fans it's "lovably sappy" – and "way better" than the "treacly" book.

### BRIDGET JONES'S DIARY | 21 | 23 | 22 | 21 |
*2001. Directed by Sharon Maguire. With Renée Zellweger, Hugh Grant, Colin Firth. 97 minutes. Rated R.*
This "everygirl" "chick flick" is a "charming" romance that logs the progress of the "fab" Zellweger, doing a "knockout job" in the title role as a "twentysomething singleton" "desperately seeking a spouse" but beleaguered by "faux pas", "weight gain" and a "perfect cad" of a boss; followers find it "hilarious yet so true" but won't commit as to whether it "nails the book" or not.

### BRIEF ENCOUNTER ◑ | 27 | 29 | 27 | 25 |
*1946. Directed by David Lean. With Celia Johnson, Trevor Howard, Stanley Holloway. 86 minutes. Not Rated.*
For a "truly romantic" fix, this "quiet" "masterpiece of yearning" from David Lean (via Noël Coward) is "right up there" in the running as the "definitive tearjerker"; the "never better" Johnson and Howard play "ordinary people" whose meeting on a commuter line develops into a "short but intense" "connection", with swells of Rachmaninoff to seal the deal; in brief, an "unforgettable" trip.

### Bringing Up Baby ◑ | 27 | 27 | 24 | 24 |
*1938. Directed by Howard Hawks. With Katharine Hepburn, Cary Grant. 102 minutes. Not Rated.*
"One continuous roar", director Hawks' "screwiest of screwball comedies" is propelled at a "frenetic pace" by the Hepburn-Grant

"chemistry" and a "tons-of-fun" scenario touching on "dinosaur bones, crazy rich folk" and a lost leopard; it's an old-school "madcap" "champ", and fans of "farce" still bring it up as the "funniest movie ever."

### Broadcast News
23 | 25 | 22 | 20

*1987. Directed by James L. Brooks. With William Hurt, Albert Brooks, Holly Hunter. 127 minutes. Rated R.*
"Appearance over substance" is the subject of this "smart" "send-up of the media" about a "love triangle" in a "career-driven", *Network*-esque TV newsroom that hums with "behind-the-scenes" one-upmanship; nominated for a slew of Oscars (but winner of none), this "ahead-of-its-time" comedy remains "totally engaging", due to the efforts of its "sharp-as-a-tack" cast.

### Broadway Danny Rose ◑
22 | 22 | 22 | 20

*1984. Directed by Woody Allen. With Woody Allen, Mia Farrow, Nick Apollo Forte. 84 minutes. Rated PG.*
Woody and Mia (in rosier days) light up this comedy about a "Mafia tootsie who melts" for the "ultimate mensch", a small-time talent agent clinging to the "underbelly" of "borscht-belt" showbiz; although infused with a "NY sensibility", some say the "shaggy-dog" plot "doesn't quite deliver."

### Brother Bear
21 | – | 21 | 23

*2003. Directed by Aaron Blaise, Bob Walker. Animated. 85 minutes. Rated G.*
"Sweet" yet "not overly sentimental", this "politically correct" Disney feature tells the tale of a boy turned into a bear, learning to "respect all living things" along the way; despite "old-fashioned" animation and a "slow-moving" pace, it redeems itself with a "message of love"; P.S. a pair of moose voiced by SCTV's McKenzie brothers provide a breath of "over-the-top" relief for grown-ups.

### Buck Privates ◑⑪
22 | 19 | 16 | 18

*1941. Directed by Arthur Lubin. With Abbott & Costello, the Andrews Sisters. 84 minutes. Not Rated.*
A coupla clowns go to boot camp and "frivolity" ensues in this "classic Abbott and Costello" comedy, which "evokes an era" thanks to the "duo's rapid-fire patter" and USO-worthy tunes by the "Andrews Sisters at their peak"; despite "patchwork" plotting, it "ranks up there" in Bud and Lou's oeuvre and works as a swell "Sunday morning" indulgence.

### Buena Vista Social Club
25 | – | 24 | 24

*1999. Directed by Wim Wenders. Documentary. 101 minutes. Rated G.*
"Revelatory – and danceable" – this documentary is a "love letter to a vanishing breed" of musicians, "aging" vets of the "Afro-Cuban jazz" scene who volunteer "personal histories" of "trials and tribulations" in the "shadow of Castro", interspersed with "irresistible" live jams; it "builds slowly" in a haze of "washed-out tropical colors" to a narrative of "great charm" and "insight", backed by a soundtrack that's as "captivating" as they come.

### Bug's Life, A
24 | – | 22 | 26

*1998. Directed by John Lasseter, Andrew Stanton. Animated. 96 minutes. Rated G.*
"Even parents" bug out on the "mind-blowing creativity" of the Disney/Pixar team's "step-ahead animation" in this "cute" parable

of "insect politics" rendered in "sharp, colorful" computer graphics that "look incredible", even if the "social satire" is "geared for kids"; most maintain it's "superior to *Antz*" and advise sticking around for the fake outtakes as the credits roll (the "best part").

### Bugsy
18 | 19 | 18 | 19

*1991. Directed by Barry Levinson. With Warren Beatty, Annette Bening, Harvey Keitel, Ben Kingsley. 135 minutes. Rated R.*
"Long but fascinating", this bio of mobster Bugsy Siegel (the "gangster who created Las Vegas out of desert dust") is a "graphic" film about high-rolling "lowlifes"; though a few yawn it's a "Beatty vanity project", at least the "bewitching cinematography" makes the already "beautiful cast even more ravishing"; fave line: "why don't you run outside and jerk yourself a soda?"

### Bull Durham
22 | 22 | 22 | 20

*1988. Directed by Ron Shelton. With Kevin Costner, Susan Sarandon, Tim Robbins. 108 minutes. Rated R.*
"Life and love in minor-league baseball" equal "diverting" comedy in this "funny and realistic" sports pic, juiced by "sexy", "laid-back acting" from Sarandon and Costner, a "great pair" out to take the "American spirit" into extra innings; fans cheer it on as a "smart home run" that's "one of the best" of the hardball yarns.

### Bullets Over Broadway
21 | 23 | 21 | 21

*1994. Directed by Woody Allen. With John Cusack, Dianne Wiest, Jennifer Tilly, Chazz Palminteri. 98 minutes. Rated R.*
A "quirky, colorful" shot of "period" atmosphere, this "backstage comedy" concerns a Jazz Age dramatist and a "gangster who rewrites his Broadway play"; it's "likable" enough for its "witty dialogue" and "over-the-top" cast, though as usual for a "post-*Hannah*" Allen opus, some wish it were "just a little funnier."

### Bullitt
22 | 20 | 20 | 24

*1968. Directed by Peter Yates. With Steve McQueen, Robert Vaughn, Jacqueline Bisset. 113 minutes. Rated PG.*
Arguably "the mother of all cop films", this "solid" action thriller stars an "icy-cool" McQueen, "acting by not acting" as a no-bull SFPD detective who takes on a corrupt system; set in Frisco "before too many high-rises" arrived, it's famed for a "definitive car chase" ("wheee!") that's "still the best" after "countless" knockoffs, though some find the ride "pretty straightforward" plotwise.

### Bus Stop
21 | 21 | 20 | 20

*1956. Directed by Joshua Logan. With Marilyn Monroe, Don Murray, Eileen Heckart. 96 minutes. Not Rated.*
Proving herself "at home on the range", Monroe brings "depth" to romantic comedy as a "vulnerable" "Western chantoosie" with "impossible dreams" adrift in an otherwise "slightly sappy" tale of a cowpoke's "crazy love" (via a William Inge play); though Marilyn proves she's more than "just a pretty face", skeptics of her "serious actress" mode say they "want to get off."

### BUTCH CASSIDY & THE SUNDANCE KID ✉ ⓤ
26 | 26 | 25 | 25

*1969. Directed by George Roy Hill. With Paul Newman, Robert Redford, Katharine Ross. 110 minutes. Rated PG.*
"Compulsive charmers" Newman and Redford play a pair of wisecracking, "magnetic" "antiheroes" trying to stay ahead of

the law in this "outstanding" Western "buddy movie", loaded with "adventure and humor"; it fuses a "snappy" script, Burt Bacharach soundtrack and "too many classic scenes to count" into a "sentimental favorite" that's "never boring" from start to "unforgettable" finish.

### Bye Bye Birdie          19 | 18 | 18 | 20

*1963. Directed by George Sidney. With Janet Leigh, Dick Van Dyke, Ann-Margret. 112 minutes. Rated G.*

The high "fun quotient" bolsters this "upbeat" musical from the "long-ago world" of 1963, a look at the hoopla surrounding an Elvis-like singer's farewell gig before he goes off to the army; though Ann-Margret is "one heck of a talented sex kitten" doing some athletic song-and-dance numbers that – whew! – "stay with you", detractors wave it off as "cheesy" fare that's "woefully dated now."

### Cabaret ✉          26 | 25 | 25 | 27

*1972. Directed by Bob Fosse. With Liza Minnelli, Michael York, Joel Grey. 124 minutes. Rated PG.*

Comprised of equal parts "love, angst", "singing, dancing and Nazis", this "seminal modern musical" set in pre-WWII Berlin is a "touchstone" of the genre that "hasn't lost its luster"; old chums cheer Fosse's "superb direction" and the "starmaking performances" from Minnelli and Grey (who all took home Oscars), and even though the mood of the piece can career from "dark" to "raunchy", it's always "fun to watch."

### Cabinet of Dr. Caligari, The ◑          26 | 21 | 24 | 26

*1921. Directed by Robert Wiene. With Conrad Veidt, Werner Kraus. 67 minutes. Not Rated.*

"They don't get any freakier" than this "fascinating antique", a "menacingly atmospheric" silent horror flick that uses "German expressionism" and "twisted sets" to kindle a "nightmare" tale of murder told by a "tortured mind"; "stark, powerful" and "spooky" right down to the pioneering "surprise ending", it's "still being imitated" and still makes many modern chillers "look lame."

### Cactus Flower          ▽ 17 | 20 | 18 | 17

*1969. Directed by Gene Saks. With Walter Matthau, Ingrid Bergman, Goldie Hawn. 103 minutes. Rated PG.*

This "cute" if "dated" comedy about the affairs of a philandering dentist might be "romantic fluff", but it's redeemed by a "strong cast", particularly the "radiant" Bergman and the "delightful", Oscar-winning Hawn "in her screen debut"; sticklers say "even Matthau can't save" the "weak story", though "he does try."

### Caddyshack ⓤ          24 | 20 | 19 | 19

*1980. Directed by Harold Ramis. With Chevy Chase, Rodney Dangerfield, Bill Murray. 99 minutes. Rated R.*

"Dumb as it is", this "goofy" comedy of "golfers gone amok" is a "classic" of "unironic" (some say "sophomoric") humor featuring a "priceless" ensemble cast and a fake gopher; "ok, it's a guy thing", but it "stands the test of time" as "oft-quoted" "mindless fun."

### Caine Mutiny, The          27 | 28 | 26 | 23

*1954. Directed by Edward Dmytryk. With Humphrey Bogart, Jose Ferrer, Van Johnson. 124 minutes. Not Rated.*

This "briny" blend of "powerful wartime story" and "engrossing" courtroom drama gets its ballast from Bogart's "brilliant", "pullout-all-the-stops" turn as Queeg, the "demented sea captain" compulsively "click, click, clicking" a set of "steel balls"; the "classic script" follows a "totally believable" high-seas rebellion to a court-martial and is "must-see" material for maritime mavens.

### Calendar Girls
23 | 25 | 23 | 22

*2003. Directed by Nigel Cole. With Helen Mirren, Julie Walters, John Alderton. 108 minutes. Rated PG-13.*
"Older can be beautiful" is the "serious message behind the tea and scones" of this comic tale of "plucky", middle-aged English gals who pose for a nude calendar to raise funds for a cancer center; the "talent-laden cast" does a "charming" job with this "female version of *The Full Monty*", and let's face it, "who doesn't love Helen Mirren naked?"; wags note certain parts "sag" a bit.

### Camelot
21 | 21 | 23 | 23

*1967. Directed by Joshua Logan. With Richard Harris, Vanessa Redgrave, Franco Nero. 179 minutes. Rated G.*
Lerner and Loewe's Broadway musical of the "well-worn" King Arthur legend receives "faithful" treatment in this tale of pomp and "passion in medieval England"; admirers of the "gorgeous" sets and "beautiful music" sing its praises as a "magical" "diversion", though dissenters take a tilt at the "ponderous" "excess" and note "no one in the cast can carry a tune."

### Candidate, The ✉
20 | 22 | 22 | 20

*1972. Directed by Michael Ritchie. With Robert Redford, Peter Boyle, Melvyn Douglas. 109 minutes. Rated PG.*
A "prescient" civics lesson, this political drama tracks a "social activist seduced into selling his soul" when he runs for the Senate from California; a "most convincing" Redford leads the pack of "top-notch performances" as the novice campaigner who's "in far over his head", presenting an "accurate" if "cynical view" of the process that registers as "timely" over 30 years later.

### Cape Fear ◑
25 | 26 | 26 | 23

*1962. Directed by J. Lee Thompson. With Gregory Peck, Robert Mitchum, Polly Bergen. 105 minutes. Not Rated.*
It's high tide for "rage and revenge" in this "doozy" of a noir thriller, a real "nail-biter" starring Peck as an upright dad who "gets down in the gutter" to protect his family from a "deeply frightening" ex-con, at large in the marsh and "as evil as they come"; most rate it "scarier than the remake", "without the histrionics."

### Cape Fear
20 | 24 | 21 | 20

*1991. Directed by Martin Scorsese. With Robert De Niro, Nick Nolte, Jessica Lange, Juliette Lewis. 128 minutes. Rated R.*
Count on "fear for sure" as Scorsese's "well-done" redo of the killer '62 thriller heads for "over-the-top territory", working up "sustained suspense" as a "terrifying" De Niro "has a ball" portraying a vengeance-bent "wacko"; it's an "edge-of-your-seat" ride, with the "cameos" from the "previous cast" that are a "nice touch."

### Captain Blood ◑
23 | 21 | 20 | 21

*1935. Directed by Michael Curtiz. With Errol Flynn, Olivia de Havilland, Basil Rathbone. 119 minutes. Not Rated.*
Avast, there's "salty" "popcorn fun" aplenty in this "smashing" swashbuckler, featuring "Flynn's first starring role" as an enslaved wretch who becomes a "devil-may-care" pirate of the Caribbean;

armchair buccaneers jump on board for the "roguish" baddies, "high-seas action" and "men in tights", not minding that the old vessel is "on the creaky side."

### Captains Courageous ✉◑∅    25 | 26 | 24 | 21

*1937. Directed by Victor Fleming. With Spencer Tracy, Freddie Bartholomew, Lionel Barrymore. 115 minutes. Not Rated.*
Fashioned from a Kipling tale that's "every boy's dream of excitement", this "tearjerker"-cum–adventure story stars Bartholomew as a bratty rich kid who's rescued at sea and matures under the helm of a salty sailor, the Oscar-winning Tracy; the lad's "highly touching" transformation is conveyed through "phenomenal" acting that's "too often forgotten."

### Carnal Knowledge    22 | 26 | 21 | 21

*1971. Directed by Mike Nichols. With Jack Nicholson, Candice Bergen, Art Garfunkel, Ann-Margret. 98 minutes. Rated R.*
"Literate people talk dirty" in this "bitter but engrossing" look at "two self-absorbed buddies who measure life in terms of their sexual conquests", and though these "pretty sad characters" can be "hard to watch", the "perfect cast" expertly evokes its theme of "innocence lost"; still, the jaded jeer what was "bold for its time" is now rather "tame."

### Carousel    24 | 22 | 22 | 25

*1956. Directed by Henry King. With Gordon MacRae, Shirley Jones, Cameron Mitchell. 128 minutes. Not Rated.*
"Girl meets wrong boy" at the traveling show in this silver screen go-round of Rodgers and Hammerstein's "sentimental" musical, which draws on a "lovely" score and "fine cast" of "first-rate" singers to spin a tale that's "romantic, sad" and "not always pretty"; while it's regarded as a "neglected great" to devotees, it's also seen as a squandering of "talent" on a "corny", "tarnished-with-age" storyline.

### Carrie ⓤ    22 | 22 | 23 | 21

*1976. Directed by Brian De Palma. With Sissy Spacek, Piper Laurie, Amy Irving, John Travolta. 98 minutes. Rated R.*
"Stephen King done right", this "bloody good" horror pic headlines Spacek as a "bug-eyed" "telekinetic outcast" (with a "nut bar" of a mom) who repays the "casual cruelty of high-schoolers" with a prom-night "flip-out" that's gorier than a bucket of "pig's blood"; with "character-oriented" carnage that's a cut above "shock schlock", it's "white knuckles all the way" to that "grabber" of an ending.

### Casablanca ✉◑    29 | 28 | 28 | 27

*1942. Directed by Michael Curtiz. With Humphrey Bogart, Ingrid Bergman, Paul Henreid, Claude Rains. 102 minutes. Rated PG.*
We'll always have the "magic" of this "most compelling" of romances, a showcase for "legendary" turns from an "enigmatic" Bogart, "radiant" Bergman and "top-shelf" supporting cast set against the "unforgettable" backdrop of WWII occupied North Africa; the "fast-paced" plot of passion and "intrigue" is an "unsurpassed" model of good, "old-fashioned storytelling" and a bona fide "runner-up to Shakespeare" for "classic lines" – there's no choice but to "play it again and again."

### Casino
**21 | 24 | 21 | 22 |**

*1995. Directed by Martin Scorsese. With Robert De Niro, Sharon Stone, Joe Pesci. 178 minutes. Rated R.*

A crash course in "pre-corporate casino management", this "flashy" crime saga of "mob life" in "seedy Vegas" relates a "dark" tale that deals out "violence, drugs and self-loathing" in spades; proponents lay their money down for De Niro as a dapper hood, Pesci's "insane mob guy" bit and a "sizzling" Stone proving she "can actually act"; still, those who yawn it's "way too long" say bets are off, since they could be "watching *Goodfellas* instead."

### Casper
**15 | 14 | 15 | 19 |**

*1995. Directed by Brad Silberling. With Christina Ricci, Bill Pullman, Cathy Moriarty. 100 minutes. Rated PG.*

The "special effects are worth the ticket price" of this "typical family movie" "appropriate for all ages" that's also notable for its "really cute" title character, a ghost who's referred to as 'living impaired'; though some say the "sappy" storyline's "charmless", at least it's "not annoyingly adorable."

### Cast Away
**20 | 25 | 18 | 23 |**

*2000. Directed by Robert Zemeckis. With Tom Hanks, Helen Hunt. 143 minutes. Rated PG-13.*

"Hanks does Crusoe" in this "well-made" adventure based on Tom's "almost-one-man show" as a "pudgy FedEx" pilot marooned after a crash landing and forced to "slim down", don a "loincloth" and start "talking to a volleyball"; though "feeling his loneliness" may be "inspiring", foes say the action's beached by "slow-moving" stretches and a "trite" windup that's too "predictable."

### Cat Ballou ✉
**21 | 22 | 19 | 20 |**

*1965. Directed by Elliot Silverstein. With Lee Marvin, Jane Fonda, Michael Callan. 97 minutes. Not Rated.*

"Not your typical Western", this comic oater "with a heart" stars Fonda as a righteous lady outlaw but is stolen by Oscar-winner Marvin, who horses around in two roles, including that of a whiskey-addled gunslinger; a "hoot in its day", it's nearing its ninth life but is still "fun to watch."

### Catch Me If You Can
**23 | 24 | 25 | 24 |**

*2002. Directed by Steven Spielberg. With Leonardo DiCaprio, Tom Hanks, Christopher Walken. 141 minutes. Rated PG-13.*

Spielberg's "witty, fast-paced" "cat-and-mouse game" ("based on a true story" about a charming con man) is "mischievous, delicious fun from the delightful opening credits until the final frame", with "lots of '60s color" and "awesome acting" by the "engaging DiCaprio" and "rock-solid" Hanks; it's an "exciting, wild ride" that shows us "sometimes crime *does* pay."

### Cat on a Hot Tin Roof
**25 | 27 | 24 | 23 |**

*1958. Directed by Richard Brooks. With Elizabeth Taylor, Paul Newman, Burl Ives. 108 minutes. Not Rated.*

"Man, these people have problems": "steamy Liz" "in that white slip" and a "dynamite" Newman "couldn't possibly look better" as they "burn up the screen" in this "sex-soaked" Tennessee Williams drama of "love, rejection" and "Southern family politics"; the "towering" Ives presides as the ragin' Big Daddy, adding an "incredibly interesting" *Lear*-like thread to all that "eye candy."

### Cat People
**16 | 17 | 18 | 18**

*1982. Directed by Paul Schrader. With Nastassja Kinski, Malcolm McDowell, John Heard, Annette O'Toole. 118 minutes. Rated R.*
"Pretty on the eye if fuzzy on the brain", this "atmospheric" remake of the 1942 "Simone Simon cult classic" is a "stylish but forgettable" fantasy having to do with panthers and "sexual politics"; fans purr about its "creepy", "feline performances" and "nifty special effects", but seen-it-alls say the "David Bowie theme song" is the "best thing about this movie."

### Celluloid Closet, The
**25 | – | 25 | 24**

*1995. Directed by Robert Epstein, Jeff Friedman. Documentary. 102 minutes. Rated R.*
Learn to "appreciate" certain classics in a "whole new" way via this documentary "revelation" that traces "gay themes and undercurrents" in Hollywood history using film clips and "insightful" interviews; it takes an "unsparing look at prejudice" that's also a "very entertaining" glimpse into a "crowded closet" – even if some wish there were more than "mild surprises behind the door."

### Charade
**26 | 25 | 26 | 25**

*1963. Directed by Stanley Donen. With Cary Grant, Audrey Hepburn, Walter Matthau. 113 minutes. Not Rated.*
Expect "plenty of plot twists" in this "quintessential romantic comedy/thriller" (the "best Hitchcock flick that Hitchcock didn't make") about the scramble for a missing fortune; its very "easy-on-the-eyes" stars, "luscious Paris" scenery, magical "Mancini melodies" and "Audrey's fab wardrobe" make for "perfect" moviemaking – "murder was never so much fun."

### Chariots of Fire ✉
**26 | 25 | 25 | 25**

*1981. Directed by Hugh Hudson. With Ben Cross, Ian Charleson, Ian Holm. 123 minutes. Rated PG.*
Remembered for "running off with" a Best Picture Oscar, this "inspiring" drama paces itself in "superb" style as it follows the "trials and triumph" of a British track team bound for the 1924 Olympics; thanks to "uplifting" legwork and a very "hummable" soundtrack, it breaks the tape as a "never boring" movie.

### Charly ✉
**21 | 25 | 22 | 17**

*1968. Directed by Ralph Nelson. With Cliff Robertson, Claire Bloom, Leon Janney. 103 minutes. Rated PG.*
A bright idea grafting drama onto a "believable" sci-fi scenario, this "original" flick gives Best Actor honoree Robertson a chance to "shine" in his "best performance" as a "man who goes from retardation to genius and back again" after a round of brain surgery; tutor Bloom adds romantic interest to make the doings "supremely touching" – "if a bit sappy" for cynics.

### Chasing Amy
**20 | 19 | 20 | 17**

*1997. Directed by Kevin Smith. With Ben Affleck, Joey Lauren Adams, Jason Lee. 111 minutes. Rated R.*
Director Smith's trademarks – "Jersey-speak", "coarse humor", "semi-realistic situations" – are all apparent in this "offbeat" romantic comedy, featuring Affleck in the role of a comic-book scribe bewitched by a lesbian with a "nails-on-chalkboard" voice; it "rocks" fans with an "entertainingly different" mix of

"smart" talk and "slacker cool", but foes claim it's a "sentimental" ode to "geek life" that's "not really funny."

### Cheaper By the Dozen ⓤ
22 | 22 | 23 | 19

*1950. Directed by Walter Lang. With Clifton Webb, Jeanne Crain, Myrna Loy. 85 minutes. Not Rated.*
Set at the turn of the last century, this "warm family comedy" relates the "wonderful", fact-based story of a pair of efficiency experts bringing up 12 "cute" children, with a "droll" Webb stealing the show as the "pompous" head of the brood; sure, it strays into "precious" territory but oldsters attest it "wears well over time."

### CHICAGO ✉
27 | 26 | 25 | 29

*2002. Directed by Rob Marshall. With Renée Zellweger, Catherine Zeta-Jones, Richard Gere, Queen Latifah. 113 minutes. Rated PG-13.*
"Bob Fosse would have been proud" of this "absolutely brilliant" adaptation of his boffo Broadway "tale of murder, greed and corruption" in 1920s Chicago; "astounded" surveyors swear this "razzle-dazzle" "visual masterpiece" "deserved every Oscar it won" thanks to its "phenomenal acting", "sexy cinematography", "spine-tingling music" ("who knew the big three could sing?") and "major dance moves that'll leave you gasping for air"; even critics who complain of "miscasting" and "MTV camerawork" hope it sparks a "return to old-fashioned movie musicals."

### Chicken Run
23 | – | 23 | 27

*2000. Directed by Peter Lord, Nick Park. Animated. 84 minutes. Rated G.*
Pure "poultry in motion", this "ingenious", "touching" barnyard saga uses "fantastic" claymation to portray a "darn appealing" bunch of British fowl and their "valiant struggle" to get off the farm; "subtle references" make it a "hilarious take" on all the *Stalag 17*–style POW pics, so while kids can enjoy the "innocent" animated escapade, it "doesn't chicken out" on "tongue-in-cheek", grown-up undertones; in an eggshell, a "good run for the money."

### Children of a Lesser God ✉
23 | 25 | 22 | 21

*1986. Directed by Randa Haines. With Marlee Matlin, William Hurt, Piper Laurie. 119 minutes. Rated R.*
This "touching" drama "does justice to the original play" on the strength of "sexy, compelling" turns from Hurt as a speech teacher at a school for the deaf and Best Actress winner Matlin, "signing throughout" as a hearing-impaired woman with a complex past; expect "moving scenes" as their intimacy develops, and though an "enjoyable" intro to the "deaf community", it might be a "little overdramatized."

### CHILDREN OF PARADISE ❶🅵
28 | 27 | 27 | 26

*1946. Directed by Marcel Carné. With Arletty, Jean-Louis Barrault, Pierre Renoir. 190 minutes. Not Rated.*
Filmed in France "under the noses of the Nazis", this "legendary" romance "lovingly re-creates 1840s Paris" in a "multilayered" story of a "lovesick" mime's passion for a vampish stage siren; built on "profound" themes and "stylized" performances (that come off as "melodramatic" but are rich with "beauty and feeling"), it "continues to fascinate" as a "masterpiece of world cinema" and the big screen's "greatest tribute to live theater."

### China Syndrome, The

22 | 25 | 24 | 20

*1979. Directed by James Bridges. With Jack Lemmon, Jane Fonda, Michael Douglas. 122 minutes. Rated PG.*
The going gets "scary" as a nuclear power facility heads for meltdown in this "intelligent thriller" with a "solid" cast, including a "terrific" Lemmon as the plant supervisor and "Fonda at her peak" as a frustrated TV reporter; the "could-happen" story is "well-crafted", but conservatives contend that the "melodramatic" matchup of "bad-guy corporate players" against "good-guy idealists" makes it into the "definitive liberal" "message film."

### CHINATOWN ✉ ❶

27 | 28 | 26 | 26

*1974. Directed by Roman Polanski. With Jack Nicholson, Faye Dunaway, John Huston. 131 minutes. Rated R.*
This "taut drama" about "stolen water" and "bottled-up emotion" in 1930s LA is a "nearly perfect" exercise in "Technicolor film noir" that's simultaneously "funny, bleak and knowing"; credit the "dynamite" cast, "ravishingly beautiful" cinematography and "superb script" (that ends with a "shocking", "untypical-Hollywood ending") for its success; most memorable scene: Dunaway's "slap"-happy "she's-my-sister-she's-my-daughter" tour de force.

### CHOCOLAT

22 | 24 | 22 | 23

*2000. Directed by Lasse Hallström. With Juliette Binoche, Alfred Molina, Johnny Depp. 121 minutes. Rated PG-13.*
A "yummy escape" "bordering on a fairy tale", this "funny" romance finds "lovely" "rebel spirit" Binoche pitted against "petty-minded villagers" when she opens a chocolate shop in a French hamlet and takes up with Depp; the blend of a "beautiful setting" mixed with some "uplifting whimsy" makes for one "tasty bonbon."

### CHRISTMAS CAROL, A ◐

27 | 26 | 28 | 23

*1951. Directed by Brian Desmond Hurst. With Alastair Sim, Kathleen Harrison, Mervyn Johns. 86 minutes. Not Rated.*
"Sim is the best Scrooge ever" in this Dickens of a "holiday delight", a "magical adaptation" of the "timeless" fable concerning a rich old paragon of "grouchiness" transformed by a Yuletide visit from a posse of ghosts; cherished as "superb" family fare that "inspires" without drowning in the "happily-ever-after tone" of other versions, it has fans replaying it "religiously" because there's "no way" to do "Christmas without it."

### Christmas Story, A

26 | 23 | 27 | 22

*1983. Directed by Bob Clark. With Peter Billingsley, Melinda Dillon, Darren McGavin. 94 minutes. Rated PG.*
A "sweet but not sugary" look at the "debacle that's Christmas in America", this "irresistible" family fave takes a "fond glimpse back" with a "funny-till-it-hurts" "exposition of a '40s childhood" centered on a kid bent on a "BB gun" under the tree; "most rewatchable" and "quotable" thanks to its "excellent cast and script", it's "good clean fun" for all ages and now widely deemed a seasonal "must."

### Cider House Rules, The ✉

22 | 24 | 23 | 22

*1999. Directed by Lasse Hallström. With Tobey Maguire, Charlize Theron, Michael Caine. 126 minutes. Rated PG-13.*
Presenting "life choices" in a '30s-era Maine orphanage, this "thought-provoking tearjerker" is a story of "compassion" with

some "tough subject matter sneaked in" that gives Maguire his "breakout role" and proves "Caine really can act"; despite a few objections to the "cloying" tone and "watered-down" treatment of John Irving's novel, "satisfied" customers rule it an "absorbing" "feel-good" flick that "doesn't pander to the Hallmark crowd."

### Cinderella
26 | – | 25 | 26

*1950. Directed by Clyde Geronimi, Wilfred Jackson, Hamilton Luske. Animated. 74 minutes. Rated G.*

"You know the drill": "breathtaking" animation from "Disney's golden age" merges with the stuff "countless girlish dreams" are made of in this "beautiful fantasy" about an "overworked, abused orphan" who bags her Prince Charming, with a little help from her fairy godmother and some "industrious", very finely feathered friends; if "short on characterization", it remains an "old-fashioned favorite" that's a shoe-in to be a "classic for generations to come."

### Cinderella Liberty ∅
19 | 23 | 20 | 17

*1973. Directed by Mark Rydell. With James Caan, Marsha Mason, Kirk Calloway. 117 minutes. Rated R.*

"Great chemistry" between the leads buoys this "honest" but "often-overlooked" romance about a lonesome shore-patrol swabbie who falls for a "tender-hearted prostitute" and becomes a real father figure to her "mixed-race son"; an "excellent" Caan plays well against Mason's "sympathetic" portrayal of the "hooker who doesn't know any other way to live"; all in all, a shipshape effort.

### Cinema Paradiso ✉ 🅵
26 | 26 | 26 | 25

*1988. Directed by Giuseppe Tornatore. With Philippe Noiret, Jacques Perrin. 123 minutes. Rated R.*

This Italian "heart-warmer" is an "endearing" look at "love and loss" as well as a "nostalgic valentine" to the "magic of cinema"; based on the "utterly charming" story of a "projectionist in the local movie house" who "mentors a fatherless child", it rolls a "colorful" cast, "*bellissimo*" camerawork and a "lovely" score into an "engrossing", frankly "sentimental" film.

### CITIZEN KANE ✉◑
28 | 27 | 27 | 28

*1941. Directed by Orson Welles. With Orson Welles, Joseph Cotten, Agnes Moorehead, Everett Sloane. 119 minutes. Rated PG.*

"Loosely based on the life of William Randolph Hearst", this "magnum opus" about a "ruthless megalomaniac" who "mourns the loss of his innocent childhood" is an "undisputed masterpiece" that's "often imitated, never duplicated" and "as fresh as ever"; starring and directed by wunderkind Welles, it "revolutionized the cinema" and forever changed the meaning of the word "rosebud" – "by comparison, all other films are home movies."

### CITY LIGHTS ◑
28 | 28 | 26 | 25

*1931. Directed by Charles Chaplin. With Charles Chaplin, Virginia Cherrill. 87 minutes. Not Rated.*

"Humor, pathos and poignancy" make this silent "Chaplin masterpiece" glow with "old-fashioned sentimentality" as the Little Tramp's "devotion for a blind flower girl" leads to a series of "classic" sequences; from famed bits like the "balletic boxing match" to the "heartbreaking" closing, this early flicker is a testament to a master "on top of his game."

### CITY OF GOD 🇫
26 | 25 | 26 | 25

*2003. Directed by Kátia Lund, Fernando Meirelles. With Matheus Nachtergaele, Seu Jorge. 130 minutes. Rated R.*

"Even those who are allergic to subtitles" will be more than "captivated" by this "shattering portrait" of "street kids in Brazil" who "grow up to become a gang of murderous drug dealers"; it's a "harrowing, gut-wrenching" "tour de force" that's "dynamically acted" by "nonactors" and made "edgy and fresh" by "hypnotic visuals"; the "extreme violence and brutality" may "leave you feeling ill", but "you can't look away."

### City Slickers 🆄
20 | 20 | 20 | 19

*1991. Directed by Ron Underwood. With Billy Crystal, Daniel Stern, Jack Palance. 112 minutes. Rated PG-13.*

"Yee-haw!"; a "super" Crystal rides high in this "tons-of-fun" "buddy comedy" about three NYers who go west for a dude-ranch vacation and wind up having a "midlife crisis during a cattle drive"; the "right-on" cast (particularly the "just-too-funny Palance") has a way with "wisdom and great one-liners", rounding up applause for "good fun" that doesn't shy from its "moving" side.

### Clear and Present Danger
20 | 21 | 22 | 20

*1994. Directed by Phillip Noyce. With Harrison Ford, Willem Dafoe, Anne Archer. 141 minutes. Rated PG-13.*

Clearly "great popcorn fodder", this "provocative action" flick is "one of the better Clancy adaptations", with Ford in "fine form" reprising his role as "what-a-man" CIA agent Jack Ryan going mano a mano with a Colombian dope cartel; though some call it "escapist stuff", it's so "exciting" and "patriotic", you can't help but root for this "smart movie hero" who "really kicks butt."

### Cleopatra
19 | 18 | 19 | 25

*1963. Directed by Joseph L. Mankiewicz. With Elizabeth Taylor, Richard Burton, Rex Harrison. 192 minutes. Not Rated.*

"Grand, gaudy and tons of fun", this epic bio of the queen of the Nile (renowned for "breaking all production-cost records") is either a "guilty pleasure" or an "incredible waste of time"; devotees dig its "huge scale", over-the-top "entertainment" value and Liz's "exquisite" beauty, but cynics nix the flick's "bloated" look and "draggy" pace, advising that you "hit the clicker" immediately after Cleo's "showstopping entrance into Rome."

### Clerks ◑
23 | 17 | 22 | 16

*1994. Directed by Kevin Smith. With Brian O'Halloran, Jeff Anderson, Marilyn Ghigliotti. 92 minutes. Rated R.*

"Crude" acting and "bottom-of-the-barrel production" values are redeemed by "wicked black humor" and "inspired", "raunchy" dialogue in this "microbudget indie" effort, a "fast-paced" comedy that pumps life into the "dead-end job" scene with a "realistic" look at "minimart" wage slavery; the "first foray" in Smith's "New Jersey series", it's a "slacker" "cult classic" that's "painfully funny" but unsafe for the "squeamish."

### Client, The
17 | 19 | 19 | 18

*1994. Directed by Joel Schumacher. With Susan Sarandon, Tommy Lee Jones, Brad Renfro. 120 minutes. Rated PG-13.*

Ok, it's "not great literature or art", but this adaptation of the John Grisham best-seller makes for a "good evening of entertainment" with its "linear story" of a youngster fleeing mobsters *and* the FBI; though too "predictable" for some, the "enjoyable Sarandon" and "impressive Renfro" keep things "interesting" enough.

### Clockwork Orange, A
25 | 24 | 24 | 25

*1971. Directed by Stanley Kubrick. With Malcolm McDowell, Patrick Magee. 137 minutes. Rated R.*

"Not for the weak of heart", this "ingenious Kubrick" cult parable is a "bold", "nightmarish" "mix of sex, ultraviolence" and "mind control" set in a "freaky", "futuristic" Britain; following the travails of "unhinged" "bad boy" McDowell (the "sinister yet strangely likable" head of a "vicious gang of droogies") through his "chilling" crimes to his "brainwashing" rehab, it threads "brilliant visuals" and "twisted" "social satire" into "riveting", "artful stuff" – helped by a bit of the old "Ludwig van."

### Close Encounters of the Third Kind
24 | 22 | 25 | 27

*1977. Directed by Steven Spielberg. With Richard Dreyfuss, François Truffaut, Teri Garr. 135 minutes. Rated PG.*

"It's ok to believe in UFOs" thanks to this "landmark" sci-fi "spectacle", a "mesmerizing", "believable contact film" wherein Spielberg's "sense of wonder" first embraces the "aliens-come-to-earth" formula; the "hopeful" plotline involves a race to "figure it all out" when strange signals arrive from the sky, and the result is a "mind-blowing" "visual treat" with plenty of "heart" (and "mountains of mashed potatoes") that delivers a "jaw-dropping" climax with a "sentimental streak" a light-year wide.

### Clueless
21 | 19 | 20 | 20

*1995. Directed by Amy Heckerling. With Alicia Silverstone, Paul Rudd, Brittany Murphy. 97 minutes. Rated PG-13.*

Totally "sneaky-smart", this "lively" "update of Emma" with a "90210" twist is a "winning" comedy about LA's "spoiled rich" kids and stars a "delightful", "not-quite-acting" Silverstone, who juggles romantic uncertainty, a variety of "Valley catch phrases" and a "'90s" wardrobe "to die for"; despite a few hints of "fluff" – "whatever" – it offers "pure enjoyment" as a "pivotal teen movie" and some of the "sharpest" "bubblegum" out there.

### Coach Carter
21 | 22 | 21 | 20

*2005. Directed by Thomas Carter. With Samuel L. Jackson. 136 minutes. Rated PG-13.*

"Reliably cool" Jackson hits nothin' but net with this "inspiring" tale ("based on a true story") of a "get-tough" high school hoops coach who leads his "underdog" squad to the Big Game; sure, the "feel-good" outcome may be "a bit predictable", but at the final buzzer fans cheer the "valuable" stay-in-school message, not to mention those "slam 'n' jam" B-ball scenes.

### Coal Miner's Daughter ✉
24 | 27 | 23 | 22

*1980. Directed by Michael Apted. With Sissy Spacek, Tommy Lee Jones, Levon Helm. 125 minutes. Rated PG.*

Kentucky moonshine and "bravura performances" brighten this "charming biopic" of country crooner Loretta Lynn, led by the Oscar-winning Spacek as the daughter of Appalachia who "makes it huge" in Nashville; a down-home, "down-to-earth fairy tale", its "realistic portrayal" of a star's "rise to fame" and bout with burnout plays like an "interesting" C&W take on *Behind the Music*.

### Cocoanuts, The ◑     24 | 22 | 19 | 19
*1929. Directed by Robert Florey, Joseph Santley. With the Marx Brothers, Kay Francis. 96 minutes. Not Rated.*
Never mind the "technical primitiveness", this first Marx Brothers comedy is as "zany" as their later work; though this "crude" rendering of the sibs' Broadway show is burdened with "trite musical numbers" and a "weak" story involving Florida real estate, die-hard Marxists say ya "gotta love" it as an "intriguing mess" that's at worst a guarantee of "better things to come."

### Cocoon ⑪     20 | 21 | 21 | 20
*1985. Directed by Ron Howard. With Don Ameche, Wilford Brimley, Hume Cronyn. 117 minutes. Rated PG-13.*
"Old duffers" meet "pod people" in this "warm" sci-fi tale, which spins a "clever story" of an intergalactic meet-up between extraterrestrials and Florida rest-home residents, whose backyard pool becomes a fountain of youth; the "delightful" setup and "complete characters" give some of Hollywood's elder statesmen room to "romp", while director Howard makes it all "credible" – if a bit too "warm and cuddly" for some.

### Cold Mountain     22 | 24 | 22 | 26
*2003. Directed by Anthony Minghella. With Jude Law, Nicole Kidman, Renée Zellweger. 152 minutes. Rated R.*
The "cinematic equivalent of a coffee table book", this "beautifully shot" Civil War saga of separated lovers "adapted from Homer's *Odyssey*" stars a "smokin'" Law opposite a "too-beautiful" Kidman, ever the "fashion plate" when she's "supposed to be starving"; never mind the too-"long" running time, "watching-the-grass-grow" pacing and controversy over Renée's Oscar win ("much deserved" vs. "Granny Clampett"), at the very least, this one is certainly "worth falling asleep on the sofa for."

### Collateral     21 | 24 | 21 | 22
*2004. Directed by Michael Mann. With Tom Cruise, Jamie Foxx, Jada Pinkett Smith. 120 minutes. Rated R.*
Cruise sports a silver hairdo and plays "against type" as a "psychopathic" contract killer pitted against Foxx's "unassuming everyman" for one "nightmare evening" in this "taut", "edge-of-your-seat" thriller from "master-of-moods" auteur Mann; devotees say the "incongruous plot", "tacked-on romance" and "generic conclusion" are "forgivable" due to the "morally challenging" situations – and "LA never looked so beautiful and dangerous."

### Collector, The     ▽ 23 | 26 | 23 | 22
*1965. Directed by William Wyler. With Terence Stamp, Samantha Eggar. 119 minutes. Not Rated.*
A "deeply disturbed recluse" kidnaps a "lovely young woman" in this "chilling story of obsession" adapted from John Fowles' "devastating" first novel; "terrific acting by Stamp and Eggar" keeps folks "fascinated", and if this "creepy stalker film" can be "hard to watch" at times, it's still "wonderfully done."

### Color of Money, The ✉     16 | 21 | 16 | 17
*1986. Directed by Martin Scorsese. With Paul Newman, Tom Cruise, Mary Elizabeth Mastrantonio. 119 minutes. Rated R.*
Something different from Martin Scorsese, this "generation-later" "follow-up to *The Hustler*" details how a washed-up billiards baron

molds an up-and-comer into his protégé; though somewhat "predictable", "excellent acting" from the "powerhouse Cruise" and the "finely tuned", Oscar-winning Newman "saves it."

### Color Purple, The 26 | 27 | 26 | 25
*1985. Directed by Steven Spielberg. With Whoopi Goldberg, Danny Glover, Oprah Winfrey. 154 minutes. Rated PG-13.*
A "heartfelt" reading of Alice Walker's "breakthrough" best-seller, this "moving" drama of "empowerment" "really hits home" with its depiction of a "post-slavery black family" in the Deep South and a wronged woman's "redemption and liberation"; the "breathtaking" lenswork, "Goldberg's best-ever showing" and a "brilliant" supporting cast ("Oprah can act!") make for a "teary" "triumph" that some cite as "Oscar's biggest snub."

### Coming Home ✉ 23 | 26 | 23 | 21
*1978. Directed by Hal Ashby. With Jane Fonda, Jon Voight, Bruce Dern, Penelope Milford. 126 minutes. Rated R.*
"Jon and Jane are magic together" in this "ultimate anti-war message" drama–cum–love triangle involving a paraplegic Vietnam vet, an "inconveniently married" hospital volunteer and a gung-ho marine; expect "moving performances" (Voight and Fonda took home Oscars) and "loads of emotion" that manage to convey a "coming of age for both the characters – and the times."

### Coming to America 18 | 18 | 17 | 17
*1988. Directed by John Landis. With Eddie Murphy, Arsenio Hall, James Earl Jones. 116 minutes. Rated R.*
"Sidesplitting", "multiple-character tour de force" showcasing the talents of "total riot" Murphy and "hilarious" Hall in a "goofy", "fish-out-of-water" comedy about an African prince who logically "heads to Queens" to find a royal mate; hard-core groupies who can "repeat the whole movie by heart" reveal their favorite scene: "pre-*ER* Eriq Le Salle's Soul Glow" routine.

### Con Air 14 | 15 | 14 | 18
*1997. Directed by Simon West. With Nicolas Cage, John Cusack, John Malkovich, Steve Buscemi. 115 minutes. Rated R.*
"Hardened criminals" en route to a "high-security prison" skyjack their plane in this "popcorn action flick" that's a "no-brainer" if you're ready for an "enjoyably obnoxious" experience; foes protest this "testosteronefest" has "little plot" and "just-collecting-a-paycheck" acting, but worst of all is Cage's "horrific mullet."

### Conan the Barbarian ⑪ 16 | 9 | 15 | 18
*1982. Directed by John Milius. With Arnold Schwarzenegger, James Earl Jones. 129 minutes. Rated R.*
The flick that "brought Arnold to everyone's attention", this "archetypal sword-and-sorcery fantasy" about a "barbarian butt-kicker" is "all a teenage boy could want" in a movie, conjuring up a pulpy, "no-holds-barred world of lust and vengeance"; even though Schwarzenegger's "acting isn't that great" – it was "before he learned to talk" – his "muscles are expressive" enough.

### Conformist, The 🄵∅ 26 | 26 | 27 | 26
*1971. Directed by Bernardo Bertolucci. With Jean-Louis Trintignant, Stefania Sandrelli, Dominique Sanda. 115 minutes. Rated R.*
Director "Bertolucci is at his absolute best" in this "supercool, superstylized" Italian psychological drama set in the '30s about an

"emotionally troubled civil servant" turned "fascist agent"; nonconformists warn "beware the dubbed version" but concur that Vittorio Storaro's "haunting" cinematography transcends dialogue; hottest moment: that "erotic tango" between Sanda and Sandrelli.

### Contact
20 | 21 | 20 | 22

*1997. Directed by Robert Zemeckis. With Jodie Foster, Matthew McConaughey, Tom Skerritt. 153 minutes. Rated PG.*
This "thinking person's" sci-fi flick asks the "Big Question" – "are we alone" in the universe?; true believers cite the "excellent special effects", "fascinating" story and a fine Foster "near the top of her form", but the alienated dismiss it as "long-winded" and "preachy", opting to "read Carl Sagan's excellent book" instead.

### Contender, The
19 | 23 | 20 | 19

*2000. Directed by Rod Lurie. With Joan Allen, Gary Oldman, Jeff Bridges, Christian Slater. 126 minutes. Rated R.*
In this Clinton White House–ish "Washington soap opera" (with enough "twists and turns" to keep you "guessing till the end"), a "scrappy" female pol "stays true to her principles" at great cost to her reputation and career; though Allen is "superb" and Bridges would make a "fine" real-life prez, some pundits protest the drama's "tackling of big issues" as "overblown melodrama."

### Conversation, The
25 | 26 | 25 | 23

*1974. Directed by Francis Ford Coppola. With Gene Hackman, John Cazale, Frederic Forrest. 113 minutes. Rated PG.*
A "brilliant" thriller about a "paranoid" surveillance specialist who comes undone, this "little-known" Coppola feature features a "virtuoso performance by Hackman", whose gradual "deterioration is amazing" (there's also an appearance by a very young Harrison Ford); though a bit "slow-moving", the script is so "superbly constructed" that "if this flick doesn't put you on edge, nothing will."

### Cooler, The
22 | 27 | 22 | 21

*2003. Directed by Wayne Kramer. With William H. Macy, Maria Bello, Alec Baldwin. 101 minutes. Rated R.*
"Losing is winning" for the perpetually "unlucky" title character in this "quirky" dramedy about a Vegas shill hired by a casino to "jinx high-rollers' winning streaks"; an "unglamorous" spin on the usual gambling yarn, it boasts "riveting acting" and a "believable love story", though some say the "gratuitous violence" and Macy's "racy" nude scenes are more of a "crapshoot."

### Cool Hand Luke
26 | 27 | 24 | 22

*1967. Directed by Stuart Rosenberg. With Paul Newman, George Kennedy, Strother Martin. 126 minutes. Not Rated.*
"One of the best movie lines ever" ('what we have here is a failure to communicate') and that "famous hard-boiled egg eating scene" make this "damn great" Deep South prison drama memorable – not to mention the efforts of "consummate pro" Newman playing one cool con on a "chain gang", abetted by a "strong" Kennedy, who grabbed an Oscar for his supporting work.

### Cool Runnings
18 | 16 | 21 | 17

*1993. Directed by Jon Turteltaub. With John Candy, Doug E. Doug, Leon, Malik Yoba. 98 minutes. Rated PG.*
Granted, it might be "silly", but this "cute", "underrated" comedy "based on the true" tale of the '88 Olympics' "Jamaican bobsled

team" is "fun for the whole family" (despite "a bit too much profanity"); cheerleaders say its "come-from-behind" story will "touch anyone's heart", particularly those who "miss John Candy."

### Cousin, Cousine 🇫 ∅ — 21 | 20 | 21 | 19
*1975. Directed by Jean-Charles Tacchella. With Marie-Christine Barrault, Victor Lanoux. 95 minutes. Rated R.*
This "sweet but naughty" French farce about romantically involved cousins-by-marriage offers a "refreshing" take on family dynamics; while some say it's "much better than the American" remake (*Cousins*), those suffering from memory lapses "can't recall anything" except – *zut alors!* – Barrault's "naked breasts."

### Crash — 26 | 27 | 26 | 25
*2004. Directed by Paul Haggis. With Sandra Bullock, Don Cheadle, Matt Dillon, Brendan Fraser, Terrence Dashon Howard, Ludacris, Thandie Newton, Ryan Phillippe. 113 minutes. Rated R.*
"Everyone's a little bit racist" according to this "provocative treatment" of "prejudice in America", with a "tightly wound" tapestry of "intertwined lives" in LA that "damn near hits the mark" attempting to "break down stereotypes" and "make you rethink your values"; with a "dream-team cast" enlivening the "incredible writing", expect to collide with some "tough", "wonderfully unpredictable" scenes that deliver a "powerful message."

### Cries and Whispers 🇫 — 26 | 28 | 24 | 26
*1972. Directed by Ingmar Bergman. With Harriet Andersson, Liv Ullmann, Ingrid Thulin. 106 minutes. Rated R.*
"Compelling is an understatement" when it comes to this "tortured masterpiece", a "raw", "close-in study of three sisters and their prickly relationship" that's "quintessential Bergman"; although it's "well acted" and "handsomely mounted", its depiction of "pain" is so "hard to watch" that some ask "are you sure 'angst' isn't a Swedish word?"

### Crimes and Misdemeanors — 26 | 26 | 25 | 24
*1989. Directed by Woody Allen. With Woody Allen, Mia Farrow, Anjelica Huston, Martin Landau. 107 minutes. Rated PG-13.*
"Crime does pay" in this "deeply serious" Allen dramedy with dual plotlines, one about a murderous philanderer, the other a "socially inept" filmmaker; "ruthlessly truthful", it manages to be alternately "scathing", "thought-provoking" and "hilarious", with "dead-on casting" and an "expert" scenario to boot.

### Crimson Tide — 21 | 24 | 22 | 22
*1995. Directed by Tony Scott. With Denzel Washington, Gene Hackman, George Dzundza. 116 minutes. Rated R.*
"Gripping", "tightly plotted" action flick relating the "macho machinations aboard a submarine" as two officers square off over a nuclear launch that could trigger an "unprovoked war"; given the "smart", "thought-provoking" acting of "big-screen titans" Washington and Hackman, you can expect a "first-rate" ride, even if some shrug it off as a "*Hunt for Red October* wannabe."

### Crocodile Dundee 🈁 — 17 | 14 | 17 | 16
*1986. Directed by Peter Faiman. With Paul Hogan, Linda Kozlowski. 98 minutes. Rated PG-13.*
This "surprise hit from Down Under" is a classic "fish-out-of-water" comedy about a transplanted Aussie "clashing with the ways of the

modern world"; though critics split on Hogan's appeal – "charming" vs. "better in Subaru commercials" – overall, it's "lightweight" fun.

**Crouching Tiger, Hidden Dragon**  `24 23 21 28`
*2000. Directed by Ang Lee. With Chow Yun-Fat, Michelle Yeoh, Zhang Ziyi. 120 minutes. Rated PG-13.*
Whether it's a "kung fu chick flick", a "thinking person's" martial arts film or "'chop-socky' translated into art", this "surreal" fantasy is full of "eye-popping fight sequences" that are half "ballet", half "Bruce Lee"; most memorable for its "strong female characters" and that "encounter in the bamboo forest", it's nothing less than a "breath of fresh air on the stale movie landscape."

**Crying Game, The** ✉ `22 24 24 20`
*1992. Directed by Neil Jordan. With Stephen Rea, Miranda Richardson, Jaye Davidson. 112 minutes. Rated R.*
"Violence and pathos" are served in the "right amounts" in this "disturbing" British drama about an "IRA recruit who's not really committed to his cause"; most famed for its whopper of a "surprise twist" (that leaves some "still flabbergasted"), this "intense vision of terrorism" offers enough nuanced "questions about race, sex and country" to justify a Best Screenplay Oscar.

**Damn Yankees** `24 23 23 24`
*1958. Directed by George Abbott, Stanley Donen. With Gwen Verdon, Tab Hunter, Ray Walston. 111 minutes. Not Rated.*
This screen adaptation of the Faust-influenced Broadway musical recounts how a "man makes a pact with the devil" to guarantee that the "Washington Senators win the pennant"; reprising their stage roles, Walston is at his "evil best" as Lucifer, while the "too-rarely-seen" Verdon gets what she wants as his sidekick, Lola; it's a "perfect evocation of the national optimism of the '50s" with a "great score" and a bonus: "Bob Fosse's mambo."

**Dancer in the Dark** `22 23 20 22`
*2000. Directed by Lars von Trier. With Björk, Catherine Deneuve, David Morse. 140 minutes. Rated R.*
A "musical like no other", this "dynamic" if "depressing" film "pushes the genre to the limit" in its account of an immigrant Czech "factory worker going blind who finds redemption only in music"; while foes find it "difficult to watch" – "even painful" – artistes laud its "wondrously strange" feel and praise pop star Björk's "amazing acting chops" and "compelling" vocal work.

**Dances with Wolves** ✉ `23 20 22 25`
*1990. Directed by Kevin Costner. With Kevin Costner, Mary McDonnell, Graham Greene. 183 minutes. Rated PG-13.*
For once, American Indians are portrayed in a "human light" in this "picturesque, sweeping epic" about a Civil War soldier who goes West, joins the Sioux and finds love along the way; although "beautifully shot" and quite the Oscar magnet (seven statuettes, including Best Picture), this "guy flick that women love" has critics citing a "monotonous", way-"too-long" running time.

**Dangerous Liaisons** ✉ `24 26 24 26`
*1988. Directed by Stephen Frears. With Glenn Close, John Malkovich, Michelle Pfeiffer. 119 minutes. Rated R.*
"Malkovich quietly chews up the scenery" opposite "perfectly evil" "ice queen" Close in this "flawless" drama set in "decadent", 17th-

century France rife with "treachery, betrayal and sexual games" among the "upper classes" ("no wonder the peasants revolted"); still, its "sumptuous production" and Oscar-winning screenplay make the "manipulating" characters more palatable.

### Dark Crystal, The
24 | – | 24 | 26

*1982. Directed by Jim Henson, Frank Oz. With puppet characters. 93 minutes. Rated PG.*
"Sinister muppets" take the stage in this "classic" "all-puppet feature", a "magical fairy tale" with an "otherworldly good and evil" storyline that represents the "culmination of Jim Henson's imagination"; while the "stunning visuals" please crowds, some warn that the "dark" plot "may be too scary" for smaller fry.

### Dark Victory ❶
25 | 27 | 23 | 23

*1939. Directed by Edmund Goulding. With Bette Davis, George Brent, Humphrey Bogart. 104 minutes. Not Rated.*
"Sensational" Bette at her "Warner Brothers peak" "turns camp into classic" in this melodramatic "tearjerker" about an heiress who's got everything – including a brain tumor; sob sisters say it's "worth every hanky" for Davis' "valiant" turn (one of the "best performances of 1939") and keep their eye out for a "young Ronald Reagan" in a supporting role.

### DAS BOOT ⊞
28 | 26 | 26 | 27

*1982. Directed by Wolfgang Petersen. With Jürgen Prochnow, Herbert Grönemeyer. 149 minutes. Rated R.*
When it comes to "underwater über alles" action, it's hard to top this "sweaty, claustrophobic" saga of "doomed German sailors" engaged in a "battle of egos" in a U-boat at the "bottom of the ocean"; though it's almost an "anti-recruiting film" given its "harrowing" realism, it exhibits enough "depth" to prove that "fear has no nationality" – you'll almost "root for" the Nazis.

### Dave
21 | 22 | 22 | 20

*1993. Directed by Ivan Reitman. With Kevin Kline, Sigourney Weaver, Frank Langella. 110 minutes. Rated PG-13.*
"Kline's adorable, as usual" in this "funny" political satire about an average "doofus" who looks so much like the President that he's asked to pinch-hit and winds up putting "faith back in government"; a latter-day "*Mr. Smith Goes to Washington*", this comedy has a "serious message", though conspiracy theorists say the message is "proof that liberals really do run Hollywood."

### David Copperfield ❶∅
▽ 27 | 26 | 27 | 25

*1935. Directed by George Cukor. With Freddie Bartholomew, W.C. Fields, Lionel Barrymore. 130 minutes. Not Rated.*
"One of the gems" of the Hollywood versions of "classic novels", this "wonderfully atmospheric", "very Dickensian" production may be a bit "creaky", though ultimately most of its "scenes are truly effective"; credit the "brilliant acting" from the MGM "repertory company", an "inspired" bunch headed up by Fields, whose "agile, hilarious" performance as Mr. Micawber is a "joy to watch."

### Day at the Races, A ❶
24 | 21 | 20 | 19

*1937. Directed by Sam Wood. With the Marx Brothers, Maureen O'Sullivan, Margaret Dumont. 111 minutes. Not Rated.*
The "Marx Brothers at their zenith of zaniness" horse around in this "very funny" comedy about a veterinarian turned human

doctor; though some say it's a "slightly second-tier" also-ran (only "sporadically funny" and even a tad "racist"), it was nevertheless one of the boys' "biggest box office hits."

### Day for Night ✉     27 | 25 | 25 | 25

*1973. Directed by François Truffaut. With Jacqueline Bisset, Valentina Cortese, Jean-Pierre Léaud. 115 minutes. Rated PG.*
"Truffaut's homage to American filmmaking", this "quintessential movie about making movies" "perfectly captures" all the "behind-the-scenes" "neuroses" and "joy" from an insider's point of view; though it shows the director "at his lightest", the "magical" result was both "charming" and "wacky" enough for it to take home a Best Foreign Language picture Oscar.

### Days of Heaven    23 | 21 | 20 | 25

*1978. Directed by Terrence Malick. With Richard Gere, Brooke Adams, Sam Shepard. 95 minutes. Rated PG.*
"Underseen but not underappreciated", this "gorgeous" if "bleak" drama detailing a love triangle between two dirt-poor migrant workers and a loaded landowner "broke new ground" in its use of "beautiful cinematography" to take the place of conventional exposition; though it "speaks volumes without much dialogue", low-attention-span types yawn "not terribly compelling."

### Days of Wine and Roses ◑    27 | 28 | 25 | 24

*1962. Directed by Blake Edwards. With Jack Lemmon, Lee Remick, Charles Bickford. 117 minutes. Not Rated.*
For a "tough look" at a "serious issue", this "harrowing" drama about the "ravages of alcoholism" was a "huge breakthrough in its day" and remains "relevant" thanks to "tear-your-heart-out" performances from Lemmon and Remick as "desperate" young marrieds "lost in the bottom of the bottle"; "Henry Mancini's haunting title song" won the Oscar and "says it all."

### Day the Earth Stood Still, The ◑    25 | 20 | 26 | 21

*1951. Directed by Robert Wise. With Michael Rennie, Patricia Neal, Sam Jaffe. 92 minutes. Rated G.*
"Fifties-era real-life fears about the fate of humanity" are the backbone of this "Cold War sci-fi" flick about a "benevolent alien" invasion of Washington DC; sure, the "less-is-more special effects" seem "dated" and "primitive by today's standards", but the "underlying message" – "world peace or else!" – makes this one "very enlightened for its time."

### Dead Again    22 | 24 | 24 | 22

*1991. Directed by Kenneth Branagh. With Kenneth Branagh, Andy Garcia, Emma Thompson. 107 minutes. Rated R.*
There are "good twists and mind tricks" aplenty in this "stylish, pseudo-noir thriller" about a detective drawn into a decades-old murder mystery; deadheads dig its "riveting performances", "Dali-esque imagery" and that "wonderful twist at the end", swearing you'll never look at a "pair of scissors" the same way after seeing this "over-the-top" "nail-biter."

### Dead Man Walking ✉    23 | 26 | 23 | 21

*1995. Directed by Tim Robbins. With Susan Sarandon, Sean Penn, Robert Prosky. 122 minutes. Rated R.*
"Based on a true story", this "enlightening" study of capital punishment is also a "profound lesson in human compassion"

thanks to "poignant" turns from a "riveting" Penn as a "condemned killer" and the Oscar-winning Sarandon as a nun bent on leading him to "redemption"; although "unsettling and disturbing" overall, the picture "provides both sides of the death-penalty argument" in an "objective", "unflinching" manner.

### Dead Poets Society ✉ | 24 | 25 | 24 | 23 |
*1989. Directed by Peter Weir. With Robin Williams, Robert Sean Leonard, Ethan Hawke. 128 minutes. Rated PG.*
"Living with rules" vs. "living with passion" gets the big-screen treatment in this "uplifting" drama about an "inspirational teacher" who admonishes his students with a ringing "'carpe diem!'"; thanks to the Oscar-winning screenplay and Williams' ultra-"convincing" turn as the "influential mentor", many say this "wake-up call" of a movie should be "mandatory classroom viewing."

### Dead Ringers | 18 | 23 | 19 | 19 |
*1988. Directed by David Cronenberg. With Jeremy Irons, Geneviève Bujold. 115 minutes. Rated R.*
Ok, it's "beyond weird", but this "cold, clinical" tale of "twin gynecologists" "descending into madness" strikes followers of things "depraved" as a "deliciously creepy" picture, given its fascination with "prescription drugs", "kinky sex" and some mighty "bizarre" surgical instruments; despite Irons' "astounding dual performance", very vocal opponents call it "really offensive" with "no redeeming value", maybe the "ickiest movie ever"; proceed at your own risk.

### Death on the Nile | 19 | 20 | 23 | 21 |
*1978. Directed by John Guillermin. With Peter Ustinov, Bette Davis, Angela Lansbury. 140 minutes. Rated PG.*
"Everyone looks properly shifty-eyed and guilty" in this "decent" enough adaptation of the Agatha Christie whodunit that takes place on a cruise down the River Nile; though foes grouse it's a "lightweight" "follow-up to *Murder on the Orient Express*", cast with "out-of-work actors", fans find it "suspenseful" enough and single out the "outrageous" Lansbury and Oscar-winning costumes for praise.

### Death Wish ⓾ | 16 | 14 | 17 | 15 |
*1974. Directed by Michael Winner. With Charles Bronson, Hope Lange, Vincent Gardenia. 93 minutes. Rated R.*
"Brash, politically incorrect and extremely macho", this '70s "revenge fantasy" was quite "scary" (and controversial) in its time, given its story of a "do-gooder" architect turned vicious "vigilante" after the murder of his wife; in the role that made him a star, Bronson is "more bad-ass than Clint Eastwood ever was", although four sequels later some say "he should have stopped after the first one."

### Deconstructing Harry | 16 | 19 | 17 | 17 |
*1997. Directed by Woody Allen. With Woody Allen, Richard Benjamin, Kirstie Alley, Judy Davis. 96 minutes. Rated R.*
"Uncompromising self-examination" is the heart of this "dark" Woody Allen film about a "neurotic" novelist who uses his life as fodder for his writing; though the finicky fuss about his "treatment of women" and "abundance of dirty-mouthed" talk, fans call it his "strongest work in the last decade"; favorite character: Robin Williams' (literally) "unfocused" actor.

## Deep, The
17 | 16 | 17 | 19

*1977. Directed by Peter Yates. With Robert Shaw, Jacqueline Bisset, Nick Nolte. 123 minutes. Rated PG.*
From the "same era" that gave us *Jaws* comes this "underwater" adventure about "dangerous sunken treasure", a damp "guilty pleasure" best remembered for that "infamous" image of "Jackie Bisset in a sopping-wet T-shirt"; though "not a match" for Peter Benchley's best-selling novel, it's still "solid", "cheesy fun."

## Deep Impact
15 | 14 | 15 | 19

*1998. Directed by Mimi Leder. With Robert Duvall, Téa Leoni, Elijah Wood, Vanessa Redgrave. 120 minutes. Rated PG-13.*
Impending "mass destruction" (via a comet plummeting toward the earth) is the subject of this "world-coming-to-an-end" "disaster flick", a "strangely moving" endeavor portraying "people preparing for a known death"; though there are comparisons to *Armageddon*'s "similar storyline", "this one has heart, a brain and a bonus – no bad Bruce Willis performance."

## Deer Hunter, The
26 | 28 | 24 | 24

*1978. Directed by Michael Cimino. With Robert De Niro, Christopher Walken, Meryl Streep, John Cazale, John Savage. 183 minutes. Rated R.*
"Ordinary guys from an ordinary American town" undergo the "ravages" of Vietnam in this "unforgettable war film", a "deeply moving", "epic-in-every-way" work that netted five Oscars (including Best Picture); brace yourself for "tough-as-nails" performances from De Niro and Walken, some "profound" if "heavy-handed symbolism" plotwise and a wrenching "Russian roulette scene" that will "leave you drained"; P.S. it also features "someone new named Streep."

## Deliverance
25 | 26 | 25 | 23

*1972. Directed by John Boorman. With Jon Voight, Burt Reynolds, Ned Beatty, Ronny Cox. 109 minutes. Rated R.*
This "allegorical nightmare" about four "city slickers" on a "weekend canoe trip" "did for camping in the woods what *Jaws* did for swimming in the ocean", mainly because of that infamous "squeal-like-a-pig" "rape scene" (to the tune of "those damn 'Dueling Banjos'"); more important, it also "proves that thought and testosterone can coexist" and "debunks the long-held myth that Reynolds can't act."

## Desperately Seeking Susan
15 | 13 | 14 | 13

*1985. Directed by Susan Seidelman. With Rosanna Arquette, Madonna, Aidan Quinn. 104 minutes. Rated PG-13.*
This "quintessential '80s" flick set in NYC's SoHo has to do with a case of mistaken identity but is best known as Madonna's "breakout vehicle" (despite Arquette's "underappreciated" starring role); though the verdict on the Material Girl's thespian abilities is lukewarm – she "basically plays herself" – the picture's still "fun."

## Diabolique
26 | 25 | 28 | 23

*1955. Directed by Henri-Georges Clouzot. With Simone Signoret, Véra Clouzot. 116 minutes. Not Rated.*
"Leave it to the French" to serve up this "nasty little thriller" about a murderous love triangle set in a boarding school that "scares the

socks" off surveyors; granted, it "looks pretty primitive today", but ultimately "Signoret still smolders", the "clever plot twists" keep coming and "whoa, what an ending!"

### Dial M for Murder
25 | 24 | 27 | 24

*1954. Directed by Alfred Hitchcock. With Ray Milland, Grace Kelly, Robert Cummings. 105 minutes. Rated PG.*
A "jilted husband seeks revenge on his philandering wife" in this "taut" Hitchcock thriller, a "stagey story" transformed into a "suspenseful" movie (fun fact: it was "originally shot in 3-D"); actingwise, "Kelly shines", Milland is "subtly sinister" and Cummings "drags down every scene he appears in."

### Diamonds Are Forever
20 | 18 | 18 | 21

*1971. Directed by Guy Hamilton. With Sean Connery, Jill St. John, Charles Gray. 125 minutes. Rated PG.*
"007 goes Vegas, baby" in this sixth installment of the series, chock-full of the usual "gadgets" and gals, including the "hot", high-"cheekboned" St. John; in his next-to-last appearance as the stirred-but-never-shaken spy, Connery's at his "dashing, womanizing best" while Gray, as a "hilarious Howard Hughes type", makes a "great villain"; still, Fleming fanatics fret it's "one of the sillier" in the canon.

### Diary of Anne Frank, The ◑
23 | 23 | 26 | 21

*1959. Directed by George Stevens. With Millie Perkins, Shelley Winters, Richard Beymer. 180 minutes. Not Rated.*
"Every young person should see" this true story of a Jewish family hiding from the Nazis in an Amsterdam attic that "brings to life a dark time in history"; "man's inhumanity to man" is depicted "from a child's point of view" and "though we know the outcome", the "suspense" is truly "heartbreaking."

### Die Another Day ⑪
19 | 17 | 16 | 23

*2002. Directed by Lee Tamahori. With Pierce Brosnan, Halle Berry, Toby Stephens. 133 minutes. Rated PG-13.*
Equipped with "everything you expect from a James Bond film", this 20th installment sports "cool gadgets", "fast cars", "easy-on-the-eyes" stars and "Schwarzenegger-like one-liners" in a story that has something to do with the "current political crisis with North Korea"; despite quibbles about an "absurd plot" and "too many CGI effects", diehards declare there's nothing wrong with the "yummy" Halle and her "homage-to-Ursula-Andress" bikini.

### Die Hard ⑪
23 | 19 | 22 | 24

*1988. Directed by John McTiernan. With Bruce Willis, Bonnie Bedelia, Alan Rickman. 131 minutes. Rated R.*
This "flawless" "granddaddy of the '80s action" flick spawned "countless imitations but no equals" thanks to its "thrill-a-minute" mix of suspense, explosions and "comic one-liners"; die-hard diehards tout Willis' "ass-kicking" turn as a "loser whom fate requires to be a hero" as well as "chic bad guy" Rickman, who supplies the "cool quips and fashion tips."

### Diner
25 | 25 | 23 | 22

*1982. Directed by Barry Levinson. With Steve Guttenberg, Mickey Rourke, Kevin Bacon, Ellen Barkin. 110 minutes. Rated R.*
Levinson's first Baltimore drama "centers on the lives of a group of '50s high school grads" "who spent their youth in diners"; a

"finely observed" "guy flick" that's both "smart and funny", it features a "wonderful ensemble cast" that delivers the snappy patter so "brilliantly" it served as a "springboard" for the careers of "many future stars."

### Dinner at Eight ◑                                    ▽ 27 | 27 | 26 | 25

*1933. Directed by George Cukor. With Marie Dressler, John Barrymore, Jean Harlow. 113 minutes. Not Rated.*
It seems as if "every star at MGM appears" in this frothy dramedy about a social-climbing hostess' "high society" dinner party where nothing goes as planned; look for plenty of "art deco sparkle" productionwise, a "joy" of a script and "suave, understated" performances from Dressler and John Barrymore; biggest surprise: Harlow's "snappy" turn as a gum-popping, gold-digging hussy.

### Dinosaur                                            19 | – | 17 | 24

*2000. Directed by Eric Leighton, Ralph Zondag. Animated. 82 minutes. Rated PG.*
"Kids interested in dinosaurs" dig this Disney flick for its "extraordinary animation", "wonderful music" and "fabulous" meteor shower scene; but despite some "exciting moments", soreheads lament that it's "lacking in the plot department" and not much more than a "dull remake of *The Land Before Time*."

### Dirty Dancing                                       21 | 17 | 20 | 20

*1987. Directed by Emile Ardolino. With Patrick Swayze, Jennifer Grey, Jerry Orbach. 96 minutes. Rated PG-13.*
Whether it's a "girls'-night-in" "entertainment" or a "Sunday afternoon vacation", this "cult classic" is the cinematic equivalent of "comfort food" and even works as an "excellent date movie" after all these years; its "heart-melting story" centers on the romance between "hot, sexy teen dream" Swayze and "cute gamine" Grey, who "shake their booties" just "like the Solid Gold dancers" used to do to pop hits in a "'60s Catskills resort."

### Dirty Dozen, The                                    21 | 19 | 22 | 20

*1967. Directed by Robert Aldrich. With Lee Marvin, Ernest Borgnine, Charles Bronson. 145 minutes. Not Rated.*
This "delightful" war adventure exudes a "healthy dose of cynicism" in telling the tale of a "merry band of cutthroats" "brought together to do good in WWII"; the "early-in-their-careers" actors are "awesome", "super-macho" types (particularly "ultimate tough guy" Marvin playing as their leader), while the "rough-and-tumble", action-packed plot still seems "fun after all these years."

### Dirty Harry ⑪                                       21 | 18 | 20 | 19

*1971. Directed by Don Siegel. With Clint Eastwood, Harry Guardino, Reni Santoni. 102 minutes. Rated R.*
Clint's at his "steely-eyed, gravelly voiced best" in this "modern cop" flick that "struck a chord in the '70s" and "created a fast-and-furious" subgenre "solid" enough to "spawn a host of imitators"; throw in some "great views of San Francisco" and a moodily "muted jazz score" and you just might "feel lucky, punk."

### Dirty Pretty Things                                 23 | 24 | 24 | 21

*2003. Directed by Stephen Frears. With Chiwetel Ejiofor, Audrey Tautou, Sergi López. 97 minutes. Rated R.*
London's illegal "immigrant underworld" goes under the microscope in this "atmospheric", "suspenseful" crime thriller

detailing "shady goings-on" (think prostitution, drug dealing and "macabre" trafficking in human organs) at a "swanky UK hotel"; the "low-budget look" works well with the "gritty performances", "thought-provoking" scenario and "unexpected ending."

### Discreet Charm of the Bourgeoisie, The ✉ 🅵
24 | 23 | 23 | 22

*1972. Directed by Luis Buñuel. With Fernando Rey, Delphine Seyrig, Stéphane Audran. 102 minutes. Rated PG.*
"Controversial" in its day, this Oscar-winning "satirical portrait of the French bourgeoisie" tells the "elliptical" tale of "six people in search of a hot meal" who are "confounded at every turn" by bizarre goings-on; Buñuel serves up enough "dream-within-a-dream sequences" to turn this dark comedy into a "thoughtful, surreal delight" that further enhances his reputation as the "Dali of cinema."

### Diva 🅵
24 | 20 | 24 | 24

*1982. Directed by Jean-Jacques Beineix. With Wilhelmenia Fernandez, Frederic Andrei. 123 minutes. Rated R.*
Perhaps the "greatest opera/action flick ever", this "oh-so-stylish" French thriller creates a "complicated world" about a "scooter-riding kid" obsessed by a "reclusive soprano"; "glorious to look at", with "wonderful images of Paris", it's most memorable for that "fast-paced motorcycle chase" in the Métro.

### D.O.A. ◑
22 | 22 | 26 | 21

*1950. Directed by Rudolph Maté. With Edmond O'Brien, Pamela Britton, Luther Adler. 83 minutes. Not Rated.*
"One of the best opening lines" – "I want to report a murder . . . mine" – sets in motion the "intriguing plot" of this "elaborate time-runs-backward" drama in which an "innocent man must find his own killer before he dies"; set against a backdrop of "great location shots of LA and San Francisco", it's "gritty, bleak" noir that's "compelling as hell", even if a few deadbeats declare it "promises more than it delivers."

### Doctor Zhivago ✉
27 | 26 | 26 | 28

*1965. Directed by David Lean. With Omar Sharif, Julie Christie, Geraldine Chaplin, Rod Steiger. 197 minutes. Rated PG-13.*
Lean's "timeless" – others say "long" – Oscar-winning evocation of Boris Pasternak's "sweeping" novel of "love and war" is the "epic to end all epics", merging "brilliant historical storytelling" with "romantic extravaganza"; set during the Russian Revolution, it "humanized the USSR during the Cold War" due to the "tear-jerking" relationship between Christie and Sharif – though its "balalaika"-heavy theme song and the scenes in that "winter wonderland" of an "ice palace" resonate most.

### Dog Day Afternoon ✉
24 | 27 | 22 | 20

*1975. Directed by Sidney Lumet. With Al Pacino, John Cazale, Chris Sarandon, Charles Durning. 124 minutes. Rated R.*
This "funny/sad" true tale of a botched "bank heist" committed by "hapless" amateurs is transformed into a "deep, character-driven" example of director Lumet "at his best"; expect "great performances from the entire cast" (from the nervous bank tellers "right down to the pizza delivery guy"), with particular kudos to an "ass-kicking" Pacino and a "brilliant" Sarandon as his gay lover.

**Donnie Brasco**  20 | 24 | 22 | 20
*1997. Directed by Mike Newell. With Al Pacino, Johnny Depp, Anne Heche. 127 minutes. Rated R.*
In this true story, an undercover FBI agent "befriends the man he's supposed to entrap" and takes you "inside the inner workings of the mob" to reveal a "more realistic side to the underworld"; a "sympathetic", "nuanced" Pacino does the "gangster-as-loser" thing right, while Depp's titular turn is similarly "excellent"; like the 'family' it portrays, this one "never lets go of you."

**Don't Look Back ◑**  ▽ 25 | – | 20 | 23
*1967. Directed by D.A. Pennebaker. Documentary. With Bob Dylan, Joan Baez, Donovan. 96 minutes. Not Rated.*
This "revealing" "slice of musical history" "captures the young Bob Dylan in all his contradictory charm and churlishness" as an "artist in transition" and is an "indelible" "reminder of what all the fuss was about"; perhaps the "most referenced" rockumentary ever, "it's improved with time" and includes one of the "first music videos" ever: the famed cue-cards clip for 'Subterranean Homesick Blues.'

**Do the Right Thing**  23 | 23 | 22 | 21
*1989. Directed by Spike Lee. With Spike Lee, Danny Aiello, Ossie Davis, Ruby Dee. 120 minutes. Rated R.*
"Italian-American pizza parlor owners in Brooklyn" and the "African-American community who patronize the shop" clash "on the hottest day of the year" in this "anatomy of a race riot" from Spike Lee, who "deftly balances tragedy with comedy" to telegraph a "message as clear as black and white" that still "resonates years later."

**DOUBLE INDEMNITY ◑**  28 | 27 | 28 | 25
*1944. Directed by Billy Wilder. With Fred MacMurray, Barbara Stanwyck, Edward G. Robinson. 107 minutes. Not Rated.*
"From the chiaroscuro settings to the world-weary voiceover", Wilder's "refreshingly sour" slice of "hard-boiled" noir "sets the standard for the genre"; the story of "another dumb cluck done in by a woman", it features a "fast-talking" MacMurray, a "knockout" Stanwyck ("love the anklet") and a "fantastic" Robinson, with enough plot "twists" and sly "killer banter" to make it the cinematic equivalent of "bonded bourbon"; best scene: shopping at the "supermarket."

**Double Jeopardy**  16 | 18 | 19 | 18
*1999. Directed by Bruce Beresford. With Tommy Lee Jones, Ashley Judd, Annabeth Gish. 105 minutes. Rated R.*
"Diverting" enough, this "clever" thriller finds Judd playing a "kick-ass bitch" wrongfully imprisoned for murder and hell-bent on "revenge"; legal eagles rule it's "completely implausible" (even its title "premise is false") and add that "Jones' cop thing is getting old", but it's "enjoyable nonetheless" if you like "a lot of twists."

**Down and Out in Beverly Hills**  17 | 19 | 17 | 17
*1986. Directed by Paul Mazursky. With Nick Nolte, Richard Dreyfuss, Bette Midler. 103 minutes. Rated R.*
The "Jean Renoir classic" *Bondu Saved from Drowning* is "given an American spin" in this "spoof of the upper class", Beverly Hills–style, wherein a "bum interacts in the lives of a wealthy family"

with "hilarious" results; Bette's "divine" as a "neurotic wife who undergoes an amazing transformation", and even if the humor verges on the "crude", it's still "winning" enough.

### Dracula ◐ �m�
24 | 21 | 23 | 20

*1931. Directed by Tod Browning. With Bela Lugosi, Helen Chandler, Dwight Frye. 75 minutes. Not Rated.*
Granted, the "special effects are nonexistent", but this "definitive Dracula" is still "scarier than anything made today", leaving "plenty of room for imagination" thanks to Lugosi's "riveting" take on the "immortal vampire"; though it uses music sparingly to evoke an "eerie atmosphere", a new, souped-up DVD with a "Philip Glass score" is highly touted; best line: "I never drink . . . wine."

### Dracula
20 | 19 | 22 | 25

*1992. Directed by Francis Ford Coppola. With Gary Oldman, Winona Ryder, Anthony Hopkins, Keanu Reeves. 130 minutes. Rated R.*
"You can sink your teeth" into Coppola's "highly underrated" "retelling of Bram Stoker's tale" of a "lovelorn", bloodthirsty Romanian count; "stylish" costumes, Oscar-winning sets, a "stunning" Oldman and the spectacle of "Tom Waits eating bugs" make for "visionary" moviemaking, even if some nix the "laughable miscasting" of Reeves.

### Dr. Dolittle ⑪
16 | 17 | 17 | 18

*1998. Directed by Betty Thomas. With Eddie Murphy, Ossie Davis, Peter Boyle. 85 minutes. Rated PG-13.*
Both "kids and kids at heart" "crack up" over this "priceless" Murphy vehicle in which he "shines" playing a doc who can "talk to animals"; based vaguely on Hugh Lofting's "perennially popular" children's stories, this update employs state-of-the-art animatronics and computer graphics to make the animalspeak both realistic and "entertaining."

### Dressed to Kill
20 | 22 | 19 | 20

*1980. Directed by Brian De Palma. With Michael Caine, Angie Dickinson, Nancy Allen. 105 minutes. Rated R.*
"Swirling camerawork, split screens, tracking shots that go on for miles" – yup, it's another "stylishly bloody" De Palma thriller, replete with "violent slashings, sensuous showers and sexual confusion" as it tells the adventures of a "happy hooker, an unhappy housewife and a shrink"; though an "inspiring" Angie provides the "sexy" "goose bumps", foes say it's "too derivative of Hitchcock."

### Driving Miss Daisy ✉
24 | 27 | 23 | 22

*1989. Directed by Bruce Beresford. With Morgan Freeman, Jessica Tandy, Dan Aykroyd. 99 minutes. Rated PG.*
"Race relations" in the South and the "loss of dignity" that can come with aging are "wonderfully depicted" in this "heartwarming" story of an "unconventional friendship" between a matriarch and her chauffeur; the "sterling" Tandy and Freeman exhibit "incredible onscreen chemistry" (she drove home with an Oscar) in this "uplifting yet down-to-earth" drama.

### Dr. No
23 | 20 | 22 | 23

*1963. Directed by Terence Young. With Sean Connery, Ursula Andress, Jack Lord. 110 minutes. Rated PG.*
The "first Bond outing" is a "lean and mean" thriller "unhindere by political correctness", with "fewer gadgets" and gals tha

**vote at zagat.com**

usual (though the image of Andress in that "white bikini" is "seared forever onto many a man's brain"); while the "dashing" Connery "makes it all look effortless", "purists" note this "unadulterated" "template" is the "closest they ever came to Ian Fleming's vision."

## DR. STRANGELOVE ◑     28 | 28 | 27 | 26
*1964. Directed by Stanley Kubrick. With Peter Sellers, George C. Scott, Sterling Hayden. 93 minutes. Rated PG.*
"Nuclear annihilation was never funnier" than in Kubrick's "stinging Cold War satire", a "chillingly comic" examination of "distressingly familiar government officials" and their "precious bodily fluids"; as members of "our military at work", Scott is "magnificent" and Sellers "phenomenal" (in "three, count 'em, roles"), while "Slim Pickens riding the bomb" remains one of the cinema's most indelible images; doomsday devotees dub it "apocalypse now and forever."

## Drugstore Cowboy     19 | 21 | 19 | 18
*1989. Directed by Gus Van Sant. With Matt Dillon, Kelly Lynch, James Le Gros. 100 minutes. Rated R.*
Van Sant's grittily "accurate depiction" of narcotics addicts robbing drugstores for drugs is loaded with "precise, unexpected performances" and a surprise bonus: William Burroughs as a junkie ex-priest; though habit-ues hail it as a "highly original dark comedy", nonsupporters say it "doesn't hold up well."

## DUCK SOUP ◑     27 | 25 | 23 | 22
*1933. Directed by Leo McCarey. With the Marx Brothers, Margaret Dumont. 70 minutes. Not Rated.*
"Hail, hail Freedonia" cry fans of the "anarchic" Marx foursome, whose trademark "lunacy" is at its "peak" in this "political satire" about a "mythical dictatorship"; "absurdly funny" – it includes the "legendary mirror scene with Groucho and Harpo" – it's the brothers' "finest hour" and voted top of the Marxes in this *Survey*.

## Dumb and Dumber ⊕     15 | 16 | 12 | 14
*1994. Directed by Peter Farrelly, Bobby Farrelly. With Jim Carrey, Jeff Daniels, Lauren Holly. 106 minutes. Rated PG-13.*
No duh, the "title says it all" in this maiden effort from the Farrelly brothers, a "gross-out" "guilty pleasure" about a "moronic duo" "traveling cross country" with a briefcase stuffed with cash; fans say the "vulgar" antics (think "potty jokes", "disgusting noises") "grow on you", though foes sneer the "puerile", "not-for-adults" storyline makes for the "ultimate" in "lowbrow humor."

## Dumbo     24 | – | 23 | 24
*1941. Directed by Ben Sharpsteen. Animated. 64 minutes. Rated G.*
"Elephants fly" in this "short but sweet" animated Disney classic message movie "about the importance of being yourself"; though the politically correct disparage its "racist undertones" and find it "too sad" for smaller fry, fans laud its "fabulous", Oscar-winning score and "unforgettable sequences" – particularly the "tripped-out" "hallucination" of those pink pachyderms on parade.

## Easter Parade     22 | 21 | 17 | 24
*1948. Directed by Charles Walters. With Judy Garland, Fred Astaire, Ann Miller. 107 minutes. Not Rated.*
"It isn't really Easter" till you've watched this "grand Irving Berlin musical" boasting 17 songs and "lots of frills upon it" – including

Fred and Judy at their "singing and dancing best" in their "only screen appearance together"; the slender story has Astaire trying to make a star out of chorus girl Garland, but this "wonderful" MGM "showcase" transcends its plot with sheer star power.

### East of Eden
24 | 27 | 24 | 23

*1955. Directed by Elia Kazan. With James Dean, Julie Harris, Raymond Massey, Jo Van Fleet. 115 minutes. Not Rated.*
An "unforgettable" Dean eats "every actor on the set for breakfast" in his "searing" big-screen debut as the "proverbial bad seed" in this adaptation of John Steinbeck's tale of "sibling rivalry"; sure, there are also "beautiful" CinemaScope panoramas and an Oscar-winning turn from Van Fleet, but Jimmy makes it "memorable" – "to think he only made three films is amazing."

### Easy Rider
23 | 23 | 20 | 20

*1969. Directed by Dennis Hopper. With Peter Fonda, Dennis Hopper, Jack Nicholson. 94 minutes. Rated R.*
"Sex, drugs and rock 'n' roll" explode on the silver screen in this "seminal" "road movie" that "defined a generation" by capturing the essence of the "tumultuous" '60s; famed for "Nicholson's starmaking performance" and Hopper's "manic", "revolutionary" direction, this "trippy" "time capsule" might have also "invented the music video" thanks to that "amazing soundtrack"; still, Gen-Y types protest it "doesn't hold up" today, unless you "get high" first.

### Eat Drink Man Woman 🇫
25 | 24 | 24 | 24

*1994. Directed by Ang Lee. With Sihung Lung, Wu Chien-Lien, Yang Kuei-Mei, Wang Yu-Wen. 123 minutes. Not Rated.*
Gourmands eat up this "tasty" Taiwanese look at a "different culture" that tells the story of a traditional "Asian father who shows his love by cooking for his daughters"; director Lee's "visual feast" contrasts "ticklish relationships" with "stupendous food scenes" so adroitly that many "get hungry just thinking about it."

### Eating Raoul
18 | 18 | 21 | 15

*1982. Directed by Paul Bartel. With Paul Bartel, Mary Woronov, Robert Beltran. 90 minutes. Rated R.*
"Not everyone can stomach" this "blacker-than-black" "bizarro" "cult" comedy, but there's agreement that its "absurd" plot (about a Moral Majority–esque couple luring swingers to their deaths) is the "trailer-park" version of "*Sweeney Todd*"; "kind of sick", this "deadpan" "low-budget" "B movie" is also kind of "fun" – and "probably for grown-ups only."

### Educating Rita
18 | 21 | 19 | 18

*1983. Directed by Lewis Gilbert. With Michael Caine, Julie Walters. 110 minutes. Rated PG-13.*
Caine and Walters exhibit "great chemistry" in this "interesting" tale of an "alcoholic professor" who tutors a "working-class" gal; though the "pseudo-*Pygmalion*" plot "isn't quite convincing" for some, others relate perfectly to the "believable" title character, a "woman who won't allow herself to be held back by social class."

### Edward Scissorhands
21 | 22 | 22 | 24

*1990. Directed by Tim Burton. With Johnny Depp, Winona Ryder, Dianne Wiest. 100 minutes. Rated PG-13.*
Burton's "oddball" opus spins a "delightfully bent" "love story" around an ultimate "outsider" – a "misfit boy with garden tools

for hands" – living in "conformist suburbia"; "Depp shows he has the big-screen stuff" (and "makes a hell of a topiary"), while the "primary-colored" art direction creates an "alternative universe disturbingly close to home"; best line: Wiest's perky "Avon calling!"

### Ed Wood ◑    20 | 23 | 19 | 21
*1994. Directed by Tim Burton. With Johnny Depp, Martin Landau, Sarah Jessica Parker. 127 minutes. Rated R.*
"Schlockmeister" director Ed Wood gets the full Tim Burton treatment in this "loving tribute" that's also an "entertaining glimpse into grade Z filmmaking"; look for an "enthusiastic", "totally sympathetic" Depp in the title role opposite an Oscar-winning Landau as a "drugged-out" Bela Lugosi – "never before have the talentless been so brilliantly rendered by the talented."

### 8½ ✉◑🇫    26 | 26 | 24 | 26
*1963. Directed by Federico Fellini. With Marcello Mastroianni, Claudia Cardinale, Anouk Aimée. 145 minutes. Not Rated.*
"Navel-gazing has never been more profound" than in this "semi-autobiographical" "Italian masterpiece" from the "extraordinary" Fellini about a blocked "director trying to make a film" by using his "life as material for his work"; told in "stream of consciousness", it also features "luscious" art direction and a "career-defining turn by Mastroianni" – no wonder many call this "heartfelt" flick the "definitive movie about movies."

### 8 Mile    19 | 18 | 17 | 19
*2002. Directed by Curtis Hanson. With Eminem, Kim Basinger, Brittany Murphy, Mekhi Phifer. 110 minutes. Rated R.*
Take "*Rocky*", add "*Purple Rain*", "go to Detroit" and top it off with "sweet freestyle scenes", and you've got this "quality" "retread" of the "poor-boy-claws-his-way-out-of-the-hood" story; while Eminem's "semi-autobiographical" performance is ("surprise!") "raw and touching", this "gritty flick" (and its "7 mile"–long string of "F-words") gets truly "compelling" in the last "rap-off."

### El Cid ∅    19 | 16 | 20 | 23
*1961. Directed by Anthony Mann. With Charlton Heston, Sophia Loren, Raf Vallone. 182 minutes. Not Rated.*
This early '60s epic is a "guy's delight" that finds Heston once again inhabiting the skin of a "larger-than-life" figure, this time the legendary 11th-century Spaniard who defended his country against the Moors; "lots of action" elates thrill-seekers, though foes lambaste it as "bombastic and overblown."

### Election    22 | 24 | 22 | 20
*1999. Directed by Alexander Payne. With Reese Witherspoon, Matthew Broderick. 103 minutes. Rated R.*
"Student council elections" as an "allegory for real political life" underscore this "whip-smart" "black comedy" about a "goody two-shoes" "high-school overachiever" and a teacher bent on putting a stop to her rise; voters find "no fraud" in this "spot-on" "social satire", adding that "unless you were home-schooled, you'll relate."

### Elephant Man, The ◑    24 | 27 | 25 | 23
*1980. Directed by David Lynch. With Anthony Hopkins, John Hurt, Anne Bancroft. 125 minutes. Rated PG.*
The "dignity in deformity" is defined in this "unflinching" true story about a "Victorian-era" freak who "tests the compassion of

a horrified society"; "brilliant acting and makeup" make it a "gloriously Gothic" "voyage into the human heart" – a "perfect match of director and material", it will "touch you deep inside."

### Elf
21 | 21 | 20 | 20

*2003. Directed by Jon Favreau. With Will Ferrell, James Caan, Bob Newhart, Zooey Deschanel. 95 minutes. Rated PG.*
Imbued with the "real spirit of Christmas", this "surprisingly sweet-natured" holiday comedy stars "funny man Ferrell" as a "human being raised by elves" at the North Pole who travels to NYC to find his birth parents; granted, there's "nothing to tax your mind" in this "old-fashioned romp", but Will's a "hoot", "Deschanel looks gorgeous" and the "deadpan" Newhart is "consistently hilarious."

### Elizabeth
24 | 27 | 23 | 26

*1998. Directed by Shekhar Kapur. With Cate Blanchett, Geoffrey Rush, Joseph Fiennes. 124 minutes. Rated R.*
"Captivating" Cate displays "unbelievable range" in this bio of England's "Virgin Queen" that follows her progress from "lusty young woman" to "ice-cold, calculating icon"; though it "feels like a fantasy version of Elizabeth I's life" to skeptics, scholars swear it's "historically on the mark", with "beautiful sets", "excellent costume design" and a "gripping" storyline.

### Elmer Gantry ✉
25 | 27 | 24 | 23

*1960. Directed by Richard Brooks. With Burt Lancaster, Jean Simmons, Shirley Jones. 146 minutes. Not Rated.*
Disciples of this "rip-roaring" adaptation of the Sinclair Lewis novel testify that Lancaster's Oscar-winning, "fire-and-brimstone" performance as a "street preacher"–cum–"con man" in a "hypocritical" traveling ministry is the "best of his career" (while some "get religion" watching Jones' take on a jilted prostitute); its "excellent script" detailing a "flesh vs. the spirit" conflict also took home a statuette.

### Elvira Madigan 🄵
20 | 19 | 20 | 24

*1967. Directed by Bo Widerberg. With Pia Degermark, Thommy Berggren. 91 minutes. Rated PG.*
Both "visually stunning" and "wonderfully dated", this Swedish sobfest recounts the "heartbreaking" affair between "two AWOL lovers" – a tightrope walker and a married army officer – who are "beautiful" and, of course, "doomed"; although memorable for its "lovely scenery" and the Mozart piano concerto it popularized, it's forgettable to those who see it as "tiresome" "romantic fluff."

### Emma
22 | 23 | 23 | 24

*1996. Directed by Douglas McGrath. With Gwyneth Paltrow, Jeremy Northam, Greta Scacchi. 121 minutes. Rated PG.*
Jane Austen's "charming" story of "matchmaking at its best and worst" gets an "engaging" spin in this "delightful period piece" starring a "perfect" Paltrow opposite a "laconically charming" Northam; its "cheery" tone and dryly "humorous approach" make it a natural to "watch back-to-back with *Clueless*, since they're both based on the same novel."

### Emperor's New Groove, The
20 | – | 18 | 20

*2000. Directed by Mark Dindal. Animated. 78 minutes. Rated G.*
A "selfish, smart-mouthed emperor becomes a llama" with extremely humbling results in this "quirky", "overlooked cartoon"

that effortlessly merges both "standard and CGI animation" with "superb voice acting"; sure, aesthetes complain of a "low-budget", "slapped-together" look, but most find it "highly entertaining" with "lots of great gags" and a script that's "actually funny."

### Empire of the Sun

| | | | |
|---|---|---|---|
| 25 | 23 | 24 | 26 |

*1987. Directed by Steven Spielberg. With Christian Bale, John Malkovich. 154 minutes. Rated PG.*
Perhaps Spielberg's most "underappreciated" picture, this "touching story of a British child's internment in a World War II Japanese prison camp" is an "ambitious" epic replete with "dazzling" acting, "David Lean–worthy" imagery and an "especially moving John Williams score"; maybe the "storyline drags" a bit midway, but overall its "sheer power" supplies the "magic moments."

### Enchanted April ∅

| | | | |
|---|---|---|---|
| 24 | 26 | 22 | 25 |

*1992. Directed by Mike Newell. With Joan Plowright, Miranda Richardson, Josie Lawrence. 95 minutes. Rated PG.*
For a "wonderfully rich pick-me-up", take a look at this "genteel" "getaway" of a movie about four "risk-taking" women who decide to "leave their dreary English lives behind" and are "transformed" during an April vacation in "lush, sunny" Tuscany; the perfect "antidote to winter", it's "more complex than it first appears", and Plowright's "terrific performance" will brighten any "rainy day."

### End of the Affair, The

| | | | |
|---|---|---|---|
| 20 | 24 | 20 | 22 |

*1999. Directed by Neil Jordan. With Ralph Fiennes, Julianne Moore, Stephen Rea. 102 minutes. Rated R.*
"Faith, love and loss" underlie this "terrific" adaptation of Graham Greene's "tragic romance" set in "rainy" WWII London about a "conflicted, adulterous Englishwoman" and her "jealous, angry lover"; this "difficult story" succeeds thanks to a "flashback"-heavy, "multilayered" scenario and "wonderful screen chemistry" between a "powerful" Fiennes and a "smoldering" Moore modeling "glamorous slips and retro suits."

### Enemy of the State

| | | | |
|---|---|---|---|
| 19 | 19 | 20 | 21 |

*1998. Directed by Tony Scott. With Will Smith, Gene Hackman, Jon Voight. 131 minutes. Rated R.*
"Privacy and civil liberties" issues take center stage in this ultra-"engaging", ultra-"paranoid" thriller about "Big Brother"–ish "government agents" pursuing a DC lawyer who's unwittingly holding an incriminating videotape; so "fast moving" that there's barely time to "catch your breath", it mixes "high-tech" effects with a "low-concept" idea to come up with something that's "very exciting" indeed.

### English Patient, The ✉

| | | | |
|---|---|---|---|
| 22 | 24 | 21 | 25 |

*1996. Directed by Anthony Minghella. With Ralph Fiennes, Juliette Binoche, Kristin Scott Thomas. 160 minutes. Rated R.*
"Love it or hate it", there's no question that this "lush" WWII romance (winner of nine Oscars) boasts an "old-Hollywood scope", swoonworthy cinematography, "brilliant writing" and "magnetic" performances from Fiennes and Scott Thomas as star-crossed lovers "in the desert sands of North Africa"; but those who "agree with Elaine on *Seinfeld*" claim this patient

requires "patience", thanks to a pace so "laborious" that it's "recommended for treating insomnia."

### Enron: The Smartest Guys in the Room
`25` `–` `26` `22`

*2005. Directed by Alex Gibney. Documentary. 109 minutes. Not Rated.*
Learn how "arrogant corruption" and "greed run amok" led to the collapse of energy trader Enron's "house of cards" in this "compelling" documentary that "reveals the downside of American corporate culture"; "full of information", it reduces a "complicated", "numbers-centered" scheme into an "easy-to-follow" account that manages to both "disgust and fascinate", without resorting to "Michael Moore hysteria."

### Enter the Dragon
`23` `16` `17` `20`

*1973. Directed by Robert Clouse. With Bruce Lee, John Saxon, Jim Kelly. 98 minutes. Rated R.*
"Martial arts" mavens maintain that this "all-time best kung fu" flicker is "butt-kicker" Lee's "magnum opus", the "standard by which all karate films are judged"; sure, the "production's cheesy" and its "James Bond" "rip-off" plot is "unoriginal", but the "balletic, ballistic" fight scenes are so "spectacular" that this one "spawned many forgettable imitators" – not to mention many "video games."

### Eraserhead ◖
`21` `17` `17` `19`

*1977. Directed by David Lynch. With Jack Nance, Charlotte Stewart. 90 minutes. Not Rated.*
Director Lynch's "trippy", "dread-inducing" debut is an "eerie glimpse of a marriage gone horribly awry" that "replicates the logic of a nightmare" (i.e. "you don't know what's going on half the time"); gird yourself for some "disturbing pictures, disturbing music" and "no discernable plot", but at least this "cult classic" is "willing to take risks."

### Erin Brockovich ✉
`21` `23` `23` `21`

*2000. Directed by Steven Soderbergh. With Julia Roberts, Albert Finney, Aaron Eckhart. 130 minutes. Rated R.*
"Roberts proves her worth" with a "boffo", Oscar-winning turn in this "uplifting", "push-up bra"–laden true story about "standing up to a big corporation and winning"; ok, its "socially conscious", "don't-mess-with-the-little-people" screenplay might owe a lot to "*Norma Rae*", but ultimately this "polished production" works as both a "star vehicle and a compelling story."

### Escape from New York ⑪
`15` `13` `17` `18`

*1981. Directed by John Carpenter. With Kurt Russell, Lee Van Cleef, Ernest Borgnine. 99 minutes. Rated R.*
A "hoot and a half", this "tongue-in-cheek" action-adventurer is set in "post-apocalyptic" Manhattan that has morphed into a maximum security prison where the President is being held hostage; to the rescue comes Russell as Snake Plissken, a "cartoon character" but still a "very appealing hero", who manages to keep the "novel premise amusing" enough to make for some "silly", "cheesy fun."

### Eternal Sunshine of the Spotless Mind
`23` `24` `24` `23`

*2004. Directed by Michel Gondry. With Jim Carrey, Kate Winslet, Tom Wilkinson, Mark Ruffalo, Kirsten Dunst. 108 minutes. Rated R.*
A "one-of-a-kind experience", this "quirky, deeply romantic" fantasy follows a "balanced" Carrey and "winning" Winslet as

broken-up lovers who biologically erase their memories of each other, then struggle to erase the erasure; though "not likely to be everyone's cup of tea", the "zany", "head-trip" script is "cerebral", "comical" and "complex" (given a "juggled time sequence" à la "*Memento*"), yet skillfully steered by director Gondry's "deft hand."

### E.T. THE EXTRA-TERRESTRIAL    26 | 22 | 26 | 27

*1982. Directed by Steven Spielberg. With Dee Wallace, Henry Thomas, Drew Barrymore. 115 minutes. Rated PG.*
Arguably the "*Wizard of Oz* for a brand-new generation", this "irresistible" sci-fi "fairy tale" is the "endearing story of a boy", the "cutest alien of all time" and their attempts to "phone home"; there's agreement that Spielberg's "incredibly imaginative" "genius strikes again", managing to express "every human emotion in less than two hours", so gather the "entire family" along with a "big bowl of Reese's Pieces" and get ready for some "true magic."

### Evil Dead, The ⑪    22 | 14 | 18 | 17

*1982. Directed by Sam Raimi. With Bruce Campbell, Ellen Sandweiss, Betsy Baker. 85 minutes. Rated NC-17.*
"Not for the weak-stomached", this "scary, scary, scary" "gorefest" with "abundant blood" and lots of "energy" is "dumb", "campy horror at its best"; alright, the acting's "questionable", the dialogue "lame", the story "hackneyed" and the effects very "low-budget", but it "blows Hollywood blockbusters away" because it's "so much fun."

### Evita    19 | 17 | 21 | 24

*1996. Directed by Alan Parker. With Madonna, Antonio Banderas, Jonathan Pryce. 134 minutes. Rated PG.*
"Sleazy politics come alive" in this "visually rich" celluloid version of the Andrew Lloyd Webber stage musical based on the life of Argentina's Eva Peron, an all-singing, dialogue-free production that seems to some like an "extended MTV video"; though surveyors split on Madonna's title turn ("surprisingly good" vs. "doesn't have the chops"), the "smoldering", "powerful" Banderas is a hit and overall this "entertaining" epic is at the very least "watchable."

### Exodus    23 | 23 | 26 | 25

*1960. Directed by Otto Preminger. With Paul Newman, Eva Marie Saint, Sal Mineo. 210 minutes. Not Rated.*
An "all-star cast" drives this story of the "founding of modern Israel", a "stunning", "satisfying" Preminger epic "faithfully" adapted from Leon Uris' best-seller; fans single out the star turn from a "too-gorgeous-for-words" Newman "in his prime", and if the plot has some "bathos" mixed into its "high drama", it's ultimately a "moving" moving picture.

### Exorcist, The ✉⑪    25 | 24 | 26 | 25

*1973. Directed by William Friedkin. With Ellen Burstyn, Max von Sydow, Linda Blair. 122 minutes. Rated R.*
"Horror and religion" collide in this "head-spinning", "nightmare-inducing" "shocker" about a child possessed by the devil that "grossed out America" with its "revolting" language and that infamous "pea-soup vomit scene"; though some say it's "slid into camp" over the years, most maintain it's still "one of the scariest

movies ever" – but stick to the "original" cut that's much more "terrifying" than the recent 'restored' reissue.

### Fabulous Baker Boys, The
20 | 22 | 18 | 19

*1989. Directed by Steven Kloves. With Jeff Bridges, Michelle Pfeiffer, Beau Bridges. 114 minutes. Rated R.*

"Sibling rivalry" gets "compelling" treatment in this "great date movie" about two "journeyman musicians" competing for the attentions of their "slinky, sexy" girl singer; the Bridges brothers exude the "art of cool" and Pfeiffer "slithers around so deliciously" that no one minds that this "slice-of-life" story "doesn't go anywhere", given the "enjoyable" ride; most memorable scene, no question: Michelle "draped over a piano" crooning 'Makin' Whoopee' – "who knew she could sing?"

### Face/Off
18 | 19 | 18 | 21

*1997. Directed by John Woo. With John Travolta, Nicolas Cage, Joan Allen, Gina Gershon. 138 minutes. Rated R.*

"Hong Kong auteur" John Woo "goes Hollywood" in this "hyperkinetic" action flick that "fires on all pistons", despite an "unashamedly preposterous scenario" in which "over-the-top" archenemies Travolta and Cage "switch places" (and faces); be prepared for "twists and turns galore", "lots of violence" and enough "mindless fun" to put this one at the very top of your "guilty pleasures list."

### Fahrenheit 451
21 | 19 | 25 | 19

*1966. Directed by François Truffaut. With Oskar Werner, Julie Christie, Cyril Cusack. 110 minutes. Not Rated.*

"Truffaut's first English-language picture" is an "excellent adaptation" of Ray Bradbury's "Big Brother"–ish sci-fi novel, a "social commentary" about "censorship by book burning" in the not-too-distant future (the title is the temperature at which paper ignites); though zealots praise the "thoughtful" presentation of an "important topic", nonbelievers flame it as "plodding" and suggest you "read the book" instead.

### Fahrenheit 9/11
21 | – | 22 | 19

*2004. Directed by Michael Moore. Documentary. 122 minutes. Rated R.*

Conveyed "with all the subtlety of a carpet bombing", Moore's "unapologetically biased" polemic against George W. Bush's "policies and leadership" elicits passionate praise and bitter condemnation alike, with defenders calling it a "daring exposé" of the "real truth" and foes crying it's a "complete fraud on every level"; though unlikely to "change your opinion", it's still a "must-see for anyone remotely interested in what's going on in the Washington world of today."

### Fail-Safe ◐
24 | 25 | 26 | 21

*1964. Directed by Sidney Lumet. With Henry Fonda, Walter Matthau, Larry Hagman. 112 minutes. Not Rated.*

The "Cold War gets hot" in this "chilling", "hypnotic" nuclear-war melodrama about an American President forced to make some "horrifying choices" as an atom bomb hurtles its way toward Moscow; devotees note that the storyline is strikingly similar to that of *Dr. Strangelove* (though decidedly laugh-free) but insist its "what if?" plot is especially "gripping – and hopefully not prophetic."

### Fame
**21 | 18 | 21 | 20**
*1980. Directed by Alan Parker. With Irene Cara, Lee Curreri, Eddie Barth, Laura Dean. 134 minutes. Rated R.*
"Little girls who sing in front of the mirror" relate to this "feel-good" musical set in "NY's High School of Performing Arts", where "talented", "leg warmer–wearing teenagers" spend their days "dancing in the streets" and "struggling for fame"; ok, it's a bit "overdone" and "very dated now", but "crank up the volume" and you'll "enjoy the energy" all the same.

### Family Man, The
**16 | 17 | 18 | 17**
*2000. Directed by Brett Ratner. With Nicolas Cage, Téa Leoni, Don Cheadle. 125 minutes. Rated PG-13.*
A "harried, unmarried exec wakes up with a new life and family" in this "what-if?" picture, an "update of *It's a Wonderful Life*" that may be "a bit far-fetched" but still "questions all the choices we make"; Leoni is "adorable", Cage "more affecting than expected" and despite the "slow" pace, most leave "believing wholeheartedly in true love."

### Fanny and Alexander
**26 | 25 | 25 | 26**
*1982. Directed by Ingmar Bergman. With Pernilla Allwin, Bertil Guve, Gunn Wallgren. 188 minutes. Rated R.*
"Proof that Bergman wasn't miserable all the time", this "semi-autobiographical look back at his childhood" in Sweden "told from two siblings' point of view" features the "master" "at his most accessible"; sure, the "pacing's slow" and the film "long" (in fact, it's a pared-down version of a six-hour TV miniseries), yet the overall "visual magnificence" makes for something "rich and interesting."

### FANTASIA ⓪
**28 | – | – | 29**
*1940. Directed by Ben Sharpsteen et al. Animated. 120 minutes. Rated G.*
Disney's "magnificent merger" of "mind-blowing" animation with a symphonic orchestra conducted by "maestro Leopold Stokowski" is a piece of "unbeatably creative" "eye candy" that's "never been equaled"; though a "flop when it first came out", it was later revived as a "'60s head movie" (thanks to trippy sequences like those "dancing hippos in tutus" and "Mickey Mouse as the sorcerer's apprentice"); modernists maintain this "original music video" remains a "perfect way to introduce a child to classical" sounds.

### Fantasia 2000
**24 | – | – | 27**
*1999. Directed by James Algar et al. Animated. 75 minutes. Rated G.*
The "perfect companion" to the 1940 "classic", this "worthy" sequel marrying animation to music of great composers is "terrific Disney" that might be "more for adults than kids" for a change; it "keeps the spirit of the original beautifully" (right down to the "cloying celebrity" intros to each vignette), and although the "flamingo-with-the-yo-yo" scene enthralls many, the "best segment" is "'Rhapsody in Blue' via Al Hirschfeld."

### Fantastic Voyage
**19 | 12 | 23 | 21**
*1966. Directed by Richard Fleischer. With Stephen Boyd, Raquel Welch, Edmond O'Brien. 100 minutes. Rated PG.*
"Outrageous in its day", this sci-fi fantasy for "thinking" folks "still wows" the wide-eyed with its story about scientists shrunken and then "injected into a human body" to repair a blood clot; despite

"wooden acting" and a "dumb ending", the "special effects are impressive for its time" – and Raquel sure looks swell in and out of that skintight diving outfit.

### Farewell My Concubine 🇫     25 | 26 | 24 | 26 |
*1993. Directed by Chen Kaige. With Leslie Cheung, Gong Li, Zhang Feng-Yi. 171 minutes. Rated R.*
"Worthy of David Lean on every level", this "sumptuous", "epic achievement" traces a complex friendship between two Peking Opera singers over a "fascinating sweep of history" from the '30s to the '70s; "stunning both visually and emotionally", it boasts "superb acting" and "outstanding scenery", but make sure to sit up straight: its "overlong" running time can be "draining."

### Far From Heaven     24 | 27 | 23 | 26 |
*2002. Directed by Todd Haynes. With Julianne Moore, Dennis Quaid, Dennis Haysbert. 107 minutes. Rated PG-13.*
Haynes' "gorgeous homage to director Douglas Sirk's '50s melodramas" takes a "grippingly bittersweet" look at the "reality of the suburban picket-fence dream" and "genteel Northern racism"; though the pace is "slow" and the story "a little weak", it remains a "must-see" thanks to "flawless performances" from Moore and Quaid as well as "colorful", "stunning cinematography" that "captures the time period with brilliance" – the "costumes alone are close to heaven."

### Fargo ✉     25 | 27 | 25 | 25 |
*1996. Directed by Joel Coen. With Frances McDormand, William H. Macy, Steve Buscemi. 98 minutes. Rated R.*
This "comic noir" treatment of "crime in the heartland" shows "how funny Minnesota can be" in the hands of the Coen brothers, who "spin a folksy", violent yarn that makes the "outrageous seem everyday" and the "mundane interesting"; but the pièce de résistance is McDormand's "deadpan", Oscar-winning turn as a "pregnant" "crime-stopper" whose "goofy dialogue" alone is – "you betcha" – worth the price of admission.

### Fast Times at Ridgemont High     22 | 19 | 21 | 18 |
*1982. Directed by Amy Heckerling. With Sean Penn, Judge Reinhold, Jennifer Jason Leigh. 92 minutes. Rated R.*
One of the "crown jewels of the teen-comedy" genre, this "totally killer" "coming-of-age" "favorite" is an indelible "snapshot of the '80s" that made a star of Penn in the immortal role of "surfer stoner dude" Jeff Spicoli; adapted from Cameron Crowe's book, it showcases a "sprawling cast in interweaving stories" (like a kind of "teenage *Nashville*") and, among other things, "inspired a generation of in-school pizza orderers"; best "gratuitous scene": "Phoebe Cates on the diving board."

### Fatal Attraction     22 | 23 | 23 | 21 |
*1987. Directed by Adrian Lyne. With Michael Douglas, Glenn Close, Anne Archer. 119 minutes. Rated R.*
"Anyone contemplating an extramarital affair" should take a hard look at this "genuinely creepy" "cautionary tale", dominated by a "demented" Close as a "licentious hubby's worst nightmare"; though the plot "goes overboard" occasionally and Douglas "plays the same character as in 47 other movies", the picture had tremendous "cultural impact" in its day and is "still hair-raising" – particularly the "yikes"-inducing "boiled-bunny" scene.

### Father of the Bride ◐ Ⅱ
**23 | 25 | 21 | 20**
*1950. Directed by Vincente Minnelli. With Spencer Tracy, Joan Bennett, Elizabeth Taylor. 92 minutes. Not Rated.*
Hollywood legends Tracy (in the "harried" title role) and Taylor (as the bride) walk down the aisle together in this "heartwarming" chestnut about the "havoc surrounding the planning of a wedding"; while most vow it's something that "all fathers and daughters should watch" together, a few pronounce it "dated and slow."

### Father of the Bride Ⅱ
**20 | 20 | 19 | 20**
*1991. Directed by Charles Shyer. With Steve Martin, Diane Keaton, Martin Short. 105 minutes. Rated PG.*
"Faster-moving than the original", this "thoroughly engaging" comedy captures the "chaos of wedding planning" thanks to a "hilarious" Martin (as the "clueless dad") and an equally "hysterical" Short; sure, it can be "tame" and rather "silly", but ultimately it goes down "like soothing chocolate pudding"; better yet, it "won't inflict pain on guys", even though it's a bona fide "chick flick."

### Fear and Loathing in Las Vegas
**15 | 20 | 15 | 18**
*1998. Directed by Terry Gilliam. With Johnny Depp, Benicio Del Toro, Craig Bierko. 119 minutes. Rated R.*
"You'll either love or loathe" this "whirlwind cult film", a "faithful adaptation" of Hunter S. Thompson's "unadaptable" book detailing his "psychedelic" escapades in Las Vegas; despite kudos for Depp and Del Toro's "bizarre but authentic" performances, loathers find the film "essentially unpleasant" with "no plot", just a bunch of "idiots doing drugs."

### Ferris Bueller's Day Off
**23 | 22 | 23 | 21**
*1986. Directed by John Hughes. With Matthew Broderick, Alan Ruck, Mia Sara. 98 minutes. Rated PG-13.*
"Every teenager's fantasy" of "ditching high school" for the day is realized in this "brilliant comedy" about a "sly slacker" on the loose in Chicago who "gets away with everything" and "does it with style"; the "smug-mugged" Broderick exudes "bravado" in the role that "launched his career", while "underappreciated" director Hughes offhandedly produces a picture so "influential" that it "belongs in a time capsule of the '80s."

### Few Good Men, A
**23 | 26 | 23 | 22**
*1992. Directed by Rob Reiner. With Tom Cruise, Jack Nicholson, Demi Moore, Kevin Bacon. 138 minutes. Rated R.*
"Star-driven", "crackerjack courtroom drama" about a military murder investigation that's both "intelligent and entertaining"; no question, there are more than a few good performances, especially the "adorable-as-ever" Cruise in a "gritty", change-of-pace role playing against Nicholson's "riveting" if "pompous" marine colonel, who delivers the picture's most "infamous line: 'you can't handle the truth.'"

### Fiddler on the Roof
**26 | 25 | 27 | 26**
*1971. Directed by Norman Jewison. With Topol, Leonard Frey, Norma Crane. 181 minutes. Rated G.*
One of the "last of the epic musicals", this "uplifting" adaptation of the "Broadway classic" finds "wide-screen resonance" in its

"memorable" score and "elaborate production" values; despite the unmusical subject matter (19th-century "Jews fleeing the pogroms"), it's still a "joyous" film that's as "moving as a moving picture can be."

### Field of Dreams
22 | 21 | 23 | 22

*1989. Directed by Phil Alden Robinson. With Kevin Costner, Amy Madigan, Ray Liotta, James Earl Jones. 107 minutes. Rated PG.*

"Even non–sports fans can love" this "feel-good" fantasy/drama about "baseball, ghosts" and "one man's search to find himself" in an Iowa cornfield; its "realistic sporting sequences, great storyline" and "touching" Costner turn ("before he lost it") make for a flick that "gets better every time you see it"; even those who find it too "sentimental" agree it's a "must-see for any father and son."

### Fifth Element, The
19 | 15 | 19 | 23

*1997. Directed by Luc Besson. With Bruce Willis, Gary Oldman, Milla Jovovich. 126 minutes. Rated PG-13.*

"Hyperkinetic", "loud" and "fast-paced", this "slick" sci-fi "actionfest" is about as substantial as a "big ball of cotton candy, but a hoot nonetheless"; sure, "Willis saves the planet – again" – but in this "loopy" "send-up of the genre", the "tongue-in-cheek" plot plays a distinct second fiddle to the "visually spectacular" effects; still, shirkers shrug it off as a "messy example of why more isn't always better."

### Fight Club
23 | 25 | 24 | 24

*1999. Directed by David Fincher. With Brad Pitt, Edward Norton, Helena Bonham Carter. 139 minutes. Rated R.*

"Love-it-or-hate-it" moviemaking is alive and well in this "testosterone-ridden" "cult classic" that uses "top-notch effects", "twisted humor" and a "killer" soundtrack in its depiction of "ultraviolent, disenfranchised males"; an "amazing Norton" and "underrated Pitt" provide the fireworks in this "gore"-drenched drama, with a "surprise finish" that's either "mind-blowing" or "nonsensical", depending on who's talking.

### FINDING NEMO
28 | – | 25 | 29

*2003. Directed by Andrew Stanton, Lee Unkrich. Animated. 100 minutes. Rated G.*

"No matter what your age", you'll be "riveted to your seat" by this "Pixar masterpiece" about a "neurotic father fish searching for his son" in a "beautifully rendered undersea world"; voters insist it's "one of the best animated films of all time", blending "superb visual effects" with a "touching" yet "hilarious script" (laced with "adult references that the tots will certainly miss") and "fully developed, brilliantly voiced characters."

### Finding Neverland
25 | 27 | 24 | 26

*2004. Directed by Marc Forster. With Johnny Depp, Kate Winslet, Julie Christie. 106 minutes. Rated PG.*

"Even if you're a rock-hearted cynic", get out your handkerchiefs for this "pixie dust–coated", "semi-biographical" reflection on *Peter Pan* playwright J.M. Barrie's "fantastic imagination" and the people who inspired it; "do-no-wrong" Depp and Winslet "fly high" with "stellar performances", though most agree it's the "adorable child" actors who "steal the show" demonstrating the "simple power of play."

### Finian's Rainbow
∇ 20 | 19 | 19 | 20

*1968. Directed by Francis Ford Coppola. With Fred Astaire, Petula Clark, Tommy Steele, Keenan Wynn. 141 minutes. Rated G.*
This "last musical" starring "lighter-than-air Fred Astaire" was "directed by Francis Ford Coppola, of all people", who supplies an "inventive" take on the genre in this story of Irish folks (and a leprechaun) transplanted to a small Southern town; although "dated" to a few, it's "underrated" to others.

### Firm, The
17 | 17 | 20 | 18

*1993. Directed by Sydney Pollack. With Tom Cruise, Jeanne Tripplehorn, Gene Hackman. 154 minutes. Rated R.*
"Nail-biters" say this "slick" adaptation of John Grisham's "solid" best-seller about an "honest lawyer and his evil employers" succeeds mainly because of its "quirky supporting performances"; but foes argue this "not-too-thrilling thriller" "rarely lives up to the book", particularly since they went and "changed the ending."

### First Blood: Rambo ⓫
18 | 13 | 19 | 18

*1982. Directed by Ted Kotcheff. With Sylvester Stallone, Richard Crenna, Brian Dennehy. 97 minutes. Rated R.*
A "great kick-butt movie" "bolstered by a muscular score", this "simplistic but satisfying revenge tale" about a Vietnam vet harassed by small-town cops "delivers some punch"; the "studly", "steroidal" Stallone makes a bloody decent "action god", if not a silver-tongued thespian ("he should never talk"), though compadres caution it's his "last good movie before getting lost in sequel land."

### First Wives Club, The
17 | 19 | 18 | 17

*1996. Directed by Hugh Wilson. With Bette Midler, Goldie Hawn, Diane Keaton, Maggie Smith. 102 minutes. Rated PG.*
The "heavyweight talent" of its "all-star cast" made this "lightweight battle-of-the-sexes farce", a revenge comedy pitting "strong women" against "rotten men", into a big hit at the box office; still, foes say it's as "fluffy as Goldie's lips", citing a "ridiculous plot" that's an "embarrassment for all involved"; P.S. it's "not a good date movie" either.

### Fish Called Wanda, A
23 | 24 | 22 | 21

*1988. Directed by Charles Crichton. With John Cleese, Jamie Lee Curtis, Kevin Kline. 108 minutes. Rated R.*
It's easy getting hooked on this "nonstop", "kitchen-sink comedy" about a heist perpetrated by a "bumbling gang" portrayed by a "few chaps of Python fame" as well as the "show-stealing", Oscar-winning Kline; be prepared for "lots of giggles", but "forget political correctness", as "stutterers" and some unfortunate "goldfish" are gleefully abused.

### Fisher King, The
21 | 24 | 21 | 21

*1991. Directed by Terry Gilliam. With Jeff Bridges, Robin Williams, Mercedes Ruehl, Amanda Plummer. 137 minutes. Rated R.*
Grail-seekers gravitate to this "strange" mix of "comedy, fantasy and drama", a "powerful" story of a high-flying radio shock jock who falls to earth only to be rescued by a homeless man; some find the plot "confusing" and "a little too out there", but loyal subjects say the "incredible visual effects in the Grand Central Station" scene alone "make it worth watching."

### Fistful of Dollars, A ⑪
19 | 17 | 18 | 17

*1967. Directed by Sergio Leone. With Clint Eastwood, Marianne Koch, Mario Brega. 99 minutes. Rated R.*
The "pasta flows" in this "early spaghetti Western" as Clint "defines coolness" with his "prototypical" "Man With No Name" caught between two rival families; though a "couple notches down from *The Good, the Bad and the Ugly*" ("maybe something was lost in the translation"), this "classic" is "still fun" on a rainy day.

### Five Easy Pieces
24 | 27 | 22 | 21

*1970. Directed by Bob Rafelson. With Jack Nicholson, Karen Black, Lois Smith. 96 minutes. Rated R.*
"Nicholson's at the height of his powers" in this "deliberately paced character study" about "disaffection", "wasted ambition and dreams" that's a "must-see" for die-hard Jack fans; it "captures the restlessness of its era" with an expert "mix of comedy and serious drama" – and offers explicit instructions on "how not to be a waitress" in that "unforgettable chicken-salad sandwich" scene.

### 5,000 Fingers of Dr. T., The
∇ 21 | 15 | 21 | 24

*1953. Directed by Roy Rowland. With Tommy Rettig, Hans Conried, Peter Lind Hayes. 88 minutes. Not Rated.*
"Imaginative, absurd, trippy and a million other crazy things", this "ahead-of-its-time" musical "written by Dr. Seuss" depicts a "bizarre world" where a boy battles a piano teacher bent on world domination; though this "quirky little masterpiece" boasts a "growing cult following", it might be a little too "dark" and "frightening" for smaller fry.

### Flashdance
16 | 14 | 15 | 18

*1983. Directed by Adrian Lyne. With Jennifer Beals, Michael Nouri. 96 minutes. Rated R.*
"Break dancing, leg warmers and sweatshirts worn off the shoulder" got their start in this "breakthrough" musical about a "Cinderella"-esque steel worker yearning to be a ballerina; granted, the "politically incorrect" story is "somewhat lacking", yet this "guilty pleasure" features a "soundtrack that nails the early '80s" and was "one of the highest grossing films" of its time – "what a feeling", indeed.

### Fletch ⑪
19 | 18 | 18 | 16

*1985. Directed by Michael Ritchie. With Chevy Chase, Joe Don Baker, Tim Matheson. 98 minutes. Rated PG.*
This "goofball" "cult" comedy represents "Chase's peak" in his "ultimate" role as an "undercover reporter who changes his ID more often than his underwear"; fools for "tomfoolery" swear it's "possibly the most quotable movie" ever, thanks to a flurry of "great one-liners" that only get "funnier every time you see it."

### Flight of the Phoenix, The
25 | 26 | 24 | 21

*1965. Directed by Robert Aldrich. With James Stewart, Richard Attenborough, Peter Finch. 147 minutes. Not Rated.*
"Jimmy Stewart can fly anything" and does in this post–*Spirit of St. Louis* adventure flicker about a desert plane crash that leaves its survivors facing a "seemingly hopeless future"; "realistically shot" and "brilliantly acted", it's a "feel-good", "can-do" kind of picture "without violence" that "really stays with you."

### Fly, The ⓫
`20 | 18 | 22 | 18`

*1958. Directed by Kurt Neumann. With Vincent Price, David Hedison, Patricia Owens. 94 minutes. Not Rated.*

The "golden age of B movies" lives on in this wonderfully "camp classic" about a scientist "who pushes the envelope too far and becomes a fly"; fans buzz it remains "truly horrifying", especially that "unforgettable" shot of our hero "stuck in the spider's web" ("*help me!*") that "makes up for any quaintness in the execution."

### Fly, The ⓫
`16 | 17 | 17 | 20`

*1986. Directed by David Cronenberg. With Jeff Goldblum, Geena Davis. 96 minutes. Rated R.*

A "reinterpretation, not a rehash" of the "campy original", this "graphic, gruesome" remake explores Cronenberg's "obsession about the relationship between biology and technology"; sure, "special effects rule the day" here, yet there's also an "effective" love story amid the otherwise "dark" doings.

### Fly Away Home
`22 | 20 | 24 | 24`

*1996. Directed by Carroll Ballard. With Anna Paquin, Jeff Daniels, Dana Delany. 107 minutes. Rated PG.*

Get out your "biggest bowl of popcorn" for this "deeply felt family film" about a young girl, her estranged dad and the flock of baby geese she takes under her wing; fans "honk" about its "captivating story" and "beautiful" Canadian scenery, saying it's "not just for kids", but rather a "quite uplifting", "lovely movie for all."

### Fog of War, The
`26 | – | 25 | 23`

*2003. Directed by Errol Morris. Documentary. 95 minutes. Rated PG-13.*

"Controversial" former U.S. Secretary of Defense Robert S. McNamara recounts his involvement in WWII and the Cuban missile crisis, as well as his role as one of the "architects of the Vietnam War", in this "eye-opening", Oscar-winning documentary that's "amazingly relevant considering the current political climate"; director Morris' "fascinating yet maddening" work underscores McNamara's "brilliance and fallibility" while "neither condemning nor excusing him entirely."

### Footloose
`17 | 15 | 16 | 17`

*1984. Directed by Herbert Ross. With Kevin Bacon, Lori Singer, John Lithgow, Dianne Wiest. 107 minutes. Rated PG.*

A "town that's banned dancing" is the setting for this "classic '80s rebellion flick", a "guilty pleasure" that "started it all for Kevin Bacon" and is best remembered for its hit-heavy soundtrack and "jumping" theme song; though "silly fluff" to detractors, it's "all-around fun" for "toe-tappers" who "take it for what it is."

### Forbidden Planet
`25 | 18 | 25 | 24`

*1956. Directed by Fred M. Wilcox. With Walter Pidgeon, Anne Francis, Leslie Nielsen. 98 minutes. Rated G.*

Its long-before-digital FX "may seem quaint" today, but this "top-notch psychological thriller" represents the "true start of the sci-fi genre" to many; despite a compelling storyline "based on Shakespeare's *Tempest*" and some halfway decent acting from the humans, "Robby the Robot is the real star" here.

### FORREST GUMP ⊠
24 | 26 | 24 | 25

*1994. Directed by Robert Zemeckis. With Tom Hanks, Robin Wright, Gary Sinise. 142 minutes. Rated PG-13.*

"Even macho guys" get misty over this "sentimental" story of "hope and perseverance" that explores recent American history through the "unlikely eyes" of a "simple-minded", Zelig-like hero (the "triumphant", Oscar-winning Hanks); though picky viewers find "not much assortment in this box of chocolates", they're overruled by "enchanted" believers who say its "basic good-heartedness" makes it "remarkably touching."

### Fort Apache ◑
23 | 22 | 23 | 22

*1948. Directed by John Ford. With John Wayne, Henry Fonda, Shirley Temple, Ward Bond. 125 minutes. Not Rated.*

This "great" Golden-Age-of-Hollywood Western is the first of the Ford trilogy that both mythologized and humanized the cavalry; Fonda's effectively "cast against type" as a by-the-numbers commander who takes over a frontier fort and can't connect with his men or the local Indians, while Wayne is "perfect" as the more understanding captain with whom he clashes; tame for the TV generation, its fight scenes are "remarkable for its era."

### Fortune Cookie, The ◑
▽ 21 | 25 | 20 | 19

*1966. Directed by Billy Wilder. With Walter Matthau, Jack Lemmon. 125 minutes. Not Rated.*

The first (and many say the "best") pairing of the Lemmon-Matthau combo", this biting black comedy via Billy Wilder takes aim at our litigious society in its story of a sports cameraman faking an injury in exchange for insurance money; a "top-notch script" intertwining "big laughs" and "nonstop snickers" keeps things moving at a fast clip, even if the ending "veers uncomfortably between drama and humor."

### 48 HRS. ⓾
19 | 18 | 18 | 17

*1982. Directed by Walter Hill. With Nick Nolte, Eddie Murphy, Annette O'Toole. 92 minutes. Rated R.*

The "blueprint" for "buddy action flicks", this "entertaining" crime thriller about a "surly white cop teaming up with a loud-mouthed black convict" features "stroke-of-genius" casting pairing Nolte and Murphy; ok, it's "brainless fun" and a "little too violent", but worth catching for Eddie's "starmaking" screen debut alone – especially his "great rendition of 'Roxanne.'"

### 42nd Street ◑
24 | 18 | 20 | 26

*1933. Directed by Lloyd Bacon. With Ruby Keeler, Ginger Rogers, Bebe Daniels. 89 minutes. Not Rated.*

Alright, it's a "bit corny by modern standards", but this "brassy" "mother of all backstage musicals" showcases choreographer "Busby Berkeley at his glossy best" applying his "inventive" genius to all those "dancing feet"; "every actress' dream" come true, it's a real "classic", so just ignore the "hackneyed" plot and Keeler's "clunky" footwork.

### For Whom the Bell Tolls
25 | 26 | 26 | 22

*1943. Directed by Sam Wood. With Gary Cooper, Ingrid Bergman, Katina Paxinou. 170 minutes. Not Rated.*

Fans swear this adaptation of Hemingway's Pulitzer Prize–winner about an American fighting fascism in '30s Spain "gets every single nuance right", starting with its "poignant", "old-fashioned love story" right down to the very convincing battle sequences; though a minority dubs it "schmaltz in macho drag", it strikes a chord as a "true classic by any measure" for most bell-ringers.

### For Your Eyes Only

| 18 | 16 | 18 | 21 |

*1981. Directed by John Glen. With Roger Moore, Carole Bouquet, Topol, Julian Glover. 127 minutes. Rated PG.*

A "solid" entry in the Bond blitz, this spy flicker focuses less on "supergadgets" and more on Moore, leading many to label it his "best" outing as the ever-suave 007; the "realistic villains", "exotic locations" and "jaw-dropping" ski chases entice "even die-hard nonfans" – although the "fight scenes are never believable."

### Foul Play

| 21 | 19 | 20 | 19 |

*1978. Directed by Colin Higgins. With Goldie Hawn, Chevy Chase, Dudley Moore. 116 minutes. Rated PG.*

Goldie "at her cute, giggly best" and a "terrific" Chevy make a "charming couple" in this "lightweight murder mystery" that's a loose "takeoff on Hitchcock's *The Man Who Knew Too Much*"; its "international-assassination plot" seesaws between "hilarity and suspense", while Moore deftly walks away with the picture as a lecherous swinger with a memorably equipped bachelor pad.

### Fountainhead, The ❶∅

| ▽ 22 | 21 | 23 | 20 |

*1949. Directed by King Vidor. With Gary Cooper, Patricia Neal, Raymond Massey. 114 minutes. Not Rated.*

Ayn Rand's mammoth novel "brought to life", this Hollywood version fortunately "doesn't take six months to watch" as it profiles the life of an independent, "Frank Lloyd Wright"–esque architect intent on being a "genuine individual"; foes find it too talky and "hokey" (except for the "delicious Neal") and advise you "read the book before seeing the movie."

### 400 BLOWS, THE ❶Ⅱ🅵

| 27 | 26 | 25 | 24 |

*1959. Directed by François Truffaut. With Jean-Pierre Léaud, Robert Beauvais. 94 minutes. Not Rated.*

"Anyone who survived adolescence" can relate to this French "coming-of-age" film, a "semi-autobiographical" effort that marked Truffaut's directorial debut; as his "great alter ego", Léaud "depicts the pain and joy of growing up" in a winsomely "giddy" turn, though the picture earned its "place in film history" by "breaking a lot of rules" while demonstrating a "true love of movies."

### Four Weddings and a Funeral

| 21 | 21 | 21 | 20 |

*1994. Directed by Mike Newell. With Hugh Grant, Andie MacDowell, Kristin Scott Thomas. 117 minutes. Rated R.*

This "fabulously entertaining" marriage of "sweet and savvy" wrings "unexpected" laughs out of the "ups and downs of modern love" and "every bad wedding" you've ever endured; notable for "putting Hugh Grant on the map", it also boasts a "sparkling script" and a "quirky" ensemble cast, though the less said about the "wooden", "whiny" MacDowell the better.

### Fox and the Hound, The

| 18 | – | 19 | 18 |

*1981. Directed by Ted Berman, Richard Rich, Art Stevens. Animated. 83 minutes. Rated G.*

As the title canines become unlikely pals, kids can learn about the "meaning of friendship" from this "cute" Disney film, but it's not all tail-wagging "family" fun: the "bittersweet" tone "tugs at those heartstrings with no mercy", and bashers bark at the "copy-machine" quality of the early '80s animation.

**Frances** ▽ 22 | 28 | 23 | 20

*1982. Directed by Graeme Clifford. With Jessica Lange, Kim Stanley, Sam Shepard. 140 minutes. Rated R.*
"Disturbing" but still "quite fine", this "harrowing" biography of "Hollywood nonconformist" Frances Farmer pulls no punches in its exploration of the actress' "demons" and "society's response to her mental illness"; in the title role, Lange is "magical" (and "matched by Stanley as her mother"), but this one's "not for the timid" given its ultimately "desperate, depressing" tone.

**Frankenstein** ◑⓪ 25 | 21 | 25 | 23

*1931. Directed by James Whale. With Boris Karloff, Colin Clive, Mae Clarke. 71 minutes. Not Rated.*
The "granddaddy of all horror films" adds a touch of "pathos" and "camp" to its story of a mad scientist who "goes against nature" and builds a creature "prone to violence"; beyond monster-mashing, it also explores the "theme of loneliness" via Karloff's "heartbreaking" ghoul, and though "a bit overacted", it's still "goose-bumps time when Colin Clive shouts '*it's alive!*'"

**Freaky Friday** 18 | 17 | 21 | 16

*1977. Directed by Gary Nelson. With Barbara Harris, Jodie Foster, John Astin. 95 minutes. Rated G.*
A "kooky" idea – a teenage girl and her mom trade bodies for a day – powers this "fun" '70s "family film" that's a step up from the "usual body-swapping" comedies; thanks to a "smart script" and "brilliant" performances from Harris and Foster, some mothers and daughters watch it together for a "great bonding experience."

**Free Willy** ⓪ 17 | 14 | 18 | 18

*1993. Directed by Simon Wincer. With Jason James Richter, Lori Petty. 112 minutes. Rated PG.*
"Everyone cries at the end" of this "family favorite", the "touching" story of an unhappy street kid who befriends an unhappy "killer whale" to "inspiring" results; it's "captivating" enough to work as a good "babysitter" for the kiddies, though seen-it-all types find it too "simplistic and message-laden."

**French Connection, The** ✉⓪ 25 | 26 | 25 | 24

*1971. Directed by William Friedkin. With Gene Hackman, Roy Scheider, Fernando Rey. 104 minutes. Rated R.*
Famed for the "most harrowing car chase ever", this "seminal hard-boiled cop drama" is a "fast-paced" "exposé of the drug underworld" that's also "superbly cast and acted", starting with Hackman's "explosive", Oscar-winning turn as the tough-talking 'Popeye' Doyle; sure, it might seem "dated" to modernists, but that's "only because it's aped so frequently."

**French Lieutenant's Woman, The** 22 | 25 | 21 | 23

*1981. Directed by Karel Reisz. With Meryl Streep, Jeremy Irons, Hilton McRae. 127 minutes. Rated R.*
"Streep is fantastic" in this "original" romance detailing parallel relationships: one involving an upper-class gentleman and a lower-class lass in Victorian England, the other between the contemporary actors playing them; granted, Harold Pinter's

scenario might be "a bit confusing at the get-go", but ultimately this "excellent" adaptation of John Fowles' novel is both "really cool and worthwhile."

### Frequency
**19 | 20 | 22 | 19**

*2000. Directed by Gregory Hoblit. With Dennis Quaid, James Caviezel. 118 minutes. Rated PG-13.*

Sure, it might be "unbelievable", but this "time-travel" tale generates lots of "surprise" with its "truly original story" about a young man who talks to his late father via ham radio; despite "metropolis-size plot holes", it's still "touching", with a baseball subplot that's "especially fun" for fans of NY's 1969 "Miracle Mets."

### FRIDA
**25 | 27 | 25 | 27**

*2002. Directed by Julie Taymor. With Salma Hayek, Alfred Molina. 123 minutes. Rated R.*

"Fiery" Hayek "put her heart and soul" into this "underrated little" bio of "eccentric" Mexican artist Frida Kahlo, "and it shows"; she delivers her "finest performance", capturing the "pain, grief and personal tragedy that the painter expressed in her art" against a "visually stunning tapestry" of "color and texture" in which her "actual paintings come to life"; "wonderful" acting by Molina and an "amazing soundtrack" are more reasons "not to miss it."

### Friday Night Lights
**21 | 21 | 21 | 20**

*2004. Directed by Peter Berg. With Billy Bob Thornton, Derek Luke, Jay Hernandez. 118 minutes. Rated PG-13.*

"Football fanatics" feel the "mojo" of this "gritty", "documentary-style" look at a Texas town's "bigger than life" devotion to high school gridiron; as an "embattled" coach preaching "love for the game", Thornton shows his "versatility", but some Monday morning quarterbacks are "unimpressed with the character development" and the "headache-inducing" camerawork.

### Friday the 13th Ⓤ
**16 | 9 | 15 | 13**

*1980. Directed by Sean S. Cunningham. With Betsy Palmer, Adrienne King, Harry Crosby. 95 minutes. Rated R.*

The "granddaddy of modern-day horror films", this "cult slasher flick" "spawned an entire franchise" of "wretched sequels" that don't hold a candle to its "unrelenting creepiness"; set in a summer camp populated by "stupid, horny teenagers" who "scream a lot", it might "succeed more on a comedic level" today, but that "twist at the end" still "scares the hell" out of everybody.

### Fried Green Tomatoes
**23 | 25 | 23 | 22**

*1991. Directed by Jon Avnet. With Kathy Bates, Jessica Tandy, Mary Stuart Masterson. 130 minutes. Rated PG-13.*

"Southern-fried memories" are the basis of this "heartwarming" dramedy detailing how a "pathetic excuse for a woman" transforms herself into a "take-charge wonder"; its "sweet story" might feature a dash of "male bashing", but it's "genuinely touching and involving" – no wonder many fried-food fans find this "feel-good" "tear-jerking" "chick flick" so gosh darn "yummy."

### Friendly Persuasion
**▽ 24 | 25 | 24 | 23**

*1956. Directed by William Wyler. With Gary Cooper, Dorothy McGuire, Anthony Perkins. 140 minutes. Not Rated.*

"One for thy heart", this story of "Quakers during the Civil War" "trying to be pacifists" is an "all-around solid" picture thanks to a "strong storyline"; its "endearing characters" include the ultra-"believable" Cooper (the "Harrison Ford of his time") as well as a "moving" McGuire and Oscar-nominated Perkins.

**From Here to Eternity** ✉◐   26 | 27 | 24 | 24
*1953. Directed by Fred Zinnemann. With Burt Lancaster, Montgomery Clift, Deborah Kerr, Frank Sinatra, Donna Reed. 118 minutes. Not Rated.*
Based on James Jones' "powerful" novel, this "gold standard" of war dramas depicts military life in Honolulu's Pearl Harbor just before the Japanese attack; the "all-star cast" (including an Oscar-winning "Ol' Blue Eyes") and a "technically brilliant" production make this a "compelling classic" – though it's best remembered for Burt and Deborah's iconic "kissing-on-the-beach" scene.

**From Russia With Love**   23 | 21 | 23 | 23
*1964. Directed by Terence Young. With Sean Connery, Robert Shaw, Lotte Lenya. 115 minutes. Rated PG.*
Ride the "Orient Express from Istanbul to Venice" – with plenty of stops for "exotic locales", "scantily clad" gals and "great fight scenes" – in this early James Bonder; the "formula never works better" thanks to an "incomparable" Connery pitted against "non-cartoon" villains, especially Lenya at her most "sadomasochistic."

**Front Page, The** ◐   ▽ 22 | 19 | 21 | 15
*1931. Directed by Lewis Milestone. With Adolphe Menjou, Pat O'Brien, Edward Everett Horton. 101 minutes. Not Rated.*
Based on the timeless stage comedy from Ben Hecht and Charles MacArthur, this zany satire of tabloid journalism is propelled by a fast-moving plot delivered with rapid-fire, overlapping dialogue; since it's an early talkie, it hasn't aged well, but the story was well-regarded enough to inspire three remakes, including *His Girl Friday,* arguably the best of the bunch.

**Fugitive, The**   23 | 24 | 24 | 23
*1993. Directed by Andrew Davis. With Harrison Ford, Tommy Lee Jones, Sela Ward, Julianne Moore. 127 minutes. Rated PG-13.*
From the "ultimate adrenaline rush" of the opening "train wreck" to the "smashing grand finale" to "on the edge of your seat" throughout this "thinking person's action flick", based on the "long-ago" TV series about a doctor unjustly accused of murder; the "cat-and-mouse" plot lends a "Hitchcockian" feel to the proceedings, while Ford and Jones deliver "pitch-perfect performances."

**Full Metal Jacket**   24 | 25 | 22 | 25
*1987. Directed by Stanley Kubrick. With Matthew Modine, Adam Baldwin, Vincent D'Onofrio. 116 minutes. Rated R.*
"Kubrick does Vietnam" in this "intense" war picture that's really "two amazing films in one": first up is the "disturbingly funny" depiction of "boot-camp" basic training, followed by an abrupt about-face to the "total hell" of the front-line war; "first-rate production and acting" keep things "compelling" throughout, even if peaceniks feel the "uneven" second half is a tad too "violent."

**Full Monty, The**   22 | 22 | 24 | 19
*1997. Directed by Peter Cattaneo. With Robert Carlyle, Mark Addy, Tom Wilkinson. 91 minutes. Rated R.*
Out-of-work, out-of-shape blokes put together a "Chippendale's-type" strip act as a "creative response to unemployment" in this "riotous" English comedy that mixes "bumps and grinds" with

"serious social themes"; its "enthusiastic" if "unknown" ensemble cast shake their booties to a "terrific" pop soundtrack, though most prefer it "with subtitles" to decipher those "British accents."

### Funny Face
24 | 24 | 21 | 25

*1957. Directed by Stanley Donen. With Audrey Hepburn, Fred Astaire, Kay Thompson. 103 minutes. Not Rated.*
"Cinderella" goes to Paris in this "fashion industry musical" wherein a "gracefully aging", "debonair" Astaire turns a "bookish" Hepburn into an "ethereal", "luminous" supermodel; despite "no story to speak of", it's "thoroughly enchanting" thanks to "magic" dancing and Gershwin's "s'wonderfully" "dreamy" score; best number: Thompson's "steal-the-movie" rendition of 'Think Pink.'

### Funny Girl ✉ⅰ
26 | 25 | 24 | 26

*1968. Directed by William Wyler. With Barbra Streisand, Omar Sharif, Walter Pidgeon. 151 minutes. Rated G.*
"Hello, gorgeous!"; Babs' "big movie debut" in one of the "last great traditional Hollywood musicals" made her the "greatest star" thanks to some "chutzpah", some "charm" and a voice "like buttah"; indeed, her Oscar-winning turn as comedienne Fanny Brice is so "socko" that it's easy to ignore the "schmaltzy" plot about the "man who got away."

### Funny Lady
15 | 17 | 14 | 18

*1975. Directed by Herbert Ross. With Barbra Streisand, James Caan, Omar Sharif. 136 minutes. Rated PG.*
This "not-as-good follow-up to *Funny Girl*" (they should have "quit while they were ahead") strikes some as a Streisand "vanity production" trying to "milk the success" of the original, with "everything in excess – except the story and acting"; on the positive side, there are a couple of "sparkling Kander and Ebb" tunes.

### Funny Thing Happened on the Way to the Forum, A
22 | 22 | 21 | 20

*1966. Directed by Richard Lester. With Zero Mostel, Phil Silvers, Buster Keaton. 99 minutes. Not Rated.*
For "comedy tonight", try this "total farce" of a musical that depicts Ancient Rome as a freewheeling toga party; sure, "Zero's the greatest" at provoking "laugh after laugh", but fans of the "quite different" stage version find it "stupid" "schlock" with "a lot lost in the translation to the screen."

### Gallipoli
25 | 25 | 25 | 24

*1981. Directed by Peter Weir. With Mel Gibson, Mark Lee, Bill Kerr, David Argue. 110 minutes. Rated PG.*
A "fresh-faced" Gibson "comes of age" as an actor in this "oh-so-sad war movie" about a "disastrous WWI" battle in Turkey that points up the "pointlessness" of combat; "one of the best of the Australian New Wave" films, it winds up with a "10-hanky tragic ending" that "tugs at the heartstrings without being corny."

### GANDHI ✉
27 | 28 | 27 | 27

*1982. Directed by Richard Attenborough. With Ben Kingsley, Candice Bergen, Edward Fox. 188 minutes. Rated PG.*
"Big Hollywood at its best", this "meticulously detailed" bio of the Indian leader is "*The Ten Commandments* of the '80s", "long but riveting" and "emotionally wrenching"; Kingsley's "searing", Oscar-winning portrayal of the figure "who brought the British

Empire to its knees" is the movie's "glorious centerpiece", and if a few find it "ponderous" and "overblown", there's no debate that it "captures the spiritual essence of the man perfectly."

### Gangs of New York    21 | 23 | 20 | 25
*2002. Directed by Martin Scorsese. With Leonardo DiCaprio, Daniel Day-Lewis, Cameron Diaz. 166 minutes. Rated R.*
The "corrupt world" of "Civil War–era New York" is the backdrop for this "bloody good" "love and revenge" picture via Martin Scorsese that's "overwhelming visually" but "wholly uneven" plotwise; cynics skewer the "unnecessary violence", "moldy love story" and "way too long" running time, while fans counter Day-Lewis' "vivid" performance is the picture's "saving grace"; in sum, "flawed, but worth it."

### Garden of the Finzi-Continis, The ✉🄵  25 | 24 | 27 | 25
*1971. Directed by Vittorio De Sica. With Dominique Sanda, Lino Capolicchio, Helmut Berger. 94 minutes. Rated R.*
"Complacency leads to disaster" in this "haunting" WWII drama about "upper-class Italian Jews" who "close their eyes to the looming evil" of fascism by believing that "money and position will insulate them"; "gripping and emotional", it's notable for making the "beautiful" young Sanda a star.

### Garden State    22 | 23 | 21 | 20
*2004. Directed by Zach Braff. With Zach Braff, Natalie Portman, Peter Sarsgaard. 102 minutes. Rated R.*
Think of it as "*The Graduate* for a new century": this "quirky" dramedy directed, written and starring Zach Braff is pitched to "disillusioned twentysomethings" with its depiction of the ultimate "quarter-life crisis sufferer"; despite mixed notices for the "enchanting" (or "annoying") Portman and catcalls for that "fake Hollywood ending", it's worth renting for the "kick-ass soundtrack" alone.

### Gaslight ✉◑    26 | 27 | 26 | 24
*1944. Directed by George Cukor. With Ingrid Bergman, Charles Boyer, Joseph Cotten. 114 minutes. Not Rated.*
Anything but light, this "high-tension" thriller stars a "glowing", Oscar-winning Bergman as a newlywed who thinks she's "going insane – or is she?"; "mesmerized" fans say the "original" storyline "maintains the suspense to the end", helped by an atmospheric "Victorian setting" and a particularly "villainous villain" in Boyer; P.S. look for a "very young Angela Lansbury" in her screen debut.

### Gay Divorcee, The ◑∅    ▽ 22 | 19 | 17 | 23
*1934. Directed by Mark Sandrich. With Fred Astaire, Ginger Rogers, Edward Everett Horton. 107 minutes. Not Rated.*
"No one could dance like Fred and Ginger", and this footloose '30s musical "whirls" with production numbers "par excellence" as Rogers plays a spouse untying the knot in high style as Astaire duly falls into step; the "silly story" is trumped by the "dreamy" tunes and, of course, that terpsichorean team-up "can't be beat."

### GENERAL, THE ◑    28 | 27 | 26 | 27
*1927. Directed by Clyde Bruckman, Buster Keaton. With Buster Keaton, Marion Mack. 75 minutes. Not Rated.*
One of the "most remarkable" silent films, this pioneering effort "establishes gags still used today" in its story of a Civil War–era

Southern engineer in relentless, hapless pursuit of a stolen locomotive; the "Great Stoneface's" most "ambitious" work, it also incorporates some "amazing physical comedy" (Keaton "does all his own stunts") that must be "seen to be believed."

### Gentleman's Agreement ✉◑ ▽ 25 | 26 | 27 | 23
*1947. Directed by Elia Kazan. With Gregory Peck, Dorothy McGuire, Celeste Holm. 118 minutes. Not Rated.*
A once-"controversial exposé" of "American anti-Semitism", this "earnest" "message drama" offers Peck in a "wonderfully emotional" turn as an investigative reporter who passes himself off as Jewish and becomes a first-hand witness to "subtle prejudice"; if the final result seems a bit "dated" and "simplistic" today, it's still "interesting" as an early attempt at social criticism.

### Gentlemen Prefer Blondes 23 | 21 | 20 | 24
*1953. Directed by Howard Hawks. With Jane Russell, Marilyn Monroe, Charles Coburn. 91 minutes. Rated PG.*
You'll probably prefer Monroe's "ingenious, ingenuous" "dumb blonde" to the "nonexistent storyline" in this "guilty-pleasure" musical comedy, a "deliciously over-the-top" story of "gold diggers" on the make made all the more vivid in "spectacular Technicolor"; it's "one for the time capsule", if only for Marilyn's "dazzling", iconic rendition of 'Diamonds Are a Girl's Best Friend.'

### George of the Jungle 17 | 16 | 16 | 17
*1997. Directed by Sam Weisman. With Brendan Fraser, Leslie Mann, Thomas Haden Church. 91 minutes. Rated PG.*
Young chimps and big apes who "remember the cartoon" have "goofy fun" with this comedy featuring "Fraser in a loincloth" as a "moronic", secondhand Tarzan; cynics say Disney grabs for the vine and "falls short", but it is "surprisingly entertaining", even if the theme ditty will stay "in your head for days."

### Ghost ✉ 21 | 21 | 22 | 21
*1990. Directed by Jerry Zucker. With Patrick Swayze, Demi Moore, Whoopi Goldberg. 128 minutes. Rated PG-13.*
There's "action for the boys and romance for the girls" in this comic "tearjerker" that's got "hot date movie" written all over it; sure, its story of a dead man watching over his surviving lover is "improbable" (and "sappy and manipulative", according to cynics), yet Moore and Swayze make it seem so "sexy", while the "priceless", Oscar-winning Goldberg "delivers the laughs."

### Ghost and Mrs. Muir, The ◑ 24 | 25 | 25 | 22
*1947. Directed by Joseph L. Mankiewicz. With Rex Harrison, Gene Tierney, George Sanders. 104 minutes. Not Rated.*
This "timeless" fantasy details the unlikely "love story" between a widow and a "crusty old" sea captain who's "full of life" – even though he's a ghost; the "otherworldly" romance that ensues avoids being "sentimental goop" thanks to "superb performances" from Tierney, Harrison and little "eight-year-old Natalie Wood."

### Ghostbusters ⑪ 21 | 18 | 21 | 23
*1984. Directed by Ivan Reitman. With Bill Murray, Dan Aykroyd, Sigourney Weaver, Harold Ramis. 107 minutes. Rated PG.*
"Kooky, spooky" and flat-out "funny", this "classic '80s" "sci-fi comedy" about 'paranormal investigators' banishing ghosts from NYC is "one of the best stupid movies ever", so "not much

thinking is required"; "wonderful special effects" and a brilliantly "sarcastic Murray" are its highlights, though its most lasting achievement is that it "made the word 'slime' into a verb."

### Ghost World    23 | 26 | 22 | 21

*2001. Directed by Terry Zwigoff. With Thora Birch, Steve Buscemi, Scarlett Johansson. 111 minutes. Rated R.*
A "witty" look at two "nonconformist" girls in a "homogenized" suburb, this "random" comedy is a "nice departure from the typical teen angst film"; the "quirky" characters sport "great thrift-store clothes", while the "phenomenal Buscemi" is "pitch-perfect."

### Giant ✉    24 | 23 | 24 | 24

*1956. Directed by George Stevens. With Elizabeth Taylor, Rock Hudson, James Dean, Dennis Hopper. 201 minutes. Rated G.*
As "sprawling" as the Lone Star state itself, this "all-out wonderful" Texas "epic" about money, love and oil "burns with star power", featuring some mighty "big names" – Liz, Rock and Jimmy (in his last role) – "in their prime"; cynics say this "way too long" example of "Hollywood bloat" is just "cornball hooey", but fans insist this "colossal '50s production" "holds your interest."

### Gigi ✉    24 | 23 | 23 | 26

*1958. Directed by Vincente Minnelli. With Leslie Caron, Maurice Chevalier, Louis Jourdan. 119 minutes. Rated G.*
"Thank heaven" for this "fine rendering" of Lerner and Loewe, an "unorthodox love story" about a "turn-of-the-century" Parisian courtesan and the client who wants to marry her; winner of nine Oscars, this "stunner" boasts a "radiant" Caron, suave Jourdan, "*amusant*" Chevalier and "top-notch production values", so even if the end result might look like a "lavish" wad of "cotton candy", "just give in" and enjoy it.

### Gilda ◑    24 | 23 | 21 | 23

*1946. Directed by Charles Vidor. With Rita Hayworth, Glenn Ford, George Macready. 110 minutes. Not Rated.*
Noir was never more "delectable" than in this "solid" love triangle starring a "delicious" "Hayworth in her signature role" as the "glamorous", hair-tossing Gilda; though her "modified striptease" in the 'Put the Blame on Mame' number is the "only reason to see it" for some, others find enough "mystery and suspense" to make it "memorable."

### Gimme Shelter    25 | – | 21 | 22

*1970. Directed by Albert Maysles, David Maysles, Charlotte Zwerin. Documentary. With the Rolling Stones. 91 minutes. Rated R.*
Originally commissioned by the Rolling Stones as a "simple concert" flick, this "rockumentary" took on a "darker side" after filmmakers inadvertently recorded a "real murder" at the group's infamous Altamont gig; the result is a "grim, gritty look" at the "turbulent '60s" "spiraling out of control", with a "complicated storyline" and "classic" soundtrack that put modern "music videos to shame"; hottest moment: the "amazing" Tina Turner at the mike.

### Girl, Interrupted    18 | 22 | 18 | 18

*1999. Directed by James Mangold. With Winona Ryder, Angelina Jolie, Brittany Murphy. 127 minutes. Rated R.*
"Haunting if overwrought" drama providing a "hair-raising glimpse" inside a mental institution headlining a "convincing" Ryder as a

"troubled" patient, though Jolie "steals the show" (and an Oscar) portraying the "sexiest crazy person" ever captured on film; fans insist it's a "compelling" "emotional trip", but others say it's so insanely "soapy" that it "should have been a 'Cosmo' article."

### Girl with a Pearl Earring
21 | 23 | 19 | 25

*2003. Directed by Peter Webber. With Colin Firth, Scarlett Johansson, Tom Wilkinson. 95 minutes. Rated PG-13.*
A "true art movie", this "beautifully photographed" period piece set in 17th-century "bourgeois Holland" is based on a Vermeer painting (and a recent novel) of the same name and explores the artist's "possible relationship" with a "lovely muse" played by Johansson, "who wows with her nearly wordless performance" as his "shy", "entrancing" servant; though the "slow" pacing is "like watching paint dry", enough "sexual tension abounds" to keep the interest level up.

### GLADIATOR ⊠
23 | 23 | 22 | 27

*2000. Directed by Ridley Scott. With Russell Crowe, Joaquin Phoenix, Oliver Reed, Richard Harris. 155 minutes. Rated R.*
"Everything a big Hollywood blockbuster should be", this "old-fashioned" "sword-and-sandal" extravaganza features lots of "action, adventure and backstabbing" in its story of a Roman general turned wretched slave; the "intense", Oscar-winning Crowe oozes "testosterone" and the "lavish re-creation of Ancient Rome" brings the "Coliseum to life", but thumbs-downers dismiss it as "bombastic beefcake."

### Glengarry Glen Ross
23 | 27 | 22 | 20

*1992. Directed by James Foley. With Al Pacino, Jack Lemmon, Ed Harris, Alec Baldwin. 100 minutes. Rated R.*
"High-pressure" real-estate salesmen "with an axe about to fall on their jobs" get the David Mamet treatment in this "dark", "lacerating drama" about the "predatory world of business"; its "talky", expletive-laden scenario can be "intensely disturbing", but ultimately it "shows what can be done with a small cast, limited sets and Godzilla talent."

### Glory
25 | 26 | 26 | 26

*1989. Directed by Edward Zwick. With Matthew Broderick, Denzel Washington, Morgan Freeman. 122 minutes. Rated R.*
Based on the "true tale" about the "first black Civil War regiment and the white Union officer who led them", this "period piece" is a fine "evocation of a story few people know"; expect "great battle scenes", even if it "doesn't end the way you want it to."

### GODFATHER, THE ⊠❶
29 | 29 | 29 | 29

*1972. Directed by Francis Ford Coppola. With Marlon Brando, Al Pacino, Diane Keaton, Robert Duvall, James Caan, John Cazale. 175 minutes. Rated R.*
Perhaps the "best three hours you can spend sitting still", this "ultimate gangster film" and "cultural phenomenon" is ranked both Top Overall and Most Popular film in this *Survey*; an "absolutely flawless" "American epic", it recounts the "operatic" lives of the Corleone family via an "intricate" plot, "bravura photography" and "iconic performances" from Brando and Pacino; in fact, the end result is so "killer" that "nothing else comes close – except maybe the sequel"; favorite line: "leave the gun, take the cannoli."

### GODFATHER PART II, THE ✉Ⓤ
`29` `29` `28` `29`

*1974. Directed by Francis Ford Coppola. With Al Pacino, Robert Duvall, Diane Keaton, Robert De Niro, John Cazale. 200 minutes. Rated R.*

A "real rarity – a sequel as good as the original" – this "true masterpiece" "stands on its own laurels" as it "delves deeper into the Corleone family" saga; a "moody meditation on the emptiness of power", its "complex" plot "masterfully intercuts" two stories separated by a half-century into a "taut", "heartbreaking tale of innocence lost", and though "never overshadowing its big brother", it just might be "even more subtle and sublime"; most chilling moment: the "kiss between Michael and Fredo."

### Godfather Part III, The
`16` `18` `16` `21`

*1990. Directed by Francis Ford Coppola. With Al Pacino, Diane Keaton, Talia Shire, Andy Garcia. 161 minutes. Rated R.*

"Conspiracy, mayhem, opera, revenge": the "prime American" crime "saga" concludes with this "flawed" but "watchable" sequel as Pacino's don Michael aims to take the Corleones legit, despite beefs from both the old guard and his own clan; though it's a "must-see" for diehards, some say the "forced" plotting and "miscasting" ("two words: Sofia Coppola") are a "disgrace to the Family"; in short, it doesn't fill the "enormous shoes" of I and II.

### Gods and Monsters ✉
`23` `27` `23` `22`

*1998. Directed by Bill Condon. With Ian McKellen, Brendan Fraser, Lynn Redgrave. 105 minutes. Rated R.*

McKellen's "brilliant" performance is the backbone of this "innovative biopic" detailing an "encounter between a hedge clipper and a has-been" moviemaker that's based on the life of 1930s "gay director" James Whale; partisans point to the Oscar-winning script as proof of why "indie films are such a delight."

### Gods Must Be Crazy, The Ⓤ
`22` `17` `23` `18`

*1981. Directed by Jamie Uys. With Marius Weyers, Sandra Prinsloo, N!xau. 109 minutes. Rated PG.*

"Consumerism meets primitive African bushmen" when a Coke bottle "falls out of the sky" in this "cult" "culture-clash" comedy that "proves you don't need a big Hollywood budget" to be "original and witty"; despite bare-bones production and middling acting, this "diamond in the rough" still exhibits "universal appeal" thanks to "creative" ideas and "more sight gags than the Marx Brothers."

### Godzilla ◑Ⓤ
`16` `10` `16` `14`

*1956. Directed by Terry Morse, Ishiro Honda. With Raymond Burr, Takashi Shimura. 80 minutes. Not Rated.*

The menace of the atom age hovers over this sci-fi "classic" about a colossal, radiation-spawned lizard who rises up to become the "prototypical city-destroying" beast, doing the "monster mash" through a model-train-gauge Tokyo; "laugh if you want" at the "camp-to-the-max" "Japanese footage" (with "Burr spliced in"), but the "bleak, creepy" A-bomb "echoes" throughout still have a "hold over our imaginations."

### Going My Way ✉◑
∇ `21` `19` `21` `18`

*1944. Directed by Leo McCarey. With Bing Crosby, Barry Fitzgerald, Risë Stevens. 126 minutes. Not Rated.*

"Sing along with Bing" in this "hokey but pleasant" musical drama showcasing Crosby "at his best" as a "popular priest" with heavenly pipes who converts a parish house choir to his feel-good philosophy; though multiple Oscars came its way, it looks "very dated" now since they "stopped making" this brand of "engaging schmaltz" "long ago."

### GoldenEye
19 | 19 | 19 | 23

*1995. Directed by Martin Campbell. With Pierce Brosnan, Sean Bean, Famke Janssen. 130 minutes. Rated PG-13.*
"Born to play the part" of the "never-fazed secret agent", Brosnan brings the 007 "franchise" "back from the dead" with a "suave" turn opposite Janssen's "great villainess" in this "modern Bond" flick; though the "convoluted storyline" about globe-busting weaponry in post-Soviet Russia is a "little clunky", overall it "gets the job done" with "outstanding action", "amazing special effects" and a "refreshing lack of hokeyness."

### Goldfinger
26 | 23 | 25 | 25

*1964. Directed by Guy Hamilton. With Sean Connery, Honor Blackman, Gert Frobe. 112 minutes. Rated PG.*
Rated the Top 007 picture in this *Survey*, this "classic" has it all: "formidable villains", the "coolest gadgets", an "out-of-this-world", "robbing-Fort-Knox" plot, a "fabulous theme song" "belted out by Shirley Bassey" and perhaps the "best-named" babe of them all, the one-and-only "Pussy Galore"; most memorable exchange: "do you expect me to talk? – no, Mr. Bond, I expect you to *die!*"

### Gold Rush, The ◑
▽ 28 | 28 | 26 | 27

*1925. Directed by Charles Chaplin. With Charles Chaplin, Mack Swain. 82 minutes. Not Rated.*
Chaplin's "amazing talent" (as a writer, director and actor) is evident in this "brilliant" silent flicker, featuring the Little Tramp as a prospector "fighting the elements in the Klondike" and "overcoming all hurdles to get the girl" – and the gold; rife with "classic sequences" (the "bread-roll dance", the boiled "shoe for dinner", the cabin teetering on the edge of a cliff), it doesn't need dialogue "to evoke both laughter and pathos" – indeed, over 80 years later, many report a "lasting emotional impact."

### GONE WITH THE WIND ✉
28 | 27 | 27 | 29

*1939. Directed by Victor Fleming. With Clark Gable, Vivien Leigh, Leslie Howard, Olivia de Havilland, Hattie McDaniel, Butterfly McQueen. 238 minutes. Rated G.*
A bona fide piece of "American pop culture", this Civil War melodrama based on Margaret Mitchell's "beloved" book is a "timeless", "sweeping" saga of love and loss in dwindling Dixieland; frankly, legions of admirers "do give a damn", rating it an "epic with a capital E" for its incredibly "beautiful production", "amazing" costumes and "perfect cast", especially Gable's "dashing" Rhett and Leigh's "performance of a lifetime" as the "feisty", "fiddle-dee-deeing" Scarlett; sure, it's a "long sit", yet in the end this "gorgeous triumph" "still thrills."

### Goodbye, Columbus
19 | 19 | 20 | 19

*1969. Directed by Larry Peerce. With Richard Benjamin, Ali MacGraw, Jack Klugman. 102 minutes. Rated PG.*
Based on Philip Roth's once-provocative novella, this frank romantic comedy "might seem dated" now, but nostalgists remember its "good performances", especially MacGraw's tour-

de-force turn as a "crush"-worthy "Jewish princess"; foes say that it "should have been better", considering the source material.

### Goodbye Girl, The ✉     21 | 23 | 20 | 20

*1977. Directed by Herbert Ross. With Richard Dreyfuss, Marsha Mason, Paul Benedict. 110 minutes. Rated PG.*

"Exactly what a romantic comedy should be", this "feel-good movie" is about a "likable", lovelorn single mom forced to share an apartment with an unlikable, "lovable actor"; one of "Neil Simon's best" screenplays, this surprise hit garnered a clutch of Oscar nominations and won one for Dreyfuss' "charismatic" turn.

### Goodbye, Mr. Chips ✉◐     ▽ 25 | 25 | 25 | 22

*1939. Directed by Sam Wood. With Robert Donat, Greer Garson, Paul Henreid. 114 minutes. Not Rated.*

More proof for the theory that "1939 was the best film year ever", this "touching" tale depicting 40 years in the life of everyone's "favorite" British schoolmaster is an unabashedly "sentimental story that will leave nary an eye dry"; credit "wonderful turns" from Garson (in her screen debut) and Donat (who copped an Oscar) for making this "classic" "withstand the test of time."

### GOODFELLAS     27 | 27 | 26 | 25

*1990. Directed by Martin Scorsese. With Robert De Niro, Ray Liotta, Joe Pesci. 146 minutes. Rated R.*

"Not for the faint of heart", "mob-master" Scorsese's "harrowing modern gangster" classic careens from "hysterically funny to terrifyingly violent" owing to an "electrifying" screenplay based on the true story of "'made' guys and greed" that reveals "mobsters as human beings" – albeit "vicious and heartless" ones; "beautiful lensing" and "stellar performances" make this one boil with "brutal power."

### Good Morning, Vietnam     22 | 24 | 22 | 22

*1987. Directed by Barry Levinson. With Robin Williams, Forest Whitaker, Bruno Kirby. 119 minutes. Rated R.*

Get a "different perspective on the Vietnam war" from this "bittersweet" tale of an army radio DJ in Saigon that "strikes just the right balance between comedy and drama", capturing the "reality" while still provoking beaucoup "laughs"; Williams "at his manic best" not only supplies the expected "hilarious ad-libbing" but shows off some "impressive acting skills" too.

### Good, the Bad and the Ugly, The     24 | 21 | 23 | 23

*1967. Directed by Sergio Leone. With Clint Eastwood, Lee Van Cleef, Eli Wallach. 161 minutes. Rated R.*

A "delicious spaghetti Western" drenched in "tasty dramatic marinara sauce", this Clint-essential "Man-With-No-Name" oater about a trio of Civil War–era gunmen battling over Confederate treasure is a "true classic"; sure, Eastwood's "penetrating glare" is "hypnotic", but some say Wallach "steals the show" by injecting some "subtle comedy" into the mix, while composer Ennio Morricone's "memorable score" will "stick in your head for days."

### Good Will Hunting ✉     24 | 25 | 24 | 22

*1997. Directed by Gus Van Sant. With Robin Williams, Matt Damon, Ben Affleck. 126 minutes. Rated R.*

Written by the "then-unknown" team of Damon and Affleck, this "intelligent" drama is built on an "uplifting", "powerful" screenplay about a "troubled petty criminal" who's coincidentally a "brilliant math genius"; its "searing yet subtle" performances include an Oscar-winning turn from Williams at his "most moving", and though the ill-willed badmouth it as "predictable", overall most folks "like them apples."

### Goonies, The
23 | 19 | 23 | 21

*1985. Directed by Richard Donner. With Sean Astin, Josh Brolin, Corey Feldman. 114 minutes. Rated PG.*
One of the "best kids' adventures ever", this "smart, finely crafted" "family movie" about a gang of "pre-teen treasure hunters" who wield "go-go gadgets" and thwart bad guys is a fun "roller-coaster ride" "for all ages" (and a bona fide "nostalgia" trip for "Gen-Xers"); ok, it may have "some flaws", but at least it "doesn't take itself too seriously."

### Gorillas in the Mist
19 | 21 | 20 | 21

*1988. Directed by Michael Apted. With Sigourney Weaver, Bryan Brown, Julie Harris. 129 minutes. Rated PG-13.*
"African jungles" supply the "beautiful setting" in this bio of primatologist Dian Fossey, the story of a complex woman who abandons humanity in favor of a group of endangered mountain gorillas; Weaver delivers a "great performance", the special effects blend real and artificial apes seamlessly and the "ending will stay with you."

### Gosford Park ✉
23 | 27 | 21 | 25

*2001. Directed by Robert Altman. With Clive Owen, Alan Bates, Maggie Smith, Helen Mirren, Kristin Scott Thomas. 137 minutes. Rated R.*
"Agatha Christie meets *Upstairs, Downstairs*" in this "jolly good show" of a "whodunit" that's an "insightful", "behind-the-scenes skewering of the British class system" set in a "'30s country estate"; "one of Altman's best", it boasts "rich atmosphere", "scintillating dialogue" and a "bloody great" ensemble cast all "acting up a storm", and if contrarians complain about its "convoluted", "hard-to-follow" plot, fans claim it "gets better every time you see it."

### GRADUATE, THE ✉
27 | 27 | 26 | 24

*1967. Directed by Mike Nichols. With Dustin Hoffman, Anne Bancroft, Katharine Ross. 105 minutes. Rated PG.*
*The* "benchmark coming-of-age comedy", this "knowing" look at a "confused young man" and his "older seductress" is the "definitive '60s alienation" flick and "somehow never ages"; credit its "witty script", Mike Nichols' "ahead-of-its-time direction", a "groovy" Simon-and-Garfunkel soundtrack and "superb" turns from the "fab" Hoffman and the "unforgettable" Bancroft as – "koo-koo-ka-choo" – Mrs. Robinson; best word: "plastics."

### Grand Canyon
18 | 21 | 18 | 18

*1991. Directed by Lawrence Kasdan. With Danny Glover, Kevin Kline, Steve Martin, Mary McDonnell. 134 minutes. Rated R.*
In this ambitious "meaning-of-life" drama, director Kasdan brings together a group of "average people leading average lives" to tell some "extraordinary stories" about "destiny and hope"; though some find the "fragmented", "confusing" result too "out there", most allow that this "surprisingly moving" moving picture "just misses being great."

### Grand Hotel ✉◑     ▽ 24 | 25 | 22 | 25

*1932. Directed by Edmund Goulding. With Greta Garbo, John Barrymore, Joan Crawford, Lionel Barrymore. 112 minutes. Not Rated.*

"Intertwined lives" are the basis of this star-studded "early MGM talkie", one of the first multicharacter dramas set in a hotel; in addition to its "sumptuous" production and "literate" screenplay, it's endured thanks to a "brilliant" cast, particularly an "amazing Crawford", the "show-stealing" Barrymores and the "breathtaking Garbo", who utters her most famous line here: "I vant to be alone."

### GRAND ILLUSION ◑🄵     28 | 28 | 27 | 26

*1938. Directed by Jean Renoir. With Jean Gabin, Erich von Stroheim, Pierre Fresnay. 114 minutes. Not Rated.*

"It's no illusion": this "compelling" WWI "masterpiece" has "inspired generations" with its "crushing portrayal of the futility of war" and is "still as powerful as ever"; director Renoir "shows how it should be done" in this "ahead-of-its-time" picture that's on "everyone's greatest list" simply because it "touches on every human emotion."

### GRAPES OF WRATH, THE ✉◑     28 | 28 | 28 | 25

*1940. Directed by John Ford. With Henry Fonda, Jane Darwell, John Carradine. 128 minutes. Not Rated.*

"Every frame is a work of art" in this "faithful rendition" of Steinbeck's "eloquent" novel about dispossessed Depression-era farmers living through "desperate" times; quite possibly "Ford's best", it's a "classic for a reason" and "ranks high on the list of great American films" as an "important statement about life", the "depth of man's sorrow and the zenith of man's spirit."

### Grease ⑪     23 | 19 | 21 | 23

*1978. Directed by Randal Kleiser. With John Travolta, Olivia Newton-John, Stockard Channing. 110 minutes. Rated PG.*

"Fun" is the word for this "campy" comedy "classic", a "high-energy" "adaptation of the Broadway musical" that's a "'70s take on a "hokey '50s" story enacted by some of the "oldest high-school students ever"; still, the "hunky Travolta" and "stunning Newton-John" "light up the screen", and the "slick production" numbers are so "irresistible" that "cult followers" watch this "guilty pleasure" "over and over."

### Great Dictator, The ◑     26 | 27 | 25 | 23

*1940. Directed by Charles Chaplin. With Charles Chaplin, Jack Oakie, Paulette Goddard. 124 minutes. Not Rated.*

The normally "silent Chaplin" "fearlessly" takes "aim at Hitler" in this rare talkie, a "scathing satire of fascist tyranny" in which he "plays two roles": a Jewish barber and "rabid" dictator Adenoid Hynkel, a "brilliant parody" of Der Führer; although "overly sentimental" and "preachy" to some, most find this "masterpiece of physical comedy" "thought-provoking and perpetually relevant."

### GREAT ESCAPE, THE     27 | 26 | 27 | 26

*1963. Directed by John Sturges. With Steve McQueen, James Garner, Richard Attenborough. 169 minutes. Not Rated.*

"Guy movies don't get any better" than this "absorbing" "prison break" flick "based on a true escape" from a WWII "German war camp"; featuring McQueen backed up by an "all-star" ensemble, it also boasts "excellent writing", a "hummable score" and "flawless action" scenes, including the "best motorcycle scene ever filmed"; though on the "long" side, it's "worth every minute."

### Great Race, The
20 | 18 | 20 | 20

*1965. Directed by Blake Edwards. With Jack Lemmon, Tony Curtis, Natalie Wood, Peter Falk. 150 minutes. Not Rated.*

Director Edwards revs up the engines in this "kitschy" "family" comedy about a turn-of-the-century auto race from NY to Paris, with plenty of "must-see" settings along the way; a tip-top cast supplies "over-the-top" performances, but the pièce de résistance is the "best pie fight in movie history"; in a word, it's a "hoot."

### Great Santini, The
22 | 27 | 21 | 21

*1979. Directed by Lewis John Carlino. With Robert Duvall, Blythe Danner, Michael O'Keefe. 115 minutes. Rated PG.*

"Adapted from the painful Pat Conroy novel", this intense "dissection" of a "dysfunctional family" offers a "look inside the mind" of a "domineering marine – "outstandingly" played by the "frighteningly good Duvall" – who treats his wife and kids like soldiers under his command; you'll "love him or hate him (or maybe both)", but in any event his "imperfect life" will "stay with you."

### Greed ❍∅
▽ 28 | 27 | 27 | 29

*1925. Directed by Erich Von Stroheim. With Gibson Gowland, ZaSu Pitts, Jean Hersholt. 140 minutes. Not Rated.*

Originally "exceedingly long" (clocking in at 10 hours), this silent "tour de force" from Erich von Stroheim is famous for the studio's "hatchet job" to trim it to a commercially viable length; still, even in a "truncated" form, this "dark masterpiece" about a down-and-out dentist and his lottery-winning wife remains an exercise in "gritty realism", right down to that "stunning finale" in Death Valley.

### Green Mile, The
23 | 25 | 23 | 24

*1999. Directed by Frank Darabont. With Tom Hanks, David Morse, Michael Clarke Duncan. 188 minutes. Rated R.*

Stephen King's "harrowing" serial novel is now "wonderfully translated to the screen" in this "disturbing drama" that "tugs at your emotions" with its "touching depiction" of "humanity at its best and worst"; despite "fine acting", this "very long" Mile makes some "wish it was an hour shorter."

### Gremlins ⓤ
19 | 14 | 20 | 20

*1984. Directed by Joe Dante. With Zach Galligan, Phoebe Cates, Hoyt Axton. 106 minutes. Rated PG.*

This "black comedy" features a "cuddly", "too-cute-for-words" pet who breeds "scary" offspring when exposed to bright light, water or being "fed after midnight"; although "lots of fun", some parents warn "proceed with caution": it has a "dark side", i.e. those "mean-spirited", "nightmare"-inducing gremlins who are too violent for smaller fry.

### Greystoke: The Legend of Tarzan
15 | 14 | 17 | 19

*1984. Directed by Hugh Hudson. With Christopher Lambert, Andie MacDowell, Ian Holm. 130 minutes. Rated PG.*

Don't expect much monkey business in this "lush" drama, a "compelling retelling" of Edgar Rice Burroughs' ape-man tale that adds class-system critique and "animal welfare overtones" to the mix; there's plenty of "gorgeous" scenery as Lambert's

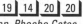

jungle-bred hunk is introduced into English aristocracy, but even though it's "pretty to look at", many see an "overlong mess."

### Grifters, The          22 | 26 | 23 | 21
*1990. Directed by Stephen Frears. With Anjelica Huston, John Cusack, Annette Bening. 119 minutes. Rated R.*
Despite "soulless characters" and a "cynical" theme, this very "adult" piece of "hard-core film noir" is a "first-class" study of "lowlife culture" (the "twisted" plot concerns a "mommy and her long-lost son who are reunited" only to "go down in flames"); while the "film gels" around the "powerhouse work of all three leads", some say the "real star" is "Donald Westlake's superb" script.

### Groundhog Day          22 | 20 | 24 | 20
*1993. Directed by Harold Ramis. With Bill Murray, Andie MacDowell, Chris Elliott. 101 minutes. Rated PG.*
An "intelligent existential romp", this "literate comedy" has an "original concept": a "jerk" is forced to "live the same day over and over until he gets it right" and "becomes a lovable man"; ok, it's a "one-joke premise" that gets "tedious", but for most it "works like a charm" thanks to the "hilarious" Murray, who exchanges his "usual smart-ass" persona for something "surprisingly deep."

### Grumpy Old Men ⓤ          21 | 24 | 20 | 20
*1993. Directed by Donald Petrie. With Jack Lemmon, Walter Matthau, Ann-Margret. 103 minutes. Rated PG-13.*
Though "made for the *Murder, She Wrote*" set, this "lighthearted comedy" works for both "young and old", reuniting the "classic Matthau-and-Lemmon" team playing retired Minnesotans "vying for the affections" of a "comely" new neighbor (the "not-hard-to-watch Ann-Margret"); sure, "we've seen it all before", but these "well-loved icons" still provoke a "ton of laughs."

### Guess Who's Coming to Dinner ✉          25 | 27 | 25 | 22
*1967. Directed by Stanley Kramer. With Spencer Tracy, Sidney Poitier, Katharine Hepburn. 108 minutes. Not Rated.*
"Daring for its day", this '60s "commentary on race relations" is the "final film of Hollywood's finest couple", "class acts Hepburn and Tracy", at their most "powerful"; sure, its "controversial subject" of "interracial marriage" might seem a bit "stagy" and "dated" now, but its "poignant and charming" treatment assures that the "issues remain" relevant.

### Gunfight at the O.K. Corral          20 | 21 | 20 | 21
*1957. Directed by John Sturges. With Burt Lancaster, Kirk Douglas, Rhonda Fleming. 122 minutes. Not Rated.*
Always "entertaining", this Western recounts the famed 19th-century shoot-out between rival gangs in Tombstone, AZ; despite two Hollywood icons "playing off each other wonderfully" – the rugged Lancaster and the cleft-chinned Douglas – foes fume this "too-long" production doesn't "move the way it should."

### Gunga Din ◖          25 | 24 | 25 | 24
*1939. Directed by George Stevens. With Cary Grant, Victor McLaglen, Douglas Fairbanks Jr. 117 minutes. Not Rated.*
This "rousing adventure flick" from "Hollywood's golden age" recounts the "golden age of the British Empire" via the "story of three soldiers in imperial India" and the titular native lad who befriends them; some snappy "byplay between Grant, McLaglen

and Fairbanks" makes it a "buddy film" prototype, though a few are troubled by the "superior", "racist attitude" of the colonialists.

### Guns of Navarone, The ⑪
23 | 22 | 24 | 23

*1961. Directed by J. Lee Thompson. With Gregory Peck, David Niven, Anthony Quinn. 158 minutes. Rated PG.*
"Even people who hate war movies love" this "star-studded" production about WWII Allied commandos plotting to destroy Nazi artillery; "pounding" suspense and a "splendid cast" put this action-adventurer "head-and-shoulders above" the rest – and that "climactic sequence" will have you "holding your breath."

### Guys and Dolls
24 | 21 | 24 | 24

*1955. Directed by Joseph L. Mankiewicz. With Marlon Brando, Jean Simmons, Frank Sinatra. 150 minutes. Not Rated.*
"Brando sings!" in this "colorful" musical rendition of the "Damon Runyon stories" about "gamblers, evangelists" and racehorses, all dolled up into one "heavyweight" extravaganza set around Times Square, rife with "catchy tunes" and "showstopping" numbers; foes think Marlon's "miscast", pointing to his "bored", "sexually smug" rendition of 'Luck Be a Lady.'

### Gypsy
20 | 21 | 22 | 22

*1962. Directed by Mervyn LeRoy. With Rosalind Russell, Natalie Wood, Karl Malden. 143 minutes. Not Rated.*
"Stripper Gypsy Rose Lee's life" is the basis of this "terrific" musical biography about the "original backstage mother" and her "passionate" efforts to mold her kids into stars; ok, it's "kind of windy" and Wood (in the title role) "doesn't really strip", while the "brilliant miscasting" of a "shrill" Russell leads many to say the part "should have gone to Ethel Merman", who delivered the "real goods" on Broadway.

### Hair
20 | 18 | 21 | 21

*1979. Directed by Milos Forman. With John Savage, Treat Williams, Beverly D'Angelo. 121 minutes. Rated PG.*
The groovy "Broadway musical" that "defined the psychedelic '60s" gets a "terrific" big-screen transfer in this story of a draftee bound for Vietnam dallying with Central Park hippies; even though "Treat's a treat" in a role that "epitomizes the loving craziness" of the time, some say the "flower-child imagery" is "sadly faded."

### Hairspray
19 | 17 | 18 | 18

*1988. Directed by John Waters. With Divine, Ricki Lake, Sonny Bono, Ruth Brown, Debbie Harry. 91 minutes. Rated PG.*
"Grab a can of Aquanet" and get ready to "shake a tailfeather": this "hilariously campy" story of a "fat girl who lives to dance" is underground director Waters' "mainstream" ode to his "beloved Baltimore" in the '60s and his "most family-friendly" flick (it even "unflinchingly looks at racism"); though "Divine's divine" and the "absolutely perfect" Lake wears her "big hair" well, "deviant" devotees hedge it's "kind of tame, but still fun."

### Halloween ⑪
22 | 16 | 20 | 19

*1978. Directed by John Carpenter. With Donald Pleasence, Jamie Lee Curtis. 91 minutes. Rated R.*
"Changing the face of horror movies forever", this "almost bloodless chiller shows that gore doesn't equal terror" as it depicts a "masked psycho stalker" who preys on "rowdy teens";

despite "zero-budget" production values and so-so acting (but mighty "great screaming by Jamie Lee"), this "influential" "slasher" flick spawned a slew of sequels and "still holds up."

### Hamlet ⊠◑     ▽ 26 | 28 | 28 | 23
*1948. Directed by Laurence Olivier. With Laurence Olivier, Eileen Herlie, Basil Sydney, Jean Simmons. 153 minutes. Not Rated.*
"Probably the best Shakespeare film ever made with the greatest Shakespearean actor", this Oscar-winning epic is a "brilliantly visual" take on the Bard's "greatest drama"; director/producer/star Olivier does Hamlet as a blond "as only he can do it", and if the action scenes are less vivid than in other versions, overall it's still considered "unfailingly great."

### Hamlet     24 | 26 | 26 | 25
*1996. Directed by Kenneth Branagh. With Kenneth Branagh, Julie Christie, Derek Jacobi. 242 minutes. Rated PG-13.*
This oft-done (maybe "overdone") Shakespearean tragedy gets "expansive" treatment from "modern master" Branagh, who uses the Bard's full text, resulting in a "four-hour adaptation"; though "engrossing, suspenseful" and "beautifully reimagined" to fans, those who say "enough already" call it "*too much* of a good thing."

### Hand That Rocks the Cradle, The     16 | 16 | 17 | 16
*1992. Directed by Curtis Hanson. With Annabella Sciorra, Rebecca De Mornay. 110 minutes. Rated R.*
It's De Mornay who "rocks" as the "world's most warped nanny" nursing a "psychopathic" grudge in this "well-done" thriller, a "real nail-biter" despite "huge plot holes" and "overwrought" situations; the ultimate in "working-mom paranoia", it delivers a "chilling" moral: "always check references!"

### Hannah and Her Sisters ⊠     24 | 25 | 23 | 23
*1986. Directed by Woody Allen. With Mia Farrow, Barbara Hershey, Dianne Wiest. 103 minutes. Rated PG-13.*
A "nice balance of jokes and philosophy", this "pertinent" romantic comedy about three sisters and their "struggle with the meaning of life" "brims with so much intelligence and heart" that many call it "Allen's most life-affirming" picture; featuring "all-around wonderful" acting, it's a "valentine" to "NYers in all their neurotic glory" that manages to "convey a message without tempering the laugh-out-loud humor."

### Hannibal ⑪     15 | 21 | 14 | 19
*2001. Directed by Ridley Scott. With Anthony Hopkins, Julianne Moore, Ray Liotta, Gary Oldman. 131 minutes. Rated R.*
Sure, it's "not the same without Jodie", but this "grisly" *Silence of the Lambs* sequel lets the "fascinating" Hopkins chew the scenery as a refined psycho dreaded for his "wry comments" – "bon appétit!" – and "unspeakable" cravings; buckets of "baroque gore" help distract from the "inferior story", yet many say it "crosses the line" into a "pointless ickfest" with a "tasteless (no pun intended)" climax better suited to "*Fear Factor*."

### Happiness     23 | 25 | 22 | 20
*1998. Directed by Todd Solondz. With Jane Adams, Jon Lovitz, Philip Seymour Hoffman. 134 minutes. Not Rated.*
Forget the "truly ironic title": this extremely "dark" "feel-bad" comedy is "*American Beauty* with a lot more acid" and so

"unrelentingly bleak" that it's "not for the faint of heart"; given some "taboo subject matter", the unhappy call it a "sicko train wreck" that's "probably the worst first-date movie ever", but fans tout its "brave" if "perverted" take on the "middle classes."

### Hard Day's Night, A ◑
24 | 19 | 19 | 24

*1964. Directed by Richard Lester. With the Beatles, Wilfrid Brambell. 87 minutes. Rated G.*
"Before there was MTV", there was this "best rock movie ever", an "ahead-of-its-time" "groundbreaker" shot with documentary-style "quick edits" that brilliantly convey the "lunacy" and the "pure joy of Beatlemania" in the "days of innocence"; it's "still a film of wonder", and, of course, there's that "incredible soundtrack" of "Fab Four" classics.

### Harold and Maude
25 | 25 | 25 | 21

*1972. Directed by Hal Ashby. With Ruth Gordon, Bud Cort, Vivian Pickles. 91 minutes. Rated PG.*
Ok, it "starts with a hanging", but this "counterculture cult classic gets funnier", managing to be both "morbid" and "absurdly wonderful" in its "May-December story" of a "death-obsessed" kid who finds love with a "free-spirited old lady"; while "not for everyone", this "original" features a "phenomenal" Gordon and a "gem" of a "Cat Stevens soundtrack."

### Harry Potter
### and the Chamber of Secrets Ⅱ
24 | 22 | 24 | 27

*2002. Directed by Chris Columbus. With Daniel Radcliffe, Rupert Grint, Emma Watson, Kenneth Branagh. 161 minutes. Rated PG.*
This "rare spectacular sequel" is "much darker and scarier than the first", but "fantastic fantasy fare for the family" nevertheless and an "excellent adaptation of the book" "within the limits of time"; the special effects are "amazing", of course, and "the young stars have grown into their roles and do an even better job" this time around, but fans who "can't wait for the next one" admit that "Dumbledore is going to be tough to replace."

### Harry Potter
### and the Prisoner of Azkaban
24 | 22 | 25 | 27

*2004. Directed by Alfonso Cuarón. With Daniel Radcliffe, Rupert Grint, Emma Watson. 141 minutes. Rated PG.*
Rowling's third installment in the "beloved" series of children's books about a triumvirate of young wizards is "as wonderful and fanciful as the others", with particularly "fabulous production values"; featuring just the "right touch of menace and darkness" to win over "older moviegoers", it has appeal for all ages, but since the "kids are growing up", some wonder "will Harry have a beard in the next one?"

### Harry Potter
### and the Sorcerer's Stone Ⅱ
24 | 23 | 25 | 27

*2001. Directed by Chris Columbus. With Daniel Radcliffe, Rupert Grint, Emma Watson. 152 minutes. Rated PG.*
It's "Hogwarts brought to magic life": this "reverent" screen adaptation of the ultra-"popular children's book" about a school for young witches and wizards is simply "spellbinding" – nothing less than a "21st-century *Wizard of Oz*"; fans zero in on the "eye-popping special effects", "outstanding" ensemble cast and "perfect" scenario that "gets every character right", "just like

you imagined them"; still, the "length and scariness factors" might mean it's "wasted on little kids."

### Harvey ◑   26 | 27 | 25 | 22
*1950. Directed by Henry Koster. With James Stewart, Josephine Hull, Peggy Dow. 104 minutes. Not Rated.*
"So sweet and genuine that it's never become dated", this ever "classic comedy" concerning an "adorable sot" and his "imaginary six-foot rabbit" is such an "enchanting, grown-up fairy tale" that the "word 'heartwarming' was coined for it"; "delightful performances" elevate this "feel-good" flick into the "can't-miss" category.

### Hatari!   21 | 17 | 18 | 23
*1962. Directed by Howard Hawks. With John Wayne, Hardy Kruger, Elsa Martinelli. 157 minutes. Not Rated.*
"Great African location shots" and a "fab" Henry Mancini score make this "somewhat forgotten" action/adventurer "better than its reputation" (even if its rather "dull" plot about "wild animal" trappers lacks "political correctness"); though it's a "lesser" vehicle for the "bigger-than-life" Wayne, at least the "beautiful photography" supplies some real "entertainment value."

### Heat   22 | 25 | 19 | 22
*1995. Directed by Michael Mann. With Al Pacino, Robert De Niro, Val Kilmer, Jon Voight. 171 minutes. Rated R.*
"Both the cop and robber are heroes" in this "operatic" crime epic, a "star-studded killfest" that's cinematically historic, since "legends" Pacino and De Niro are "finally on-screen together" (their "face-to-face" "coffeehouse scene" is a "knockout"); yet "despite a captivating cast and storyline", "they could have done a better job in the editing room" – "there's a perfect two-hour movie" lurking in this sprawling, 171-minute marathon.

### Heathers   21 | 19 | 22 | 18
*1989. Directed by Micheal Lehmann. With Winona Ryder, Christian Slater, Shannen Doherty. 102 minutes. Rated R.*
The "pinnacle of '80s dark humor" – maybe even "before its time" – this "out-there" "black comedy" is "twisted" and "proud of it" as it provides an important lesson in "teen peer pressure": "popularity can kill"; though "not for everyone" (especially the "lighthearted or light-stomached"), it did "launch Slater's and Ryder's careers", and the "deliciously biting dialogue is full of comebacks you wish you'd thought of."

### Heaven Can Wait   21 | 19 | 22 | 19
*1978. Directed by Warren Beatty, Buck Henry. With Warren Beatty, Julie Christie, Dyan Cannon. 101 minutes. Rated PG.*
An "enjoyable remake of *Here Comes Mr. Jordan*", this comedy-fantasy mix of true love and the afterlife is kind of "far-fetched, but it works"; sure, "Buck Henry's script is as good as the original" and a "likable" Beatty at least "tries to be sincere", but the "hysterical" Charles Grodin "steals the show."

### Heavenly Creatures   24 | 25 | 26 | 24
*1994. Directed by Peter Jackson. With Kate Winslet, Melanie Lynskey, Clive Merrison. 99 minutes. Rated R.*
One part "fantasy", one part "true crime", this "absolutely riveting" drama about two teens plotting "matricide" is a "surreal", "haunting descent into the imagination" as it details an

"attachment that turns deadly"; Winslet's "career-launching" performance is so "astounding" that some say "*this* is the movie" that the *Titanic* star "should have gotten an Oscar nomination for."

### Heavy Metal ⓤ                    20 | – | – | 21

*1981. Directed by Gerald Potterton. Animated. 86 minutes. Rated R.*
"Based on the sci-fi comic book of the same name", this "cult" cartoon "classic" is a novel "departure for animation", given its "adult-oriented" content and "heavy metal" score; some shrug it "wavers between entertaining and dull", since this "strung-together anthology" of hard-rock-flavored "vignettes" is more than "a little choppy" (it "makes no sense without alcohol").

### Hello, Dolly!                    20 | 19 | 20 | 23

*1969. Directed by Gene Kelly. With Barbra Streisand, Walter Matthau, Michael Crawford. 146 minutes. Rated G.*
This "big, over-the-top" musical concerning a turn-of-the-century matchmaker is a "colorful" romp with all the "beautiful music from the Broadway show"; but goodbye Charlies call it an "overblown spectacle", citing "one of the most unappealing romantic couplings imaginable": a "miscast" Streisand ("who knew Dolly Levi was 25 years old?") playing opposite an "embarrassing" Matthau.

### Help!                    19 | 16 | 15 | 20

*1965. Directed by Richard Lester. With the Beatles, Leo McKern, Eleanor Bron. 90 minutes. Rated G.*
"Sing along with the hits from 1965" that enliven this "zany musical comedy", a "perfectly enjoyable" if "silly John-Paul-George-and-Ringo romp" that's really not much more than a "platform to take advantage of the Beatles' popularity"; still, the "story's ok" ("at least there's a plot this time"), the international "locations are great" and, "of course, the soundtrack is terrific."

### Henry & June                    ▽ 18 | 21 | 19 | 19

*1990. Directed by Philip Kaufman. With Fred Ward, Uma Thurman, Maria de Medeiros. 136 minutes. Rated NC-17.*
"Not for the prudish", this "lushly produced" drama explores the libidinous "literary underbelly" of Paris in the '30s, where burgeoning bohemian scribe Henry Miller, his alluring wife June and their groupie Anaïs Nin indulge in a steamy triangle fueled by "curiosity and lust"; an ultra-"erotic lesbian love scene" helped tag this "perverse gem" with the "first NC-17 rating" ever.

### Henry V                    26 | 28 | 27 | 26

*1989. Directed by Kenneth Branagh. With Kenneth Branagh, Derek Jacobi. 137 minutes. Rated PG-13.*
"Brush up on your Shakespeare" via this "revisionist" adaptation of the Bard's "difficult" history play about an English monarch at war with France; "both spectacular and approachable", it makes the 17th-century dialogue "completely understandable to modern ears", and first-time director Branagh's "lavish, lusty" brio is so "brilliant" that many acolytes ask "Sir Laurence who?"

### Hercules                    17 | – | 17 | 21

*1997. Directed by Ron Clements, John Musker. Animated. 92 minutes. Rated G.*
To "Disney-fy" Greek mythology risks the wrath of Zeus, but this "witty", "well-told" animated saga is "elevated" Olympusward by a "strong voice cast", "great songs" and enough "jokes for

adults" to make for "stylish family fun" with "an edge"; like its brawny hero fending off superhuman foes, it "stands up well" and marks a "departure from the usual formula."

### Hero 🅕
25 | 22 | 23 | 27

*2004. Directed by Zhang Yimou. With Jet Li, Zhang Ziyi. 99 minutes. Rated PG-13.*
"Not your typical martial-arts movie", this Chinese "homage to *Rashomon*" told from multiple perspectives in "non-linear" format explodes with "luscious visuals", "chop-'em-up kung fu" fight scenes and even some "noble" performances ("Jet Li can act!"); still, while fans see a "thought-provoking" epic about "politics, loyalty and truth", a few Sinophobes can't help but read a "propaganda" message in the "nationalist storyline."

### Hidalgo
20 | 21 | 21 | 23

*2004. Directed by Joe Johnston. With Viggo Mortensen, Omar Sharif. 136 minutes. Rated PG-13.*
"*The Little Engine That Could* meets *Lawrence of Arabia*" with "not quite epic" results in this "old-fashioned" story about an "underdog" cowboy undertaking a 3,000-mile horse race across the North African desert; while the scenery's "sumptuous" and Viggo's a "god" as the "handsome daredevil hero", neigh-sayers say the plot's "weak" and the running time "a little long."

### High Anxiety ∅
21 | 19 | 19 | 19

*1977. Directed by Mel Brooks. With Mel Brooks, Madeline Kahn, Cloris Leachman. 94 minutes. Rated PG.*
"Hitch would have laughed" at this "totally goofy" comic homage from the "totally insane" Mel Brooks that's a "send-up" of the Hitchcockian oeuvre, particularly *Psycho* and *Vertigo*; only problem is, "you must know the material he's spoofing in order to get the jokes" or else this "silly" picture "doesn't really hang together."

### HIGH NOON ✉◗
28 | 26 | 26 | 25

*1952. Directed by Fred Zinnemann. With Gary Cooper, Grace Kelly, Lloyd Bridges. 85 minutes. Not Rated.*
Voted the "best Western" in this *Survey*, this "tense drama" filmed in "real time" "breaks the mold" by combining all the "grit of the West" with a "strong comment on the McCarthyist '50s" and a touch of "Greek drama" to boot; as a "single-minded sheriff" with "principles", Cooper took home an Oscar, though many admit they're drawn to this "classic" "allegory" for its "theme song" alone; in short, it's "absolutely tops" – nothing else "comes close."

### High Plains Drifter
18 | 19 | 20 | 19

*1972. Directed by Clint Eastwood. With Clint Eastwood, Verna Bloom, Marianna Hill. 105 minutes. Rated R.*
"Perennial badass" Eastwood plays a "violent" "avenging angel" in this "powerful" if by-the-numbers Western in which "everyone gets what they deserve"; connoisseurs say it's Clint's "defining moment", though the less enamored rate it an "acquired taste", "not up to the standard of some of his others."

### High Sierra ◗
▽ 23 | 25 | 23 | 19

*1941. Directed by Raoul Walsh. With Humphrey Bogart, Ida Lupino, Alan Curtis. 100 minutes. Not Rated.*
Hard-boiled with a heart, this "gritty gangster pic" features a sneering Bogie in a "part made for him" as a "bad crook gone

worse" who puts on a "tough" front to cover up the sentimental sap underneath; noir connoisseurs call it "dated but great", heaping high praise on Lupino's incredibly "hot" performance.

### High Society
23 | 22 | 22 | 23

*1956. Directed by Charles Walters. With Bing Crosby, Grace Kelly, Frank Sinatra, Celeste Holm. 107 minutes. Not Rated.*
"What a swell party" is this Cole Porter "musical rendition of *The Philadelphia Story*", a "sophisticated comedy of manners" set in a "Newport mansion" inhabited by some "fantastic talent": a "gorgeous Grace", "swingin' Bing" and "delightful Sinatra"; sure, the original might be "far superior" plotwise, but fans dub this "softer" take the "Tiffany" of the singing-and-dancing genre.

### Hilary and Jackie
21 | 26 | 22 | 21

*1998. Directed by Anand Tucker. With Emily Watson, Rachel Griffiths, David Morrissey. 121 minutes. Rated R.*
"Poignant and touching", this "overlooked" biodrama tells the true story of the prickly "relationship between two sisters", one a cellist who's "battling MS" as well as other "personal" demons; "outstanding lead performances from Watson and Griffiths" lend appeal to more than just "classical music fans", though some say it can be "difficult to watch", given the "tragic" storyline.

### His Girl Friday ◑
26 | 28 | 24 | 22

*1940. Directed by Howard Hawks. With Cary Grant, Rosalind Russell, Ralph Bellamy. 92 minutes. Not Rated.*
"Pay attention" now: the "superfast-moving plot" "comes at you at 100 mph" in this "biting" screwball comedy that's a "wonderful adaptation" of "*The Front Page*"; Grant and Russell "snap and crackle" as a "newspaper editor and star reporter chasing the story of a lifetime – and each other" – and if the "breakneck speed" of this zippy "roller-coaster ride" can be "exhausting", the payoff is "absolute hilarity."

### Hitch
21 | 21 | 20 | 20

*2005. Directed by Andy Tennant. With Will Smith, Eva Mendes, Kevin James. 118 minutes. Rated PG-13.*
A "charismatic" "date doctor" tutoring a "down-on-his-luck guy" on the "NYC singles scene" loses his cool in the face of true love in this "light" romantic comedy; while a tad "trite and silly" for those who disparage the "no-brainer" "Hollywood heart-tugger" ending, it's "no disappointment" for chuckleheads thanks to that "unforgettable dance scene."

### Hoffa
∇ 16 | 22 | 17 | 17

*1992. Directed by Danny DeVito. With Jack Nicholson, Danny DeVito, Armand Assante. 140 minutes. Rated R.*
DeVito's laborious, "uneven" drama delivers a "real dose of reality" as it traces the rise and demise of notorious union boss Jimmy Hoffa, who uses rough justice and mob connections to win the Teamsters their due; though it's "very well-acted and photographed", critics call it an overlong, "flawed" piece of work.

### Holes
23 | 23 | 24 | 22

*2003. Directed by Andrew Davis. With Sigourney Weaver, Jon Voight, Tim Blake Nelson. 117 minutes. Rated PG.*
The "wonderful children's book" about a boy punished for a crime he didn't commit has been "faithfully adapted" into this "excellent

movie for the whole family"; a "creative, interesting story",
"outstanding" performances by "old pros" and "young actors"
alike and an "awesome soundtrack" that will keep "the kids
singing all week" add up to a "highly entertaining" two hours.

### Holiday Inn ◐ — 23 | 20 | 20 | 23

*1942. Directed by Mark Sandrich. With Bing Crosby, Fred Astaire, Marjorie Reynolds. 100 minutes. Not Rated.*
"Crooner Bing" and "hoofer Astaire" are "rivals" in this "lively"
"musical romance" that's chock-full of "Irving Berlin favorites"
but most remembered for introducing 'White Christmas'; sure, the
plot's pretty "lightweight", but at least the songs of this "holiday
bonbon" will "stick in your brain well into the new year."

### Home Alone ⑪ — 19 | 17 | 20 | 19

*1990. Directed by Chris Columbus. With Macaulay Culkin, Joe Pesci, Daniel Stern. 103 minutes. Rated PG.*
"Every parent's nightmare" – and "every child's fantasy" – this
"ultimate sleepover movie" made Culkin a star as a "self-sufficient
kid who defends himself against robbers" after his vacation-
bound family accidentally "leaves him at home"; though its "loony
premise" is "full of sight gags", some warn it can be too "violent"
for smaller fry: "this is Bugs Bunny vs. Yosemite Sam for real."

### Honey, I Shrunk the Kids ⑪ — 16 | 14 | 18 | 19

*1989. Directed by Joe Johnston. With Rick Moranis, Matt Frewer, Marcia Strassman. 101 minutes. Rated PG.*
A "cute", "creative idea" that "grows on you", this "wacky
family" comedy concerns a "friendly mad scientist" dad whose
"experiments go awry" when his kids are zapped down to sub-
pint size; with "inventive" special effects to "overcome lame
acting", it's "always good for some laughs", though most shrink
from the "next two installments."

### Hook — 17 | 18 | 17 | 21

*1991. Directed by Steven Spielberg. With Robin Williams, Dustin Hoffman, Julia Roberts. 144 minutes. Rated PG.*
Presenting "Peter Pan if he grew up", this "clever" '90s "twist"
on the adventure finds Williams' cynical adult Peter activating his
"inner child" for a rematch with Hoffman's "memorable" Hook; if
often a "pleasure to watch", it's also panned as a "bloated", "PC
version" of the fairy tale and "one of Spielberg's rare mistakes."

### Hoop Dreams — 26 | – | 26 | 23

*1994. Directed by Steve James. Documentary. 170 minutes. Rated PG-13.*
"Two young athletes who dream of NBA fame" as a way "to escape
the inner city" are the subjects of this "gritty" documentary, a
"slam-dunk exposé" of "naive boys" that's "quite moving" if a
"tad long"; "superb editing" makes it feel more like a "drama"
than a real-life story, but don't look for a "Hollywood ending": this
one's so "devastatingly real", it just might "break your heart."

### Hoosiers — 23 | 22 | 24 | 19

*1986. Directed by David Anspaugh. With Gene Hackman, Barbara Hershey, Dennis Hopper. 114 minutes. Rated PG.*
A modern-day "David and Goliath on the basketball court", this
"inspirational" "classic of the small-town-team-rises-up genre"
is a "corporate team builder" kind of flick; as the "motivational"
but "down-and-out coach trying to make a comeback in the

boonies", Hackman captures the spirit of "rural" hoops culture and supplies this "underdog story" with some "real heart."

### Horse Feathers ❶
24 | 22 | 20 | 18

*1932. Directed by Norman Z. McLeod. With the Marx Brothers, Thelma Todd. 68 minutes. Not Rated.*
"One of the Marxes' zaniest comedies" showcases the boys in "peak form" in a college setting, in which Groucho is the incoming university president; expect the usual "breezy lunacy" "based on years of vaudeville antics" – especially the "hilarious" "French-farcical wooing of Todd" – and ignore that "abrupt ending."

### Horse Whisperer, The
17 | 19 | 18 | 20

*1998. Directed by Robert Redford. With Robert Redford, Kristin Scott Thomas, Sam Neill. 169 minutes. Rated PG-13.*
"Redford and horses" are "so right" together in this "tearjerker" romance, with Bob taking a "real star turn" as a Montana cowpoke whose way with the "healing process" sweeps city gal Scott Thomas right out of her saddle; it's all "uplifting", "tender" and "lovingly" shot, and if some bridle at the "boring", "interminable" pace, stay awake and you'll "learn a lot about horses."

### HOTEL RWANDA
28 | 28 | 28 | 26

*2004. Directed by Terry George. With Don Cheadle, Sophie Okonedo, Joaquin Phoenix, Nick Nolte. 121 minutes. Rated PG-13.*
A "heartwrenching" reminder of the "horrors" committed during the 1994 Rwandan genocide ("a modern-day Holocaust"), this "true story" of a hotel manager who "helped save 1,200 lives" eschews "preachy" moralizing and overt carnage in order to emphasize the "redemptive" notion that "courage can turn the tide"; the "magnificent" Cheadle and "brilliant" supporting cast "do a great service" to this "important piece of history", inspiring "much hope" that such an "appalling" tragedy "doesn't happen again."

### Hound of the Baskervilles, The ❶
▽ 21 | 21 | 24 | 19

*1939. Directed by Sidney Lanfield. With Basil Rathbone, Nigel Bruce, Richard Greene. 80 minutes. Not Rated.*
Critics call this the "most successful" take on Arthur Conan Doyle's "classic" thriller, featuring Rathbone's "quintessential" Sherlock Holmes sleuthing around an English castle; it's "must" viewing for detective devotees, complete with "campy" ambiance and "over-the-top" emoting.

### Hours, The ✉
25 | 28 | 24 | 25

*2002. Directed by Stephen Daldry. With Nicole Kidman, Julianne Moore, Meryl Streep, Ed Harris. 114 minutes. Rated PG-13.*
There's "no action, only acting" in this "intelligent, challenging" adaptation of the "brilliant" book about three women of different generations whose "not perfect" lives are linked by a Virginia Woolf novel – and the "acting by all three leading ladies" "deserved an Oscar" (Kidman "won by a nose"); "don't watch it if you're in a good mood", however, because it's "hopelessly depressing" and "so slow moving it should have been called *The Days*."

### House of Flying Daggers 🇫
24 | 22 | 21 | 27

*2004. Directed by Zhang Yimou. With Takeshi Kaneshiro, Zhang Ziyi, Andy Lau. 119 minutes. Rated PG-13.*
"Exhilarating fight sequences" and "feast-for-the-eyes" scenery team up with a "tearjerker" story of "star-crossed lovers" in this

"outstanding" Chinese epic from "virtuoso" director Zhang that kicks the martial arts genre to "new heights"; still, visual beauty aside, not everyone's flying high over the kung-fusing plot (with "more twists and turns than the Yangtze River"), ditto the seemingly "interminable" ending.

### House of Games
24 | 23 | 27 | 21

*1987. Directed by David Mamet. With Lindsay Crouse, Joe Mantegna, Lilia Skala. 102 minutes. Rated R.*
"Cold characters and clipped conversations" make this "mind-bending thriller" pure Mamet "at his most manipulative"; its "twisty" con-game plot (something like "*The Sting*," all grown-up") "keeps you guessing", and though the dialogue reminds some critics of "cartoons talking", it's "chilling on many levels", with a "head-spinning" ending that stays with you "long after the movie's over."

### House of Sand and Fog
23 | 27 | 22 | 23

*2003. Directed by Vadim Perelman. With Jennifer Connelly, Ben Kingsley, Shoreh Aghdashloo. 126 minutes. Rated R.*
A "brilliant rendering" of the "moral stand-off" between a "slacker who loses her home" and a "desperate" Iranian who purchases it for his exiled family, this "taut", "heart-wrenching" drama explores "everything that the American dream is – and isn't"; "balanced directing" and "amazingly nuanced performances" by Kingsley, Connelly and Aghdashloo turn this inherently "dour material" into a "gripping", "haunting" tragedy.

### House of Wax
21 | 18 | 21 | 20

*1953. Directed by Andre de Toth. With Vincent Price, Frank Lovejoy, Phyllis Kirk. 90 minutes. Rated PG.*
"Look out for the giant vat of wax!": this "entertaining" "horror melodrama" was one of the first flicks made in 3-D, but modern-day fans say it's "still fun" "even without the glasses"; featuring a "priceless Price", a "chiller"-diller story and "atmospheric", "gaslight-era" settings, it's ever the "stuff of nightmares" and always "spooky."

### Howards End
22 | 26 | 21 | 25

*1992. Directed by James Ivory. With Anthony Hopkins, Emma Thompson, Helena Bonham Carter. 140 minutes. Rated PG.*
"Another Merchant-Ivory masterpiece", this "period piece" adaptation of the E.M. Forster novel concerns a "snobby upper-class" British family scheming to cut an interloper out of their mother's will; though Anglophiles laud the lovely cinematography and appearances by "some of the best actors of our time" (including a "superb" Hopkins and Oscar-winning Thompson), phobes fret it's "way too slow."

### How the Grinch Stole Christmas
17 | 18 | 19 | 23

*2000. Directed by Ron Howard. With Jim Carrey, Jeffrey Tambor, Christine Baranski. 105 minutes. Rated PG.*
Dr. Seuss gets the "grand production" treatment in this mighty "enjoyable" comedy featuring "great visuals" and a "scary" Carrey as a "perfect Grinch" plotting Yuletide vengeance on the "über-commercialized" "world of the Whos"; while it's hailed as a "holiday keeper" that stands "heart to heart" with the "classic cartoon", some viewers see a "heavy-handed" effort that's a few sizes too "overinflated."

### How the West Was Won ✉     ▽ 22 | 20 | 21 | 25

*1963. Directed by John Ford, Henry Hathaway, George Marshall. With Gregory Peck, Henry Fonda, James Stewart, George Peppard, Carroll Baker, Eli Wallach. 162 minutes. Rated G.*
A "true epic" that feels like "five films in one", this "sprawling Western" boasts an "all-star cast" hitting the trail to follow "compelling storylines" ranging from the Civil War to a prairie-schooner drive, all in blazing "Cinerama"; the "long overview" of the "taming" of the territories makes for a grand, "sweeping tale" that's "plenty entertaining", but see it in "wide-screen" or else "don't bother."

### How to Marry a Millionaire     22 | 20 | 19 | 22

*1953. Directed by Jean Negulesco. With Betty Grable, Marilyn Monroe, Lauren Bacall. 95 minutes. Not Rated.*
"Fabulous gowns and mink coats are the stars" of this "rather entertaining" romantic comedy, a "guilty pleasure" about three gold diggers on the loose in Manhattan; "Lauren and Marilyn are charming in their own ways", while its "fascinating look" at women's roles in "'50s society" makes many feminists sigh "thank goodness for progress."

### Hunchback of Notre Dame, The ◑     ▽ 26 | 27 | 26 | 25

*1939. Directed by William Dieterle. With Charles Laughton, Cedric Hardwicke, Maureen O'Hara. 116 minutes. Not Rated.*
One of the more "remarkable" adaptations of the much-filmed Victor Hugo novel of 15th-century Paris, this "timeless" picture about a hunchback's love for a gypsy girl garners praise for its "terrific story and wonderful production"; in the flashy title role, the "spectacular" Laughton gives Lon Chaney's 1923 silent performance a run for its money; best word: "sanctuary!"

### Hunchback of Notre Dame, The     19 | – | 19 | 21

*1996. Directed by Gary Trousdale, Kirk Wise. Animated. 91 minutes. Rated G.*
"Disney does Victor Hugo" in this "underrated" bell-ringer that's "edgier than most animated fluff" and thus "more rewarding" for adults, given its "opera"-esque feel and "dark subtleties"; but cynics nix it as a bit "too sinister for children" and fear that the "forgettable songs" and "stupid talking gargoyles" must have the author "turning in his grave."

### Hunger, The     20 | 21 | 20 | 20

*1983. Directed by Tony Scott. With Catherine Deneuve, David Bowie, Susan Sarandon. 100 minutes. Rated R.*
Deliciously "scary and erotic", this "stylish" "modern-day vampire film" "gets the blood moving" with a "to-die-for cast", including a "surprisingly effective Bowie" opposite Deneuve and Sarandon as two very "hot" vamps ("Buffy wouldn't stand a chance against them"); a pop Goth score by Bauhaus helps the atmospherics, but ultimately this one's best remembered for that notorious "lesbian" interlude.

### Hunt for Red October, The     24 | 24 | 25 | 24

*1990. Directed by John McTiernan. With Sean Connery, Alec Baldwin, Scott Glenn. 134 minutes. Rated PG.*
The "first and best Jack Ryan thriller", this "entertaining" "Cold War guy flick" about a "renegade Russian submarine captain"

combines "heart-pounding" suspense with "characters you can root for" (i.e. the "powerhouse" Connery and "holding-his-own" Baldwin); the "twisting plot" supplies enough "white-knuckle" moments to make it every bit "as good as the book."

### Hurricane, The
`21 | 26 | 21 | 21`

*1999. Directed by Norman Jewison. With Denzel Washington, Liev Schreiber. 145 minutes. Rated R.*
Denzel's "excellent", "Oscar-worthy" performance is the glue in this true story about a hardscrabble middleweight boxer wrongly convicted of a triple murder; alternately "exciting and poignant", the script "really emphasizes human emotion", but it's Washington's "tremendous" performance that makes this miscarriage-of-justice movie so moving.

### Hustler, The ◐ Ⅱ
`25 | 26 | 24 | 22`

*1961. Directed by Robert Rossen. With Paul Newman, Jackie Gleason, Piper Laurie. 134 minutes. Not Rated.*
"Dark, tense and beautifully delivered", this "ultimate movie about winning" is also a "love poem to the game of pool", featuring "Newman on a roll" opposite Gleason in a rare dramatic turn that nearly "steals the picture"; it's "convincing", "gripping" stuff, and though Paul reprised the character of Eddie Felson in *The Color of Money*, connoisseurs claim this first take is so "much better."

### I Am Sam
`21 | 25 | 21 | 21`

*2001. Directed by Jessie Nelson. With Sean Penn, Michelle Pfeiffer, Dakota Fanning. 132 minutes. Rated PG-13.*
Nary an emotion's left untouched in this "enjoyable, if predictable tearjerker" about a "mentally handicapped man's struggle to raise his child"; while it does "make one ponder the rights of the retarded", it's basically "a Barney movie for grown-ups" abetted by an "amazing soundtrack of Beatles remakes"; what saves it are the "luminous performances" from a "poignant" Penn and Fanning as "his darling daughter" ("I want one like her").

### Ice Age
`23 | – | 21 | 25`

*2002. Directed by Chris Wedge, Carlos Saldanha. Animated. 81 minutes. Rated G.*
The "oddest combination" of ice-age mammals sets out to save a little girl in this "cute", "cross-generational animated flick" featuring a "perfectly chosen" "all-star" vocal cast (e.g. Ray Romano as a "whiney" woolly mammoth); although it's "not up to the current high animated film standards", the "laugh-out-loud funny" script and "well-done graphics" certainly "won't leave you cold."

### Igby Goes Down
`20 | 23 | 19 | 19`

*2002. Directed by Burr Steers. With Kieran Culkin, Claire Danes, Jeff Goldblum, Amanda Peet, Ryan Phillippe, Bill Pullman, Susan Sarandon. 97 minutes. Rated R.*
"Hints of *Catcher in the Rye*" permeate this "quirky" coming-of-ager featuring the "terrific" Culkin ("Macaulay, eat your heart out") as a Caulfield-esque "dispossessed teen" coping with his "rich, dysfunctional family" and other "messed-up" metropolitans; its "touching moments" and "fabulously dark" flourishes unfold at a "slow" pace that "loses energy" at times, so stay alert to "pick up where it's going."

### Il Postino ▣
24 | 25 | 24 | 24

*1995. Directed by Michael Radford. With Massimo Troisi, Philippe Noiret. 108 minutes. Rated PG.*

A "charming" mix of "poetry and postal services", this "small treasure" "could only have been made in Italy", given its "lyrical", "humble" airs; the "sweet tale" of a "simple" postman "with the heart of a poet", it manages to be both a "great love story" and a "haunting" tale of "inspiration", with "bravura" acting and "beautiful scenery" that come together for "winning" moviemaking.

### Imitation of Life
21 | 22 | 23 | 22

*1959. Directed by Douglas Sirk. With Lana Turner, John Gavin, Sandra Dee. 125 minutes. Not Rated.*

Bring "two boxes of Kleenex" before viewing this melodramatic Turner vehicle, a "classy" if "campy" "B movie" about a black woman who passes for white; a remake of the 1934 Claudette Colbert "tearjerker", this time around it's "all gussied up in pretty color" with the "racial theme toned down", leading realists to rate it a "ridiculous", "sudsy" soap opera.

### Importance of Being Earnest
21 | 23 | 23 | 22

*2002. Directed by Oliver Parker. With Rupert Everett, Colin Firth, Frances O'Connor, Reese Witherspoon, Judi Dench. 97 minutes. Rated PG.*

This "undemanding" production of Oscar Wilde's "comedy of mistaken identities, romance and your typical weekend at an English manor" scores with "gorgeous sets" and "wonderful" acting from a "cast that looks like they're enjoying themselves"; but purists who prefer the "perfect 1952 version" insist the "magically funny play didn't need 'opening up'" by the screenwriter.

### In America
26 | 27 | 25 | 24

*2003. Directed by Jim Sheridan. With Paddy Considine, Samantha Morton, Djimon Hounsou. 107 minutes. Rated PG-13.*

Sheridan's "beautiful" retelling of the "immigrants-come-to-NY" story is brought to life by an "exceptional ensemble" cast in this "small movie with a big heart"; while its "bittersweet" scenario of a poor Irish family trying to "rebuild after the tragic loss" of a child has many "crying like babies", it's executed so "brilliantly" that even the dry-eyed concur it's "without a single false moment."

### In & Out
17 | 19 | 17 | 17

*1997. Directed by Frank Oz. With Kevin Kline, Joan Cusack, Matt Dillon, Tom Selleck. 90 minutes. Rated PG-13.*

"Is he gay or not?", that is the question: a Midwestern drama teacher protests too much after being outed at the Oscars in this "lighthearted" comedy that's like an extended "*Saturday Night Live* skit"; though "well-acted" by an ace "ensemble cast", it's Kline's "inspired" lead – capped by a "scene-stealing boogie session" – that's the "very funny" payoff.

### In Cold Blood ◑
25 | 26 | 26 | 22

*1967. Directed by Richard Brooks. With Robert Blake, Scott Wilson, John Forsythe. 134 minutes. Rated R.*

Brooks' "brilliant" adaptation of Truman Capote's "true-crime" "spellbinder" is "one of the most chilling films" about random murders ever made ("remember when not showing blood was more scary than showing it?"); shot "in almost documentary style" and all the more frightening thanks to Quincy Jones' evocative score, it "still works today" as "powerful" albeit "disturbing" moviemaking.

### Incredibles, The                                    26 | – | 25 | 28
*2004. Directed by Brad Bird. Animated. 115 minutes. Rated PG.*
"Not everyone can be Batman", and this animated Pixar satire "with brains" depicts the everyday "humdrum" lives of "has-been superheroes" suddenly drawn into an "edge-of-your-seat" rescue; it's "not just for kids" what with its "existential take on superherodom", though its "stunning animation" and "witty" set pieces (the "Jack Jack attack", that "show-stealing costumer") appeal to "all ages"; in fact, its "old-fashioned" message – the "family comes first" – makes many "love cartoons again."

### Independence Day                                    19 | 16 | 18 | 24
*1996. Directed by Roland Emmerich. With Will Smith, Bill Pullman, Jeff Goldblum. 145 minutes. Rated PG-13.*
"*E.T.* with an attitude", this "ultimate flying-saucer movie" might be a "remake of *War of the Worlds*" and "splashy trash" with a "plot as thin as a dime" that's "all noise and no substance", but at least it "doesn't take itself too seriously"; so grab some "popcorn" and hold on for a "helluva lot of fun."

### Indiana Jones and the Last Crusade            24 | 23 | 23 | 26
*1989. Directed by Steven Spielberg. With Harrison Ford, Sean Connery, Denholm Elliott. 127 minutes. Rated PG-13.*
"Almost as good as the first" installment, this third foray in the "Indy adventure" series is a "search-for-the-Holy-Grail" tale that alternates "lighthearted humor" with plenty of "gee-whiz", "close-call action sequences"; Ford is the "perfect hero", but Connery (as his dad) "takes the cake" in this fond salute to "old-fashioned Saturday afternoon movie serials" "brought up to date."

### Indiana Jones and the                             22 | 21 | 21 | 25
### Temple of Doom Ⓤ
*1984. Directed by Steven Spielberg. With Harrison Ford, Kate Capshaw, Quan Ke Huy. 118 minutes. Rated PG.*
"Ford rules the day and saves the world" – again – in this "take-me-away" action/adventure story, the "follow-up to *Raiders*" that "goes more for shock value than the original" (though as exhilaratingly "over the top" as ever); still, doomsayers say its "hooey"-heavy plot and "dark feel" can be "far too grisly for younger viewers", dismissing it as a "blip in the trilogy"; most indelible image: those "chilled monkey brains."

### Indochine ✉Ⓕ                                      23 | 25 | 23 | 25
*1992. Directed by Régis Wargnier. With Catherine Deneuve, Vincent Perez. 152 minutes. Rated PG-13.*
A "haunting", "epic" tale of French Indochina, this Foreign Language Oscar winner details an "enthralling romance" played out against the background of a country in turmoil; as a "beautiful" plantation owner, Deneuve "looks smashing in great clothes", though some say the end result is a "little too picture perfect."

### Inherit the Wind Ⓞ                               26 | 28 | 27 | 22
*1960. Directed by Stanley Kramer. With Spencer Tracy, Fredric March, Gene Kelly. 128 minutes. Rated PG.*
"You'll go ape" for this "superb" "fictionalized account of the Scopes monkey trial", based on the true story of a teacher trying

to bring Darwin into his Tennessee classroom; a "magnificent Tracy and March" are "at the top of their game" trying to "reconcile creationism with evolution" in this "relevant thought-provoker" that many call the "ultimate in intelligent courtroom drama."

### In-Laws, The
24 | 24 | 24 | 20

*1979. Directed by Arthur Hiller. With Peter Falk, Alan Arkin, Richard Libertini. 103 minutes. Rated PG-13.*

If you have any "weird" relatives-by-marriage, you'll "laugh out loud" at this "sidesplitting" comedy pitting a "chameleonic Falk" against a "befuddled Arkin" ("one of the great pairings of the cinema") as about-to-be in-laws; "totally unpredictable", it's "worth watching" if only to "find out where *Meet the Parents* came from."

### Innerspace
15 | 15 | 18 | 17

*1987. Directed by Joe Dante. With Dennis Quaid, Martin Short, Meg Ryan, Kevin McCarthy. 120 minutes. Rated PG.*

Far-out FX and "likable" characters keep this "charming" entry in the "comedy sci-fi category" inneresting as Quaid's top-gun pilot is shrunken and inadvertently sent into the bloodstream of nerdy clerk Short, who's "never been better"; the "cute-as-always" Ryan rounds out the cast for an excursion that's lightweight but "quite funny" as crackpot "fantasy" goes.

### Insider, The
25 | 28 | 25 | 23

*1999. Directed by Michael Mann. With Al Pacino, Russell Crowe, Christopher Plummer. 157 minutes. Rated R.*

Crowe turns in a "quietly intense" performance (while Pacino is intense but definitely not quiet), in this dramatic thriller about a tobacco company "whistle-blower" trying to "do the right thing no matter what the consequences"; although a "disillusioning behind-the-scenes look" at "big business, the media and public opinion", it's "absolutely riveting" and an "inspirational" profile in "courage."

### Interpreter, The
20 | 23 | 20 | 22

*2005. Directed by Sydney Pollack. With Nicole Kidman, Sean Penn. 128 minutes. Rated PG-13.*

A "United Nations interpreter overhears something she shouldn't and ends up under Secret Service protection" in this "promising" if "predictable" political thriller; while Kidman does the "classic movie heroine" thing well and Penn "seems to get better with age", the real star of the picture might be the "awe-inspiring" UN – this is the "first film shot inside the building."

### Interview with the Vampire
19 | 19 | 20 | 22

*1994. Directed by Neil Jordan. With Tom Cruise, Brad Pitt, Antonio Banderas, Christian Slater. 123 minutes. Rated R.*

"Cover up your neck"; this "entertaining Gothic horror flick about a maladjusted trio of immortal vampires" is "almost as good" as Anne Rice's "overwrought" best-selling book; sure, it might be "too beautiful" for words and they "could have cut out some of the gore", but with "pretty boys" Brad, Tom and Antonio playing "yummy bloodsuckers", "what's not to like?"

### In the Bedroom
22 | 26 | 20 | 21

*2001. Directed by Todd Field. With Sissy Spacek, Tom Wilkinson, Marisa Tomei. 130 minutes. Rated R.*

"Less is more" in this "intense" drama about murder, revenge and family "dysfunction" that's the kind of picture in which the "silences say more than any of the dialogue"; though "Spacek and Wilkinson are superb" and "first-time director" Field "does an amazing job", critics sigh it's a "made-for-Lifetime movie" that's "dark, depressing and 20 minutes too long."

### In the Company of Men
21 | 23 | 22 | 17
*1997. Directed by Neil LaBute. With Aaron Eckhart, Stacy Edwards, Matt Malloy. 95 minutes. Rated R.*
A "manipulative", "seriously despicable" loser abuses his "power over men and women alike" and "plays them for fools" in this "nasty little" drama that unflinchingly depicts the "evil that lurks in the hearts of men"; even those who "left the movie with a scowl" and "felt like they needed a shower" afterward admit being "strangely affected" by this "underwatched work."

### In the Heat of the Night  
24 | 27 | 24 | 22
*1967. Directed by Norman Jewison. With Sidney Poitier, Rod Steiger, Warren Oates. 109 minutes. Rated PG.*
The "faint smell of honeysuckle hangs over" this "excellent" crime drama, a "brave statement on race relations" about a "black Yankee cop" suspected of murder in a small Southern town; it "generated a fair amount of controversy in its day" and was quite the Oscar magnet, taking home five statuettes including Best Picture and Best Actor for the "perfect Steiger."

### In the Line of Fire
20 | 20 | 21 | 19
*1993. Directed by Wolfgang Petersen. With Clint Eastwood, John Malkovich, Rene Russo. 128 minutes. Rated R.*
"Eastwood is perfect" as an "aging but resourceful" Secret Service agent – "vulnerable, tough and world-weary" – battling a "would-be Presidential assassin" in this "solid action" thriller; throw in a "truly creepy" Malkovich as the "coldly reptilian" villain and you have a "completely engrossing" flick that's more than "effective", right up to the "suspenseful climax."

### In the Name of the Father
23 | 25 | 24 | 21
*1993. Directed by Jim Sheridan. With Daniel Day-Lewis, Emma Thompson, Pete Postlethwaite. 133 minutes. Rated R.*
This "shattering" look at "desperate times" in Northern Ireland is a "riveting" true story about a "father and son jailed for a crime they did not commit"; "Day-Lewis is mesmerizing" and "totally believable" in this "troubling" account of "love and respect" amid a "terrible civil war."

### Intolerance ◑
▽ 27 | 23 | 24 | 28
*1918. Directed by D.W. Griffith. With Lillian Gish, Mae Marsh, Constance Talmadge. 178 minutes. Not Rated.*
"D.W. Griffith's apology" for the racist subtext in his earlier film, *Birth of a Nation,* is this "monumental" silent "landmark", which intercuts four tales of intolerance set respectively in Babylon, Calvary, 15th-century France and contemporary California; the result is "grandiosity glorified" on a scale of "sheer staggering size" never seen before, and arguably the birth of "epic" filmmaking.

### Invasion of the Body Snatchers ◑
24 | 19 | 25 | 19
*1956. Directed by Don Siegel. With Kevin McCarthy, Dana Wynter, Larry Gates. 80 minutes. Not Rated.*
"Don't fall asleep!"; this '50s slice of "paranoid science fiction" posits that there are "alien pod people among us" "plotting to

take over our hearts and minds"; alright, it's a "classic Red Scare parable", but "still perfectly effective today" despite "wooden acting" and that studio-enforced optimistic ending.

### Invasion of the Body Snatchers          19 | 18 | 21 | 18
*1978. Directed by Philip Kaufman. With Donald Sutherland, Brooke Adams, Jeff Goldblum. 115 minutes. Rated PG.*
You'll be "looking for pods in the basement" after seeing this "thought-provoking", "very different" remake of the "classic" sci-fi thriller about an insidious alien invasion; this time around, the McCarthyist subtext has been replaced by 'Me Decade' pop psychobabble, and even if "less fun" than the original, it's still pretty darn "scary."

### Invisible Man, The ◑⓫          22 | 20 | 21 | 20
*1933. Directed by James Whale. With Claude Rains, Gloria Stuart, William Harrigan. 71 minutes. Not Rated.*
"Fabulous effects" ("especially for its time") and some slyly "campy" moments make this "classic" creature feature worthy of "every movie lover's repertoire"; the tale of an inventor whose invisibility serum transforms him into a crazed killer, it stars an engrossing Rains in the "scary" title role, whose amazing acting has more to do with vocalizing than visibility.

### Iris          ▽ 23 | 27 | 20 | 20
*2001. Directed by Richard Eyre. With Judi Dench, Kate Winslet, Jim Broadbent. 90 minutes. Rated R.*
This "beautifully done" bio of English writer Iris Murdoch and her "spiral" into "frightening illness" shines with "amazing acting" and bookish wit; "flashbacks" follow her from a "sweet" Oxford courtship to later years when the "superb" Dench "realistically portrays" the onset of Alzheimer's in a "sad but finally uplifting" tribute to "true" fidelity.

### Irma La Douce          21 | 23 | 20 | 21
*1963. Directed by Billy Wilder. With Shirley MacLaine, Jack Lemmon, Lou Jacobi. 147 minutes. Not Rated.*
A surprisingly "sweet" comedy from the acerbic Billy Wilder, this story of an honest Parisian cop who falls for a prostitute, becomes her unwilling pimp, then schemes to keep her off the streets is "funny and well done"; MacLaine plays the "hooker with a heart of gold" perfectly, while Lemmon mugs winningly in a dual role.

### Iron Giant, The          24 | – | 25 | 25
*1999. Directed by Brad Bird. Animated. 86 minutes. Rated PG.*
"Markedly different from other animated films", this story of a "quirky boy and an enormous robot from outer space" is both a "sly satire of the '50s" and a "message" flick about "tolerance and non-violence"; "criminally underrated" (it "slipped through the cracks due to poor marketing"), it's "entertaining and deserves to be seen."

### Italian Job, The          22 | 19 | 21 | 24
*2003. Directed by F. Gary Gray. With Mark Wahlberg, Edward Norton, Charlize Theron. 111 minutes. Rated PG-13.*
The "Mini Cooper is the real star" of this "edge-of-your-seat" remake that "fires on most, if not all, cylinders", as a "fast-moving", "action-packed" "heist film" "filled with plot twists, maniacal car chases", "high-tech gadgets" and "timely pop-

culture references"; while "not at all thought-provoking", it's "everything a summer movie should be."

### IT HAPPENED ONE NIGHT ✉◑          28 | 28 | 26 | 25

*1934. Directed by Frank Capra. With Clark Gable, Claudette Colbert. 105 minutes. Not Rated.*
"Gable and Colbert are swell together" in this "great Depression spirit-lifter", the "mother of all screwball comedies" about a "wisecracking tabloid reporter" and a "snooty heiress" "on the run"; the first picture to "sweep all the major Oscars", it was also considered rather "racy for its time": indeed, Gable's baring of his chest in the "walls of Jericho" sequence sent the "undershirt industry" into a tizzy.

### It's a Mad Mad Mad Mad World          24 | 21 | 22 | 23

*1963. Directed by Stanley Kramer. With Spencer Tracy, Milton Berle, Sid Caesar, Buddy Hackett, Mickey Rooney, Ethel Merman, Edie Adams, Jonathan Winters. 192 minutes. Rated G.*
The ultimate "car comedy", this "sprawling gut-buster" features a "huge cast" of "crème de la crème" comedians in an "every-man-for-himself" "race to find a hidden fortune"; sure, it's a "long long long long movie", but it's "still terrifically entertaining" with plenty of "silly slapstick" and "great cameos" to keep things lively; best moment: "Jonathan Winters tearing up the gas station."

### IT'S A WONDERFUL LIFE ◑          27 | 27 | 27 | 25

*1946. Directed by Frank Capra. With James Stewart, Donna Reed, Henry Travers. 130 minutes. Not Rated.*
"Nobody tells a story like Capra", and this "inspirational" film "strikes a fundamental chord with lots of people" via its "small-town" tale about a "good guy" coping with "hard times" and proving "how one life can make a difference"; sure, it's a "little schmaltzy" and "surprisingly dark", but most say "it's a wonderful picture" and "Christmas wouldn't be Christmas without it" – even if you've seen it a "million times" on TV.

### Jagged Edge          22 | 22 | 22 | 20

*1985. Directed by Richard Marquand. With Glenn Close, Jeff Bridges, Peter Coyote. 108 minutes. Rated R.*
This "entertaining murder" thriller tells the tale of a "grisly homicide, a sensational trial and a forbidden love affair"; "great performances" from "'80s diva" Close (as a lawyer with principles) and Bridges (as the client endowed with troubling "charm") keep it so "exciting" that you'll be "guessing to the very end."

### James and the Giant Peach          20 | – | 20 | 24

*1996. Directed by Henry Selick. Animated. 79 minutes. Rated PG.*
"Fantastic effects", a kinetic visual style and bushels of "charm" give this "quirky" cartoon a "different look from the typical animated movie"; the story of a boy and a house-size fruit, it blends "live-action" shots with animation, though the result is "too edgy" and "bizarre" for those who claim Roald Dahl's "book is much better."

### Jane Eyre ◑⊘          25 | 27 | 26 | 22

*1944. Directed by Robert Stevenson. With Orson Welles, Joan Fontaine, Margaret O'Brien. 97 minutes. Not Rated.*
A "moody rendition of the Brontë novel", this "damn good" Gothic romance concerns a "frail" governess, a rich landowner and a houseful of dark secrets; expect plenty of "gloom and doom from

the get-go" followed by atmospheric "shadows" and "Orson scowling" throughout – but as for that "disappointingly contrived ending", blame the author, not Hollywood.

### Jaws ❶ | 26 | 22 | 25 | 26
*1975. Directed by Steven Spielberg. With Roy Scheider, Robert Shaw, Richard Dreyfuss. 124 minutes. Rated PG-13.*
"Sink your teeth" into this "classic summer" scarefest that "gets the adrenaline pumping", since it's got "everything": "horrifying shark attacks", "missing limbs", "crackling" John Williams music and even "fully developed characters"; it "launched the Spielberg juggernaut" by cleverly "making you fear what you don't see", and if the title character looks a bit dated today, the "seasick" wonder "will it ever be safe to go back in the water?"

### JEAN DE FLORETTE ❷ 🅵 | 27 | 27 | 26 | 26
*1987. Directed by Claude Berri. With Yves Montand, Gérard Depardieu. 120 minutes. Rated PG.*
"As Balzacian as French cinema can get", this "epic" drama about farmers feuding over a natural spring in the "pastoral paradise of Provence" is "stunningly beautiful" and "totally compelling"; since it's only the "first half of a genuinely tragic tale", "make sure to see *Manon of the Spring*" (its sequel) afterward to get the full scope of this truly "unforgettable story."

### Jeremiah Johnson | 23 | 21 | 23 | 22
*1972. Directed by Sydney Pollack. With Robert Redford, Will Geer, Stefan Gierasch. 108 minutes. Rated PG.*
"One of the earliest Westerns to change the movie stereotypes of Indian ways", this saga relates the story of an American soldier turned "mountain man" and his pitched, emotional battle with Crow Nation warriors; a precursor of *Dances with Wolves*, it showcases Redford "at his best" and is a "classic" to true believers.

### Jerk, The | 22 | 21 | 19 | 18
*1979. Directed by Carl Reiner. With Steve Martin, Bernadette Peters, Catlin Adams. 94 minutes. Rated R.*
Opening with "one of the best lines ever" – "I was born a poor black child" – this "absolutely hysterical" "rags-to-riches-to-rags" comedy captures the "wacky early Steve Martin" in all his "zany" glory (with ample support from Peters as his "sweetly naive love interest"); some say it's "silly", but "that's exactly the point."

### Jerry Maguire | 21 | 22 | 21 | 20
*1996. Directed by Cameron Crowe. With Tom Cruise, Cuba Gooding Jr., Renée Zellweger, Jonathan Lipnicki. 138 minutes. Rated R.*
A "gutsy sports agent" "sees the light" and "rediscovers his soul" in this "crowd-pleasing" dramedy that blends "football and love" into an "honest", "better-than-average" brew; in the "tailor-made" title role, "Tom terrific" plays "Mr. Show Me the Money" with excellent backup from the Oscar-winning Gooding and "little kid" Lipnicki (who "steals the movie"); best line: "you had me at hello."

### Jesus Christ Superstar | 21 | 18 | 22 | 21
*1973. Directed by Norman Jewison. With Ted Neeley, Carl Anderson, Yvonne Elliman. 108 minutes. Rated G.*
"Old flower children" find religion in this "visually arresting" "rock opera", a "fantastic" depiction of "Christ's humanity" featuring

"hottie" Neeley in the title role and possibly the "best Andrew Lloyd Webber score" ever; heretics say it's "overindulgent" and "not as good as the stage show", speculating that the "cast was stoned the entire time" and thus it all "made sense to them."

### JFK | 19 | 20 | 20 | 21 |
*1991. Directed by Oliver Stone. With Kevin Costner, Kevin Bacon, Tommy Lee Jones, Gary Oldman. 189 minutes. Rated R.*
This "riveting", "revisionist" "conspiracy theory" drama about "what really happened on November 22, 1963" is, at the very least, a look at "what might have happened"; zealots swear it "makes a pretty good case" and delivers some "pull-out-all-the-stops" punches, but debunkers dub it "powerful paranoia" with "too many ifs, buts and maybes to be credible"; in the end, "whether truth or fiction", it remains as "controversial" as ever.

### Journey to the Center of the Earth | 19 | 16 | 21 | 18 |
*1959. Directed by Henry Levin. With James Mason, Pat Boone, Arlene Dahl. 132 minutes. Rated G.*
"Bernard Herrmann's score lends enchantment" to this very "enjoyable" production based on "Jules Verne's fantastical tale" of underground exploration that's a "fun" sci-fi "romp" worth seeking out in a "widescreen" format; sure, it's a tad "hokey", but kids like its "Disney-esque" flavor and "superior special effects."

### Judgment at Nuremberg ✉️◑ | 26 | 27 | 25 | 22 |
*1961. Directed by Stanley Kramer. With Spencer Tracy, Burt Lancaster, Richard Widmark. 178 minutes. Not Rated.*
Based on the "historic" 1948 Nazi war criminal trials, this "excellent courtroom drama" "asks some tough questions" and boasts "uniformly fine" players "often cast against type", as well as a "brilliant", Oscar-winning script; though the issues it raises are "unsettling", it remains a "relevant flick that everyone should see."

### Jules and Jim ◑🇫 | 24 | 26 | 24 | 23 |
*1962. Directed by François Truffaut. With Jeanne Moreau, Oskar Werner, Henri Serre. 100 minutes. Not Rated.*
One of the "milestones of the French New Wave", this charming "Truffaut masterpiece" is the "ultimate" "love triangle", wherein Moreau's "enigmatic beauty" makes her the "elusive muse" of two best friends; the "chemistry" between the players is "haunting and lyrical", and though that "bad-dream" ending is mighty "sad", the "fascinating story" proves "how complicated life can be."

### Julia ✉️∅ | ▽ 24 | 26 | 25 | 23 |
*1977. Directed by Fred Zinnemann. With Jane Fonda, Vanessa Redgrave, Jason Robards. 118 minutes. Rated PG.*
"Fonda and Redgrave are radiant" in this "fascinating" drama, a "superb pairing of two actresses" cast as playwright Lillian Hellman and her "beloved childhood friend" Julia, a lefty resisting the Nazis in '30s Europe; fans applaud the "nervous" suspense and "moving" moments in this "frightening portrayal" of fraught times.

### Juliet of the Spirits 🇫 | ▽ 24 | 24 | 21 | 26 |
*1965. Directed by Federico Fellini. With Giulietta Masina, Mario Pisu, Sandra Milo. 142 minutes. Not Rated.*
"Fellini's first color feature", this "dreamlike" tale is the story of an unhappy housewife who escapes her "dreary marriage" and slides into "fantasy" after a séance; it "still haunts" fans who

dub it a "vivid" look at the power of "imagination", thanks to the performance of the director's "likable" real-life wife Masina, along with a "surrealistic platter" of "fascinating" character actors.

### Jumanji
18 | 18 | 19 | 22

*1995. Directed by Joe Johnston. With Robin Williams, Bonnie Hunt, Kirsten Dunst. 104 minutes. Rated PG.*
"You'll see rolling dice in a whole different light" after a look at this "smartly done" adventure fantasy about a "mysterious board game" that swallows a young boy and coughs him up a quarter-century later – "along with a number of rampaging animals"; despite a "very cool concept" with "lots of action" and "loud CGI effects", it's "too scary for younger children" and ultimately might be a "better theme-park ride than movie."

### Jungle Book, The
▽ 24 | 22 | 25 | 25

*1942. Directed by Zoltan Korda. With Sabu, Joseph Calleia, Rosemary DeCamp. 109 minutes. Not Rated.*
Talk to the animals: this "great children's movie" is a picturesque take on the Kipling yarn of Mowgli, a lad reared by wolves who returns to village life only to face mercenary types hot on the scent of hidden riches; it's a wild eyeful of "classic" family fare that even outdoes "one of the best Disneys", the Mouse House's animated version made 25 years later.

### Jungle Book, The
23 | – | 23 | 24

*1967. Directed by Wolfgang Reitherman. Animated. 78 minutes. Rated G.*
Kipling's "Tarzan-like character and all his friends" pop up in this "charming" Disney cartoon that "makes an impression" with a "crowd-pleasing" story full of "family fun"; it might not be the studio's "best animation", but its "enchanting" soundtrack has enough "delightful songs" to make for a thing of "pure joy."

### Jurassic Park
22 | 16 | 22 | 27

*1993. Directed by Steven Spielberg. With Sam Neill, Laura Dern, Jeff Goldblum. 127 minutes. Rated PG-13.*
"Humans are upstaged by dinosaurs" in this sci-fi "thrill ride" from the "astounding" Spielberg set in an extinct-creatures-come-to-life theme park that's "every child's dream come true"; don't expect much from the "lame story" and "weak" actors (nothing more than "dinochow"), but hold on for "white-knuckle", "roller-coaster" pacing and "astounding special effects" so "truly frightening" that they "might scare younger viewers."

### Karate Kid, The ⑪
19 | 16 | 20 | 17

*1984. Directed by John G. Avildsen. With Ralph Macchio, Pat Morita, Elisabeth Shue. 126 minutes. Rated PG.*
"*Rocky* for teenagers", this "classic" "underdog-wins-the-day story" matches a "kid finding it hard to fit in" with a martial-arts "mentor" who teaches him control through "discipline and loyalty"; balancing "solid values" with "doses of action", this "not-typical teen movie" has the "coming-of-age" thing down pat while being "inspiring" and "entertaining throughout."

### Key Largo ◑
26 | 26 | 23 | 23

*1948. Directed by John Huston. With Humphrey Bogart, Edward G. Robinson, Lauren Bacall. 101 minutes. Not Rated.*
"Tough guys and dolls bring back the golden Warner Brothers days" in this "hard-hitting" noir showcase about a group held

hostage by a "super-rat" of a gangster – until "anti-hero" Bogart shows up; near the "top of Huston's body of work", it features a "highly suspenseful" plot, "stellar performances" and some "vintage" Bogie and Bacall moments – "'nuff said."

### Kid Stays in the Picture, The
21 – 22 20

*2002. Directed by Nanette Burstein, Brett Morgen. Documentary. 93 minutes. Rated R.*
The "rise and fall" of legendary producer/studio head Robert Evans (*Chinatown, The Godfather, Rosemary's Baby*) gets the big-screen treatment in this "stylish documentary", an "only-in-America story" that's "narrated by the subject himself"; although "self-congratulatory propaganda" to some, most find it a "fascinating", "inside" look at moviemaking – "if you can get past Evans' enormous ego", that is.

### Kill Bill Vol. 1 🎖
23 22 21 25

*2003. Directed by Quentin Tarantino. With Uma Thurman, Lucy Liu, Vivica A. Fox, Sonny Chiba. 111 minutes. Rated R.*
"Violence and gore abound" in this "over-the-top", "occasionally ridiculous" first installment of Quentin Tarantino's two-part salute to "comic strips", "spaghetti westerns" and "grindhouse kung fu flicks"; starring a "butt-kicking" Uma as a "revenge"-seeking "killing machine", it's "not for everyone" what with all the "spurting blood", "flying limbs" and "gross sound effects", but thrill freaks purr its "adrenaline" rush is simply "cool as heck" – provided you "check your brains at the door" before viewing.

### Kill Bill Vol. 2
25 24 24 26

*2004. Directed by Quentin Tarantino. With Uma Thurman, David Carradine, Michael Madsen, Daryl Hannah. 136 minutes. Rated R.*
A continuation that "improves upon the original", this "gentler cousin" of the "obscenely graphic" *Vol. 1* features "less red food coloring" and more "character development", while remaining a "wickedly referential" homage to martial arts movies; as the ever-vengeful assassin, Thurman still "burns bright" and despite "trademark" Tarantino dialogue that gets a bit "long-winded", fans say there's a "true heart beating at the center of all the fighting" that lends "emotional heft" to both parts.

### Killers, The ◑
25 25 25 23

*1946. Directed by Robert Siodmak. With Burt Lancaster, Ava Gardner, Edmond O'Brien. 105 minutes. Not Rated.*
"Lancaster makes a powerful film debut" backed up by an "outstanding" Gardner in this "riveting" flick "expanded from the Hemingway short story" about a mysterious small-town murder and its aftermath; it gets to the "core of film noir" through a burbling mix of "moral ambiguity, sexual tension and crime."

### Killing Fields, The
26 26 27 25

*1984. Directed by Roland Joffé. With Sam Waterston, Haing S. Ngor, John Malkovich. 141 minutes. Rated R.*
"Friendship is tested by war" in this "harrowing" true story "told through the eyes of a journalist" relating the "atrocities in Cambodia" and the "horrors of the Khmer Rouge" following the U.S. pullout from Vietnam; "worthy Oscar-winner Ngor" (a real-life survivor of this "holocaust") turns in an "honest" performance that "will move you to tears" and "make you think" a lot.

### Kind Hearts and Coronets ◑          26 | 28 | 26 | 24
*1949. Directed by Robert Hamer. With Alec Guinness, Dennis Price, Valerie Hobson. 106 minutes. Not Rated.*
For "quintessential" "English humor" that "gets better with each viewing", check out this "matchless black comedy" about the disinherited scion of a noble family who tries to achieve dukedom through serial murder; in an inspired twist, his victims – all eight of them – are played by the one-and-only Alec Guinness, whose spot-on performance squarely places this one on the "forever best list."

### King and I, The ✉          27 | 26 | 25 | 27
*1956. Directed by Walter Lang. With Yul Brynner, Deborah Kerr, Rita Moreno. 133 minutes. Rated G.*
The "'Shall We Dance' scene" alone is "worth the price of admission" to this regally "sumptuous" version of Rodgers and Hammerstein's "terrific, old-fashioned" Broadway musical; though it may be "historically inaccurate", "who cares?" given the "stunning production", "gorgeous score" and "totally engaging" team of the "lovely Kerr" "getting to know" Oscar-winner Brynner.

### King Kong ◑⓫∅          25 | 15 | 24 | 24
*1933. Directed by Merian C. Cooper, Ernest B. Schoedsack. With Fay Wray, Robert Armstrong, Bruce Cabot. 100 minutes. Rated PG.*
This "granddaddy of all monster flicks" "still rules the roost" as an "essential piece of cinema history" and the inspiration for "countless" imitators; ok, the "stop-motion" special effects are "Stone Age stuff by today's standards", but this "warped beauty-and-the-beast saga" remains memorable for its "indelible" imagery, that iconic "climax atop the Empire State Building" and most of all for the "irreplaceable" Fay Wray, "filmdom's finest screamer."

### King of Comedy, The          23 | 26 | 23 | 21
*1983. Directed by Martin Scorsese. With Robert De Niro, Jerry Lewis, Sandra Bernhard. 101 minutes. Rated PG.*
"Sharp, insightful and totally original", this pitch-black comedy about a wannabe comedian and the talk-show host he stalks is a different kind of "De Niro psycho flick" that's "complex and unsettling, but kind of fun"; as the stalkee, Lewis is both "funny and sad" ("maybe the French do know something"), and the picture itself is the "most underrated of Scorsese's career."

### King Solomon's Mines          20 | 18 | 20 | 22
*1950. Directed by Compton Bennett, Andrew Marton. With Stewart Granger, Deborah Kerr. 103 minutes. Not Rated.*
"Location filming on the beautiful African continent" is the raison d'être of this H. Rider Haggard "chestnut" that's "hardly the most realistic" action flick, but a "good enough rendition" for most; it delivers some "romance" (via its "matinee idol" marquee names) and some "camp" (that "noble savages" subtext), but whether it's truly "Indiana Jones *before* Indiana Jones" is your call.

### Kinsey          22 | 26 | 22 | 22
*2004. Directed by Bill Condon. With Liam Neeson, Laura Linney, Chris O'Donnell, Peter Sarsgaard, Timothy Hutton. 118 minutes. Rated R.*
"Kinky", "controversial" sex therapist Alfred Kinsey is the subject of this "racy", "pulls-no-punches" biopic that details "how the sexual revolution started" as well as "how far we've progressed

and how far we have to go"; Neeson is "arousing" and Linney ever the "acting goddess", but overall what's "provocative and poignant" to some is "sterile and congratulatory" to others; P.S. "don't watch it with your parents."

### Kissing Jessica Stein
21 | 20 | 21 | 19

*2001. Directed by Charles Herman-Wurmfeld. With Jennifer Westfeldt, Heather Juergensen, Tovah Feldshuh. 97 minutes. Rated R.*
"Single women relate" to this "new-age chick flick", a "quirky romantic comedy" about a "funny, likable" gal "discouraged by the dating scene" who embarks on a lesbian affair; it's rendered in such a "sensitive" way that it "transcends moral objections" (i.e. it "won't offend your mother"), and even if "not profound", it's sure "sweet and solid."

### Kiss Me Kate
24 | 21 | 24 | 25

*1953. Directed by George Sidney. With Howard Keel, Kathryn Grayson, Ann Miller. 109 minutes. Not Rated.*
"Cole Porter's Broadway smash" gets the "Hollywood treatment" in this "sparkling film version" that's a reworking of "*The Taming of the Shrew*"; even though the "principals lack star power", you can still "brush up on your Shakespeare" nicely with "great musical numbers" and "exciting dancing", which come together famously in Miller's "knock-'em-dead" turn in 'Too Darn Hot.'

### Kiss of the Spider Woman ⊠∅
22 | 25 | 22 | 21

*1985. Directed by Hector Babenco. With William Hurt, Raul Julia, Sonia Braga. 120 minutes. Rated R.*
An "odd couple" – a political activist and a gay pederast – inhabit the same prison cell in this "intense drama" based on the Manuel Puig novel that deals with "love, corruption and redemption"; though "worth seeing" for its "moving" script and Hurt's Oscar-winning turn, it may be "too much" for mainstream audiences.

### Klute ⊠
20 | 23 | 21 | 19

*1971. Directed by Alan J. Pakula. With Jane Fonda, Donald Sutherland, Roy Scheider. 114 minutes. Rated R.*
Oscar-winner Fonda stars as an "unhappy hooker" in this "heart-pounding" thriller, where she's "stalked by a killer" but protected by an "excellent" Sutherland as the cop who humanizes her; it "avoids all the clichés" of the genre via a chillingly matter-of-fact script, and if a bit "forgotten", at least Jane's shag "hairdo" is memorable.

### Kramer vs. Kramer ⊠
23 | 26 | 23 | 21

*1979. Directed by Robert Benton. With Dustin Hoffman, Meryl Streep, Justin Henry. 105 minutes. Rated PG.*
"All about the acting", this "riveting drama" won Oscars for Hoffman and Streep as a married couple undergoing the "trauma of divorce and child custody"; overturning the "gender-biased view of parenting", its depiction of a growing "father-son" bond is the core of the story, though its "heart-wrenching" theme "hits you hard" – "there are no winners" in this split-up.

### Kung Fu Hustle ▣
23 | 20 | 21 | 24

*2005. Directed by Stephen Chow. With Stephen Chow, Yuen Wah, Qiu Yuen. 95 minutes. Rated R.*
"Move over Jackie Chan!": this "wildly imaginative" piece of "chop-socky" merges "mind-boggling fight choreography" with "genre-blending" aplomb in its tale of "unlikely heroes" facing

off against mobsters; its "spaghetti-western-meets-*Crouching-Tiger*" approach is equal parts "Bruce Lee, Wile E. Coyote and Quentin Tarantino", with a dash of "Bob Fosse" thrown in for good measure.

### La Cage aux Folles ❶🅵     24 | 26 | 25 | 22

*1979. Directed by Edouard Molinaro. With Michel Serrault, Ugo Tognazzi, Remy Laurent. 100 minutes. Rated R.*
"Funnier than the American remake", the "Broadway musical" and the "two sequels", this "absurd" French farce is "light-years ahead of its time" telling the story of two gay blades forced to "play it straight" in order to impress prospective in-laws; "overacted to perfection" by an "unbeatable" cast, it defines flaming "frivolity", even if a few cluck it's become "a bit faded" with time.

### L.A. Confidential ✉     26 | 27 | 25 | 26

*1997. Directed by Curtis Hanson. With Kevin Spacey, Russell Crowe, Guy Pearce, Kim Basinger. 138 minutes. Rated R.*
"Every nuance is perfect" in this "steamy" period crime drama, an "explosive exposé" about "crooks, hookers" and "police corruption" in '50s LA that's "sharp", "detailed" and "violent as hell"; though it "made a star of Crowe", the overall "dead-on casting" advances the "case for an ensemble acting award", while the "smart", Oscar-winning script has "all the grit" of a "film noir" classic, boosted by "21st-century production values."

### La Dolce Vita ❶🅵     25 | 25 | 23 | 25

*1961. Directed by Federico Fellini. With Marcello Mastroianni, Anita Ekberg, Anouk Aimée. 167 minutes. Not Rated.*
"Celebrity-obsessed culture" goes under the microscope in this "scandalous" study of "decadence", "damnation and redemption" as seen in '60s Rome through the eyes of a jaded gossip columnist (Mastroianni "at his best") fed up with the "sweet life"; arguably "Fellini's most famous" film, it's a "decidedly unglamorous look at glamour" that "introduced the word 'paparazzi'" into the world lexicon; most iconic scene: "Ekberg in the Trevi Fountain."

### Lady and the Tramp     26 | – | 24 | 25

*1955. Directed by Wilfred Jackson, Hamilton Luske, Clyde Geronimi. Animated. 75 minutes. Rated G.*
Puppy love gets a "gorgeous vintage Disney" spin in this "cute" canine romance awash in "lush animation" and lensed in "beautiful" CinemaScope; doggy devotees adore its fetching characters, "endearing story" and "great songs" ("highlighted by Peggy Lee's" sultry rendition of 'He's a Tramp'), though the most unforgettable moment has to be its "famous spaghetti kiss."

### LADY EVE, THE ❶     28 | 28 | 27 | 26

*1941. Directed by Preston Sturges. With Barbara Stanwyck, Henry Fonda, Charles Coburn. 97 minutes. Not Rated.*
"Steamy innuendo" and "wacky pratfalls" coexist in this "smart" Preston Sturges "romp" about a "scheming con artist" out to snare an "unsuspecting" "wealthy geek", aided by an "outstanding supporting cast" of "cardsharps"; a "sassy", "shameless" Stanwyck does "that sultry thing" so well that Fonda's "bumbling rube" "doesn't stand a chance" in this "slyly amusing" screwball comedy that many pronounce "perfect."

### Lady from Shanghai, The ◐    25 | 23 | 22 | 26
*1948. Directed by Orson Welles. With Orson Welles, Rita Hayworth, Everett Sloane. 87 minutes. Not Rated.*
"Another Orson Welles achievement", this "bravura" "B movie" is "completely enjoyable" for many, thanks to some memorable "stand-out scenes": the "shootout in the hall of mirrors", "Rita Hayworth speaking Chinese"; still, skeptics shrug the plot is a "confusing mess" that "looks like it's been cut to death."

### Lady Sings the Blues ∅    ∇ 20 | 21 | 21 | 19
*1972. Directed by Sidney J. Furie. With Diana Ross, Billy Dee Williams, Richard Pryor. 144 minutes. Rated R.*
"Sad yet real", this biography of songbird Billie Holiday moves to the tempo of the "commanding" Miss Ross' body-and-soul performance; following Lady Day from hard times to the big time to her "strung-out" decline, it "holds you from beginning to end", though for diva devotees it's Diana who's the "best part."

### Lady Vanishes, The ◐    ∇ 25 | 24 | 26 | 24
*1938. Directed by Alfred Hitchcock. With Margaret Lockwood, Michael Redgrave, Dame May Whitty. 97 minutes. Not Rated.*
A first-class ticket to "intrigue", this "crackerjack Hitchcock classic" finds the master at his "most fleet" and "fascinating", cooking up a "sublime combination" of the comic and the thrilling; its story of a strange disappearance on a train full of "memorable characters" is such "sheer entertainment" that even those who "know the ending" "never tire" of jumping back aboard.

### La Femme Nikita 🄵    23 | 22 | 24 | 23
*1991. Directed by Luc Besson. With Anne Parillaud, Jean-Hugues Anglade, Jeanne Moreau. 115 minutes. Rated R.*
The "intelligent foreign film" gets a "violent jolt of adrenaline" in this "fast-paced" but "thought-provoking" "tough chick" flick about a punk junkie turned professional assassin; as the "kick-ass" lead, the "mesmerizing" Parillaud performs "spectacular stunts" that "hold your attention" so completely that it's more than "worth the effort to read the subtitles."

### Last Emperor, The ✉    26 | 24 | 25 | 28
*1987. Directed by Bernardo Bertolucci. With John Lone, Joan Chen, Peter O'Toole. 160 minutes. Rated PG-13.*
"Truly an epic, and a darned good one" at that, this "sweeping", "large-scale" bio tells the story of China's "final monarch" from his ascent to the throne at age three through war, occupation and "revolutionary changes" in his kingdom; credit "lavish" sets, "spectacular scenery" and "outstanding" acting by Lone and O'Toole for its winning an impressive "nine Academy Awards"; P.S. several versions exist, but all are on the "long" side.

### Last of the Mohicans, The    22 | 22 | 22 | 25
*1992. Directed by Michael Mann. With Daniel Day-Lewis, Madeleine Stowe, Russell Means. 122 minutes. Rated R.*
For a "realistic portrayal of the French and Indian War", this "historical adventure set in the battle-torn American colonies" doesn't stint on the "barbarism", though they're tempered by "beautiful scenery" and an "incredible score"; "truly evil villains and larger-than-life heroes" make this "wonderful realization of James Fenimore Cooper's book" "top-notch filmmaking."

**L.A. Story**                                                20 | 20 | 20 | 19
*1991. Directed by Mick Jackson. With Steve Martin, Victoria
Tennant, Sarah Jessica Parker. 95 minutes. Rated PG-13.*
"Every LA stereotype is played for laughs" in this "on-point"
romantic comedy that's a "biting" if "loving put-down" of the
"outrageous city" where people "really do drive down the road to
get the mail"; Martin's "effortlessly intelligent" script throws
"wacky" curves – and foretells the Starbucks invasion with its
priceless "half-caff-triple-shot-no-foam-cappuccino" scene.

**Last Picture Show, The** ❶⓫                                23 | 23 | 23 | 22
*1971. Directed by Peter Bogdanovich. With Timothy Bottoms, Jeff
Bridges, Cybill Shepherd, Ben Johnson. 118 minutes. Rated R.*
This "gritty portrait of a small Texas town on the brink of extinction"
is "stunningly realized" in Bogdanovich's "masterpiece" that
captures the loss so well "you can practically hear the death
rattle"; the "birthplace of many new stars", it features some
mighty "raw performances" from its "marvelous ensemble", a
"strong script" and ultra-"realistic production values"; in short,
it's a "lovely" if "sad" tribute to "something intrinsically American."

**LA STRADA** ✉❶◨                                            27 | 28 | 26 | 25
*1956. Directed by Federico Fellini. With Giulietta Masina, Anthony
Quinn, Richard Basehart. 108 minutes. Not Rated.*
Set in a "traveling circus", Fellini's "parable of goodness thwarted
by cruelty" pairs a "strongman who's all muscle and no heart"
with a "peasant girl who's nothing but heart"; the "waiflike"
Masina is "luminous" opposite a "surprisingly good" Quinn, and
combined with "beautiful imagery" and "sad" "music that will
stay with you", it's plain to see why this "masterwork" won the
very first Best Foreign Film Oscar.

**Last Samurai, The**                                        23 | 23 | 22 | 27
*2003. Directed by Edward Zwick. With Tom Cruise, Ken
Watanabe, Tony Goldwyn. 154 minutes. Rated R.*
"Shogun" meets "Dances with Wolves" in this "rousing" epic,
wherein a haunted, "drunken Civil War vet" goes to feudal Japan to
fight the samurai and is instead taken hostage by their "honor and
spirit"; while Cruise garners an equivocal appraisal ("bang-up job"
vs. "doesn't cut it"), "Watanabe wildly outshines him" as the "noble,
betrayed" samurai leader; despite "slow pacing" and way "too
much blood", this "clash of cultures" still swells with "sweeping
vistas", "beautiful cinematography" and "amazing fight scenes."

**Last Seduction, The** ⓫                                     22 | 24 | 22 | 20
*1994. Directed by John Dahl. With Linda Fiorentino, Peter Berg,
Bill Pullman. 110 minutes. Rated R.*
"Fiorentino sizzles" as a "bad"-to-the-bone "femme fatale" in
this "deliciously wicked" neo-noir crime thriller about a "very
sexy" gal who rips off her husband and takes cover with a love-
struck doofus; sure, it's "low budget" and there may be more than
a few "holes in the plot", but "man, what a ride!"

**Last Tango in Paris**                                       17 | 20 | 15 | 19
*1973. Directed by Bernardo Bertolucci. With Marlon Brando,
Maria Schneider. 129 minutes. Rated NC-17.*
Definitely not about dance lessons, this "evocative blend" of
the "romantic" and the "erotic" presents a "graphically sexual"

Parisian pas de deux between a "compelling" Brando and a limber Schneider; scenes that "seemed steamy then" may come off as "pointless" now, but Marlon's "at his best" "mumbling in two languages" and dreaming up "risqué" ways to "use butter."

**Last Temptation of Christ, The**  22 | 23 | 25 | 22
*1988. Directed by Martin Scorsese. With Willem Dafoe, Harvey Keitel, Barbara Hershey. 164 minutes. Rated R.*
"Controversial" with a big C, this "intriguing" drama "reexamines Christian faith" by portraying "one of the most humanizing perspectives on Jesus" ever filmed; of course, those "rigid on the Scriptures" consider it blasphemous (and it's still not available in certain video chains to this day), but believers say this "absorbing", "important" Scorsese drama must "be seen to be criticized."

**Last Waltz, The**  26 | – | 20 | 26
*1978. Directed by Martin Scorsese. Documentary. With The Band. 117 minutes. Rated PG.*
In the running for "best concert movie of all time", this renowned documentary "captures the end of a rock 'n' roll era" in its recording of The Band's last gasp, abetted by a musical "dream team" that includes, among others, Bob Dylan, Eric Clapton, Joni Mitchell, Muddy Waters, Neil Young and Van Morrison; it's "clearly a labor of love from Scorsese" that "shouldn't be this good, but it is."

**Laura ❶**  27 | 25 | 27 | 26
*1944. Directed by Otto Preminger. With Gene Tierney, Dana Andrews, Clifton Webb. 88 minutes. Not Rated.*
A "suspenseful, elegant whodunit with a twist" – the "detective falls in love with the murder victim" – this "chic" take on film noir provides plenty of "romantic goose bumps" owing to the simmering "chemistry" between the "brooding" Andrews and "exquisite" Tierney; throw in some "haunting music" and a "nicely paced" if somewhat "silly plot", and the result is "Preminger's best flick."

**Lavender Hill Mob, The ✉❶**  25 | 26 | 23 | 22
*1951. Directed by Charles Crichton. With Alec Guinness, Stanley Holloway. 78 minutes. Not Rated.*
"Wittily whimsical", this British comic "gem" helped introduce Alec Guinness – an "actor's actor with the most expressive raised eyebrow in film" – to America; the caper-gone-awry story involving a milquetoast bank clerk who dreams up the "perfect crime" is "delightfully funny" thanks to its "wonderful" script.

**L'Avventura ❶F**  ∇ 24 | 23 | 22 | 24
*1961. Directed by Michelangelo Antonioni. With Gabriele Ferzetti, Monica Vitti, Lea Massari. 145 minutes. Not Rated.*
A real art-house "landmark" and one of "Antonioni's most accessible" films, this "minimalist masterwork" follows a jaded playboy as he hunts for his missing mistress on a Mediterranean isle; its "stark visual and intellectual" values are hailed as "revolutionary", though literalists wading through the "ennui" come up "baffled and confused."

**LAWRENCE OF ARABIA ✉**  29 | 28 | 27 | 29
*1962. Directed by David Lean. With Peter O'Toole, Omar Sharif, Alec Guinness. 222 minutes. Rated PG.*
The "biggest epic of them all", this bio of WWI British soldier T.E. Lawrence "sets the standard for large-scale filmmaking" with its

"stunning" desert cinematography, "suspense by the duneful" and "stupendous cast", led by the "perfect" O'Toole; thanks to Lean's "painterly techniques", the "background is as consistently amazing as the foreground" in this "gold standard" of an Oscar magnet that "demands to be seen on the big screen."

### League of Their Own, A                20 | 20 | 22 | 20 |
*1992. Directed by Penny Marshall. With Geena Davis, Tom Hanks, Madonna, Lori Petty, Rosie O'Donnell. 128 minutes. Rated PG.*
"There's no crying in baseball", though this "nostalgic gem" about a WWII women's team has fans praising its "fantastic" ensemble cast ("even Madonna is good"); "bringing back the innocence" of simpler times, this "piece of history" might have a "sentimental epilogue", but its "feel-good" aura makes it "highly rewatchable."

### Leaving Las Vegas ✉                20 | 24 | 18 | 18 |
*1995. Directed by Mike Figgis. With Nicolas Cage, Elisabeth Shue, Julian Sands. 111 minutes. Rated R.*
"Disturbing", "depressing" and "painful to watch", this "tragic love story" between a "suicidal alcoholic" and a "burned-out prostitute" is still "brilliant in all aspects", leaving viewers "emotionally drained"; while giddy fans agree the "damn good" Cage "deservedly won the Oscar" for his "best work thus far", soberer sorts call this "feel-bad" flick the "ultimate downer."

### Legally Blonde ⓤ                19 | 20 | 17 | 19 |
*2001. Directed by Robert Luketic. With Reese Witherspoon, Luke Wilson. 96 minutes. Rated PG-13.*
The near-unanimous verdict on this "*Clueless*-goes-to-law-school" comedy: "cute-as-a-button" Witherspoon is "irresistible" as a "Valley Girl" "bursting the stereotype" and proving that "anyone can achieve their dream"; though most jurors decree that "even an intellectual can like" this "pink puffball of a movie", some say "there ought to be a law" against such "derivative piffle."

### Legend                18 | 15 | 18 | 22 |
*1986. Directed by Ridley Scott. With Tom Cruise, Mia Sara, Tim Curry, David Bennent. 94 minutes. Rated PG.*
"Fantasy" fanatics adore this "mythical" tale of a quest to rescue an "innocent princess" and free the "last remaining unicorn" by a group of "bumbling elves" and a "forest boy"; while it's atmospheric enough to be a "guilty pleasure" for some, "dippy" dialogue makes it a "winner in the unintentional humor" department for others.

### Legends of the Fall                20 | 21 | 20 | 23 |
*1994. Directed by Edward Zwick. With Brad Pitt, Anthony Hopkins, Aidan Quinn, Julia Ormond. 133 minutes. Rated R.*
This "sweeping epic" set in "untamed 19th-century America" chronicles "one family's struggle in times of political turmoil" and the "moving" story of a woman "tragically passed between three brothers"; sure, a few label it "pretentious" and "no threat to the best Westerns", but there are no complaints about the "fantastic scenery" – and "nothing beats Pitt riding in on that horse!"

### Lethal Weapon ⓤ                21 | 19 | 20 | 21 |
*1987. Directed by Richard Donner. With Mel Gibson, Danny Glover, Gary Busey. 112 minutes. Rated R.*
"Top-notch" action peppered with "plenty of laughs" establishes this "classic buddy" flick as the "first and best of the franchise"

(three sequels and counting); as "hard-bitten, job-weary" LA detectives, Gibson and Glover are "at the top of their form" with such "tremendous chemistry" that the picture became the "model for '80s cop movies", a "classic" of the genre.

### Letter, The ◑          ▽ 25 | 28 | 26 | 25
*1940. Directed by William Wyler. With Bette Davis, Herbert Marshall, Gale Sondergaard. 95 minutes. Not Rated.*
"Bette shines" as a cool customer in torrid British Malaya in this "superb" drama based on Somerset Maugham's story of a planter's wife who goes postal on her paramour; replete with "tinkling chimes and clouded full moons", the "exotic ambiance" lends "scary impact" to the proceedings, while Davis' "incredible" chops set the "standard for judging acting to this day."

### Liar Liar          16 | 17 | 16 | 16
*1997. Directed by Tom Shadyac. With Jim Carrey, Maura Tierney, Justin Cooper. 87 minutes. Rated PG-13.*
Critics quibble over this "Carrey vehicle" about a lawyer compelled to tell the truth for 24 hours for the sake of his child; while some laud the star's "hilarious", "effective" performance shaded with some "poignant, non-hammy" moments, cynics nix the "not believable" (verging on "boring") story.

### Lifeboat ◑          25 | 26 | 25 | 22
*1944. Directed by Alfred Hitchcock. With Tallulah Bankhead, William Bendix, Walter Slezak. 96 minutes. Not Rated.*
"Can a one-set movie hold your attention?": this "fascinating Hitchcock" war-era thriller does, providing "more drama per square inch", since the "entire picture takes place in a small lifeboat"; among the "bickering crew of castaways", Bankhead is "superb, dahling", but blink and you'll miss the director's "inspired" cameo.

### LIFE IS BEAUTIFUL ✉🇫          27 | 27 | 27 | 25
*1998. Directed by Roberto Benigni. With Roberto Benigni, Nicoletta Braschi. 118 minutes. Rated PG-13.*
Simultaneously "heart-wrenching" and "uplifting", this story about an Italian family's attempt to shelter their son from the Holocaust is a "bittersweet fable about the triumph of the human spirit"; Oscar-winner Benigni provides an "emotional roller-coaster ride" with some "inspired comedic" touches, and though some "uncomfortable" viewers suggest a "trivialization" of a very serious subject, most agree "if you don't shed a tear, you're not human."

### Life of Brian          23 | 21 | 23 | 20
*1979. Directed by Terry Jones. With Monty Python. 94 minutes. Rated R.*
"Profane, sacrilegious and really funny", this "hysterical" "cult classic" about a Holy Land sad sack mistaken for the Messiah is "as bitingly original a spoof as has ever been made" and "probably one of God's favorites"; only "Monty Python at their finest" could "get away with" the final scene that "sends you off singing 'Always Look on the Bright Side of Life.'"

### Life of David Gale          21 | 24 | 22 | 20
*2003. Directed by Alan Parker. With Kevin Spacey, Kate Winslet, Laura Linney. 130 minutes. Rated R.*
Expect a "great shocker at the end" of this "compelling" capital punishment drama, "but getting there has some pretty dull moments"; "surprised" surveyors "love the twists and turns",

while those who "figured things out ahead of time" find the story "predictable" and "contrived", but "interesting nonetheless."

### Like Water for Chocolate 🅵          25 | 24 | 25 | 25

*1993. Directed by Alfonso Arau. With Lumi Cavazos, Marco Leonardi. 123 minutes. Rated R.*

"Ahh, food and sex" make a "lip-smacking" combination in this "mouthwatering" Mexican "foodie classic" that serves up an "eccentric" love story that's "as pleasing to the eye as it is to the palate"; "deliciously true to the novel", it offers "magical realism at its best" and, "like a warm dessert", leaves one feeling so "content and hopeful" that many show up for "another helping."

### Lili ⊘          ∇ 23 | 23 | 23 | 23

*1953. Directed by Charles Walters. With Leslie Caron, Mel Ferrer, Jean-Pierre Aumont. 81 minutes. Rated G.*

Walking a tightrope between "deep whimsy" and "endearing" drama, this ringside look at an "innocent" orphan follows "ultimate waif" Caron as she joins the circus; enlivened by "one song" and some occasional dancing, the story is almost "too cute", but an "outstanding" cast ensures it will "turn on the tears every time."

### Lilies of the Field ⊠◑          25 | 26 | 24 | 23

*1963. Directed by Ralph Nelson. With Sidney Poitier, Lilia Skala, Stanley Adams. 94 minutes. Not Rated.*

With his "flawless" performance in this "quiet, simple" tale about a handyman who helps refugee nuns build a chapel, Poitier became the first African-American to win a lead-role Oscar and also helped "open up racial dialogue" in the Civil Rights era; the film's many admirers hail a "sweet story" told with "heart and charm" that delivers a "lesson in dignity and trust."

### Lilo & Stitch          23 | – | 22 | 24

*2002. Directed by Chris Sanders, Dean DeBlois. Animated. 85 minutes. Rated PG.*

"Different from the usual Disney stuff", this "adorable" animated tale features a "spunky" orphaned Hawaiian girl who adopts a "lovable" blue 'dog' that turns out to be a space alien; it's a "heartwarming story" with "great life lessons" about "love", the "meaning of family" and "finding your place in the world", as well as "laughs from beginning to end" and an Elvis-infused soundtrack; "beautiful watercolor backdrops" give the film its "distinctive look."

### LION IN WINTER, THE ⊠          28 | 29 | 27 | 26

*1968. Directed by Anthony Harvey. With Peter O'Toole, Katharine Hepburn. 134 minutes. Rated PG.*

Hepburn and O'Toole give "performances so brilliant your eyes will hurt" as "two titans battling each other and history" in this "intelligent, delicious" drama that reigns as "one of the best historical films ever made"; indeed, this "masterful" look at Henry II and Eleanor of Aquitaine (the original "dysfunctional royal family") is so "superb" that it earned Kate her third Oscar, as well as statuettes for its "sparkling" screenplay and score.

### Lion King, The          25 | – | 25 | 27

*1994. Directed by Roger Allers, Rob Minkoff. Animated. 89 minutes. Rated G.*

*Hakuna Matata!*: this "crowning achievement" garners roars of approval as one of "Disney's best" thanks to its "breakthrough

154          **subscribe to zagat.com**

animation techniques", "toe-tapping" music and "exceptional voice characterizations by Matthew Broderick and Jeremy Irons"; though this "heartwarming" tale about an exiled lion cub (sort of the "same story as *Bambi*") is "touching" and often "comedic", the film has some bona fide "scary moments" and "may be too intense" for smaller fry.

### Little Big Man 24 | 25 | 24 | 23

*1970. Directed by Arthur Penn. With Dustin Hoffman, Faye Dunaway, Chief Dan George. 147 minutes. Rated PG.*
A "rousing" Wild West "saga", this "memorable period piece" concerns a "Forrest Gump–like" character with a knack for popping up at "famous historical moments"; plaudits go to its "engrossing blend of humor and drama" and "great" performances by George and Hoffman ("truly the man of 1,000 faces") – indeed, it's "one of the best looks at Native Americans" ever portrayed in moviedom.

### Little Foxes, The ◑ ▽ 25 | 27 | 23 | 24

*1941. Directed by William Wyler. With Bette Davis, Herbert Marshall, Teresa Wright, Dan Duryea. 116 minutes. Not Rated.*
All the "power" of Lillian Hellman's "bitter little" stage drama is apparent in this "excellent" film adaptation via William Wyler, a showcase for "Bette at her bitchy best" as the mercenary missus in a shifty Southern family; the sly scheming and deadly betrayal make for such a bang-up "lesson in acting" that many wonder "why don't they make movies like this anymore."

### Little Mermaid, The 24 | – | 23 | 25

*1989. Directed by Ron Clements, John Musker. Animated. 82 minutes. Rated G.*
This "first of the great second wave of Disney classics" manages to "hold its own against *Cinderella* and *Snow White*", what with its delightful cartoon "critters", "witty dialogue" and "upbeat", Oscar-winning music that "made animation sing again"; sure, feminists discern a "sexist message" ("why does the woman have to change for the man?"), but in the end "how could you not love this adorable redheaded mermaid?"

### Little Princess, A ▽ 26 | 24 | 25 | 26

*1995. Directed by Alfonso Cuarón. With Liesel Matthews, Eleanor Bron. 97 minutes. Rated G.*
"Shirley Temple's version has nothing on" this "sumptuous", "perfectly played" family fable of a "pampered" boarding-school lass with "mystical" leanings who goes from "riches to rags and back" after her dragoon dad is declared dead during WWI; though it attracts less than the "attention it deserves", loyalists label it a "top-flight tearjerker."

### Little Shop of Horrors 19 | 19 | 20 | 21

*1986. Directed by Frank Oz. With Rick Moranis, Ellen Greene, Steve Martin. 94 minutes. Rated PG-13.*
If "campy" "sci-fi musicals" ring your bell, this "twisted" tale about a boy, a girl and a "smart-ass, man-eating plant" (based on an old Roger Corman B-movie) "ranks right up there with *The Rocky Horror Picture Show* as a cult classic"; credit the "great cast" and "humorously dark score" for the ensuing "goofy fun"; most "priceless" moment: Martin's "sadistic dentist" treating "masochist patient" Bill Murray.

### Little Women                21 | 23 | 24 | 21
*1994. Directed by Gillian Armstrong. With Winona Ryder, Susan Sarandon. 115 minutes. Rated PG.*
Surveyors are split on this "feminist" adaptation of Louisa May Alcott's classic novel about a Civil War–era family: partisans of George Cukor's 1933 version dismiss this remake as "unnecessary", harrumphing that "Ryder can't compare to Katharine Hepburn", yet others swear it's "worth watching" for Sarandon's performance alone; there's no debate, however, that its "great message" – about a "family loving each other no matter what" – is "very well done."

### Live and Let Die            19 | 17 | 20 | 21
*1973. Directed by Guy Hamilton. With Roger Moore, Jane Seymour, Yaphet Kotto. 119 minutes. Rated PG.*
Expect "beautiful women, fast cars", "snakes, voodoo and Yaphet Kotto" in this "exotic" James Bond caper set in the Caribbean and the "sultry South"; "nonstop" action sequences ("particularly the bayou boat chase"), "humor that's shaken (not stirred)" and Moore's first 007 impersonation make it worth watching – even if Sean Connery loyalists label it the "beginning of the decline."

### Local Hero                  26 | 24 | 26 | 23
*1983. Directed by Bill Forsyth. With Burt Lancaster, Peter Riegert, Peter Capaldi. 111 minutes. Rated PG.*
"The little people triumph over the money people" in this "understated but brilliant" comedy contrasting the differences between a "quaint Scottish town" and the "corporate world"; its "engaging characters", "quirky" storyline and Mark Knopfler's "great soundtrack" make for such "bighearted", "whimsical" fun that many argue it "deserves a larger following."

### Lock, Stock and Two Smoking Barrels   23 | 22 | 25 | 23
*1998. Directed by Guy Ritchie. With Jason Flemyng, Dexter Fletcher, Nick Moran. 105 minutes. Rated R.*
"First-time director" Ritchie does a "brilliant job co-opting every gangster flick cliché" in this "violent but riveting" thriller that's a "Cockney" take on *Pulp Fiction*; agreed, it's "hard to understand the accents", but the "acting, setting and soundtrack are dead-on" and "super plot surprises" abound; all in all, this "fun romp with guns" is "lean", mean and "wonderfully produced."

### Lolita ◑                    24 | 24 | 24 | 23
*1962. Directed by Stanley Kubrick. With James Mason, Sue Lyon, Shelley Winters, Peter Sellers. 152 minutes. Not Rated.*
Though this "fine adaptation of the Nabokov classic" might be somewhat "sanitized" ("it was made in 1962, after all"), it's still "slyly dirty" enough for its very adult subject, a middle-aged man's obsession with a barely teenaged girl; though ageists argue Lyon is "too old" for the title role, there still are plenty of "choice moments" supplied by an "extremely funny" Sellers and Winters, who "gives the performance of her life."

### Lone Star                   25 | 25 | 25 | 22
*1996. Directed by John Sayles. With Kris Kristofferson, Matthew McConaughey, Chris Cooper. 135 minutes. Rated R.*
Director Sayles' "overlooked masterpiece" is a "flawless murder mystery that digs deep into the American psyche" and "takes a hard look at race relations"; following the discovery of a buried

skeleton in a small Texas town, the plot goes through "more twists and turns than the Rio Grande" but still "works on multiple levels" as it "seamlessly interweaves multiple characters" – and that "ending will make your jaw drop."

### Longest Day, The ◑                    24 | 20 | 25 | 26

*1962. Directed by Ken Annakin, Andrew Marton et al. With John Wayne, Rod Steiger. 180 minutes. Rated G.*
As far as "war-as-spectacle" epics go, this "sweeping" saga of the Normandy invasion sets the "standard by which all others are measured"; D-day devotees dig the "superb dedication to detail" and "all-star cast" that "really gets into their characters" thanks to a script that "includes the point of view of everyone involved"; still, foes snipe "too many cameos" turn it into a "cattle call."

### Longest Yard, The                     17 | 15 | 18 | 16

*1974. Directed by Robert Aldrich. With Burt Reynolds, Eddie Albert, Michael Conrad. 121 minutes. Rated R.*
A "guy's movie" Hall of Famer, this "prison football comedy" stars Reynolds as a pro quarterback sent to the big house only to "lead a Heisman-quality cast" of roughneck convicts in a game against the guards; scoring many "memorable lines", it has "Mean Machine" mavens ruling it "arguably the best" pigskin pic ever.

### Looking for Mr. Goodbar ∅            18 | 21 | 19 | 18

*1977. Directed by Richard Brooks. With Diane Keaton, Tuesday Weld, Richard Gere. 135 minutes. Rated R.*
Powered by Keaton's "brilliant" turn as a "sexually repressed" teacher by day who "trolls the bars by night", this "sobering tale of '70s promiscuity" is a "dark primer for single women" that "sends chills down your spine" – with a "gruesome ending" delivered "like a sledgehammer upside the head."

### Lord of the Flies ◑           ▽ 21 | 17 | 25 | 19

*1963. Directed by Peter Brook. With James Aubrey, Tom Chapin, Hugh Edwards. 90 minutes. Not Rated.*
The last word in youth gone wild, this "powerful" take on novelist William Golding's "modern classic" finds a pack of marooned British schoolboys slipping into "disturbing" behavior as barbarity overtakes breeding; the "realistic" style makes for an "unsettling" drama with bonus "social commentary buried within", though some savage the "incompetent acting" and sniff "read the book instead."

### Lord of the Rings, The                15 | – | 22 | 16

*1978. Directed by Ralph Bakshi. Animated. 132 minutes. Rated PG.*
Graphics guru Bakshi's animated take on Tolkien is no "Fritz the Hobbit": it's "true to the books" in presenting the elfin Frodo's "epic" face-off with the forces of evil (even if it's "too bad" the "truncated storyline" "breaks off halfway" into the trilogy); but others say that this "muddled" "travesty" often "looks ridiculous" – "thank God for Peter Jackson."

### LORD OF THE RINGS:                     27 | 25 | 27 | 29
### THE FELLOWSHIP OF THE RING 🄪

*2001. Directed by Peter Jackson. With Elijah Wood, Ian McKellen, Viggo Mortensen, Sean Astin, Liv Tyler. 178 minutes. Rated PG-13.*
This "enthralling", "true-to-the-book" retelling of Tolkien's classic epic "transcends the genre" and "sets the benchmark for fantasy films to come" with its "lovingly crafted" visualization of Middle

Earth; despite a somewhat "slow beginning", "three hours of brilliant bliss" ensue that are "exhilaratingly" perfect, "right down to the hairy Hobbit feet."

### LORD OF THE RINGS: THE RETURN OF THE KING ✉
28 | 26 | 27 | 29

*2003. Directed by Peter Jackson. With Elijah Wood, Ian McKellen, Viggo Mortensen, Sean Astin, Liv Tyler. 201 minutes. Rated PG-13.*
Jackson "should be knighted" for this "history-making", Oscar-grabbing finale to the "superlative trilogy", a "paean to the goodness of good" in the Fellowship's "united allegiance against evil"; it "lives up to the hoopla" from its two "faithfully rendered" predecessors thanks to "mythic sweep and grandeur" and a "cast obviously devoted to the picture"; in sum, this "masterpiece" is a "cinematic monument" to Tolkien's original fantasy, capped by a "long ending" that nonetheless draws a "big round of applause."

### LORD OF THE RINGS: THE TWO TOWERS ⑪
27 | 25 | 26 | 29

*2002. Directed by Peter Jackson. With Elijah Wood, Ian McKellen, Viggo Mortensen, Sean Astin, Liv Tyler. 179 minutes. Rated PG-13.*
There's "much less exposition" and much "more testosterone" in the second "gripping" installment of the Tolkien trilogy, which "starts right where the last one ended"; grab a "comfortable chair" and brace yourself for three hours of "flawless special effects" ("Gollum rocks"), "wonderful" acting by "hot guys", "epic battles the likes of which have never before been captured on celluloid" and an "amazing storyline" that really "does justice" to the book.

### Lost Horizon ◑
25 | 24 | 26 | 22

*1937. Directed by Frank Capra. With Ronald Colman, Jane Wyatt, Margo, Sam Jaffe. 138 minutes. Not Rated.*
A "nostalgic reminder of Hollywood's Golden Age", this "moving" adaptation of James Hilton's best-seller still "casts a spell" thanks to an "irresistible" conceit, the utopia known as "Shangri-la"; sure, this "fairy tale" of a picture may seem rather "quaint" and "dated" now, but Colman's performance is "as contemporary as if it were made today."

### Lost in America
20 | 20 | 21 | 17

*1985. Directed by Albert Brooks. With Albert Brooks, Julie Hagerty, Garry Marshall. 91 minutes. Rated R.*
Brooks' "seriously underrated" satire about a yuppie couple who chuck it all and hit the road is dryly "hilarious" filmmaking boasting what may be the "funniest first 45 minutes in movie history"; though a few lost souls protest the "premise doesn't quite get there", the majority reports the "situations, characters and jokes are all in sync."

### Lost in Translation ✉
21 | 24 | 19 | 21

*2003. Directed by Sofia Coppola. With Bill Murray, Scarlett Johansson. 102 minutes. Rated R.*
"Not much happens" in this "poignant" look at a young woman and a "has-been" movie star who meet out of "boredom and insomnia" in a Tokyo hotel; admirers say it's "eminently watchable" thanks to "talented" writer/director Coppola (it must "run in the family") as well as the "surprising chemistry" between the "world-weary" Murray and "enigmatic" Johansson; still, "baffled" viewers want

to know "what the hoopla is all about" – and especially "what he whispers at the end"; best scene: the "Suntory commercial."

### Lost Weekend, The ✉◗ ∇ 23 | 25 | 23 | 21

*1945. Directed by Billy Wilder. With Ray Milland, Jane Wyman, Phillip Terry. 101 minutes. Not Rated.*
"Strong" stuff served neat, this "smart", sobering drama depicts the "terrifying inner world" of an alcoholic who "lives only" for the bottle, starring Milland in a "top-shelf", Oscar-winning turn as a barfly on a bender careening from double bourbons to detox to the d.t.'s; some maintain it "should be required viewing" at AA meetings – it's the "scariest movie of all time if you drink."

### Love Actually 22 | 23 | 21 | 22

*2003. Directed by Richard Curtis. With Hugh Grant, Liam Neeson, Colin Firth, Laura Linney, Emma Thompson, Alan Rickman, Keira Knightley, Bill Nighy. 135 minutes. Rated R.*
"Intertwining" vignettes of lovesick Londoners meeting up "cute" and breaking up "sad" form the core of this "walk-away-smiling" romantic comedy; while Brit chick flick fans are "delighted" by the "great ensemble" with a special nod to the habitually "charming" Grant, those finding it "not that good actually" zap its "saccharine", "scattershot" script as barely "tolerable fluff."

### Love Bug, The ⏏ 18 | 15 | 16 | 17

*1969. Directed by Robert Stevenson. With Dean Jones, Michele Lee, Buddy Hackett. 107 minutes. Rated G.*
"They don't get much sillier" than this "imaginative" Disney "oldie" about Herbie, a "sweet"-talking VW bug that supplies boomers with plenty of "fond memories"; it still "stands the test of time" well enough for it to be a perennial "rainy-afternoon" rental.

### Love in the Afternoon ◗ ∇ 24 | 24 | 22 | 22

*1957. Directed by Billy Wilder. With Gary Cooper, Audrey Hepburn, Maurice Chevalier. 130 minutes. Not Rated.*
An "old-fashioned" romance set in "misty" Paree, this "witty" Wilder "treat" stars Coop as an "American playboy" who goes "mad with desire" for the much-younger Hepburn; if the "age difference" between the "odd couple" might seem "unspannable", the "bright cast" shows lots of "chemistry" – "isn't love grand?"

### Love Is a Many-Splendored Thing 22 | 23 | 22 | 21

*1955. Directed by Henry King. With Jennifer Jones, William Holden. 102 minutes. Not Rated.*
"What drama! what heartbreak!" sigh admirers of this "classic" romantic "tearjerker", an "ahead-of-its-time" tale about an affair between a "liberated" Eurasian woman and a conflicted American war correspondent; ok, it's a little "soppy" and "Jones isn't believable as a Eurasian", but the "breathtaking" Hong Kong scenery and "memorable", Oscar-winning theme song "make the whole thing worth it."

### Love Story 19 | 18 | 20 | 18

*1970. Directed by Arthur Hiller. With Ali MacGraw, Ryan O'Neal, Ray Milland. 99 minutes. Rated PG.*
"Get out the Kleenex" – this "three-hanky chick flick" about a "rich boy, a poor girl" and an incurable disease is applauded for its "adorable" leads, the "cute" O'Neal and "divine" MacGraw; critics of this "shameless" "schmaltz"-fest sneer that "love

means having to say you're sorry every five minutes", but even they admit "35 years of soggy-eyed females can't be wrong."

### M **O F**    26 | 26 | 26 | 23
*1931. Directed by Fritz Lang. With Peter Lorre, Ellen Widmann, Gustaf Gründgens. 99 minutes. Not Rated.*
Still "frightening seven decades later", this crime thriller features Lorre as a "nervous, sweaty little child killer" in a "riveting" performance that evokes "horror and pity at the same time"; set in "'30s Berlin" "plunging headlong into fascism", it's known for its "expressionistic" camerawork and montage sequences that "set the benchmark for film editing."

### Madagascar    21 | – | 19 | 24
*2005. Directed by Eric Darnell, Tom McGrath. Animated. 86 minutes. Rated PG.*
"NYC zoo animals" fly the coop and end up "in the wilds of Africa" in this "wholesome" animated feature rendered in "eye-popping colors", and with enough "zaniness for kids" (and "'in' jokes" for adults) to keep viewers of all ages happy; sure, its "uneven" storyline eventually gets "tangled" in its own nets, so it's a good thing those "penguins steal the show."

### Mad Max **⓫**    20 | 17 | 19 | 19
*1980. Directed by George Miller. With Mel Gibson, Joanne Samuel, Hugh Keays-Byrne. 93 minutes. Rated R.*
"Raw" and thrillingly "underproduced", this "seminal" tale of "post-apocalyptic", "Darwinian doom" is one of the "all-time great low-budget fantasies", done with "conviction and style"; it pits a "fabulous Mel in tight black leather" against some "truly bad bad guys" and is so "ultimately effective" that it spawned two sequels (though connoisseurs claim the first is "the best").

### Madness of King George, The    22 | 26 | 23 | 24
*1994. Directed by Nicholas Hytner. With Nigel Hawthorne, Helen Mirren, Ian Holm. 107 minutes. Rated PG-13.*
"Insightful", "worthwhile" bio of the "mad, irascible" British monarch who, among other things, lost the American colonies; though "history buffs" declare the "accuracy is debatable", there's no debate about Hawthorne's "superb" performance (that "almost makes George III sympathetic"), nor that it's "visually stunning", with an Art Direction Oscar as proof.

### Magdalene Sisters, The    25 | 26 | 26 | 23
*2003. Directed by Peter Mullan. With Anne-Marie Duff, Dorothy Duffy, Eileen Walsh, Nora-Jane Noone. 119 minutes. Rated R.*
"Quite an eye-opener", this Irish "exposé" tells the true story of young women "deemed immoral" and committed to asylums to "pay for their sins" "in the name of religion"; its "documentary-like style" and a strong cast of "little-known actors" make for "raw" filmmaking that "stays in your mind."

### Magnificent Ambersons, The **O∅**    ∇ 24 | 23 | 22 | 23
*1942. Directed by Orson Welles. With Joseph Cotten, Dolores Costello, Anne Baxter, Agnes Moorehead. 88 minutes. Not Rated.*
"In the shadow of *Citizen Kane*" stands Welles' "visually brilliant" but oft-"overlooked" follow-up, this "turn-of-the-century" drama detailing the "downfall of an Indiana family" whose spoiled scion can't "keep up with the times"; some magnificence is lost due to

the "damage done by the studio's re-editing", but admirers say this "90% masterpiece" is still "brilliant filmmaking."

### Magnificent Seven, The ⑪ | 26 | 22 | 25 | 23 |
*1960. Directed by John Sturges. With Yul Brynner, Steve McQueen, Eli Wallach, Charles Bronson. 128 minutes. Not Rated.*
"Gunfighter cool" is alive and well in this "magnificent remake" of *The Seven Samurai* that "stands on its own" despite being "translated into a Western" and cast with "big stars of the '60s"; those who "never tire of watching it" "enjoy the adventure", "love the score" and attempt to "memorize the dialogue" that's become "fodder for countless movie trivia questions."

### Magnolia | 20 | 23 | 18 | 21 |
*1999. Directed by Paul Thomas Anderson. With Tom Cruise, Julianne Moore, Philip Seymour Hoffman, Jason Robards Jr., John C. Reilly. 188 minutes. Rated R.*
"Love-it-or-hate-it" filmmaking from auteur Anderson that's either a "compelling" study of "intersecting lives" in the San Fernando Valley or a "never-ending" "letdown" about a "bunch of dysfunctional people"; still, the direction is "energetic" and "Cruise actually acts", though some ask "what's up with the frogs?"

### Malcolm X | 23 | 26 | 23 | 23 |
*1992. Directed by Spike Lee. With Denzel Washington, Angela Bassett, Al Freeman Jr. 194 minutes. Rated PG-13.*
In this "galvanizing", "probing" bio, the "transformation" of Malcolm X from "young hustler" to "outspoken" Civil Rights leader is portrayed by an "emotional" Washington in such a "bravura", "sympathetic" way that many say he was "robbed of an Oscar"; still, this "profound" film is a "time capsule of black American style" that resolutely "captivates and educates."

### MALTESE FALCON, THE ◑ | 28 | 27 | 27 | 25 |
*1941. Directed by John Huston. With Humphrey Bogart, Mary Astor, Peter Lorre. 101 minutes. Not Rated.*
The "stuff movies should be made of", this "vintage noir gem" boasts an "unforgettable Bogie" as the "hard-boiled detective" Sam Spade, plus a "blue-ribbon" supporting cast of "creeps and crooks", all searching for a mysterious "rara avis"; although its "taut script" that "runs like a Swiss watch" and "keeps you guessing to the end" is "often imitated", this "perfect rendering" of Dashiell Hammett's novel has been "never duplicated."

### Man and a Woman, A ✉⑪🅵 | 24 | 24 | 24 | 24 |
*1966. Directed by Claude Lelouch. With Anouk Aimée, Jean-Louis Trintignant. 102 minutes. Not Rated.*
For "romance par excellence", this "touching", "very French" '60s "classic" is served with "panache" and is "still worth seeing" today – indeed, the "music alone can make you fall in love"; detailing an affair between a widow and widower, it stars a "beautiful Aimée" opposite "Trintignant at his best"; "see it with someone special" and you may produce your own little sequel.

### MANCHURIAN CANDIDATE, THE ◑ | 27 | 26 | 28 | 25 |
*1962. Directed by John Frankenheimer. With Frank Sinatra, Laurence Harvey, Angela Lansbury. 126 minutes. Rated PG-13.*
As "perfectly paranoid" "Cold War" filmmaking, this provocative "conspiracy thriller" about Korean War–era "brainwashing" still

packs a "wallop" due to a "twist"-laden script and a "take-your-breath-away" ending; Sinatra and Harvey are "electrifying", but the real revelation is Lansbury as an "evil", solitaire-playing mommy.

### MAN FOR ALL SEASONS, A ✉    28 | 28 | 27 | 27
*1966. Directed by Fred Zinnemann. With Paul Scofield, Wendy Hiller, Robert Shaw. 120 minutes. Rated G.*
"Intelligent and riveting in a quiet way", this "literate" historical drama about the "conflict between conscience and convenience" between Henry VIII and Sir Thomas More garnered six Oscars, including Best Actor for the "magnificent Scofield"; a "rare film about integrity", "loyalty and betrayal", it serves as a "reminder of the days when the movies enlightened."

### Manhattan ◑    26 | 24 | 23 | 24
*1979. Directed by Woody Allen. With Woody Allen, Diane Keaton, Michael Murphy, Mariel Hemingway. 96 minutes. Rated R.*
"Even NYers get all mushy" about this "love letter to the Big Apple" filmed in "fantastic black and white" and set to a thrilling "Gershwin soundtrack"; a romance laced with "angst", it appeals to those who like their "philosophy mixed with a little comedy" and is "more fully realized than *Annie Hall*"; in a nutshell, "it can be fun to be depressive."

### Man on Fire    21 | 25 | 21 | 22
*2004. Directed by Tony Scott. With Denzel Washington, Dakota Fanning, Christopher Walken. 146 minutes. Rated R.*
"Revenge" is the emotion driving this "intense" thriller starring a "prime Denzel" as "one bad mother" bodyguard who turns "vigilante" after his charge is kidnapped; critics find the beginning "compelling" enough, but say the second half disintegrates into a "mindless shoot-'em-up" further muddied by "hyperactive" camerawork; "no lasting impact" is the final verdict.

### Man on the Moon    16 | 22 | 15 | 17
*1999. Directed by Milos Forman. With Jim Carrey, Danny DeVito, Courtney Love. 118 minutes. Rated R.*
Carrey is "better as Andy than Andy himself" in this "affecting" bio of spaced-out '70s comic Andy Kaufman, whose "funny but strange" routines conclude with an early curtain after he succumbs to cancer; though it's heckled as a "disappointing, disjointed" portrait that "doesn't shed much light" on its "complicated" subject, it's still "entertaining" for Dada comedy fans.

### Man Who Came to Dinner, The ◑∅   ▽ 26 | 27 | 25 | 23
*1942. Directed by William Keighley. With Bette Davis, Ann Sheridan, Monty Woolley. 112 minutes. Not Rated.*
Fans of "smart, hilarious" comedy relish the "unforgettable feast" in this screen treatment of Kaufman-Hart's stage play à clef, with Woolley "stealing the movie" as a "pompous radio personality" who visits a Midwestern household and "won't go home" after becoming wheelchair-bound; mixing "acid wit" with "fast-paced" dialogue, it's a "not-to-be-missed" "scream" from the "old school."

### Man Who Fell to Earth, The    18 | 18 | 20 | 17
*1976. Directed by Nicolas Roeg. With David Bowie, Rip Torn, Candy Clark. 140 minutes. Rated R.*
Followers of this "way-ahead-of-its-time" sci-fi fantasy about an extraterrestrial "searching for water" to save his planet say it's

"still relevant", citing its "inventive" storyline and "perfect casting" ("Bowie has no trouble playing a trippy alien"); however, some dismiss it as an "incoherent", "unwatchable mess" that's too "creepy and weird."

### Man Who Knew Too Much, The    24 | 24 | 25 | 24
*1956. Directed by Alfred Hitchcock. With James Stewart, Doris Day, Brenda de Banzie. 120 minutes. Rated PG.*
A "Hitchcock remake of an earlier Hitchcock" thriller, this "more commercial" version plays up the "amazing ordinariness" of its "everyman" stars as they seek their kidnapped son; for most, it's "very exciting" – especially the "unbearably suspenseful" "scene in Royal Albert Hall" – though a few "could do without" Day's "cornball" rendition of 'Que Sera, Sera' (which still snagged a Best Song Oscar).

### Man Who Shot Liberty Valance, The ◑ 25 | 24 | 25 | 23
*1962. Directed by John Ford. With John Wayne, James Stewart, Vera Miles, Lee Marvin, Edmond O'Brien. 123 minutes. Not Rated.*
The formidable Ford's "darkest Western" is illuminated by a "star-studded" cast featuring "all-time bad guy" Lee Marvin in his "finest performance", with "dynamic" backup from Wayne and Stewart; though a bit "claustrophobic" (it was filmed "mostly on Hollywood soundstages"), this is still "mythic" moviemaking that "works like a huge, sprawling novel"; biggest surprise: "Wayne loses the girl."

### Man Who Wasn't There, The ◑    21 | 25 | 19 | 25
*2001. Directed by Joel Coen. With Billy Bob Thornton, Frances McDormand, James Gandolfini. 116 minutes. Rated R.*
This "quirky, haunting" take on vintage film noir ("as only the Coen brothers can re-create it") charts the last days of a "hapless" small-town barber whose "decline is a metaphor" for nothing less than "modern alienation"; the "stylistically incredible" cinematography is "so colorful you forget it's filmed in black and white", while Thornton's titular turn nearly manages to "out-Bogart Bogart."

### Man Who Would Be King, The    25 | 26 | 26 | 25
*1975. Directed by John Huston. With Sean Connery, Michael Caine, Christopher Plummer. 129 minutes. Rated PG.*
Based on Kipling's "epic of friendship and heroism", this "classic adaptation" is a "ripsnorting", "good-time adventure" chronicling the perils of a pair of "opportunistic" "British rogues" on a "grand lark" in 19th-century colonial India; the combination of "sweeping vistas", "incandescent chemistry" between Connery and Caine and a "haunting ending" make for a "buddy flick that rises way above the genre."

### Man with the Golden Gun, The    18 | 17 | 17 | 20
*1974. Directed by Guy Hamilton. With Roger Moore, Christopher Lee, Britt Ekland. 125 minutes. Rated PG.*
"Moore almost redeems himself" in his second stab at 007 ("much better than his debut"), though Lee steals the show as a "droll" assassin boasting "three nipples" as well as a golden gun; still, despite the sizzle supplied by Ekland and some "great Asian scenery", foes dismiss it as a "disjointed, inferior" misfire in the Bond canon.

## Marathon Man
24 | 27 | 24 | 22

*1976. Directed by John Schlesinger. With Dustin Hoffman, Laurence Olivier, Roy Scheider. 125 minutes. Rated R.*

"Just when you thought it was safe to go back to the dentist" comes this "nasty" little thriller about a "totally mad", "tooth-drilling" "Nazi on the loose" hell-bent on retrieving ill-gotten loot; the "huffing, puffing" Hoffman is "superlative" as a man "drawn into something way beyond his control", while set pieces like the "whining drill" scene and the "diamond-swallowing" finale raise enough "goose bumps" to make most "swear off checkups for life."

## Maria Full of Grace 🅕
25 | 26 | 25 | 22

*2004. Directed by Joshua Marston. With Catalina Sandino Moreno, Yenny Paola Vega. 101 minutes. Rated R.*

The "horrific plight" of women desperate to "wean themselves from poverty" by becoming "pawns in the drug trade" is the "untold story" brought to light by this "raw", "impactful" indie; newcomer Moreno shows she's "full of talent" in the role of a Colombian cocaine mule, and while her near-"suicidal" mission "puts you through a wringer", it's worth it for the film's "unbleached message of hope."

## Mark of Zorro, The ◑
22 | 19 | 22 | 19

*1940. Directed by Rouben Mamoulian. With Tyrone Power, Linda Darnell, Basil Rathbone. 94 minutes. Not Rated.*

This "rousing adventure" tale of "double identity and romance" has "hardly dated" thanks to the "dashing", buckle-swashing Power's "sexy swordfighting"; "lady-in-distress" Darnell is "unbelievably lovely", "fop" Rathbone "as dastardly as ever" and a "marvelous" Alfred Newman score provides the cinematic coup de grace.

## Married to the Mob
17 | 17 | 16 | 16

*1988. Directed by Jonathan Demme. With Michelle Pfeiffer, Matthew Modine, Dean Stockwell. 103 minutes. Rated R.*

'Family' fare à la Jonathan Demme, this "quirky" comedy stars a "gorgeous" Pfeiffer playing a "small-time mobster's wife" parting with The Life after a dishonored don rubs out her hubby; "silly" but "easy to watch", it features a "fine" ensemble cast "having a great time" as well as a "don't-miss-it" cameo from "Alec Baldwin's chest hair."

## Marty ✉◑
25 | 27 | 24 | 21

*1955. Directed by Delbert Mann. With Ernest Borgnine, Betsy Blair, Esther Minciotti. 91 minutes. Not Rated.*

Ok, the story of a "sloppy butcher" who finds love with a "mousy clerk" might "never play", but this "poignant" Paddy Chayefsky drama proved naysayers wrong, garnering four Oscars (including Best Actor for Borgnine, who's "perfect" as an ordinary Brooklyn schmo); shot in black and white, its "realistic style" "never gets old" – but be prepared for a feeling of "hopelessness" throughout.

## Mary Poppins ✉
27 | 24 | 25 | 27

*1964. Directed by Robert Stevenson. With Julie Andrews, Dick Van Dyke, David Tomlinson. 140 minutes. Rated G.*

Mix a "perky" Andrews (as an "odd" nanny with "magical powers") with a "cheeky" Van Dyke, "fantastic animation" and "catchy tunes", add a "spoonful of sugar" and the result is a "super-duper" Disney "treat"; a "technical marvel of its time", this "jolly" production "makes you feel good at any age" and serves as a dandy "introduction to musicals for kids."

### MASH ✉     26 | 25 | 26 | 24
*1970. Directed by Robert Altman. With Donald Sutherland, Elliott Gould, Sally Kellerman. 116 minutes. Rated PG.*
"War is hell (and funny)" in this "groundbreaking" "black" satire about a dysfunctional Korean War medical unit that still "holds up" as "one of the smartest comedies ever written" – "once you get past all the blood", that is; maybe the "last third" goes "downhill" during the "lame" football game, but there's no doubt this is "Altman's breakthrough."

### Mask     21 | 24 | 23 | 19
*1985. Directed by Peter Bogdanovich. With Cher, Sam Elliott, Eric Stoltz. 120 minutes. Rated PG-13.*
Proof that "Cher can act", this "touching tearjerker" showcases the diva in "top form" as a single biker mom "in a tough situation with a challenged kid" who's horribly disfigured; as the "grotesque" teen who just "wants to be treated normally", an "amazing" Stoltz radiates enough "inner beauty" to remind the rest of us "how lucky we are."

### Mask, The     17 | 18 | 15 | 20
*1994. Directed by Chuck Russell. With Jim Carrey, Cameron Diaz, Peter Riegert. 101 minutes. Rated PG-13.*
A bedraggled schmo finds a magical mask that transforms him into a swinging, macho hero in this "entertaining" comedy that might hinge on a "ridiculous concept" but nevertheless "works" (thanks to Carrey's "funny" performance); though "kinda stupid" to brainiacs, fans are wowed by the "dazzling effects", including the "luminous Diaz", who makes her "delightful" screen debut here.

### Mask of Zorro, The     18 | 17 | 18 | 21
*1998. Directed by Martin Campbell. With Antonio Banderas, Catherine Zeta-Jones. 136 minutes. Rated PG-13.*
This "big-budget" spin on the "Zorro legend" provokes dueling opinions: zealots admire its "old-school movie style" ("great swordfights", "breathtaking" production values) and ask "is there a better-looking cast ever assembled?"; but critics parry it's "lightweight fluff" that might work well with "popcorn" but "doesn't hold a candle to the 1940 version."

### Master and Commander:     23 | 24 | 22 | 27
### The Far Side of the World
*2003. Directed by Peter Weir. With Russell Crowe, Paul Bettany. 138 minutes. Rated PG-13.*
For "textbook adventure filmmaking" sailing over the "bounding main", set your sights on this "visually extraordinary" nautical epic depicting "cat-and-mouse" high-sea games during the Napoleonic War; the all-male cast includes the "great-as-usual" Crowe backed up by a "strong" Bettany, but despite "incredible battle scenes", "magnificent storms" and "stellar" special effects, mutineers say the "thin" storyline and "endless frigate jargon" simply "don't hold water"; other seafarers, however, "look forward to another installment."

## MATRIX, THE ⊕     25 | 19 | 25 | 28

*1999. Directed by Andy Wachowski, Larry Wachowski. With Keanu Reeves, Laurence Fishburne, Carrie-Anne Moss. 136 minutes. Rated R.*
"Move over, *Star Wars*"; not even Reeves' "leaden" acting can sink this "mind-bending, reality-rocking" "new modern myth" of a movie that "raised the bar on special effects" and "revolutionized hand-to-hand combat in filmmaking"; even if its "intricate" plot (something about a computer hacker turned "humanity's last hope") verges on "incoherence", this "sci-fi shoot-'em-up for people with brains" just "gets better every time you see it."

## Matrix Reloaded, The ⊕     21 | 17 | 18 | 26

*2003. Directed by Andy Wachowski, Larry Wachowski. With Keanu Reeves, Carrie-Anne Moss, Laurence Fishburne, Hugo Weaving. 138 minutes. Rated R.*
The "conceptual novelty's gone", the "story is not as compelling as the original" and it "could have benefited from some editing", yet the "sexier" second installment of the "groundbreaking" sci-fi trilogy is still "worth a watch" for its "eye candy galore" – "off-the-charts special effects", "take-your-breath-away fight scenes" and a "car-chase scene that just blows your mind"; now if only there were "a *Matrix for Dummies* to explain what happened."

## Matrix Revolutions, The     15 | 14 | 13 | 23

*2003. Directed by Andy Wachowski, Larry Wachowski. With Keanu Reeves, Laurence Fishburne, Carrie-Ann Moss. 129 minutes. Rated R.*
This "less than stellar end" to the martial-arts/sci-fi trilogy features the same "over-the-top CGI effects" and "garbled-but-intriguing philosophy" as the preceding installments, but this time out there's "too much action and not enough thought"; in fact, it's such a "letdown" to a series that "started with so much potential" that many think "they should have stopped after the first one."

## Maverick     18 | 20 | 17 | 19

*1994. Directed by Richard Donner. With Mel Gibson, Jodie Foster, James Garner. 127 minutes. Rated PG.*
As TV shows morphed into movies go, this "laid-back Western" based on ABC's '50s series "works well" by loading the deck with "escapism", "modern twists" and Gibson as a "tall, dark stranger" who's "having more fun than the audience"; but it's the "effortless style" of Garner (the original Maverick) that wins big.

## McCabe & Mrs. Miller     23 | 23 | 23 | 24

*1971. Directed by Robert Altman. With Warren Beatty, Julie Christie, Shelley Duvall. 120 minutes. Rated R.*
Decidedly "not for conventional Western" fans, this "brilliantly directed", "postmodern deconstruction" of the genre "eliminates the clichés" and "faithfully re-creates what the West was really like": namely, "harsh, cruel and lacking true heroes"; despite one major drawback – "you can't understand what anyone is saying" – it's more than evident that the leads are "impossibly in love."

## Mean Streets     ∇ 24 | 27 | 22 | 22

*1973. Directed by Martin Scorsese. With Harvey Keitel, Robert De Niro. 110 minutes. Rated R.*
"Gritty and graphic before that became the norm", Scorsese's breakout drama of hoods in the 'hood "rings with truth" as a "definitive slice of NY", with Keitel out to "make it in the mob"

in spite of "Catholic guilt" and ties to De Niro's "unforgettable" loose-cannon "loser"; it's a "grim" but "passionate" study of streetwise style, including some "pioneering" use of "oldies but goodies" on the soundtrack.

### Meatballs Ⓞ
18 | 15 | 17 | 14

*1979. Directed by Ivan Reitman. With Bill Murray, Harvey Atkin, Kate Lynch. 99 minutes. Rated PG.*

A pre-"*Caddyshack*" Murray plays a wisecracking "summer camp counselor everyone would love to have" in this "underrated", lowbrow "comedy staple", later "ruined" by three sequels; ok, it might be a "little dated" and "poor production quality" detracts, but overall it conveys the "experience every camper hopes for."

### Mediterraneo ✉️🎬∅
21 | 21 | 20 | 23

*1991. Directed by Gabriele Salvatores. With Diego Abatantuono, Claudio Bigagli. 96 minutes. Rated R.*

Sure, this "sweet" comedy about a group of WWII Italian soldiers "stranded" on a Greek isle is a "trifle", but the "beautiful cinematography" and "sweep-you-away" soundtrack nicely complement its assortment of "cute characters"; some report the story "drags in some parts" (resulting in "awkward" scenes), but it offers enough "great escapism" to make for a primo "date flick."

### Meet Me in St. Louis
26 | 24 | 23 | 26

*1944. Directed by Vincente Minnelli. With Judy Garland, Margaret O'Brien, Mary Astor. 113 minutes. Not Rated.*

Clang, clang, clang, here comes Garland "at her radiant finest" as a girl who "adores the boy next door" in this musical "treasure" about a "turn-of-the-century" American family; fans laud its "sumptuous" Technicolor production and "unforgettable" tunes, while brainiacs hint it's "darker and deeper than its rep suggests."

### Meet the Parents Ⓞ
19 | 21 | 19 | 19

*2000. Directed by Jay Roach. With Robert De Niro, Ben Stiller, Blythe Danner. 108 minutes. Rated PG-13.*

"Every guy's worst nightmare" about being introduced to his "prospective in-laws" comes true in this very "watchable" comedy that succeeds mainly because of the "brilliant pairing of Stiller and De Niro"; though the unamused frown it "relies too much on slapstick" and repeats the "same joke for two hours straight", most say it "pinpoints" an "all-too-real" situation.

### MEMENTO
26 | 25 | 27 | 25

*2000. Directed by Christopher Nolan. With Guy Pearce, Carrie-Anne Moss. 113 minutes. Rated R.*

"Bring your brain to the theater, you'll need it" for this "exquisitely existential" "mind-bender" about a man who loses his "short-term memory" following his wife's murder; it "turns traditional narrative on its head" by telling the story "in reverse" – so it may "require several viewings to get it all straight"; though there's applause for the "stunning" Pearce, befuddled folks "still trying to figure it out" wail it's too "gnisufnoc."

### Men in Black Ⓞ
21 | 20 | 21 | 24

*1997. Directed by Barry Sonnenfeld. With Tommy Lee Jones, Will Smith, Linda Fiorentino. 98 minutes. Rated PG-13.*

"Wisecracking" Smith and "deadpan" Jones show "great chemistry" as they battle "slime, aliens and explosions" in this "action-packed" sci-fi "blockbuster" that's "delicious fun"; a "kids' movie for adults", it's a "hugely enjoyable spoof" that some find "silly" and may be a "little gross."

## METROPOLIS ◑
27 | 22 | 24 | 28

*1927. Directed by Fritz Lang. With Alfred Abel, Gustav Froelich, Brigitte Helm. 153 minutes. Not Rated.*

A "visionary" film of "magnitude, imagination and depth", this "sci-fi social commentary" about "oppression and uprising" set in a "futuristic city" "still retains its visual impact" seven decades later; indeed, Lang's "man-versus-machine" story (embodied by a "fetishized woman robot") remains "revolutionary in every sense of the word" – this is a "movie everybody should watch at least once."

## Metropolitan ∅
▽ 20 | 19 | 20 | 17

*1990. Directed by Whit Stillman. With Carolyn Farina, Edward Clements, Christopher Eigeman. 98 minutes. Rated PG-13.*

The "young and the privileged" in "present-day NY" get the Jane Austen treatment in this "charming" "coming-of-age" comedy with an "exciting young cast" spouting "intensely dry", "droll" dialogue; those fascinated by "rich kids and their problems" say it's one part "Woody Allen", one part "George Plimpton."

## Midnight Cowboy ✉
26 | 28 | 24 | 24

*1969. Directed by John Schlesinger. With Dustin Hoffman, Jon Voight, Sylvia Miles. 113 minutes. Rated R.*

"Still as gritty as ever", this "unvarnished look at NYC street life" is a "touching" if "depressing" depiction of a pair of "down-and-out" losers "spiraling downward" that turns the "buddy-flick concept" on its ear; the first "X-rated" film to take Best Picture honors (and since re-rated), it continues to wow with "inner beauty", "haunting music" and "brilliant" turns from Hoffman and Voight – and that "ending on the bus is unforgettable."

## Midnight Express ✉
24 | 24 | 25 | 22

*1978. Directed by Alan Parker. With Brad Davis, Randy Quaid, John Hurt. 120 minutes. Rated R.*

This "frighteningly realistic" drama about a not-so-innocent American abroad imprisoned for smuggling hash "should be required viewing for teens and travelers", even though this "eye-opener" might "induce nightmares for years to come"; it probably "did more to stop kids from doing drugs" than all of "Nancy Reagan's efforts" combined.

## Mighty Aphrodite
18 | 21 | 18 | 18

*1995. Directed by Woody Allen. With Woody Allen, Mira Sorvino, Michael Rapaport. 98 minutes. Rated R.*

Maybe "not as incisive" as Allen's "best", this "minor Woody" work still exudes "inventive charm" in its story of a man seeking the biological mother of his adopted child; throw in an "inspired Greek chorus" providing commentary and Sorvino's Oscar-winning turn as a "ditzy hooker", and the result is "painless fun."

## Mighty Wind, A
23 | 26 | 21 | 23

*2003. Directed by Christopher Guest. With Bob Balaban, Christopher Guest, John Michael Higgins, Eugene Levy. 91 minutes. Rated PG-13.*

"You'll have almost as much fun as the cast" watching this "hysterical mockumentary" about the "'60s folk music scene" full of "priceless material", a "hilarious cast of characters" and "lots of hidden humor"; while "not as good as *Best in Show*", "anything by Guest is better than most everyone else's work."

### Mildred Pierce ✉◗

26 | 25 | 25 | 24

*1945. Directed by Michael Curtiz. With Joan Crawford, Jack Carson, Ann Blyth, Eve Arden. 111 minutes. Not Rated.*
Oscar-winner Crawford is in "full weeper bloom" (with "shoulder pads for days" and "star lighting to make sure you get the point") in this noir "sudser" based on the James M. Cain novel about a "mother who sacrifices everything for her daughter"; "camp" followers crack up over Arden's "witty repartee" (which "would put any drag queen to shame") and "rent it as a double feature with *Mommie Dearest* for full impact."

### Miller's Crossing

22 | 23 | 22 | 22

*1990. Directed by Joel Coen. With Gabriel Byrne, Albert Finney, Marcia Gay Harden. 115 minutes. Rated R.*
"Don't give the high hat" to this "subtle", "criminally underrated" early Coen brothers "gem" about a gangland war between Irish and Italian mobsters that proves "betrayal can come back to haunt you"; devotees declare it "deserves to be up there with *Goodfellas*", given the worthiness of the "broody" Byrne, "knockout Finney" and "deliciously tangled" plot "larded with obscure underworld slang."

### MILLION DOLLAR BABY ✉

27 | 28 | 25 | 26

*2004. Directed by Clint Eastwood. With Clint Eastwood, Hilary Swank, Morgan Freeman. 132 minutes. Rated PG-13.*
What begins as a boxing "Cinderella story" about a "guilt-racked coach" mentoring a "determined female fighter" takes a "sharp turn" and becomes a "profound" meditation on "significant moral dilemmas" in this "knockout" Oscar magnet from "powerhouse" actor/director Eastwood; a "flawless Swank" and "quietly brilliant" Freeman round out the cast in this "simple", "less-is-more" production, with a "surprise" ending that "leaves you breathless."

### Minority Report

21 | 20 | 22 | 25

*2002. Directed by Steven Spielberg. With Tom Cruise, Colin Farrell, Samantha Morton, Max Von Sydow. 145 minutes. Rated PG-13.*
"Cruise and Spielberg are a great combo" in this "intelligent, exciting" sci-fi thriller with "stunning visual effects" and "a mind-bending premise" – catching murderers before they commit the actual crime; though the "original, chilling storyline" "moves at lightning speed", it's "hard to follow at times", making it more difficult to detect the "holes in the plot"; bottom line: "better than the box office would indicate."

### Miracle

24 | 23 | 26 | 24

*2004. Directed by Gavin O'Connor. With Kurt Russell, Patricia Clarkson. 135 minutes. Rated PG.*
Although most already "know the ending", this "feel-good" "insider's look" at the U.S. hockey team's quest for gold at the 1980 Olympics keeps athletic supporters "riveted" with its taut "they-shoot-they-score" script; indeed, Kurt's "commanding performance" and the "realistic moments on and off the ice" keep its "inspirational" themes resonating long afterwards – "way to go, team."

### Miracle on 34th Street ✉◑    25 | 23 | 26 | 23
*1947. Directed by George Seaton. With Maureen O'Hara, Natalie Wood, Edmund Gwenn. 96 minutes. Not Rated.*
It "can't be Christmas" without a screening of this "schmaltzy", "charming fantasy" that embodies a "child's belief in Santa Claus" so well that it's become an enduring "seasonal favorite" for "every generation"; true believers say the Oscar-winning screenplay is the key behind this "perfect" "holiday classic" that puts the remakes to shame.

### Miracle Worker, The ✉◑    25 | 28 | 24 | 22
*1962. Directed by Arthur Penn. With Anne Bancroft, Patty Duke, Victor Jory, Inga Swenson. 106 minutes. Not Rated.*
"Beautifully transferred from stage to screen" by director Penn, this "moving" account of deaf-and-blind Helen Keller and her teacher Annie Sullivan garnered Oscars for both leads (who reprised their Broadway roles); while Duke is undeniably "superb", it's Bancroft who "dominates" this "fiercely acted", "exceptional" film; most memorable moment: at the water pump.

### Misery ✉    21 | 24 | 23 | 19
*1990. Directed by Rob Reiner. With James Caan, Kathy Bates, Richard Farnsworth. 107 minutes. Rated R.*
This "freaky" yarn about an injured writer "rescued" from a snowstorm by a "seriously deranged" fan is a "hobbling", "cracking-with-tension" experience that really "packs a wallop"; Oscar-winner Bates is beyond "mesmerizing" as the seriously "obsessed", "sledgehammer-swinging" captor opposite Caan's "excellent", hapless hostage, though diehards say the real credit goes to Reiner's "great hand when it comes to directing Stephen King stories."

### Miss Congeniality    15 | 16 | 15 | 16
*2000. Directed by Donald Petrie. With Sandra Bullock, Michael Caine, Benjamin Bratt. 109 minutes. Rated PG-13.*
Action comedy meets "chick flick" in this "lighthearted send-up" of beauty-contest culture starring Bullock at her most "adorable" as a "tomboy FBI agent" who goes undercover as cheesecake in a national pageant; ok, it's "slight" and "sophomoric", but in the eyes of most beholders it's "endearing fun" – despite the absence of "Bert Parks."

### Mission, The    24 | 24 | 22 | 25
*1986. Directed by Roland Joffé. With Robert De Niro, Jeremy Irons, Liam Neeson. 126 minutes. Rated PG.*
"Beautifully shot", Oscar-winning cinematography nearly steals the show in this "intriguing drama" about an 18th-century struggle between missionaries and mercenaries over the riches of South America; even though evangelist Irons and reformed slave trader De Niro turn out their usual "amazing" work, unfazed foes feel Ennio Morricone's "soundtrack is far better" than the picture itself.

### Mission: Impossible ⓸    16 | 15 | 15 | 21
*1996. Directed by Brian De Palma. With Tom Cruise, Jon Voight, Ving Rhames. 110 minutes. Rated PG-13.*
Many "convoluted" plot "twists" make this "tense", "James Bond–ish" action/adventurer a "watchable" if "highly confusing" picture; while diehards "drool" over the "never-looking-better"

Tom in an "all-black DKNY-ish outfit" performing "amazing stunts", purists pronounce it "not as good as the TV show" and bawl "bring back Peter Graves."

### Mississippi Burning
23 | 24 | 23 | 22

*1988. Directed by Alan Parker. With Gene Hackman, Willem Dafoe, Frances McDormand. 128 minutes. Rated R.*
A "story that needed to be told", this "powerful" depiction of '60s "racial unrest" focuses on an investigation of the murder of three Civil Rights workers; yet despite an "all-too-real glimpse of life in the Deep South", critics say it overemphasizes "white hate" to the point that there are few "speaking parts for black actors."

### Mister Roberts ⑪
27 | 27 | 24 | 23

*1955. Directed by John Ford, Mervyn LeRoy. With Henry Fonda, James Cagney, Jack Lemmon. 123 minutes. Not Rated.*
A Broadway hit transposed to the big screen, this "heartfelt" story about the misadventures of a WWII supply ship crew delivers "wonderful acting all around", from the "unforgettable" Cagney to the "perfect" Fonda and "no-slouch" Lemmon; a "great wartime comedy with a serious side", it leaves even tough guys with a "lump in their throat."

### MODERN TIMES ◑
28 | 26 | 26 | 25

*1936. Directed by Charles Chaplin. With Charles Chaplin, Paulette Goddard. 87 minutes. Not Rated.*
"Timelessly funny and resonant", this "man-vs.-machine" story runs on a "blend of slapstick and pathos" guaranteed to make you "smile . . . though your heart is breaking"; there's "little dialogue" (save for Chaplin's "singing waiter" "gibberish number"), but his "heartwarming" performance and sharp "swipes at the age of technology" transcend words; in short, this one's a "must-see in *these* times."

### Mommie Dearest
17 | 19 | 16 | 17

*1981. Directed by Frank Perry. With Faye Dunaway, Diana Scarwid, Steve Forrest. 129 minutes. Rated PG.*
Right up there in the "camp classic" pantheon is this look at "ice lady" Joan Crawford and her adopted daughter Christina that's notorious for Dunaway's "uncanny", "over-the-top" title performance, a truly "scary" imagining of the "horror of being a fading star"; though some call it "exploitive", "bitter stuff", others insist it's "absorbing" and sometimes "terribly funny"; most quoted line: "*no more wire hangers!*"

### Monkey Business ◑
▽ 25 | 24 | 19 | 20

*1931. Directed by Norman Z. McLeod. With the Marx Brothers, Thelma Todd. 77 minutes. Not Rated.*
This "early" Marx Brothers' "Hollywood vehicle" is both "solidly entertaining" and "suitably anarchic" as the sibs stow away on a luxury liner and much "hilarious" "shipboard mayhem" ensues; though maybe "not quite their best" work, this "could be their looniest" of all – especially Harpo's "Punch and Judy" riff.

### Mon Oncle ✉🇫
▽ 25 | 24 | 22 | 24

*1958. Directed by Jacques Tati. With Jacques Tati, Jean-Pierre Zola. 110 minutes. Not Rated.*
A trove of "very French" folly to "tickle your brain" and "set you giggling", this "delightful" comedy has Tati reprising his "sad-sack"

Hulot act as he "bumbles through life" in a series of "superb gags and set pieces"; his "everyman-as-a-buffoon" shtick is a trusty "chuckle producer", while the underlying "commentary on modernity gone awry" is "really funny" too.

### Monsoon Wedding 🇫     24 | 23 | 23 | 23

*2002. Directed by Mira Nair. With Naseeruddin Shah, Lillete Dubey, Shefali Shetty, Vasundhara Das, Parvin Dabas. 114 minutes. Rated R.*

A "feast for the funny bone, eyes and mind", this "charming" dramedy about a "dysfunctional" Indian family and the wedding of their daughter "proves that all families are the same no matter the ethnicity"; it's "a bit slow", but the "colorful cinematography" and "fantastic music" will make you "want to see it again."

### Monster ✉     24 | 29 | 24 | 22

*2003. Directed by Patty Jenkins. With Charlize Theron, Christina Ricci. 109 minutes. Rated R.*

"Frighteningly believable" and thus "tough to watch", this bio of serial murderess Aileen Wuornos "pushes all the emotional buttons" thanks to a "complete immersion" in the role by the Oscar-winning, "makeup"-slathered Theron (with ample backup from the "unsung" Ricci as her girlfriend); though "not as gruesome as it could have been", this "downer" does deliver enough imagery so "violent" that many vow to "never pick up a hitchhiker again."

### Monster's Ball ✉     22 | 26 | 21 | 21

*2001. Directed by Marc Forster. With Billy Bob Thornton, Halle Berry. 111 minutes. Rated R.*

A "redneck" prison guard and the widow of an inmate he helped execute fall in love in this "disturbingly good" drama, a "gritty depiction" of "two lost souls"; the "slow-moving" story sometimes seems "strained, but is redeemed by the acting" of a deglamorized, Oscar-winning Berry and a "solid" Thornton, who display "great chemistry" during that "steamy sex scene."

### Monsters, Inc.     26 | – | 25 | 28

*2001. Directed by Peter Docter, David Silverman, Lee Unkrich. Animated. 92 minutes. Rated G.*

"Pixar does it again" with this "innovative" "animation gem" that "shows kids that the monsters in their closets are really harmless"; this time around, the "*Toy Story*" tech team alloy an "original" plot, "amazing attention to detail" and "ugly" but "cute" characters to create an "endearing" entertainment that works "for adults" too; P.S. the "blow-you-away" "flying door" sequence has got "theme-park ride" written all over it.

### Monty Python & the Holy Grail     26 | 22 | 23 | 21

*1975. Directed by Terry Gilliam, Terry Jones. With Monty Python. 91 minutes. Rated PG.*

By dint of "sheer tasteless genius", this "absurdly wacky" "burlesque of the King Arthur legend" turns "historic reverence" on its ear and rules among "true" Pythonettes as the "movie of a thousand quotes" ("bring out your dead!"); granted, it may be comprised of a series of "strung-together skits" involving "killer bunnies" and "knights who say 'ni'", but the array of "knee-slapping" characters provides enough "lunacy to last the ages."

## Moonraker ⓞ
### 16 | 14 | 15 | 20
*1979. Directed by Lewis Gilbert. With Roger Moore, Lois Chiles, Richard Kiel. 126 minutes. Rated PG.*
A "stiff" Roger Moore pursues the usual mad villain in this 007 picture that has a hard time living up to its "dynamite credits sequence"; most agree the "silly" scenario is "quite a stretch", what with metal-mouth "Jaws finding love" and a "laughable space battle" that "tries to cash in on *Star Wars*" but "plays more like a Bond spoof."

## Moonstruck ✉
### 24 | 25 | 24 | 22
*1987. Directed by Norman Jewison. With Cher, Nicolas Cage, Olympia Dukakis. 102 minutes. Rated PG.*
Both "Italians and wannabe Italians" fall for this "totally charming" "romp" that shows how "love can be found in the least likely places" – even Brooklyn; a "phenomenal" Cher and Cage (making *amore* at such "full throttle" that the "heat between them could peel wallpaper") combine with a "dead-on", "star-studded" ensemble to keep this "romance classic" shining bright; fave scene: the "snap-out-of-it" slap.

## Motorcycle Diaries, The 🄵
### 23 | 25 | 23 | 24
*2004. Directed by Walter Salles. With Gael García Bernal, Rodrigo de la Serna. 128 minutes. Rated R.*
Witness the "seeds of social conscience" sprouting in "young Che Guevara" in this "poetic" road picture set amid "breathtaking South American scenery"; "ogle"-icious Bernal's "marvelous" turn as the future "legendary figure" stokes the revolutionary fire despite hitting a raw nerve with a few *capitalistas* who claim this "saintly" depiction fosters too much "undeserved attention."

## Moulin Rouge
### 21 | 22 | 20 | 26
*1952. Directed by John Huston. With José Ferrer, Zsa Zsa Gabor, Colette Marchand. 119 minutes. Not Rated.*
"Drenched in color and the excitement of belle epoque Paris", this "original" look at the tortured life of artist Toulouse-Lautrec is the "lush" product of an era when "movies were movies"; Ferrer's "completely entertaining" performance as the "completely odd" painter is the glue here, even if his gloomy portrayal might be at odds with the "eye-candy" production values.

## MOULIN ROUGE!
### 23 | 23 | 20 | 27
*2001. Directed by Baz Luhrmann. With Nicole Kidman, Ewan McGregor, Jim Broadbent. 127 minutes. Rated PG-13.*
This "dizzying, decadent" "fever dream of a musical" set in "bohemian Paris" earned a clutch of Oscar nominations and may have "single-handedly revived and re-created the genre" for the "new millennium"; the ever-"ravishing" Kidman "sheds her icy image" in a "kaleidoscopic" turn as a notorious "shady lady" smitten by a "naive poet", and it turns out "McGregor can sing", but naysayers call it a "confusing", "overedited" "mishmash" that's "all glitter, no substance."

## Mouse That Roared, The ⓞ
### 23 | 23 | 24 | 19
*1959. Directed by Jack Arnold. With Peter Sellers, Jean Seberg, David Kossoff. 83 minutes. Not Rated.*
"British humor has never been better" than in this "priceless" Cold War–era import about an impoverished nation that declares

war on America, planning to lose in exchange for foreign aid; an "ingenious" satire that "pokes lots of holes" in a lot of targets, it's "worth seeing" for "Sellers' expert multiple performances alone."

### Mr. Blandings Builds His Dream House ◐
23 | 24 | 23 | 21

*1948. Directed by H.C. Potter. With Cary Grant, Myrna Loy, Melvyn Douglas. 94 minutes. Not Rated.*

"If you're thinking of building or remodeling your home", "there's no funnier movie" than this "timeless" "cautionary tale" that "proves the "perils haven't changed in the last 50 years"; "fixer-uppers" laugh along with this amusing view of the "suburban dream gone askew", most notably "Myrna's painting-the-living-room" scene.

### Mr. Holland's Opus
21 | 22 | 21 | 19

*1995. Directed by Stephen Herek. With Richard Dreyfuss, Glenne Headly. 143 minutes. Rated PG.*

"Sweet, funny and insightful", this "uplifting" opus chronicles the career of a "reluctant" high-school music teacher "who makes a difference in the lives of his students" while "struggling to come to terms with his own deaf son"; though the hard-hearted fuss it's too "preachy", most swear this "inspirational" story is worth seeing for Dreyfuss' "superb" performance alone.

### Mr. Hulot's Holiday ◐
∇ 26 | 25 | 22 | 22

*1954. Directed by Jacques Tati. With Jacques Tati, Nathalie Pascaud. 86 minutes. Not Rated.*

Right "up there with Keaton and Chaplin", Tati's "irresistible" "comic masterpiece" is bound to "take away the worst blues" with some of the "best sight gags" delivered in "almost pure mime"; when its "hilariously" maladroit title character goes to a vacation retreat, whatever "could possibly go wrong does" and the payoff's a "quirky", "low-key" "laugh riot."

### Mr. Mom ✉
18 | 18 | 20 | 17

*1983. Directed by Stan Dragoti. With Michael Keaton, Teri Garr, Martin Mull. 91 minutes. Rated PG.*

Mom and pop "switch roles" in this "fish-out-of-water" comedy detailing the misadventures of a "stay-at-home dad" reduced to "ironing grilled-cheese sandwiches" and "playing poker" with housewives for "shopping coupons"; but even though Keaton is a "likable" enough "slob" in the title role, rewinders report this "guilty pleasure" "doesn't hold up" to repeated viewings.

### Mrs. Brown
22 | 28 | 23 | 23

*1997. Directed by John Madden. With Judi Dench, Billy Connolly, Geoffrey Palmer. 103 minutes. Rated PG.*

"Not widely seen", this "intelligent" drama detailing the platonic relationship between Queen Victoria and her groomsman shows that "even the most hardened heart can be changed by love"; naturally, many say that the "amazing" Dench is "the reason to see it", given her "poignant" performance, though the "intriguing" plot and "subtle" work from Connolly are equally "wonderful."

### Mrs. Doubtfire
20 | 23 | 20 | 20

*1993. Directed by Chris Columbus. With Robin Williams, Sally Field, Pierce Brosnan. 125 minutes. Rated PG-13.*

This "laugh-out-loud" story of a man attempting to "win back his ex and kids" by impersonating a "nanny" manages to be "over-the-top", "subversive" and "endearing" all at once; sure, doubters snipe the "far-fetched" screenplay "can't decide if it's a farce or a tearjerker", but it's agreed that "riot" Williams is "at his manic best" when in "drag."

### Mr. Smith Goes to Washington ◑    26 | 27 | 25 | 22 |
*1939. Directed by Frank Capra. With James Stewart, Jean Arthur, Claude Rains. 125 minutes. Not Rated.*
"As American as two slices of apple pie", Frank Capra's "rousing" "political fairy tale" about "one man's belief in goodness" and his eventual "triumph" "appeals to the idealist in each of us"; "corny", perhaps, but "you can't help but be moved" by Stewart waging the "filibuster to beat all filibusters" – and proving "you *can* beat City Hall."

### Mulan    23 | – | 23 | 24 |
*1998. Directed by Tony Bancroft, Barry Cook. Animated. 88 minutes. Rated G.*
An "underrated" rarity, this "gorgeously realized" animated "Chinese folk tale" features a Disney heroine "who can carry a movie on her own"; its mix of "family honor" and "women power" make it "good for a girl's self-esteem", while "just the right balance of seriousness and humor" "sends its message without preaching."

### Mulholland Dr.    20 | 22 | 19 | 22 |
*2001. Directed by David Lynch. With Naomi Watts, Laura Harring, Justin Theroux. 145 minutes. Rated R.*
"Another confusing but consuming Lynch production", this "intriguing", "utterly disquieting" "portrait of Hollywood losers" "requires contemplation" since it's "hard to follow"; sure, fans say its "smoldering" leads are so "beautiful" that their presence alone makes the film "visually worth it", but cynics feel "totally ripped off" by this "weird" "nonsense."

### Mummy, The ◑    ▽ 22 | 20 | 21 | 19 |
*1932. Directed by Karl Freund. With Boris Karloff, Zita Johann. 72 minutes. Not Rated.*
Fresh out of his Frankenstein boots, "master" of fear Karloff wraps himself around the role of an ancient Egyptian priest who's revived when foolhardy explorers open his crypt in this "standout" horror flick; indeed, Boris is "so very creepy" that many say this "original" version of the oft-filmed tale is still the "best."

### Mummy, The ⓤ    19 | 16 | 18 | 24 |
*1999. Directed by Stephen Sommers. With Brendan Fraser, Rachel Weisz. 124 minutes. Rated PG-13.*
Archeologists ravage Egyptian tombs to disastrous results in this "cornball" "modern B movie" featuring "fancy CGI effects" and a plot that lurches between "scary and funny"; but foes who dis its "ridiculous" premise suggest you "rent the original – *Raiders of the Lost Ark.*"

### Muppet Movie, The ⓤ    24 | 23 | 23 | 25 |
*1979. Directed by James Frawley. With Charles Durning, Austin Pendleton. 97 minutes. Rated G.*
"You're never too old" to enjoy this "goofy" but "utterly delightful" romp that might unleash your "inner kid" thanks to some "wonderful puppetry" abetted by an array of star-studded cameos from everyone from Milton Berle to Steve Martin; fans say it's the

"best" of the Muppet oeuvre, crediting the "genius" of "national treasure" Jim Henson for the "successful transition" of *Sesame Street*'s denizens to the big screen.

### Murder by Death
21 | 21 | 22 | 19

*1976. Directed by Robert Moore. With Peter Falk, Peter Sellers, Maggie Smith, Alec Guinness. 94 minutes. Rated PG.*
A "kooky lampoon that hits the spot", this Neil Simon–penned whodunit "spoof" places a "diverse" group of private eyes in a castle where murder ensues; given the efforts of a Charlie Chan–esque Sellers and a Bogart-channeling Falk, this "madcap" exercise is a "must-see satire for mystery lovers", even if some turn up evidence of too many "good actors playing useless parts."

### Murder on the Orient Express
23 | 23 | 26 | 24

*1974. Directed by Sidney Lumet. With Albert Finney, Lauren Bacall, Ingrid Bergman. 128 minutes. Rated PG.*
"Agatha Christie hasn't been done better" than in this "fascinatingly complex, lushly produced" Hercule Poirot mystery set onboard the Orient Express; boasting a "crisply directed" "all-star" ensemble cast that "looks like they're having the time of their lives", this "luxuriously funny" "perfect thriller" certainly "won't bore you" – and "you'll never guess whodunit."

### Music Man, The
25 | 24 | 25 | 26

*1962. Directed by Morton DaCosta. With Robert Preston, Shirley Jones, Buddy Hackett. 151 minutes. Rated G.*
Making an "exquisite, seamless transition" from Broadway to the silver screen", this slice of "pure Americana" about a "traveling con man" let loose in River City, Iowa, hits "classic" notes with its "catchy" Meredith Willson score; thanks to a "tour-de-force" turn by a "mesmerizing" Preston, this "family treat" "never grows old."

### Mutiny on the Bounty
25 | 25 | 25 | 23

*1935. Directed by Frank Lloyd. With Charles Laughton, Clark Gable, Franchot Tone. 132 minutes. Not Rated.*
Despite being "a bit creaky" after all these years, this original version of a legendary clash of egos on the high seas remains "the one and only" simply because "you don't get acting like this anymore": Laughton is darn "grand" as "definitive villain" Captain Bligh, and "Gable is, well, Gable" as Mr. Christian, his second-in-command.

### Mutiny on the Bounty ∅
22 | 24 | 24 | 22

*1962. Directed by Lewis Milestone. With Marlon Brando, Trevor Howard, Richard Harris. 178 minutes. Not Rated.*
Ultra-"fabulous scenery" that will surely make you "want to move to Tahiti" and a "cast of thousands" collide in this "big-budget" MGM remake about an uprising at sea; Brando turns in "one of his most controversial roles" as a "foppish" Fletcher Christian, even if foes harrumph "I'll take Gable."

### My Beautiful Laundrette
∇ 21 | 22 | 21 | 19

*1985. Directed by Stephen Frears. With Daniel Day-Lewis, Gordon Warnecke. 98 minutes. Rated R.*
This "highly original" drama of "modern London" puts race and assimilation through a "wonderfully up-front" spin cycle in its

story of "smart", "entrepreneurial" immigrants vs. the nativist "lower classes"; amid the many "honest" moments that come out in the wash is the "daring" bond between Warnecke's go-getting Pakistani and Day-Lewis' tough hooligan, resulting in some "steamy gay kissing."

### My Best Friend's Wedding
**19 | 19 | 19 | 19**

*1997. Directed by P.J. Hogan. With Julia Roberts, Dermot Mulroney, Rupert Everett. 105 minutes. Rated PG-13.*
There's "no thinking required" in this "enjoyable if predictable" "chick flick" about a single gal bent on preventing her best male friend from getting hitched; while a "surprisingly funny Roberts" and "yummy Everett" "chew up the scenery" entertainingly, those through with love find this "anti-romance" "contrived" and "obvious" – except for the "'Say a Little Prayer'" sing-along.

### My Big Fat Greek Wedding
**23 | 22 | 23 | 21**

*2002. Directed by Joel Zwick. With Nia Vardalos, John Corbett, Lainie Kazan. 96 minutes. Rated PG.*
It "doesn't matter whether you are Greek, Jewish, Italian or Albanian" – "we all see our crazy relatives up on the screen" in this "absolutely hilarious" "feel-good" look at Hellenic matrimony featuring a "likable cast of characters that you grow to love despite all their quirks"; critics claim "too much big fat hype", but they're outvoted by fans who "will never look at Windex the same way again."

### My Bodyguard
**18 | 18 | 19 | 16**

*1980. Directed by Tony Bill. With Chris Makepeace, Adam Baldwin, Matt Dillon. 96 minutes. Rated PG.*
The "ultimate teenage revenge fantasy", this "feel-good" flick about an "underdog" high-schooler who hires a tough classmate to protect him from a bully "rings true" with "anyone who was ever picked on"; sure, there's a "silly, irrelevant" subplot about "eccentric grown-ups", but overall this "endearing" "coming-of-age saga" is "well done."

### My Cousin Vinny
**22 | 24 | 21 | 19**

*1992. Directed by Jonathan Lynn. With Joe Pesci, Ralph Macchio, Marisa Tomei. 120 minutes. Rated R.*
"Fuhgeddaboudit": this "laugh-out-loud", "quotable" "courtroom classic" about a novice "Noo Yawk lawyer" representing his cousin in an Alabama murder trial is a "cleverly written" comic look at "Southern justice"; a "perfect" Pesci "carries the show", amply assisted by Tomei, who earned a "well-deserved Oscar" just by "making a Brooklyn accent the sexiest sound around"; P.S. it works best with "ordered-in pizza."

### My Dinner with Andre
**21 | 21 | 18 | 19**

*1981. Directed by Louis Malle. With Wallace Shawn, Andre Gregory. 110 minutes. Not Rated.*
Who'd have thought a movie that "consists entirely of a dinner conversation" between two acquaintances could keep you entertained for two hours?; although with talk "spanning every philosophical topic" that "captures the magic in the ordinary", Shawn and Gregory do just that; "remarkable for how little it works with", this "simple, unpretentious" art-house hit is "oddly fascinating" to those who wish their own dining companions "could be as interesting."

### MY FAIR LADY ✉    27 | 27 | 27 | 27
*1964. Directed by George Cukor. With Audrey Hepburn, Rex Harrison, Stanley Holloway. 170 minutes. Rated G.*
"Hollywood couldn't have done a better job" than this "grand, classy" version of Broadway's Lerner and Loewe musical "based on *Pygmalion*"; a "breathtaking" (but "dubbed") Hepburn is "incomparable" as the Cockney "guttersnipe turned into a lady", while Oscar-winner Harrison "at his tweedy best" plays her "superior yet vulnerable" teacher; "infectious" tunes and costumes that "leave you weak-kneed" ("those hats!") make this "luscious production" all the more "loverly."

### My Favorite Year    22 | 25 | 22 | 20
*1982. Directed by Richard Benjamin. With Peter O'Toole, Mark Linn-Baker, Jessica Harper. 92 minutes. Rated PG.*
This "winning comedy" about the "early days of TV" involves a boozy matinee idol's appearance on a program that's a "great riff on the old Sid Caesar show"; although "O'Toole playing a drunk might not be a stretch", he "nails every nuance", turning this "affectionate period piece" into "one of the funniest movies no one has ever seen."

### My Girl ⓘ    20 | 18 | 19 | 18
*1991. Directed by Howard Zieff. With Dan Aykroyd, Jamie Lee Curtis, Anna Chlumsky. 102 minutes. Rated PG.*
Get out your handkerchiefs: this "make-you-cry" dramedy pulls out all the stops in its depiction of a motherless girl dealing with emotional awakening (and her father's new girlfriend); Chlumsky's "sweet", "heart-wrenching" turn nails the "innocence and complexity of childhood" so well that many would like to "have her as a daughter."

### My Left Foot ✉    25 | 28 | 25 | 23
*1989. Directed by Jim Sheridan. With Daniel Day-Lewis, Brenda Fricker, Hugh O'Conor. 98 minutes. Rated R.*
It "could have been sappy and overly sentimental", but this "stereotype-smashing" true account of an Irish man born with cerebral palsy is "handled with unvarnished dignity" thanks to the Oscar-winning Day-Lewis, who "maintains the contorted body and emotional scars" of his condition so adeptly that "you forget you're watching an actor"; "very moving", this film's a "beacon of light for all."

### My Life As a Dog 🇫    25 | 24 | 25 | 22
*1987. Directed by Lasse Hallström. With Anton Glanzelius, Melinda Kinnaman. 101 minutes. Rated PG-13.*
"For once, an adult really gets into a child's head" in this "enchanting" Swedish "coming-of-age" drama that devotees deem director "Hallström's best"; the "puckish" lead is both "complex" and "cute", his fellow villagers "wacky" and the story "heart-tugging" without a "single false note" – no wonder many say it's "goose bump–worthy."

### My Man Godfrey ◑    25 | 25 | 23 | 21
*1936. Directed by Gregory La Cava. With William Powell, Carole Lombard, Eugene Pallette. 94 minutes. Not Rated.*
As an "unconventional love-struck heiress", Lombard displays "impeccable timing" opposite the "masterful" Powell as the

"hobo hired to be the family butler" in this "ultimate screwball comedy", the standard by which "all others are measured"; of course, the "fast-paced", fast-talking "plot is absurd" (that's "precisely the point"), but the "charming" principals "make it look convincing."

### My Own Private Idaho          19 | 21 | 19 | 19
*1991. Directed by Gus Van Sant. With River Phoenix, Keanu Reeves, William Richert. 102 minutes. Rated R.*
"Beautiful boys" work the streets of Portland in this "original modern romance" about a "narcoleptic hustler" (Phoenix, in a "heartbreaking" turn) who falls for a "man he can never have"; once the plot drifts off into a "pretentious" takeoff of "Henry IV", some say it becomes "overreaching" and downright "depressing", but still there are "enough good moments to make it worthwhile."

### Mystic Pizza          17 | 18 | 17 | 15
*1988. Directed by Donald Petrie. With Annabeth Gish, Julia Roberts, Lili Taylor. 104 minutes. Rated R.*
"Female friendships" and young romance are examined in this "coming-of-age charmer" set in a New England pizza parlor, an "authentic slice of life" that's also a "great Sunday afternoon chick flick"; notable for being "Julia's first major movie", it's "very fluffy", though its "sweetness" is very "winning."

### Mystic River ✉          26 | 28 | 25 | 25
*2003. Directed by Clint Eastwood. With Sean Penn, Tim Robbins, Kevin Bacon, Laurence Fishburne, Marcia Gay Harden, Laura Linney. 137 minutes. Rated R.*
"Lots of angst and anger" lie beneath this "bleak" tale of childhood buddies reunited as adults in the aftermath of a murder; it really "packs a wallop" thanks to a "pitch-perfect", "all-star" ensemble (with special kudos to Oscar winners Penn and Robbins for their "kick-in-the-gut" performances), not to mention Clint's "compelling" direction and "haunting score", the only dissonant note is that "slightly off-the-mark" ending.

### Naked Gun, The ⑪          20 | 17 | 17 | 18
*1988. Directed by David Zucker. With Leslie Nielsen, Priscilla Presley, George Kennedy. 85 minutes. Rated PG-13.*
This "laugh-a-minute" "cop spoof" from the minds behind *Airplane!* stars a "deadpan" Nielsen, who "raises the bar for satirical comedy" with his "terrific" performance; sure, the "brilliantly dumb characters" and "loopy overlapping dialogue" are equally "riotous", but ultimately "you have to be a guy to enjoy this much stupidity"; P.S. some find it "discomfortingly amusing" when O.J. Simpson appears.

### Napoléon ❶∅          ▽ 29 | 22 | 22 | 29
*1927. Directed by Abel Gance. With Albert Dieudonné, Antonin Artaud. 235 minutes. Rated G.*
"Eye-popping even today", this bio of Napoléon Bonaparte from "audacious" director Gance is a "sweeping epic" from the silent era that had been truncated over time but then restored to its former glory; its "unsurpassed" camerawork includes shots made "from horseback" and on a "pendulum", but its "final triptych", predating widescreen photography, makes for a particularly "rousing" windup.

## Nashville
23 | 23 | 22 | 24

*1975. Directed by Robert Altman. With Ronee Blakley, Keith Carradine, Lily Tomlin. 159 minutes. Rated R.*

It's the "wonderful ensemble" cast that makes this comic "portrait of '70s America" set in Nashville "richer and funnier with every viewing"; though some find it "frustrating" ("too many people talking at once"), "black humor" fans dub it "Altman's best", with enough "interesting characters" and "smart observations" to make it the "country cousin of *Gosford Park*."

## National Lampoon's Vacation ⑪
22 | 17 | 20 | 17

*1983. Directed by Harold Ramis. With Chevy Chase, Beverly D'Angelo, Randy Quaid. 98 minutes. Rated R.*

"Bad taste has never been funnier" than in this "vacation-from-hell" comedy recounting a "dysfunctional family's" cross-country road trip; as the beleaguered dad, Chase is at the "pinnacle of his career", though many say he's upstaged by fleeting glimpses of white-"hot" "Christie Brinkley in a red sports car."

## National Velvet ⑪
24 | 24 | 24 | 22

*1945. Directed by Clarence Brown. With Elizabeth Taylor, Mickey Rooney, Anne Revere. 123 minutes. Rated G.*

The movie equivalent of "comfort food", this "classic" "coming-of-age story" about a "girl and her horse" stars a "dazzlingly young Taylor" and a "scene-stealing" Rooney in a "feel-good" parable of "surmounting obstacles to make dreams come true"; maybe it's "corny", but any young lady "who ever dreamed of having a pony" can't help but "gush" over that climatic steeplechase race.

## Natural, The
23 | 21 | 23 | 22

*1984. Directed by Barry Levinson. With Robert Redford, Robert Duvall, Glenn Close. 134 minutes. Rated PG.*

"Every Little Leaguer's favorite flick", this mix of "magic" and "major league baseball" stars a "rugged Redford" as a "middle-aged rookie" who hits a "chill"-inducing "home run into the lights"; though some sigh it's too "sentimental", fans cheer this "solid period drama" (and Randy Newman's "unforgettable score").

## Network ✉
24 | 25 | 24 | 22

*1976. Directed by Sidney Lumet. With Faye Dunaway, William Holden, Peter Finch, Beatrice Straight. 120 minutes. Rated R.*

Even 30 years later, newscaster Howard Beale's "fateful cry, 'I'm mad as hell, and I'm not going to take it anymore'" is still "relevant" to proponents of this "prophetic" dramedy about television's "battle between news and entertainment"; "expertly written" by Paddy Chayefsky and "brilliantly acted" by Finch, Dunaway and Straight (who all won Oscars), this "biting" dark comedy has surveyors citing "*Jerry Springer*" and sighing "it's all true now."

## Never on Sunday ◑
24 | 26 | 23 | 21

*1960. Directed by Jules Dassin. With Melina Mercouri, Jules Dassin. 91 minutes. Not Rated.*

A "sensuous" Mercouri became an international star after illuminating the screen in this "delightful" drama about an "earthy" Greek prostitute and an uptight American (played by director Dassin) who tries to pull a Pygmalion on her; although once "shocking" and now "delightfully dated", every-nighters could "watch it anytime – even on a Sunday."

### Never Say Never Again
`18 | 20 | 17 | 19`

*1983. Directed by Irvin Kershner. With Sean Connery, Klaus Maria Brandauer, Barbara Carrera. 134 minutes. Rated PG.*
Live-and-let-diehards declare it's "fun to see Connery reprise the role that made him famous (and rich)" in this "rehash of *Thunderball*" featuring an "older" though "still studly" 007 who's "stunningly" teamed with Carrera; but foes say this "disappointing" picture "shouldn't be considered a Bond film", since it lacks the "appropriate music" and panache of producer Albert Broccoli.

### New York, New York
`▽ 18 | 19 | 18 | 20`

*1977. Directed by Martin Scorsese. With Liza Minnelli, Robert De Niro, Mary Kay Place. 164 minutes. Rated PG.*
Minnelli's "perfectly cast" and in "flawless voice" in this "postmodern musical from Martin Scorsese" about married musicians yearning for "fame in the 1940s"; still, many moan "De Niro's character is so unlikable" that the "picture never works", resulting in a "forgettable muddle" – "except for a certain song."

### Night at the Opera, A ◑
`26 | 25 | 22 | 22`

*1935. Directed by Sam Wood. With the Marx Brothers, Kitty Carlisle, Margaret Dumont. 96 minutes. Not Rated.*
"Inspired insanity" meets "Marxist lunacy" in this "nutty" comedy (the "origin of the term 'laugh riot'") from the brothers Marx, wherein Groucho persuades a social-climbing Dumont to invest in an opera production; fans fast-forward through the "saccharine musical moments" in favor of the "verbal dazzle" of the "contract routine", the "baseball-in-the-orchestra-pit" bit and, of course, that "not-to-be-believed stateroom scene."

### Nightmare Before Christmas, The
`24 | – | 22 | 28`

*1993. Directed by Henry Selick. Animated. 76 minutes. Rated PG.*
The "perfect antidote to the holidays" may well be this "magical", "macabre masterpiece" of stop-motion animation that ideally epitomizes the "bizarre genius" of producer Tim Burton; with a "cool story" – Halloween meets Christmas – "interesting characters" and "Danny Elfman's great score", it's a "must-see for kids of all ages."

### Nightmare on Elm Street, A ⓫
`19 | 14 | 19 | 18`

*1984. Directed by Wes Craven. With John Saxon, Ronee Blakley, Johnny Depp. 91 minutes. Rated R.*
Built around the "concept that your nightmares are real", this "original splatter" flick "did for sleeping what *Jaws* did for swimming" thanks to Freddy Krueger, its "pizza-faced" villain who sports "knives for fingers"; over 20 years later, this "darn scary" picture is now recognized as a "modern horror classic."

### NIGHT OF THE HUNTER, THE ◑
`27 | 28 | 25 | 26`

*1955. Directed by Charles Laughton. With Robert Mitchum, Shelley Winters, Lillian Gish. 93 minutes. Not Rated.*
Playing a "semi-psychotic preacher" "personifying pure evil", the "mesmerizing" Mitchum "terrorizes a bunch of kids" (and "invents tattooed knuckles") in this "strange" film noir frightfest; it's a "pity this was Laughton's only directorial" effort, given the "exquisite cinematography" and "unforgettable" performances that add up to "stunningly innovative cinema."

### Night of the Living Dead ◐Ⓤ    `22` `13` `19` `16`
*1968. Directed by George A. Romero. With Duane Jones, Judith O'Dea, Russ Streiner. 96 minutes. Not Rated.*
Director Romero "does zombies right" in this "zero-budget" indie "landmark" that proves that even "schlocky" special effects, a "shabby storyline" and "bad acting" can produce what living dead–heads call the "scariest movie ever made"; the "grainy black-and-white film used adds to the creepy aura", right down to the "freak-you-out", "pj-wetting" finale.

### NIGHTS OF CABIRIA ✉◑Ⓕ    `27` `28` `25` `24`
*1957. Directed by Federico Fellini. With Giulietta Masina, François Périer. 117 minutes. Not Rated.*
"Post-WWII Italy" as seen "through the eyes of a streetwalker" is the premise of this "simple, heartfelt" drama that's one of Fellini's "most moving" (and least "bizarre") films; as the "lovable girl of the streets", the "radiant" Masina is nothing less than a "female Charlie Chaplin", rendering an "amazing" performance that "ranges from tragedy to transcendence to flat-out comedy."

### 9½ Weeks Ⓤ    `15` `15` `15` `16`
*1986. Directed by Adrian Lyne. With Mickey Rourke, Kim Basinger. 113 minutes. Rated R.*
"Groundbreaking for its time", this "steamy" rendering of an "obsessive relationship" remains a definite "third-date movie", what with the "twisted" Rourke and "hot! hot! hot!" Basinger engaged in "kinky sex" via blindfolds, "ice cubes" and peanut shells; still, bluenoses find it "dreary, numbing" "softcore porn" that's nowhere near "as sexy as *An Officer and a Gentleman*."

### 1900 Ⓕ∅    ▽ `22` `24` `19` `23`
*1976. Directed by Bernardo Bertolucci. With Robert De Niro, Gérard Depardieu, Burt Lancaster. 243 minutes. Rated R.*
This "sweeping epic" from Bernardo Bertolucci is a "sumptuous", "fascinating study of Italian society and politics in the first half of the 20th century"; "finely acted" by De Niro (playing an aristocrat) and Depardieu (as a proletariat labor leader), it might be "a bit long and self-indulgent", but most find its "operatic form" and "meticulous" camerawork completely "involving."

### 9 to 5    `18` `18` `19` `17`
*1980. Directed by Colin Higgins. With Jane Fonda, Lily Tomlin, Dolly Parton, Dabney Coleman. 110 minutes. Rated PG.*
"Every secretary's dream" of "getting even with the boss" comes true in this "silly comedy", a "feminist classic" with a "relevant message" (though chauvinists snicker it's "proof that women's lib can be sexist too"); still, its "strong" protagonists exhibit "amazing chemistry" and Parton's theme song sure is "catchy."

### Ninotchka ◐    ▽ `25` `26` `24` `22`
*1939. Directed by Ernst Lubitsch. With Greta Garbo, Melvyn Douglas, Ina Claire. 110 minutes. Not Rated.*
This "great American comedy" depicts Soviet comrades seduced by capitalism, but is best known as the picture in which "Garbo laughs" for the first time on-screen; playing a "woman who follows her heart rather than the Communist manifesto", she's "smooth and sexy" spouting "incredibly funny dialogue" courtesy of a group of ace scenarists including Billy Wilder.

### Norma Rae ✉

24 | 27 | 24 | 21

*1979. Directed by Martin Ritt. With Sally Field, Beau Bridges, Ron Leibman, Pat Hingle. 110 minutes. Rated PG.*
A "stirring tale about ordinary people", this "uplifting" drama "based on a true story" is a "painfully accurate look" at a "courageous" mill worker's "fight for justice" when caught between "unions and management"; in the title role, the "superb" Field really "earned her Oscar", and the "image of her holding up that sign" has become iconically "indelible."

### NORTH BY NORTHWEST

28 | 26 | 27 | 27

*1959. Directed by Alfred Hitchcock. With Cary Grant, Eva Marie Saint, James Mason. 136 minutes. Not Rated.*
"James Bond, eat your heart out" – "no one is cooler than Cary Grant" in this "incredibly stylish" Hitchcock thriller, a "twisting story of mistaken identity" set "all over the country" involving a "cool blonde", a "smooth villain" and a "malevolent crop duster"; despite some "holes in the script", there's distraction via that "exhilarating" climb down Mount Rushmore and the "double entendre" scenario (e.g. the "train entering a tunnel" at the climax).

### Nosferatu ◑

▽ 26 | 22 | 23 | 24

*1922. Directed by F.W. Murnau. With Max Schreck, Gustav von Wangenheim, Greta Schroeder. 84 minutes. Not Rated.*
"Still creepy after all these years", this "important German horror film" (an "unauthorized version of *Dracula*") is "one spooky" silent flick that can "evoke terror" thanks to the "genuinely scary Schreck"; it's the "most poetic of vampire films" and the "standard that others are measured against – and usually found lacking."

### Notebook, The

23 | 24 | 24 | 23

*2004. Directed by Nick Cassavetes. With Ryan Gosling, Rachel McAdams, James Garner, Gena Rowlands. 123 minutes. Rated PG-13.*
Sweet enough to "dissolve a tooth", this "hauntingly beautiful" sob-o-rama based on the Nicholas Sparks best-seller might be the "ultimate chick flick", a "testament to the awesome power of love" as it endures "through the ages"; naturally, the dry-eyed cry "corny", but even they credit the "genuinely sad Alzheimer's storyline" for addressing an issue that's "not often given attention."

### Nothing Sacred

▽ 23 | 23 | 20 | 20

*1937. Directed by William Wellman. With Carole Lombard, Fredric March. 75 minutes. Not Rated.*
The "notion of celebrity is lampooned" in this nutty screwball comedy, the story of a woman diagnosed with a terminal disease who's feted by a newspaper in exchange for her exclusive story – only to find out that she's been misdiagnosed; it's way "ahead of its time" in its arch analysis of the fame game alone.

### No Time for Sergeants ◑∅

23 | 22 | 22 | 19

*1958. Directed by Mervyn LeRoy. With Andy Griffith, Myron McCornick, Nick Adams. 119 minutes. Not Rated.*
Managing to be "endearing without being annoying", Griffith "delivers the goods" in this "hilarious" comedy about a "dim hayseed who nearly destroys the U.S. Air Force", abetted by "perfect foil" Don Knotts; the infamous "toilet-seat scene" is a "display of American ingenuity" at its finest.

## NOTORIOUS ◑
27 | 27 | 26 | 26

*1946. Directed by Alfred Hitchcock. With Cary Grant, Ingrid Bergman, Claude Rains. 101 minutes. Not Rated.*

"Fetching" Ingrid Bergman "goes under the sheets for her country and gets Cary Grant as a reward" in this "brilliantly subversive" Hitchcock spy thriller featuring equal parts of "suspense", "suspicion", "hurt pride" and "Nazis too"; best remembered for the leads' "lingering, smoldering love scene", it also boasts "top-notch" supporting work from Rains, who has the best line: "mother, I'm married to an American agent."

## Notting Hill
19 | 19 | 18 | 19

*1999. Directed by Roger Michell. With Julia Roberts, Hugh Grant, Rhys Ifans. 124 minutes. Rated PG-13.*

"Straight-up chick flick" about a "hair-flicking" movie star who finds love with an "endearing" bookseller; though rotters relate it's "formulaic" (with "Roberts playing herself" and Grant in his "stammering ingénue" mode), at least the supporting cast is "brilliantly funny"; the London scenery provides the "charm."

## No Way Out
20 | 19 | 23 | 19

*1987. Directed by Roger Donaldson. With Kevin Costner, Gene Hackman, Sean Young. 114 minutes. Rated R.*

Perhaps "Costner's finest hour", this "entirely enjoyable military thriller" offers "wonderful intrigue" in its way-out plot, something to do with the KGB, the Pentagon, the backseat of a limousine and a classy call girl (the "very hot" Young); while coolly "tense" throughout, the "unexpected", "twisty" ending is still a "shocker."

## Now, Voyager ◑
27 | 28 | 26 | 25

*1942. Directed by Irving Rapper. With Bette Davis, Paul Henreid, Claude Rains. 117 minutes. Not Rated.*

"Break out the hankies" – this "chick flick extraordinaire" features "the moon, the stars and Bette Davis", who effects an "appealing transformation" as an "old maid" defecting from a "demanding mother" to find kismet with a "perfect" Henreid; though the "two-cigarette scene" is decidedly un-PC today, it's become a "sacred" (and paradoxically "life-affirming") moment in this "classy" "mature love story."

## Nurse Betty
15 | 18 | 15 | 15

*2000. Directed by Neil LaBute. With Renée Zellweger, Morgan Freeman, Chris Rock. 108 minutes. Rated R.*

"Entertaining" but "unconventional", this "quirky black comedy" top-lines Zellweger as a "clueless blonde" soap opera buff pursued by vicious hitmen; foes find the wild mix of comedy and gore too "incongruous" and "unnecessarily violent" ("what planet did the screenwriter come from?"), and even fans admit it's "not for everyone" – just those who appreciate "inventive" filmmaking.

## Nutty Professor, The
21 | 19 | 18 | 18

*1963. Directed by Jerry Lewis. With Jerry Lewis, Stella Stevens, Del Moore. 107 minutes. Not Rated.*

Jerry's "finest hour", this "can't-be-improved-upon" "wacky" comedy concerns a nerdy college prof who is transformed from Dr. Jerk-yll into Mr. Hyde after guzzling an exotic tonic; fans find it "sweet", foes shrug "typical Lewis shtick" and deep thinkers deem it a "metaphor for the monsters inside the greatest comedians."

### Nutty Professor, The ⓤ
15 | 18 | 14 | 18

*1996. Directed by Tom Shadyac. With Eddie Murphy, Jada Pinkett, James Coburn. 95 minutes. Rated PG-13.*

This "competent remake" of the Jerry Lewis comedy features Murphy in "amazingly versatile" mode, playing a seriously overweight professor (in a "great fat suit") in addition to six other minor characters; it may be "more sentimental and less sharp" than the original – and "probably not appreciated by the French" – but those "dinner table scenes" are "wet-your-pants funny."

### O Brother, Where Art Thou?
22 | 23 | 22 | 24

*2000. Directed by Joel Coen. With George Clooney, John Turturro, Tim Blake Nelson, John Goodman. 106 minutes. Rated PG-13.*

"Who else but the Coen brothers could mix Greek mythology, bluegrass and George Clooney?" ask fans of this picaresque, "perversely funny" satire "based on Homer's *Odyssey*" that details the adventures of three Depression-era "hayseeds" who bust out of prison; though a bit too "highbrow" for some, the "beautiful period detail" and "best roots music soundtrack ever" keep this "sweet" if "strange" genre-bender accessible.

### Ocean's Eleven
16 | 15 | 19 | 18

*1960. Directed by Lewis Milestone. With Frank Sinatra, Dean Martin, Sammy Davis, Jr., Peter Lawford. 127 minutes. Not Rated.*

A "guilty pleasure to be sure", this "original version" of the casino heist caper features the "Rat Pack at their best" in a fab "1960 Las Vegas" setting ("when all the buildings were one story"); sure, it may be a bit "slow" in the beginning, but the look is "so stylish", the cast "so cool" and the ending so "clever" that it's always "entertaining."

### Ocean's Eleven
19 | 19 | 19 | 22

*2001. Directed by Steven Soderbergh. With George Clooney, Brad Pitt, Andy Garcia. 116 minutes. Rated PG-13.*

"Fluffy fun" that "goes down smooth like a good martini", this "breezy caper" flick is "more lively than the original" version with its "great shots of Vegas", "never-a-dull-moment" plot and "lots of eye candy for the ladies"; ok, it might be "really silly", but the "slick", "all-star cast" and "genius director du jour Soderbergh" serve up something "wonderfully entertaining."

### Octopussy ⓤ
17 | 15 | 16 | 19

*1983. Directed by John Glen. With Roger Moore, Maud Adams, Louis Jourdan. 130 minutes. Rated PG.*

James Bond goes to India in this "over-the-top" feature whose "name lets you know how silly it is"; it might have a rather "basic", "assembly-line" formula, a "hokey" script and a star "getting too old for the part", but fans say it's worth seeing just for a glimpse of 007 masquerading "as a clown."

### Odd Couple, The ⓤ
25 | 27 | 25 | 21

*1968. Directed by Gene Saks. With Jack Lemmon, Walter Matthau, John Fiedler. 105 minutes. Rated G.*

Lemmon and Matthau are "brilliant" in this "timeless" Neil Simon "classic" (which spawned a sequel and a TV series) that poses the question 'can two divorced men share an apartment without driving each other crazy?'; the ensuing dilemma makes for "unbeatable" comedy that'll make your "sides hurt from laughter."

### Officer and a Gentleman, An
22 | 21 | 21 | 20

*1982. Directed by Taylor Hackford. With Richard Gere, Debra Winger, David Keith. 122 minutes. Rated R.*

"What gal doesn't dream" of Richard Gere "sweeping" her into his arms and lifting her up where she belongs?; this "quintessential" '80s "date movie" provides plenty of fodder for "guilty-pleasure" fantasizing with its love story between a "young enlisted man" and a "poor" working girl, even if foes pan it as "a bit lame" and advise "fast-forward to the last scene that makes the rest worthwhile."

### Oh, God! ⓤ
17 | 17 | 18 | 16

*1977. Directed by Carl Reiner. With George Burns, John Denver, Teri Garr, Paul Sorvino. 104 minutes. Rated PG.*

For pure "entertainment value", it's tough to top this "irresistible" comedy about an average Joe chosen by God to spread His word; believers say Burns is "perfectly cast" in the title role ("he's old enough to be God") and Denver as his disciple is "surprisingly effective", but even though this "humanist" picture is "worth a watch", it "didn't deserve to launch a series of follow-ups."

### Oklahoma!
24 | 22 | 23 | 25

*1955. Directed by Fred Zinnemann. With Gordon MacRae, Shirley Jones, Gloria Grahame. 145 minutes. Rated G.*

"Every song" in this "sprawling" Rodgers and Hammerstein musical/Western "makes you want to sing along" with the "lovely" voices of Jones and MacRae, plus there are "rousing dance numbers"; though modernists malign it as a "little dated", for most it's a whole lot "more than O-K", it's a pure "C-L-A-S-S-I-C."

### Old Yeller ⓤ
24 | 20 | 24 | 20

*1957. Directed by Robert Stevenson. With Dorothy McGuire, Fess Parker, Tommy Kirk. 83 minutes. Rated G.*

"You can't help but cry your eyes out" after watching this "outstanding" Disney "tearjerker" about a "boy and his big yellow dog"; if a few find the acting "formulaic" and the plot "sappy", most agree it's an "all-time" children's "standard" that even adults "never tire of watching" – despite that gosh-darned "sad ending."

### Oliver! ✉
24 | 23 | 24 | 26

*1968. Directed by Carol Reed. With Mark Lester, Ron Moody, Shani Wallis, Oliver Reed. 153 minutes. Rated G.*

Dickens' "bleak yet hopeful" novel is "lovingly brought to the screen" in this Oscar-winning adaptation of the "classic" stage musical; giving the "incredible" production numbers, "wonderful" score and "just-about-perfect" cast, many "English orphan" wannabes beg 'please, sir can we watch it again?'

### Omen, The ⓤ
21 | 21 | 22 | 20

*1976. Directed by Richard Donner. With Gregory Peck, Lee Remick, David Warner. 111 minutes. Rated R.*

This "genuinely spooky" thriller has a "brilliant premise" – a couple unwittingly adopts the devil's child – and features an appropriately "satanic" storyline, "eerie" music and a frightening turn by the "scariest kid ever to be in a horror movie" (Harvey Stephens); thrill-seekers also quiver in delight at its "terrifying" special effects that make the "unbelievable believable."

### Once Upon a Time in America
24 | 26 | 24 | 24

*1984. Directed by Sergio Leone. With Robert De Niro, James Woods, Elizabeth McGovern. 227 minutes. Rated R.*
Some of De Niro's "most subtle and effective" acting is on display in this "unfairly neglected" crime epic spanning four decades, which hard-core cineasts hail as "truly remarkable" when "seen in the long [227-minute] director's cut"; but despite a "top-drawer cast" and "magnificent" direction, others are less enthused about the "flawed" end result that's awash in "too much blood."

### ONE FLEW OVER THE CUCKOO'S NEST ✉
27 | 29 | 27 | 25

*1975. Directed by Milos Forman. With Jack Nicholson, Louise Fletcher, Will Sampson. 133 minutes. Rated R.*
"Life in a mental ward" gets the "stand-up-for-your-rights" treatment in this "absorbing, disturbing" and "influential" drama starring "national treasure" Nicholson at his "ornery best", backed up by an "amazing" ensemble cast; no surprise, it took five major Oscars, made Nurse Ratched a household name and is "hard to top" – folks are just plain "nuts about it."

### 101 Dalmatians
24 | – | 22 | 24

*1961. Directed by Wolfgang Reitherman, Clyde Geronimi, Hamilton Luske. Animated. 79 minutes. Rated G.*
Puppy proponents put their paws together for Pongo, Perdita and their prolific progeny when watching this "fast, funny" piece of Disney animation; its "hugely entertaining" tale of a klatch of "cute" canines outrunning über-villainess Cruella De Vil appeals to the "little kid in everyone" and makes this one an "enduring winner."

### 101 Dalmatians 🅙
18 | 19 | 19 | 22

*1996. Directed by Stephen Herek. With Glenn Close, Jeff Daniels, Joely Richardson. 103 minutes. Rated G.*
"*The* reason" to see Disney's "cute" live-action "update" of their earlier animated feature is the "over-the-top" Close as the "truly wicked" Cruella De Vil (though there's also "dry humor" courtesy of the largely British supporting cast); still, cynics nix this "wholly unnecessary remake" as "not as good as the original."

### One, Two, Three ◑
▽ 24 | 26 | 25 | 24

*1961. Directed by Billy Wilder. With James Cagney, Horst Buchholz, Pamela Tiffin. 108 minutes. Not Rated.*
"Billy Wilder scores in this Cold War comedy", a "fast and furious farce" set in Berlin about a "harried Coca-Cola executive" whose "world is collapsing around him"; Cagney's "machine-gun delivery is a scream", though diehards say the picture's "underrated" and "overshadowed" by the director's better-known films.

### On Golden Pond ✉
24 | 27 | 23 | 23

*1981. Directed by Mark Rydell. With Katharine Hepburn, Henry Fonda, Jane Fonda. 109 minutes. Rated PG.*
A "beautiful tale of growing old and looking back on life", this "brilliant" drama features the "stunning", Oscar-winning Hank and Kate "pulling out all the stops" as an elderly couple coming to terms with their child and each other over one golden summer; the "real-life tension" between the real-life father-and-daughter Fondas supplies some "electric" moments, while its timeless theme about the "strength of the human spirit" "will appeal to all."

### On Her Majesty's Secret Service   19 | 15 | 21 | 20
*1969. Directed by Peter R. Hunt. With George Lazenby, Diana Rigg, Telly Savalas. 140 minutes. Rated PG.*
"James Bond gets married" in this "respectable" flick featuring "astonishing ski chases", "Swiss Alp views" and a "believable love story" for a change; still, opinion splits on Lazenby's one-time-only turn as 007 ("wooden" vs. "formidable"), and as for the end result, it's either "underrated" or "the worst" in the series.

### On the Town   23 | 23 | 21 | 25
*1949. Directed by Stanley Donen, Gene Kelly. With Gene Kelly, Frank Sinatra, Jules Munshin. 98 minutes. Not Rated.*
Despite "wonderful dancing by Kelly" and some "funny" bits from the ensemble cast, "NYC is the real star" of this "exuberant" musical "celebrating the American spirit in the '40s"; "filmed partially on location" and juiced up by a "great Leonard Bernstein score", it follows three sailors at liberty on the town, and although rather "silly", it effortlessly radiates the "pure joy" of simpler times.

### ON THE WATERFRONT ⊠◑   28 | 29 | 26 | 26
*1954. Directed by Elia Kazan. With Marlon Brando, Karl Malden, Eva Marie Saint, Rod Steiger. 108 minutes. Not Rated.*
Most decidedly a "candidate for all-time greatest" film, this "gritty tale of corruption on the NJ docks" is a "movie to turn you onto movies", with Oscar wins for the "phenomenal Brando" (as a "washed-up", "Palookaville"-bound boxer) and a "knockout" Saint (in her screen debut); indeed, this "gutsy", "brutal masterwork" "rings so true" and is so "emotionally satisfying" that it's "nothing less than brilliant"; best line: "I coulda been a contender."

### Open City ◑F   ▽ 28 | 29 | 28 | 25
*1946. Directed by Roberto Rossellini. With Aldo Fabrizi, Anna Magnani. 105 minutes. Not Rated.*
One of the major works of Italian neorealism, this "devastating" look at occupied Rome in the 1940s shows the "devastation that war produces and how people pick up the pieces that are left"; the "unforgettable" Magnani's performance "burns in one's memory", while the picture itself is credited for reawakening American interest in modern international films.

### Operation Petticoat   19 | 19 | 18 | 19
*1959. Directed by Blake Edwards. With Cary Grant, Tony Curtis, Joan O'Brien, Dina Merrill. 124 minutes. Not Rated.*
"Feel-good" WWII comedy having to do with a Navy captain's "emergency" efforts to keep a gaggle of army nurses and a "pink submarine" afloat; despite smooth "chemistry" between Grant and Curtis resulting in some pretty "funny" situations (i.e. lots of tight-quarters gags), the unamused torpedo it as "contrived."

### Ordinary People ⊠   25 | 27 | 25 | 23
*1980. Directed by Robert Redford. With Donald Sutherland, Mary Tyler Moore, Timothy Hutton. 124 minutes. Rated R.*
"Every parent's nightmare" – the death of a child – is dissected in this "devastating" drama that goes below the "veneer of an upper-middle-class family" to plumb the "dysfunction" below; Redford's "deserving" directorial debut copped a Best Picture Oscar, but it's Moore's "playing-against-type" role as a "classy" but "coldhearted" mom that "steals the movie."

### Others, The
23 | 25 | 23 | 24

*2001. Directed by Alejandro Amenábar. With Nicole Kidman, Fionnula Flanagan. 101 minutes. Rated PG-13.*

A "dynamic" Kidman delivers an "old-school movie star turn" in this "grand ghost story" about a mother protecting her children who suffer from a rare "photosensitive" condition (an "excellent excuse to keep the house dark and murky"); "wonderfully atmospheric" and "deliciously scary", it's "highbrow horror" with a "jeepers-creepers" ending that's a "real shocker."

### Outbreak
16 | 18 | 17 | 18

*1995. Directed by Wolfgang Petersen. With Dustin Hoffman, Rene Russo, Morgan Freeman. 127 minutes. Rated R.*

"Cheer the hero and hiss the villain" in this "entertaining bio-thriller" where "time's running out" in a California community threatened by "wayward monkeys" and "airborne viruses"; in his first "action hero" role, Hoffman is "realistic" enough, but foes say the upshot is "silly" – "more bad science" – and suggest you "read *The Hot Zone* instead."

### Outlaw Josey Wales, The
25 | 23 | 24 | 23

*1976. Directed by Clint Eastwood. With Clint Eastwood, Sondra Locke, Chief Dan George. 135 minutes. Rated PG.*

Playing a renegade Confederate soldier seeking revenge after his wife and children are murdered, Eastwood is his "usual unreadable self" (though you "feel for his plight") in this "quirky" Western that's a "rural version of *Death Wish*"; fans rate it "better-than-usual Clint", given its "classic lines" and "profound issues."

### Out of Africa ✉
25 | 25 | 24 | 27

*1985. Directed by Sydney Pollack. With Meryl Streep, Robert Redford, Klaus Maria Brandauer. 150 minutes. Rated PG.*

Supporters are "spellbound" by this "splendiferous" "love story played out against the mysterious continent" starring a "radiant" Streep as Danish writer Karen Blixen (aka Isak Dinesen) and a "great-looking" Redford as her paramour; the "beauty" of Africa and "soaring score" "amplify the emotion", and even though it's a "real tearjerker", most eat up this "treat" "again and again."

### Out of Sight
21 | 21 | 21 | 22

*1998. Directed by Steven Soderbergh. With George Clooney, Jennifer Lopez, Ving Rhames. 123 minutes. Rated R.*

"Clooney and Lopez generate electricity aplenty" in this "smart caper" flick that "oozes cool" in its depiction of a "cocksure" con artist, his "eye-candy police pursuer" and "one of the sexiest love scenes" ever; a "crackling" story (via Elmore Leonard's novel) and "brilliant" direction from Soderbergh make this one an "overlooked gem."

### Out-of-Towners, The
20 | 22 | 22 | 18

*1970. Directed by Arthur Hiller. With Jack Lemmon, Sandy Dennis, Sandy Baron. 98 minutes. Rated G.*

"They don't make comedies" like this Neil Simon–scripted "classic" anymore, the saga of an Ohio couple visiting "Fun City" only to discover that it's their "worst nightmare" as they endure one "hilariously miserable" mishap after another; "Lemmon and Dennis are perfection as the tortured tourists", leading many to wonder "why they remade this movie" at all.

**Outrageous Fortune**　　　15 | 14 | 14 | 13 |
*1987. Directed by Arthur Hiller. With Shelley Long, Bette Midler,*
*Peter Coyote. 100 minutes. Rated R.*
"Midler and Long make a funny team" in this buddy comedy about
two struggling actresses tracking down a mutual boyfriend turned
espionage agent; though too "strident" and "formulaic" for some,
it's "guilty pleasure" time for those in the mood for something "silly."

**Outsiders, The**　　　22 | 21 | 22 | 19 |
*1983. Directed by Francis Ford Coppola. With C. Thomas Howell,*
*Matt Dillon, Ralph Macchio. 91 minutes. Rated PG.*
Coppola "paints a great picture" of "teen angst" in this "coming-
of-age story" that limns the "problems" between adolescent
gangs in a '50s Oklahoma hamlet; what seems like the "entire
Brat Pack" delivers such "outstanding" work that the end result is
"almost as good" as S.E. Hinton's enduring novel.

**Ox-Bow Incident, The ◑**　　　▽ 27 | 26 | 27 | 23 |
*1943. Directed by William Wellman. With Henry Fonda, Dana*
*Andrews. 75 minutes. Not Rated.*
"Decent, law-abiding folk never looked more pathetic" than in
this message Western, a "gripping story of mob violence gone
mad" that's a chilling indictment of American justice; there are no
heroes in this dark "morality tale", though the "excellent ensemble"
makes this "adaptation of the classic novel" come alive.

**Paint Your Wagon**　　　18 | 18 | 19 | 21 |
*1969. Directed by Joshua Logan. With Lee Marvin, Clint*
*Eastwood, Jean Seberg. 166 minutes. Rated PG-13.*
"See Clint sing" in this tuneful Lerner and Loewe Western that
cynics say is the "reason why musicals have had a hard time
succeeding since the '60s"; but champions claim this story of
bigamous Wild West gold miners "pokes fun at many cultures" and
believe that the "non-singer" cast "does a surprisingly good job."

**Paper Chase, The**　　　▽ 21 | 23 | 21 | 18 |
*1973. Directed by James Bridges. With Timothy Bottoms, Lindsay*
*Wagner, John Houseman. 111 minutes. Rated PG.*
The "terrors and rigors of the first year of Harvard Law School"
are revealed in this "seminal" '70s movie that re-creates the
student "rat race" in an "entertaining" way; despite "outstanding
performances by all", the Oscar-winning Houseman (as a "crusty
professor") is the "main reason to see it."

**Paper Moon ◑**　　　22 | 23 | 21 | 22 |
*1973. Directed by Peter Bogdanovich. With Ryan O'Neal, Tatum*
*O'Neal, Madeline Kahn. 102 minutes. Rated PG.*
Have "fun watching Ryan and Tatum acting together" in this
"delightful" "father/daughter bonding flick", the "charming"
story of a Depression-era con man and his equally manipulative
offspring who "drift" through the Midwest in glorious black and
white; though some say this "sweet little comedy" was "stolen by
Madeline Kahn", it was the younger O'Neal who copped the Oscar.

**Papillon**　　　26 | 27 | 26 | 24 |
*1973. Directed by Franklin J. Schaffner. With Steve McQueen,*
*Dustin Hoffman. 150 minutes. Rated R.*
It's hard to escape from this "powerful" tale of prisoners scheming
to break out of Devil's Island, the French Guiana penal colony that

makes "HBO's *Oz* look like Club Med"; a "consistently cool McQueen" and "heavyweight Hoffman" play "mistreated-but-not-defeated" inmates "determined to be free" in this "tight", taut drama that's all the more "scary" since it's "based on a true story."

### Parenthood
22 | 22 | 22 | 20

*1989. Directed by Ron Howard. With Steve Martin, Mary Steenburgen, Dianne Wiest. 124 minutes. Rated PG-13.*
"Modern family life" gets "compelling" treatment in this "harrowing if affectionate look at being a parent", a "feel-good" dramedy that confirms "you need a sense of humor" when you have kids; "smart, insightful" and briskly paced thanks to "multiple plotlines", it features "one of Martin's better performances."

### Parent Trap, The
23 | 21 | 23 | 21

*1961. Directed by David Swift. With Hayley Mills, Maureen O'Hara, Brian Keith. 129 minutes. Rated G.*
"Hayley Mills and Hayley Mills" star as "twins separated at birth plotting to bring their estranged parents together" in this "non-animated Disney classic", an "entertaining romp" that serves up "warmhearted family fare"; one of the "most remembered" movies in boomerdom, it boasts such a "timeless story" that most "stick to the original", having "no need for the remake."

### Passion of the Christ, The 🅵
22 | 23 | 21 | 23

*2004. Directed by Mel Gibson. With James Caviezel, Monica Bellucci, Maia Morgenstern. 127 minutes. Rated R.*
Echoing the "overblown controversy" surrounding its release, Mel Gibson's "brutal portrayal" of the last 12 hours of Christ's life similarly "polarizes" surveyors: proponents praise its "lengthy torture scenes" as "necessary to make the point" of "what Jesus went through", but "traumatized" viewers see a "slasher film" full of "prejudice and propaganda" that "preaches to the converted"; both sides concur it's "not for kids" (nor for subtitle-phobes, given the all-Aramaic/Latin/Hebrew dialogue).

### Patch Adams
16 | 18 | 17 | 15

*1998. Directed by Tom Shadyac. With Robin Williams, Daniel London, Monica Potter. 115 minutes. Rated PG-13.*
Laughter's the best medicine in this tale of a doctor who tries to heal patients with humor, an "inspiring" story that's both "funny and sad" but ultimately "uplifting"; eye-rollers counter that Williams "needs to get back to his roots" and avoid such "sappy" material.

### PATHS OF GLORY ◑
28 | 27 | 28 | 26

*1957. Directed by Stanley Kubrick. With Kirk Douglas, Ralph Meeker, George Macready. 86 minutes. Not Rated.*
"All the hopelessness, folly and stupidity" of WWI is "dramatically" depicted in Kubrick's "devastating" "anti-war" picture that "ruthlessly" depicts "corrupt" officers deploying "scapegoated enlisted men" as "cannon fodder"; even though this "grim" yet "moving" film is in black and white, the "story is full color", and it "really makes its point" and "stands the test of time."

### Patriot, The
21 | 21 | 21 | 23

*2000. Directed by Roland Emmerich. With Mel Gibson, Heath Ledger, Joely Richardson. 164 minutes. Rated R.*
Present-day patriots salute this "epic in the Gibson tradition" as an "inspiring portrait" of a reluctant American "hero" enmeshed

in "gruesome Revolutionary War battles"; though turncoats dismiss it as typical "Hollywood good guy/bad guy nonsense" ("Lethal Musket"), they're outvoted by partisans who "feel liberated" by this "heartfelt" history jazzed up with some "entertainment value."

### Patriot Games
21 | 21 | 22 | 21

*1992. Directed by Phillip Noyce. With Harrison Ford, Anne Archer, Patrick Bergin. 117 minutes. Rated R.*
"Harrison gets cool again" as a "humble hero whose life is turned upside down by a crazed IRA terrorist" in this "slick" action-adventurer known for its "mind-spinning chase across oceans and freeways"; though it's as "thrilling on the screen as on the written page", traitors contend it's "cookie-cutter espionage" and say that Alec Baldwin is the "more believable Jack Ryan."

### PATTON ✉
27 | 28 | 26 | 27

*1970. Directed by Franklin J. Schaffner. With George C. Scott, Karl Malden. 170 minutes. Rated PG.*
Legions salute "one of the best biopics ever made", this "hauntingly mounted character study" of fabled WWII General Patton, who's "superbly fleshed out" as both "monstrous and human"; though there's "lots of drama" throughout, it "doesn't get much better than that opening speech" by "Old Blood and Guts", probably the most "memorable" scene; P.S. the "convincing" portrayal won Scott an Oscar, which he famously rejected.

### Pawnbroker, The ◗
26 | 28 | 24 | 22

*1965. Directed by Sidney Lumet. With Rod Steiger, Geraldine Fitzgerald. 116 minutes. Not Rated.*
This "disturbing", "depressing message picture", expertly rendered in "chilling black and white", shows the "horrors of the Holocaust" by focusing on one survivor, the owner of a Harlem pawnshop; in "one of the all-time great screen performances", Steiger is nothing short of "mesmerizing" in the title role – too bad it's been so "sadly neglected" over the years.

### Pee-wee's Big Adventure ⓤ
19 | 17 | 17 | 20

*1985. Directed by Tim Burton. With Paul Reubens, Elizabeth Daily, Diane Salinger. 90 minutes. Rated PG.*
"Wacky", "campy", maybe even "inspired", this comic "cult classic" is a "work of the sublime from the ridiculous" team of "twisted" director Burton and "genius" performer Reubens; though ostensibly aimed at small fry, "adults love it" too, yet the pleasure is bittersweet for those who "miss Pee-wee" and "wish for another" installment; P.S. "Large Marge is worth the price of admission."

### Peggy Sue Got Married
19 | 20 | 21 | 18

*1986. Directed by Francis Ford Coppola. With Kathleen Turner, Nicolas Cage. 104 minutes. Rated PG-13.*
Unhappily married Peggy Sue "magically enters her teenage self's world" in this "back-in-time" comedy "with a heart and a brain"; though ageists say Turner is "too old" for the role, the "original premise" and "nostalgic" mood provide ample distraction.

### Pelican Brief, The
16 | 18 | 18 | 16

*1993. Directed by Alan J. Pakula. With Julia Roberts, Denzel Washington, Sam Shepard. 141 minutes. Rated PG-13.*
In this "fast-paced" adaptation of John Grisham's best-seller, an inventive law student posits a dangerously compelling conspiracy

theory after two Supreme Court justices are murdered; while "terminally predictable" for "suspense-thriller" seekers, it has a "great team" in Julia and Denzel – even if their characters' book romance didn't make it to the silver screen.

### People vs. Larry Flynt, The
18 | 21 | 18 | 18

*1996. Directed by Milos Forman. With Woody Harrelson, Courtney Love, Edward Norton. 129 minutes. Rated R.*
Forman's "daring movie" creates an unlikely "hero" out of a "less than excellent subject", "pornographer" Larry Flynt, whose "rags-to-riches-to-ruin story" is rendered in such "heartbreaking" but "inspiring" terms that you wind up "loving the bad guy"; Harrelson is "first-rate" in the title role, Love "really can act" and you might just come away with a "whole new outlook" on smut.

### Perfect Storm, The
16 | 16 | 18 | 22

*2000. Directed by Wolfgang Petersen. With George Clooney, Mark Wahlberg, John C. Reilly. 129 minutes. Rated PG-13.*
There's "never a dull moment" in this "compelling" tale of an "ill-fated fishing boat crew" swept up in 1991's 'storm of the century'; no question, the deep-sea FX are "stunning", but the "unconvincing script" strikes some as "surprisingly shallow", "pulling the heartstrings" in a "dumbed-down", "big-budget Hollywood" way.

### Persona ❶ 🖪
∇ 28 | 29 | 25 | 25

*1967. Directed by Ingmar Bergman. With Bibi Andersson, Liv Ullmann. 81 minutes. Not Rated.*
Bergman's "plunge into the mysteries of the self" beguiles surveyors who say this "intense, very moving" film is the director's "best synthesis of symbolism and reality"; the story of a nurse and her patient (an actress who has gone mute) is "not rational but psychologically satisfying" as the two characters' identities "blend" together to make a "stunning" whole.

### Peter Pan ❶
25 | – | 25 | 25

*1953. Directed by Clyde Geronimi, Wilfred Jackson, Hamilton Luske. Animated. 76 minutes. Rated G.*
Lost boys and girls who "never want to grow up" fly to this "simple", pixie dust–peppered tale concerning the eternally youthful Peter's adventures in Neverland; a "true classic" of Disney animation from the days when "Walt was running the show", it remains enough of an "important childhood film" for latter-day critics to ask "why did they bother with a remake?"

### Peter Pan
20 | 19 | 21 | 23

*2003. Directed by P.J. Hogan. With Jeremy Sumpter, Jason Isaacs, Rachel Hurd-Wood, Lynn Redgrave. 113 minutes. Rated PG.*
"Move over, Disney": J.M. Barrie's oft-filmed children's classic gets a "beautiful live-action" retelling in this "well-done" movie that "really captures what it feels like to grow up"; a "seductive undertone" and some "darker aspects" make it a "bit more adult than previous versions", and if this puts off traditionalists ("after Mary Martin, why bother?"), most find it "thoroughly enjoyable."

### Pete's Dragon
20 | – | 20 | 21

*1977. Directed by Don Chaffey. Animated. With Helen Reddy, Jim Dale, Mickey Rooney. 128 minutes. Rated G.*
Surveyors slayed by this "Disney classic" combining both animation and live action cheer its "heartwarming" story of a

runaway orphan and his sometimes-invisible dragon companion; though fire-breathers blast it as "overlong" and "unmemorable", most agree the "kids will dig it", which is all that matters.

### Phantom of the Opera, The
21 | 20 | 23 | 26

*2004. Directed by Joel Schumacher. With Gerard Butler, Emmy Rossum, Patrick Wilson, Miranda Richardson, Minnie Driver. 143 minutes. Rated PG-13.*

Towing along its "lavish sets" and "to-die-for" tunes, Andrew Lloyd Webber's "Gothic romance" hit musical leaps onto the silver screen in this "faithful adaptation" courtesy of "over-the-top" director Schumacher; castwise, Phantom fandom is "swept away" by Rossum's "starmaking performance" as the "angelic" ingénue, though some purists wince at "hunk" Butler's "rock 'n' roll" rendition of the titular masked marauder.

### Phenomenon
18 | 18 | 19 | 17

*1996. Directed by John Turteltaub. With John Travolta, Kyra Sedgwick, Forest Whitaker. 124 minutes. Rated PG.*

This "inspirational" "tearjerker" "pulls at the heartstrings" and "makes you want to live a better, fuller life" by showcasing a "convincing" Travolta as a small-town schmo who acquires supernatural powers and becomes a benevolent hero; though the dubious dub it "new-age hooey", for many the "message is touching" and the "beautiful images" leave a "good feeling."

### Philadelphia ✉
24 | 27 | 25 | 23

*1993. Directed by Jonathan Demme. With Tom Hanks, Denzel Washington. 125 minutes. Rated PG-13.*

"Hollywood takes on AIDS" in this "extraordinarily powerful and poignant" drama that "puts a human face" on a "depressing" subject thanks to Hanks' "brave", Oscar-winning portrayal of a gay lawyer battling the "double-edged sword of discrimination and physical deterioration"; the final result resonates with "thought-provoking" issues, but don't forget to "bring the tissues – it's painful to watch."

### PHILADELPHIA STORY, THE ✉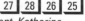
27 | 28 | 26 | 25

*1940. Directed by George Cukor. With Cary Grant, Katharine Hepburn, James Stewart. 112 minutes. Not Rated.*

For the "sheer joy" of "listening to fast, furious dialogue" that "doesn't insult your intelligence", this "laugh-out-loud" screwball "comedy of manners" provides a "wild ride"; "you'll need a scorecard to keep up" with the "banter and spark" between the "classy" Kate, "acerbic" Grant and "underplaying" Stewart, uttered in settings so "perfectly frothy" that many wish that "life was really like that."

### PIANIST, THE ✉
28 | 29 | 27 | 28

*2002. Directed by Roman Polanski. With Adrien Brody, Thomas Kretschmann. 150 minutes. Rated R.*

"Agonizing and beautiful all at once", this "haunting" true story about a concert pianist's struggle to survive in Nazi-occupied Warsaw receives raves as "Polanski's historic achievement", a "masterpiece of filmmaking" that "will stay in your mind"; Brody's "brilliant", "subdued performance" "conveys so much without hardly saying a word", while the "depiction of the horror" is "accurate and harrowing in its detail"; in sum, both the director and star "deserved to win those Oscars."

### Piano, The ✉     21 | 24 | 19 | 22
*1993. Directed by Jane Campion. With Holly Hunter, Harvey Keitel, Sam Neill. 121 minutes. Rated R.*
"Each frame could be a painting" in this "exquisitely shot" drama set in 19th-century New Zealand concerning a "mute woman" and her "search for fulfillment"; though Hunter delivers an "expressive", Oscar-winning performance (despite very "limited dialogue") opposite Keitel at his "sensual", "full-frontal" best, critics contend the "contrived" plot strikes flat notes.

### Picnic     24 | 24 | 24 | 24
*1955. Directed by Joshua Logan. With William Holden, Kim Novak, Rosalind Russell. 115 minutes. Not Rated.*
Darn "sexy for its time", this "star-crossed", "moonglow"-drenched romance relates the havoc that a "handsome drifter" wreaks upon a group of "small-town" gals; fans say it "retains its charm", since it "epitomizes the lush storytelling of the '50s", but admit it may be a "little too theatrical to appeal to today's audiences"; hottest scene, no contest: Novak and Holden's "sizzling dance on the bridge."

### Pieces of April     21 | 24 | 21 | 19
*2003. Directed by Peter Hedges. With Katie Holmes, Patricia Clarkson, Derek Luke. 80 minutes. Rated PG-13.*
A Thanksgiving dinner rife with "family dysfunction" is the setting of this "hysterical yet heartbreaking" dramedy that's "touching without being overly sentimental"; while Holmes gives a "winning performance" as the estranged title character and an "off-the-wall" cast keeps pace, the "stunning" Clarkson as her cynical, cancer-stricken mother steals this "little film with a big heart."

### Pillow Talk ✉     20 | 20 | 17 | 19
*1959. Directed by Michael Gordon. With Doris Day, Rock Hudson, Tony Randall, Thelma Ritter. 103 minutes. Not Rated.*
The "first – and best – of the Rock-Doris bedroom farces", this "gloriously goofy" romantic comedy about an "unlikely" pair who share a telephone party line is "good clean fun" with "no laugh track needed"; alright, the "setup is a bit dated" (verging on "insipid"), but more than a few fess up it's a "true guilty pleasure" that they "never tire of watching."

### Pink Flamingos     ∇ 17 | 11 | 12 | 11
*1972. Directed by John Waters. With Divine, David Lochary, Mink Stole, Edith Massey. 95 minutes. Rated NC-17.*
Watch it "at your own risk": this "cult favorite from John Waters" is the rare flick with "something to offend absolutely everyone", with a plot incorporating a "demented" drag queen, a "filthy" motor home, a "gross" half-dead chicken and topped off by an "extreme" ending too "disgusting" to relate; it's "lowbrow" and ultra "low-budget", but "mondo trasho" mavens maintain it's the "best worst movie ever made."

### Pink Panther, The ⓫     24 | 24 | 21 | 21
*1964. Directed by Blake Edwards. With Peter Sellers, David Niven, Robert Wagner. 113 minutes. Not Rated.*
"Hilarity abounds" – "starting with the opening credits" – in this "outlandish" caper, the first production by the "comedy dream team" of director Edwards and actor Sellers (in his "brilliant" debut

as "bumbling Jacques Clouseau"); "funny to this day", it marked the start of a "sequel brigade" that marched along for years afterward.

### Pinocchio
26 | – | 26 | 26

*1940. Directed by Hamilton Luske, Ben Sharpsteen. Animated. 88 minutes. Rated G.*
"Forget the wooden kid with the schnoz" (who's a bit "dull" anyway) – this "wonderful" animated fantasy is more memorable for its introduction of the "classic" character of Jiminy Cricket and its Oscar-winning song, 'When You Wish Upon a Star'; otherwise, this story of a puppet transformed into a boy still "combines some of the sweetest and scariest scenes" in all of Disneydom.

### Pirates of the Caribbean:
### The Curse of the Black Pearl
24 | 25 | 22 | 27

*2003. Directed by Gore Verbinski. With Johnny Depp, Geoffrey Rush, Orlando Bloom, Keira Knightley. 143 minutes. Rated PG-13.*
"Eat your heart out, Errol Flynn" – Johnny Depp's a real "hoot" in this Disney high seas adventure, turning in an "over-the-top" performance as a pirate captain who's half "swashbuckling", half "swish" (think "Keith Richards with a cutlass"); though it "could have been fluff" given its "audio-animatronic", "theme-park-ride" origins, this "rollicking" romp keeps the violence "stylized" and rolls out enough "impressive" FX to provide lots of "salty fun."

### Pit and the Pendulum, The
▽ 22 | 20 | 22 | 19

*1961. Directed by Roger Corman. With Vincent Price, John Kerr, Barbara Steele. 80 minutes. Not Rated.*
"Vincent Price does Edgar Allen Poe" in this low-budget "B-movie" that might bear little resemblance to the source material (save the climax), but is atmospheric and "scary" throughout; part of a series based on Poe stories, this one's the "all-time favorite" of dyed-in-the-wool Roger Corman fans.

### Place in the Sun, A ✉◗
27 | 27 | 27 | 24

*1951. Directed by George Stevens. With Montgomery Clift, Elizabeth Taylor, Shelley Winters. 122 minutes. Not Rated.*
This "classic American" love triangle from Oscar-winning director Stevens might be a "glamorized version of the Dreiser novel" but was still rather daring for its time given the unwed-mother subplot; while it's hard to miss the "radiant Clift and Taylor" (thanks to some swoonworthy giant close-ups), "poor Shelley Winters'" role as the third wheel may well be the best performance; most famous line: Liz's smoldering "'tell mama all.'"

### Places in the Heart ✉
20 | 22 | 20 | 18

*1984. Directed by Robert Benton. With Sally Field, Lindsay Crouse, Ed Harris, Danny Glover. 112 minutes. Rated PG.*
Softhearted souls really, really like this "moving Depression-era tale" of a Texas "woman alone with kids, a farm, a mortgage" and, thankfully, plenty of "courage"; though both Field and screenwriter Benton snagged Oscars for this "heartwarming" study, the hard-hearted nix it as too "depressing."

### Planet of the Apes ❶
23 | 20 | 25 | 23

*1968. Directed by Franklin J. Schaffner. With Charlton Heston, Roddy McDowall, Kim Hunter. 112 minutes. Rated G.*
"Darwin would have loved" this "thought-provoking" stew of "science fiction and pop culture" about an American astronaut

who crashes on a simian-ruled planet; Heston's "brawny", "over-the-top" performance brings equal parts "paranoid power" and "Republican campiness" to the leading role, while that "wallop" of an ending remains one of the "most talked-about ever."

### Platoon ✉    25 | 25 | 24 | 26

*1986. Directed by Oliver Stone. With Tom Berenger, Willem Dafoe, Charlie Sheen. 120 minutes. Rated R.*

"Disturbing" yet "unforgettable", this "almost-too-real" war picture offers a "raw" view of the Vietnam conflict as seen "through the eyes of a recruit just arrived in the jungle"; granted, it "fails to offer the slightest glimmer of hope", but it "captures the desperation" of battle "better than any other movie", with a clutch of Oscars (including Best Picture and Best Director) to prove it.

### Player, The    23 | 23 | 23 | 22

*1992. Directed by Robert Altman. With Tim Robbins, Greta Scacchi, Fred Ward. 124 minutes. Rated R.*

"People who love movies about movies" love this "scathing satire" of "cutthroat" Hollywood, "perfectly directed" by "genius" Altman; cineasts cite the "excellent opening shot" (eight minutes "without a cut") and the "wonderful all-star cameo" appearances peppered throughout, but zero in on Robbins' "marvelous" portrayal of a "ne'er-do-well producer" as the real standout.

### Play It Again, Sam    22 | 21 | 23 | 20

*1972. Directed by Herbert Ross. With Woody Allen, Diane Keaton, Tony Roberts. 85 minutes. Rated PG.*

Woody's "wonderful" in this "fine early comedy" adapted from his Broadway hit about a lovelorn film critic so enamored with *Casablanca* that he conjures up an imaginary Bogie for advice; though this spoof "works on every level" for "hard-core" Allen fans, purists protest there's one major problem: "he didn't direct it."

### Play Misty for Me    22 | 20 | 23 | 19

*1971. Directed by Clint Eastwood. With Clint Eastwood, Jessica Walter, Donna Mills. 102 minutes. Rated R.*

The "original, much creepier" version of "*Fatal Attraction*", this "scary", "suspenseful" erotic thriller concerns a 'Misty'-spinning DJ "stalked by a deranged radio listener" (who supplies the "jump-out-at-you" moments); fans "get a thrill" out of Eastwood playing the "hunted instead of the hunter" for a change and dub his directorial debut "must-see" material.

### Pleasantville    20 | 21 | 22 | 23

*1998. Directed by Gary Ross. With Tobey Maguire, Jeff Daniels, Joan Allen, Reese Witherspoon. 124 minutes. Rated PG-13.*

"Two modern teens" are magically transported into the "world of a '50s sitcom" in this "totally disarming" parable about "American family" life that's enlivened by some "high-tech tricks" (notably the "imaginative" use of "color vs. black and white"); though a bit "heavy-handed" for some, its "clever premise" and "memorable Randy Newman score" make for "unique" moviemaking.

### Pocahontas    17 | – | 16 | 20

*1995. Directed by Mike Gabriel, Eric Goldberg. Animated. 82 minutes. Rated G.*

"Disney does it again" with this "subtly beautiful" animated feature about American Indians and English invaders in the Virginia colonies that might be "not historically accurate" but does offer a "great message" vis-à-vis tolerance and true love; if too "bland and preachy" for some, at least the "music's exceptional."

**Polar Express, The** 21 | 20 | 21 | 25
*2004. Directed by Robert Zemeckis. Animated. With Tom Hanks. 99 minutes. Rated G.*
Showcasing an "impressive" new filming technique that drops a "CGI"-enhanced Hanks into "five roles", this "good-spirited" animated adaptation of the "classic" children's book about a little boy who "doesn't believe in Santa" is "destined to become a holiday classic"; still, concerned parents caution that while the "choo-choo magic" is "pretty to look at", there are a "few scary spots" that might creep out the "preschooler set."

**Pollock** 22 | 26 | 21 | 22
*2000. Directed by Ed Harris. With Ed Harris, Marcia Gay Harden, Amy Madigan, Jennifer Connelly. 122 minutes. Rated R.*
"Harris is uncanny" capturing the "essence of dark genius" Jackson Pollock, the "misunderstood" 20th-century artist/"self-destructive" individual who's the subject of this "unflashy" biopic; as his mate and fellow painter, "Harden matches him every step of the way" in a "deservedly Oscar-winning" performance that further transforms this "amazing life" story into a "real work of art."

**Poltergeist** Ⓤ 22 | 20 | 23 | 24
*1982. Directed by Tobe Hooper. With JoBeth Williams, Craig T. Nelson, Beatrice Straight. 114 minutes. Rated PG.*
"Half social satire, half haunted-house tale", this "vivid" "roller-coaster ride" of a horror flick has a "pure Spielberg" premise: "affluent parents and cute children" living in a home "built over a graveyard" chock-full of "pesky ghosts"; the "strong story", "ahead-of-its-time special effects" and that "little voice" squeaking "they're he-ere" still startle boo-mers over "20 years later."

**Poseidon Adventure, The** Ⓤ 19 | 18 | 20 | 22
*1972. Directed by Ronald Neame. With Gene Hackman, Ernest Borgnine, Red Buttons. 117 minutes. Rated PG.*
A "boat flips over" and the "actors flip out" in this "topsy-turvy" "granddaddy of Hollywood all-star disaster flicks" that's "more fun in a campy way than you'd expect"; sure, the "phenomenal underwater footage" and "unforgettable (if not completely subtle) performances" are "entertaining" enough, but foes sneer this "kitschy" "sinking ship" defines the "true meaning of 'all wet.'"

**Postcards from the Edge** 18 | 23 | 19 | 18
*1990. Directed by Mike Nichols. With Meryl Streep, Shirley MacLaine, Dennis Quaid. 101 minutes. Rated R.*
Edgy types tout this "Hollywood insider story" as a "terrifically funny" look at the relationship between a "recovering-druggie" movie star and her scenery-chewing movie-star mom; though both the "biting" MacLaine and "brilliant" Streep "shine", fans say that the "sharp" script is as acidly "amusing" as they come.

**Postman Always Rings Twice, The** ◑ 25 | 25 | 25 | 24
*1946. Directed by Tay Garnett. With John Garfield, Lana Turner, Cecil Kellaway. 113 minutes. Not Rated.*
Garfield and Turner "set off the smoke alarms" in this "steamy" slice of film noir, a "deliciously sinful" saga about a "married

femme fatale", a "streetwise vagabond" and their simmering affair that "boils over into murderous passion"; though this "twisting" tale of "love, betrayal" and "homicide" is pretty "wonderful", one question remains: "didn't people know about divorce in those days?"

**Postman Always Rings Twice, The**    20 | 23 | 22 | 19
*1981. Directed by Bob Rafelson. With Jack Nicholson, Jessica Lange, John Colicos. 122 minutes. Rated R.*
Maybe it's "not as good as the original", but this "decent" enough remake of the film noir classic features "real sex" scenes instead of "implied" ones, most notably that display of "countertop love" that inspired many to install "butcher blocks in their kitchens"; "Jack is as creepy as ever" and Jessica's "good" as well, though purists pout "there's too much emphasis on sex at the expense of characterization" here.

**POTEMKIN ◑**    27 | 22 | 25 | 27
*1925. Directed by Sergei Eisenstein. With Aleksandr Antonov, Vladimir Barsky. 75 minutes. Not Rated.*
Over 80 years later, cineasts are still electrified by director Eisenstein's "influential" "triumph" that "put 'montage' into the filmmaking lexicon" and "forever set the standards for camerawork"; detailing the failed 1905 uprising against the Czar, it's best known for its "often copied baby-carriage-on-the-Odessa-steps sequence" that "paved the way for edit-happy MTV directors"; indeed, it's so "exciting" that many insist it "should be mandatory moviegoing."

**Presumed Innocent**    20 | 21 | 22 | 18
*1990. Directed by Alan J. Pakula. With Harrison Ford, Brian Dennehy, Raul Julia. 127 minutes. Rated R.*
Based on Scott Turow's best-seller, this "darkly powerful courtroom thriller" concerns a Philadelphia prosecutor whose life takes a "roller-coaster" turn after he's accused of murder; jurists say its "cliff-hanger" storyline boasts a "perfect surprise ending" that "keeps you guessing up till the last frame."

**Pretty in Pink**    19 | 18 | 19 | 18
*1986. Directed by Howard Deutch. With Molly Ringwald, Harry Dean Stanton, Jon Cryer. 96 minutes. Rated PG-13.*
For a most "entertaining" "glimpse into the horrors of teenage dating", try this "Brat Pack" comedy "classic" starring Ringwald (at her late-'80s "poutiest") as an "angst"-ridden gal from the "wrong side of the tracks" who falls for a "rich preppie"; ok, it's "sappy" and "not too original", but given all the "cute touches" and that "killer soundtrack", many call it a "guilty pleasure to the nth degree."

**PRETTY WOMAN**    23 | 22 | 22 | 22
*1990. Directed by Garry Marshall. With Richard Gere, Julia Roberts, Jason Alexander. 119 minutes. Rated R.*
Despite a premise somewhere between "Cinderella" and "Eliza Doolittle", this story of a "hooker with a heart of gold" who bags "Prince Charming" is a "happily-ever-after" romance that "put Julia (and her smile) on the map"; credit the "dizzying charisma" and "palpable chemistry between its stars" for its "believability", and though the "glamorization-of-prostitution" angle turns off bluenoses, "hopeless romantics" insist it will "steal your heart."

### Pride and Prejudice ◑∅    ▽ 24 | 24 | 26 | 23
*1940. Directed by Robert Z. Leonard. With Greer Garson,*
*Laurence Olivier, Mary Boland. 118 minutes. Not Rated.*
A "lovely, headstrong heroine and a handsome haughty hero"
make "sparks fly" in this "lush", "true-to-the-book" adaptation of
the Jane Austen classic; "fabulous period costumes and sets" in
high MGM style contribute to the "splendid" feel, while "Garson
and Olivier play off each other wonderfully" – now, "that's style."

### Pride of the Yankees, The ◑    22 | 22 | 23 | 20
*1942. Directed by Sam Wood. With Gary Cooper, Teresa Wright,*
*Walter Brennan. 127 minutes. Not Rated.*
A "must" for both "baseball and Yankee fans", this "best sports"
biopic virtually guarantees a "lump in the throat" as it delineates
the life story of the "great Lou Gehrig" and his courage in the
face of death; in the title role, Cooper is so effectively "self-
effacing" that repeat viewers "cry every time" they hear
his "farewell speech."

### Primal Fear    22 | 25 | 23 | 21
*1996. Directed by Gregory Hoblit. With Richard Gere, Laura*
*Linney, Edward Norton. 129 minutes. Rated R.*
The verdict's in: an "amazing" Norton "hits a home run" in his
"stunning debut" as a "timid, stuttering" altar boy accused of
killing an archbishop in this "unsettling" murder mystery/courtroom
drama; otherwise, the "acting is on-point all around" (even "Gere
is less dull than usual"), though the performances are nearly "blown
away" by that "knock-you-for-a-loop" "surprise ending."

### Primary Colors    16 | 19 | 17 | 17
*1998. Directed by Mike Nichols. With John Travolta, Emma*
*Thompson, Kathy Bates. 143 minutes. Rated R.*
An "uncomfortable peek" into the '92 Presidential campaign, this
"tight" political comedy stars a "right-on" Travolta as a "thinly
disguised" Bill Clinton in all his "lovably infuriating" grandeur;
though hindered by "unnecessary melodrama", this "underrated"
picture works as a "good insider's view" of the "way things
probably were – and you wish they weren't."

### Prince of Egypt, The    19 | – | 19 | 23
*1998. Directed by Simon Wells, Brenda Chapman, Steve Hickner.*
*Animated. 99 minutes. Rated PG.*
Respondents part like the Red Sea over this "history/cartoon
combo" from the "then-fledgling Dreamworks": fans insist it's a
"fascinating modern Bible retelling" of the story of Moses' exodus
with the Jews from Egypt, with "terrific animation" and "beautiful
songs", but foes say it's an "overwrought" derivation of the "Disney
formula" that "lacks" in all areas "except special effects."

### Prince of Tides, The    19 | 21 | 21 | 20
*1991. Directed by Barbra Streisand. With Barbra Streisand, Nick*
*Nolte, Blythe Danner. 132 minutes. Rated R.*
In this "interesting story" about a "Southern football coach, his
dysfunctional family" and the "New York City psychiatrist who
sorts it all out", the "convincing Nolte really gives his all"; yet
despite the "lyricism" and "stunning scenery", some say the
"self-important" Babs "never should have directed herself" in
this "vanity" production.

### PRINCESS BRIDE, THE          27 | 23 | 27 | 24

*1987. Directed by Rob Reiner. With Cary Elwes, Mandy Patinkin, Robin Wright. 98 minutes. Rated PG.*

Despite the "chick-flick title", this "lighthearted" but "fractured fairy tale" defies any easy "categorization" and is admired by "even the most macho" guys for its "swordfights" and "verbal jousting"; thanks to an "intelligent" William Goldman script, "masterful" direction by Reiner and an "incredibly talented" cast, "finding a better movie is inconceivable" – "plus, it's got André the Giant."

### Princess Diaries, The          18 | 19 | 17 | 18

*2001. Directed by Garry Marshall. With Julie Andrews, Anne Hathaway, Hector Elizondo. 114 minutes. Rated G.*

It's "every girl's dream" – to discover she's "actually a princess" (albeit of "some little country you've never heard of") – and this "wholesome" "mom-and-daughter" comedy follows newcomer Hathaway's transformation from "high-school dork" to crowned head amusingly enough; but even though this "feel-good" flick appeals to the "teenager inside us all", critics complain it's a "little flat for older audiences."

### Private Benjamin          17 | 19 | 17 | 16

*1980. Directed by Howard Zieff. With Goldie Hawn, Eileen Brennan, Armand Assante. 100 minutes. Rated R.*

"Goldie's golden" in this "funny, inspirational" comedy about a newly widowed Jewish princess who comes into her own after unwittingly enlisting in the army; a "lighthearted twist on women's liberation", it "shines" with "punchy" dialogue and a "charming" cast, particularly an acerbic Brennan and a "what-a-hunk" Assante as the romantic interest.

### Prizzi's Honor          21 | 24 | 21 | 19

*1985. Directed by John Huston. With Jack Nicholson, Kathleen Turner, Anjelica Huston. 130 minutes. Rated R.*

This "terrific black comedy about a dysfunctional mob family" anticipates *The Sopranos* with "cynical", "give-and-take" dialogue delivered by the "perfect cast" (a "bright" Jack and a "stellar", Oscar-copping Anjelica); one of John Huston's "last masterpieces", this "whacked-out gangster farce" wrings laughs via a "play-it-straight" script peppered with "in-jokes"; best line: "let's do it right here on the oriental – with all the lights on."

### Producers, The ✉          26 | 26 | 26 | 23

*1968. Directed by Mel Brooks. With Zero Mostel, Gene Wilder, Kenneth Mars. 88 minutes. Rated PG.*

Flaunting "silly and shocking originality" long before the "Broadway hoopla", this "anarchic", "appallingly funny" comedy boasts Mostel and Wilder "at their best" as perps of a "Ponzi scheme" to produce an "unbelievably over-the-top" musical winningly titled *Springtime for Hitler* and cash in on its failure; it earns a standing ovation as "unrelenting", "inspired lunacy" from the "warped mind" of Mel Brooks that still "holds up" as a manic "masterpiece."

### PSYCHO ◐❚❚          28 | 26 | 27 | 27

*1960. Directed by Alfred Hitchcock. With Anthony Perkins, Vera Miles, John Gavin, Janet Leigh. 109 minutes. Rated R.*

"Generations of moviegoers started double-locking their bathroom doors" after one look at the "famous shower scene" in this "classic

Hitchcock" "psycho-logical thriller" that was "quite a shocker in its day" and "still packs a wallop" – "without the gross violence of modern flicks"; standouts include Bernard Herrmann's "scariest film score ever" and Perkins' "twitchy", "tour-de-force" performance as the ultimate "mama's boy."

**Public Enemy ◑**　　　　　　　　▽ 25 | 24 | 21 | 20

*1931. Directed by William Wellman. With James Cagney, Jean Harlow, Edward Woods, Mae Clarke. 84 minutes. Not Rated.*
"Cagney's spectacular" in this "classic '30s gangster flick" that made him a star in the role of a petty crook who evolves into a "dangerous" crime czar; the picture still delivers quite a punch, brimming with "energy", especially the famous scene in which the girlfriend gets it in the kisser with a grapefruit.

**PULP FICTION ✉**　　　　　　　　26 | 26 | 25 | 25

*1994. Directed by Quentin Tarantino. With John Travolta, Samuel L. Jackson, Uma Thurman, Bruce Willis, Amanda Plummer, Tim Roth, Ving Rhames, Harvey Keitel. 154 minutes. Rated R.*
A "pioneer of plot shuffling" and "twisty chronology", this "propulsive", "in-your-face" thriller is a "true original" with an "unpredictable storyline" and "dialogue that's like a punch in the face"; recounting the affairs of some "charming hit men", it stars a "rogues' gallery of actors" in memorable bits ("Travolta's dancing", Uma's overdose, Plummer's "psychotic rant") played out with "dark humor", "intense violence" and "foul language"; not only did it "put Tarantino on the map", it's in a "genre all by itself."

**Purple Rose of Cairo, The**　　　　　21 | 21 | 24 | 21

*1985. Directed by Woody Allen. With Mia Farrow, Jeff Daniels, Danny Aiello. 84 minutes. Rated PG.*
The Woodman rises to the occasion with this "clever", "not-self-absorbed" comedy, a "bittersweet tale" featuring "Farrow's best" work as a Depression-era moviegoer whose "fantasy world" merges with "real life" when an RKO star walks off the screen into her life; the "imaginative" plot takes an "inside-out" look at "love of the movies", with a last reel calculated to "break your heart."

**Quiet American, The**　　　　　　24 | 26 | 24 | 24

*2002. Directed by Phillip Noyce. With Michael Caine, Brendan Fraser. 101 minutes. Rated R.*
Delivering a "powerful performance", Caine demonstrates why he's "legendary" in this "highly underrated" adaptation of the Graham Greene novel about "America's involvement in the early stages of the Vietnam War"; a "terrific" Fraser, a "wonderful story" and a "lavish" re-creation of 1950s Saigon are more reasons why many say "it's a shame" this "sleeper wasn't promoted enough."

**QUIET MAN, THE ✉**　　　　　　27 | 25 | 25 | 27

*1952. Directed by John Ford. With John Wayne, Maureen O'Hara, Barry Fitzgerald. 129 minutes. Not Rated.*
"Every Irish cliché" is "alive and well" in this "romanticized" drama, starring the Duke as an American boxer who hangs up his gloves and settles in his Hibernian "ancestral home" only to be smitten by the "beautiful", "feisty" O'Hara; presenting a "postcard" Ireland populated by "enchanting townspeople", it's "witty" and – despite a wee bit o' "blarney" – judged "worthy of a yearly viewing."

**Quiz Show** | 21 | 23 | 21 | 20 |

*1994. Directed by Robert Redford. With Ralph Fiennes, John Turturro, Rob Morrow. 133 minutes. Rated PG-13.*

"America's loss of innocence" is the subtext for this "intelligent" drama chronicling the '50s TV quiz-show scandals, a "blistering" commentary on the "mania for celebrity and money"; Turturro is the cast's "bright spot" as a bought-off contestant in a rigged highbrow showdown, and nostalgists prize the "vivid picture of the era", long before *Millionaire* – the "kicker is it really happened."

**Rabbit-Proof Fence** | 26 | 25 | 26 | 24 |

*2002. Directed by Phillip Noyce. With Everlyn Sampi, Tianna Sansbury, Laura Monaghan, Kenneth Branagh. 94 minutes. Rated PG.*

Young Aboriginal girls "escape forced slavery" and trek 1,500 miles across the Australian outback to return home in this "heart-wrenching true story" "acted wonderfully" by "three unknowns"; "don't expect special effects", and make sure to "watch the credits and you'll see the real children, now in their 80s."

**Radio** | 22 | 25 | 23 | 22 |

*2003. Directed by Michael Tollin. With Cuba Gooding Jr., Ed Harris. 109 minutes. Rated PG.*

"Small-scale" and proud of it, this "inspiring" sports drama recounts the true story of a "friendly football coach" who molds a "less fortunate", mentally disabled man into a popular mascot-cum-cheerleader (played by the "outstanding" Gooding, who "loses himself in the character"); parents say its "old-fashioned, feel-good" scenario teaches "great life lessons for kids."

**Radio Days** | 23 | 23 | 23 | 23 |

*1987. Directed by Woody Allen. With Mia Farrow, Julie Kavner, Dianne Wiest. 85 minutes. Rated PG.*

Tune in for "fond memories" to this "charming" "family comedy", an "affectionate period piece" set in late-'30s Rockaway Beach, where "childhood innocence, neurotic relatives" and golden-age radio fill the airwaves in a series of "warm vignettes"; touted for "top-to-bottom acting excellence", it's a "funny", "free-form" sampler of "Allen at his sunniest" and "most enjoyable."

**Raging Bull** ✉◐ | 26 | 28 | 24 | 26 |

*1980. Directed by Martin Scorsese. With Robert De Niro, Cathy Moriarty, Joe Pesci. 129 minutes. Rated R.*

Perhaps the "best boxing movie of all time", this "riveting" biopic charts the "rise and fall" of former middleweight champion Jake LaMotta, whose toughest opponents were his own "self-destructive tendencies"; shot in "beautiful black and white", it features a "primo De Niro", and though it can be "as painful as an open wound" to watch, most feel this is "knockout" filmmaking.

**RAIDERS OF THE LOST ARK** ⑪ | 28 | 24 | 27 | 28 |

*1981. Directed by Steven Spielberg. With Harrison Ford, Karen Allen, Paul Freeman. 115 minutes. Rated PG.*

It doesn't get "more exciting" than this "benchmark" of "nonstop pulp-fiction action", Spielberg's "roller-coaster" homage to "Saturday matinee" serials that introduces the "rakish" Indiana Jones, a tweedy archaeologist with a "strapping-hero" alter ego who scraps with the Nazis over an "all-powerful artifact"; chock-full of "retro" delights like "tongue-in-cheek" humor, "improbable cliff-hanger escapes" and a "love interest" amid the "snakes, whips and guns", it's a "rousing blockbuster" that proves the "'80s weren't all bad."

### Rain Man ✉ 　　　　　25 | 27 | 24 | 23
*1988. Directed by Barry Levinson. With Dustin Hoffman, Tom Cruise, Valeria Golino. 133 minutes. Rated R.*
This Best Picture winner is an unconventional "brothers bonding" drama driven by an Oscar-winning performance from Hoffman, who's "nothing short of incredible" as a full-grown "autistic savant" blessed with an endless supply of "quirky mannerisms" and "memorable lines"; Cruise shows off his own "acting chops" as the "scheming" sibling angling for half his inheritance, bringing on showers of "insight" that clear up to let a "feel-good" resolution shine through.

### Raising Arizona 　　　　　23 | 23 | 23 | 21
*1987. Directed by Joel Coen. With Nicolas Cage, Holly Hunter, John Goodman. 94 minutes. Rated PG-13.*
For a "completely original" and truly "bizarre" screwball comedy, check out this "hilarious white-trash" "cult classic" about a "childless", "criminal-class" couple (a policewoman married to a "failed convenience-store thief") that kidnaps a kid; Cage and Hunter are drolly "deadpan" delivering "dialogue that can't be beat", while the plot is typical Coen brothers: "goofy", "quirky" and gosh "darn funny."

### RAN 🅵 　　　　　27 | 25 | 27 | 29
*1985. Directed by Akira Kurosawa. With Tatsuya Nakadai, Mieko Harada, Daisuke Ryu. 160 minutes. Rated R.*
"Big, bold and beautiful", Kurosawa's "swan song" shows his "deft touch" intact in this "expansive retelling of *King Lear*" transformed into a "riveting" samurai "epic" involving a Shogun warlord whose decision to sheath his sword leads to intra-clan "betrayals"; suitably "Shakespearean" in scale, with "stunning" depictions of "feudal society" and "incredible battle scenes", it's "slow"-running pacewise but most hail it as "brilliant almost beyond belief."

### Ransom 　　　　　16 | 18 | 17 | 17
*1996. Directed by Ron Howard. With Mel Gibson, Rene Russo, Gary Sinise, Lili Taylor. 120 minutes. Rated R.*
"Gripping", "sustained suspense" is tempered with "much emotion" in this "dark" tale of a kidnapped child, starring "Mel in a suit" as a "conflicted" dad; though some bluff-callers deem it "overblown" and "formulaic", others swear by its "realistic" tension that's "scary to every parent out there."

### RASHOMON 🅞🅕 　　　　　29 | 27 | 29 | 25
*1951. Directed by Akira Kurosawa. With Toshiro Mifune, Machiko Kyo, Masayuki Mori. 88 minutes. Not Rated.*
Surely "truth is in the eye of the beholder", but most agree that Akira Kurosawa's "superb head-twister" of a Japanese drama should be "required viewing"; aided by "exquisite" camerawork and "fine medieval embellishments", it's a "simple story" about an ambush in the forest told from "four different points of view", proving that "self-interest" amounts to "nine-tenths of everything"; in sum, this "seminal" tale has been tirelessly "copied but never equaled."

### Ray ✉                                                    26 | 29 | 25 | 26
*2004. Directed by Taylor Hackford. With Jamie Foxx. 152 minutes.*
*Rated PG-13.*
"Foxx almost disappears into the person of Ray Charles" in this
"phenomenal" bio-"tribute" to the "legendary musician", nabbing a
"well-deserved" Oscar for his "foot-stomping", "heartrending"
portrayal of the superstar that's so convincing you'll "forget who
you're really watching"; fans agree the "uncompromising" look
at the soul man's "boozing, drugs and womanizing" is right on key,
with additional hoorays going out to that "marvelous soundtrack."

### Reality Bites                                            19 | 18 | 18 | 17
*1994. Directed by Ben Stiller. With Winona Ryder, Ethan Hawke,*
*Janeane Garofalo. 99 minutes. Rated PG-13.*
"Escape with the losers" in this romantic comedy of "post-college"
Gen-X existence as Winona and company find themselves "going
nowhere" but obliged to deal when faced with "job woes", tainted
love and "utter annoyance with life"; vets of the day say as a
"portrayal of MTV and other pop-culture" touchstones, "nothing
represents the '90s more accurately."

### Real Women Have Curves                                   21 | 22 | 21 | 19
*2002. Directed by Patricia Cardoso. With America Ferrera, Lupe*
*Ontiveros, Ingrid Oliu, George Lopez. 90 minutes. Rated PG-13.*
Those with "less-than-supermodel bodies" – "which is about
99 percent of the population" – will especially enjoy this
"inspirational" coming-of-age story about a "courageous" Latina
teen "who isn't a size eight" "caught between family traditions
and modern mores"; "there need to be more movies" like this
"celebration of women."

### REAR WINDOW                                              28 | 27 | 28 | 27
*1954. Directed by Alfred Hitchcock. With James Stewart, Grace*
*Kelly, Thelma Ritter. 112 minutes. Rated PG.*
"Voyeurism" meets "suspense" in this "snooper's dream" about
a "wheelchair-bound" photographer "spying on his neighbors"
and trying to "trap a killer" while fending off his girlfriend, who's
tempting him into "another trap – marriage"; while the "crisp
script" and "great NY set" draw huzzahs, fans tout its "perfectly
cast" leads, the "solid" Stewart and "deeelicious" Kelly; so many
find it "unsurpassed" that it was voted the top Hitchcock flick
in this *Survey*.

### Rebecca ✉◐                                               27 | 27 | 27 | 25
*1940. Directed by Alfred Hitchcock. With Laurence Olivier, Joan*
*Fontaine, Judith Anderson. 130 minutes. Not Rated.*
Based on Daphne du Maurier's "ultimate romance novel",
"Hitchcock's first American film" is a "dark, moody" tale of a
woman living in the shadow of her new husband's old wife;
"haunting" and "eerily captivating", it showcases an "excellent"
Olivier and a "gorgeous" Fontaine, but it's the "over-the-top"
Anderson who's the real "hoot" here.

### Rebel Without a Cause                                    24 | 24 | 21 | 22
*1955. Directed by Nicholas Ray. With James Dean, Natalie Wood,*
*Sal Mineo. 111 minutes. Not Rated.*
A "lost generation lives on" in this "terse drama" of "disaffected
youth" and "family conflict", which elevated Dean to "icon" status

as a "rebellious" juvenile delinquent who leads a "great cast" as they cope with "hope, fear and love" in the "inchoate LA" of the '50s; if all that acting out is a bit "dated", most maintain it "lives up to its rep" as the "ultimate" ode to "teen alienation."

### Red River ◐

26 | 25 | 25 | 27

*1948. Directed by Howard Hawks. With John Wayne, Montgomery Clift, Joanne Dru. 133 minutes. Not Rated.*
"Perhaps the grandest" Western of all, this cowpuncher "classic" breaks into a gallop when "lots of hunky men" saddle up for a dangerous cattle drive along the Chisholm Trail; Wayne "excels in an unsympathetic role" as a "stolid" rancher who turns against Monty, who "holds his own" as a buckaroo of "brooding sensitivity"; the result is a horn-lock that fans brand a grade-A prime "rewatcher."

### Reds ✉∅

21 | 21 | 20 | 22

*1981. Directed by Warren Beatty. With Warren Beatty, Diane Keaton, Jack Nicholson. 194 minutes. Rated PG.*
Agitprop meets "epic romance" in this "impressive" bio of writers John Reed and Louise Bryant that chronicles their courtship and activities as bolshie sympathizers during the Russian Revolution; "Beatty's labor of love" celebrating "American radicalism", it's an "excellent re-creation" of the time, framed by "remembrances" of "largely forgotten men and women", but "major themes" or no, critics say this "big production" is "too long to keep you interested."

### Red Shoes, The

26 | 24 | 24 | 26

*1948. Directed by Michael Powell, Emeric Pressburger. With Anton Walbrook, Moira Shearer. 133 minutes. Not Rated.*
With a tip of the slipper to Hans Christian Andersen, this "ageless" drama of "romance and ballet" "takes a fairy tale and creates magic" around the story of a young dancer who joins a celebrated troupe only to enter into a pas de deux with a composer; "sumptuous" staging and "dreamy choreography" make it a terpsichorean "benchmark", and fans "love every bit of it."

### Red Violin, The 🅵

24 | 23 | 24 | 24

*1999. Directed by François Girard. With Samuel L. Jackson, Greta Scacchi. 131 minutes. Rated R.*
A "symphony" recounting the "many tales of a violin's life", this "intricate" drama "follows the path" of a "fabulous instrument" from its creation in Renaissance Italy though various owners, countries and epochs, up to Jackson's encounter as a present-day appraiser; in spite of "art-house" airs, boosters bow to a "twisting" story that "keeps you guessing" – backed by a really "stunning" soundtrack featuring "real music by a real composer."

### Remains of the Day, The

24 | 27 | 23 | 25

*1993. Directed by James Ivory. With Anthony Hopkins, Emma Thompson, Christopher Reeve. 138 minutes. Rated PG.*
"If you loved *Howards End*", you'll dig this "complex and entertaining" drama of "two fragile souls" on a British estate in the late '30s; "repressed" head butler Hopkins "puts duty above all else", even his yen for housekeeper Thompson, and both give "precise, controlled performances" filled with "gripping silences" to suit its "nuanced" story of "unfulfilled love", "class-system" bias and the "obtuseness of the upper crust" – just "don't expect action."

### Remember the Titans
**20 | 21 | 21 | 19**

*2000. Directed by Boaz Yakin. With Denzel Washington, Will Patton, Wood Harris. 113 minutes. Rated PG.*

"Denzel is the man" to knock a ball team into shape while tackling "racial fault lines" in this "inspirational" family drama about a black high-school coach taking over a newly integrated football squad; if the "feel-good" theme of "tolerance and social understanding" on and off the field plays out as "hokey" and "about as deep as astroturf", fans "cheer anyway" for a "sleeper" that never fumbles its underlying "hope."

### Repo Man
**17 | 15 | 17 | 16**

*1984. Directed by Alex Cox. With Harry Dean Stanton, Emilio Estevez. 92 minutes. Rated R.*

A "cult classic with a serious following", this "wacko" comedy "captures the nihilism of the '80s punk scene" in its story of lowlifes repossessing cars and chasing after UFO's; with lots of "throwaway gags", "quotable lines" and an "overlooked soundtrack", this "silly delight" is proudly "over the edge" and "hard to resist."

### Repulsion ○∅
**▽ 25 | 27 | 24 | 23**

*1965. Directed by Roman Polanski. With Catherine Deneuve, Ian Hendry. 105 minutes. Not Rated.*

Polanski's first English-language feature, this "disturbing" psychological thriller top bills an "unbeatable" Deneuve as an unstable young woman slowly descending into madness; although made on a shoestring budget, it's still really "frightening" in its "depiction of insanity from the inside out" and is already showing "definite cult potential."

### Requiem for a Dream
**25 | 27 | 24 | 25**

*2000. Directed by Darren Aronofsky. With Ellen Burstyn, Jared Leto, Jennifer Connelly. 102 minutes. Not Rated.*

"Heavy" and "altogether devastating", this "bleak" "druggy" drama "spirals into the depths of hell" on the back of some "scary", strung-out imagery and Burstyn's "amazing" turn as a magenta-maned diet-pill popper with a none-too-swift junkie son; a "stomach-churning" depiction of "major drug use" that pushes Aronofsky to the "cutting edge" of "directing talents", it's "not subtle" but lingers like a "brilliant", "unnerving nightmare" – "be prepared" for some "grueling" going.

### Rescuers, The ⑪
**▽ 20 | – | 21 | 20**

*1977. Directed by Wolfgang Reitherman, John Lounsbery, Art Stevens. Animated. 76 minutes. Rated G.*

A "must-see for every child", this animated Disney feature stars a pair of "adorable" mice bent on rescuing a kidnapped little girl; although maybe not at the top of the Mouse House pantheon, it's still "cute and fun" with memorable voicework from Bob Newhart, Eva Gabor and Geraldine Page.

### Reservoir Dogs
**24 | 25 | 24 | 22**

*1992. Directed by Quentin Tarantino. With Harvey Keitel, Tim Roth, Michael Madsen, Steve Buscemi. 99 minutes. Rated R.*

The Tarantino "template" for a "new" style of crime thriller splices "hip, sharp" dialogue with "hard-core violence" as a "dream cast" sporting two-tone threads turns a jewel heist into a "riveting" "bloody spectacle"; the "clever" script relies on diced chronology, "sly riffs" on pop culture and "psychological twists" to lend heart to the "vicious" gang, though many howl the "nasty" bits ("ear removal", anyone?) are still "painful to watch."

### Reversal of Fortune ✉ ▽ 19 | 24 | 19 | 18
*1990. Directed by Barbet Schroeder. With Jeremy Irons, Glenn Close, Ron Silver. 120 minutes. Rated R.*
"You can't make this stuff up" – Oscar-winner Irons is "totally mesmerizing" in his "smarmy" take on the real-life Claus von Bulow, the high-society ladies' man accused of sending his heiress wife into an irreversible coma; Close and Silver also deliver the goods in this "solid" picture whose only drawback is "not having the ending that you want."

### Right Stuff, The 26 | 24 | 26 | 26
*1983. Directed by Philip Kaufman. With Sam Shepard, Scott Glenn, Ed Harris. 193 minutes. Rated PG.*
"Exuberant", "involving" and "proud to be American", this "triumphant" drama "never flags" in launching Tom Wolfe's "snarky yet sincere" "epic of the space age" onto the big screen; a "retelling of true events" surrounding the evolution of test pilots into astronauts in the Mercury program, it takes "historical" stuff and pushes the envelope with "adventure, humor" and a cast that's "A-ok in every way."

### Rio Bravo ▽ 23 | 22 | 23 | 23
*1959. Directed by Howard Hawks. With John Wayne, Dean Martin, Ricky Nelson. 141 minutes. Not Rated.*
"As Westerns go", this "entertaining" oater from the Hawks/ Wayne team is an "expert reshuffling" of the plot elements of "*High Noon*", the story of a sheriff trying to hold a prisoner against a threatening mob virtually alone; though the picture was remade as *El Dorado* (and later as *Rio Lobo*), aficionados say the original is the "best version."

### Risky Business 20 | 18 | 19 | 18
*1983. Directed by Paul Brickman. With Tom Cruise, Rebecca De Mornay, Bronson Pinchot. 98 minutes. Rated R.*
"Every boy's dream" comes true in this "smart, sexy" "coming-of-age" comedy, with Cruise as the high-schooler who turns chez suburbia into party central when his parents leave town – only to fall into "the arms of a beautiful hooker" and venture into the brothel business; it's a "funny" jibe at "upper-middle-class teenage life" with some "raging hormones" thrown in, and that celebrated scene of "Tom dancing in his Jockeys" is nothing short of "starmaking."

### River Runs Through It, A 22 | 23 | 21 | 25
*1992. Directed by Robert Redford. With Brad Pitt, Craig Sheffer, Tom Skerritt. 123 minutes. Rated PG.*
Sounding "deep" waters with a "pastoral" tale of "life as we no longer know it", Redford's "elegiac" drama of "family bonds" takes a "moving", "candid" look at the sibling rivalry between two small-town minister's sons; the "smooth" pace is set by the stars' "subtle emotion" and "striking" cinematography that captures the "Montana wilderness" in all of its full "majesty", though some clock-watchers find the running time a bit "too slow."

### Road to Perdition 23 | 26 | 22 | 25 |
*2002. Directed by Sam Mendes. With Tom Hanks, Paul Newman, Daniel Craig, Jude Law. 117 minutes. Rated R.*
"Hanks proves his versatility" in this "evocative period piece", playing a "cold-blooded hit man" for the Irish mafia during the Depression; the "intense journey" is "impeccably done", with Newman in "stellar form", Oscar-winning cinematography that will "take your breath away" (notably that "tommy gun scene in the rain") and "top-notch screenwriting" that "stays true to the novel."

### Road Warrior, The ⓤ 22 | 18 | 21 | 20 |
*1982. Directed by George Miller. With Mel Gibson, Bruce Spence, Mike Preston. 94 minutes. Rated R.*
"Road rage" kicks into overdrive in this "raw Aussie action flick", with "lean, mean" Gibson "at his baddest" as Mad Max, a "lone, reluctant cowboy" cruising a "post-apocalyptic" wasteland and upholding his "own brand of justice"; set in a "nihilistic" near-future when barbaric gangs comb the desert pestering decent folk for petrol, its combo of an "intriguing" setup and "incredible car stunts" makes it a "visceral" "cult favorite"; gas up.

### Robe, The ⓤ ▽ 19 | 19 | 20 | 21 |
*1953. Directed by Henry Koster. With Richard Burton, Jean Simmons, Victor Mature. 135 minutes. Not Rated.*
"Burton reigns" as a Roman centurion who oversees the crucifixion, then wins Christ's robe in a dice game in this '50s "religious movie" that inspired a slew of biblical flicks; most memorable for being the first feature shot in CinemaScope, it's "big" in every way, though some ask "can it really be an epic without Charlton Heston?"

### Robin and Marian ▽ 21 | 24 | 23 | 22 |
*1976. Directed by Richard Lester. With Sean Connery, Audrey Hepburn, Robert Shaw. 106 minutes. Rated PG.*
In "Robin Hood's later years" he resumes his affair with Maid Marian in this "wistful wisp" of a tale worth seeing for the "casting" alone; the "sadness of time passing is palpable" (right down to that "darkly romantic ending"), and if it's mainly a "woman's film", there's still "enough swordplay" to keep the guys happy.

### Robin Hood: Prince of Thieves 16 | 14 | 17 | 18 |
*1991. Directed by Kevin Reynolds. With Kevin Costner, Morgan Freeman, Alan Rickman. 138 minutes. Rated PG-13.*
This retelling of the spurned-lord-turned-benevolent-thief legend is "surprisingly original", with a "super villain" and enough "tongue-in-cheek" antics to "keep it moving"; but Costner's "now-you-hear-it, now-you-don't English accent" and other "inaccuracies" make holdouts hold out for "Errol Flynn."

### RoboCop ⓤ 16 | 13 | 17 | 19 |
*1987. Directed by Paul Verhoeven. With Peter Weller, Nancy Allen, Ronny Cox. 103 minutes. Rated R.*
"Ruthlessly smart and satirical", this "novel" sci-fi adventure flick tells the story of a cop killed in the line of duty then brought back to life as a bio-mechanical robot; alternately "violent and hilarious", this "live-action comic book" is a "thought-provoking look" at a "techno vigilante" and a heck of a lot "better than it should have been."

**Robots** | 20 | – | 19 | 24 |
*2005. Directed by Chris Wedge, Carlos Saldanha. Animated.*
*91 minutes. Not Rated.*
"Dazzling", "Rube Goldberg-esque" animation "keeps the whole family entertained" in this "simple", "heartfelt" 'toon about a young 'droid who "leaves home to chase a dream" in the big city; ok, the "ho-hum" "fish out of water" plotline is "as mechanical as the characters", 'bot at least it's got an "uplifting", "you-can-do-anything-you-put-your-mind-to" message for the kids.

**Rock, The** | 20 | 21 | 20 | 22 |
*1996. Directed by Michael Bay. With Sean Connery, Nicolas Cage, Ed Harris. 136 minutes. Rated R.*
Find out who's got the biggest "fireballs" in this very "noisy testosterone fix", bringing "slick", "edge-of-your-seat action" to Alcatraz as "crusty" ex-spy Connery and "bumbling" weapons-expert Cage penetrate the prison walls to stop a mad general from blitzing the Bay Area with nerve gas; fans find the pair "amazing together", and despite the highly "not-likely" scenario, the "awesome locale" and "great FX" ensure a "kick-ass" good time.

**Rocky**  | 25 | 20 | 25 | 21 |
*1976. Directed by John G. Avildsen. With Sylvester Stallone, Talia Shire, Burt Young. 119 minutes. Rated PG.*
This "red-blooded" ring drama (and Oscar champ) "goes the distance" with an "underdog-makes-good" theme as "two-bit" boxer Sly "wins over everyone's heart" when he "gets his shot" at the title, works up "lots of sweat" and "finds true love" along the way; though part "hokey" "Hollywood fantasy", it's also a "stirring confidence-booster" that packs an everlasting "wallop."

**Rocky Horror Picture Show, The** | 21 | 18 | 19 | 22 |
*1975. Directed by Jim Sharman. With Tim Curry, Susan Sarandon, Barry Bostwick. 100 minutes. Rated R.*
"Beyond weird" to the uninitiated, this "camp classic" rock 'n' roll musical is famed for the "floor show" put on at "midnight screenings" by costumed carousers who pronounce it the "best trash ever"; a "pure B-movie" spoof involving a pair of innocents who stumble into the lair of a "sweet transvestite", it's "silly" but "entertaining on its own bizarre level", so "get out your toast, rice and lighter" and "sing along" with this "legendary mess."

**Roger & Me** | 24 | – | 24 | 20 |
*1989. Directed by Michael Moore. Documentary. 91 minutes. Rated R.*
"Laugh and cringe" at this salvo of "guerrilla filmmaking", an "eye-opening" documentary chronicling both the "disintegration" of a Michigan town after its GM plant pulls up stakes and "squeaky wheel" Moore's "quest to confront" the corporation's CEO; the "too-real" footage is "drop-dead funny" yet "sobering" ("rabbit lovers beware"), and if a few find the "irreverent" tone "annoying", progressives everywhere hail it as a "vital exposé" of the "new global economy" and a "stirring" fanfare for the "common man."

**Romancing the Stone** Ⓤ | 20 | 19 | 21 | 20 |
*1984. Directed by Robert Zemeckis. With Michael Douglas, Kathleen Turner, Danny DeVito. 105 minutes. Rated PG-13.*
This "poor man's *Raiders of the Lost Ark*" turns a "lighthearted" adventure into a "fast-paced crowd-pleaser", with Turner cast as

a "nerdy" romance novelist who hooks up with "tongue-in-cheek hero" Douglas down South America way; the two are "quite the duo", and some "humorous action sequences" with archrival DeVito "trying to keep up" make for "durable escapism."

### Roman Holiday ✉◗     27 | 26 | 25 | 25
*1953. Directed by William Wyler. With Gregory Peck, Audrey Hepburn. 118 minutes. Not Rated.*
A "date movie without equal", this "frothy", "witty romance" presents a "radiant" Hepburn as the "rebellious" "gamine princess" with a "pixie cut" who plays hooky in the Eternal City, escorted by "charming", "not-so-hard-boiled reporter" Peck; helped along by "wondrous Roman scenery", their "coy" exchanges lead things on their natural "exhilarating" course, making for a "captivating fantasy" that draws to a "bittersweet", "refreshingly realistic" ending ("awww!").

### Romeo and Juliet     26 | 24 | 27 | 26
*1968. Directed by Franco Zeffirelli. With Olivia Hussey, Leonard Whiting. 138 minutes. Rated PG.*
"Achingly beautiful" and played with "youthful vigor", this "faithful Zeffirelli" reading renders the "grand" romance of star-crossed love so "accessible" that "even boys cry" during the tragic last act; the "classic" production stays "true to the Bard" with "so-cute" teenage actors and "gorgeous" sets, pleasing "purists" as the "definitive film version" and surviving as the odds-on favorite to be the Shakespeare everyone's "made to watch in school."

### Romeo + Juliet     19 | 17 | 22 | 23
*1996. Directed by Baz Luhrmann. With Leonardo DiCaprio, Claire Danes, John Leguizamo. 120 minutes. Rated PG-13.*
Flash master Luhrmann presents the ageless romance "in a different light" in this "daring updating", a "kinetic visual feast" that aims to please the "MTV generation" with "pop music" and "creative" modern-day staging; Leo and Claire lend the lovers "teen-idol" allure, and if some sniff at "style over substance" and say the "acting seriously lacks", those who are "ok with extravagance" find it "effective" and "really cool."

### Rookie, The     22 | 22 | 23 | 20
*2002. Directed by John Lee Hancock. With Dennis Quaid, Rachel Griffiths, Brian Cox. 127 minutes. Rated G.*
Quaid "hits a grand slam" as an over-the-hill major-league baseball rookie in this "feel-good movie for the whole family to enjoy" and "learn from"; it's a true story (with a "little Disney sprinkled on it") "that shows the importance of following your dreams" "even when it seems too late"; critics have just one quibble: it "drags on longer than a low-scoring doubleheader."

### Room with a View, A ✉     26 | 26 | 24 | 27
*1986. Directed by James Ivory. With Maggie Smith, Helena Bonham Carter, Denholm Elliott. 117 minutes. Not Rated.*
"Florence looks like heaven" in this "crisp" costume drama about a "proper Victorian girl's" sightseeing tour that's considerably perked up by "friendships that form in a pensione", leading to her "romantic awakening"; the "brilliant acting" brings "wit and energy" to a "sunny" "study of class and character" that finds all kinds of room for "superb fin de siècle" touches and "seductive" shots of the Italian landscape.

**Rope**                                22 | 21 | 23 | 22
*1948. Directed by Alfred Hitchcock. With Farley Granger, James Stewart, John Dall. 80 minutes. Rated PG.*
"One word – Hitchcock" – draws film buffs to this "chilling" reworking of the Leopold and Loeb murder case that's told with a "compelling gimmick": it was "shot entirely on one set" and "runs in real time"; though a few snore "slow and stagy", at least the master's "eye to detail" makes it an "interesting curiosity."

**Rose, The**                            19 | 23 | 18 | 18
*1979. Directed by Mark Rydell. With Bette Midler, Alan Bates, Frederic Forrest. 125 minutes. Rated R.*
The "mesmerizing" Miss M makes the "most stunning movie debut since Streisand" in this rock-chanteuse drama, a "homage" to the wild-at-heart chronicling the life and times of a "self-destructive Janis Joplin type" as she barrels down the road to ruin; groupies who insist Midler's "strong performance" should have "won the Oscar" find consolation in that "great title song."

**Rosemary's Baby** ⓜ                     24 | 25 | 25 | 22
*1968. Directed by Roman Polanski. With Mia Farrow, John Cassavetes, Ruth Gordon. 136 minutes. Rated R.*
A "glamorous horror" flick about a "naive" housewife duped into bearing "Satan's child", this "gut-wrenching classic" still "scares the hell out" of nearly everybody; "pro-choice" types tout Farrow's "amazing" turn (and "faaabulous haircut") as well as Polanski's "very faithful adaptation" of Ira Levin's novel, but everyone says that the "devilishly good", Oscar-winning Gordon "steals the show."

**Roxanne**                              21 | 21 | 21 | 19
*1987. Directed by Fred Schepisi. With Steve Martin, Daryl Hannah, Rick Rossovich. 107 minutes. Rated PG.*
Schnoz aficionados consider this "amusing" romance the "quintessential Martin vehicle": a "modernization" of *Cyrano de Bergerac* concerning a fire chief cursed with a prodigious proboscis but blessed with a "grab bag of comic devices" with which he helps a surrogate court the highly "watchable" Hannah; though some find it too "cute", "God nose" it's a "good-natured" yarn with a "ton of heart."

**Royal Tenenbaums, The**                20 | 24 | 18 | 21
*2001. Directed by Wes Anderson. With Gene Hackman, Anjelica Huston, Ben Stiller, Gwyneth Paltrow. 109 minutes. Rated R.*
This "very black" yet colorful "character-driven" comedy delineates the "humorous side of dysfunctionality" within a "wacky family of overachievers"; while the "Oscar-worthy" script and "stellar ensemble cast" draw applause, some shrug it's a "movie about nothing" that's "too clever" and "cynical" – the "reviewers liked it more than I did."

**Rules of the Game, The** ⦿🅕          ▽ 27 | 24 | 25 | 26
*1939. Directed by Jean Renoir. With Marcel Dalio, Nora Gregor, Mila Parély. 110 minutes. Not Rated.*
"Always on the short list of the greatest films ever made" is this "scathing indictment of the French upper class" from "master" filmmaker Renoir, which "takes place at a weekend retreat in the country" and contrasts the romantic entanglements of both rich and poor alike; although "perfectly written, filmed and acted", it

was not a hit in its initial release, and only garnered its rep after resurfacing at a film festival 20 years later.

### Runaway Jury
20 | 22 | 21 | 20

*2003. Directed by Gary Fleder. With John Cusack, Gene Hackman, Dustin Hoffman. 127 minutes. Rated PG-13.*

"Liberal Hollywood goes after the gun industry" in this courtroom drama pitting a "jury-stacking lawyer" against a "righteous underdog"; ok, it "doesn't follow the storyline" of its John Grisham origins, but devotees dig watching "old pros Hackman and Hoffman square off" just the same – even if they appear together onscreen in "just one scene."

### Runaway Train
21 | 22 | 20 | 21

*1985. Directed by Andrei Konchalovsky. With Jon Voight, Eric Roberts, Rebecca de Mornay. 111 minutes. Rated R.*

"Surprisingly" stimulating despite "cheapish production values", this "stark", "existential actioner" keeps onlookers "enthralled" with a "twist on the prison-break" scenario as a freight train carrying a pair of fugitive cons careens through the Alaskan wild ("bring a parka") while the law looks on; though "over the top" enough to nearly hop the rails, this "bleak masterwork" also offers "powerful" acting and "dark" themes.

### Run Lola Run 🇫
23 | 21 | 24 | 24

*1999. Directed by Tom Tykwer. With Franka Potente, Moritz Bleibtreu, Herbert Knaup. 81 minutes. Rated R.*

There's "never a dull moment" in this "amped-up" German import involving the "sweat-dripping" effort of a fleet-footed fräulein to hustle a big pile of cash to save her boyfriend from a nasty mobster; "strongly driven" by an "adrenaline"-pumping "techno soundtrack" and "video-game" vibe, the "breathless" "nonlinear" narrative forges "different perspectives" and "time repeats" into a "pulse-pounding" "original" that's as "ultra-watchable" as it is "quirky."

### Rush Hour ⑪
19 | 17 | 16 | 20

*1998. Directed by Brett Ratner. With Jackie Chan, Chris Tucker, Tom Wilkinson. 97 minutes. Rated PG-13.*

Formula "fluff" with "all the right moves", this actioner finds time for "comic relief" as a crime-fighting pair of "exact opposites" teams up to rescue a kidnapped kid; "high-kicking" Chan breaks out with some "inventive chop-socky sequences" and "exhilarating" stunts while playing it straight alongside outspoken "wild man" Tucker, so even if the "plot's not much", the "buddy pairing" offers enough crowd-pleasing "chemistry" to translate into "loads of fun."

### Rushmore
23 | 25 | 22 | 22

*1998. Directed by Wes Anderson. With Jason Schwartzman, Olivia Williams, Bill Murray. 93 minutes. Rated R.*

A monument of "quality quirkiness", this "unabashedly unusual" comedy stars Schwartzman as an "arrogant and clever" but "dysfunctional" scholarship student at an elite prep school whose "coming of age" takes many a "droll" twist when he befriends a rich alumnus and falls for a teacher; the "smart", "character-driven" script is "expertly acted", leading to high marks for a "winning gem" with "real heart" "beneath the smarminess" – and how about that "killer soundtrack"?

## Russians Are Coming, The Russians Are Coming, The
21 | 21 | 22 | 20

*1966. Directed by Norman Jewison. With Alan Arkin, John Phillip Law, Jonathan Winters. 120 minutes. Not Rated.*
Da, comrades, this "classic '60s comedy" is a "Cold War satire" that offers a "sweet take" on a paranoid period as a Red Navy sub goes aground off the Massachusetts coast and Soviet swabbie Arkin is sent into a Nantucket-like island community for a rescue boat, setting off rumors of an invasion; *Strangelove* it ain't, but the "very funny" situations are still "worth the time."

## Ruthless People
20 | 19 | 19 | 17

*1986. Directed by David Zucker, Jerry Zucker, Jim Abrahams. With Danny DeVito, Bette Midler. 93 minutes. Rated R.*
*Echt* '80s in its send-up of "pure greed", this pretty "crass" but "sidesplitting" black comedy gets going when a couple of "inept kidnappers" snatch Midler (carrying on at her "bitchy best") and demand ransom from DeVito, a "standout" as the "crude", double-dealing "spandex king" husband scheming to rid himself of a despised spouse; "lots of plot twists" ensue in a "silly", "hilarious" caper that anyone with a cynical side shouldn't overlook.

## Ryan's Daughter ⊘
∇ 22 | 23 | 23 | 24

*1970. Directed by David Lean. With Robert Mitchum, Trevor Howard, Sarah Miles, John Mills. 176 minutes. Rated PG.*
"Love and infidelity" are played out against a "magnificent Irish seacoast setting" in this "epic tearjerker" via David Lean, a "weak-in-the-knees romance" that's "gorgeously filmed" and set to memorably "haunting music"; its "bracing scenery" and truly "powerful" story – depicting "love as steadfastness rather than a cheap emotion" – lead many to call it "underrated."

## Sabrina ◐
25 | 25 | 25 | 23

*1954. Directed by Billy Wilder. With Humphrey Bogart, Audrey Hepburn, William Holden. 113 minutes. Not Rated.*
Like an order of "first-class everything", this "delicious" "rags-to-riches" romance sparkles with "wit and couture" as an "ethereal" Hepburn plays a "beguiling", love-struck chauffeur's daughter in a "little black dress"; the "modern Cinderella" scenario finds Bogie in a "comedic role" as an all-business heir determined to beat out his "younger playboy brother" for Audrey's affections; as for Harrison Ford's 1995 remake, loyalists "consider it blasphemy."

## Same Time, Next Year
22 | 24 | 25 | 21

*1978. Directed by Robert Mulligan. With Ellen Burstyn, Alan Alda, Ivan Bonar. 119 minutes. Rated PG.*
Expect to go from "laughter to tears and back again" in this "decade-spanning romance", featuring "convincing" turns from Alda and Burstyn as a couple of "married lovers who meet once a year"; adapted from the stage, the "annual adultery" device tracks the two as they "change with the times", making for "sweet", "warm" entertainment – even if it does "promote affairs."

## Sand Pebbles, The
24 | 26 | 25 | 24

*1966. Directed by Robert Wise. With Steve McQueen, Richard Crenna, Richard Attenborough, Candice Bergen. 179 minutes. Rated PG-13.*
An "epic of China" told from the point of view of Yank sailors knee-deep in the revolutionary turmoil of 1926, this "powerful,

pertinent" war drama features "authentic hero" McQueen "smoldering in top form" as a "tough-guy" Navy mechanic "with a heart of gold", manning an American patrol boat; if the tale "meanders like the Yellow River", it's still a "must-see" for History Channel addicts.

### Santa Clause, The ⓤ    19 | 17 | 19 | 19
*1994. Directed by John Pasquin. With Tim Allen, Judge Reinhold, Wendy Crewson. 97 minutes. Rated PG.*
"Corny in a good way", this holiday comedy packages the "fantastic" with the "real world" when exec Allen takes over the reins from an abruptly retired Kris Kringle, mysteriously begins "fattening" and meets with complications in the custody of his young son; though it sleds along on a "sappy story", consensus calls it rather "original" as far as Yuletide yarns go.

### Saturday Night Fever ⓤ    22 | 19 | 20 | 22
*1977. Directed by John Badham. With John Travolta, Karen Lynn Gorney. 118 minutes. Rated R.*
A paean to "polyester", this romance defines the "days of disco" with an "electric" Travolta as the blow-dried mook who lives to "look good" and "shake his groove thing" but has to boogie to "improve his life" when love comes to town; iconic "dance scenes" accentuate an "affecting" story with "dark" undercurrents that "perfectly evokes" "real life in Brooklyn" circa '77, even if some survivors of those "cheesy times" "feel embarrassed" about it now.

### Save the Last Dance    17 | 17 | 17 | 17
*2001. Directed by Thomas Carter. With Julia Stiles, Sean Patrick Thomas, Kerry Washington. 112 minutes. Rated PG-13.*
This "modern star-crossed-lovers" saga stars Stiles as a suburban teen transferred to an inner-city school where she falls into an interracial "across-the-tracks romance"; though the "textbook" set-ups "could have been more inventive", the picture imparts a "good message", abetted by a "great soundtrack", some "fancy footwork" and a climactic "hip-hop 'n' classical ballet."

### SAVING PRIVATE RYAN ✉    26 | 26 | 24 | 28
*1998. Directed by Steven Spielberg. With Tom Hanks, Tom Sizemore, Edward Burns. 170 minutes. Rated R.*
"As intense as it gets", Steven Spielberg's "celluloid monument" to WWII evokes the fear of war with "in-your-face" footage like the "devastating" opening, a "masterful" montage of "graphic" death and mayhem on a D-day beachhead; thereafter Hanks leads a "superbly" cast unit through no-man's-land on a "compelling" quest for a missing grunt, and despite sniping that "the story bogs down", it's a "wrenching" oh-"so-real" reminder that "war is hell."

### Scarface    22 | 23 | 22 | 22
*1983. Directed by Brian De Palma. With Al Pacino, Steven Bauer, Michelle Pfeiffer. 170 minutes. Rated R.*
"Raw and fun all at once", this "benchmark" crime thriller about a Miami-based "Latin drug ring" is ultra-"intense" and "extravagantly bloody" ("close your eyes when they bring out that chainsaw!"); addicts attest that it's worth seeing for Pacino's "over-the-top" turn as the "kind of bad guy you could really like", but the unmoved sneer it's "ultimately unredeeming" – and too "profane" to boot ("how many times can you say the F-word?").

### Scenes from a Marriage ⬛  ▽ 24 | 27 | 22 | 22

*1973. Directed by Ingmar Bergman. With Liv Ullmann, Erland Josephson, Bibi Andersson. 168 minutes. Rated PG.*
Originally a six-hour TV miniseries pared down to feature length, this still "powerful" portrayal of a "marriage breaking down" via Ingmar Bergman is a "real, poignant" tale told with such "rich execution" that it might "scare off all but the bravest from the altar"; though "hard to take for its intensity", this "talkathon" is worth seeing for its simply "astonishing performances."

### Scent of a Woman ✉  21 | 25 | 21 | 21

*1992. Directed by Martin Brest. With Al Pacino, Chris O'Donnell, Philip Seymour Hoffman. 157 minutes. Rated R.*
Pacino's "bravura" Best Actor bit has him cast as a retired military man compensating for his visual impairment with an "abrasive personality" and "foghorn" pipes as he drags his "meek" preppy babysitter along for a wild weekend in the Naked City; where cynics see "hokum" that "tends to drag", fans of the "too-fabulous" Al find it worthwhile "for the tango scene" alone.

### SCHINDLER'S LIST ✉◑  29 | 29 | 28 | 29

*1993. Directed by Steven Spielberg. With Liam Neeson, Ben Kingsley, Ralph Fiennes. 197 minutes. Rated R.*
Embarking on a "tour-de-force" "journey through a dark period", Spielberg's "direct", "painful" wartime drama "crystallizes" the "real-life horror" of the Holocaust in "stunning quasi-documentary" black-and-white, with Neeson as the man of "moral conscience" dealing with the Nazis in "shattering" circumstances; "beyond moving" and "tough to watch" in spite of its "understatement" and "touches of grace", it's a top Oscar honoree that's all-but-unanimously cited as "unforgettable required viewing."

### School of Rock  20 | 20 | 20 | 19

*2003. Directed by Richard Linklater. With Jack Black, Joan Cusack. 108 minutes. Rated PG-13.*
"Jack Black's manic zeal" takes center stage in this comedy about a "selfish wannabe" pop star who learns "selflessness" and turns a "bunch of buttoned-up prep schoolers" into "rock monsters"; it's "cute" and "sappy" in a "predictable", "family-friendly" way, but the "infectious energy" embodies the "irreverent spirit of classic rock" well enough to appeal to "young and old alike."

### Scream ⓤ  20 | 16 | 21 | 19

*1996. Directed by Wes Craven. With David Arquette, Neve Campbell, Courteney Cox. 111 minutes. Rated R.*
In an "aptly titled" entry, *Nightmare on Elm Street*'s Wes Craven "revives" the horror genre by aiming "clever potshots" at a host of hackneyed "slasher-film" clichés, lending a "humorously self-aware twist" to a "fast-paced" story of a "slice-and-dice" psycho at large among suburban teens; sure, the picture "makes fun of itself", but it's still "scary stuff" that sets a suitably "bloody and gross" precedent for a "slew of imitators."

### Seabiscuit  25 | 25 | 25 | 26

*2003. Directed by Gary Ross. With Tobey Maguire, Jeff Bridges, Chris Cooper. 141 minutes. Rated PG-13.*
Set against the "backdrop of the Great Depression", this "winning" adaptation of Laura Hillenbrand's best-selling pony tale trots out an

"old-fashioned" story about a "little horse that could"; "moving" turns from Maguire, Bridges and Cooper (as jockey, owner and trainer) and "beautifully photographed", "suspenseful" racing sequences evoke cheers, even if a few find this gelding's gait a tad "slow", saying "it misses greatness by a nose."

### SEARCHERS, THE
27 | 25 | 27 | 27

*1956. Directed by John Ford. With John Wayne, Jeffrey Hunter, Vera Miles. 120 minutes. Not Rated.*
"Not just a shoot-'em-up", this "thinking person's" Western boasts "peak" work from Wayne, who delivers a "gripping" portrayal of a "brooding" Civil War vet obsessed with tracking down his niece, abducted by Comanches; with its "spectacular" backdrops and "controversial" handling of "kinship and racism", it's much praised as "Ford's masterpiece", "perhaps the finest in the genre."

### Secondhand Lions
22 | 25 | 22 | 22

*2003. Directed by Tim McCanlies. With Michael Caine, Robert Duvall, Haley Joel Osment. 109 minutes. Rated PG.*
A young boy spends the summer in the "middle of nowhere" with his "eccentric uncles" in this "family-friendly", "feel-good" flicker that teaches "moral lessons about integrity and honor", yet is still "fun to watch"; as two "grumpy old men" weaving "tall tales from truth", Caine and Duvall exhibit "perfect timing", despite a somewhat "corny", "predictable" premise.

### Secretary
21 | 24 | 20 | 19

*2002. Directed by Steven Shainberg. With James Spader, Maggie Gyllenhaal. 104 minutes. Rated R.*
A "repressed" attorney "takes out his do-as-I-say delights on his all-too-willing secretary" in this "brilliant black comedy" (or is it a "kinky love story"?) that "makes you realize there's someone for everyone"; "hilarious characters", "interesting plot twists" and "superb acting" add up to an "ass-spanking good time."

### Secret of NIMH, The ⑪
24 | – | 25 | 24

*1982. Directed by Don Bluth. Animated. 82 minutes. Rated G.*
From the all-pro pens of "former Disney artists" comes this "freaky", oft-"forgotten" "alternative to sugar-coated" animation, a "beautifully drawn gem" of a barnyard yarn about a mama mouse desperately seeking a new nest for her brood; the "captivating" depiction of farm life comes with "character development" and an "interesting" story designed to appeal to the "adult" in everyone.

### Secrets and Lies
24 | 27 | 24 | 22

*1996. Directed by Mike Leigh. With Brenda Blethyn, Marianne Jean-Baptiste. 136 minutes. Rated R.*
Bad boy Leigh turns "accessible" in this "smart", "solid British drama" of "long-lost" family ties concerning a young black Londoner who "searches out her biological mother" only to find out that mum may be a working-class white woman; led by Blethyn's "pure, honest performance", the principals do a "terrific job" of making this tale "involving" and "heartbreaking."

### Sense and Sensibility ✉
26 | 27 | 26 | 26

*1995. Directed by Ang Lee. With Emma Thompson, Alan Rickman, Kate Winslet, Hugh Grant. 136 minutes. Rated PG.*
"Jane Austen would have liked" this "bittersweet" story of two husband-hunting sisters that "captures the true flavor" of her

novel "with wit and honesty" largely due to a "strong", Oscar-winning script from the "so-fine" Emma Thompson; sensitive types tout the "beautiful" scenery, director Lee's "brilliant" job and an ensemble cast that "rises to the occasion" – "this is what moviemaking should be."

### Sergeant York ✉️ ◐ ⊘                        ▽ 24 | 24 | 23 | 21
*1941. Directed by Howard Hawks. With Gary Cooper, Walter Brennan, Joan Leslie. 134 minutes. Not Rated.*
A "true story that needs no amplification", this "satisfying" biopic stars an Oscar-winning Cooper as the pacifist who became WWI's most decorated soldier after single-handedly dismantling an enemy regiment; a "complex" piece of pro-war propaganda, it's also a "great depiction" of a man of "quiet inner strength."

### Serpico                                      23 | 26 | 24 | 21
*1973. Directed by Sidney Lumet. With Al Pacino, John Randolph, Tony Roberts. 129 minutes. Rated R.*
Honesty "doesn't pay" in this "gritty" true story starring a "superb" Pacino as a whistle-blowing NYPD do-gooder who becomes a "man alone" when his exposure of "cop corruption" threatens to bring down the whole city; if all the "raw emotion" can grow "frustrating" and the milieu seems "a bit dated", it remains arresting as a "compelling commentary on the times."

### Seven                                        23 | 23 | 24 | 23
*1995. Directed by David Fincher. With Brad Pitt, Morgan Freeman, Kevin Spacey. 123 minutes. Rated R.*
All the "elegant nastiness" of a "guided tour through hell" surfaces in this "macabre psychological thriller" about two big-city detectives on the trail of an "ingenious" serial killer who dreams up "genuinely disturbing" torments "based on the seven deadly sins"; an "unrelenting" dose of "creepy modern noir" at its "darkest", it's wickedly "riveting" and "impressive" but "hard-to-take" and "gruesome" – with "no happy ending."

### Seven Beauties 🄵                             ▽ 25 | 26 | 24 | 23
*1976. Directed by Lina Wertmüller. With Giancarlo Giannini, Fernando Rey, Shirley Stoler. 115 minutes. Rated R.*
Wertmüller's "extraordinary" exploration of "survival in WWII" stars Giannini as a Chaplin-esque romeo trying to stay alive in a German concentration camp; a "brilliant" "amalgam of comedy and drama", it's a "powerful introduction to foreign filmmaking."

### Seven Brides for Seven Brothers              24 | 20 | 21 | 25
*1954. Directed by Stanley Donen. With Howard Keel, Jane Powell, Russ Tamblyn. 103 minutes. Rated G.*
Ok, it's "low on feasibility", but this "down-home" musical of "seven eligible backwoodsmen looking for love" with a septet of hillbilly "Sabine women" strikes "pure gold" with its "great Johnny Mercer" tunes and "extraordinary" choreography; fans dig its "exuberant" production numbers so "athletic" they "make dance macho", particularly that "barn-raising scene."

### Seven Days in May ◐                          26 | 24 | 28 | 22
*1964. Directed by John Frankenheimer. With Burt Lancaster, Kirk Douglas, Fredric March. 118 minutes. Not Rated.*
"It could happen here", or so says this "riveting 'what-if' drama", a "scary" Cold War story about disgruntled Pentagon brass who

lay plans for a "military takeover"; soldiering along with "well-plotted" plausibility and "Douglas and Lancaster turning up the star heat", it's a "powerful nail-biter" that "political junkies" consider – gulp – "as timely today as ever."

## SEVEN SAMURAI, THE ❶🅵   | 29 | 27 | 28 | 27 |
*1956. Directed by Akira Kurosawa. With Toshiro Mifune, Takashi Shimura. 203 minutes. Not Rated.*
Credited with "defining its own genre", Kurosawa's "awesome", "pivotal" Japanese adventure introduces the "original magnificent seven" as old-time samurai "warrior-heroes" who rise to the defense of a village menaced by a "vicious band of marauders"; the "epic running time melts away" before the "exciting" display of "honor", "courage" and "classic swordplay", and though there are "countless" reworkings, connoisseurs claim this "way-cool prototype" is "far superior."

## 1776   | 22 | 22 | 24 | 23 |
*1972. Directed by Peter H. Hunt. With William Daniels, Howard da Silva, Blythe Danner. 142 minutes. Rated G.*
Put away the books and take an "entertaining shortcut" to U.S. history via this "faithful" rendering of the Broadway musical, a "patriotic pageant" wherein periwigged radicals assemble in Philly and wrangle over the Declaration of Independence, backed up by "wonderful music and lyrics"; it's a "smart", "informative" way to "put a face" on "those lovable founding fathers", and they turn out to be "such great singers" – "who knew?"

## SEVENTH SEAL, THE ❶🅵   | 27 | 27 | 26 | 26 |
*1957. Directed by Ingmar Bergman. With Max von Sydow, Gunnar Björnstrand, Nils Poppe. 96 minutes. Not Rated.*
An utterly foreign flick and staple of "college days", Bergman's "challenging" drama is a "dark allegory" with von Sydow as a "knight returning from the Crusades to plague-swept Europe" only to hunker down for a high-stakes "chess game with Death"; as a "cerebral" meditation on the "meaning of existence", it seals the deal with "some of the greatest visuals ever" and a "symbolic story" that "makes everything else look like a game of checkers."

## 7th Voyage of Sinbad, The   | 20 | 12 | 20 | 22 |
*1958. Directed by Nathan Juran. With Kerwin Mathews, Kathryn Grant, Torin Thatcher. 88 minutes. Rated G.*
"Amazing for its time", this "delightful" adventure "throwback" "makes myth real without computers" using '50s-era FX to summon up a host of "lovingly created monsters"; ok, the "Saturday-matinee" storyline is "standard cheese", but it's a "fondly remembered fantasy" for fans who happily "take it for what it is."

## Seven Year Itch, The   | 23 | 23 | 20 | 20 |
*1955. Directed by Billy Wilder. With Marilyn Monroe, Tom Ewell, Evelyn Keyes. 105 minutes. Not Rated.*
Marilyn's billowing-dress "subway-grate scene" is the iconic moment in this "enjoyable" comedy, which finds "ordinary guy" Ewell "on his own" when the wife and kiddies split for summer vacation simultaneous with the arrival of his new neighbor, a most "memorable" Monroe in full "innocent-sexpot" mode, who brings on a major "midlife crisis"; sure, the repartee seems "dated and stagy", but it can still tickle the "funny" bone.

### Sex, Lies and Videotape
19 | 20 | 20 | 18

*1989. Directed by Steven Soderbergh. With James Spader, Andie MacDowell, Peter Gallagher. 98 minutes. Rated R.*
Wounded libidos fight the "battles of the sexes" in this "fresh take" on the "deterioration of relationships", a "simple", "well-crafted" drama about a college chum visiting an unhappily married couple and getting some spicy tell-all on tape; it's an "intelligent" look at the "permissive age" heated up by erotic "suspense" more than "actual" on-screen whoopee, though those who spurn "loser" characters find it "hard to care about."

### Shadow of the Vampire
20 | 25 | 20 | 23

*2000. Directed by E. Elias Merhige. With John Malkovich, Willem Dafoe, Cary Elwes. 92 minutes. Rated R.*
Maybe it's "not scary", but this "unusual", "behind-the-scenes" drama does apply a few shadowy "touches of horror" as it chronicles the "legendary production" of the fiendish '20s masterwork *Nosferatu*; Dafoe does a "great job" vamping as an undead actor with an "evil" hankering for hemoglobin, but foes call it a "disappointing" "art-house mess" that's "not sharp" enough to draw blood.

### Shakespeare in Love ✉
24 | 25 | 24 | 26

*1998. Directed by John Madden. With Gwyneth Paltrow, Geoffrey Rush, Joseph Fiennes, Judi Dench. 122 minutes. Rated R.*
"Whether it be true or not", this "lush, literate" romance is a "good-humored confection" that "lights up the screen" with "adorable" performances from Fiennes (an "ink-stained" Elizabethan scribe) whose "writer's block" is cleared by the "exquisitely attired" Paltrow (his not-so-secret admirer); a "rich" depiction of the age "laced with dialogue" from the plays, it's a "captivating", "rip-roaring" ride that's "accessible at any level."

### Shampoo
16 | 16 | 15 | 16

*1975. Directed by Hal Ashby. With Warren Beatty, Julie Christie, Goldie Hawn, Lee Grant, Carrie Fisher. 109 minutes. Rated R.*
Starring a "state-of-the-art Warren Beatty at his prettiest", this bedroom farce unfolds over election day, 1968, and follows the "hysterical" ups and downs of a randy hairdresser bouncing around Beverly Hills; both Christie and Hawn are a "blast", the premise is "very funny" and the "bittersweet" ending is a "touching" surprise.

### Shane
26 | 25 | 25 | 25

*1953. Directed by George Stevens. With Alan Ladd, Jean Arthur, Van Heflin. 118 minutes. Not Rated.*
There's "always a nuance to savor" in this "towering", "classic" Western, telling the "mythical American" tale of a "world-weary gunslinger forced out of retirement" when he sides with a homesteader family menaced by "ruthless cattle ranchers"; the "poignant" setup pays off with a "great finale" as Ladd walks tall in a showdown with "no-good" varmint Jack Palance, leading many oater voters to name it "best" in the West.

### Shattered Glass
21 | 23 | 24 | 19

*2003. Directed by Billy Ray. With Hayden Christensen, Peter Sarsgaard, Chloë Sevigny. 95 minutes. Rated PG-13.*
A "smart surprise" reminiscent of "*All the President's Men*", this true story about a "gifted journalist who self-destructs" after

"making up articles for the *New Republic*" is an "engrossing", behind-the-scenes look at "how the media manipulates what the public sees"; though it "drags a tad", Christensen delivers a "surprisingly mature performance" – "why couldn't he do that in *Star Wars*?"

### Shaun of the Dead
22 | 19 | 22 | 20

*2004. Directed by Edgar Wright. With Simon Pegg, Kate Ashfield, Nick Frost. 99 minutes. Not Rated.*
Leave it to "those crazy Brits" to concoct this "groovy" "send-up of zombie movies" combining equal doses of "campy fun" and "all-out horror bloodbath" to give you "giggles with your chills"; geeks advise watching some "George Romero flicks" first to "get all the references", but if that's not doable, "a few pints of ale" should be sufficient to prime your "brainnnnssss."

### SHAWSHANK REDEMPTION, THE
28 | 28 | 28 | 27

*1994. Directed by Frank Darabont. With Tim Robbins, Morgan Freeman, Bob Gunton. 142 minutes. Rated R.*
Finding the "stirring" in the stir and big hearts in the big house, this "first-rate" "gripper" of a prison drama goes behind the walls of a "dismal" state pen to follow fellow lifers Robbins and Freeman on a "long, dark journey" that pits "friendship", "ingenuity and inner strength" against a "brutal, corrupt system"; besides the "marvelous acting", there's a last-reel "surprise" to add a "feel-good factor" and even some "hope."

### She Wore a Yellow Ribbon
24 | 22 | 23 | 25

*1949. Directed by John Ford. With John Wayne, Joanne Dru, John Agar, Ben Johnson. 103 minutes. Not Rated.*
Ford's second bugle blast in his "cavalry trilogy" finds the director "at his best" in a tribute to the "honor and tradition" of horse soldiers posted to the ever-fleeting frontier; the Duke is typically "bigger than life" as a stiff-brimmed but sympathetic old man about to hang up his hat after a career in Injun territory, all portrayed against boundlessly "beautiful" big-sky scenery – "what else does a Western need?"

### Shine ✉
22 | 25 | 21 | 21

*1996. Directed by Scott Hicks. With Geoffrey Rush, Armin Mueller-Stahl, Lynn Redgrave. 105 minutes. Rated PG-13.*
"Mad musician makes good" in this "enlightening", "uplifting true story" about a gifted Australian pianist who succeeds in the shadow of an inflexible father but succumbs to a "harrowing" bout with schizophrenia – only to return to the bench for a midlife comeback; Rush's "compelling" turn keeps things uptempo, and if some dub it an "overrated curiosity", more offer bravos for a portrait that "shines" from first movement to last.

### Shining, The
25 | 26 | 25 | 25

*1980. Directed by Stanley Kubrick. With Jack Nicholson, Shelley Duvall, Scatman Crothers. 146 minutes. Rated R.*
The "supernatural and psychotic" collide in this "revolutionary horror film", a "downright scary" story from the Stephen King novel about a "snowbound caretaker of an old hotel" running amok; though voters agree that the "elevator scene", "Diane Arbus twin girls" and "gloriously unhinged Nicholson" all shine, Duvall gets mixed marks: "intensely annoying" vs. "profoundly brilliant"; best line, no contest: "heeere's Johnny!"

### Shipping News, The
18 | 21 | 17 | 21

*2001. Directed by Lasse Hallström. With Kevin Spacey, Julianne Moore, Judi Dench. 111 minutes. Rated R.*

Based on the best-selling book, this drama tells the "strange story" of a "hopeless mope" doing drudge work at a small-town gazette who gets a "second chance" when his wife dies and he ships out to the Newfoundland coast; though it's praised as "ultimately optimistic", foes torpedo the "overblown", "contrived" production as a "lackluster" Miramax bid for the Oscar race.

### Shirley Valentine ∅
24 | 24 | 23 | 20

*1989. Directed by Lewis Gilbert. With Pauline Collins, Tom Conti, Alison Steadman. 108 minutes. Rated R.*

A real "charmer" with a "Liverpudlian accent", this "spirited" comedy sends a "terrific message" with its "sweet midlife fantasy" of a "bored English housewife" who flees to the Aegean "looking for love" and nets Greek sailor Conti; adapted from the "superb" stage show, it "loses nothing in the translation" as a "wise" celebration of "independence and self-respect."

### SHOAH ▣
28 | – | 28 | 26

*1985. Directed by Claude Lanzmann. Documentary. 563 minutes. Not Rated.*

"Not a film to watch casually", this documentary addresses the "horror of the Holocaust" through "first-hand accounts" as a "necessary antidote" to "one of the worst episodes in human history"; Lanzmann uses witnesses from both sides of the "barbed-wire fence" to record their "intense", "shattering" memories of an entire society's "complicity", and "emotions pour out" over "eight hours of painful viewing" that are "impossibly sad and difficult" – but "worth all of it."

### Shot in the Dark, A ⬤
23 | 22 | 20 | 20

*1964. Directed by Blake Edwards. With Peter Sellers, Elke Sommer, George Sanders. 102 minutes. Rated PG.*

Sort of a cub *Pink Panther*, this "laugh-aloud funny" comedy features a "brilliant" Sellers as the clueless Inspector Clouseau, bumbling his way through a "delicious red-herring salad" of a plot that finds him assigned to solve a murder pinned on a Parisian chambermaid; if the "charmingly quirky" setup has its "slow" moments, the "master" makes it watchable "for his accent alone."

### Show Boat
23 | 20 | 24 | 25

*1951. Directed by George Sidney. With Kathryn Grayson, Ava Gardner, Howard Keel. 107 minutes. Not Rated.*

The "schmaltzy" but "fabulous" hit from the Broadway boards gets the "brightest Technicolor" treatment in this "sterling MGM musical" about a showgirl's "sentimental" entanglement with a riverboat gambler; the big wheel paddles along to "unforgettable" songs, "solid production numbers" and hoofers who "dance up a storm", and if purists prefer 1936's "glory-days" version, most can't help lovin' dat "beautiful, melodic" spectacle.

### SHREK ⬤
26 | – | 25 | 28

*2001. Directed by Andrew Adamson, Vicky Jenson. Animated. 90 minutes. Rated PG.*

They "added a category" on Oscar night to honor this "playfully creative original" that uses "exceptional" CGI animation and "great voicing" to rework a "hoary storyline" about an ogre saving a princess into "highly entertaining" fare; it challenges the "Disney fairy-tale formula" with adult-level "parody" and "inside jokes" underscored with a "positive message" for all.

### SHREK 2
26 | – | 24 | 28

*2004. Directed by Andrew Adamson, Kelly Asbury, Conrad Vernon. Animated. 92 minutes. Rated PG.*

"Another ogre-achiever", this "worthy sequel" once again features "incredible animation so lifelike you forget it's animation", "star voice actors" (Mike Myers, Eddie Murphy, Cameron Diaz) and a "laugh-out-loud" love story that sends up classic fairy-tale films; the "sly" satire and "clever" dialogue are "as much fun for adults as for the kids", and new addition Antonio Banderas – "purrfect as Puss 'n' Boots" – nearly "steals the movie."

### Sid & Nancy
18 | 20 | 18 | 16

*1986. Directed by Alex Cox. With Gary Oldman, Chloe Webb, David Hayman. 112 minutes. Rated R.*

An "absolutely demented but totally compelling love story", this "gripping" slice of "rock history" details the rise and fall of the "Sex Pistols' wildest member", featuring a "convincing Oldman" as Sid Vicious and the "scarily real" Webb as his "crazy girlfriend"; though the story of their downward, drug-laden spiral is not for the faint-hearted, groupies dig it 'cause it's "dark, ugly and vibrant all at once."

### Sideways
23 | 26 | 22 | 22

*2004. Directed by Alexander Payne. With Paul Giamatti, Thomas Haden Church, Virginia Madsen, Sandra Oh. 123 minutes. Rated R.*

Oenophiles toast this "intoxicatingly hilarious" road tripper pitting Giamatti's "shlub" against Church's "crack-up" for a Bacchian weekend of "middle-age angst"–inspired "debauchery" in "scenic California wine country"; the "literate", Oscar-winning script uncorks some "wonderfully painful" scenes that are "so real" it's "like watching a train wreck", though a few whine it's just a "mundane soaper" with as much depth as a "glass of merlot."

### Signs
18 | 20 | 18 | 20

*2002. Directed by M. Night Shyamalan. With Mel Gibson, Joaquin Phoenix, Rory Culkin. 106 minutes. Rated PG-13.*

Farmer Mel Gibson finds weird "crop circles" in his cornfields in this "paranormal" thriller from M. Night Shyamalan that delivers a "good number of jump-out-of-your-seat moments"; some say it's a really a "religious movie disguised as science fiction" ("I've coughed up scarier things"), yet there's a "creepy realness" about it that keeps the mood "tense."

### SILENCE OF THE LAMBS, THE ✉ ⓤ
27 | 28 | 27 | 26

*1991. Directed by Jonathan Demme. With Jodie Foster, Anthony Hopkins, Scott Glenn. 118 minutes. Rated R.*

Every subsequent "psych-profiling" flick owes something to this "masterful", "profoundly creepy" thriller that combines "heart-thumping suspense" with "premier" performances as Foster, an FBI greenhorn on a serial-killer hunt, is drawn into "intense mind games" with the "soft-spoken" madman Hopkins; its "well-deserved Oscars" speak for its "twisted", "truly terrifying" achievement, though some say it "gives fava beans a bad name."

### Silkwood
22 | 26 | 25 | 21

*1983. Directed by Mike Nichols. With Meryl Streep, Kurt Russell, Cher, Craig T. Nelson. 131 minutes. Rated R.*

This "somewhat forgotten" drama generates a "great deal of tension" telling the fact-based story of a whistle-blowing nuclear plant worker who comes to a "mysterious end" when she tries to go public with hazardous goings-on at the facility; lit up by "terrific acting" from "marvelous" Meryl and "eye-opener" Cher, it's a "moving" picture of blue-collar good guys vs. white-collar baddies.

### Silverado
24 | 24 | 23 | 24

*1985. Directed by Lawrence Kasdan. With Kevin Kline, Scott Glenn, Kevin Costner. 127 minutes. Rated PG-13.*

Boys, the "fun Western" rides again in this "well-made" "modern horse opera", a "true homage" that "throws in all the clichés" and delivers some "slick sequences" and "great one-liners" of its own; a "tremendous" cast "manages to upstage the glorious scenery", though it's best appreciated on the "biggest screen you can find."

### Silver Streak
19 | 19 | 18 | 19

*1976. Directed by Arthur Hiller. With Gene Wilder, Richard Pryor, Jill Clayburgh. 114 minutes. Rated PG.*

"One of the best comedy teams on film" gets its "first pairing" in this "slick takeoff" on Hitchcock-style "train capers", featuring Wilder in the "amusing" role of an innocent railroaded in an art-world murder only to find himself on the run along with the "beyond-funny" Pryor; devotees call it "enjoyable" and "underappreciated."

### Simple Plan, A
19 | 22 | 22 | 19

*1998. Directed by Sam Raimi. With Bill Paxton, Bridget Fonda, Billy Bob Thornton. 121 minutes. Rated R.*

B-movie maestro Raimi's "entry into respectable filmdom" is a "well-paced thriller" with a "convincing" scenario about a rustic threesome in the backwoods who stumble upon a wrecked plane and a bag of cash; "plot-twisting" and "suspense" ensue as lives "unravel" in a "tragic" parable of the "evils of ill-gotten gain" that makes it the "*Treasure of the Sierra Madre*" for the "*Fargo*" crowd.

### Sin City
22 | 21 | 20 | 26

*2005. Directed by Frank Miller, Robert Rodriguez, Quentin Tarantino. With Bruce Willis, Mickey Rourke, Jessica Alba, Clive Owen, Elijah Wood. 124 minutes. Not Rated.*

"Not for the faint of heart", this "sin-tillating" noir take on a pulp comic book series is "gritty" and "ultra-violent", with a "meandering storyline" played out in a "wonderful" mix of black-and-white live action and colorful "comic animation"; a "'roided-up Rourke" makes his "comeback", Wood does "Frodo-turned-psycho" and a "scantily clad" Alba does tricks with a "lasso."

### SINGIN' IN THE RAIN
28 | 26 | 25 | 28

*1952. Directed by Stanley Donen, Gene Kelly. With Gene Kelly, Donald O'Connor, Debbie Reynolds. 103 minutes. Rated G.*

"Giddy", "wet and wonderful", this "timeless" musical brightens the worst day with an "exuberant" "something-for-everyone" blend of "quintessential" song and dance, "satire" and a "sappy, funny love story"; the "flawless" Kelly plays a silent movie star in a "sweet send-up" of Hollywood's early talkie days and effortlessly executes the puddle-hopping "title number", leaving fans "awed."

---

### Single White Female
16 | 18 | 17 | 15

*1992. Directed by Barbet Schroeder. With Bridget Fonda, Jennifer Jason Leigh, Steven Weber. 107 minutes. Rated R.*

"Watch your back!": this "roommate-from-hell thriller" "keeps you on edge" with its "sick vulgarity" and mounting "suspense"; though the trading-identities storyline might be "derivative", the picture's still "full of surprises" and "done well" enough to "make you think it could actually happen"; P.S. brace yourself for a particularly "nasty ending."

### Sister Act Ⓤ
18 | 18 | 17 | 17

*1992. Directed by Emile Ardolino. With Whoopi Goldberg, Maggie Smith, Kathy Najimy. 100 minutes. Rated PG.*

Whoopi gets a witness protection program in this "engaging" "fish-out-of-water comedy" about a lounge diva who sings for the cops after her beau commits homicide, only to find herself stashed in "nun other than" a convent; the verdict: a "guilty pleasure" that rises above the "run of the mill" with "cool" musical interludes.

### Six Degrees of Separation
21 | 24 | 23 | 20

*1993. Directed by Fred Schepisi. With Will Smith, Stockard Channing, Donald Sutherland. 112 minutes. Rated R.*

"Great performances" ensure this "intriguing" "stage-to-screen" drama "adjusts quite nicely" to celluloid as a "sublime" Channing offers an encore of her theatrical role opposite a "young" Smith in the "challenging" part of a "charming hustler" posing as Sidney Poitier's son; it draws applause as a "clever" critique of "moneyed values" that's "surprisingly strong."

### Sixteen Candles
22 | 18 | 21 | 19

*1984. Directed by John Hughes. With Molly Ringwald, Justin Henry, Anthony Michael Hall. 93 minutes. Rated PG.*

"Ringwald will steal your heart" in this "sweet coming-of-age classic", a "day-in-the-life" comedy that conveys the "teen angst" of high school, "first love and puberty" as seen through the eyes of a 16-year-old "birthday girl whom everyone forgot"; though its "damn funny" "Brat Pack" cast "characterizes the '80s to a tee", modernists who love this "brilliant" send-up "can still relate to it."

### Sixth Sense, The
26 | 25 | 27 | 25

*1999. Directed by M. Night Shyamalan. With Bruce Willis, Haley Joel Osment, Toni Collette. 107 minutes. Rated PG-13.*

A "tricky" one, this mega-hit thriller "surprises even the most astute" with its "perfectly crafted story" of a troubled boy with an "unwelcome gift" who finds a friend in Willis, leading to "really spooky" plot developments; it's hailed as an "unpredictable" sensation that rewards with "white-knuckle jolts" and a "stunning" "O. Henry"–esque ending.

### Slap Shot Ⓤ
22 | 18 | 19 | 17

*1977. Directed by George Roy Hill. With Paul Newman, Michael Ontkean, Strother Martin. 122 minutes. Rated R.*

Right up there with the "funniest sports flicks", this puckish comedy finds "Newman on skates" as the "foul-mouthed coach" of a "dark horse" minor-league hockey team with a "strange way" of turning every face-off into a riot on ice; it "epitomizes the goonery" of the high-sticking '70s, resulting in "crazy", "profane" and "fairly violent" fare that hard-core fans "cannot live without."

### Sleeper
23 | 19 | 23 | 20

*1973. Directed by Woody Allen. With Woody Allen, Diane Keaton, John Beck. 89 minutes. Rated PG.*
Orwell's wake-up call has nothing on this "inspired sci-fi spoof", a "hilarious" comedy of a nebbishy NYer who's cryogenically preserved then "defrosted in the future"; "laced with fast-paced verbal" cracks, it's "vintage" Allen at his "goofiest" and "most slapsticky" in a romp that generates "nonstop laughs" – the "orgasmatron alone is worth the price of admission."

### Sleeping Beauty
25 | – | 23 | 25

*1959. Directed by Clyde Geronimi. Animated. 75 minutes. Rated G.*
No snooze among the "old Disney greats", this "lushly animated" "princess movie" has a trio of good fairies protecting the titular knockout from an evil spell by zapping her into a sound nap, interrupted only after her true love battles it out with filmdom's most fearsome dragon lady; the very wicked witch may be "too scary for the little ones", but most say this "classic" only "gets better with age."

### Sleeping with the Enemy
17 | 18 | 18 | 17

*1991. Directed by Joseph Ruben. With Julia Roberts, Patrick Bergin, Kevin Anderson. 99 minutes. Rated R.*
"Harrowing scenes of spousal abuse" supply the "scary edge" in this "Julia Roberts vehicle" about a "murderous husband and the wife determined to get away from him"; though it strikes a few as "overwrought and cartoonish", this thriller makes others "think long and hard" about a problem that could be "more common than we think."

### Sleepless in Seattle
21 | 22 | 22 | 21

*1993. Directed by Nora Ephron. With Tom Hanks, Meg Ryan, Rosie O'Donnell. 105 minutes. Rated PG.*
Although pretty "predictable", this Ephron romance "works", renewing faith in the "soul-mate concept" as the "perfectly cast", "totally lovable" Hanks and Ryan make "a great match" in the story of a woman who pursues a lonely-hearts stranger cross country; sure, this "toothache-sweet trifle" is "a bit far-fetched" ("at least Harry *met* Sally"), but it's also a "funny", "male-tolerable chick flick" that's likely to spring eternal for "hopeless romantics."

### Sleepy Hollow
17 | 18 | 17 | 23

*1999. Directed by Tim Burton. With Johnny Depp, Christina Ricci, Miranda Richardson. 105 minutes. Rated R.*
All your "decapitation entertainment needs will be fulfilled" in this "engrossing" rendition of Washington Irving's "headless horseman fable", a "funny but gory" ride from Tim Burton that's a "wonderful update of the Hammer horror films"; Depp is "daringly unconventional", and the "eye-popping" cinematography is "visually splendid" – so it's alright to nod off during that "big Hollywood action finale."

### Sleuth
25 | 28 | 26 | 23

*1972. Directed by Joseph L. Mankiewicz. With Laurence Olivier, Michael Caine. 138 minutes. Rated PG.*
It's no mystery why this suspense thriller based on the Broadway smash adapts "wonderfully to film": "masters-at-work" Olivier

226　　　　　　　　　　　　　　　subscribe to zagat.com

and Caine offer "witty", "subtle" work as a cuckolded writer and his rival engaged in a calculated confrontation in an English country manor; the "creative" story builds "numerous plot twists" that cross and double-cross, and "two of the greatest" muster up some of the liveliest back-and-forth volleys ever seen "outside of Wimbledon."

### Sling Blade ✉                     25 | 27 | 25 | 22
*1996. Directed by Billy Bob Thornton. With Billy Bob Thornton, Dwight Yoakam, J.T. Walsh. 135 minutes. Rated R.*
"Too convincing" in the role that lands him "on the map", "creepy Billy Bob" is "brilliantly believable" in this "tragedy from the real world" playing a slow-witted country boy who's sprung from the state booby hatch and taken in by a single mom; a "unique, touching" drama of man trouble, it "earns every accolade" with "excellent acting" and an "unforgettable punch" at the climax.

### Smokey and the Bandit ⊕          16 | 13 | 15 | 15
*1977. Directed by Hal Needham. With Burt Reynolds, Sally Field, Jackie Gleason. 96 minutes. Rated PG.*
This "good ol' boys car chase" comedy is a rootin' tootin' good "road movie" about a cross-country "race against time"; sure, it's "corny", "cheaply made" stuff based on what appears to be a completely improvised script, but in the end, it's plain that "everyone's having fun", particularly the "dynamite duo" of Reynolds and Field.

### Snatch                             21 | 23 | 22 | 22
*2000. Directed by Guy Ritchie. With Benicio Del Toro, Dennis Farina, Brad Pitt. 104 minutes. Rated R.*
Fittingly "splashy" fare from Mr. Madonna, director Ritchie's sophomore effort is a "relentless crime comedy" with a substantial cast of "wild" London gangsters who follow "interacting storylines" in a "quick-witted" "mix-'em-up heist" caper centered around a stolen diamond; the results are "bloody hilarious", and though you might need "subtitles" to decipher Pitt's "crazy-man accent", at least it's "never boring."

### SNOW WHITE & THE SEVEN DWARFS   27 | – | 26 | 27
*1937. Directed by David Hand. Animated. 83 minutes. Rated G.*
The "one that started it all", this "true classic" is the "*Citizen Kane* of animation", the "first full-length feature" from the Disney drawing boards and "still the finest" of them all; this tale of a fair maiden hiding in the forest with a band of "cute little guys" to escape a "terrifying wicked queen" is a "masterpiece" of "charm, simplicity and beauty" that continues to "entertain generations" and leave 'em humming "hi ho, hi ho!"

### SOME LIKE IT HOT ◑               28 | 27 | 26 | 26
*1959. Directed by Billy Wilder. With Marilyn Monroe, Tony Curtis, Jack Lemmon, Joe E. Brown. 120 minutes. Rated PG.*
"Cross-dressing was never so hilarious" as in this "legendary" "laff riot" about "two patsies on the run from the mob" who don dresses and join an all-girl band as part of their escape plan; thanks to Wilder's "sure touch" and the "sidesplitting" script's "countless priceless scenes" ("Lemmon with the maracas", "Curtis' riff on Cary Grant", Monroe "running wild"), this is one hot contender for the "greatest comedy ever made" – with the "best closing line" in moviedom: "nobody's perfect."

### Something's Gotta Give
`23 | 26 | 22 | 23`
*2003. Directed by Nancy Meyers. With Jack Nicholson, Diane Keaton, Keanu Reeves. 128 minutes. Rated PG-13.*
"People over 50 having sex" is the novel premise of this "middle-aged" romantic comedy positing that "growing old can be fun"; cynics nix the "lousy title" and "predictable", "sitcom-lite" plot, but the "*Architectural Digest*–worthy" settings and mighty "excellent chemistry" between Jack and Diane make it go down easy for "mature audiences"; just ignore the "lame", "too-bad-she-wound-up-with-the-wrong-guy" ending.

### Song of the South ∅
`23 | – | 22 | 26`
*1946. Directed by Wilfred Jackson, Harve Foster. Animated. With Ruth Warrick, James Baskett. 94 minutes. Rated G.*
Yup, it's "corny and dated", but "Disney's version of the Uncle Remus stories" is also "one of the earliest" to offer an "animation–live action mix" as a young boy encounters Brers Rabbit, Fox and Bear; its "controversial" stereotyping of plantation life means it's currently "missing in action" on DVD, but music lovers say it will always be "tough to top 'Zip-A-Dee-Doo-Dah.'"

### Sophie's Choice ✉
`26 | 28 | 26 | 24`
*1982. Directed by Alan J. Pakula. With Meryl Streep, Kevin Kline, Peter MacNicol. 150 minutes. Rated R.*
A "luminous" Streep with a "faint Polish accent" "shows her stuff" in this "haunting", highly "emotional" drama, which draws its "powerful story" from William Styron's novel about an Auschwitz survivor; though "wrenching" at points, it's a "compelling tour de force" that many see as Oscar-winner Meryl's "finest" hour.

### SOUND OF MUSIC, THE ✉
`28 | 25 | 27 | 28`
*1965. Directed by Robert Wise. With Julie Andrews, Christopher Plummer, Eleanor Parker. 174 minutes. Rated G.*
Everyone has an Alp-size "soft spot" for this "schmaltzy" Rodgers and Hammerstein musical, wherein a "charming" governess marries into a "do-re-mi" singing family and "stands on principle" after the Huns invade; the only Best Picture winner to feature "nuns, Nazis" and "kids in lederhosen", it's "shamelessly saccharine" but loved for its "uplifting" story, "fantastic" songs and "lush" scenery.

### South Pacific
`24 | 22 | 24 | 25`
*1958. Directed by Joshua Logan. With Mitzi Gaynor, Rossano Brazzi, John Kerr. 151 minutes. Not Rated.*
"Incomparable music" washes up in a "tropical paradise" in this Rodgers and Hammerstein songfest, which finds American sea dogs and dames living and loving and singing along to "beautiful orchestrations" on a WWII Pacific atoll; though a huge hit in its day owing to those "eternal" tunes, some say it "doesn't hold up" anymore, pointing to the "filtered camera gels" that drown meaningful moments in "gaudy Technicolor" tints.

### South Park
`20 | – | 19 | 16`
*1999. Directed by Trey Parker. Animated. 81 minutes. Rated R.*
Don't "blame Canada" for this "tasteless" full-length treatment of the "rude, crude" TV series, a "very un-PC" "equal-opportunity offender" with a "raunchy" mix of "lowbrow" laffs and "catchy" musical interludes; "rated R for a reason", it's "unbelievably funny" but "not for the kiddies" or "faint-of-heart" adults.

### Spaceballs
**18 | 15 | 17 | 17**

*1987. Directed by Mel Brooks. With Mel Brooks, John Candy, Rick Moranis. 96 minutes. Rated PG.*

"Brooks strikes again" in this "goofy takeoff on *Star Wars*" that skewers sci-fi as a couple of space cowboys rocket to the rescue of a princess, setting up "cornball" gags that are the "hysterical" stuff of Mel's genre parodies; though hard-core fans find it "gets funnier every time", those unamused by the "tired", "obvious" humor contend it's "hard to believe" this is the work of a "genius."

### Space Jam
**16 | – | 14 | 19**

*1996. Directed by Joe Pytka. Animated. With Michael Jordan, Wayne Knight, Charles Barkley. 87 minutes. Rated PG.*

The "Looney Tunes get their own movie" in this "fun fantasy" in which Bugs and crew play b-ball with über-hoopster Jordan and other stars to free themselves from alien kidnappers; despite "so-so" acting and storytelling, the "surprisingly good" matching of animation and live action makes this one "fun for the whole family."

### Spartacus
**26 | 24 | 25 | 26**

*1960. Directed by Stanley Kubrick. With Kirk Douglas, Laurence Olivier, Jean Simmons. 184 minutes. Rated PG-13.*

"Elevated" by its "sweeping vision" and "superb all-star cast", Kubrick's "impressive" epic headlines Douglas as the "virile" leader of a "slave revolt against Rome"; pairing a "psychologically complex" story with plenty of "gory but good" action, it's an "exciting" box-office big-timer that's "matched by few" in the "classic" spectacle sweeps.

### Speed ⑪
**18 | 14 | 19 | 20**

*1994. Directed by Jan de Bont. With Keanu Reeves, Dennis Hopper, Sandra Bullock. 116 minutes. Rated R.*

"*Die Hard* on a bus" is the "inanely simple" premise behind this "fast-moving" "high-concept actioner", with "sweetheart" Bullock and "studly SWAT boy" Reeves making a "cute and feisty" twosome as they find themselves "trapped" on a "tense", "nonstop" "thrill ride" aboard a "runaway bus" wired to "go boom"; though it's dismissed as "lightweight bubblegum" with "wooden" line readings from "Mr. Whoa", at least there's "no letup."

### Spellbound ◑
**24 | 25 | 23 | 24**

*1945. Directed by Alfred Hitchcock. With Gregory Peck, Ingrid Bergman, Leo G. Carroll. 111 minutes. Not Rated.*

One of the first mainstream movies to tackle psychiatry, this "outstanding" Hitchcock thriller deals with unlocking a "repressed memory", and the "perfect Bergman" and "gorgeous Peck" are a "good match" as doctor and patient; but despite touches like the "ahead-of-its-time dream sequences" designed by Salvador Dali, some analysts dismiss it as "dated Freudian nonsense."

### Spider-Man ⑪
**21 | 19 | 20 | 25**

*2002. Directed by Sam Raimi. With Tobey Maguire, Willem Dafoe, Kirsten Dunst, James Franco. 121 minutes. Rated PG-13.*

Comic-book mavens marvel at how well this "adaptation captures the spirit of the original" – a literally "loopy tale" of "spider bites boy" (Maguire), who sprouts superpowers and "spins around town on threads", battling "campy, cackling nemesis" Dafoe and kissing "hot" honey Dunst upside down; heroes hail the "CGI effects "seamlessly woven" into the "action-packed visuals" but hiss the "wooden acting and predictable plot"; overall, it's caught most folks "in its web."

### Spider-Man 2          22 | 20 | 21 | 26
*2004. Directed by Sam Raimi. With Tobey Maguire, Kirsten Dunst, James Franco, Alfred Molina. 127 minutes. Rated PG-13.*
"Spidey tries to hang up his tights" and "live his own life" only to be bugged by "super villain" Doc Ock in this comic-book movie follow-up that's "as good as the original"; expect the usual "jaw-dropping" FX plus a "deeper" exploration of the webslinger's struggles with "guilt, sacrifice" and "love", and get ready for "further sequels" 'cause this franchise has legs.

### Spirit: Stallion of the Cimarron          21 | – | 21 | 23
*2002. Directed by Kelly Asbury, Lorna Cook. Animated. 83 minutes. Rated G.*
A "gorgeous" combination of hand-drawn and computer animation "elevates" this "charming tearjerker" about a "spirited wild stallion and man's hapless efforts to tame him"; it's "great for kids and adults who grew up watching old Westerns", with "endearing characters" and a "sad" but "beautiful storyline."

### SPIRITED AWAY 🄵          27 | – | 25 | 28
*2002. Directed by Hayao Miyazaki. Animated. 125 minutes. Rated PG.*
"Master storyteller" Miyazaki's "inventive", "visually stunning" Japanese version of "*The Wizard of Oz*" meets "*Alice in Wonderland*" "transcends the animation genre", bringing viewers to an "enchanted" "spirit world" filled with "bizarre characters", "unexpected sights" and "fantastic artwork"; it's "a tad long" and "has some pretty scary moments in it", so it may be best for "those 10 and up" – "unless you want to spend money on therapy" for the kids later.

### Splash 🄊          19 | 18 | 19 | 20
*1984. Directed by Ron Howard. With Tom Hanks, Daryl Hannah, John Candy. 111 minutes. Rated PG.*
More "sweet" than salty yet "not too mushy", this "fish-out-of-water love story" is an "engaging" comedy shored up by Hannah's starmaking splash as a "sexy mermaid" whom Hanks courts and transports to NYC; the fantasy is buoyed by a cast of "charming" characters "you can't help but like", including some "sterling support" from a "scene-stealing" Candy – so dive in and "enjoy."

### Splendor in the Grass ✉          25 | 25 | 24 | 22
*1961. Directed by Elia Kazan. With Natalie Wood, Warren Beatty, Zohra Lampert. 124 minutes. Not Rated.*
There's "heartbreak" in the heartland as "yearning" breeds "teen angst" in this "bittersweet" romance set in pre-Depression Kansas; the very "young" and very "gorgeous" Wood and Beatty supply some "real acting" as a "modern Romeo and Juliet" driven to "wrenching" extremes in this drama of "stolen dreams" and "lost love" that makes some sob sisters "cry just thinking about it."

### Spy Kids 🄊          19 | 17 | 19 | 21
*2001. Directed by Robert Rodriguez. With Antonio Banderas, Carla Gugino. 88 minutes. Rated PG.*
Look for "good clean spy fun" in this "appealing" family adventure that's "empowering for kids" in its story of a bungling parental pair

of agents "called back into duty", leaving it up to their "cute" tykes to "save the world"; there are plenty of "cool gadgets", so grown-ups might not want to "check their brain" after all.

### Spy Who Loved Me, The          21 | 17 | 20 | 22
*1977. Directed by Lewis Gilbert. With Roger Moore, Barbara Bach, Richard Kiel. 125 minutes. Rated PG.*
When it comes to "popcorn" action fare, "nobody does it better" than Mr. Bond, and this is "one of Moore's better outings" as 007 pursues a nuclear blackmailer and fights off the "awesome", metal-mouthed nemesis Jaws; if by now the scripts are "superfluous", it's still the leading franchise for "fast cars, fast women" in "clingy clothes" ("oh, James!") and "lots of things that blow up."

### Stagecoach ◑          27 | 24 | 26 | 25
*1939. Directed by John Ford. With John Wayne, Claire Trevor, John Carradine. 96 minutes. Not Rated.*
"Wayne's grand entrance" alone immortalizes this "archetypal" Ford Western about a group of stock frontier types "traversing hostile Indian territory" by rickety stage; featuring the young Duke in his "breakthrough role" as a fugitive convict, it rolls along on "great dialogue" and "well-acted" ensemble work interrupted by "viscerally exciting" action scenes, making it the "classic source" of countless tumbleweed "clichés."

### STALAG 17 ✉◑          27 | 26 | 27 | 24
*1953. Directed by Billy Wilder. With William Holden, Don Taylor, Otto Preminger. 120 minutes. Not Rated.*
Wilder's "wonderful" adaptation of the stage drama supplies the "intrigue" of a "psychological thriller" with some comic relief in this story starring the "properly Oscarized" Holden as a "cynical prisoner" in a WWII POW camp who's "suspected of being a German spy"; thanks to "tremendous acting" and "tense" plotting that "keeps you guessing until the end", this study of military "camaraderie" and "mob judgment" is "not to be missed."

### Stand and Deliver          20 | 22 | 22 | 17
*1988. Directed by Ramon Menendez. With Edward James Olmos, Lou Diamond Phillips. 102 minutes. Rated PG.*
Giving credit to the "common man", this "inspirational" drama presents Olmos as the real-life Jaime Escalante, a "math teacher who makes a difference" in a tough East LA school by tutoring a class of bad-attitude kids; tough graders say this "good fun flick" also scores as an "underrated" self-esteem booster.

### Stand by Me          24 | 23 | 25 | 23
*1986. Directed by Rob Reiner. With Wil Wheaton, River Phoenix, Corey Feldman. 89 minutes. Rated R.*
This "wholesome" "coming-of-ager" focuses on preadolescent "best buddies" in '50s Oregon who set out "in search of a missing boy", bonding in the face of various perils and learning about the "real stuff" along the way; a platform for "young talent", it carries a "strong message" about the "struggle to grow up."

### Stargate          18 | 17 | 20 | 22
*1994. Directed by Roland Emmerich. With Kurt Russell, James Spader, Jaye Davidson. 121 minutes. Rated PG-13.*
"Egypt" meets "outer space" in this "interesting" sci-fi flicker about a "portal" discovered in the desert that's an intergalactic

 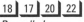

wormhole to a "distant world" enslaved by the "powerful" Egyptian god Ra; the ensuing "face-off" is long on "thoughtless action" and "terrific" pyrotechnics but "never delivers" on the "great premise."

### Star Is Born, A                          25 | 26 | 26 | 26

*1954. Directed by George Cukor. With Judy Garland, James Mason, Jack Carson. 181 minutes. Rated PG.*

"Forget the other versions": this "heartbreaking" musical drama revisits the Tinseltown parable of fickle celebrity fortunes with the "best Judy ever", showcasing her "true range" as the nobody whose rise to fame is paralleled by her big-name hubby's descent; whether laughing, singing or "turning on the waterworks", the "mesmerizing" Garland gives the "performance of her life", leaving loyalists to lament the Oscar "that got away."

### Starman                                19 | 20 | 21 | 17

*1984. Directed by John Carpenter. With Jeff Bridges, Karen Allen, Richard Jaeckel. 115 minutes. Rated PG-13.*

A spacecraft falls to Earth and an "alien and earthling fall for each other" in this "overlooked date movie"; a "first-rate" Bridges plays an "E.T. in human form" who inhabits the bod of Allen's recently deceased husband, leading to "sentimental" getting-to-know-you sessions and a "romantic" road trip that draws to a "sweet" if "predictable" conclusion.

### Starship Troopers                      15 | 9 | 15 | 21

*1997. Directed by Paul Verhoeven. With Casper Van Dien, Dina Meyer, Denise Richards. 129 minutes. Rated R.*

"Robert A. Heinlein's classic yarn" about an invasion of "big bad bugs" gets a "campy" rendering in this "full-throttle sci-fi" flick loaded with "amazing" big-budget effects; while cynics nix the "appallingly cheesy acting", "trite" plot and "pointless violence", "nonstop action" fans counter that this "critique of militarism" isn't "meant to be taken seriously."

### Star Trek II: The Wrath of Khan ⑪      23 | 19 | 24 | 24

*1982. Directed by Nicholas Meyer. With William Shatner, Leonard Nimoy, DeForest Kelley, Ricardo Montalban. 113 minutes. Rated PG.*

"Best villain + best story" = "best *Trek*": so say supporters of this "ripping" sci-fi sequel that hits warp speed when "scenery-chewing" outer-space outlaw Khan hijacks a starship and goes gunning for Admiral Kirk, back for yet one more mission with his familiar Starfleet crew; it offers all the "overblown acting" and "heart of the original", and the windup with Spock on the spot has enough "emotional punch" to "make a Trekkie out of anyone."

### Star Trek IV: The Voyage Home ⑪       21 | 17 | 21 | 23

*1986. Directed by Leonard Nimoy. With William Shatner, Leonard Nimoy, DeForest Kelley. 119 minutes. Rated PG.*

The final frontiersmen send us a "message from the future" in this "easygoing", "most accessible" of the sci-fi spin-offs, with Kirk and company "letting their hair down" to indulge in "tongue-in-cheek" interplay as they travel backward through the centuries to join a modern-day "scientific babe" in a mission to "save the whales"; it's a little "lightweight" despite the "timely ecological" theme, but as with the other "even-numbered" entries in the series, the voyaging is "not at all bad."

## STAR WARS ⑪
28 | 22 | 28 | 29

(aka Star Wars Episode IV: A New Hope)
*1977. Directed by George Lucas. With Mark Hamill, Harrison Ford, Carrie Fisher. 121 minutes. Rated PG.*
Lucas' "Force is strong" in this "visionary" blockbuster, the "quantum leap" that "redefined sci-fi" and established a "dynasty" by locating the "universal" in a "galaxy far, far away", where "original" "critters" and "futuristic samurais" side with a put-upon princess against an evil Empire; building to a "black hats/white hats" showdown, it's an "entertaining" mix of "modern myth" and "thrill-and-a-half" FX; subsequent space operas "can't touch" it.

### Star Wars Episode I: The Phantom Menace ⑪
18 | 16 | 18 | 26

*1999. Directed by George Lucas. With Liam Neeson, Ewan McGregor, Natalie Portman. 133 minutes. Rated PG.*
"After all the hype", here's the "good-looking" sci-fi prequel, which finds an earlier Jedi generation aiding a "planet under blockade" while setting some backstories straight as Obi-Wan and Skywalker *père* are groomed for knighthood; though denounced as a "giant misstep" that makes do with "so-so" storytelling while "pandering to the kiddies" with CGI "overkill" and "irritating" cast members ("why Jar Jar?"), "it's still *Star Wars*", and many "escapists" welcome it as a "worthy addition."

### Star Wars Episode II: Attack of the Clones ⑪
17 | 13 | 16 | 24

*2002. Directed by George Lucas. With Hayden Christensen, Ewan McGregor, Natalie Portman. 143 minutes. Rated PG.*
Unmoved by thunderous legions jeering the "magic is missing", franchise faithfuls stand by this "impressive" second act of the prequel trilogy, lauding its "mesmerizing visuals", "foreboding" moods and "many-questions-answered" plotlines; of course, even diehards don't deny Anakin and Padmé's courtship is a "cardboard"-acted, "dire attempt at romance", yet it's all "worthwhile" for the "showstopping" scene when Yoda fights.

### Star Wars Episode III: Revenge of the Sith
23 | 16 | 23 | 28

*2005. Directed by George Lucas. With Hayden Christensen, Ewan McGregor, Ian McDiarmid, Natalie Portman. 140 minutes. Rated PG-13.*
"Even though you know" how it wraps up, seeing the "missing pieces of the puzzle" fall into place brings "closure" to a generation of fans who've waited "20-plus years" to learn how Jedi "badass" Anakin Skywalker falls from grace and "becomes Darth Vader" in this "very dark", "epic conclusion" to the beloved space saga; piling on more "dazzling" FX and "campy acting" than ever, it's the "stronger story" this time 'round ("it took Lucas three tries") that explains why it's widely considered "the best of the prequels."

### STAR WARS EPISODE V: THE EMPIRE STRIKES BACK ⑪
26 | 21 | 26 | 28

*1980. Directed by Irvin Kershner. With Mark Hamill, Harrison Ford, Carrie Fisher, Billy Dee Williams. 124 minutes. Rated PG.*
The "darkest of the *Star Wars* series", this "worthy" first sequel features more "depth" in its characterizations and the "best storyline so far", "revealing many important secrets" as the

"cosmic struggle continues"; "blissfully free of wooden dialogue", it might be the "most adult" of the "original trilogy", while that open-ended "cliff-hanger" of a finale makes for a suitably "spectacular" windup.

### Star Wars Episode VI: Return of the Jedi
24 | 20 | 23 | 28

*1983. Directed by Richard Marquand. With Mark Hamill, Harrison Ford, Carrie Fisher, Billy Dee Williams. 134 minutes. Rated PG.*
Either a "worthy sequel" or "leftovers", this "wrap-up" episode of the *Star Wars* original trilogy finds the now-classic cast "comfortable in their roles", mugging their way through a "patented good-wins-over-evil storyline" with ample space for "cool special effects" and an "amazing final battle"; loyalists say the force is with it, but skeptics see a "weak entry" overrun with "cute, furry Ewoks", foreshadowing "toy tie-ins" and the "beginnings of Jar Jar."

### Station Agent, The
25 | 27 | 23 | 23

*2003. Directed by Thomas McCarthy. With Peter Dinklage, Patricia Clarkson, Bobby Cannavale. 88 minutes. Rated R.*
"Putting the *Q* in quirky and the *S* in subtle", this "quiet little film" also puts the *I* in indie with its "arty" but "restrained" portrayal of the unlikely friendship between three "eccentrics" in rural New Jersey; while "not much happens" in this "meandering character study", a "great ensemble performance" (especially little person Dinklage's "charisma"-laden turn as a train enthusiast) makes for a "funny", "poignant" flick that "never falls off the track."

### Steel Magnolias
24 | 25 | 24 | 23

*1989. Directed by Herbert Ross. With Sally Field, Dolly Parton, Shirley MacLaine, Daryl Hannah. 117 minutes. Rated PG.*
Break out the "Kleenex" for this "estrogen"-soaked drama, a "major tearjerker" smothered in "Southern-fried flavor", dashed with "laughs" and "memorable one-liners" and played "to the hilt and then some" by a "talented" bunch of "adorable" all-star "belles"; the story of "best girlfriends" in a Looziana beauty parlor bonding through "thick and thin", it's "captivating", "well-made" and "weepy" enough to qualify as the "ultimate chick flick."

### St. Elmo's Fire
17 | 17 | 17 | 17

*1985. Directed by Joel Schumacher. With Rob Lowe, Demi Moore, Andrew McCarthy, Judd Nelson. 110 minutes. Rated R.*
This "nostalgic" '80s "cult classic" starring the "Brat Pack at its finest" addresses "issues faced in life just after college"; sure, there are some "weak spots" and a few moments that are now "unintentionally hilarious", but overall, it remains a "favorite" "coming-of-age flick", like "*The Big Chill* for Generation X."

### STING, THE ✉Ⅱ
27 | 26 | 27 | 26

*1973. Directed by George Roy Hill. With Paul Newman, Robert Redford, Robert Shaw. 129 minutes. Rated PG.*
"Deftly" charming its way to Best Picture honors, this "classy" comedy "caper" "succeeds in spades" as a "likable", "fast-paced" vehicle for Newman and Redford, radiating "great rapport" as a pair of grifters playing a gangster for a sucker in Depression-era Chicago; a "funny, intriguing" "period piece" set to "elegant" Joplin rags, it raises the "suspense" stakes with "masterful" plotting and a final "zinger" that saves the sharpest sting for last.

**Stir Crazy**  ▽ 18 | 19 | 16 | 16
*1980. Directed by Sidney Poitier. With Gene Wilder, Richard Pryor, JoBeth Williams. 111 minutes. Rated R.*
The second "outing from the estimable team of Pryor and Wilder" (after the successful *Silver Streak*), this buddy comedy concerns two wrongly imprisoned jokers out to clear their name; though some consider it somewhat downhill from the comedians' first matchup, it was popular enough to spawn a TV sitcom.

**Stop Making Sense**  25 | – | 14 | 24
*1984. Directed by Jonathan Demme. Documentary. With the Talking Heads. 88 minutes. Not Rated.*
"Turn up the sound", because Demme's "alterna-rockumentary" presents a "superior" show from new wave faves the Talking Heads in their "heyday", burning down the house with "energetic music"; the flick proves the "exception to the rule that concerts don't translate" to the big screen and finds bandleader "David Byrne in top form", "swaying" in his trademark "enormous suit."

**Straight Story, The**  24 | 27 | 22 | 21
*1999. Directed by David Lynch. With Richard Farnsworth, Sissy Spacek, Jane Galloway. 111 minutes. Rated G.*
The "only G-rated" effort from malaise-meister Lynch goes straight for the heart in this "odd" but "compelling" drama of a septuagenarian "who rides his John Deere" power mower cross country to mend fences with his infirm brother; this "interesting" "character study" is polished into an "absolute gem" by "brilliant performances" and a "lovely" meditation on the "ending of the life cycle", but be warned that "travel by tractor" can be a "slow" ride.

**Strangers on a Train** ◑  26 | 24 | 27 | 24
*1951. Directed by Alfred Hitchcock. With Farley Granger, Robert Walker, Ruth Roman. 101 minutes. Rated PG.*
Be careful "what you wish for" is the underlying theme of this "fascinating", "forward-thinking" Hitchcock thriller wherein a flippant "promise to exchange murders" spirals out of control into a "dark tale of unwanted bedfellows"; "spine-tingler" aficionados single out Walker's "chilling" turn as a "wacko" mama's boy, and among many "tense moments", the "carousel finale still amazes."

**STREETCAR NAMED DESIRE, A** ✉◑  27 | 28 | 26 | 25
*1951. Directed by Elia Kazan. With Vivien Leigh, Marlon Brando, Kim Hunter, Karl Malden. 125 minutes. Rated PG.*
Destined to "hold great forever", this "brilliant interpretation" of Tennessee Williams' "overwrought classic" showcases the "amazing" Brando "exploding onto the scene" ("hey, *Stella!*") in the "legendary" role of a "rugged" slob who engages in "shattering" "psychological warfare" with his delicate sister-in-law (the "wonderful", "so-sad" Leigh); fans say it's worth watching if only for a look at the "virile" Marlon when he was "still acting."

**Strictly Ballroom**  23 | 21 | 23 | 22
*1992. Directed by Baz Luhrmann. With Paul Mercurio, Tara Morice, Bill Hunter. 94 minutes. Rated PG.*
This "quirky" dose of "flash and flamenco" is a surprise charmer of a romantic comedy pairing a "hot" Aussie hoofer with an "ugly duckling", who proceed to shake up a dance championship with

the question "to tango or not to tango?"; a "delightful send-up" of the "viciousness of the competitive ballroom circuit", it amuses with "well-executed" moves, even if onlookers "kinda know" how the strictly by-the-numbers story will turn out.

### Stripes
21 | 18 | 18 | 18

*1981. Directed by Ivan Reitman. With Bill Murray, Harold Ramis, Warren Oates. 101 minutes. Rated R.*

"Red-blooded guys" are quick to salute this "service comedy" starring "cynical" Murray as a goldbricking civilian who joins the Army and endures basic training with the idea that it's "all about laughs"; with a "strong comic cast" and gags ranging from the truly "hilarious" to the sublimely "ridiculous", it ranks as "one of the funniest" in its class, though deserters say it "bogs down" midway and caution it's "no *Caddyshack*" – and "that's a fact, Jack."

### Stuart Little Ⓤ
19 | 18 | 19 | 21

*1999. Directed by Rob Minkoff. With Geena Davis, Hugh Laurie, Jonathan Lipnicki. 84 minutes. Rated PG.*

Adapted from E.B. White's "sweet" children's classic, this "cute production" craftily combines "amazing animation" and live action to tell the tale of an "adorable" "talking mouse" who's adopted by humans only to be claimed by a couple of rodents posing as his "birth parents"; most can't help "lovin'" its "warm" "poignancy", though a few whiskers twitch at the "piffle"-ridden plot that "mangles the original" into a flick "only a little kid could like."

### Sullivan's Travels ◑
▽ 27 | 25 | 25 | 25

*1941. Directed by Preston Sturges. With Joel McCrea, Veronica Lake, William Demarest. 90 minutes. Not Rated.*

A Depression-era movie director suffering from a "mid-career crisis" "develops a conscience" and decides to shoot a truly "serious film" in this "profound comedy" from Preston Sturges; the result is a delightfully "inspirational" flick that not only has "something important to say about America", but also is one of the "best pictures ever made about Hollywood – even though it hardly takes place there."

### Summer of '42
21 | 19 | 23 | 19

*1971. Directed by Robert Mulligan. With Jennifer O'Neill, Gary Grimes, Jerry Houser. 103 minutes. Rated R.*

Sentimental yearning and raging hormones drive this "coming-of-age" romance, which finds a trio of "pubescent boys" spending the first summer after Pearl Harbor goofing off until one of them hooks up with a young soldier's widow, who's "grasping at life"; the combination of "humor" and "heartbreak" is also a "moving" remembrance of a "time of war", while the Oscar-winning score alone is "worth the price of admission."

### SUNSET BOULEVARD ✉◑
28 | 28 | 27 | 27

*1950. Directed by Billy Wilder. With William Holden, Gloria Swanson, Erich Von Stroheim. 110 minutes. Not Rated.*

"Some of the greatest dialogue ever" (most famously, "I'm ready for my close-up, Mr. DeMille") graces this hybrid of "Gothic" and "film noir", a "scabrous take on Hollywood" from the standpoint of a "struggling screenwriter" trying to "resurrect the career of a silent movie star" who's "not exactly in touch with reality"; given Wilder's "acerbic" direction, an "'in'-joke"–laced script and "pitch-perfect" performances from a "larger-than-life Swanson" and "hunky Holden", "who needs a musical version?"

### Sunshine Boys, The
21 23 19 18

*1975. Directed by Herbert Ross. With Walter Matthau, George Burns, Richard Benjamin. 111 minutes. Rated PG.*

The radiant screen rendition of Neil Simon's Broadway comedy presents Matthau and Burns (who reappears after decades offscreen and snags an Oscar) as a couple of crusty "vaudeville greats who must work together" on a TV reunion show, even though they're given to much bickering; the "funny story" makes for surefire yuks, but razzers report the act as a whole is "not so bright."

### Superman ⅠⅠ
22 19 22 23

*1978. Directed by Richard Donner. With Christopher Reeve, Margot Kidder, Gene Hackman. 143 minutes. Rated PG.*

"You'll really believe a man can fly" after a look at this "ahead-of-its-time" superhero fantasy, the "delightful", "campy" saga of a survivor from a doomed planet who grows up to be a "man of steel"; even if the "comic-book sensibility" is "a little silly" and the line readings "stiff", a super "heart shines through" as Reeve turns in the "definitive", "true-blue portrayal" of "all things good" – when he's not "sizing up telephone booths", that is.

### Super Size Me
24 – 24 21

*2004. Directed by Morgan Spurlock. Documentary. 96 minutes. Rated G.*

Near-"suicide by gluttony" is both "disturbing" and "funny" in this "crowd-pleasing documentary" wherein director/star Spurlock submits himself to an all-McDonald's diet for a full month; although "not the most researched study of fast food" and perhaps "lacking in nutritional substance", this "eye-opening, stomach-churning" "wake-up call" still might send you running for a "piece of fruit."

### Suspect
∇ 19 19 20 18

*1987. Directed by Peter Yates. With Cher, Dennis Quaid, Liam Neeson. 121 minutes. Rated R.*

Cher's an ambitious public defender in this "courtroom thriller" about a high-level conspiracy involving a slick lobbyist, a dead Supreme Court justice and a deaf-and-dumb homeless man; though "predictable" and only "relatively involving" to the suspicious, others say it "keeps you wondering" until the "surprise ending."

### Sweet Charity
20 21 19 23

*1969. Directed by Bob Fosse. With Shirley MacLaine, John McMartin, Chita Rivera. 149 minutes. Rated G.*

"Fosse's directorial debut" adapts a boffo Broadway show into an "exciting" musical featuring "MacLaine at her best" as a honey of a dance-hall damsel; look for "over-the-top production numbers" (especially Chita's raucous 'Big Spender') with "memorable staging" and "great tunes", and if the "quirky" story "drifts" when the music stops, charitable types cheer the players for "trying with all their might."

### Sweet Hereafter, The
24 25 23 23

*1997. Directed by Atom Egoyan. With Ian Holm, Sarah Polley, Bruce Greenwood. 112 minutes. Rated R.*

"Haunting" in a "somber" way, this adaptation of Russell Banks' novel is a "beautifully shot", "terribly moving" drama about the "aftermath of a small-town tragedy" and the "dysfunction" it lays bare; the "terrific cast" led by Holm and Polley sees the burg's "delicate balance" upset when a group of children die in a bus crash, and the camera lends a "hypnotic" feel to material that's "smart" but "shrouded in sadness."

### SWEET SMELL OF SUCCESS, THE ◑    27 | 28 | 26 | 26
*1957. Directed by Alexander Mackendrick. With Burt Lancaster, Tony Curtis, Martin Milner. 96 minutes. Not Rated.*
A "cookie full of arsenic" soaked in "hydrochloric acid", this extra-"tasty" morsel of "moody noir" unearths the "seamy side" of showbiz with its "cynical" "character study" of the "slimy" sorts working the "publicity end": a "superb" Lancaster as a "brutal", Winchell-esque columnist and the "unctuous Curtis" as his publicist toady; brace yourself for "crackling dialogue" and some "beyond beautiful" NYC "nighttime shots" in this "timeless" but never "more timely" picture.

### Swept Away 𝔽    24 | 24 | 24 | 24
*1975. Directed by Lina Wertmüller. With Mariangela Melato, Giancarlo Giannini. 116 minutes. Rated R.*
Stranding strangers on a "sunbaked isle" long "before the arrival of *Survivor*", Wertmüller's "unforgettable" Italian comedy "steams up the screen" as a snobbish socialite and a coarsely "expressive" boatman develop a "passionate" "love/hate relationship" alone on a Mediterranean cay; the satire "speaks volumes" as a "comment on class" and the "battle of the sexes", though there's a strong undercurrent of "violence" running beneath the beautiful "scenery."

### Swimming Pool    20 | 23 | 20 | 20
*2003. Directed by François Ozon. With Charlotte Rampling, Ludivine Sagnier, Charles Dance. 103 minutes. Rated R.*
A burnt-out "older British woman" and a "slutty French girl" share a house in the south of France in this "plenty sexy" psychological thriller that delineates some "wonderfully uncomfortable" "generational differences"; while the "cryptic" climax leaves cynics perplexed – "could someone please explain the ending?" – boobs say it's "worth renting for the nudity" alone.

### Swingers    23 | 22 | 23 | 20
*1996. Directed by Doug Liman. With Jon Favreau, Vince Vaughn, Heather Graham. 96 minutes. Rated R.*
"Hooking up in the '90s" gets a "hilarious" but "realistic" spin in this "hip, kinetic" buddy comedy–cum–"cultural phenomenon" about two single guys "finding their mojo" on the "Los Angeles dating scene"; it's "immensely funny", universally "accurate in defining a generation" and "'so money' that it spawned its very own vernacular."

### Swiss Family Robinson    ∇ 23 | 18 | 25 | 22
*1960. Directed by Ken Annakin. With John Mills, Dorothy McGuire, James MacArthur. 126 minutes. Rated G.*
"Action, romance, adventure and comedy" coexist amiably in this "absolute classic" from Walt Disney, a story of castaways shipwrecked on a tropical isle that "bears little resemblance to the novel"; an exercise in "good, clean fun", it's everything a "family movie should be", and that "terrific" treehouse set "still fascinates" smaller fry.

### Take the Money and Run
21 | 18 | 21 | 17

*1969. Directed by Woody Allen. With Woody Allen, Janet Margolin, Marcel Hillaire. 85 minutes. Rated R.*
Woody's "first full-fledged feature" wings it with "pure slapstick" and "typical" self-deprecating shtick, depicting the escapades of a "hopeless nerd bank robber" into a phony documentary that's "basically a series of blackouts and sketches"; though a bit "threadbare" in between the "patches of brilliance", it packs in enough "anarchy and whimsy" to foretell things to come.

### Talented Mr. Ripley, The
18 | 21 | 19 | 21

*1999. Directed by Anthony Minghella. With Matt Damon, Jude Law, Gwyneth Paltrow. 139 minutes. Rated R.*
A "lush thriller of mistaken identity" set in '50s Europe, this "unsettling", "underrated" study of a murderous "schmuck-turned-socialite" stars Damon as the "slippery" title character (in a performance that's either "unnervingly good" or totally "botched"); while the "disturbing storyline" played out against "spectacular scenery" enthralls many, critics see little talent in its "lack of warmth" and way-"too-long" running time.

### TALK TO HER ✉ 🄵
26 | 26 | 26 | 25

*2002. Directed by Pedro Almodóvar. With Javier Cámara, Darío Grandinetti, Leonor Watling, Rosario Flores, Geraldine Chaplin. 112 minutes. Rated R.*
"Don't think about it too much and it will captivate you" advise fans of this "brilliant piece of art" by the "risk-taking" Almodóvar, a "haunting", "highly original" "drama, comedy and mystery all in one" about "two women who have fallen into comas and the men who love them"; a "wonderful cast" tackles a "provocative" "multilayered storyline" that "allows fantasy to play with reality" – "finally, a film for mature audiences!"

### Tarzan
22 | – | 21 | 24

*1999. Directed by Chris Buck, Kevin Lima. Animated. 88 minutes. Rated G.*
Some of "Disney's best work" "re-creates the magic" of a "classic" in this tale of man and monkey swinging through life via "phenomenally innovative" animation; a "fast-paced adventure" that takes time out for "character" but "keeps things relatively lighthearted", it adds some "thoughtful modern" angles and a "great score", including an Oscar-winning song from Phil Collins.

### Tarzan the Ape Man ◑ ⑪
21 | 16 | 21 | 18

*1932. Directed by W.S. Van Dyke. With Johnny Weissmuller, Maureen O'Sullivan. 99 minutes. Not Rated.*
An "old-fashioned" fave among the "first real adventure films", this "memorable" intersection of Hollywood and vine finds a Brit lady Jane abducted by the ape-bred hero only to civilize him (and catch a bit of jungle fever herself); Olympic swimmer Weissmuller brings "definitive" bravura to the title character, and thus this "campy" but "trendsetting original" "holds up better" than all the sequels you can shake a banana at.

### TAXI DRIVER
27 | 29 | 25 | 25

*1976. Directed by Martin Scorsese. With Robert De Niro, Jodie Foster, Harvey Keitel, Cybill Shepherd. 113 minutes. Rated R.*
Confirming "non-NYers' greatest fears" about the "brutal underbelly" of "modern urban life", Scorsese's vividly "cerebral"

thriller rolls through "sleazy" streets and "neon" nights charged by De Niro's "monumental performance" as a "creepy", insomniac hack – "you talking to me?" – whose live-wire issues build to "harrowing" magnum force in the "steam-filled" city; overall, its depiction of "urban decay, rage and alienation" is "top-class" but "lurid" and very "intense."

### 10　　　　　　　　　　　　17 | 16 | 16 | 17
*1979. Directed by Blake Edwards. With Dudley Moore, Julie Andrews, Bo Derek, Robert Webber. 122 minutes. Rated R.*
This "midlife crisis movie for men" might be "silly" and "rather dated", but will always be a "time capsule of the American dream, circa 1979" thanks to one iconic image: "Derek in cornrows" bouncing on the beach in "slow motion" to the accompaniment of "Ravel's 'Bolero'"; sure, it has about as much depth as the "*Sports Illustrated* swimsuit issue", but it's "still funny" and proves that "short guys can be sexy."

### Ten Commandments, The　　　　24 | 21 | 25 | 27
*1956. Directed by Cecil B. DeMille. With Charlton Heston, Yul Brynner, Anne Baxter, Edward G. Robinson. 220 minutes. Rated G.*
"Let it be written" that DeMille's "over-the-top" biblical blockbuster is the "epic of all epics", a "Cliffs Notes" account of Exodus built on "Heston's finest" role as the "one and only Moses", performer of "monumental" miracles on land and Red Sea; though "fantastic sets" and Brynner's "badass" Egyptian king distract from the "kitschy" script and "overblown" production, it's "entertaining" enough to keep a "cast of thousands" in "constant circulation."

### Terminator, The ⓤ　　　　　24 | 18 | 24 | 24
*1984. Directed by James Cameron. With Arnold Schwarzenegger, Michael Biehn, Linda Hamilton. 108 minutes. Rated R.*
Buckle up for Cameron's "unstoppable breakthrough", this sci-fi/action "genre-maker" about an "evil cyborg sent from the future" to wreak havoc on the past via Ah-nuld's "seriously scary presence" alone; it "doesn't disappoint" in dispensing "awesome" "violent" mayhem all over '80s LA, and its most famous line – "I'll be back" – was a harbinger of the sequels to come.

### Terms of Endearment ✉ⓤ　　　25 | 26 | 24 | 22
*1983. Directed by James L. Brooks. With Shirley MacLaine, Debra Winger, Jack Nicholson. 132 minutes. Rated PG.*
A "four-hanky tearjerker" "worth its weight in Kleenex", this "engrossing" "weepie with a spine" starts off comically enough depicting a "tangled mother-daughter relationship" but takes a "serious" turn in the second act when "life-and-death" issues arise; quite the Oscar magnet, it took home Best Picture honors as well as statuettes for the "amazing" MacLaine and Nicholson, who's a "hoot" as the former astronaut who lives next door.

### Texas Chainsaw Massacre, The ⓤ　　17 | 13 | 17 | 15
*1974. Directed by Tobe Hooper. With Marilyn Burns, Allen Danziger, Paul A. Partain. 83 minutes. Rated R.*
Something "like a car wreck", this "alternately repulsive and fascinating" "slashfest" is the "nightmarish" story of innocent folk "falling prey to a cannibalistic family" and is "creepy beyond belief" despite "surprisingly little overt gore"; aficionados call it the "Casablanca of horror films" notwithstanding the "low-budget" looks and "bad acting" – but "truly amazing screaming."

### That's Entertainment! ⓫    `25` `–` `–` `25`
*1974. Directed by Jack Haley Jr. Documentary. With Gene Kelly, Fred Astaire. 127 minutes. Rated G.*
This "remarkable survey of MGM musicals" lays out a "delicious", "crème-de-la-crème" buffet of glorious "old clips" set up with "narration by some mighty big stars"; showcasing the likes of Kelly and Astaire at their "thrilling" peak, this compilation is "desert-island" viewing and an "entertaining introduction" for young folks to the bygone days of "real talent."

### Thelma & Louise ✉    `23` `25` `23` `21`
*1991. Directed by Ridley Scott. With Susan Sarandon, Geena Davis, Brad Pitt, Harvey Keitel. 129 minutes. Rated R.*
A "high-powered" "girl-power" flick focusing on a "feminist crime spree", this "groundbreaking" display of "female macho" "rocks" as two everyday gals "finally get back" at the men who've wronged them by becoming "devil-may-care outlaws" on the lam; the "superb storyline" and "stellar performances" keep things "involving" right up to the "heartbreaking", *Butch Cassidy*–esque "bad ending."

### There's Something About Mary    `21` `19` `20` `19`
*1998. Directed by Bobby Farrelly, Peter Farrelly. With Cameron Diaz, Matt Dillon, Ben Stiller. 119 minutes. Rated R.*
Proceed "at your own risk" as the "ultra-crude" Farrelly brothers "push the limits" of "gross-out comedy" in this "tacky laugh riot" about a "loser with a heart of gold" and the "good-sport" girl he loves that's an "oh-my-gosh" compendium of "high-school humor" and "vulgar" "sight gags" (the "dog", the "zipper", the "hair gel"); but foes moan this movie "made by morons for morons" is "even dumber than *Dumb and Dumber*."

### They Shoot Horses, Don't They?    `21` `24` `22` `21`
*1969. Directed by Sydney Pollack. With Jane Fonda, Michael Sarrazin, Susannah York. 120 minutes. Rated PG.*
"Jane Fonda at her world-weariest" provides the glue in this "classic" Depression drama about "desperate" marathon dancers frantically trying to make a buck; though the story's "small" and the sentiments grim, its ensemble cast is "unforgettable" – particularly the "superlative" Gig Young, who copped an Oscar for the role of the slimy emcee.

### Thief of Bagdad, The ◑    ▽ `25` `24` `23` `24`
*1924. Directed by Raoul Walsh. With Douglas Fairbanks, Snitz Edwards, Julanne Johnston. 155 minutes. Not Rated.*
This Arabian Nights fantasy is a "definitive swashbuckler", featuring an "athletic" Fairbanks "at his best" as a charming rogue seeking a princess' hand; one of the most expensive silent movies ever made, it's a "lavish" spectacle with sets by William Cameron Menzies that are "still amazing by today's standards"; in short, it's simply "great."

### Thing, The ◑    `23` `19` `25` `19`
(aka The Thing from Another World)
*1951. Directed by Christian Nyby. With Kenneth Tobey, Margaret Sheridan. 87 minutes. Not Rated.*
This "serious" '50s sci-fi suspenser "still holds up" as a "smart" "flying-saucer" shocker about a group of scientists driven to

"creepy" extremes in a "claustrophobic, paranoid" encounter with a murderous alien found frozen in the Arctic ice; despite "skimpy" special effects, the "tight script" builds enough "tension" to frighten the "daylights" out of fans, who spurn the "gory remake" – there's nothing like "the real *Thing*."

### Thing, The
23 | 19 | 23 | 23

*1982. Directed by John Carpenter. With Kurt Russell, Wilford Brimley, David Clennon. 109 minutes. Rated R.*
"Chills" abound in Carpenter's "excellent remake of the '51 classic", wherein the Antarctic's most "frigid science outpost" is beset by a "horrible alien" capable of disguising itself in human form; an "imaginative" contribution to the "sci-fi/horror pantheon", it supplies enough "true suspense" to keep the audience "guessing" as the "paranoia" mounts.

### THIN MAN, THE ◑ ⑪
26 | 25 | 23 | 23

*1934. Directed by W.S. Van Dyke. With William Powell, Myrna Loy, Maureen O'Sullivan. 93 minutes. Not Rated.*
"Break out the martini glasses": "mystery meets screwball comedy" in this "snazzy" flicker featuring "cool detective" Nick Charles and his "classy wife", Nora, "drinking like fish" and "fluidly" spouting "snappy dialogue" ("double entendre, anyone?") as they investigate a murder; the "suave, sexy fun" is so "cosmopolitan" and "wonderfully evocative of the '30s" that it seems unsporting to point out that the "whodunit" plot is a bit thin.

### Thin Red Line, The
19 | 21 | 17 | 22

*1998. Directed by Terrence Malick. With Sean Penn, George Clooney, John Cusack. 170 minutes. Rated R.*
Malick's "experimental war epic" is made for those who "enjoy thinking about big questions", with Penn exuding "gravity" as a sarge facing the front lines at Guadalcanal with a "star-studded" company of "common soldiers"; "stunning visuals" "attempt to poeticize" the "horror and beauty" of battle and warfare's "emotional effects", though detractors grunt it's "incoherent."

### THIRD MAN, THE ◑
28 | 28 | 27 | 28

*1949. Directed by Carol Reed. With Joseph Cotten, Alida Valli, Orson Welles, Trevor Howard. 104 minutes. Not Rated.*
"Oh, that zither!"; this "masterful" piece of "postwar" noir simmers with shadowy "intrigue" as an "alienated" Cotten encounters "romance" and "betrayal" while searching "bombed-out" Vienna for a "mysterious" black marketeer (played by Welles, who makes the most of a "small" role with an "arresting" entrance); graced with "expressionist" lensing, Graham Greene's "clever, dark script" and a "memorable" final fade, it's hailed as "all-around perfect."

### Thirteen
21 | 26 | 22 | 19

*2003. Directed by Catherine Hardwicke. With Holly Hunter, Evan Rachel Wood, Nikki Reed. 100 minutes. Rated R.*
"You won't want to let your kids out of the house" after a gander at this "disturbing" cautionary tale about a pair of "troubled" 13-year-olds who are "harder to control than Mike Tyson"; while critics hiss the "clichéd", "after-school-special" script and "weak ending", far more applaud this "wake-up call" for telling it like it is "without sugar coating."

### 39 Steps, The ◐
27 | 25 | 27 | 24

*1935. Directed by Alfred Hitchcock. With Robert Donat, Madeleine Carroll. 86 minutes. Not Rated.*

"You can't go wrong" with this "classic" "British period" Hitchcock nail-biter, a "virtuoso" "thriller diller" wherein an "innocent man wrongly accused" of murder tries to clear his name amid "chase scenes, foreign spy intrigue and romance" (with a woman he winds up "handcuffed" to); sure, the "dated" special effects are on the low-tech side, but this "tense mystery" delivers enough suspense to "keep you on the edge of your seat."

### This Is Spinal Tap
26 | 24 | 25 | 22

*1984. Directed by Rob Reiner. With Christopher Guest, Michael McKean, Rob Reiner. 82 minutes. Rated R.*

"VH1's *Behind the Music*" pales before this "hysterical" "rock mockumentary", an "unbelievably authentic-feeling send-up" of the music industry and superstar "pretensions" that follows an "aging heavy-metal band" taking its act on the road; the "stellar cast" plays an "unforgettable" group of clueless musicians, simulating a "sidesplitting insider's view" that's alarmingly "like the real thing" – except "every single second is funny."

### Thomas Crown Affair, The
23 | 23 | 24 | 22

*1968. Directed by Norman Jewison. With Steve McQueen, Faye Dunaway, Paul Burke. 102 minutes. Rated R.*

This "slick", "grown-up romance" offers a "cat-and-mouse" plot as millionaire McQueen engineers a bank heist for kicks until he encounters Dunaway, a "knockout" insurance sleuth in mad pursuit; their "smoldering", "high-tension" affair is a "stylish" standoff down to the final "checkmate" in that famed chess match, and as for the remake, "do not accept imitations."

### Thoroughly Modern Millie
18 | 19 | 16 | 21

*1967. Directed by George Roy Hill. With Julie Andrews, Mary Tyler Moore, Carol Channing. 138 minutes. Rated G.*

"Roaring '20s" razzle-dazzle makes this musical comedy an "absolute hoot", with "Andrews at her peak" as a big-city rookie trying to land a man; it's played as a "slapstick farce set to song and dance" that alternates new tunes with "flapper-era" standards, and if "silly fluff", all that "jazzy fun" is "entertaining nonetheless."

### Three Coins in the Fountain
▽ 20 | 20 | 20 | 21

*1954. Directed by Jean Negulesco. With Clifton Webb, Dorothy McGuire, Jean Peters, Louis Jourdan. 102 minutes. Not Rated.*

"Rome at its best" is the real "star" of this "good old-fashioned love story" about three husband-hunters making coin-tossing wishes in the Trevi Fountain; it's every 1950s "female's dream" and still "so much emotional fun" that it's easy to ignore the correspondingly overripe 1950s "sentimentality."

### Three Faces of Eve, The ✉◐
24 | 27 | 24 | 20

*1957. Directed by Nunnally Johnson. With Joanne Woodward, David Wayne, Lee J. Cobb. 91 minutes. Not Rated.*

"Incredible" Oscar-winner Woodward delivers a "tour-de-force" turn in this "multiple-personality genre film", an "interesting drama" about a "woman tormented" by triple identities; switching from subdued homemaker to brazen party girl, Woodward does a "stellar" job of "bringing all three characters to life."

### Three Kings    20 | 21 | 21 | 22
*1999. Directed by David O. Russell. With George Clooney, Mark Wahlberg, Ice Cube. 114 minutes. Rated R.*
Opening at the close of Desert Storm, this "bold and different" war flick offers a combo of "crackerjack action" and "surprisingly good" acting as "irreverent army guy" Clooney launches a "chase for stolen Kuwaiti gold" that morphs into a "morality tale" midway through; the "insightful" scenario and "creative" visuals make it royally "enjoyable on many levels", though a few are "not impressed" by the "chaotic storyline" and "preachy dialogue."

### Three Men and a Baby ⓤ    16 | 15 | 17 | 16
*1987. Directed by Leonard Nimoy. With Tom Selleck, Steve Guttenberg, Ted Danson. 102 minutes. Rated PG.*
Like the title implies, "three men care for a baby girl" in this "big-hearted" comedy with a "charming ensemble" cast that makes most viewers "laugh and feel good"; the unamused suggest you "bring insulin" or hold out for the "much better" original French film on which it's based: *Three Men and a Cradle*.

### Three Musketeers, The ⓤ    22 | 22 | 22 | 23
*1974. Directed by Richard Lester. With Oliver Reed, Richard Chamberlain, Michael York. 105 minutes. Rated PG.*
A "rollicking rendition" of the Dumas classic, this "rousing" "old-fashioned" adventure "stays faithful" to the original tale but spices up the swordplay with "slapstick" and "bawdy" humor as a brave band of swashbucklers defends the queen's honor against that crooked cardinal; the "lavish" 17th-century sets and all-for-one "charm" of the "great cast" ensure its place as the "quintessential" version by which all others "shall be judged."

### Thunderball    22 | 21 | 21 | 23
*1965. Directed by Terence Young. With Sean Connery, Claudine Auger, Adolfo Celi. 130 minutes. Rated PG.*
Bringing the "basic Bond formula" to the Bahamas, this swimming entry in the superspy series has Connery breaking out his arsenal of "gadgets" and dry wisecracks against the "very real threat" of stolen nukes held for ransom; the "nonstop action" and "incredible underwater fight sequences" made it a thunderous success in its day, and if now "underappreciated", connoisseurs nevertheless rank it "near the top" of the 007 oeuvre.

### Tie Me Up! Tie Me Down! ☻    20 | 21 | 20 | 20
*1990. Directed by Pedro Almodóvar. With Victoria Abril, Antonio Banderas, Loles Leon. 111 minutes. Rated NC-17.*
"Madcap" director Almodóvar strikes again in this naughty knotty comedy about a kidnapped, trussed-up B-movie star that's a cross between "*The Collector*" and a soft-core bondage flick; its "sexy", "vivid characters" and "nice" Ennio Morricone soundtrack further spice up a storyline that's already "hysterically funny."

### Time After Time    23 | 23 | 25 | 21
*1979. Directed by Nicholas Meyer. With Malcolm McDowell, Mary Steenburgen, David Warner. 112 minutes. Rated PG.*
A "clever" bit of "brainy entertainment", this "charming" sci-fi thriller recounts "H.G. Wells chasing Jack the Ripper to modern-day San Francisco" via a "functioning time machine"; a "witty" romp expertly blending "romantic" interludes between McDowell

and Steenburgen with "suspenseful" sequencing, it's "well worth seeing" for Warner's "helluva performance" alone.

### Time Bandits
21 | 19 | 23 | 22

*1981. Directed by Terry Gilliam. With John Cleese, Sean Connery, Shelley Duvall. 116 minutes. Rated PG.*

Gilliam's "warped-mind" "genius" shines in this "bittersweet" time-travel fantasy about the "classic struggle between good and evil", with a sprawling cast that includes a "band of midgets", a "fantastic villain" and a parade of "delightful" cameos; though the visual effects may be showing their age, there are still enough "juicy moments" to justify its "cult-classic" status.

### Time Machine, The
22 | 17 | 26 | 23

*1960. Directed by George Pal. With Rod Taylor, Alan Young, Yvette Mimieux. 103 minutes. Rated G.*

"Faithful to both the letter and spirit of H.G. Wells' novel", this "granddaddy of time-travel movies" concerning a 19th-century scientist flabbergasted by the future is "nicely paced" and "fondly remembered" for its "thought-provoking storyline" and "good special effects for the era" (which won an Oscar); though the "remake isn't bad", the "much-better" original is the real "gem."

### Time to Kill, A
18 | 18 | 22 | 19

*1996. Directed by Joel Schumacher. With Matthew McConaughey, Sandra Bullock, Samuel L. Jackson. 149 minutes. Rated R.*

"Very adult" and "suspenseful to the end", this "hard-hitting" Mississippi courtroom drama about racist violence and retribution is a "solid adaptation of the John Grisham novel"; despite the very "Hollywood ending", it's "captivating" thanks to "intelligent" turns from Bullock and McConaughey ("his best role").

### Tin Drum, The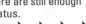
▽ 23 | 24 | 24 | 23

*1979. Directed by Volker Schlöndorff. With David Bennent, Mario Adorf, Angela Winkler. 142 minutes. Rated R.*

A "fine social commentary" about apathy and "life in Nazi Germany", this "disturbing" allegorical drama about a young boy who refuses to grow old "preserves the spirit of Günter Grass' novel" while charting the rise and fall of the Third Reich; the "well-deserved winner of the Best Foreign Film Oscar", it's a "surreal" work that remains "vivid and haunting" a generation later.

### Titanic ✉
19 | 16 | 18 | 26

*1997. Directed by James Cameron. With Leonardo DiCaprio, Kate Winslet, Billy Zane. 194 minutes. Rated PG-13.*

Ok, it's "not highbrow stuff", but this "over-the-top spectacular" detailing a "doomed love story" aboard a "doomed ocean liner" thrills with "dazzling" special effects, including a "fantastic" "re-creation of the original ship" and icebergs so real "you can almost touch them"; some torpedo the "shallow" "cardboard characters", "soap opera"–esque script and "weak acting" as "all wet", and whether it's "deserving of its Oscars" – all 11 of them – is still hotly debated.

### To Be or Not to Be ◐
▽ 25 | 25 | 25 | 23

*1942. Directed by Ernst Lubitsch. With Carole Lombard, Jack Benny, Robert Stack. 99 minutes. Not Rated.*

"Life in Nazi-occupied Europe" becomes "exhilarating comedy" in this "funny but poignant" war story, an "oft-overlooked gem" via the ever "clever" Ernst Lubitsch; playing married actors, Benny and Lombard supply "barrels of laughs" – particularly when Jack "does to Shakespeare what the Germans are doing to Poland."

### To Catch a Thief
**25 | 25 | 24 | 25**

*1955. Directed by Alfred Hitchcock. With Grace Kelly, Cary Grant, Jesse Royce Landis. 106 minutes. Not Rated.*

"Slick, sophisticated and oh-so-cool", this romantic thriller may be "Hitchcock lite", but Grant and Kelly provide plenty of "dazzle" in an amusing trifle about a cat burglar prowling the south of France; maybe the "plot is secondary" to the "enjoyable scenery" and "fab clothes", but there's snappy patter aplenty, notably Grace's classic picnic query "would you prefer a leg or a breast?"

### To Die For
**18 | 21 | 19 | 18**

*1995. Directed by Gus Van Sant. With Nicole Kidman, Matt Dillon, Joaquin Phoenix. 106 minutes. Rated R.*

A "true tabloid story" becomes "cuttingly observed satire" in this drama about "America's obsession with fame", a "wicked black comedy" due to "Buck Henry's brilliant script" and Van Sant's "incisive" direction; in her "most original role", Kidman "positively shines" as an "ambitious" TV weathergirl "trying to get ahead in her job and out of her marriage" – many say her performance alone is the "reason to see it."

### To Have and Have Not ◐
**26 | 27 | 24 | 24**

*1944. Directed by Howard Hawks. With Humphrey Bogart, Lauren Bacall, Walter Brennan. 100 minutes. Not Rated.*

Bacall (in her screen debut) teams with future real-life hubby Bogart to "define star chemistry" in this dramatization of the Hemingway novel about WWII resistance runners; Martinique supplies a sultry backdrop for the two stars to "smolder", especially when Lauren "steams up the screen" with her legendary question "you know how to whistle, don't you?"

### TO KILL A MOCKINGBIRD ✉◐
**29 | 29 | 29 | 26**

*1962. Directed by Robert Mulligan. With Gregory Peck, Mary Badham, Robert Duvall. 129 minutes. Not Rated.*

"After all these years", this Southern courtroom drama about racism and prejudice "told from the point of view of a young girl" "still packs the same emotional punch"; kudos go to Oscar-winning screenwriter Horton Foote "for not having strayed" from Harper Lee's "original text", and to an "im-peck-able" Peck at his "peak" as the "dad we wish we had"; in short, "Hollywood got this one right."

### Tombstone
**21 | 22 | 21 | 21**

*1993. Directed by George P. Cosmatos. With Kurt Russell, Val Kilmer, Sam Elliott. 130 minutes. Rated R.*

More than an ok rendition of the "O.K. Corral story", this "slick retelling" brings legends Wyatt Earp and Doc Holliday up to date with plenty of good old "modern-day violence"; starring a pistol-packing Russell and "fun-to-watch" Kilmer, it's a "worthy" enough stab at pure "entertainment" – "even if you don't like Westerns."

### Tom Jones ✉
**25 | 24 | 24 | 25**

*1963. Directed by Tony Richardson. With Albert Finney, Susannah York, Hugh Griffith. 121 minutes. Not Rated.*

"Richly crafted and craftily acted" – with four Oscars to prove it – this hilariously "bawdy" "period piece par excellence" might be set in 18th-century England but moodwise is more like a "snapshot of the Swinging '60s"; devotees are ever smitten with its "clever script", "lively direction" and Finney's "lusty" title turn, while gourmands eat up that "sexy food-seduction scene."

### Tommy
16 | 14 | 16 | 20

*1975. Directed by Ken Russell. With Roger Daltrey, Ann-Margret, Oliver Reed, Elton John. 111 minutes. Rated PG.*
The Who's "seminal rock opera" goes Hollywood in this "over-the-top feast for the senses" that divides voters: ravers revel in the "great score", "Tina Turner as the Acid Queen" and that "scene with Ann-Margret and the baked beans", but bashers bawl it's a "disservice to both musicals and rock 'n' roll."

### Tomorrow Never Dies
20 | 20 | 17 | 21

*1997. Directed by Roger Spottiswoode. With Pierce Brosnan, Jonathan Pryce, Michelle Yeoh. 119 minutes. Rated PG-13.*
". . . and neither does James" joke 007 junkies of the juggernaut's 18th entry, wherein "Brosnan fills Connery's" custom-made shoes and "brings back" the secret agent's "cruel streak"; the "thoughtful plot" (something about a mad "media magnate" bent on starting WWIII) is buoyed by "high-tech special effects", though Bond-girl watchers say the picture belongs to the "fabulous" Yeoh.

### Tootsie
25 | 27 | 24 | 23

*1982. Directed by Sydney Pollack. With Dustin Hoffman, Jessica Lange, Bill Murray, Teri Garr. 119 minutes. Rated PG.*
"Cross-dressing doesn't get much better" than this "brilliantly funny" comedy about a long-"struggling actor" who finally achieves success – "as an actress"; though Hoffman might be "one ugly" broad, his "sublime", "think-out-of-the-box" performance mixing "humor with humanity" is beautiful, while a "slick" but "unpredictable script" and an "outstanding" supporting cast make this one a "keeper, not a renter."

### TOP GUN
22 | 18 | 20 | 24

*1986. Directed by Tony Scott. With Tom Cruise, Kelly McGillis, Val Kilmer. 110 minutes. Rated PG.*
"Sexy fighter pilots" populate this "absolutely irresistible" "'80s action icon", a roiling mix of "noise", "romance" and "aerial maneuvers"; Cruise "looks great in uniform" and that "volleyball scene" sure is "hot", but foes dis the "hokey" plot and "intermittent acting" and can't fathom why it's so "inexplicably popular."

### TOP HAT ◑
27 | 23 | 21 | 26

*1935. Directed by Mark Sandrich. With Fred Astaire, Ginger Rogers, Edward Everett Horton. 101 minutes. Not Rated.*
"Heaven, I'm in heaven" sigh fans of this "classic '30s musical" spotlighting the big-city charms of a "debonair Astaire" opposite a "feather"-gowned Rogers; sure, there's an "all-hit Irving Berlin score", "amazing production numbers" and a "witty French farce of a script", but in the end, it's "Fred and Ginger dancing cheek-to-cheek" that catapults it to "sublime"-ville.

### Topkapi
24 | 22 | 25 | 21

*1964. Directed by Jules Dassin. With Melina Mercouri, Peter Ustinov. 119 minutes. Not Rated.*
Director "Dassin's '60s caper holds up well", managing to "avoid clichés the same way" its jewel-thief cast "avoid traps" as they

engineer a heist in Istanbul; owing to a "clever script" and some "beautifully drawn characters" (like the "sophisticated" Mercouri and "priceless", "Oscar-winning" Ustinov), this "taut" thriller/comedy is reminiscent of an erstwhile "*Mission: Impossible*."

### Topper ❶⓶
20 | 21 | 21 | 19

*1937. Directed by Norman Z. McLeod. With Roland Young, Constance Bennett, Cary Grant. 97 minutes. Not Rated.*
Grant and Bennett "never miss a beat" in this "smart" romantic comedy about a pair of martini-swilling, madcap ghosts who must do a good deed to go to heaven; expect lots of laughs when the "delightful" phantoms select uptight banker Cosmo Topper as the beneficiary of their largesse in this "lighthearted" bit of "whimsy."

### Topsy-Turvy
23 | 25 | 23 | 26

*1999. Directed by Mike Leigh. With Jim Broadbent, Allan Corduner, Timothy Spall. 160 minutes. Rated R.*
This "finely observed story about the stormy partnership of Gilbert and Sullivan" provides a "window into the Victorian age" as well as a "fascinating" glimpse into the "creative process" via a subplot about the first staging of *The Mikado*; "superb" acting (with an especially "grand Broadbent") and a "gorgeous production" make it a "joy to watch" for most, though a few yawn "boring."

### Tora! Tora! Tora!
23 | 19 | 25 | 24

*1970. Directed by Richard Fleischer, Kinji Fukasaku, Toshio Masuda. With Martin Balsam, Jason Robards, Joseph Cotten. 144 minutes. Rated G.*
Surveyors split on this "intricate" war chronicle of the "Japanese attack on Pearl Harbor": defenders say this "ultimate docudrama" is "well done historically", citing its "bilingual plotlines" and over-the-top "stunning" special effects, but curmudgeons counter it's a "comic-book" look at the tragedy.

### To Sir, With Love ⓶
22 | 23 | 24 | 20

*1967. Directed by James Clavell. With Sidney Poitier, Judy Geeson, Christian Roberts. 105 minutes. Not Rated.*
The "always-excellent" Poitier stars in this "nice little piece of '60s" nostalgia as a "London high school teacher" passing on life lessons to "inner-city punks"; "sweet" and "timeless", it deals with "still-relevant" issues – "race, family conflicts, respect for authority" – in a "genuinely moving" fashion, and Lulu's smashing rendition of the title song "makes the movie."

### Total Recall
18 | 14 | 21 | 22

*1990. Directed by Paul Verhoeven. With Arnold Schwarzenegger, Rachel Ticotin, Sharon Stone. 113 minutes. Rated R.*
"One of Ah-nuld's better" efforts may be this "exciting sci-fi adventure" flick, one of those "is-it-all-a-dream" stories about a secret agent implanted with someone else's memory chip; filmed "just before the age of digital effects" dawned, this "visual tour de force" inspires diverse reactions – "original" vs. "mediocre" – though pacifists are peeved by all that "gratuitous violence."

### Touch of Evil ❶
26 | 24 | 25 | 26

*1958. Directed by Orson Welles. With Charlton Heston, Janet Leigh, Orson Welles. 95 minutes. Rated PG-13.*
"Proof that Welles was more than a one-hit wonder", this "rococo" "pinnacle of film noir" stars the director as a "bloated" Texas border town cop feuding with his south-of-the-border counterpart (Heston

in "Mexican blackface"); among its many memorable touches are the "sweeping" opening sequence and the "effortless scene-stealing" by Marlene Dietrich, who has the picture's best line: "lay off the candy bars"; P.S. the "restored version" is "much better" than the original release.

### Towering Inferno, The
18 | 17 | 18 | 22

*1974. Directed by John Guillermin, Irwin Allen. With Steve McQueen, Paul Newman, William Holden. 165 minutes. Rated PG.*
"Make sure you know where all the exits are" before settling into this "big, bad '70s disaster" flick starring a skyscraper, a fire and a "rogues' gallery of great actors"; although the "passable" "special effects were top-drawer for its time", cynical sorts snort it's more of a "made-for-TV movie" by modern standards.

### Toy Story ⓘ
27 | – | 25 | 28

*1995. Directed by John Lasseter. Animated. 81 minutes. Rated G.*
Ushering in a "new era of animation" with "breakthrough" computer-generated effects, this Pixar-produced "instant classic" is a bona fide "technical wonder"; its "humorous" storyline, "lovable characters" and the "great concept" of walking, talking toys add up to a picture that's not only "equally entertaining for adults and kids" but also "deserving of the franchise it started."

### Trading Places
23 | 22 | 23 | 20

*1983. Directed by John Landis. With Dan Aykroyd, Eddie Murphy, Jamie Lee Curtis. 118 minutes. Rated R.*
This "hysterical" treatment of the "classic" "rags-to-riches" "switcheroo" has "pauper" Murphy turned into "prince" Aykroyd and vice-versa; "quickly paced and never boring", it's memorable for "early vintage" Eddie moments, some "funny" business from Dan and the spectacle of Jamie Lee's "exposed breasts."

### Traffic ✉
23 | 24 | 23 | 25

*2000. Directed by Steven Soderbergh. With Michael Douglas, Benicio Del Toro, Catherine Zeta-Jones. 147 minutes. Rated R.*
Maybe "more realistic than you want", this "eye-opening portrait of the drug wars" is "poignant, intelligent" and "troubling", using "multiple storylines" to create a "stunning" hybrid of "thriller" and "cautionary tale"; the "amazing use of color", "documentary-like handheld" camerawork and Del Toro's deft, Oscar-winning turn all get the green light, though the highest praise is reserved for its "absolutely brilliant" director.

### Training Day ✉
20 | 27 | 19 | 22

*2001. Directed by Antoine Fuqua. With Denzel Washington, Ethan Hawke, Scott Glenn, Tom Berenger. 120 minutes. Rated R.*
"Denzel shows his scary side" as a "profoundly bad" LA cop with "charisma" in his Oscar-winning role as a detective who has "one day to teach the ropes" to a "rookie" (played by a "holding-his-own" Hawke); the "twisting" plot "grabs you from the very beginning" and takes you on one "wild ride."

### Trainspotting
22 | 22 | 20 | 22

*1996. Directed by Danny Boyle. With Ewan McGregor, Ewen Bremner, Robert Carlyle. 94 minutes. Rated R.*
"Giddy and witty" but also "harrowing and intense", this "graphic" British drama depicting the "daily life of drug addicts" has a

"kinetic rawness" about it that "gets right under your skin"; while "not for everyone", its "quirky" cinematography and "outstanding" '80s pop score make for "reality-check" viewing, but bring an "interpreter" – the "Scottish accents are thick."

## TREASURE OF THE SIERRA MADRE, THE ✉◐    27 | 27 | 26 | 24
*1948. Directed by John Huston. With Humphrey Bogart, Walter Huston, Tim Holt. 126 minutes. Not Rated.*
"Human nature poisoned by greed" is the theme of this "old-fashioned" "treasure hunt", a "wonderful adventure" that won Oscars for the father-and-son Hustons; Bogart exudes "masculine energy" showing "what gold will do to a man" in an "unforgettably powerful" performance that devolves into "paranoia" – and as for the "stunning" black-and-white photography, purists say "we don't need no stinkin' color."

## Triplets of Belleville, The 🇫    24 | – | 23 | 26
*2003. Directed by Sylvain Chomet. Animated. 80 minutes. Rated PG-13.*
"Trippy and funny in a way that American animation isn't", this "art house" French cartoon sure "ain't Disney" with its "surreal" plot, "stylized" illustration and "nearly dialogue-free" soundtrack; having something to do with a kidnapped bicyclist rescued by his "grandmère", an "amazing" dog and the "wacky" Triplets of Belleville, it's both "innovative" and "offbeat", and probably more "for adults" than small fry.

## TRIUMPH OF THE WILL ◐🇫    27 | – | 17 | 27
*1935. Directed by Leni Riefenstahl. Documentary. 114 minutes. Not Rated.*
"Perhaps the most powerful (and immoral) documentary" ever made, this "Leni Riefenstahl masterpiece" was commissioned to honor Germany's 1934 National Socialist Party Congress and the metaphorical "enthronement of Hitler"; the "superb" camerawork leads reluctant admirers to admit this "artful" propaganda piece is indeed a "triumph of filmmaking", if not subject matter.

## Tron    18 | 14 | 18 | 22
*1982. Directed by Steven Lisberger. With Jeff Bridges, Bruce Boxleitner, David Warner. 96 minutes. Rated PG.*
Wired types tout this "underappreciated forerunner to today's special-effects" extravaganzas by dubbing it the "first real geek movie", owing to a storyline that posits what could happen "if you got sucked into your Nintendo"; ok, it could be a tad "dated" now, but it was the "coolest thing since sliced bread when it came out."

## Troy    19 | 19 | 20 | 25
*2004. Directed by Wolfgang Petersen. With Brad Pitt, Orlando Bloom, Eric Bana. 163 minutes. Rated R.*
Homer's *Iliad* gets the "Hollywood treatment" in this "genuine epic" featuring lots of "oiled", "well-tanned" dudes in "miniskirts" engaged in battles that bear distinct "similarities to WWF wrestling"; wags say Brad's performance is the "only thing more wooden than the Trojan horse" ("too much buff, not enough substance"), but there's applause for the "action-packed" script and "excellent production values."

### True Grit ✉ ⑪
22 | 23 | 21 | 22

*1969. Directed by Henry Hathaway. With John Wayne, Glen Campbell, Kim Darby. 128 minutes. Rated G.*

"Another Western for your library", this "classic" oater is made "especially for Wayne fans" because the Duke took home his first (and only) Oscar here; otherwise, it's standard stuff about a vengeful lawman, though early-in-their-career performances by Dennis Hopper and Robert Duvall keep things lively.

### True Lies
19 | 16 | 20 | 22

*1994. Directed by James Cameron. With Arnold Schwarzenegger, Jamie Lee Curtis. 144 minutes. Rated R.*

"Arnold is Bond, James Bond" in this "tongue-in-cheek" spy flicker that's a "wonderful combo" of "comedy, action and intrigue"; as his "frumpy wife" turned "drop-dead gorgeous" siren, Jamie Lee is "smoking", while Tom Arnold's a "gas" as the "not-so-super secret-agent sidekick"; throw in "lots of explosions and weapons" and you've got a true "blockbuster" "blastfest."

### Truman Show, The
21 | 22 | 23 | 22

*1998. Directed by Peter Weir. With Jim Carrey, Laura Linney, Ed Harris. 103 minutes. Rated PG.*

This "original", "thought-provoking" fantasy/comedy offers a "departure" for Carrey, who's "unusually restrained" (i.e. "doesn't act like a moron") in the role of an unwitting star of a 24/7 reality TV show set in a "phony world"; though some lookers find "little content" among all the "hype", intellectuals enthuse that this "Big Brother"–ish allegory leaves you "questioning what reality is."

### Truth or Dare
15 | – | 14 | 17

*1991. Directed by Alek Keshishian. Documentary. With Madonna. 118 minutes. Rated R.*

"Ardent Madonna fanatics" say this "behind-the-scenes" documentary of her 1990 tour, a "warts-and-all" portrayal of the superstar "not striking a pose", is "better than it has any right to be"; but knockers claim this "self-absorbed" "vanity project" is just "mugging for the camera", save for the cameo by Warren Beatty, who "looks appropriately embarrassed as her latest boy toy"; most amusing scene: "talking to Daddy on the phone."

### Tucker: The Man and His Dream
20 | 21 | 23 | 21

*1988. Directed by Francis Ford Coppola. With Jeff Bridges, Joan Allen, Martin Landau. 110 minutes. Rated PG.*

For a "revealing look beneath the hood of the American auto industry", this "colorful", "stylish" film features a "terrific" Bridges in the sort of "true-ish story" of a "visionary '40s car maker and his sad defeat" at the hands of competitors and politicians; Coppola-ficionados say this "underrated" film "deserves more notice."

### 12 ANGRY MEN ◗
28 | 28 | 27 | 23

*1957. Directed by Sidney Lumet. With Henry Fonda, Martin Balsam, Lee J. Cobb, E.G. Marshall. 96 minutes. Not Rated.*

"Human nature at its best and worst" is on display in this "brilliant courtroom drama" depicting the "hidden agendas" of jurors deciding the fate of a murder defendant; thanks to its "taut" script and an "unforgettable Fonda", this "study of American democracy" is alternately "suspenseful and compelling."

**Twelve Monkeys**  22 | 23 | 24 | 23
*1995. Directed by Terry Gilliam. With Bruce Willis, Madeleine Stowe, Brad Pitt. 129 minutes. Rated R.*
Gilliam's "master-of-the-bizarre" status is reinforced by this "complex", "super-ingenious" time-travel tale about the "release of a deadly virus" followed by a "post-apocalyptic" attempt to "save the world"; the sets are "dazzling", Brad 'n' Bruce prove they can "actually act" and if the "*Terminator*-meets-*Brazil*" sci-fi storyline is "confusing", it's "wonderfully" so.

**Twelve O'Clock High** ◐  26 | 25 | 26 | 23
*1949. Directed by Henry King. With Gregory Peck, Hugh Marlowe, Dean Jagger. 132 minutes. Not Rated.*
"Peck is marvelous" as a WWII Brigadier General "placing terrible pressure on young American pilots" in this "accurate" depiction of the "burdens of command" and the "human side of war"; a "perfect screenplay" "rooted in historical reality" "manipulates the tension" right up to the compelling climax.

**28 Days Later**  18 | 17 | 19 | 18
*2002. Directed by Danny Boyle. With Cillian Murphy, Naomie Harris. 113 minutes. Rated R.*
"Modern-day horror" gets some "low-budget twists" in this "seriously scary" British import that "reinvents the zombie flick for the new millennium" in its story of a "viral disaster" that threatens civilization; while surveyors split on its digital video cinematography ("cool and grainy" versus "looks like it was shot with a bad camcorder"), most agree that the finale "wimps out" – although the DVD includes a number of "alternate endings."

**25th Hour**  21 | 25 | 20 | 21
*2002. Directed by Spike Lee. With Edward Norton, Philip Seymour Hoffman, Barry Pepper. 135 minutes. Rated R.*
A drug dealer "with one day left before prison turns to his friends for comfort" in this "captivating film that's even more poignant given its tribute to post-9/11 NYC"; it's "not your typical Spike Lee, but still one of his best" thanks to "superb ensemble acting"; still, some say "it seemed like it was 25 hours long."

**21 Grams**  22 | 27 | 21 | 21
*2003. Directed by Alejandro González Iñárritu. With Sean Penn, Naomi Watts, Benicio Del Toro. 124 minutes. Rated R.*
"Not an easy watch", this "disturbing take on love and loss" details the lives of three people who meet as the result of a deadly accident; its "nonlinear storyline" told via "flashbacks and flashforwards" (à la "*Memento*" and "*Pulp Fiction*") might be "intriguing" to some and "confusing" to others, but the "stellar" ensemble supplies enough "brain candy" to make for "compelling" viewing; in sum, be ready for an "emotionally draining downer" that's "moving, intelligent" and guaranteed to "keep you guessing."

**20,000 Leagues Under the Sea**  22 | 18 | 25 | 23
*1954. Directed by Richard Fleischer. With Kirk Douglas, James Mason, Peter Lorre. 127 minutes. Rated G.*
"Disney's live-action adaptation of the Jules Verne classic" is a "fabulous" undersea adventure starring a "singing", "tight shorts"–wearing Douglas as the heroic 19th-century seafarer who battles both Captain Nemo and a "scary giant squid" who "should have

received an Oscar"; even though the special effects look "cheesy" today, overall it's a "real old-fashioned hoot."

### Twister
**15 | 14 | 14 | 22**

*1996. Directed by Jan de Bont. With Helen Hunt, Bill Paxton, Cary Elwes, Jami Gertz. 114 minutes. Rated PG-13.*

"Mother nature" runs amok in this "far-fetched disaster movie" about Midwestern meteorologists tracking tornados; though the "fancy computer effects" make the "awesome" twisters "look so real", the "sleepwalking" actors and "easily forgettable" story with "no concern for logic" lead some to snore "major bore."

### Two for the Road ∅
**24 | 27 | 24 | 24**

*1967. Directed by Stanley Donen. With Albert Finney, Audrey Hepburn. 111 minutes. Not Rated.*

"Love isn't always easy" in this "bittersweet travelogue of the ups and downs of a married couple" that "jumps back and forth in time" as they "find, lose and rekindle" their relationship; Audrey's at her "most charming" and "marvelous together" with Finney amid all that "unmatched European scenery"; meanwhile, the "mesmerizing, melodious" Mancini music "sustains the mood."

### 2001: A SPACE ODYSSEY ⑪
**26 | 19 | 24 | 27**

*1968. Directed by Stanley Kubrick. With Keir Dullea, Gary Lockwood, William Sylvester. 139 minutes. Rated G.*

The "*Citizen Kane* of science-fiction films", this "era-defining" Kubrick interpretation of an Arthur C. Clarke story "changed movies forever" with its "haunting view" of a future world of "machine domination"; sure, some modernists find it "slow" and "ponderous", but even those who have "no clue what it all means" say this "coldly magnificent" epic is "undeniably influential" – and add "you'll never hear Strauss' 'Blue Danube Waltz' the same way again"; P.S. "don't bother trying to figure out the ending."

### 2010
**16 | 16 | 17 | 20**

*1984. Directed by Peter Hyams. With Roy Scheider, John Lithgow, Helen Mirren, Bob Balaban. 114 minutes. Rated PG.*

"High-quality special effects" make this sequel to *2001* "relatively worthwhile", not to mention "less confusing", since a "more linear plot" "helps to explain the original storyline"; but foes insist it's "not in the same league at all", merely a "workmanlike" effort with "no transcendence", though admitting it "had an awful lot to live up to."

### Two Women ✉❶❒
**▽ 25 | 28 | 25 | 22**

*1961. Directed by Vittorio De Sica. With Sophia Loren, Eleanora Brown, Raf Vallone. 99 minutes. Not Rated.*

The "horror of war" from a "woman's viewpoint" is delineated in this "heartbreaking" Italian drama where a "protective mother and her daughter" bond after being "brutally raped" by a gang of soldiers; best remembered for Sophia's "riveting" performance, it's a "very emotional" film that's "seldom seen these days."

### U-571
**17 | 17 | 19 | 21**

*2000. Directed by Jonathan Mostow. With Matthew McConaughey, Bill Paxton, Harvey Keitel. 116 minutes. Rated PG-13.*

This "tense" World War II "submarine flick" brings out plenty "claustrophobia" in its story of a tightly quartered American c

duking it out with a German U-boat under high seas; while it's "ne
*Das Boot*" (given "so-so acting" and a "could-have-been-better"
storyline "full of obvious holes"), it's still a "rousing", bona
fide guy movie.

### Umbrellas of Cherbourg, The 𝔽    24 | 22 | 21 | 26
*1964. Directed by Jacques Demy. With Catherine Deneuve, Nino
Castelnuovo. 87 minutes. Not Rated.*
Ultra-"bright Technicolor" and "captivating" music from Michel
Legrand provide the uplift in this "sad story" of love in vain, an
idiosyncratic French bonbon that's "entirely sung" (a "risky"
proposition that ultimately "works"); starring a "fetching young
Deneuve", it has the "courage" to turn a potentially "cheesy"
premise into "inspiring" filmmaking.

### Unbearable Lightness of Being, The    21 | 24 | 21 | 21
*1988. Directed by Philip Kaufman. With Daniel Day-Lewis, Juliette
Binoche, Lena Olin. 171 minutes. Rated R.*
"Romance amid revolution" is the theme of this erudite picture
about the "erotic" misadventures of a young Czech surgeon
swept up in the '68 Russian invasion of Prague; while the light-
headed like the "hottie" cast's "compelling" work, cynics sneer
this "yawner" "leaves a lot to be desired" and suggest the title be
cut to just plain "*Unbearable.*"

### Unbreakable    16 | 19 | 17 | 19
*2000. Directed by M. Night Shyamalan. With Bruce Willis, Samuel L.
Jackson, Robin Wright Penn. 107 minutes. Rated PG-13.*
Ok, it's "hard to live up to *The Sixth Sense*", but this solid follow-
up from the Shyamalan/Willis team "keeps you wondering all
the time" with its "intriguing" story of a "man struggling with
immortality"; though surveyors split on the end result (a "noble
failure" vs. "terribly underrated"), holdouts insist it "warrants more
than one viewing" to be fully appreciated.

### Uncle Buck    17 | 18 | 17 | 17
*1989. Directed by John Hughes. With John Candy, Amy Madigan,
Jean Louisa Kelly. 100 minutes. Rated PG.*
"Among John Candy's best", most "lovable" roles is his heavy-
duty turn as a "derelict turned babysitter" in this lightweight
comedy; while the "movie itself is just ok", the "funny dialogue"
and heroic oafishness of the lead prevail – and an appearance by
a pre–*Home Alone* Macaulay Culkin adds to its family appeal.

### Under Siege Ⓤ    15 | 11 | 14 | 16
*1992. Directed by Andrew Davis. With Steven Seagal, Tommy Lee
Jones, Gary Busey. 102 minutes. Rated R.*
Think "*Die Hard* on a battleship" to get the gist of this "graphically
violent" Seagal vehicle where he "kicks some serious ass" to keep
his "reputation afloat"; maybe the plot about lunatic villains thieving
nukes is "moronic", but at least the "kill-first-ask-questions-later"
sensibility is "entertainingly dumb."

### Under the Tuscan Sun    19 | 20 | 18 | 22
*2003. Directed by Audrey Wells. With Diane Lane, Sandra Oh,
Raoul Bova. 113 minutes. Rated PG-13.*
newly divorced woman buys a house in "picturesque Tuscany"
start her life anew and "find herself" in this "coming-into-bloom"
ure, a "feel-good" chick flick worth seeing for Lane's "warm,

enuine performance" alone; ok, "it isn't *Enchanted April*" and there's "not much storyline", but it's still "sweet and fun."

### Unfaithful
21 | 24 | 20 | 20

*2002. Directed by Adrian Lyne. With Diane Lane, Richard Gere, Olivier Martinez. 124 minutes. Rated R.*
Diane Lane is "spectacular" and "so convincing" as a modern housewife "torn between guilt and thrills as she embarks on an affair" with a "hot" stranger, and Richard Gere delivers the "most mature, nuanced performance of his career" as the "cuckold" in this "unexpectedly intense film" that's "disturbing in its credibility"; "now if only they'd found a better plot" and a less "lame" ending.

### Unforgiven ✉
26 | 26 | 24 | 25

*1992. Directed by Clint Eastwood. With Clint Eastwood, Gene Hackman, Morgan Freeman. 131 minutes. Rated R.*
"Clint directs, Clint scores, Clint wins" a Best Picture statuette with this "grim" "anti-Western" that manages to "revise every convention and cliché of the genre" with a "superb script" and cast of "unforgivable", "unforgettable" characters; indeed, it's so "powerful" and "dark", you'll find "no white hats here."

### Unmarried Woman, An ∅
20 | 25 | 21 | 19

*1978. Directed by Paul Mazursky. With Jill Clayburgh, Alan Bates, Michael Murphy. 130 minutes. Rated R.*
This "very-much-of-its-time" portrait of a "New Yorkey" divorcée "in transition" offers a "thoughtful", "emotional" examination of a '70s "woman's lib"–style romance; the picture broke "new ground" when originally released, thanks to the "excellent" Clayburgh as the recently "single" gal, though postfeminists posit it may "seem dated now."

### Unsinkable Molly Brown, The
21 | 20 | 20 | 21

*1964. Directed by Charles Walters. With Debbie Reynolds, Harve Presnell, Ed Begley. 128 minutes. Not Rated.*
"Think of it as the last big" MGM musical and "you'll be in for a good evening's entertainment" with this "rollicking" bio of a turn-of-the-century "bawdy broad who wants it all and gets it"; warblers adore the "rip-roarin'" Reynolds in the title role, who drowns all doubts about how "she got the name 'unsinkable.'"

### Untouchables, The
22 | 22 | 22 | 22

*1987. Directed by Brian De Palma. With Kevin Costner, Sean Connery, Robert De Niro. 119 minutes. Rated R.*
"Sassy" '30s crime drama recounting the epic "good-vs.-evil" struggle between Eliot Ness and Al Capone, as interpreted by Costner and De Niro (wearing "amazing Armani suits" that nearly upstage them); while this "period piece" has "exciting action" and "style to spare", the most "compelling" work comes from the Oscar-winning Connery as a streetwise copper.

### Upside of Anger, The
22 | 26 | 21 | 22

*2005. Directed by Mike Binder. With Joan Allen, Kevin Costner, Erika Christensen, Evan Rachel Wood, Keri Russell. 118 minutes. Rated R.*
"Rage and depression" are about to overwhelm an abandoned housewife when a "washed-up baseball player" steps up to the plate to "suffer by her side" in this "acute observation" "real people"; it pairs the "amazing" Allen with a "hang-loos

Costner, but apart from the "great screen chemistry", there's a downside: that "difficult-to-swallow" "surprise" ending.

### Urban Cowboy
18 | 17 | 16 | 17

*1980. Directed by James Bridges. With John Travolta, Debra Winger, Scott Glenn. 132 minutes. Rated PG.*
Travolta "in tight jeans" plays opposite Winger at her most "adorable" in this "highly watchable" honky-tonk romance about "beer-swigging", "mechanical bull–riding" men and the women who love them; although Debra nearly "steals the show", she's almost bested by an appealing Houston setting.

### USUAL SUSPECTS, THE ✉
27 | 28 | 28 | 25

*1995. Directed by Bryan Singer. With Gabriel Byrne, Kevin Spacey, Benicio Del Toro, Stephen Baldwin. 106 minutes. Rated R.*
"Don't blink" or you'll risk missing one of the many "imaginative" twists in this "tricky-as-hell" "instant classic" that may be one of the finest "whodunit" "thrill rides" ever made; fans "watch it at least twice" to absorb the "brilliant" story, admire the "flawless" Spacey and figure out what the heck "Benicio's saying"; as for that "unpredictable finale", you'll "never see it coming."

### Vera Drake
24 | 28 | 25 | 23

*2004. Directed by Mike Leigh. With Imelda Staunton. 125 minutes. Rated R.*
Wherever you stand on Roe vs. Wade, it's "hard not to be moved" by this "devastating portrait" of a "well-meaning abortionist who runs afoul of the law" in '50s London; "delicate" direction by Leigh keeps the "polarizing" material in check, while "flawless" performances by a "magnificent" ensemble (particularly Staunton's "unforgettable" title turn) ensure there's "never a false moment."

### Verdict, The
23 | 25 | 23 | 20

*1982. Directed by Sidney Lumet. With Paul Newman, Charlotte Rampling, Jack Warden. 129 minutes. Rated R.*
A "David-vs.-Goliath" legal struggle is the underpinning of this "underrated" courtroom drama about a "burned-out lawyer trying one last case to keep from going under"; Newman's "intense", "tour-de-force" turn is one of his "greatest" roles (leaving many "stunned" that the Oscar eluded him), while the "mesmerizing" Rampling "excels" as the love interest.

### VERTIGO
27 | 26 | 27 | 26

*1958. Directed by Alfred Hitchcock. With James Stewart, Kim Novak, Tom Helmore. 128 minutes. Rated PG.*
"Don't look down": this "dizzyingly complex" thriller offers lots of "twists and turns" as it details the "haunting" tale of an "obsessive" man who "tries to mold a woman into a vision of his lost love"; many call it "Hitchcock's crowning achievement" thanks to a Bernard Herrmann score that's "like perfume" as well as "spellbinding" work from a "bewitching Novak" and "Stewart at his darkest"; as for that "fever dream" of a plot, "it's not supposed to make sense."

### Very Long Engagement, A 🇫
22 | 24 | 22 | 25

*2004. Directed by Jean-Pierre Jeunet. With Audrey Tautou, Gaspard Ulliel. 134 minutes. Rated R.*
Amélie's "dynamic duo" (director Jeunet and "radiant" actress Tautou) reunite for this "beautifully done" French war saga whose

graphic" depictions of WWI trenches are tempered by a "tearful" story of "lost love"; with "so many characters", the "complex storyline" can be "hard to follow" and "takes time" to develop, leaving some to retitle it "*A Very Long Movie*."

### Victor/Victoria
23 | 24 | 23 | 23

*1982. Directed by Blake Edwards. With Julie Andrews, James Garner, Robert Preston. 132 minutes. Rated PG.*

"What a hoot!" holler fans who "never tire of watching" this "hilarious" musical farce about Parisian nightlife denizens in the '30s; "Andrews lights up the screen" as the titular double-crossed cross-dresser, while Leslie Ann Warren's fabulous floozie is deliciously "over-the-top"; in sum, this "fast-paced", "madcap" tale of "jazz-age gender bending" is "just plain fun."

### Village of the Damned ❶⓿
∇ 21 | 19 | 22 | 19

*1960. Directed by Wolf Rilla. With George Sanders, Barbara Shelley, Michael Gwynn. 78 minutes. Not Rated.*

An "unfortunate town" becomes host to an army of "alien children" with funny eyeballs in this "spooky" British sci-fi flick that "succeeds without a lot of fancy effects"; ever "cool" over 45 years later, it still "creeps out" viewers ("whoever thought kids could be so scary?") who advise "don't bother with the '95 version."

### WAGES OF FEAR ❶🄵
27 | 26 | 27 | 24

*1953. Directed by Henri-Georges Clouzot. With Yves Montand, Charles Vanel. 148 minutes. Not Rated.*

"Fasten your seatbelts for a bumpy" ride via this "nerve-racking" "nail-biter" about "down-and-outers" racing a "nitroglycerine-loaded truck" across the mountains of South America; Clouzot's knack for "oh-my-God" suspense and "social commentary" makes it one of the "best art-house action" flicks around.

### Wag the Dog
19 | 22 | 22 | 19

*1997. Directed by Barry Levinson. With Dustin Hoffman, Robert De Niro, Anne Heche. 97 minutes. Rated R.*

Pundits praise this "biting black comedy" that "makes light (and dark) of media-oriented politics" via a "surreal" story about a "nonexistent war created by the government to divert attention" from a presidential scandal; though some wonder if it's a "documentary", others tout this "underrated" political satire for Hoffman and De Niro's "standout" turns.

### Waiting for Guffman
25 | 26 | 24 | 23

*1996. Directed by Christopher Guest. With Christopher Guest, Eugene Levy, Fred Willard, Catherine O'Hara. 84 minutes. Rated R.*

"Anyone who loves the theater and loves to laugh" shouldn't miss this "hilarious" mockumentary about "community theater in the boonies" courtesy of "comic genius" Guest and his "usual incredibly talented ensemble"; it's a "laugh riot from the first frame to the last", with "classic" scenes you'll "quote lines from" – "I'm still searching for *My Dinner with Andre* action figures."

### Wait Until Dark
25 | 26 | 27 | 23

*1967. Directed by Terence Young. With Audrey Hepburn, Alan Arkin, Richard Crenna. 107 minutes. Not Rated.*

This "unforgettable" thriller posits a "simple, nerve-shattering premise": a blind woman, all alone in her apartment, in a "gam of cat-and-mouse" with a "brutal psychopath"; gird yourself f an "eerie Henry Mancini soundtrack" and a "twists-and-turns" laden scenario with "one particularly electrifying moment" that's guaranteed to "have you out of your seat."

### Wall Street ✉                     22 | 23 | 22 | 21
1987. Directed by Oliver Stone. With Michael Douglas, Charlie Sheen, Martin Sheen. 125 minutes. Rated R.
"Greed is good" in this "quintessential insider's view" of the "go-go '80s" as personified by "ruthless financier" Gordon Gecko, an "ever-so-cool" piece of "Wall Street slime", "brilliantly executed" by the Oscar-winning Douglas; the "world of high finance" in all its "moneymaking" excess is captured here "like in no other film."

### War of the Roses, The                17 | 20 | 17 | 18
1989. Directed by Danny DeVito. With Michael Douglas, Kathleen Turner, Danny DeVito. 116 minutes. Rated R.
"You need a slightly off-color sense of humor" (namely, "black") to enjoy this "daring" comedy about the "disintegration of a marriage" and subsequent "over-the-top divorce shenanigans"; still, the "materialism, ego and folly" are played out with such a "mean-spirited", "venomous edge" that some find it "completely depressing and charmless."

### War of the Worlds, The               23 | 16 | 24 | 23
1953. Directed by Byron Haskin. With Gene Barry, Ann Robinson, Les Tremayne. 85 minutes. Rated G.
Although the "Orson Welles radio broadcast" is "more famous", this "faithful" filming of the H.G. Wells "sci-fi classic" still clearly telegraphs its "frightening premise" of Martians run amok on Planet Earth; ok, it may be a bit "overstated" and "unintentionally funny today", but boob-tubers tune in "every time it's on television."

### Wayne's World ⑪                   17 | 14 | 15 | 15
1992. Directed by Penelope Spheeris. With Mike Myers, Dana Carvey, Rob Lowe. 95 minutes. Rated PG-13.
"One of the few Saturday Night Live skits to soar in a longer format", this parody of local access cable TV shows is an "inventive", "mindless" romp that was one of the biggest box office comedies of the '90s; it's also the breakout for the pre–Austin Powers Myers, who gives an "awesome" rendition of "stupidity at its finest."

### Way We Were, The                   24 | 25 | 25 | 23
1973. Directed by Sydney Pollack. With Barbra Streisand, Robert Redford, Bradford Dillman. 118 minutes. Rated PG.
"Still a tearjerker after all these years", this "improbable romance" pits a "brainy" Jewish girl opposite a "golden Wasp boy" and "tugs every heartstring available" in its "realistic" depiction of their "ill-fated" affair; Streisand and Redford "at their peak" are "beyond delicious" together, though the most indelible "memories" involve the "famous final scene" at the "Plaza Hotel" with that "sad", Oscar-winning song playing in the background.

### Wedding Banquet, The 🄵              22 | 21 | 25 | 21
1993. Directed by Ang Lee. With Winston Chao, May Chin, Mitchell Lichtenstein. 106 minutes. Rated R.
"Family dynamics" get a "touching" twist in this "gently told" Taiwanese tale about a "marriage of convenience" between a "gay man" hoping to make his parents happy and his green card–seeking bride; this "funny charade" comes to a climax at the

ular feast, where "unconditional love" comes "out of the closet"
n a "warmhearted" if "bittersweet finale."

### Wedding Singer, The
17 | 16 | 16 | 16

*1998. Directed by Frank Coraci. With Adam Sandler, Drew Barrymore. 96 minutes. Rated PG-13.*
Take a "blast to the past" via this romantic comedy set in the "suburban '80s" whose real stars are its rocking retro soundtrack and obligatory "tasteless fashion" parade; beyond that, it's a "cute if insipid" "chick flick" about a down-and-out wedding singer, "dejected love" and its "sweet" redemption.

### Welcome to the Dollhouse
22 | 21 | 21 | 19

*1995. Directed by Todd Solondz. With Heather Matarazzo, Matthew Faber, Eric Mabius. 88 minutes. Rated R.*
A "dead-on look at the horrors" of junior high, this "scathing" study of a "dorky adolescent" "hits close to home" thanks to an "eerily real" performance by Matarazzo as the "picked-on" protagonist; both "cruelly funny" and "disturbingly accurate", it makes some oldsters "worry about young people today."

### WEST SIDE STORY ✉
27 | 24 | 27 | 27

*1961. Directed by Robert Wise, Jerome Robbins. With Natalie Wood, Richard Beymer, Rita Moreno, George Chakiris. 151 minutes. Not Rated.*
Starting with that "opening bird's-eye view of Manhattan", this "remarkable musical" that transposes "*Romeo and Juliet*" to "urban" turf is "sheer perfection" thanks to "fiery acting", Robbins' "superb" streetwise choreography and the "dynamic" Leonard Bernstein/Stephen Sondheim score; sure, Beymer might be "miscast" and it's "too bad they wouldn't let Natalie sing", but otherwise this Oscar magnet – 10 statuettes including Best Picture – is "forever fabulous."

### Westworld ⑪
19 | 16 | 21 | 20

*1973. Directed by Michael Crichton. With Yul Brynner, Richard Benjamin, James Brolin. 88 minutes. Rated PG.*
You can "see where *Jurassic Park* came from" in this sci-fi thriller whose "irresistible premise" involves a futuristic resort where vacationers live out their Wild West fantasies with robot stand-ins; though sharp-shooters say Brynner is "perfect" as an "android gunslinger" gone haywire, cynics ponder the idea of a "wooden actor playing an automaton."

### Whale Rider
25 | 26 | 24 | 24

*2003. Directed by Niki Caro. With Keisha Castle-Hughes, Rawiri Paratene, Vicki Haughton. 101 minutes. Rated PG-13.*
Featuring "no stars, no explosions and no CGI effects", this nonetheless "powerful" film tells the "captivating" story of a Maori girl's struggle to help her tribe balance "tradition and the 21st century"; a "refreshing", family-friendly slice of "edutainment" complete with "beautiful" New Zealand vistas and "phenomenal" work by "up-and-comer" Castle-Hughes, this "achingly sad" story will "leave your soul touched."

### What About Bob?
18 | 19 | 18 | 17

*1991. Directed by Frank Oz. With Bill Murray, Richard Dreyfus Julie Hagerty. 99 minutes. Rated PG.*
Proving that "life is indeed baby steps", this "dark" comedy ab "shrink driven nuts" by a "psycho patient" pairs the "scre"

Murray with the "hilarious" Dreyfuss; though the picture might .
"as irritating as it is funny", your "sides will hurt" from laughter
all the same.

### What Dreams May Come
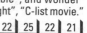
16 | 17 | 15 | 24

*1998. Directed by Vincent Ward. With Robin Williams, Cuba
Gooding Jr., Annabella Sciorra. 113 minutes. Rated PG-13.*
"Extremely pleasing to the eye", this "beautiful fantasy of the
afterlife" "based on the touching Richard Matheson novel" finds
Williams desperately trying to rescue his wife's soul from the
underworld; but realists report a "sappy", "schmaltzy script" and
sum this one up as "visually exquisite, but little else."

### Whatever Happened to Baby Jane? ◑
22 | 25 | 23 | 21

*1962. Directed by Robert Aldrich. With Bette Davis, Joan
Crawford, Victor Buono. 134 minutes. Not Rated.*
"Campy and creepy", this "classic" exercise in Grand Guignol is
the last hurrah of Hollywood's "two queen bees" in a "frightening"
story of the "hate-hate relationship" between a pair of movie-star
sisters; expect an "audacious" Crawford facing off against an
"over-the-top" Davis, whose "grotesque" appearance is "too
scary to think about" for too long; most memorable scene: Joan's
"rat à-la-carte" din-din.

### What Lies Beneath
16 | 18 | 16 | 18

*2000. Directed by Robert Zemeckis. With Harrison Ford, Michelle
Pfeiffer, Diana Scarwid. 126 minutes. Rated PG-13.*
This "chilling" "Hitchcockian" thriller about a "sinister ghost" at
loose in the house is a "slick" endeavor, with enough "scary
moments" to "make you jump" out of your seat; but foes find the
"cable-TV-caliber script" "silly" and "predictable", and wonder
what "A-list actors" are doing in this "overwrought", "C-list movie."

### What's Eating Gilbert Grape
22 | 25 | 22 | 21

*1993. Directed by Lasse Hallström. With Johnny Depp, Juliette Lewis,
Leonardo DiCaprio, Mary Steenburgen. 118 minutes. Rated PG-13.*
An "original" study of an ultra-"dysfunctional" family, this "weirdly
winning" dramedy features a "quietly intense" Depp opposite a
"brilliant" DiCaprio "before he became a celebrity teen idol"; its
"loving look at two fringe groups – the obese and the mentally
challenged" – turns this "quirky" "coming-of-age" tale into
"surprisingly good" moviemaking.

### What's Love Got to Do with It
22 | 26 | 22 | 21

*1993. Directed by Brian Gibson. With Angela Bassett, Laurence
Fishburne. 118 minutes. Rated R.*
That Tina Turner "never did anything nice and easy" is plain to
see in this "perfect" biopic depicting how a "gifted" gal "got the
strength to move on" from an abusive marriage to super-duper
stardom; in a picture that's "all about the acting", Bassett is
"outstanding", but be warned that it can be "painful to watch."

### What's Up, Doc?
21 | 20 | 21 | 20

*1972. Directed by Peter Bogdanovich. With Barbra Streisand,
Ryan O'Neal, Madeline Kahn. 94 minutes. Rated G.*
"Streisand's like butter" in this "zany" "modern screwball
comedy" "reminiscent of *Bringing Up Baby*" wherein some
terrific Ryan-Babs chemistry" is brought to bear on a nutty
line involving "igneous rocks", identical plaid suitcases and

...ntastic comic car chase through San Francisco"; P.S. "Kahn's ...cream" in her film debut.

### What Women Want
`15 | 17 | 17 | 16`
*2000. Directed by Nancy Meyers. With Mel Gibson, Helen Hunt, Marisa Tomei. 126 minutes. Rated PG-13.*
A misogynist is redeemed after becoming superhumanly "sensitized" to women's inner monologues in this "enjoyably light" chick flick; while it might "miss the mark" due to "predictable" plotting, it's an "original concept" that's "worth it just to see" "Mad Max Mel struggle with pantyhose."

### WHEN HARRY MET SALLY . . .
`26 | 25 | 25 | 24`
*1989. Directed by Rob Reiner. With Billy Crystal, Meg Ryan, Carrie Fisher, Bruno Kirby. 96 minutes. Rated R.*
"Can a man and a woman be just friends?"; this romantic comedy – the "king of all date movies" – attempts to answer that question as it details a "terrific take on relationships" that "rings true for many"; written by Nora Ephron as an "ode to Manhattan", it stars an "adorable", "pre-pixie cut" Ryan opposite a "perfect" Crystal, both "forever remembered" for the "infamous orgasm scene" in Katz's Deli that inspired one of the best lines in moviedom: "I'll have what she's having."

### While You Were Sleeping
`18 | 19 | 20 | 18`
*1995. Directed by Jon Turteltaub. With Sandra Bullock, Bill Pullman, Peter Gallagher. 103 minutes. Rated PG.*
"Token-booth worker" Bullock "falls in love with two brothers" in this "tender" romantic comedy, an "engaging", "Cinderella"-like "fairy tale" trading on "mistaken identity"; sure, it's "feel-good fluff", but the "unique storyline", "sweet" performances and "great chemistry" between the leads add up to an "all-around cute movie."

### White Christmas
`25 | 21 | 22 | 24`
*1954. Directed by Michael Curtiz. With Bing Crosby, Danny Kaye, Rosemary Clooney. 120 minutes. Not Rated.*
"It wouldn't be Christmas" without a peek at this "sentimental" favorite, a virtual holiday "requirement" with "all the trimmings": "wonderful dance numbers", "essential" Irving Berlin tunes and "Der Bingle" crooning "kringle jingles"; in short, this "classic" is so "charming", it's almost "un-American not to love it"; P.S. sticklers note that Bing originally "made the title song famous in *Holiday Inn*."

### White Heat ◑
`25 | 28 | 24 | 23`
*1949. Directed by Raoul Walsh. With James Cagney, Virginia Mayo, Edmond O'Brien. 114 minutes. Not Rated.*
One part "descent into madness", one part "valentine to mom", this schizophrenic, noirish thriller represents the "classic gangster film refined to the nth degree"; as a "homicidal nut job" "mama's boy", Cagney turns in one of his "greatest performances", though the flick's most remembered for the "best last line in movie history": 'made it, ma! top of the world!'

### Who Framed Roger Rabbit
`24 | – | 23 | 27`
*1988. Directed by Robert Zemeckis. Animated. With Bob Hoskin... Christopher Lloyd. 103 minutes. Rated PG.*
This "one-of-a-kind treat" featuring a "glorious mix of live ac... and animation" boasts an all-star cartoon cast, with appeara... by every 'toon from Mickey to Woody (though the "sedu...

Jessica Rabbit runs away with the picture); set in the Hollyw
of yore, the "classic" noir plot has Hoskins investigating a murc
case, with "wonderfully entertaining" results.

**Who's Afraid of Virginia Woolf?** ✉ ◐ | 25 | 27 | 25 | 23 |
*1966. Directed by Mike Nichols. With Elizabeth Taylor, Richard
Burton, George Segal, Sandy Dennis. 134 minutes. Not Rated.*
Maybe "Liz made up to look frumpy is a laugh", but otherwise this
"scalding adaptation" of Edward Albee's "masterpiece" about an
"unraveling marriage" is pretty serious stuff, "brilliantly acted"
and "brutally honest"; it's "funny and mean and sad" all at once –
"never has a play been converted into a movie" with such "power."

**WILD BUNCH, THE** | 27 | 26 | 25 | 27 |
*1969. Directed by Sam Peckinpah. With William Holden, Ernest
Borgnine, Robert Ryan. 134 minutes. Rated R.*
Not for the faint of heart, this "blood-and-guts" Peckinpah "epic" is
a "Western to end all Westerns" that "transcends the genre" with
an "in-your-face style" that turns "violence into poetry"; starring
Holden as the leader of a band of "honorable outlaws", it depicts a
"changing world" at the "end of an era" in "unsentimental" terms
and manages to be both "noble and perverse at the same time."

**Wild Strawberries** ◐ 🇫 | 26 | 26 | 24 | 25 |
*1959. Directed by Ingmar Bergman. With Victor Sjöström, Bibi
Andersson, Ingrid Thulin. 91 minutes. Not Rated.*
"Essential Bergman" that's not just for art movie mavens, this
"elegiac" "road film about life, death and redemption" "continues
to hold up well"; a "bittersweet" story of an "elderly doctor who
learns how to love at the last minute of his life", it's ultimately
"cathartic and hopeful", even if it occasionally displays the
director's signature "depressive" streak.

**Willow** | 20 | 18 | 20 | 22 |
*1988. Directed by Ron Howard. With Val Kilmer, Joanne Whalley,
Warwick Davis. 130 minutes. Rated PG.*
"If you like *Princess Bride*", you'll like this "wonderfully escapist"
fantasy featuring "appealing" characters in a sword-and-sorcery
story that "seems familiar" to those who dub it a "*Lord of the Rings*"
clone; "Kilmer's gorgeous" and there's plenty of "excitement",
but some say that it's a "formulaic disappointment."

**Willy Wonka and the Chocolate Factory** | 26 | 22 | 26 | 26 |
*1971. Directed by Mel Stuart. With Gene Wilder, Jack Albertson,
Peter Ostrum. 100 minutes. Rated G.*
Chocoholics cheer this "delicious family classic" adeptly adapted
from the "brilliant Roald Dahl book" about an "underdog" kid who
gets a "once-in-a-lifetime" chance to tour a "curious candy
factory"; it's such a "blast to watch" (thanks to "psychedelic"
sets, "imaginative" vignettes and "great songs") that it's almost
become a "rite of passage" for the stroller set.

**Wind and the Lion, The** | 24 | 25 | 24 | 24 |
*1975. Directed by John Milius. With Sean Connery, Candice
Bergen, Brian Keith. 119 minutes. Rated PG.*
⸱is "old-fashioned, character-driven adventure" about an Arab
⸱eftain's abduction of an American widow is loosely "based
⸱real incident during Teddy Roosevelt's presidency"; despite
⸱wonderful desert romance" that blooms between the

narismatic" Connery and "watchable" Bergen, there's "still
nough action for the guys" in this "obscure history lesson."

### Winged Migration
26 | – | 21 | 28

*2003. Directed by Jacques Perrin, Jacques Cluzaud, Michel
Debats. Documentary. 98 minutes. Rated G.*
"Soar with the birds" in this "breathtaking" documentary whose
"amazing camerawork" puts you shoulder-to-wing with "flocks
flying" around the globe on their "moving" migratory journeys; a
"masterpiece" that will "awaken your appreciation" of nature's
"avian heroes", it "should be required viewing" for budding
environmentalists and cinematographers alike; P.S. one welcome
feature: there's "no bad acting."

### Wings of Desire ❶⓫🅵
24 | 24 | 22 | 25

*1988. Directed by Wim Wenders. With Bruno Ganz, Solveig
Dommartin. 127 minutes. Rated PG-13.*
A "charming meditation" about the "angels who watch over us",
"longing to be human", this "haunting" German film "celebrates
the human condition"; "dreamy cinematography" and an "amazing"
cast elevate it to "pure poetry" – but don't "judge it by its self-
conscious remake", Hollywood's "unfortunate" *City of Angels.*

### Witches of Eastwick, The
17 | 20 | 18 | 18

*1987. Directed by George Miller. With Jack Nicholson, Cher,
Susan Sarandon, Michelle Pfeiffer. 118 minutes. Rated R.*
Three small-town gals take on the devil himself in this "funny
but disturbing" comedy, a variation on the "beauty-and-the-
beast" theme based on the John Updike novel; no surprise, a
"wicked Jack" walks away with the picture, triumphing over
the occasionally "weird storyline" and "bizarre" denouement.

### Witness ✉
23 | 24 | 23 | 22

*1985. Directed by Peter Weir. With Harrison Ford, Kelly McGillis,
Lukas Haas. 112 minutes. Rated R.*
"One of Weir's finest", this "quiet" film offers a "sensitive
portrayal" of a "small Amish community" that "collides with the
violent outside world" in the aftermath of a murder; the actors
have "perfect pitch" (particularly the "workmanlike" Ford, who
"sizzles" against the "luminous McGillis"), and even if the story's
somewhat "improbable", its overall "excellence sneaks up on you."

### WITNESS FOR THE PROSECUTION ❶
27 | 28 | 28 | 25

*1957. Directed by Billy Wilder. With Tyrone Power, Marlene
Dietrich, Charles Laughton. 116 minutes. Not Rated.*
Perhaps the "best murder mystery ever", this "Agatha Christie
puzzler" is one of "Wilder's wiliest", featuring "two legends" – an
"incredible" Laughton and an "outstanding" Dietrich – along with
a courtroom-full of "compelling characterizations"; the dialogue
"crackles" and the "plot twists and double twists" right up to the
"still shocking ending."

### WIZARD OF OZ, THE
28 | 26 | 28 | 29

*1939. Directed by Victor Fleming. With Judy Garland, Ray Bolger,
Jack Haley, Bert Lahr. 101 minutes. Rated G.*
A "star is born" – the "iconic" "Judy, Judy, Judy" – in this
"timeless", "transporting" musical about a Kansas girl "of
see the Wizard" that's been "adored for decades" thank
its "tremendous" cast, "glorious", "rainbow"-hued score a

"inspired" moments involving a pair of "ruby slippers", a pack "scary flying monkeys" and that "magical", "hello-Technicolor transition; in Toto, this "landmark in family entertainment" is the ultimate proof that "there's no place like home."

### Wolf Man, The ◑Ⅱ                          20 | 19 | 22 | 19
*1941. Directed by George Waggner. With Lon Chaney Jr., Claude Rains, Ralph Bellamy. 70 minutes. Not Rated.*
This "classic Universal monster" flicker set the "standard for fright" in its day with a hair-raising mix of ominous gypsies, howling werewolves and foreboding full moons; a "superb" Chaney stars as the fuzzy-faced lead, though a few howl about his "hammy" acting chops and "special effects that look damn silly" now.

### WOMAN OF THE YEAR ✉◑               27 | 28 | 26 | 26
*1942. Directed by George Stevens. With Katharine Hepburn, Spencer Tracy, Fay Bainter. 114 minutes. Not Rated.*
The "war between the sexes was never more fun" than in this first matchup of legendary duo Hepburn and Tracy in what some call the "best" of their eight films together; its Oscar-winning script pits the "right-on" Kate as an "ahead-of-her-time" foreign correspondent against Spence's laid-back sportswriter, but the hands-down winner in this battle of wills is clearly the audience.

### Women, The ◑                        ▽ 27 | 26 | 26 | 25
*1939. Directed by George Cukor. With Norma Shearer, Joan Crawford, Rosalind Russell, Paulette Goddard. 133 minutes. Not Rated.*
"*Meow!*": a "wonderful wallow" in "fabulous bitchiness", this "marvelous" MGM adaptation of Clare Boothe Luce's "clever" stage play about high-society divorcées boasts an all-star, all-gal cast rattling off "extraordinary fast-paced" dialogue; though the constant "cattiness" can be a turnoff, it's still "required viewing" for "chick flick" and camp followers.

### Women on the Verge
### of a Nervous Breakdown 🇫            24 | 24 | 23 | 22
*1988. Directed by Pedro Almodóvar. With Carmen Maura, Antonio Banderas. 90 minutes. Rated R.*
Forget the "depressing" title: this "campy", "door-slamming farce" "put director Almodóvar on the map" and is one of the "funniest foreign films" ever made; a "wacky" story of "neurotic characters with different agendas", it also introduced "eye-candy Banderas to the Western world."

### Wonder Boys                          21 | 24 | 21 | 20
*2000. Directed by Curtis Hanson. With Michael Douglas, Tobey Maguire, Frances McDormand. 111 minutes. Rated R.*
Douglas shines in this "intelligent" if "overlooked" dramedy as a "humpy-shlumpy" college professor stultified by writer's block compounded by a "midlife crisis"; a "funny, smart and caring" piece of moviemaking, it supplies "many different interwoven storylines" – though calculators say its "parts prove greater than the sum of the whole."

### Woodsman, The                        21 | 27 | 21 | 20
*2004. Directed by Nicole Kassell. With Kevin Bacon, Kyra Sedgwick. minutes. Rated R.*
*uring far afield from his* Footloose *beginnings, Bacon earns marks" for his "daring" turn as a "recovering pedophile"*

sperately "seeking a second chance" in this "honorably
alistic" indie character study; fans warn if you're not in the
mood to "feel sorry for" a "fragile" child molester, this one's
gonna be "hard to watch."

### Woodstock
24 | – | 21 | 23

*1970. Directed by Michael Wadleigh. Documentary. With Jimi Hendrix, The Who. 184 minutes. Rated R.*

"Drop out, turn on and tune in" to this "seminal pop-culture event", a "groundbreaking" rockumentary about the fabled "peace-and-love" concert that's a "near-perfect snapshot" of the era, "minus the bad acid"; though ticked-off "tie-dyed flower children" sniff the "split-screen stuff gets old" and find "too much mud and not enough Hendrix", peaceniks maintain that this "marathon" movie provides "evidence that the summer of love was no pipe dream."

### Working Girl
20 | 20 | 21 | 19

*1988. Directed by Mike Nichols. With Melanie Griffith, Harrison Ford, Sigourney Weaver. 109 minutes. Rated R.*

"Workplace revenge" was never funnier than in this "Cinderella-by-way-of-Wall-Street" "chick flick" that "empowers every woman who's had to put up with a difficult boss"; Griffith's at her "dumb girl/smart girl best", Weaver's "delightfully loathsome" and Ford's "adorable" "not playing an action hero for a change"; favorite line: "I've got a head for business and a bod for sin."

### World According to Garp, The
21 | 23 | 22 | 19

*1982. Directed by George Roy Hill. With Robin Williams, Mary Beth Hurt, Glenn Close. 131 minutes. Rated R.*

An "unforgettable", "modern-day fairy tale" full of "bizarre characters", this adaptation of John Irving's best-seller relates the "weird life" of T.S. Garp, beginning with his conception "when his mother sleeps with a man on his death bed"; though "unusual" is putting it mildly, this "unforgettable" tale is ultimately "affecting."

### World Is Not Enough, The
19 | 19 | 18 | 21

*1999. Directed by Michael Apted. With Pierce Brosnan, Denise Richards. 128 minutes. Rated PG-13.*

Though admittedly "pure escapism", 007's 19th trip to the big screen divides voters: fans vow that Pierce is "as good as Sean", but foes growl that "gadgets have replaced characterization and plot" and snicker at the "ludicrous" Richards playing a "short-shorts–wearing nuclear physicist."

### Wuthering Heights ◐
27 | 27 | 27 | 24

*1939. Directed by William Wyler. With Laurence Olivier, Merle Oberon, David Niven. 103 minutes. Not Rated.*

This "Gothic romance" is a "charter" member of the "pantheon" of silver screen weepies and the "ultimate" adaptation of the Brontë tale; Olivier's "soulful brooding" as a spurned, lower-caste lover is so "brilliantly intense" that it's inspired generations of maidens to "waste away from heartbreak on the moors" ever after.

### X-Files, The
17 | 17 | 16 | 19

*1998. Directed by Rob Bowman. With David Duchovny, Gillian Anderson, Martin Landau. 120 minutes. Rated PG-13.*

Both "fans and novices appreciate" this blockbuster adaptat
of the TV series that's "just like the show" but with some "tw
and an "occasional dirty word" thrown in; it doesn't "answ

questions" and may be "muddled, disappointing" stuff to connoisseurs, but it does "serve as a bridge between season. with some "catchy" moments.

### X-Men ❷

| 19 | 18 | 18 | 23 |

*2000. Directed by Bryan Singer. With Patrick Stewart, Hugh Jackman, Ian McKellen, Halle Berry, James Marsden. 104 minutes. Rated PG-13.*

Even those "who've never read the comic book" chime in with their "ringing endorsement" of this "true-to-the-source" adaptation of the Marvel sci-fi series; most memorable for Jackman's "starmaking turn", it's such an obvious "setup for a franchise" that many "popcorn" eaters are hungrily "awaiting the sequels."

### X2: X-Men United

| 24 | 21 | 22 | 27 |

*2003. Directed by Bryan Singer. With Patrick Stewart, Hugh Jackman, Ian McKellen, Halle Berry, Brian Cox. 133 minutes. Rated PG-13.*

"Finally, a sequel to sink your claws into": this "X-cellent" follow-up "tops the mediocre original" "in just about every way" – a "better storyline", "intriguing new characters", a "deservedly bigger role" for the "buff", "brooding" Jackman and "mega-cool special effects" . . . "what a bigger budget will do for a movie"; "can't wait for the next one – and there *will* be a next one."

### Yankee Doodle Dandy ✉◐

| 25 | 25 | 23 | 25 |

*1942. Directed by Michael Curtiz. With James Cagney, Joan Leslie, Walter Huston. 126 minutes. Not Rated.*

"Flag-waving", "red-white-and-blue" musical bio of the "all-American" showman George M. Cohan, starring Cagney in full "hoofer" bloom; the story's "whitewashed", but after a few bars of its "patriotic tunes" you'll understand why the "4th of July wouldn't be the same without it."

### Year of Living Dangerously, The

| 24 | 25 | 25 | 24 |

*1983. Directed by Peter Weir. With Mel Gibson, Sigourney Weaver, Linda Hunt. 117 minutes. Rated PG.*

An outbreak of "civil war" during the "Sukarno regime" in '60s Indonesia comes alive in this "captivating" "political" drama following a journalist who's covering the conflict; though the "compelling" Gibson and Weaver cast "steamy sparks", Hunt took home an Oscar for her "tour-de-force", "gender-bending role" in this "tense" thriller.

### Yellow Submarine

| 22 | – | 18 | 23 |

*1968. Directed by George Dunning. Animated. 90 minutes. Rated G.*

"Contagiously fun", this "lighthearted" "hallucination" of a cartoon supplies "eye-popping" "psychedelic" imagery aplenty in recounting a story about the Fab Four's battle to save Pepperland from the Blue Meanies; though the "actual Beatles don't provide" the speaking parts, their performance on the "foot-tapping" soundtrack is "more than enough" – and the music "won't drive parents crazy."

### Yentl ∅

| 18 | 19 | 19 | 20 |

*⁊83. Directed by Barbra Streisand. With Barbra Streisand, ⁊ndy Patinkin, Amy Irving. 132 minutes. Rated PG.*

Streisand" does it all – "acts, sings and directs" – in this ⁊rrated", "impeccably made" musical about a turn-of-the-

...ntury Jewish girl masquerading as a "boy in order to study ...e Talmud"; though foes call it Babs at her "self-indulgent worst", ...ans counter her "incredible talent" and "amazing attention to detail" make this "emotionally stirring" picture "deserving of more credit."

### Yojimbo ❶⓫🅕

▽ 27 | 27 | 25 | 25

*1961. Directed by Akira Kurosawa. With Toshiro Mifune, Tatsuya Nakadai. 110 minutes. Not Rated.*

"Kurosawa's classic samurai film" stars Mifune as the "ultimate antihero" who "plays both sides" of a village feud between a silk merchant and a sake merchant, and then watches as the depraved "warring factions" destroy each other; the "inspiration" for myriad remakes (*A Fistful of Dollars, Last Man Standing*, etc.), this "far superior" original clearly "shows how great this director really is."

### You Can Count on Me

23 | 26 | 22 | 20

*2000. Directed by Kenneth Lonergan. With Laura Linney, Mark Ruffalo, Rory Culkin, Matthew Broderick, John Tenney. 109 minutes. Rated R.*

Freshman director Lonergan "doesn't take a false step" in this "compelling", "character-driven" indie film about the "family bonds" between a "messed-up brother and sister" and the divergent paths their lives have taken; you can count on lots of "terrific acting" (with a "breakout performance from Linney") and a "lifelike lack of final resolution" that makes this a "sleeper with a heart."

### YOUNG FRANKENSTEIN ❶

27 | 26 | 25 | 25

*1974. Directed by Mel Brooks. With Gene Wilder, Peter Boyle, Marty Feldman, Madeline Kahn, Cloris Leachman. 108 minutes. Rated PG.*

"Frankenstein Sr. would be proud" of this "insanely hysterical" "spoof of the Mary Shelley" horror classic that's Mel Brooks' "high-water mark" ("who else would have the monster" perform 'Puttin' on the Ritz' wearing a tuxedo?"); Wilder is "pure genius" in the title role backed up by an "endlessly amusing" cast of characters spouting some of the "most quoted" dialogue in movie history; best line: a toss-up between "walk this way", "what knockers" and "hump? what hump?"; best song: Kahn's rendition of 'Ah! Sweet Mystery of Life', no contest.

### Young Guns ⓫

15 | 12 | 15 | 17

*1988. Directed by Christopher Cain. With Emilio Estevez, Kiefer Sutherland, Lou Diamond Phillips, Charlie Sheen. 107 minutes. Rated R.*

This "good Wild West romp 'n' stomp flick" featuring the "Brat Pack" in all their glory chronicles the beginnings of Billy the Kid's felonious career with his band of misfits, the Regulators; though "hardly the best movie ever", it works when you're in the mood for "interesting escapist fun."

### You Only Live Twice

22 | 21 | 20 | 22

*1967. Directed by Lewis Gilbert. With Sean Connery, Mie Ham... Donald Pleasence. 117 minutes. Rated PG.*

"Despite the absurdity of a six-foot-plus Scotsman as a s... Japan", diehards declare this espionage flicker one of the "... Connery Bonds", given its amusing "'60s Tokyo" settings

"great Nancy Sinatra" theme song; ok, it might be "cheesy" a
"doesn't age well", but camp followers claim that's what makes
"all the more fun now."

### You've Got Mail
18 | 20 | 18 | 18

*1998. Directed by Nora Ephron. With Tom Hanks, Meg Ryan,
Parker Posey, Greg Kinnear, Jean Stapleton. 119 minutes.
Rated PG.*

Manhattan's "Upper West Side looks like Paris" in this "feel-
good" romantic comedy, a "remake of *The Shop Around the
Corner*" updated to "today's techie, e-mail-ish world"; though a
tad too "cutesy pie" and "predictable" for cynics, "chick flick"
fans find it "enchanting" thanks to that "great chemistry between
Hanks and Ryan."

### Y Tu Mamá También 🖪
24 | 24 | 23 | 21

*2002. Directed by Alfonso Cuarón. With Maribel Verdu,
Gael García Bernal, Diego Luna, Diana Bracho. 105 minutes.
Rated R.*

Two "upper-middle-class Mexican boys" "learn the facts of life"
and then some from a "sexy older woman" during a road trip
"that takes some unexpected turns" in this *muy caliente* "coming-
of-age" character study; some say "everything takes a back seat
(no pun intended)" to the "very explicit sex scenes" – whew! –
but more cerebral types see it more as a "passionate film about
life, youth and love" that's "far greater than the sum of its parts."

### Z ✉🖪
26 | 25 | 26 | 24

*1969. Directed by Costa-Gavras. With Yves Montand, Irene
Papas, Jean-Louis Trintignant, Jacques Perrin. 127 minutes.
Rated PG.*

Unfortunately all "too true", this fact-based account of the
assassination of a left-leaning scientist in a right-wing country
is a crackerjack "political thriller" that's "deeply affecting"
and "not easy to watch"; Montand is "nothing less than
superb" in the title role, while director Costa-Gavras makes
this "documentary-like" "exposé" of corruption "captivating
from the first scene."

### Zelig ◑
20 | 20 | 21 | 21

*1983. Directed by Woody Allen. With Woody Allen, Mia Farrow.
79 minutes. Rated PG.*

What could be "Forrest Gump's ancestor" is the much "more
charming (and neurotic) Zelig", a human chameleon who somehow
manages to play a prominent role in 20th-century world events
with "dryly comedic" results; it's an unusual, "technically complex"
outing for the usually straightforward Allen that "warps history"
by "digitally" inserting our hero into vintage "newsreel footage",
but cynics say this "curiosity piece" has only "one clever idea"
and "should have been funnier."

### Zorba the Greek ◑
25 | 27 | 25 | 23

*1964. Directed by Michael Cacoyannis. With Anthony Quinn, Alan
Bates, Irene Papas, Lila Kedrova, Georges Foundas. 142 minutes.
ot Rated.*

re's ex-zorba-tant praise for this "still-fresh" drama about
nglishman visiting Crete on an existential quest, only to fall
the spell of a "person full of passion", the "flamboyant"
Quinn's "breakout" performance, plus some "memorable"

...he music and dancing, keep this "feel-good" "affirmation of ..." so "exciting and entertaining" that repeaters faithfully "see every year."

### Zulu ⓤ

| 24 | 24 | 25 | 24 |

*1964. Directed by Cy Endfield. With Stanley Baker, Jack Hawkins, Michael Caine. 138 minutes. Not Rated.*

The "true story of valor in the face of incredible odds", this "epic treatment of a 19th-century British military disaster" is played out against the "broad canvas of Africa" and features an "unknown Caine" in his "first big film"; "visually and viscerally stunning", it's "historically accurate without sacrificing dramatic appeal", and the "tension's unrelenting."

# Indexes

DECADES
GENRES/SPECIAL FEATURES

# DECADES

## 1910s/1920s

Birth of a Nation
Cabinet of Dr. Caligari
Cocoanuts, The
General, The
Gold Rush
Greed
Intolerance
Metropolis
Napoléon
Nosferatu
Potemkin
Thief of Bagdad

## 1930s

Adventures of Robin Hood
Alexander Nevsky
All Quiet on the Western Front
Angels with Dirty Faces
Animal Crackers
Awful Truth
Beau Geste
Blue Angel
Bride of Frankenstein
Bringing Up Baby
Captain Blood
Captains Courageous
City Lights
Dark Victory
David Copperfield
Day at the Races
Dinner at Eight
Dracula
Duck Soup
42nd Street
Frankenstein
Front Page
Gay Divorcee
Gone with the Wind
Goodbye, Mr. Chips
Grand Hotel
Grand Illusion
Gunga Din
Horse Feathers
Hound of the Baskervilles
Hunchback/Notre Dame
Invisible Man

It Happened One Night
King Kong
Lady Vanishes
Lost Horizon
M
Modern Times
Monkey Business
Mr. Smith Goes to Washington
Mummy, The
Mutiny on the Bounty
My Man Godfrey
Night at the Opera
Ninotchka
Nothing Sacred
Public Enemy
Rules of the Game
Snow White
Stagecoach
Tarzan the Ape Man
Thin Man
39 Steps
Top Hat
Topper
Triumph of the Will
Wizard of Oz
Women, The
Wuthering Heights

## 1940s

Adam's Rib
All the King's Men
Arsenic and Old Lace
Bambi
Beauty/Beast
Best Years of Our Lives
Bicycle Thief
Big Sleep
Bishop's Wife
Brief Encounter
Buck Privates
Casablanca
Children of Paradise
Citizen Kane
Double Indemnity
Dumbo
Easter Parade
Fantasia
Fort Apache

For Whom the Bell Tolls
Fountainhead, The
Gaslight
Gentleman's Agreement
Ghost and Mrs. Muir
Gilda
Going My Way
Grapes of Wrath
Great Dictator
Hamlet
High Sierra
His Girl Friday
Holiday Inn
It's a Wonderful Life
Jane Eyre
Jungle Book
Key Largo
Killers, The
Kind Hearts and Coronets
Lady Eve
Lady from Shanghai
Laura
Letter, The
Lifeboat
Little Foxes
Lost Weekend
Magnificent Ambersons
Maltese Falcon
Man Who Came to Dinner
Mark of Zorro
Meet Me in St. Louis
Mildred Pierce
Miracle on 34th Street
Mr. Blandings
National Velvet
Notorious
Now, Voyager
On the Town
Open City
Ox-Bow Incident
Philadelphia Story
Pinocchio
Postman Always Rings Twice
Pride and Prejudice
Pride of the Yankees
Rebecca
Red River
Red Shoes
Rope
Sergeant York

She Wore a Yellow Ribbon
Song of the South
Spellbound
Sullivan's Travels
Third Man
To Be or Not to Be
To Have and Have Not
Treasure of the Sierra Madre
Twelve O'Clock High
White Heat
Wolf Man
Woman of the Year
Yankee Doodle Dandy

## 1950s

Affair to Remember
African Queen
Alice in Wonderland
All About Eve
American in Paris
Anastasia
Anatomy of a Murder
Around the World in 80 Days
Asphalt Jungle
Auntie Mame
Bad Day at Black Rock
Bad Seed
Band Wagon
Bell, Book and Candle
Ben-Hur
Big Heat
Blackboard Jungle
Black Orpheus
Born Yesterday
Bridge on the River Kwai
Bus Stop
Caine Mutiny
Carousel
Cat on a Hot Tin Roof ·
Cheaper By the Dozen
Christmas Carol
Cinderella
Damn Yankees
Day the Earth Stood Still
Diabolique
Dial M for Murder
Diary of Anne Frank
D.O.A.
East of Eden
Father of the Bride

## Decades

5,000 Fingers of Dr. T.
Fly, The
Forbidden Planet
400 Blows
Friendly Persuasion
From Here to Eternity
Funny Face
Gentlemen Prefer Blondes
Giant
Gigi
Godzilla
Gunfight at the O.K. Corral
Guys and Dolls
Harvey
High Noon
High Society
House of Wax
How to Marry a Millionaire
Imitation of Life
Invasion/Body Snatchers
Journey to the Center
King and I
King Solomon's Mines
Kiss Me Kate
Lady and the Tramp
La Strada
Lavender Hill Mob
Lili
Love in the Afternoon
Love Is a Many-Splendored
Man Who Knew Too Much
Marty
Mister Roberts
Mon Oncle
Moulin Rouge
Mouse That Roared
Mr. Hulot's Holiday
Night of the Hunter
Nights of Cabiria
North by Northwest
No Time for Sergeants
Oklahoma!
Old Yeller
On the Waterfront
Operation Petticoat
Paths of Glory
Peter Pan
Picnic
Pillow Talk

Place in the Sun
Quiet Man
Rashomon
Rear Window
Rebel Without a Cause
Rio Bravo
Robe, The
Roman Holiday
Sabrina
Searchers, The
Seven Brides/Seven Brothers
Seven Samurai
Seventh Seal
7th Voyage of Sinbad
Seven Year Itch
Shane
Show Boat
Singin' in the Rain
Sleeping Beauty
Some Like It Hot
South Pacific
Stalag 17
Star Is Born
Strangers on a Train
Streetcar Named Desire
Sunset Boulevard
Sweet Smell of Success
Ten Commandments
Thing, The
Three Coins in the Fountain
Three Faces of Eve
To Catch a Thief
Touch of Evil
12 Angry Men
20,000 Leagues Under the Sea
Vertigo
Wages of Fear
War of the Worlds
White Christmas
Wild Strawberries
Witness for the Prosecution

### 1960s
Absent-Minded Professor
Alamo, The
Alfie
Apartment, The
Battle of Algiers
Becket
Bedazzled

e de Jour
ls Are Ringing
irdman of Alcatraz
Birds, The
Blowup
Bob & Carol & Ted & Alice
Bonnie and Clyde
Born Free
Breakfast at Tiffany's
Breathless
Bullitt
Butch Cassidy/Sundance Kid
Bye Bye Birdie
Cactus Flower
Camelot
Cape Fear
Cat Ballou
Charade
Charly
Cleopatra
Collector, The
Cool Hand Luke
Days of Wine and Roses
Dirty Dozen
Doctor Zhivago
Don't Look Back
Dr. No
Dr. Strangelove
Easy Rider
8½
El Cid
Elmer Gantry
Elvira Madigan
Exodus
Fahrenheit 451
Fail-Safe
Fantastic Voyage
Finian's Rainbow
Fistful of Dollars
Flight of the Phoenix
Fortune Cookie
From Russia With Love
Funny Girl
Funny Thing Happened...
Goldfinger
Goodbye, Columbus
Good, the Bad and the Ugly
Graduate, The
Great Escape

Great Race
Guess Who's Coming . . .
Guns of Navarone
Gypsy
Hard Day's Night
Hatari!
Hello, Dolly!
Help!
How the West Was Won
Hustler, The
In Cold Blood
Inherit the Wind
In the Heat of the Night
Irma La Douce
It's a Mad Mad Mad World
Judgment at Nuremberg
Jules and Jim
Juliet of the Spirits
Jungle Book
La Dolce Vita
L'Avventura
Lawrence of Arabia
Lilies of the Field
Lion in Winter
Lolita
Longest Day
Lord of the Flies
Love Bug
Magnificent Seven
Man and a Woman, A
Manchurian Candidate
Man for All Seasons
Man Who Shot Liberty Valance
Mary Poppins
Midnight Cowboy
Miracle Worker
Music Man
Mutiny on the Bounty
My Fair Lady
Never on Sunday
Night of the Living Dead
Nutty Professor
Ocean's Eleven
Odd Couple
Oliver!
101 Dalmatians
One, Two, Three
On Her Majesty's Secret
    Service

**vote at zagat.com**

Paint Your Wagon
Parent Trap
Pawnbroker, The
Persona
Pink Panther
Pit and the Pendulum
Planet of the Apes
Producers, The
Psycho
Repulsion
Romeo and Juliet
Rosemary's Baby
Russians Are Coming...
Sand Pebbles
Seven Days in May
Shot in the Dark
Sound of Music
Spartacus
Splendor in the Grass
Sweet Charity
Swiss Family Robinson
Take the Money and Run
They Shoot Horses, Don't They?
Thomas Crown Affair
Thoroughly Modern Millie
Thunderball
Time Machine
To Kill a Mockingbird
Tom Jones
Topkapi
To Sir, With Love
True Grit
Two for the Road
2001: A Space Odyssey
Two Women
Umbrellas of Cherbourg
Unsinkable Molly Brown
Village of the Damned
Wait Until Dark
West Side Story
Whatever Happened to ...
Who's Afraid of Virginia . . .
Wild Bunch
Yellow Submarine
Yojimbo
You Only Live Twice

‎ba the Greek

## 1970s

Airport
Alice Doesn't Live Here
Alien
All That Jazz
All the President's Men
Amarcord
American Graffiti
Andromeda Strain
Animal House
Annie Hall
Apocalypse Now
Apprenticeship/Duddy Kravitz
Badlands
Bad News Bears
Bananas
Bang the Drum Slowly
Barry Lyndon
Being There
Benji
Black Stallion
Blazing Saddles
Breaking Away
Cabaret
Candidate, The
Carnal Knowledge
Carrie
China Syndrome
Chinatown
Cinderella Liberty
Clockwork Orange
Close Encounters
Coming Home
Conformist, The
Conversation, The
Cousin, Cousine
Cries and Whispers
Day for Night
Days of Heaven
Death on the Nile
Death Wish
Deep, The
Deer Hunter
Deliverance
Diamonds Are Forever
Dirty Harry
Discreet Charm
Dog Day Afternoon
Enter the Dragon

...serhead
...orcist, The
...iddler on the Roof
Five Easy Pieces
Foul Play
Freaky Friday
French Connection
Funny Lady
Garden of the Finzi-Continis
Gimme Shelter
Godfather
Godfather Part II
Goodbye Girl
Grease
Great Santini
Hair
Halloween
Harold and Maude
Heaven Can Wait
High Anxiety
High Plains Drifter
In-Laws, The
Invasion/Body Snatchers
Jaws
Jeremiah Johnson
Jerk, The
Jesus Christ Superstar
Julia
Klute
Kramer vs. Kramer
La Cage aux Folles
Lady Sings the Blues
Last Picture Show
Last Tango in Paris
Last Waltz
Life of Brian
Little Big Man
Live and Let Die
Longest Yard
Looking for Mr. Goodbar
Lord of the Rings
Love Story
Manhattan
Man Who Fell to Earth
Man Who Would Be King
Man with the Golden Gun
Marathon Man
MASH
McCabe & Mrs. Miller

Mean Streets
Meatballs
Midnight Express
Monty Python/Holy Grail
Moonraker
Muppet Movie
Murder by Death
Murder on the Orient Express
Nashville
Network
New York, New York
1900
Norma Rae
Oh, God!
Omen, The
One Flew Over Cuckoo's Nest
Outlaw Josey Wales
Out-of-Towners
Paper Chase
Paper Moon
Papillon
Patton
Pete's Dragon
Pink Flamingos
Play It Again, Sam
Play Misty for Me
Poseidon Adventure
Rescuers, The
Robin and Marian
Rocky
Rocky Horror Picture Show
Rose, The
Ryan's Daughter
Same Time, Next Year
Saturday Night Fever
Scenes from a Marriage
Serpico
Seven Beauties
1776
Shampoo
Silver Streak
Slap Shot
Sleeper
Sleuth
Smokey and the Bandit
Spy Who Loved Me
Star Wars
Sting, The
Summer of '42

Sunshine Boys
Superman
Swept Away
Taxi Driver
10
Texas Chainsaw Massacre
That's Entertainment!
Three Musketeers
Time After Time
Tin Drum
Tommy
Tora! Tora! Tora!
Towering Inferno
Unmarried Woman
Way We Were
Westworld
What's Up, Doc?
Willy Wonka/Chocolate Factory
Wind and the Lion
Woodstock
Young Frankenstein

## 1980s

Absence of Malice
Abyss, The
Accidental Tourist
Accused, The
After Hours
Agnes of God
Airplane!
Akira
Aliens
All Dogs Go to Heaven
Altered States
Amadeus
American Tail
American Werewolf in London
Annie
Arthur
Atlantic City
Au Revoir Les Enfants
Babette's Feast
Baby Boom
Back to the Future
Barfly
Batman
  eetlejuice
  verly Hills Cop

  hill

Bill & Ted's
Blade Runner
Blood Simple
Blues Brothers
Blue Velvet
Body Heat
Born on the Fourth of July
Brazil
Breaker Morant
Breakfast Club
Broadcast News
Broadway Danny Rose
Bull Durham
Caddyshack
Cat People
Chariots of Fire
Children of a Lesser God
Christmas Story
Cinema Paradiso
Coal Miner's Daughter
Cocoon
Color of Money
Color Purple
Coming to America
Conan the Barbarian
Crimes and Misdemeanors
Crocodile Dundee
Dangerous Liaisons
Dark Crystal
Das Boot
Dead Poets Society
Dead Ringers
Desperately Seeking Susan
Die Hard
Diner
Dirty Dancing
Diva
Do the Right Thing
Down and Out in Beverly Hills
Dressed to Kill
Driving Miss Daisy
Drugstore Cowboy
Eating Raoul
Educating Rita
Elephant Man
Empire of the Sun
Escape from New York
E.T. The Extra-Terrestrial
Evil Dead

| | |
|---|---|
| ...abulous Baker Boys | Last Temptation of Christ |
| Fame | Legend |
| Fanny and Alexander | Lethal Weapon |
| Fast Times at Ridgemont High | Little Mermaid |
| Fatal Attraction | Little Shop of Horrors |
| Ferris Bueller's Day Off | Local Hero |
| Field of Dreams | Lost in America |
| First Blood: Rambo | Mad Max |
| Fish Called Wanda | Married to the Mob |
| Flashdance | Mask |
| Fletch | Mission, The |
| Fly, The | Mississippi Burning |
| Footloose | Mommie Dearest |
| 48 HRS. | Moonstruck |
| For Your Eyes Only | Mr. Mom |
| Fox and the Hound | My Beautiful Laundrette |
| Frances | My Bodyguard |
| French Lieutenant's Woman | My Dinner with Andre |
| Friday the 13th | My Favorite Year |
| Full Metal Jacket | My Left Foot |
| Gallipoli | My Life As a Dog |
| Gandhi | Mystic Pizza |
| Ghostbusters | Naked Gun |
| Glory | National Lampoon's Vacation |
| Gods Must Be Crazy | Natural, The |
| Good Morning, Vietnam | Never Say Never Again |
| Goonies, The | Nightmare on Elm Street |
| Gorillas in the Mist | 9½ Weeks |
| Gremlins | 9 to 5 |
| Greystoke | No Way Out |
| Hairspray | Octopussy |
| Hannah and Her Sisters | Officer and a Gentleman |
| Heathers | Once Upon a Time in America |
| Heavy Metal | On Golden Pond |
| Henry V | Ordinary People |
| Honey, I Shrunk the Kids | Out of Africa |
| Hoosiers | Outrageous Fortune |
| House of Games | Outsiders, The |
| Hunger, The | Parenthood |
| Indiana Jones/Last Crusade | Pee-wee's Big Adventure |
| Indiana Jones/Temple of Doom | Peggy Sue Got Married |
| Innerspace | Places in the Heart |
| Jagged Edge | Platoon |
| Jean de Florette | Poltergeist |
| Karate Kid | Postman Always Rings Twice |
| Killing Fields | Pretty in Pink |
| King of Comedy | Princess Bride |
| Kiss of the Spider Woman | Private Benjamin |
| Last Emperor | Prizzi's Honor |

Purple Rose of Cairo
Radio Days
Raging Bull
Raiders of the Lost Ark
Rain Man
Raising Arizona
Ran
Reds
Repo Man
Right Stuff
Risky Business
Road Warrior
RoboCop
Roger & Me
Romancing the Stone
Room with a View
Roxanne
Runaway Train
Ruthless People
Scarface
Secret of NIMH
Sex, Lies and Videotape
Shining, The
Shirley Valentine
Shoah
Sid & Nancy
Silkwood
Silverado
Sixteen Candles
Sophie's Choice
Spaceballs
Splash
Stand and Deliver
Stand by Me
Starman
Star Trek II
Star Trek IV
Star Wars V/Empire Strikes
  Back
Star Wars VI/Return of Jedi
Steel Magnolias
St. Elmo's Fire
Stir Crazy
Stop Making Sense
Stripes
ˆuspect
ˌrminator, The
ˌns of Endearment
ˌ, The

This Is Spinal Tap
Three Men and a Baby
Time Bandits
Tootsie
Top Gun
Trading Places
Tron
Tucker
2010
Unbearable Lightness of Being
Uncle Buck
Untouchables, The
Urban Cowboy
Verdict, The
Victor/Victoria
Wall Street
War of the Roses
When Harry Met Sally . . .
Who Framed Roger Rabbit
Willow
Wings of Desire
Witches of Eastwick
Witness
Women on the Verge
Working Girl
World According to Garp
Year of Living Dangerously
Yentl
Young Guns
Zelig

## 1990s
Ace Ventura
Addams Family
Adventures of Priscilla
Affliction
Age of Innocence
Air Force One
Aladdin
All About My Mother
American Beauty
American History X
American Pie
American President
Amistad
Analyze This
Anastasia
Anna and the King
Antonia's Line
Antz

Apollo 13
Armageddon
As Good As It Gets
Austin Powers
Awakenings
Babe
Backdraft
Barton Fink
Basic Instinct
Basquiat
Batman Returns
Beauty/Beast
Beethoven
Being John Malkovich
Big Lebowski
Big Night
Birdcage, The
Boogie Nights
Boys Don't Cry
Boys on the Side
Boyz N the Hood
Braveheart
Breaking the Waves
Bridges of Madison County
Buena Vista Social Club
Bug's Life
Bugsy
Bullets Over Broadway
Cape Fear
Casino
Casper
Celluloid Closet
Chasing Amy
Cider House Rules
City Slickers
Clear and Present Danger
Clerks
Client, The
Clueless
Con Air
Contact
Cool Runnings
Crimson Tide
Crying Game
Dances with Wolves
Dave
Dead Again
Dead Man Walking
Deconstructing Harry

Deep Impact
Donnie Brasco
Double Jeopardy
Dracula
Dr. Dolittle
Dumb and Dumber
Eat Drink Man Woman
Edward Scissorhands
Ed Wood
Election
Elizabeth
Emma
Enchanted April
End of the Affair
Enemy of the State
English Patient
Evita
Face/Off
Fantasia 2000
Farewell My Concubine
Fargo
Father of the Bride
Fear and Loathing in Las Vegas
Few Good Men, A
Fifth Element
Fight Club
Firm, The
First Wives Club
Fisher King
Fly Away Home
Forrest Gump
Four Weddings and a Funeral
Free Willy
Fried Green Tomatoes
Fugitive, The
Full Monty
George of the Jungle
Ghost
Girl, Interrupted
Glengarry Glen Ross
Godfather Part III
Gods and Monsters
GoldenEye
Goodfellas
Good Will Hunting
Grand Canyon
Green Mile
Grifters, The
Groundhog Day

| | |
|---|---|
| Grumpy Old Men | Madness of King George |
| Hamlet (1996) | Magnolia |
| Hand That Rocks the Cradle | Malcolm X |
| Happiness | Man on the Moon |
| Heat | Mask, The |
| Heavenly Creatures | Mask of Zorro |
| Henry & June | Matrix, The |
| Hercules | Maverick |
| Hilary and Jackie | Mediterraneo |
| Hoffa | Men in Black |
| Home Alone | Metropolitan |
| Hook | Mighty Aphrodite |
| Hoop Dreams | Miller's Crossing |
| Horse Whisperer | Misery |
| Howards End | Mission: Impossible |
| Hunchback/Notre Dame | Mr. Holland's Opus |
| Hunt for Red October | Mrs. Brown |
| Hurricane, The | Mrs. Doubtfire |
| Il Postino | Mulan |
| In & Out | Mummy, The |
| Independence Day | My Best Friend's Wedding |
| Indochine | My Cousin Vinny |
| Insider, The | My Girl |
| Interview with the Vampire | My Own Private Idaho |
| In the Company of Men | Nightmare Before Christmas |
| In the Line of Fire | Notting Hill |
| In the Name of the Father | Nutty Professor |
| Iron Giant | 101 Dalmatians |
| James and the Giant Peach | Outbreak |
| Jerry Maguire | Out of Sight |
| JFK | Patch Adams |
| Jumanji | Patriot Games |
| Jurassic Park | Pelican Brief |
| L.A. Confidential | People vs. Larry Flynt |
| La Femme Nikita | Phenomenon |
| Last of the Mohicans | Philadelphia |
| L.A. Story | Piano, The |
| Last Seduction | Player, The |
| League of Their Own | Pleasantville |
| Leaving Las Vegas | Pocahontas |
| Legends of the Fall | Postcards from the Edge |
| Liar Liar | Presumed Innocent |
| Life Is Beautiful | Pretty Woman |
| Like Water for Chocolate | Primal Fear |
| Lion King | Primary Colors |
| ittle Princess | Prince of Egypt |
| tle Women | Prince of Tides |
| k, Stock and Two . . . | Pulp Fiction |
| Star | Quiz Show |

...som
...ality Bites
...ed Violin
Remains of the Day
Reservoir Dogs
Reversal of Fortune
River Runs Through It
Robin Hood: Prince of Thieves
Rock, The
Romeo + Juliet
Run Lola Run
Rush Hour
Rushmore
Santa Clause
Saving Private Ryan
Scent of a Woman
Schindler's List
Scream
Secrets and Lies
Sense and Sensibility
Seven
Shakespeare in Love
Shawshank Redemption
Shine
Silence of the Lambs
Simple Plan
Single White Female
Sister Act
Six Degrees of Separation
Sixth Sense
Sleeping with the Enemy
Sleepless in Seattle
Sleepy Hollow
Sling Blade
South Park
Space Jam
Speed
Stargate
Starship Troopers
Star Wars I/Phantom Menace
Straight Story
Strictly Ballroom
Stuart Little
Sweet Hereafter
Swingers
Talented Mr. Ripley
Tarzan
Thelma & Louise
There's Something About Mary

Thin Red Line
Three Kings
Tie Me Up! Tie Me Down!
Time to Kill
Titanic
To Die For
Tombstone
Tomorrow Never Dies
Topsy-Turvy
Total Recall
Toy Story
Trainspotting
True Lies
Truman Show
Truth or Dare
Twelve Monkeys
Twister
Under Siege
Unforgiven
Usual Suspects
Wag the Dog
Waiting for Guffman
Wayne's World
Wedding Banquet
Wedding Singer
Welcome to the Dollhouse
What About Bob?
What Dreams May Come
What's Eating Gilbert Grape
What's Love Got to Do with It
While You Were Sleeping
World Is Not Enough
X-Files, The
You've Got Mail

## 2000s

About a Boy
About Schmidt
Adaptation
A.I.: Artificial Intelligence
Almost Famous
Along Came a Spider
Amélie
American Splendor
Antwone Fisher
Atlantis
Aviator, The
Bad Education
Bad Santa
Beautiful Mind

Before Night Falls
Before Sunset
Being Julia
Bend It Like Beckham
Best in Show
Big Fish
Billy Elliot
Black Hawk Down
Bourne Identity
Bourne Supremacy
Bowling for Columbine
Bridget Jones's Diary
Brother Bear
Calendar Girls
Cast Away
Catch Me If You Can
Chicago
Chicken Run
Chocolat
City of God
Coach Carter
Cold Mountain
Collateral
Contender, The
Cooler, The
Crash
Crouching Tiger
Dancer in the Dark
Die Another Day
Dinosaur
Dirty Pretty Things
8 Mile
Elf
Emperor's New Groove
Enron/Smartest Guys in Room
Erin Brockovich
Eternal Sunshine
Fahrenheit 9/11
Family Man
Far From Heaven
Finding Nemo
Finding Neverland
Fog of War
Frequency
Frida
Friday Night Lights
~ngs of New York
~den State
~t World

Girl with a Pearl Earring
Gladiator
Gosford Park
Hannibal
Harry Potter/Chamber of
   Secrets
Harry Potter/Sorcerer's Stone
Harry Potter/Prisoner of
   Azkaban
Hero
Hidalgo
Hitch
Holes
Hotel Rwanda
Hours, The
House of Flying Daggers
House of Sand and Fog
How the Grinch Stole Christmas
I Am Sam
Ice Age
Igby Goes Down
Importance of Being Earnest
In America
Incredibles, The
Interpreter, The
In the Bedroom
Iris
Italian Job
Kid Stays in the Picture
Kill Bill Vol. 1
Kill Bill Vol. 2
Kinsey
Kissing Jessica Stein
Kung Fu Hustle
Last Samurai
Legally Blonde
Life of David Gale
Lilo & Stitch
Lord of the Rings/Fellowship
Lord of the Rings/Two Towers
Lord of the Rings/Return
Lost in Translation
Love Actually
Madagascar
Magdalene Sisters
Man on Fire
Man Who Wasn't There
Maria Full of Grace
Master and Commander

...atrix Reloaded
...latrix Revolutions
Meet the Parents
Memento
Mighty Wind
Million Dollar Baby
Minority Report
Miracle
Miss Congeniality
Monsoon Wedding
Monster
Monster's Ball
Monsters, Inc.
Motorcycle Diaries
Moulin Rouge!
Mulholland Dr.
My Big Fat Greek Wedding
Mystic River
Notebook, The
Nurse Betty
O Brother, Where Art Thou?
Ocean's Eleven
Others, The
Passion of the Christ
Patriot, The
Perfect Storm
Peter Pan
Phantom of the Opera
Pianist, The
Pieces of April
Pirates of the Caribbean
Polar Express
Pollock
Princess Diaries
Quiet American
Rabbit-Proof Fence
Radio
Ray
Real Women Have Curves
Remember the Titans
Requiem for a Dream
Road to Perdition
Robots
Rookie, The
Royal Tenenbaums
Runaway Jury
Save the Last Dance
School of Rock
Seabiscuit

Secondhand Lions
Secretary
Shadow of the Vampire
Shattered Glass
Shaun of the Dead
Shipping News
Shrek
Shrek 2
Sideways
Signs
Sin City
Snatch
Something's Gotta Give
Spider-Man
Spider-Man 2
Spirit: Stallion of the Cimarron
Spirited Away
Spy Kids
Star Wars II/Attack of Clones
Star Wars III/Revenge of Sith
Station Agent
Super Size Me
Swimming Pool
Talk to Her
Thirteen
Traffic
Training Day
Triplets of Belleville
Troy
28 Days Later
25th Hour
21 Grams
U-571
Unbreakable
Under the Tuscan Sun
Unfaithful
Upside of Anger
Vera Drake
Very Long Engagement
Whale Rider
What Lies Beneath
What Women Want
Winged Migration
Wonder Boys
Woodsman, The
X-Men
X2: X-Men United
You Can Count on Me
Y Tu Mamá También

## GENRES/SPECIAL FEATURES

### Action/Adventure

Adventures of Robin Hood
Around the World in 80 Days
Backdraft
Batman
Batman Returns
Benji
Beverly Hills Cop
Black Stallion
Bourne Identity
Bourne Supremacy
Captain Blood
Captains Courageous
Cast Away
Catch Me If You Can
Con Air
Conan the Barbarian
Contact
Crimson Tide
Crocodile Dundee
Crouching Tiger
Deep, The
Deep Impact
Deliverance
Die Hard
Easy Rider
Enter the Dragon
Evil Dead
Face/Off
Fantastic Voyage
Fifth Element
First Blood: Rambo
Flight of the Phoenix
Fly Away Home
Gladiator
Gods Must Be Crazy
Goonies, The
Great Escape
Great Race
Greystoke
Hatari!
Hero
Hidalgo
House of Flying Daggers
Independence Day
Indiana Jones/Last Crusade
Indiana Jones/Temple of Doom

Journey to the Center
Jumanji
Jurassic Park
Kill Bill Vol. 1
Kill Bill Vol. 2
King Kong
King Solomon's Mines
Kung Fu Hustle
Last Samurai
Lawrence of Arabia
Legend
Lethal Weapon
Longest Yard
Lord of the Rings/Fellowship
Lord of the Rings/Two Towers
Lord of the Rings/Return
Mad Max
Magnificent Seven
Man Who Would Be King
Mark of Zorro
Mask of Zorro
Master and Commander
Matrix, The
Matrix Reloaded
Matrix Revolutions
Men in Black
Minority Report
Mission, The
Mummy, The (1999)
Mutiny on the Bounty (1935)
Mutiny on the Bounty (1962)
Papillon
Peter Pan
Pirates of the Caribbean
Planet of the Apes
Poseidon Adventure
Raiders of the Lost Ark
Rio Bravo
Road Warrior
Robin and Marian
Robin Hood: Prince of Thieves
RoboCop
Rocky
Romancing the Stone
Romeo + Juliet
Rush Hour
Seven Samurai

Voyage of Sinbad
Smokey and the Bandit
Spartacus
Spider-Man
Spider-Man 2
Spy Kids
Stargate
Starship Troopers
Star Trek II
Star Trek IV
Star Wars
Star Wars I/Phantom Menace
Star Wars II/Attack of Clones
Star Wars III/Revenge of Sith
Star Wars V/Empire Strikes
   Back
Star Wars VI/Return of Jedi
Superman
Swiss Family Robinson
Tarzan the Ape Man
Terminator, The
Thief of Bagdad
Three Kings
Three Musketeers
Time Machine
Top Gun
Topkapi
Total Recall
Treasure of the Sierra Madre
Tron
Troy
True Lies
Twister
Under Siege
Wages of Fear
War of the Worlds
Wind and the Lion
X-Men
X2: X-Men United
Yojimbo
Young Guns
Zulu

## Adults Only
American History X
Bad Education
Bad Seed
Basic Instinct
Belle de Jour
Blue Velvet

Body Heat
Boogie Nights
Dead Ringers
Grifters, The
Happiness
Henry & June
Hunger, The
Kill Bill Vol. 1
Kill Bill Vol. 2
Last Tango in Paris
Last Temptation of Christ
Lolita
Looking for Mr. Goodbar
Midnight Cowboy
Monster
Passion of the Christ
Pink Flamingos
Requiem for a Dream
Reservoir Dogs
Secretary
Woodsman, The

## Americana
Alamo, The
All the King's Men
American Graffiti
Amistad
Badlands
Best Years of Our Lives
Blue Velvet
Bull Durham
Cheaper By the Dozen
Christmas Story
Dances with Wolves
Days of Heaven
East of Eden
Far From Heaven
Forrest Gump
Friday Night Lights
Friendly Persuasion
Giant
Grapes of Wrath
Guys and Dolls
It's a Wonderful Life
Last Picture Show
League of Their Own
Meet Me in St. Louis
Mr. Smith Goes to Was'
Music Man
Nashville

Natural, The
O Brother, Where Art Thou?
Oklahoma!
Old Yeller
Picnic
Places in the Heart
Pleasantville
Radio Days
River Runs Through It
Seabiscuit
1776
Stand by Me
Straight Story
Summer of '42
To Kill a Mockingbird
Tucker
Yankee Doodle Dandy

## Animated

(* Not for children)
Akira*
Aladdin
Alice in Wonderland
All Dogs Go to Heaven
American Tail
Anastasia (1997)
Antz
Atlantis
Bambi
Beauty/Beast (1991)
Brother Bear
Bug's Life
Chicken Run
Cinderella
Dinosaur
Dumbo
Emperor's New Groove
Fantasia
Fantasia 2000
Finding Nemo
Fox and the Hound
Heavy Metal*
Hercules
Hunchback/Notre Dame
Ice Age
Incredibles, The
Iron Giant
James and the Giant Peach
Jungle Book (1967)
Lady and the Tramp

Lilo & Stitch
Lion King
Little Mermaid
Lord of the Rings
Madagascar
Monsters, Inc.
Mulan
Nightmare Before Christmas
101 Dalmatians (1961)
Peter Pan
Pete's Dragon
Pinocchio
Pocahontas
Polar Express
Prince of Egypt
Rescuers, The
Robots
Secret of NIMH
Shrek
Shrek 2
Sleeping Beauty
Snow White
Song of the South
South Park*
Space Jam
Spirit: Stallion of the Cimarron
Spirited Away
Tarzan
Toy Story
Triplets of Belleville*
Who Framed Roger Rabbit
Yellow Submarine

## Biographies

Alexander Nevsky
Amadeus
American Splendor
Anastasia (1956)
Antwone Fisher
Aviator, The
Basquiat
Becket
Before Night Falls
Birdman of Alcatraz
Bonnie and Clyde
Born Free
Born on the Fourth of July
Boys Don't Cry
Bugsy

Cleopatra
Coal Miner's Daughter
Diary of Anne Frank
Ed Wood
Elephant Man
Elizabeth
Evita
Finding Neverland
Frances
Frida
Funny Girl
Funny Lady
Gandhi
Gods and Monsters
Gorillas in the Mist
Gypsy
Henry & June
Hoffa
Hurricane, The
Iris
Julia
Kid Stays in the Picture
Kinsey
Lady Sings the Blues
Last Emperor
Lawrence of Arabia
Madness of King George
Malcolm X
Man for All Seasons
Man on the Moon
Miracle Worker
Mommie Dearest
Motorcycle Diaries
Mrs. Brown
Napoléon
Patch Adams
Patton
People vs. Larry Flynt
Pocahontas
Pollock
Pride of the Yankees
Raging Bull
Ray
Reds
Reversal of Fortune
Sergeant York
Sid & Nancy
Tucker
What's Love Got to Do with It

Yankee Doodle Dandy
Young Guns

## Black Comedies
After Hours
Arsenic and Old Lace
Bad Santa
Beetlejuice
Being John Malkovich
Being There
Brazil
Clerks
Discreet Charm
Dr. Strangelove
Eating Raoul
Ed Wood
Election
Fear and Loathing in Las Vegas
Fortune Cookie
Groundhog Day
Happiness
Harold and Maude
Heathers
Kind Hearts and Coronets
Life of Brian
Lolita
MASH
Monty Python/Holy Grail
Nurse Betty
Pink Flamingos
Prizzi's Honor
Producers, The
Royal Tenenbaums
Russians Are Coming...
Ruthless People
Secretary
Time Bandits
To Die For
Wag the Dog
War of the Roses
Welcome to the Dollhouse
What About Bob?

## Box-Office Bonanzas
(Annual highest grossing
movies with year of releas)
Aladdin (1992)
Armageddon (1998)
Back to the Future (198)
Bambi (1942)

## Genres/Special Features

Batman (1989)
Ben-Hur (1959)
Best Years of Our Lives (1946)
Birth of a Nation (1915)
Blazing Saddles (1974)
Bridge on the River Kwai (1957)
Butch Cassidy/Sundance Kid (1969)
Cleopatra (1963)
E.T. The Extra-Terrestrial (1982)
Exorcist, The (1973)
Forrest Gump (1994)
French Connection (1971)
Funny Girl (1968)
Ghostbusters (1984)
Godfather (1972)
Going My Way (1944)
Gone with the Wind (1939)
Graduate, The (1967)
Grease (1978)
Harry Potter/Sorcerer's Stone (2001)
Home Alone (1990)
Honey, I Shrunk the Kids (1989)
How the Grinch Stole Christmas (2000)
Independence Day (1996)
Jaws (1975)
Jurassic Park (1993)
King Kong (1933)
King Solomon's Mines (1950)
Kramer vs. Kramer (1979)
Lawrence of Arabia (1962)
Lord of the Rings/Return (2003)
Love Story (1970)
Mary Poppins (1964)
Mister Roberts (1955)
Night at the Opera (1935)
Raiders of the Lost Ark (1981)
Rain Man (1988)
Red River (1948)
Robe, The (1953)
Robin Hood: Prince of Thieves (1991)
cky (1976)
ng Private Ryan (1998)
ant York (1941)
 (2004)
hite (1937)

Sound of Music (1965)
South Pacific (1958)
Spartacus (1960)
Spider-Man (2002)
Star Wars (1977)
Star Wars I/Phantom Menace (1999)
Star Wars III/Revenge of Sith (2005)
Star Wars V/Empire Strikes Back (1980)
Star Wars VI/Return of Jedi (1983)
Ten Commandments (1956)
Thin Man (1934)
Three Men and a Baby (1987)
Titanic (1997)
Top Gun (1986)
Toy Story (1995)
Twister (1996)
Under Siege (1992)
West Side Story (1961)
White Christmas (1954)

### Buddy Films
About a Boy
Blues Brothers
Breaking Away
Butch Cassidy/Sundance Kid
City Slickers
Easy Rider
48 HRS.
Ghost World
Gunga Din
Lethal Weapon
Man Who Would Be King
Mean Streets
Men in Black
Midnight Cowboy
Motorcycle Diaries
Odd Couple
Outrageous Fortune
Rush Hour
Stir Crazy
Swingers
Thelma & Louise

### Camp Classics
Adventures of Priscilla
Auntie Mame

...dcage, The
...ride of Frankenstein
Conan the Barbarian
Eating Raoul
Evil Dead
Fly, The (1958)
Gentlemen Prefer Blondes
Godzilla
Grease
Hairspray
How to Marry a Millionaire
Imitation of Life
La Cage aux Folles
Little Shop of Horrors
Mildred Pierce
Mommie Dearest
9½ Weeks
Pee-wee's Big Adventure
Pillow Talk
Pink Flamingos
Poseidon Adventure
Rocky Horror Picture Show
Texas Chainsaw Massacre
Whatever Happened to ...
Women, The
Women on the Verge

## Capers

Asphalt Jungle
Catch Me If You Can
Fish Called Wanda
Italian Job
Lavender Hill Mob
Lock, Stock and Two ...
Ocean's Eleven (1960)
Ocean's Eleven
Out of Sight
Pink Panther
Reservoir Dogs
Ruthless People
Silver Streak
Snatch
Sting, The
Thomas Crown Affair
Topkapi

## Chick Flicks

(See also Romance)
Affair to Remember
Amélie

Baby Boom
Boys on the Side
Breakfast at Tiffany's
Bridges of Madison County
Bridget Jones's Diary
Calendar Girls
Clueless
Desperately Seeking Susan
Dirty Dancing
Enchanted April
English Patient
Father of the Bride (1991)
First Wives Club
Four Weddings and a Funeral
Fried Green Tomatoes
Funny Face
Ghost
Kissing Jessica Stein
Legally Blonde
Little Women
Love Is a Many-Splendored
Love Story
Miss Congeniality
My Best Friend's Wedding
Mystic Pizza
Notting Hill
Now, Voyager
Officer and a Gentleman
Out of Africa
Outrageous Fortune
Pretty Woman
Pride and Prejudice
Private Benjamin
Real Women Have Curves
Roman Holiday
Sense and Sensibility
Shakespeare in Love
Sleepless in Seattle
Something's Gotta Give
Splendor in the Grass
Steel Magnolias
Terms of Endearment
Thelma & Louise
Under the Tuscan Sun
Unmarried Woman
Way We Were
What Women Want
When Harry Met Sally .
Women, The

Working Girl
You've Got Mail

## Children/Family
(See also Animated)
Annie
Bad News Bears
Beethoven
Big
Black Stallion
Born Free
Casper
Christmas Carol
Christmas Story
Cool Runnings
Dark Crystal
David Copperfield
Dr. Dolittle
Elf
E.T. The Extra-Terrestrial
Father of the Bride (1950)
Father of the Bride (1991)
Fly Away Home
Freaky Friday
Free Willy
George of the Jungle
Goonies, The
Great Race
Harry Potter/Chamber of
    Secrets
Harry Potter/Sorcerer's Stone
Harry Potter/Prisoner of
    Azkaban
Hidalgo
Holes
Honey, I Shrunk the Kids
Hook
How the Grinch Stole Christmas
It's a Wonderful Life
Journey to the Center
Jungle Book (1942)
Lili
Little Princess
Love Bug
Mary Poppins
Mrs. Doubtfire
National Velvet
Heller

101 Dalmatians (1996)
Parent Trap
Pee-wee's Big Adventure
Peter Pan
Princess Bride
Princess Diaries
Remember the Titans
Rookie, The
Santa Clause
Sound of Music
Spy Kids
Stuart Little
Swiss Family Robinson
Three Men and a Baby
Tron
20,000 Leagues Under the Sea
Whale Rider
Willow
Willy Wonka/Chocolate Factory
Wizard of Oz

## City Settings
**LA Stories**
Adaptation
Barfly
Barton Fink
Beverly Hills Cop
Big Sleep
Boyz N the Hood
Chinatown
Clueless
Crash
D.O.A.
Down and Out in Beverly Hills
Ed Wood
Gods and Monsters
Grand Canyon
L.A. Confidential
L.A. Story
Mulholland Dr.
Player, The
Postcards from the Edge
Pretty Woman
Princess Diaries
Reservoir Dogs
Shampoo
Singin' in the Rain
Sunset Boulevard
Swingers

**Vegas Stories**
gsy
Casino
Cooler, The
Diamonds Are Forever
Fear and Loathing in Las Vegas
Leaving Las Vegas
Ocean's Eleven (1960)
Ocean's Eleven

**London Stories**
About a Boy
Alfie
American Werewolf in London
Austin Powers
Bedazzled
Blowup
Bridget Jones's Diary
Elephant Man
End of the Affair
Fish Called Wanda
Gaslight
Lock, Stock and Two . . .
Love Actually
Man Who Knew Too Much
Mary Poppins
My Fair Lady
Notting Hill
Oliver!
101 Dalmatians (1996)
Patriot Games
Secrets and Lies
Snatch
28 Days Later

**New York Stories**
Affair to Remember
After Hours
Age of Innocence
All About Eve
All That Jazz
Angels with Dirty Faces
Annie Hall
Apartment, The
Arthur
Basquiat
Bells Are Ringing
Big
Breakfast at Tiffany's
Broadway Danny Rose
Bullets Over Broadway

Crimes and Misdemeanors
Crocodile Dundee
Death Wish
Desperately Seeking Susan
Dog Day Afternoon
Donnie Brasco
Do the Right Thing
Dressed to Kill
Elf
Escape from New York
Fame
Fisher King
42nd Street
French Connection
Gangs of New York
Ghostbusters
Godfather
Godfather Part II
Guys and Dolls
Hair
Hannah and Her Sisters
Hitch
Hustler, The
Igby Goes Down
Interpreter, The
King Kong
King of Comedy
Kissing Jessica Stein
Klute
Madagascar
Manhattan
Marathon Man
Marty
Mean Streets
Midnight Cowboy
Mighty Aphrodite
Miracle on 34th Street
Moonstruck
My Favorite Year
Network
New York, New York
Odd Couple
Once Upon a Time in America
On the Town
On the Waterfront
Out-of-Towners
Pawnbroker, The
Pieces of April
Pollock

Prizzi's Honor
Quiz Show
Radio Days
Ransom
Rear Window
Rosemary's Baby
Saturday Night Fever
Serpico
Six Degrees of Separation
Spider-Man
Sunshine Boys
Sweet Smell of Success
Taxi Driver
Tootsie
25th Hour
Unfaithful
Unmarried Woman
Wall Street
West Side Story
When Harry Met Sally . . .
Working Girl
You've Got Mail

**Paris Stories**
Amélie
American in Paris
Before Sunset
Belle de Jour
Bourne Identity
Breathless
Charade
Children of Paradise
Discreet Charm
Diva
400 Blows
Funny Face
Gigi
Henry & June
Hunchback/Notre Dame
Irma La Douce
Last Tango in Paris
Love in the Afternoon
Moulin Rouge (1952)
Moulin Rouge! (2001)
Victor/Victoria

**ome Stories**
n-Hur
cle Thief
atra
Thing Happened...

Gladiator
La Dolce Vita
Open City
Roman Holiday
Spartacus
Talented Mr. Ripley
Three Coins in the Fountain

**San Francisco Stories**
Basic Instinct
Birdman of Alcatraz
Birds, The
Bullitt
Conversation, The
Dead Man Walking
Dirty Harry
48 HRS.
Foul Play
Invasion/Body Snatchers (1978)
Jagged Edge
Love Bug
Rock, The
Time After Time
Towering Inferno
Vertigo
What's Up, Doc?

## Comedies
(See also Black Comedies,
Dramedies, Screwball
Comedies)
Absent-Minded Professor
Ace Ventura
Adam's Rib
Addams Family
Adventures of Priscilla
Airplane!
Amarcord
American Pie
American Werewolf in London
Analyze This
Animal House
Annie Hall
Apprenticeship/Duddy Kravitz
Arthur
Auntie Mame
Austin Powers
Babe
Baby Boom
Bad News Bears
Bananas

dazzled
Beethoven
Bell, Book and Candle
Best in Show
Beverly Hills Cop
Big
Big Lebowski
Bill & Ted's
Birdcage, The
Bishop's Wife
Blazing Saddles
Breakfast Club
Bridget Jones's Diary
Broadway Danny Rose
Bullets Over Broadway
Cactus Flower
Caddyshack
Cat Ballou
Chasing Amy
Cheaper By the Dozen
City Slickers
Clueless
Coming to America
Cool Runnings
Crocodile Dundee
Dave
Deconstructing Harry
Desperately Seeking Susan
Down and Out in Beverly Hills
Dr. Dolittle
Dumb and Dumber
Eat Drink Man Woman
Elf
Emma
Family Man
Fast Times at Ridgemont High
Father of the Bride (1950)
Father of the Bride (1991)
Ferris Bueller's Day Off
First Wives Club
Fish Called Wanda
Fletch
Foul Play
Four Weddings and a Funeral
Freaky Friday
Full Monty
General, The
George of the Jungle
Ghostbusters

Gods Must Be Crazy
Gold Rush
Goodbye, Columbus
Goodbye Girl
Graduate, The
Great Dictator
Great Race
Gremlins
Grumpy Old Men
Hairspray
Harvey
Hatari!
High Anxiety
Hitch
Home Alone
Honey, I Shrunk the Kids
How to Marry a Millionaire
Importance of Being Earnest
In & Out
Innerspace
It's a Mad Mad Mad World
Jerk, The
Jungle Book (1967)
Kissing Jessica Stein
Kung Fu Hustle
La Cage aux Folles
L.A. Story
Lavender Hill Mob
Legally Blonde
Liar Liar
Little Big Man
Local Hero
Lost in America
Love Actually
Love Bug
Manhattan
Man Who Came to Dinner
Married to the Mob
Mask, The
Maverick
Meatballs
Mediterraneo
Meet the Parents
Mighty Aphrodite
Mighty Wind
Miss Congeniality
Mister Roberts
Modern Times
Monkey Business

**vote at zagat.com**

Mon Oncle
Mouse That Roared
Mr. Blandings
Mr. Hulot's Holiday
Mr. Mom
Mrs. Doubtfire
Muppet Movie
Murder by Death
My Best Friend's Wedding
My Big Fat Greek Wedding
My Cousin Vinny
My Favorite Year
Naked Gun
National Lampoon's Vacation
9 to 5
No Time for Sergeants
Notting Hill
Nutty Professor (1963)
Nutty Professor (1996)
O Brother, Where Art Thou?
Odd Couple
Oh, God!
One, Two, Three
Operation Petticoat
Out-of-Towners
Outrageous Fortune
Parent Trap
Pee-wee's Big Adventure
Peggy Sue Got Married
Pillow Talk
Pink Panther
Play It Again, Sam
Postcards from the Edge
Pretty in Pink
Pretty Woman
Princess Diaries
Private Benjamin
Purple Rose of Cairo
Radio Days
Repo Man
Risky Business
Roxanne
Rush Hour
Santa Clause
School of Rock
Seven Year Itch
Shampoo
Shaun of the Dead
My Bloody Valentine

Shot in the Dark
Silver Streak
Sister Act
Sixteen Candles
Slap Shot
Sleeper
Sleepless in Seattle
Smokey and the Bandit
Some Like It Hot
Something's Gotta Give
South Park
Spaceballs
Stir Crazy
Strictly Ballroom
Stripes
Sunshine Boys
Swingers
Take the Money and Run
10
There's Something About Mary
This Is Spinal Tap
Three Men and a Baby
Tie Me Up! Tie Me Down!
Tom Jones
Tootsie
Topkapi
Topper
Trading Places
Two for the Road
Uncle Buck
Unmarried Woman
Waiting for Guffman
Wayne's World
Wedding Banquet
Wedding Singer
What Women Want
When Harry Met Sally . . .
While You Were Sleeping
Witches of Eastwick
Woman of the Year
Working Girl
Young Frankenstein
You've Got Mail
Zelig

**Comic Book Adaptations**
Addams Family
Akira
American Splendor

Annie
Batman
Batman Returns
Casper
Ghost World
Heavy Metal
Men in Black
Road to Perdition
Sin City
Spider-Man
Spider-Man 2
Superman
X-Men
X2: X-Men United

## Crime
(See also Film Noir)
Anatomy of a Murder
Angels with Dirty Faces
Arsenic and Old Lace
Badlands
Big Lebowski
Bonnie and Clyde
Boyz N the Hood
Bugsy
Casino
Chicago
City of God
Clockwork Orange
Death on the Nile
Diabolique
Dial M for Murder
Dirty Harry
Dirty Pretty Things
Dog Day Afternoon
Donnie Brasco
Fargo
Fletch
48 HRS.
French Connection
Gangs of New York
Godfather
Godfather Part II
Godfather Part III
Goodfellas
Heat
Heavenly Creatures
Hoffa
In Cold Blood
In the Heat of the Night

Italian Job
Lavender Hill Mob
Lethal Weapon
Lock, Stock and Two . . .
M
Married to the Mob
Mean Streets
Miller's Crossing
Monster
Mystic River
Nurse Betty
Ocean's Eleven (1960)
Ocean's Eleven
Once Upon a Time in America
On the Waterfront
Out of Sight
Prizzi's Honor
Public Enemy
Pulp Fiction
Rear Window
Reservoir Dogs
Road to Perdition
Scarface
Serpico
Snatch
Sting, The
To Catch a Thief
Traffic
Training Day
25th Hour
Untouchables, The
Usual Suspects

## Cross-Dressing
Adventures of Priscilla
All About My Mother
Bad Education
Birdcage, The
Boys Don't Cry
Celluloid Closet
Crying Game
Ed Wood
Farewell My Concubine
Hairspray
Kind Hearts and Coronets
La Cage aux Folles
Life of Brian
Monty Python/Holy Grail
Mouse That Roared
Mrs. Doubtfire

Pink Flamingos
Psycho
Rocky Horror Picture Show
Some Like It Hot
Tootsie
Victor/Victoria
World According to Garp
Yentl

**Cult Films**
Adventures of Priscilla
After Hours
Akira
All About Eve
American Splendor
Barfly
Being John Malkovich
Big Lebowski
Bill & Ted's
Blade Runner
Blue Velvet
Brazil
Casablanca
Children of Paradise
Clerks
Clockwork Orange
Crying Game
Dr. Strangelove
Eating Raoul
8½
Enter the Dragon
Eraserhead
Eternal Sunshine
Evil Dead
Fantasia
Fear and Loathing in Las Vegas
Ferris Bueller's Day Off
Fight Club
5,000 Fingers of Dr. T.
Forbidden Planet
Friday the 13th
Gods Must Be Crazy
Grease
Harold and Maude
Heathers
Heavy Metal
a Wonderful Life
Bill Vol. 1
Il Vol. 2
Brian

Little Shop of Horrors
Mad Max
Manchurian Candidate
Monty Python/Holy Grail
Mulholland Dr.
My Dinner with Andre
Night of the Living Dead
Pee-wee's Big Adventure
Pink Flamingos
Princess Bride
Raising Arizona
Red Shoes
Repo Man
Repulsion
Road Warrior
Rocky Horror Picture Show
Royal Tenenbaums
Rushmore
7th Voyage of Sinbad
Shawshank Redemption
Sin City
Sound of Music
Star Wars
Texas Chainsaw Massacre
Time Bandits
28 Days Later
Village of the Damned
Waiting for Guffman
Welcome to the Dollhouse
Willy Wonka/Chocolate Factory
Wizard of Oz

**Date Movies**
Amélie
Annie Hall
Before Sunset
Big Chill
Bull Durham
Casablanca
Chocolat
Dirty Dancing
Eternal Sunshine
Fabulous Baker Boys
Four Weddings and a Funeral
Ghost
Jerry Maguire
Love Actually
Love Story
Man and a Woman, A
Mediterraneo

Moonstruck
My Big Fat Greek Wedding
Notting Hill
Officer and a Gentleman
Pretty Woman
Prince of Tides
Romancing the Stone
Roman Holiday
Romeo and Juliet
Saturday Night Fever
Shakespeare in Love
Sideways
Sleepless in Seattle
Something's Gotta Give
Starman
Strictly Ballroom
Summer of '42
Titanic
Way We Were
Wedding Singer
What Women Want
When Harry Met Sally . . .
You've Got Mail

## Disaster Flicks
(See also End of the World)
Airplane!
Airport
Backdraft
China Syndrome
Perfect Storm
Poseidon Adventure
Titanic
Towering Inferno
Twister

## Documentaries
Bowling for Columbine
Buena Vista Social Club
Celluloid Closet
Don't Look Back
Enron/Smartest Guys in Room
Fahrenheit 9/11
Fog of War
Gimme Shelter
Hoop Dreams
Kid Stays in the Picture
Last Waltz
Roger & Me
Shoah

Stop Making Sense
Super Size Me
That's Entertainment!
Triumph of the Will
Truth or Dare
Winged Migration
Woodstock

## Dramas
(See also Crime, Dramedies, Film Noir)
Absence of Malice
Accidental Tourist
Affliction
Age of Innocence
Agnes of God
Alfie
Alice Doesn't Live Here
All That Jazz
All the King's Men
All the President's Men
American History X
Amistad
Antonia's Line
Atlantic City
Au Revoir Les Enfants
Aviator, The
Awakenings
Babette's Feast
Bad Education
Bang the Drum Slowly
Barfly
Barry Lyndon
Beautiful Mind
Belle de Jour
Best Years of Our Lives
Bicycle Thief
Billy Elliot
Blackboard Jungle
Black Orpheus
Blowup
Blue Angel
Blue Velvet
Boogie Nights
Breaker Morant
Breaking Away
Breaking the Waves
Breathless
Caine Mutiny
Candidate, The

Carnal Knowledge
Cat on a Hot Tin Roof
Chariots of Fire
Charly
Children of a Lesser God
Cider House Rules
Cinderella Liberty
Cinema Paradiso
Citizen Kane
Coach Carter
Cold Mountain
Color of Money
Color Purple
Coming Home
Conformist, The
Contender, The
Conversation, The
Crash
Cries and Whispers
Crying Game
Dancer in the Dark
Dangerous Liaisons
David Copperfield
Day for Night
Days of Wine and Roses
Dead Man Walking
Dead Poets Society
Deer Hunter
Driving Miss Daisy
Drugstore Cowboy
East of Eden
Educating Rita
8½
8 Mile
Elmer Gantry
Enchanted April
End of the Affair
English Patient
Erin Brockovich
Fail-Safe
Fame
Fanny and Alexander
Far From Heaven
Few Good Men, A
Field of Dreams
Finding Neverland
Flashdance
Order of the Phoenix
House

Fountainhead, The
400 Blows
Free Willy
French Lieutenant's Woman
Friday Night Lights
Friendly Persuasion
From Here to Eternity
Garden of the Finzi-Continis
Gentleman's Agreement
Girl, Interrupted
Girl with a Pearl Earring
Glengarry Glen Ross
Goodbye, Mr. Chips
Grand Canyon
Grand Hotel
Grand Illusion
Grapes of Wrath
Great Santini
Greed
Green Mile
Greystoke
Hamlet (1948)
Hamlet (1996)
Henry V
High Noon
Hilary and Jackie
Hoosiers
Horse Whisperer
Hotel Rwanda
Hours, The
House of Games
House of Sand and Fog
Howards End
Hunchback/Notre Dame
Hustler, The
I Am Sam
Il Postino
Imitation of Life
In America
Inherit the Wind
Insider, The
In the Bedroom
In the Company of Men
In the Name of the Father
Jane Eyre
Jean de Florette
JFK
Judgment at Nuremberg
Kinsey

of the Spider Woman
amer vs. Kramer
a Dolce Vita
Last Picture Show
La Strada
Last Tango in Paris
Last Temptation of Christ
L'Avventura
Leaving Las Vegas
Lilies of the Field
Lion in Winter
Little Foxes
Little Women
Lone Star
Looking for Mr. Goodbar
Lord of the Flies
Lost Weekend
Love Is a Many-Splendored
Love Story
Magdalene Sisters
Magnificent Ambersons
Magnolia
Maria Full of Grace
Marty
Mask
McCabe & Mrs. Miller
Midnight Cowboy
Million Dollar Baby
Miracle
Miracle on 34th Street
Mission, The
Mississippi Burning
Monster's Ball
Motorcycle Diaries
Moulin Rouge (1952)
Mr. Holland's Opus
Mulholland Dr.
My Beautiful Laundrette
My Bodyguard
My Dinner with Andre
My Left Foot
My Life As a Dog
My Own Private Idaho
National Velvet
Natural, The
Never on Sunday
New York, New York
Nights of Cabiria
9½ Weeks

Norma Rae
Notebook, The
Now, Voyager
On Golden Pond
Open City
Ordinary People
Out of Africa
Outsiders, The
Ox-Bow Incident
Passion of the Christ
Paths of Glory
Pawnbroker, The
Persona
Phantom of the Opera
Phenomenon
Philadelphia
Pianist, The
Piano, The
Place in the Sun
Places in the Heart
Primal Fear
Prince of Tides
Quiet American
Quiet Man
Quiz Show
Rabbit-Proof Fence
Radio
Rain Man
Rashomon
Ray
Rebel Without a Cause
Red Shoes
Red Violin
Remains of the Day
Remember the Titans
Requiem for a Dream
Reversal of Fortune
Right Stuff
River Runs Through It
Robe, The
Rocky
Romeo and Juliet
Rookie, The
Room with a View
Rose, The
Runaway Jury
Sand Pebbles
Save the Last Dance
Scenes from a Marriage

Schindler's List
Seabiscuit
Secrets and Lies
Seven Days in May
Seventh Seal
Sex, Lies and Videotape
Shadow of the Vampire
Shattered Glass
Shawshank Redemption
Shine
Shipping News
Silkwood
Six Degrees of Separation
Sling Blade
Sophie's Choice
Splendor in the Grass
Stand and Deliver
Stand by Me
Star Is Born
Straight Story
Streetcar Named Desire
Suspect
Sweet Hereafter
Swimming Pool
Talented Mr. Ripley
Talk to Her
Taxi Driver
Thelma & Louise
They Shoot Horses, Don't They?
Thirteen
Three Faces of Eve
Time to Kill
Tin Drum
To Have and Have Not
To Kill a Mockingbird
Tommy
Topsy-Turvy
To Sir, With Love
12 Angry Men
21 Grams
2010
Two Women
Unbearable Lightness of Being
Unfaithful
Urban Cowboy
Vera Drake
Verdict, The
Very Long Engagement
Street

Whale Rider
Whatever Happened to ...
Who's Afraid of Virginia . . .
Wild Strawberries
Witness
Witness for the Prosecution
Woodsman, The
Wuthering Heights
Year of Living Dangerously
Yentl
Yojimbo
You Can Count on Me
Zorba the Greek

## Dramedies
(Part comedy, part drama)
About a Boy
About Schmidt
Adaptation
African Queen
All About Eve
All About My Mother
Almost Famous
American Beauty
American Graffiti
American Splendor
Apartment, The
As Good As It Gets
Barton Fink
Being Julia
Bend It Like Beckham
Big Chill
Big Fish
Big Night
Bob & Carol & Ted & Alice
Boys on the Side
Breakfast at Tiffany's
Broadcast News
Bull Durham
Bus Stop
Calendar Girls
Charade
City Lights
Cooler, The
Cool Hand Luke
Cousin, Cousine
Crimes and Misdemeanors
Diner
Dinner at Eight
Do the Right Thing

go
...ght Club
...isher King
Five Easy Pieces
Forrest Gump
Fried Green Tomatoes
Front Page
Garden State
Ghost World
Going My Way
Good Morning, Vietnam
Good Will Hunting
Gosford Park
Guess Who's Coming . . .
Hannah and Her Sisters
Heaven Can Wait
Igby Goes Down
Irma La Douce
It's a Wonderful Life
Jerry Maguire
Juliet of the Spirits
King of Comedy
Lady Vanishes
League of Their Own
Life Is Beautiful
Longest Yard
Lost in Translation
Love in the Afternoon
Madness of King George
Man Who Wasn't There
Metropolitan
Monsoon Wedding
Moonstruck
Mr. Smith Goes to Washington
My Girl
Mystic Pizza
Nashville
Network
Ninotchka
One Flew Over Cuckoo's Nest
Paper Chase
Paper Moon
Parenthood
Pieces of April
Player, The
Pleasantville
Pride and Prejudice
Primary Colors
Reality Bites

Real Women Have Curves
Rules of the Game
Rushmore
Sabrina
Same Time, Next Year
Scent of a Woman
Secondhand Lions
Sense and Sensibility
Seven Beauties
Shakespeare in Love
Sideways
Snatch
Stalag 17
Station Agent
Steel Magnolias
St. Elmo's Fire
Sting, The
Sullivan's Travels
Swept Away
Terms of Endearment
Three Musketeers
To Be or Not to Be
Trainspotting
Triplets of Belleville
Truman Show
Under the Tuscan Sun
Upside of Anger
What's Eating Gilbert Grape
Women, The
Wonder Boys
World According to Garp
Y Tu Mamá También

## DVD Not Available
African Queen
Apprenticeship/Duddy Kravitz
Au Revoir Les Enfants
Becket
Bedazzled
Captains Courageous
Cinderella Liberty
Conformist, The
Cousin, Cousine
David Copperfield
El Cid
Enchanted April
Fountainhead, The
Gay Divorcee
Greed
High Anxiety

Jane Eyre
Julia
King Kong
Kiss of the Spider Woman
Lady Sings the Blues
Lili
Looking for Mr. Goodbar
Magnificent Ambersons
Man Who Came to Dinner
Mediterraneo
Metropolitan
Mutiny on the Bounty (1962)
Napoléon
1900
No Time for Sergeants
Pride and Prejudice
Reds
Repulsion
Ryan's Daughter
Sergeant York
Shirley Valentine
Song of the South
Two for the Road
Unmarried Woman
Yentl

### End of the World
(See also Disaster Flicks)
A.I.: Artificial Intelligence
Andromeda Strain
Armageddon
Deep Impact
Dr. Strangelove
Escape from New York
Independence Day
Mad Max
Matrix, The
Matrix Reloaded
Matrix Revolutions
Planet of the Apes
Road Warrior
Terminator, The
28 Days Later
War of the Worlds

### Epics
Alexander Nevsky
Around the World in 80 Days
Ben-Hur
Birth of a Nation
Braveheart

Bridge on the River Kwai
Cleopatra
Dances with Wolves
Doctor Zhivago
El Cid
Empire of the Sun
Evita
Exodus
Gandhi
Giant
Gladiator
Gone with the Wind
Gunga Din
Hamlet (1996)
How the West Was Won
Intolerance
It's a Mad Mad Mad World
King Solomon's Mines
Last Emperor
Last Samurai
Lawrence of Arabia
Legends of the Fall
Longest Day
Master and Commander
Mutiny on the Bounty (1935)
Mutiny on the Bounty (1962)
Napoléon
1900
Once Upon a Time in America
Patriot, The
Ran
Reds
Robe, The
Ryan's Daughter
Sand Pebbles
Seven Samurai
Spartacus
Ten Commandments
Titanic
Tora! Tora! Tora!
Troy
Zulu

### Fantasy
Addams Family
Back to the Future
Batman
Batman Returns
Beauty/Beast (1947)
Beetlejuice
Being John Malkovich

Fish
l & Ted's
Brazil
Casper
Christmas Carol
Conan the Barbarian
Crouching Tiger
Dark Crystal
Edward Scissorhands
Eraserhead
Eternal Sunshine
Fantastic Voyage
Field of Dreams
Finian's Rainbow
Fisher King
5,000 Fingers of Dr. T.
Ghost
Ghost and Mrs. Muir
Gremlins
Harry Potter/Chamber of
   Secrets
Harry Potter/Sorcerer's Stone
Harry Potter/Prisoner of
   Azkaban
Harvey
Heaven Can Wait
Heavy Metal
Holes
Hook
How the Grinch Stole Christmas
Hunger, The
Indiana Jones/Last Crusade
Indiana Jones/Temple of Doom
Juliet of the Spirits
Jumanji
King Kong
Legend
Little Princess
Lord of the Rings
Lord of the Rings/Fellowship
Lord of the Rings/Two Towers
Lord of the Rings/Return
Lost Horizon
Mad Max
Man Who Fell to Earth
Mary Poppins
Mask, The
Miracle on 34th Street
Nightmare Before Christmas

Peggy Sue Got Married
Pete's Dragon
Phenomenon
Pirates of the Caribbean
Pleasantville
Polar Express
Princess Bride
Purple Rose of Cairo
Raiders of the Lost Ark
Repo Man
7th Voyage of Sinbad
Spider-Man
Spider-Man 2
Spirited Away
Splash
Stuart Little
Superman
Time Bandits
Topper
Truman Show
Unbreakable
What Dreams May Come
Willow
Willy Wonka/Chocolate Factory
Wings of Desire
Witches of Eastwick
Wizard of Oz

## Film Noir
Asphalt Jungle
Big Heat
Big Sleep
Blade Runner
Blood Simple
Body Heat
Cape Fear (1962)
Cape Fear (1991)
Chinatown
Dead Again
D.O.A.
Double Indemnity
Gilda
Grifters, The
High Sierra
Key Largo
Killers, The
L.A. Confidential
Lady from Shanghai
Last Seduction
Laura

Letter, The
Maltese Falcon
Man Who Wasn't There
Memento
Mildred Pierce
Night of the Hunter
Postman Always Rings Twice
Postman Always Rings Twice
  (1981)
Seven
Sin City
Strangers on a Train
Sunset Boulevard
Sweet Smell of Success
Third Man
Touch of Evil
White Heat
Who Framed Roger Rabbit

### Food-Themed
Babette's Feast
Big Night
Chocolat
Diner
Dinner at Eight
Discreet Charm
Eat Drink Man Woman
Fried Green Tomatoes
Like Water for Chocolate
My Big Fat Greek Wedding
Mystic Pizza
9½ Weeks
Super Size Me
Tom Jones
Wedding Banquet

### Foreign Films
#### Australian
Adventures of Priscilla
Babe
Breaker Morant
Crocodile Dundee
Gallipoli
Mad Max
Piano, The
Rabbit-Proof Fence
Road Warrior
?e
?ly Ballroom
? Living Dangerously

#### Brazilian
City of God
Motorcycle Diaries
#### British
About a Boy
Alfie
Barry Lyndon
Becket
Bedazzled
Bend It Like Beckham
Billy Elliot
Blowup
Born Free
Brazil
Bridge on the River Kwai
Bridget Jones's Diary
Brief Encounter
Calendar Girls
Chariots of Fire
Christmas Carol
Clockwork Orange
Crying Game
Death on the Nile
Diamonds Are Forever
Die Another Day
Dirty Pretty Things
Dr. No
Educating Rita
Elizabeth
Enchanted April
English Patient
Fahrenheit 451
For Your Eyes Only
Four Weddings and a Funeral
French Lieutenant's Woman
From Russia With Love
Full Monty
Gandhi
Girl with a Pearl Earring
GoldenEye
Goodbye, Mr. Chips
Greystoke
Hamlet (1948)
Hamlet (1996)
Hard Day's Night
Help!
Henry V
Hilary and Jackie
In America

ne Name of the Father
lling Fields
Kind Hearts and Coronets
Lady Vanishes
Lavender Hill Mob
Lawrence of Arabia
Legend
Life of Brian
Lion in Winter
Live and Let Die
Local Hero
Lock, Stock and Two . . .
Lord of the Flies
Love Actually
Madness of King George
Magdalene Sisters
Man for All Seasons
Man with the Golden Gun
Mission, The
Monty Python/Holy Grail
Moonraker
Mouse That Roared
Mrs. Brown
Murder on the Orient Express
My Beautiful Laundrette
My Left Foot
Notting Hill
Octopussy
Oliver!
On Her Majesty's Secret
   Service
Red Shoes
Remains of the Day
Repulsion
Robin and Marian
Rocky Horror Picture Show
Romeo and Juliet
Room with a View
Ryan's Daughter
Secrets and Lies
Sense and Sensibility
Shaun of the Dead
Snatch
Spy Who Loved Me
Third Man
39 Steps
Time Bandits
Tom Jones
Tommy

Tomorrow Never Dies
Topsy-Turvy
To Sir, With Love
Trainspotting
28 Days Later
Vera Drake
Village of the Damned
World Is Not Enough
Yellow Submarine
You Only Live Twice
Zulu

**Canadian**
Apprenticeship/Duddy Kravitz
Heavy Metal
Meatballs
Red Violin
Sweet Hereafter

**Chinese**
Crouching Tiger
Farewell My Concubine
Hero
House of Flying Daggers
Kung Fu Hustle

**Danish**
Babette's Feast
Breaking the Waves
Dancer in the Dark

**Dutch**
Antonia's Line

**French**
Amélie
Au Revoir Les Enfants
Beauty/Beast (1947)
Belle de Jour
Black Orpheus
Breathless
Children of Paradise
Cousin, Cousine
Day for Night
Diabolique
Discreet Charm
Diva
400 Blows
Grand Illusion
Indochine
Jean de Florette
Jules and Jim
La Cage aux Folles
La Femme Nikita

Man and a Woman, A
Mon Oncle
Mr. Hulot's Holiday
Napoléon
Pianist, The
Rules of the Game
Shoah
Swimming Pool
Triplets of Belleville
Umbrellas of Cherbourg
Very Long Engagement
Wages of Fear
Winged Migration
Z

**German**
Blue Angel
Cabinet of Dr. Caligari
Das Boot
M
Metropolis
Nosferatu
Run Lola Run
Tin Drum
Triumph of the Will
Wings of Desire

**Greek**
Never on Sunday
Zorba the Greek

**Indian**
Monsoon Wedding

**Italian**
Amarcord
Battle of Algiers
Bicycle Thief
Cinema Paradiso
Conformist, The
8½
Fistful of Dollars
Garden of the Finzi-Continis
Good, the Bad and the Ugly
Il Postino
Juliet of the Spirits
La Dolce Vita
La Strada
ast Tango in Paris
vventura
ls Beautiful
erraneo
of Cabiria

1900
Open City
Seven Beauties
Swept Away
Two Women

**Japanese**
Akira
Godzilla
Ran
Rashomon
Seven Samurai
Spirited Away
Yojimbo

**Mexican**
Like Water for Chocolate
Y Tu Mamá También

**New Zealand**
Whale Rider

**Russian**
Alexander Nevsky
Potemkin

**Spanish**
All About My Mother
Bad Education
Talk to Her
Tie Me Up! Tie Me Down!
Women on the Verge

**Swedish**
Cries and Whispers
Elvira Madigan
Fanny and Alexander
My Life As a Dog
Persona
Scenes from a Marriage
Seventh Seal
Wild Strawberries

**Taiwanese**
Eat Drink Man Woman
Wedding Banquet

## Guy Movies
(See also Sports, War)
Airplane!
Animal House
Beverly Hills Cop
Big Fish
Big Lebowski
Blazing Saddles
Blues Brothers

aker Morant
addyshack
Conan the Barbarian
Cool Hand Luke
Dances with Wolves
Diner
Dirty Harry
Dumb and Dumber
Escape from New York
Face/Off
Few Good Men, A
Fight Club
First Blood: Rambo
Fistful of Dollars
48 HRS.
French Connection
Gladiator
Goodfellas
High Plains Drifter
Hunt for Red October
Lock, Stock and Two . . .
Mad Max
Meatballs
Naked Gun
Outlaw Josey Wales
Papillon
Reservoir Dogs
Road Warrior
Rush Hour
Scarface
Serpico
Snatch
South Park
Stir Crazy
Stripes
Swingers
10
Terminator, The
Time Bandits
Top Gun
Total Recall
Under Siege
Wild Bunch
X-Men
Young Guns

## Holiday
**Christmas**
Bad Santa
Bishop's Wife
Christmas Carol
Christmas Story
Elf
Holiday Inn
How the Grinch Stole Christmas
It's a Wonderful Life
Miracle on 34th Street
Nightmare Before Christmas
Polar Express
Santa Clause
White Christmas

**Easter**
Easter Parade
Last Temptation of Christ
Passion of the Christ
Robe, The

**Independence Day**
Born on the Fourth of July
Patriot, The
1776
Yankee Doodle Dandy

## Horror
American Werewolf in London
Bride of Frankenstein
Cabinet of Dr. Caligari
Carrie
Cat People
Dracula (1931)
Dracula (1992)
Evil Dead
Exorcist, The
Fly, The (1958)
Fly, The (1986)
Frankenstein
Friday the 13th
Godzilla
Halloween
House of Wax
Hunger, The
Interview with the Vampire
Invasion/Body Snatchers (1956)
Invasion/Body Snatchers (1978)
Invisible Man
Mummy, The (1932)
Mummy, The (1999)
Nightmare on Elm Street
Night of the Living Dead
Nosferatu

Omen, The
Pit and the Pendulum
Poltergeist
Rosemary's Baby
Scream
Shadow of the Vampire
Shaun of the Dead
Shining, The
Sleepy Hollow
Texas Chainsaw Massacre
Thing, The (1951)
Thing, The (1982)
28 Days Later
Village of the Damned
Wolf Man
Young Frankenstein

### Independents
(See also Documentaries)
American Splendor
Barfly
Basquiat
Before Night Falls
Being John Malkovich
Being Julia
Benji
Blood Simple
Clerks
Cooler, The
Crash
Deconstructing Harry
Eating Raoul
Eraserhead
Evil Dead
Far From Heaven
Frida
Garden State
Girl with a Pearl Earring
Gods and Monsters
Gods Must Be Crazy
Happiness
Henry V
In the Company of Men
Kissing Jessica Stein
Lost in Translation
Metropolitan
Monster
Monster's Ball
Python/Holy Grail
Beautiful Laundrette

My Big Fat Greek Wedding
My Dinner with Andre
Night of the Living Dead
Passion of the Christ
Pieces of April
Pink Flamingos
Pollock
Real Women Have Curves
Requiem for a Dream
Reservoir Dogs
Room with a View
Secretary
Sex, Lies and Videotape
Shattered Glass
Sideways
Station Agent
Swingers
Texas Chainsaw Massacre
This Is Spinal Tap
21 Grams
Upside of Anger
Welcome to the Dollhouse
Whale Rider
Woodsman, The
You Can Count on Me

### James Bond
Diamonds Are Forever
Die Another Day
Dr. No
For Your Eyes Only
From Russia With Love
GoldenEye
Goldfinger
Live and Let Die
Man with the Golden Gun
Moonraker
Never Say Never Again
Octopussy
On Her Majesty's Secret
    Service
Spy Who Loved Me
Thunderball
Tomorrow Never Dies
World Is Not Enough
You Only Live Twice

### Literary Adaptations
About a Boy
About Schmidt

| | |
|---|---|
| cidental Tourist | Cold Mountain |
| Japtation | Collector, The |
| Adventures of Robin Hood | Color of Money |
| Affliction | Color Purple |
| Age of Innocence | Conan the Barbarian |
| A.I.: Artificial Intelligence | Contact |
| Airport | David Copperfield |
| Aladdin | Death on the Nile |
| Alice in Wonderland | Death Wish |
| All Quiet on the Western Front | Deep, The |
| All the King's Men | Deliverance |
| All the President's Men | Diamonds Are Forever |
| Along Came a Spider | Dirty Dozen |
| Altered States | Doctor Zhivago |
| Andromeda Strain | Dracula (1931) |
| Anna and the King | Dracula (1992) |
| Apprenticeship/Duddy Kravitz | Dr. Dolittle |
| Around the World in 80 Days | Dr. No |
| Babette's Feast | East of Eden |
| Barry Lyndon | Elmer Gantry |
| Beau Geste | Emma |
| Beautiful Mind | Empire of the Sun |
| Beauty/Beast (1947) | End of the Affair |
| Bedazzled | English Patient |
| Being There | Exodus |
| Ben-Hur | Exorcist, The |
| Big Fish | Fahrenheit 451 |
| Big Sleep | Fast Times at Ridgemont High |
| Black Stallion | Fear and Loathing in Las Vegas |
| Blade Runner | Firm, The |
| Bourne Identity | First Blood: Rambo |
| Bourne Supremacy | First Wives Club |
| Breakfast at Tiffany's | Fletch |
| Bridge on the River Kwai | Forbidden Planet |
| Bridges of Madison County | Forrest Gump |
| Bridget Jones's Diary | For Whom the Bell Tolls |
| Caine Mutiny | Fountainhead, The |
| Captain Blood | Frances |
| Captains Courageous | Frankenstein |
| Carrie | French Lieutenant's Woman |
| Catch Me If You Can | Fried Green Tomatoes |
| Christmas Carol | Friendly Persuasion |
| Christmas Story | From Here to Eternity |
| Cider House Rules | From Russia With Love |
| City of God | Gentleman's Agreement |
| Clear and Present Danger | Giant |
| Client, The | Gigi |
| Clockwork Orange | Girl, Interrupted |
| Clueless | Godfather |

Goldfinger
Gone with the Wind
Goodbye, Columbus
Goodbye, Mr. Chips
Graduate, The
Grand Hotel
Grapes of Wrath
Great Santini
Greed
Green Mile
Greystoke
Grifters, The
Gunga Din
Guns of Navarone
Hamlet (1948)
Hamlet (1996)
Hannibal
Harry Potter/Chamber of
   Secrets
Harry Potter/Sorcerer's Stone
Harry Potter/Prisoner of
   Azkaban
Henry & June
Henry V
High Sierra
Holes
Hook
Horse Whisperer
Hound of the Baskervilles
Hours, The
House of Sand and Fog
Howards End
How the Grinch Stole Christmas
Hunchback/Notre Dame
Hunchback/Notre Dame
Hunt for Red October
Imitation of Life
Importance of Being Earnest
In Cold Blood
Interview with the Vampire
Invisible Man
Iris
James and the Giant Peach
Jane Eyre
Jaws
an de Florette
rney to the Center

Book (1942)

Jungle Book (1967)
Jurassic Park
Killers, The
King Solomon's Mines
Kiss of the Spider Woman
Lady Vanishes
Last of the Mohicans
Last Picture Show
Laura
Like Water for Chocolate
Lili
Little Big Man
Little Princess
Little Women
Live and Let Die
Lolita
Looking for Mr. Goodbar
Lord of the Flies
Lord of the Rings
Lord of the Rings/Fellowship
Lord of the Rings/Two Towers
Lord of the Rings/Return
Lost Horizon
Lost Weekend
Love in the Afternoon
Love Story
Maltese Falcon
Manchurian Candidate
Man Who Fell to Earth
Man Who Would Be King
Man with the Golden Gun
Marathon Man
Mary Poppins
Master and Commander
Mildred Pierce
Misery
Mommie Dearest
Moonraker
Motorcycle Diaries
Murder on the Orient Express
Mutiny on the Bounty (1935)
Mutiny on the Bounty (1962)
Mystic River
National Velvet
Never Say Never Again
Night of the Hunter
Nosferatu
Notebook, The
Octopussy

n, God!
Oliver!
One Flew Over Cuckoo's Nest
On Her Majesty's Secret
   Service
Ordinary People
Out of Africa
Out of Sight
Outsiders, The
Ox-Bow Incident
Paper Chase
Papillon
Passion of the Christ
Patch Adams
Patriot Games
Pelican Brief
Perfect Storm
Pianist, The
Pit and the Pendulum
Place in the Sun
Planet of the Apes
Polar Express
Postcards from the Edge
Postman Always Rings Twice
Postman Always Rings Twice
   (1981)
Presumed Innocent
Pride and Prejudice
Primary Colors
Prince of Tides
Princess Diaries
Prizzi's Honor
Quiet American
Rabbit-Proof Fence
Rebecca
Remains of the Day
Rescuers, The
Reversal of Fortune
Right Stuff
Robe, The
Romancing the Stone
Room with a View
Rosemary's Baby
Roxanne
Runaway Jury
Sense and Sensibility
Serpico
Seven Days in May
Shawshank Redemption

Shining, The
Shipping News
Sideways
Silence of the Lambs
Single White Female
Sleeping with the Enemy
Sleepy Hollow
Sophie's Choice
Spy Who Loved Me
Starship Troopers
Strangers on a Train
Sweet Hereafter
Swiss Family Robinson
Talented Mr. Ripley
Tarzan
Tarzan the Ape Man
Terms of Endearment
They Shoot Horses, Don't They?
Thin Man
Thin Red Line
Three Coins in the Fountain
Three Musketeers
Thunderball
Time Machine
Time to Kill
Tin Drum
To Have and Have Not
To Kill a Mockingbird
Tom Jones
Topper
Treasure of the Sierra Madre
Troy
25th Hour
20,000 Leagues Under the Sea
2010
Two Women
Unbearable Lightness of Being
Under the Tuscan Sun
Village of the Damned
War of the Roses
War of the Worlds
Whale Rider
What Dreams May Come
Willy Wonka/Chocolate Factory
Witches of Eastwick
Wizard of Oz
World According to Garp
Wuthering Heights
You Only Live Twice

**vote at zagat.com**

## Martial Arts

Crouching Tiger
Enter the Dragon
Hero
House of Flying Daggers
Karate Kid
Kill Bill Vol. 1
Kill Bill Vol. 2
Kung Fu Hustle
Last Samurai
Magnificent Seven
Matrix, The
Matrix Reloaded
Matrix Revolutions
Ran
Rush Hour
Seven Samurai
Yojimbo

## Movies About Movies

Adaptation
Aviator, The
Bad Education
Barton Fink
Cinema Paradiso
Day for Night
Ed Wood
8½
Frances
Kid Stays in the Picture
Mommie Dearest
Notting Hill
Player, The
Postcards from the Edge
Purple Rose of Cairo
Shadow of the Vampire
Singin' in the Rain
Star Is Born
Sullivan's Travels
Sunset Boulevard

## Musicals

All That Jazz
American in Paris
Annie
Band Wagon
ells Are Ringing
es Brothers
k Privates
ye Birdie

Cabaret
Camelot
Carousel
Chicago
Damn Yankees
Dancer in the Dark
Easter Parade
Evita
Fame
Fiddler on the Roof
Finian's Rainbow
42nd Street
Funny Face
Funny Girl
Funny Lady
Funny Thing Happened...
Gay Divorcee
Gentlemen Prefer Blondes
Gigi
Grease
Guys and Dolls
Gypsy
Hair
Hard Day's Night
Hello, Dolly!
Help!
High Society
Holiday Inn
Jesus Christ Superstar
King and I
Kiss Me Kate
Little Shop of Horrors
Mary Poppins
Meet Me in St. Louis
Moulin Rouge! (2001)
Music Man
My Fair Lady
New York, New York
Oklahoma!
Oliver!
On the Town
Paint Your Wagon
Phantom of the Opera
Rocky Horror Picture Show
Seven Brides/Seven Brothers
1776
Show Boat
Singin' in the Rain
Song of the South

und of Music
outh Pacific
Sweet Charity
That's Entertainment!
Thoroughly Modern Millie
Tommy
Top Hat
Topsy-Turvy
Umbrellas of Cherbourg
Unsinkable Molly Brown
Victor/Victoria
West Side Story
White Christmas
Wizard of Oz
Yankee Doodle Dandy
Yentl

## Occupations
### Doctors
Awakenings
Charly
Dark Victory
Dead Ringers
Dr. Dolittle
Elephant Man
Girl, Interrupted
Greed
Love Story
Marathon Man
MASH
Nurse Betty
One Flew Over Cuckoo's Nest
Outbreak
Patch Adams
Spellbound
Three Faces of Eve

### Journalists
Absence of Malice
All the President's Men
Almost Famous
Broadcast News
Chicago
China Syndrome
Citizen Kane
Fear and Loathing in Las Vegas
Fletch
Front Page
Gentleman's Agreement
Good Morning, Vietnam

Groundhog Day
His Girl Friday
Insider, The
It Happened One Night
Killing Fields
La Dolce Vita
Life of David Gale
Love Is a Many-Splendored
Mighty Aphrodite
Nashville
Network
Nothing Sacred
Pelican Brief
Philadelphia Story
Quiet American
Reds
Roger & Me
Roman Holiday
Shattered Glass
Shipping News
Superman
Sweet Smell of Success
Talk to Her
To Die For
Woman of the Year
Year of Living Dangerously

### Lawyers
Absence of Malice
Accused, The
Anatomy of a Murder
Body Heat
Breaker Morant
Caine Mutiny
Chicago
Client, The
Enemy of the State
Erin Brockovich
Few Good Men, A
Firm, The
Fortune Cookie
I Am Sam
Inherit the Wind
Jagged Edge
Judgment at Nuremberg
Kramer vs. Kramer
Legally Blonde
Liar Liar
Man for All Seasons
My Cousin Vinny

Paper Chase
Pelican Brief
Philadelphia
Presumed Innocent
Primal Fear
Reversal of Fortune
Runaway Jury
Secretary
Suspect
Time to Kill
To Kill a Mockingbird
12 Angry Men
Verdict, The
Witness for the Prosecution

**Politicians**
Air Force One
All the King's Men
All the President's Men
American President
Being There
Candidate, The
Contender, The
Dave
Evita
Fahrenheit 9/11
Gandhi
Great Dictator
JFK
Malcolm X
Manchurian Candidate
Mississippi Burning
Mrs. Brown
Mr. Smith Goes to Washington
Nashville
Pelican Brief
Primary Colors
Reds
Seven Days in May
1776
Taxi Driver
Wag the Dog
Z

**Prostitutes**
Belle de Jour
Cinderella Liberty
Dressed to Kill
Saving Raoul

Gantry

Farewell My Concubine
Irma La Douce
Klute
Leaving Las Vegas
McCabe & Mrs. Miller
Midnight Cowboy
Mighty Aphrodite
Monster
My Own Private Idaho
Never on Sunday
Nights of Cabiria
Pretty Woman
Risky Business
Sweet Charity
Taxi Driver
Trading Places

**Spies**
(See also James Bond)
Austin Powers
Bourne Identity
Bourne Supremacy
Clear and Present Danger
Conversation, The
Donnie Brasco
General, The
Hunt for Red October
In-Laws, The
La Femme Nikita
Man Who Knew Too Much
Mission: Impossible
Notorious
No Way Out
Outrageous Fortune
Patriot Games
Spy Kids
39 Steps
True Lies

**Teachers**
Anna and the King
Au Revoir Les Enfants
Beautiful Mind
Billy Elliot
Blackboard Jungle
Blue Angel
Charly
Children of a Lesser God
Coach Carter
Dead Poets Society
Diabolique

Educating Rita
Election
Fame
Goodbye, Mr. Chips
Harry Potter/Chamber of
  Secrets
Harry Potter/Sorcerer's Stone
Harry Potter/Prisoner of
  Azkaban
In & Out
Inherit the Wind
King and I
Looking for Mr. Goodbar
Miracle Worker
Mr. Holland's Opus
My Fair Lady
Nutty Professor (1963)
Nutty Professor (1996)
Oliver!
Paper Chase
Piano, The
Red Shoes
Rushmore
School of Rock
Stand and Deliver
To Sir, With Love
Wonder Boys

## Oscar Winners
### Best Picture
All About Eve (1950)
All Quiet on the Western Front
  (1930)
All the King's Men (1949)
Amadeus (1984)
American Beauty (1999)
American in Paris (1951)
Annie Hall (1977)
Apartment, The (1960)
Around the World in 80 Days
  (1956)
Beautiful Mind (2001)
Ben-Hur (1959)
Best Years of Our Lives (1946)
Braveheart (1995)
Bridge on the River Kwai (1957)
Casablanca (1943)
Chariots of Fire (1981)
Chicago (2002)

Dances with Wolves (1990)
Deer Hunter (1978)
Driving Miss Daisy (1989)
English Patient (1996)
Forrest Gump (1994)
French Connection (1971)
From Here to Eternity (1953)
Gandhi (1982)
Gentleman's Agreement (1947)
Gigi (1958)
Gladiator (2000)
Godfather (1972)
Godfather Part II (1974)
Going My Way (1944)
Gone with the Wind (1939)
Grand Hotel (1932)
Hamlet (1948)
In the Heat of the Night (1967)
It Happened One Night (1934)
Kramer vs. Kramer (1979)
Last Emperor (1987)
Lawrence of Arabia (1962)
Lord of the Rings/Return (2003)
Lost Weekend (1945)
Man for All Seasons (1966)
Marty (1955)
Midnight Cowboy (1969)
Million Dollar Baby (2004)
Mutiny on the Bounty (1935)
My Fair Lady (1964)
Oliver! (1968)
One Flew Over Cuckoo's Nest
  (1975)
On the Waterfront (1954)
Ordinary People (1980)
Out of Africa (1985)
Patton (1970)
Platoon (1986)
Rain Man (1988)
Rebecca (1940)
Rocky (1976)
Schindler's List (1993)
Shakespeare in Love (1998)
Silence of the Lambs (1991)
Sound of Music (1965)
Sting, The (1973)
Terms of Endearment (1983)
Titanic (1997)
Tom Jones (1963)

Unforgiven (1992)
West Side Story (1961)

**Best Actor**

F. Murray Abraham
  Amadeus
Roberto Benigni
  Life Is Beautiful
Humphrey Bogart
  African Queen
Ernest Borgnine
  Marty
Marlon Brando
  Godfather
  On the Waterfront
Adrien Brody
  Pianist, The
Yul Brynner
  King and I
Nicolas Cage
  Leaving Las Vegas
James Cagney
  Yankee Doodle Dandy
Gary Cooper
  High Noon
  Sergeant York
Broderick Crawford
  All the King's Men
Bing Crosby
  Going My Way
Russell Crowe
  Gladiator
Daniel Day-Lewis
  My Left Foot
Robert De Niro
  Raging Bull
Robert Donat
  Goodbye, Mr. Chips
Michael Douglas
  Wall Street
Richard Dreyfuss
  Goodbye Girl
Peter Finch
  Network
Henry Fonda
  On Golden Pond
Jamie Foxx
  Ray
  k Gable
  Happened One Night

Alec Guinness
  Bridge on the River Kwai
Gene Hackman
  French Connection
Tom Hanks
  Forrest Gump
  Philadelphia
Rex Harrison
  My Fair Lady
Charlton Heston
  Ben-Hur
Dustin Hoffman
  Kramer vs. Kramer
  Rain Man
William Holden
  Stalag 17
Anthony Hopkins
  Silence of the Lambs
William Hurt
  Kiss of the Spider Woman
Jeremy Irons
  Reversal of Fortune
Ben Kingsley
  Gandhi
Burt Lancaster
  Elmer Gantry
Fredric March
  Best Years of Our Lives
Lee Marvin
  Cat Ballou
Ray Milland
  Lost Weekend
Paul Newman
  Color of Money
Jack Nicholson
  As Good As It Gets
  One Flew Over Cuckoo's Nest
Laurence Olivier
  Hamlet (1948)
Al Pacino
  Scent of a Woman
Gregory Peck
  To Kill a Mockingbird
Sean Penn
  Mystic River
Sidney Poitier
  Lilies of the Field
Cliff Robertson
  Charly

Geoffrey Rush
  Shine
Paul Scofield
  Man for All Seasons
George C. Scott
  Patton
Kevin Spacey
  American Beauty
Rod Steiger
  In the Heat of the Night
James Stewart
  Philadelphia Story
Spencer Tracy
  Captains Courageous
Jon Voight
  Coming Home
Denzel Washington
  Training Day
John Wayne
  True Grit

**Best Actress**
Julie Andrews
  Mary Poppins
Anne Bancroft
  Miracle Worker
Kathy Bates
  Misery
Ingrid Bergman
  Anastasia (1956)
  Gaslight
Halle Berry
  Monster's Ball
Ellen Burstyn
  Alice Doesn't Live Here
Cher
  Moonstruck
Claudette Colbert
  It Happened One Night
Joan Crawford
  Mildred Pierce
Faye Dunaway
  Network
Sally Field
  Norma Rae
  Places in the Heart
Louise Fletcher
  One Flew Over Cuckoo's Nest
Jane Fonda
  Coming Home
  Klute

Jodie Foster
  Accused, The
  Silence of the Lambs
Audrey Hepburn
  Roman Holiday
Katharine Hepburn
  Guess Who's Coming . . .
  Lion in Winter
  On Golden Pond
Judy Holliday
  Born Yesterday
Holly Hunter
  Piano, The
Helen Hunt
  As Good As It Gets
Diane Keaton
  Annie Hall
Nicole Kidman
  Hours, The
Vivien Leigh
  Gone with the Wind
  Streetcar Named Desire
Sophia Loren
  Two Women
Shirley MacLaine
  Terms of Endearment
Marlee Matlin
  Children of a Lesser God
Frances McDormand
  Fargo
Liza Minnelli
  Cabaret
Gwyneth Paltrow
  Shakespeare in Love
Julia Roberts
  Erin Brockovich
Susan Sarandon
  Dead Man Walking
Sissy Spacek
  Coal Miner's Daughter
Meryl Streep
  Sophie's Choice
Barbra Streisand
  Funny Girl
Hilary Swank
  Boys Don't Cry
  Million Dollar Baby
Jessica Tandy
  Driving Miss Daisy

Elizabeth Taylor
   Who's Afraid of Virginia . . .
Charlize Theron
   Monster
Emma Thompson
   Howards End
Joanne Woodward
   Three Faces of Eve

**Best Director**
All About Eve
All Quiet on the Western Front
Amadeus
American Beauty
Annie Hall
Apartment, The
Awful Truth
Beautiful Mind
Ben-Hur
Best Years of Our Lives
Born on the Fourth of July
Braveheart
Bridge on the River Kwai
Cabaret
Casablanca
Dances with Wolves
Deer Hunter
English Patient
Forrest Gump
French Connection
From Here to Eternity
Gandhi
Gentleman's Agreement
Giant
Gigi
Godfather Part II
Going My Way
Gone with the Wind
Graduate, The
Grapes of Wrath
It Happened One Night
Kramer vs. Kramer
Last Emperor
Lawrence of Arabia
Lord of the Rings/Return
Lost Weekend
Man for All Seasons
rty
night Cowboy
Dollar Baby

My Fair Lady
Oliver!
One Flew Over Cuckoo's Nest
On the Waterfront
Ordinary People
Out of Africa
Patton
Pianist, The
Place in the Sun
Platoon
Quiet Man
Rain Man
Reds
Rocky
Saving Private Ryan
Schindler's List
Silence of the Lambs
Sound of Music
Sting, The
Terms of Endearment
Titanic
Tom Jones
Traffic
Treasure of the Sierra Madre
Unforgiven
West Side Story

**Best Screenplay**
All About Eve
Almost Famous
Amadeus
American Beauty
American in Paris
Annie Hall
Apartment, The
Around the World in 80 Days
Beautiful Mind
Becket
Best Years of Our Lives
Breaking Away
Bridge on the River Kwai
Butch Cassidy/Sundance Kid
Candidate, The
Casablanca
Chariots of Fire
Chinatown
Cider House Rules
Citizen Kane
Coming Home
Crying Game

Dances with Wolves
Dangerous Liaisons
Dead Poets Society
Doctor Zhivago
Dog Day Afternoon
Driving Miss Daisy
Elmer Gantry
Exorcist, The
Fargo
Forrest Gump
French Connection
From Here to Eternity
Gandhi
Ghost
Gigi
Godfather
Godfather Part II
Gods and Monsters
Going My Way
Gone with the Wind
Good Will Hunting
Gosford Park
Guess Who's Coming . . .
Hannah and Her Sisters
Howards End
How the West Was Won
In the Heat of the Night
It Happened One Night
Judgment at Nuremberg
Julia
Kramer vs. Kramer
L.A. Confidential
Last Emperor
Lavender Hill Mob
Lion in Winter
Lord of the Rings/Return
Lost in Translation
Lost Weekend
Man and a Woman, A
Man for All Seasons
Marty
MASH
Midnight Cowboy
Midnight Express
Miracle on 34th Street
Moonstruck
Mr. Mom
Network
One Flew Over Cuckoo's Nest

On Golden Pond
On the Waterfront
Ordinary People
Out of Africa
Patton
Philadelphia Story
Piano, The
Pillow Talk
Place in the Sun
Places in the Heart
Producers, The
Pulp Fiction
Rain Man
Roman Holiday
Room with a View
Schindler's List
Sense and Sensibility
Shakespeare in Love
Silence of the Lambs
Sling Blade
Splendor in the Grass
Sting, The
Sunset Boulevard
Talk to Her
Terms of Endearment
Thelma & Louise
To Kill a Mockingbird
Tom Jones
Traffic
Treasure of the Sierra Madre
Usual Suspects
Witness
Woman of the Year

**Best Foreign Language Film**
All About My Mother
Amarcord
Antonia's Line
Babette's Feast
Bicycle Thief
Black Orpheus
Cinema Paradiso
Crouching Tiger
Day for Night
Discreet Charm
8½
Fanny and Alexander
Garden of the Finzi-Continis
Indochine
La Strada

Life Is Beautiful
Man and a Woman, A
Mediterraneo
Mon Oncle
Nights of Cabiria
Tin Drum
Z

## Religion
Agnes of God
Bad Education
Ben-Hur
Elmer Gantry
Exorcist, The
Going My Way
Hunchback/Notre Dame
Intolerance
Jesus Christ Superstar
Last Temptation of Christ
Life of Brian
Magdalene Sisters
Oh, God!
Passion of the Christ
Prince of Egypt
Robe, The
Ten Commandments
Yentl

## Remakes
(Both versions reviewed herein)
Anastasia
Beauty/Beast
Birdcage, The
Cape Fear
Dracula
Father of the Bride
Fly, The
Front Page
Hamlet
High Society
His Girl Friday
Hook
Hunchback/Notre Dame
Invasion/Body Snatchers
Jungle Book
La Cage aux Folles
Moulin Rouge
Mummy, The
Mutiny on the Bounty

Nutty Professor
Ocean's Eleven
101 Dalmatians
Peter Pan
Philadelphia Story
Postman Always Rings Twice
Romeo and Juliet
Tarzan
Thing, The

## Rock 'n' Roll
Almost Famous
Bill & Ted's
Blues Brothers
Bye Bye Birdie
Don't Look Back
Fame
Footloose
Gimme Shelter
Grease
Hair
Hard Day's Night
Help!
Jesus Christ Superstar
Last Waltz
Rocky Horror Picture Show
Rose, The
Saturday Night Fever
School of Rock
Sid & Nancy
Stop Making Sense
This Is Spinal Tap
Tommy
Truth or Dare
Wayne's World
What's Love Got to Do with It
Woodstock
Yellow Submarine

## Romance
(See also Chick Flicks)
Accidental Tourist
Adventures of Robin Hood
African Queen
Almost Famous
American in Paris
American President
Anna and the King
Annie Hall
Apartment, The

Arthur
As Good As It Gets
Awful Truth
Barry Lyndon
Before Sunset
Bell, Book and Candle
Bishop's Wife
Breaking the Waves
Brief Encounter
Bringing Up Baby
Broadcast News
Broadway Danny Rose
Bull Durham
Bus Stop
Cactus Flower
Camelot
Carousel
Casablanca
Charade
Chasing Amy
Children of a Lesser God
Children of Paradise
Chocolat
Cinderella Liberty
Cold Mountain
Cooler, The
Cousin, Cousine
Dangerous Liaisons
Dark Victory
Days of Heaven
Doctor Zhivago
Dracula (1992)
Easter Parade
Elvira Madigan
Emma
End of the Affair
Eternal Sunshine
Fabulous Baker Boys
Family Man
Farewell My Concubine
Far From Heaven
Flashdance
For Whom the Bell Tolls
Fountainhead, The
French Lieutenant's Woman
From Here to Eternity
Garden State
Gay Divorcee
Ghost and Mrs. Muir

Gigi
Gone with the Wind
Goodbye, Columbus
Goodbye Girl
Graduate, The
Hannah and Her Sisters
Harold and Maude
Hello, Dolly!
Henry & June
His Girl Friday
Hitch
Holiday Inn
Horse Whisperer
House of Flying Daggers
How to Marry a Millionaire
Importance of Being Earnest
Indochine
It Happened One Night
Jane Eyre
Jerry Maguire
Jules and Jim
Kiss Me Kate
Lady and the Tramp
Lady Eve
L.A. Story
Last Tango in Paris
Laura
Like Water for Chocolate
Lili
Lost Horizon
Love Actually
Love in the Afternoon
Man and a Woman, A
Manhattan
Marty
Monster's Ball
Moonstruck
Moulin Rouge (1952)
Moulin Rouge! (2001)
Mrs. Brown
My Big Fat Greek Wedding
My Fair Lady
My Girl
9½ Weeks
Ninotchka
Notebook, The
Nothing Sacred
Notorious
Out of Sight

Philadelphia Story
Piano, The
Picnic
Pillow Talk
Place in the Sun
Play It Again, Sam
Pretty in Pink
Prince of Tides
Quiet Man
Reality Bites
Rebecca
Reds
Red Shoes
Remains of the Day
Robin and Marian
Romancing the Stone
Romeo and Juliet
Romeo + Juliet
Room with a View
Roxanne
Ryan's Daughter
Sabrina
Same Time, Next Year
Saturday Night Fever
Save the Last Dance
Shine
Sid & Nancy
South Pacific
Spellbound
Splash
Starman
St. Elmo's Fire
Strictly Ballroom
Summer of '42
Talk to Her
10
Thomas Crown Affair
Three Coins in the Fountain
Titanic
To Catch a Thief
To Have and Have Not
Tootsie
Top Hat
Topper
Two for the Road
Umbrellas of Cherbourg
Unbearable Lightness of Being
Upside of Anger
Urban Cowboy

Vertigo
Wedding Singer
West Side Story
What Dreams May Come
While You Were Sleeping
White Christmas
Witness
Wuthering Heights

## Sci-Fi

Abyss, The
A.I.: Artificial Intelligence
Akira
Alien
Aliens
Altered States
Andromeda Strain
Back to the Future
Blade Runner
Close Encounters
Cocoon
Contact
Day the Earth Stood Still
Deep Impact
Escape from New York
E.T. The Extra-Terrestrial
Fahrenheit 451
Fifth Element
Fly, The (1958)
Fly, The (1986)
Forbidden Planet
Frequency
Ghostbusters
Godzilla
Independence Day
Innerspace
Invasion/Body Snatchers (1956)
Invasion/Body Snatchers (1978)
Journey to the Center
Jurassic Park
Man Who Fell to Earth
Matrix, The
Matrix Reloaded
Matrix Revolutions
Men in Black
Metropolis
Minority Report
Nutty Professor (1996)
Planet of the Apes
Repo Man

RoboCop
Signs
Sleeper
Spaceballs
Stargate
Starman
Starship Troopers
Star Trek II
Star Trek IV
Star Wars
Star Wars I/Phantom Menace
Star Wars II/Attack of Clones
Star Wars III/Revenge of Sith
Star Wars V/Empire Strikes
   Back
Star Wars VI/Return of Jedi
Terminator, The
Thing, The (1951)
Thing, The (1982)
Time After Time
Time Machine
Total Recall
Tron
Twelve Monkeys
28 Days Later
20,000 Leagues Under the Sea
2001: A Space Odyssey
2010
Village of the Damned
War of the Worlds
Westworld
X-Files, The
X-Men
X2: X-Men United

## Screwball Comedies
Animal Crackers
Awful Truth
Born Yesterday
Bringing Up Baby
Cocoanuts, The
Day at the Races
Duck Soup
His Girl Friday
Horse Feathers
In-Laws, The
It Happened One Night
Lady Eve
My Man Godfrey
Night at the Opera

Nothing Sacred
Philadelphia Story
Raising Arizona
Thin Man
What's Up, Doc?
Women on the Verge

## Silent
Birth of a Nation
Cabinet of Dr. Caligari
City Lights
General, The
Gold Rush
Greed
Intolerance
Metropolis
Modern Times
Napoléon
Nosferatu
Potemkin
Thief of Bagdad

## Soundtracks
(See also Musical; * Best
Score Oscar winner)
Adventures of Robin Hood*
Aladdin*
Alexander Nevsky
Alfie
All That Jazz*
Almost Famous
Amadeus
Amarcord
American Beauty
American Graffiti
American in Paris*
Anatomy of a Murder
Around the World in 80 Days*
Barry Lyndon*
Basquiat
Beauty/Beast (1991)*
Bells Are Ringing
Ben-Hur*
Big Chill
Blackboard Jungle
Black Orpheus
Blue Velvet
Born Free*
Braveheart
Breakfast at Tiffany's*

Bridge on the River Kwai*
Brief Encounter
Buena Vista Social Club
Butch Cassidy/Sundance Kid*
Cabaret*
Camelot*
Cat Ballou
Cat People
Charade
Chariots of Fire*
Chinatown
Cinema Paradiso
Clockwork Orange
Cold Mountain
Crouching Tiger*
Damn Yankees
Dances with Wolves*
Days of Heaven
Days of Wine and Roses*
Desperately Seeking Susan
Diner
Dinosaur
Dirty Dancing
Diva
Doctor Zhivago*
Don't Look Back
Dracula (1931)
Dumbo*
Easter Parade*
Easy Rider
8½
8 Mile
El Cid
Elvira Madigan
Emma*
Empire of the Sun
English Patient*
E.T. The Extra-Terrestrial*
Exodus*
Fame*
Fantasia
Fantasia 2000
Far From Heaven
Fear and Loathing in Las Vegas
Fiddler on the Roof*
Fight Club
First Blood: Rambo
Flashdance
Footloose

Forbidden Planet
Forrest Gump
Frida*
Full Monty*
Funny Thing Happened...*
Garden State
Gigi*
Gimme Shelter
Gladiator
Godfather
Godfather Part II*
Goldfinger
Gone with the Wind
Good, the Bad and the Ugly
Graduate, The
Great Escape
Hard Day's Night
Harold and Maude
Harry Potter/Sorcerer's Stone
Hatari!
Heavy Metal
Hello, Dolly!*
High Noon*
Hunger, The
I Am Sam
Il Postino*
In Cold Blood
Irma La Douce*
Jaws*
Journey to the Center
Jungle Book (1967)
King and I*
Lady Sings the Blues
Last Emperor*
Last of the Mohicans
La Strada
Last Tango in Paris
Last Waltz
Lawrence of Arabia*
Life Is Beautiful*
Lili*
Lion in Winter*
Lion King*
Little Mermaid*
Local Hero
Lock, Stock and Two ...
Lord of the Rings/Fellowship*
Lord of the Rings/Two Towers
Lord of the Rings/Return*

Love Is a Many-Splendored*
Love Story*
Magnificent Seven
Magnolia
Man and a Woman, A
Man Who Knew Too Much
Mark of Zorro
Mary Poppins*
Mean Streets
Mediterraneo
Midnight Cowboy
Midnight Express*
Mighty Wind
Mission, The
Music Man*
My Fair Lady*
Nashville
Natural, The
Nightmare Before Christmas
Night of the Hunter
1900
North by Northwest
Now, Voyager*
O Brother, Where Art Thou?
Oklahoma!*
Oliver!*
Omen, The*
On the Town*
Out of Africa*
Phantom of the Opera
Piano, The
Pink Panther
Place in the Sun*
Pleasantville
Pocahontas
Pretty in Pink
Princess Bride
Psycho
Pulp Fiction
Raiders of the Lost Ark
Ray
Red Shoes*
Red Violin*
Repo Man
Repulsion
Rescuers, The
Right Stuff*
Rocky
Romeo and Juliet

Room with a View
Rose, The
Run Lola Run
Rushmore
Saturday Night Fever
Schindler's List*
School of Rock
Seven Brides/Seven Brothers*
7th Voyage of Sinbad
Shakespeare in Love*
Shine
Shrek
Sleepless in Seattle
Snow White
Sound of Music*
South Park
Spartacus
Spellbound*
Stagecoach*
Stand by Me
Star Trek II
Star Wars*
Star Wars V/Empire Strikes
   Back
Star Wars VI/Return of Jedi
St. Elmo's Fire
Sting, The*
Stop Making Sense
Strictly Ballroom
Summer of '42*
Sunset Boulevard*
Superman
Sweet Smell of Success
Talk to Her
Tarzan
Taxi Driver
Third Man
This Is Spinal Tap
Thoroughly Modern Millie*
Thunderball
Tie Me Up! Tie Me Down!
Titanic
To Kill a Mockingbird
Tom Jones*
Tommy
Top Gun
To Sir, With Love
Touch of Evil
Trainspotting

Truth or Dare
Two for the Road
2001: A Space Odyssey
Urban Cowboy
Vertigo
Victor/Victoria*
Wait Until Dark
Way We Were*
Wedding Singer
West Side Story*
What's Love Got to Do with It
When Harry Met Sally . . .
Wild Bunch
Willy Wonka/Chocolate Factory
Wind and the Lion
Wizard of Oz*
Woodstock
Yankee Doodle Dandy*
Yellow Submarine
Young Frankenstein
Zorba the Greek
Zulu

## Sports
### Baseball
Bad News Bears
Bang the Drum Slowly
Bull Durham
Damn Yankees
League of Their Own
Natural, The
Pride of the Yankees
Rookie, The

### Basketball
Hoop Dreams
Hoosiers
Space Jam

### Boxing
Hurricane, The
Raging Bull
Rocky

### Football
Ace Ventura
Fortune Cookie
Jerry Maguire
Longest Yard
Radio
Remember the Titans

### Hockey
Miracle
Slap Shot
### Other
Bend It Like Beckham
Chariots of Fire
Color of Money
Cool Runnings
Hustler, The
Seabiscuit

## Stage Adaptations
Amadeus
Animal Crackers
Annie
Arsenic and Old Lace
Auntie Mame
Awful Truth
Bad Seed
Becket
Bell, Book and Candle
Bells Are Ringing
Birdcage, The
Born Yesterday
Brief Encounter
Bus Stop
Bye Bye Birdie
Cabaret
Cactus Flower
Camelot
Carousel
Cat on a Hot Tin Roof
Chicago
Children of a Lesser God
Cocoanuts, The
Damn Yankees
Dial M for Murder
Diary of Anne Frank
Dinner at Eight
Driving Miss Daisy
Educating Rita
Elephant Man
Evita
Fiddler on the Roof
Finian's Rainbow
Front Page
Funny Girl
Funny Thing Happened...
Gaslight
Gay Divorcee

Glengarry Glen Ross
Grease
Guys and Dolls
Gypsy
Hair
Hamlet (1948)
Hamlet (1996)
Harvey
Hello, Dolly!
Henry V
High Society
His Girl Friday
Inherit the Wind
Irma La Douce
Jesus Christ Superstar
Key Largo
King and I
Kiss Me Kate
La Cage aux Folles
Letter, The
Lion in Winter
Little Foxes
Little Shop of Horrors
Madness of King George
Man for All Seasons
Man Who Came to Dinner
Miracle Worker
Mister Roberts
Music Man
My Fair Lady
Odd Couple
Oklahoma!
Oliver!
One, Two, Three
On Golden Pond
On the Town
Paint Your Wagon
Peter Pan
Peter Pan
Phantom of the Opera
Philadelphia Story
Picnic
Play It Again, Sam
Real Women Have Curves
Rocky Horror Picture Show
Romeo and Juliet
Rope
Roxanne
Same Time, Next Year

1776
Seven Year Itch
Shirley Valentine
Show Boat
Six Degrees of Separation
Sleuth
Sound of Music
South Pacific
Stalag 17
Steel Magnolias
Streetcar Named Desire
Sunshine Boys
Sweet Charity
Unsinkable Molly Brown
Wait Until Dark
West Side Story
Who's Afraid of Virginia . . .
Witness for the Prosecution
Women, The

## Swashbucklers

Adventures of Robin Hood
Captain Blood
Mark of Zorro
Mask of Zorro
Master and Commander
Mutiny on the Bounty (1935)
Mutiny on the Bounty (1962)
Pirates of the Caribbean
Robin and Marian
Robin Hood: Prince of Thieves
7th Voyage of Sinbad
Thief of Bagdad
Three Musketeers

## Thrillers

(See also James Bond)
Accused, The
Air Force One
Airport
Alien
Aliens
Along Came a Spider
Apollo 13
Armageddon
Bad Day at Black Rock
Bad Seed
Basic Instinct
Birds, The
Blood Simple

Body Heat
Bourne Identity
Bourne Supremacy
Bullitt
Cape Fear (1962)
Cape Fear (1991)
China Syndrome
Clear and Present Danger
Client, The
Collateral
Collector, The
Dead Again
Dead Ringers
Death Wish
Deep, The
Diabolique
Dial M for Murder
Dirty Pretty Things
Diva
Dog Day Afternoon
Double Jeopardy
Dressed to Kill
Enemy of the State
Fail-Safe
Fatal Attraction
Firm, The
Forbidden Planet
Foul Play
Frequency
Fugitive, The
Gaslight
Hand That Rocks the Cradle
Hannibal
Hound of the Baskervilles
Hunt for Red October
Insider, The
Interpreter, The
In the Line of Fire
Invasion/Body Snatchers (1956)
Invasion/Body Snatchers (1978)
Jagged Edge
Jaws
Klute
Lady Vanishes
La Femme Nikita
Last Seduction
Lifeboat
Life of David Gale
Manchurian Candidate

Man on Fire
Man Who Knew Too Much
Marathon Man
Memento
Midnight Express
Misery
Mission: Impossible
Murder on the Orient Express
Nightmare on Elm Street
Night of the Hunter
North by Northwest
Notorious
No Way Out
Omen, The
Others, The
Outbreak
Patriot Games
Pelican Brief
Perfect Storm
Play Misty for Me
Poltergeist
Poseidon Adventure
Presumed Innocent
Primal Fear
Psycho
Pulp Fiction
Ransom
Rear Window
Repulsion
Rock, The
Rope
Rosemary's Baby
Runaway Jury
Runaway Train
Run Lola Run
Seven
Seven Days in May
Signs
Silence of the Lambs
Simple Plan
Sin City
Single White Female
Sixth Sense
Sleeping with the Enemy
Sleepy Hollow
Sleuth
Speed
Spellbound
Strangers on a Train

Suspect
Swimming Pool
Talented Mr. Ripley
Taxi Driver
Texas Chainsaw Massacre
Third Man
39 Steps
Time After Time
To Catch a Thief
Towering Inferno
Training Day
Twelve Monkeys
Twister
Unbreakable
Unforgiven
Vertigo
Wages of Fear
Wait Until Dark
Westworld
Whatever Happened to ...
What Lies Beneath
X-Files, The
Z

## War

Alamo, The
Alexander Nevsky
All Quiet on the Western Front
Apocalypse Now
Battle of Algiers
Beau Geste
Black Hawk Down
Born on the Fourth of July
Braveheart
Bridge on the River Kwai
Caine Mutiny
Casablanca
Cold Mountain
Coming Home
Das Boot
Deer Hunter
Diary of Anne Frank
Dirty Dozen
El Cid
Empire of the Sun
Exodus
For Whom the Bell Tolls
Full Metal Jacket
Gallipoli
Glory

Good Morning, Vietnam
Good, the Bad and the Ugly
Grand Illusion
Great Escape
Gunga Din
Guns of Navarone
Henry V
Hotel Rwanda
Killing Fields
Last of the Mohicans
Longest Day
MASH
Mister Roberts
Open City
Paths of Glory
Patriot, The
Patton
Pianist, The
Platoon
Potemkin
Ran
Sand Pebbles
Saving Private Ryan
Schindler's List
Sergeant York
South Pacific
Stalag 17
Thin Red Line
Three Kings
Tin Drum
Tora! Tora! Tora!
Troy
Twelve O'Clock High
Two Women
U-571
Very Long Engagement
Year of Living Dangerously

## Weddings

Father of the Bride (1950)
Father of the Bride (1991)
Four Weddings and a Funeral
Godfather
In-Laws, The
Monsoon Wedding
My Best Friend's Wedding
My Big Fat Greek Wedding
Philadelphia Story
Sixteen Candles

Wedding Banquet
Wedding Singer

## Westerns
Alamo, The
Blazing Saddles
Butch Cassidy/Sundance Kid
Cat Ballou
City Slickers
Dances with Wolves
Fistful of Dollars
Fort Apache
Good, the Bad and the Ugly
Gunfight at the O.K. Corral
High Noon
High Plains Drifter
How the West Was Won
Jeremiah Johnson
Legends of the Fall
Little Big Man
Magnificent Seven
Man Who Shot Liberty Valance
Maverick
McCabe & Mrs. Miller
Oklahoma!
Outlaw Josey Wales
Ox-Bow Incident
Paint Your Wagon
Red River
Rio Bravo
Searchers, The
Shane
She Wore a Yellow Ribbon
Silverado
Spirit: Stallion of the Cimarron
Stagecoach
Tombstone
True Grit
Unforgiven
Wild Bunch
Young Guns